The Practice of U.S. Women's History

D0165681

The Practice of U.S. Women's History

Narratives, Intersections, and Dialogues

Edited by

S. JAY KLEINBERG
EILEEN BORIS
VICKI L. RUIZ

RUTGERS UNIVERSITY PRESS

NEW BRUNSWICK, NEW JERSEY, AND LONDON

LIBRARY OF CONGRESS CATALOGING-IN-PUBLICATION DATA

The practice of U.S. women's history : narratives, intersections, and dialogues /
edited by S. Jay Kleinberg, Eileen Boris, and Vicki L. Ruiz.
    p. cm.
    Includes bibliographical references and index.
    ISBN 978-0-8135-4180-8 (hardcover : alk. paper) — ISBN 978-0-8135-4181-5
    (pbk. : alk. paper)
  I. Women—United States—History.   I. Kleinberg, S. J.   II. Boris, Eileen, 1948–
III. Ruíz, Vicki.
    HQ1410.P73 2007
    305.40973—dc22   2007001046

A British Cataloging-in-Publication record for this book is available
from the British Library

Manufactured in the United States of America

CONTENTS

ACKNOWLEDGMENTS

This collection originated with a conference in London sponsored by Brunel University and the Mellon Fund of the University of Cambridge. Re-Visioning U.S. Women's History convened fifteen scholars from the United States and the United Kingdom to consider the impact of women's and gender history on standard topics in U.S. history, major themes in U.S. women's history, and fresh directions within women's history. Trevor Burnard and Inge Dornan co-organized this meeting with S. Jay Kleinberg.

S. Jay Kleinberg expresses her gratitude to the Research Committee of Brunel University and to Professor Tony Badger, Master of Clare College, Cambridge and Mellon Professor of American History, for material assistance in funding the conference. The supportive community of Americanists who are part of the British Association for American Studies and members of the Centre for American, Transatlantic, and Caribbean History at Brunel University have provided a collegial intellectual environment and shared interests. Nic, Kirsten, and Peter have been, as always, the ideal family: loving, interested, supportive, and tolerant.

Eileen Boris would like to thank Blair Hull for his generosity in endowing the Hull Chair, which she holds, and providing her with resources to pursue this project; her assistant for this book, Leandra Zarnow, who represents the best of the next generation of women's and gender historians of the United States; her other women's history graduate students at the University of California, Santa Barbara, over the last five years, Carolyn Herbst Lewis, Sandra Dawson, April Haynes, Danielle Swiontek, Carol Feinberg, Warren Wood, Andrea Gill, and Bianca Murillo; her other graduate assistants, Jill Jensen, Beth Currans, and Ellie Shermer; and Nelson Lichtenstein, whose support — and keen historical sense — make all the difference. She especially was grateful for the presence of Daniel during that weekend when Vicki and Jay came over to wrestle with turning a conference into a collection.

Vicki L. Ruiz acknowledges the feminist graduate students at the University of California, Irvine, with whom she has worked for the past five years and who are in now in the throes of writing their dissertations — Margie Brown-Coronel, Casey Christensen, Julie Cohen, and Ryan Kray. Although not her advisees, she also thanks Veronica Castillo-Muñoz, Tracy Sachtjen, and Jennifer Thigpen. This community of scholars pushes her intellectually on a daily basis and for that she is forever in their debt. And to Victor, Miguel, and Dan — thank you for all of your love and eternal patience.

Leslie Mitchner, Kendra Boileau, and the entire Rutgers University Press crew have proved delightful to work with. We also thank the anonymous readers whose constructive comments and recommendations made a substantive difference in our framing of this volume and in the revisions of individual essays.

Finally, we couldn't have completed this project without each other. A cooperative work always has its own rewards. This one was facilitated by e-mail; especially fortuitous was the time difference between London and California, which allowed Jay to send corrections and comments with which those of us on the U.S. West Coast could begin our day, and Jay, in turn, could wake up with yet another task to perform. Eileen and Vicki must thank Jay for bringing us all together and for the volume that follows. We are grateful to the patience and hard labors of our contributors, whose work we make available as they showcase the efforts of an entire field.

The Practice of U.S. Women's History

Introduction: Narratives, Intersections, and Dialogues

S. JAY KLEINBERG

EILEEN BORIS

VICKI L. RUIZ

In her classic work, *Relations of Rescue*, Peggy Pascoe reflected on history "as a kind of conversation between the past and the present in which we travel through time to examine the cultural assumptions — and possibilities of our society as well as the societies before us."[1] *The Practice of U.S. Women's History* mirrors a collective belief that writing women into the historical record has shifted and changed over time, and, with it, the practice of history. Offering gendered historiographies from an array of perspectives, *The Practice of U.S. Women's History* questions whose voices count and who decides what matters.

Each of the editors has witnessed women's history transform U.S. history. When S. Jay Kleinberg presented the paper "Technology and Women's Work" at the Organization of American Historians annual conference in the mid-1970s, one commentator opined that whatever else it was, the study of working-class women's daily routines and their access to household and municipal technology was not history. It might be sociology, but it certainly did not jibe with the commentator's understanding of historical inquiry. For Eileen Boris, the problem was which dwellings counted as part of the history of domestic architecture, though she successfully convinced her professors that slave cabins and tenement houses as well as Catharine Beecher and Charlotte Perkins Gilman belonged to the canon of American studies. Vicki L. Ruiz, as part of the first generation of Chicana historians, pieced together the lives of Mexican women cannery workers in southern California during the 1930s and 1940s, and in presenting the preliminary results of her research, she frequently had to persuade colleagues in feminist, labor, and even Chicana/o studies that these women were historical actors whose lives and legacies mattered.

From its inception, the practice of U.S. women's history had involved interrogating and challenging traditional periodization, paradigms, and practices. Where have we been and where are we going as chroniclers of a gendered American story? As historian Valerie Matsumoto reminds us, "Perhaps scholars should be reminded that we, no less than those we study, are actors in history, making choices that affect the lives of others."[2] Historians of women and gender have stretched the boundaries of the national past, even beyond a narrow concept of the nation-state, but also have engaged in a noisy conversation with each other over the subject of women's history itself.

To write a narrative of the field of U.S. women's history, we would begin with the civil rights movements of the 1960s and '70s, whose impact changed the intellectual landscape of American college campuses not only in terms of more diverse student bodies but also in terms of institutionalizing new interdisciplinary programs and departments created in response to student demand, e.g., Black, Chicana/o, Puerto Rican, Native American, Asian American, and Women's Studies. U.S. women's history emerged in this heady atmosphere of campus activism and community engagement. Early works reflected the consciousness of the women's movement, some bearing such evocative titles as *Up From the Pedestal* and *Liberating Women's History*.[3]

Many feminist scholars who came of intellectual age during this era were activists in the streets as well as the archives. As literary critic Susan Stanford Friedman has argued, "The feminist desire to 'make history' entangles the desire to effect significant and lasting change with the desire to be the historian of change. The narrative act of assigning meaning to the past potentially intervenes in the present and future construction of history."[4] The excitement of the initial research of recovery was palpable and the first collections of primary documents like Nancy F. Cott's *Root of Bitterness* and Gerda Lerner's *Black Women in White America* provided springboards for future research. Book-length studies appeared that profiled strong, independent women engaged in a greater good. In 1973 the first Berkshire Conference on the History of Women (now held every three years and the largest history conference in the world) gathered at Douglass College in Rutgers.[5] The scene was sisterhood, but for whom?

The idea of a universal womanhood predicated on a white, middle-class worldview (an idea that had so distanced many feminists of color from the mainstream women's movement) had the effect (albeit unintentional) of rendering invisible the legacies of women of color. As Ellen Carol DuBois and Vicki L. Ruiz pointed out in the introduction to the first edition of *Unequal Sisters:* "Most of the early work in U.S. women's history paid little attention to race and assumed instead a universal women's experience, defined in contrast to "man's" history. . . . In this uniracial model, the universal man of the American history was replaced with the universal woman."[6]

Inequality takes many forms and many women's historians recognized early on that gender was not the only fault line. Early work addressed differences between "the lady and the mill girl" and celebrated "the rising of the women" during the great immigrant garment strikes of the early twentieth century, but attention to class concentrated on the urban North and Midwest.[7] A "biracial model" shattered a singular vision as feminists turned their attention to the ways in which women oppressed other women, delineating power relations along lines of class and race. While historians of the planter class questioned the northern bias of the field, African American women's history exploded even the assumptions about power and authority of these other southern historians.[8] Deborah Gray White's *Ar'n't I a Woman: Female Slaves in the Plantation South* and Paula Giddings's *When and Where I Enter*, as examples, placed African American women at the center of the discipline.[9] While this model privileged a black/white binary, it remains a powerful analytical tool as evident in several essays included in this volume.

U.S. women's historians were not content to discuss among themselves the "relevance" of their research. As scholars on a mission, they organized numerous workshops across the nation during the 1970s and into the 1980s on curriculum integration, convincing colleagues that a fuller, more satisfying recounting of the American past included more than a sidebar about suffrage. Indeed, their goal was nothing less than an "integration" or "inclusion" of women throughout the teaching of the U.S. history survey. Contributionist phrases like "We were there, too" may now seem antiquated, but for the time period this claiming of legitimacy was crucial.

During the 1980s scholars who defined themselves as U.S. women's historians began to achieve major recognition in the form of coveted prizes in American history. From 1980 to 1986, Thomas Dublin, Mary Ryan, Suzanne Lebsock, and Jacqueline Jones walked away with a Bancroft, one of the highest honors for a book in U.S. history. Jones's *Labor of Love, Labor of Sorrow: Black Women, Work, and the Family from Slavery to the Present*, also a finalist for the Pulitzer prize, situated the individual experiences of black women squarely within the frame of U.S. history writ large, not as people contributing to the American past, but as people defining it.[10] However, racialized gender, the melding of race and gender into a whole distinguished from either race or gender separately, would assume alternate forms depending on the topic and the region.

Historians of the "Women's West" stood at the forefront in complicating this biracial model, noting the multiplicity of groups who called the "West" home. "Given the confluence of many cultures and races in this region — Native American, Mexican, Asian, Black, and Anglo — grappling with race at all requires a framework that has more than two positions."[11] Womanhood by itself, as Shirley Hune here observes in her chapter on Chinese Americans, "conceals how race, ethnicity, class, sexuality, citizenship, and other factors contribute to their histories and experiences."

Increasingly since the 1980s, women of color, antiracist white feminists, and lesbians — indeed, all those who in their own ways deviated from a uniracial model — demanded that scholars account not only for the many and varied women's histories but also for the inequalities between women beyond a black/white binary. Essays in this volume take this challenge seriously by not merely documenting what different groups of women did at various historical junctures. They examine not only differences in men's and women's experiences, but also differences among women. In essence, they incorporate the lessons of an intersectional feminism, in which identity encompasses multiple dimensions so that one is not merely gendered or raced or classed or abled, but all of these factors combine and refract upon each other in a *mezcla* (mixture) of self and society. In 1990 DuBois and Ruiz labeled this model "multicultural" as they called for scholars to envision "American women's history, as a series of dialectical relations among and across races and classes of women, representing diverse cultures and unequal power."[12]

The term "multicultural," however, seems a bit dated, a battered lightning rod of contested meanings. In particular, multicultural education has often been conceptualized as either a fluffy, hegemonic ploy celebrating diversity or a subversive threat to American character and culture. More importantly, for U.S. women's historians, this model seems permanently moored to the nation-state. It perhaps takes for granted identities that demand investigation into their constructions, developments, changes, and continuities, as illuminated in this volume by Ruiz's discussion of *"morena/o, blanca/o, y café con leche."*

For many scholars, a transnational paradigm holds more promise. But like the multicultural model, transnationalism has become a permeable construct, subject to many meanings from the migrations of contemporary global immigrants to the impact of empire and imperialism to transhemispheric colonial spheres of knowledge and power — with the Atlantic World and the Pacific World themselves contested designations. Ann Stoler's *Haunted by Empire: Geographies of Intimacy in North American History* points to an evolving transnational paradigm that encompasses relations of multiple subjects and differential power rooted within physical place, ideological environs, and individual bodies.[13] The saliency of cultural locations across physical and metaphorical borders remains a constant in U.S. women's history. In her chapter that follows, Leisa D. Meyer cogently frames the history of sexualities within the "multiplicity of identities and experiences of those individuals within the groups on which they focused" and suggests how institutional discourses, such as formulated in science and law, interact with understandings of ordinary people so that neither "top down" or "bottom up" approaches by themselves are wholly satisfying.

In challenging scholars of the United States, especially those who live there, to transcend the nation-state, Laura Briggs in this volume reminds us of the power of the transnational turn in narrating women's lives, especially in situating migrants and immigrants, both free and forced. Breaking out of the boundaries of the nation-state, this history must become transatlantic, transpacific, and transhemispheric to include at the very least Canada, Mexico, and the Caribbean. In short, many of the chapters in this collection complicate the very meaning of "American." As editors, we also acknowledge that the interdisciplinarity and intersectional feminism that has transformed the field owes much to rich, vibrant, and tough conversations that emerged among scholars of gender in American studies, ethnic studies, and women's studies.

The Practice of U.S. Women's History presents seventeen chapters arranged roughly chronologically, moving from early America to the present as would a survey course. But shared topics — migrations, war, work, and politics — suggest additional combinations that highlight contrasting as well as complimentary approaches. We thus invite you to read the chapters out of "order." By disrupting standard periodization, this volume emphasizes the conversational nature of historiography, the nuances and disagreements that emerge when historians reflect on each other's work. A thematic approach gives greater space to issues vital to a reconfigured U.S. women's history, such as relations between identities and spatial locations, tensions between structure and agency, and interaction between self-fashioning and cultural representation, as well as experience and discourse. In most cases, the scholarship has decentered the construct of woman in order to focus on gender as a major category of analysis. Moreover, while most subfields present a trajectory from exclusion to inclusion, from some women to multiple voices, and from women to gender, this layering of approaches has developed at different paces, generating a variegated series of conversations. The contributors to this volume come from diverse locations within the academy and span three generations of scholars.

The first four essays revisit early America, a field that now focuses on intercultural contact and conflict between Europeans, Africans, and Native Americans. Reconsidering the narrative of British settlement through the movement of voluntary, indentured, and enslaved migrants, Trevor G. Burnard and Ann M. Little locate the origins of slavery in the refusal of European women to come to the Americas. British North America was a masculine place; the economic incentives that encouraged European men were not available to their female counterparts, who had to leave family and neighborhood for uncertain rewards. To compensate for absent women, they argue, "colonial men stole the labor of African men and women."

The tension between structure and agency that informs what Burnard and Little say about reluctant migration also has dominated scholarship on Native American women. With attention to multiple gender systems and regional differences, Gail D. MacLeitch studies not only the consequences of European migration, but also how indigenous women shaped political and economic interactions between European and Native Americans. She finds fault with the declension narrative (a "women-as-victims model"), which posits that Native women lost power with European settlement. On the other hand, she also considers an emphasis on women's creative adaptation by itself inadequate as it downplays the larger destruction of Native cultures. So whether or not women gained greater independence in relation to their men from embracing Christianity and trading fur, "native people as a whole experienced growing inequality with Europeans" when imperial and colonial systems and a market economy eroded their self-sufficiency. To incorporate Native women into the history of early America, she argues, calls for showing how broad historical forces affected various tribes in comparison with each other and with European settlers.

Essays by Susan Branson and Betty Wood on the American Revolution illustrate how a historian's positionality shapes interpretation. Branson begins with historical memory and then considers European gender roles and female types, including "daughters of liberty" and "women of the Republic." She judges the extension of the Revolutionary period into the early nineteenth century as an advance in the scholarship because it features white women making "their voices heard in the street, the parlor, and the theater." Wood, in contrast, focuses on southern women of color. To judge the extent of black women's agency, Wood reconsiders sources generated by white men and official authorities, which, nonetheless, reveal "the sheer diversity of the decisions taken by, and subsequent experiences of, southern women of color," who found themselves "active, if not always voluntary, participants on both sides of the war."

While the absence of women's labor may have "vexed colonial development," as Burnard and Little contend, its myriad forms fueled the American economy. Newer scholarship on women and work in the nineteenth century challenges the once dominant paradigm of separate spheres by showing the private connected to the public. Assigning lower-paid and undervalued tasks to women, and the more despised toils to women of color, a sexual division of labor did not necessarily curtail struggles for economic and social autonomy, but most women never went on strike or felt independent by earning wages as factory operatives or schoolteachers. Instead, they undertook domestic labor, an arena where servants and slaves contested the arbitrariness of the women who benefited from their efforts. Balancing between agency and constraint, Inge Dornan and S. Jay Kleinberg compare and contrast women's work in a regional framework that considers the imposition of Anglo-American law on economic relations in newly acquired territory. Thus, they emphasize how southwestern women "developed strategies for survival and assimilation"; and, like MacLeitch, they reject any simple declension model of conquest.

As these essays suggest, war and conquest generate gendered tales. Susan-Mary Grant observes how historians, centered on military strategy, have downplayed women's participation in the Civil War and thus have misunderstood the war itself. Armies depended on the labors of wives and other camp followers on the frontlines, and the Confederacy relied on both free and enslaved women and children performing men's jobs in the fields and factories. Women may have bound "up the nation's wounds," transgressing gendered boundaries, but their labors, including the volunteerism of northern wives and daughters, failed to translate into political power. A gendered analysis goes to the larger meaning of the conflict, both in terms of differential consequences for the emancipated and vanquished and in "how war functions as a force for national cohesion" not only in its pursuit but as re-enacted in memory.[14]

Other wars followed. Women's historians, like Susan Armitage, formed part of an intellectual generation that fundamentally challenged popular and scholarly accounts of the "winning of the West." The "new" Western history replaced heroic stories of European American homesteaders with those of settlers from Asia and Mexico and stressed the interactions of peoples along a shifting borderland. Armitage traces her thirty-year attempt to exorcise Turner's Ghost, a journey that began with recovering rural white and black women's lives, but one that placed her at the forefront of mentoring younger scholars engaged in writing more inclusive histories of the "Women's West."

The incorporation of Spanish, Mexican, and Native inhabitants into the United States belongs to a larger expansionary impulse that Laura Briggs connects to imperialism. Hers is not your father's diplomatic history, but an approach that links the histories of migration and borders to the violence of U.S. military and economic intervention. Whether as a laborer in a global sweatshop, a missionary, "legitimate" wife, sex worker, or migrant seeking a different life, a gendered history of imperialism generates new scripts of cultural construction and political authority. It rewrites standard women's history subjects, like feminist movements, birth control, or domestic service, but also interrogates the ways that languages of masculinity and home shape imperialism. Briggs calls for the study of places, like Puerto Rico or Vietnam, to illuminate big processes, but cautions that writing such a history requires "multi-sited, multi-lingual, multi-archival work," familiarity with political and social theory, and engagement in a transnational conversation with scholars around the globe.

Shirley Hune provides an in-depth look at one such transnational encounter. Though historians once simply ignored Chinese American women, more recent portrayals continue to render them as victims, objects of "colonialism, capitalism, and sexist family practices." Comparing the self-fashioning of Chinese women with their representation by others as prostitutes, deviants, or pawns, she examines the place of Chinese Americans within the academy, their growing numbers as historians, and the importance of alternative methodologies for the project of Chinese American women's history. Gendered constructions mattered, not only for the decisions of immigration officials, but also for the aspirations and actions of subsequent generations of women. Their labor in family businesses and sustenance of transnational families challenges facile generalizations.

Recent research on Chinese immigration has been in the forefront of the gendering of immigration history. As Donna R. Gabaccia and Vicki L. Ruiz emphasize, transnational analysis has replaced notions of simple assimilation with "a new methodology" that interrogates the ties that migrants maintained with their homelands. In emphasizing the themes of making home, community building, memory, and citizenship, they show how a gendered immigration history charts a changing understanding of belonging. Heterosexuality and

marriage provided criteria for entrance into the country, and discourses of reproduction based on racial purity shaped nationalism itself. "Communities of
mobile people meld interior, exterior, and imagined spaces into homes where
work, family, business, and identity-formation intersect," confronting the division of private from public and emphasizing women's negotiations rather than
only their oppressions. The turn in immigration studies to questions of law and
public policy coincides with one trajectory within women's history to bring the
state back in, as later seen in the chapter by Eileen Boris and S. Jay Kleinberg.

The movement of African Americans, first to the Americas and from
bondage and then out of the rural South, offers a parallel narrative of migration
in which women make and remake communities. In the words of Leslie Brown,
"Mobility . . . has existed as a gendered exercise of freedom." However, beginning
with early twentieth century, black social scientists and other researchers identified the typical migrant as male, even though, as Brown reminds us, black women
"have outnumbered males in urban populations for about as long as there have
been cities." In taking up the challenge to rewrite the story of the Great
Migration, she locates this upheaval in a longer diasporic timeframe and refo-
cuses the discussion from "the women problem," in which women's presence
stood for sexual danger and family disintegration, to a female quest "to reclaim a
certain amount of autonomy and to undercut the kinds of gender exploitation
they had known in the past."

Communities of color understood that gender, race, class, and sexuality created fundamentally different paths to the privileges and obligations of citizenship. Vicki L. Ruiz shows this clearly in her essay on racial constructions within
Chicana/o historiography, an area certainly shaped by social and political
struggles. "From the borderlands era to the present, the fluidities embedded in
mestizaje allow for multiple constructions of subjectivities including *morena/o,
blanca/o, y café con leche*." In examining the imbrications of gender throughout
Chicana/o history, Ruiz notes how Mexican women have used the legal system
from ridding themselves of abusive husbands in the 1860s to challenging the segregation of California schools in the 1940s. They transformed wrongs into legal
rights.

The century-long battle for the vote once dominated the study of women and
citizenship; now it illuminates "nation-building and citizen-making," exposing
the racial assumptions behind those processes. Elizabeth J. Clapp considers this
historiography, including tensions between suffrage and other rights-seeking
movements. She also explores efforts by women and men of color to secure this
right well after passage of the Nineteenth Amendment. For Clapp, local studies
have allowed for a more precise charting of the push for and resistance to enfranchisement. Here, too, scholarship on the West has reinvigorated an old topic,
especially in connecting the success of suffrage to Populism and union organizing. Many women's historians remain vitally concerned with questions like
political environment, leadership, and strategies, as seen in Mary Ellen Curtin's

gendered framing of the historiography of civil rights. Suffrage historians also have begun to construct a transnational narrative that connects the fight for the Nineteenth Amendment with comparable struggles in Latin America, China, and Europe.

Social welfare history long had included women as the objects of inquiry, but feminist scholarship has cast women as policy makers as well as recipients of aid. Eileen Boris and S. Jay Kleinberg chart the trajectory of a field that exposes the fault lines of race, class, ethnicity, and geography among women as well as between women and men. In the early twentieth century, maternalist reformers sought to reorder the households of the poor, while recipients of their largesse fought to use both private philanthropy and state provision for their own ends. Indeed, the protests of poor women, defined as racial and class others and judged as sexual deviants, shaped the making of the welfare state into the late twentieth century. But it has not been enough merely to write women back into this narrative. A racialized, gendered perspective shows the ways that social policy reinforced inequalities based on race, gender, age, employment, and marital status.

The most well-known American political movement of the twentieth century was the African American civil rights struggle. In reassessing women's leadership and activism during "the long civil rights movement," Mary Ellen Curtin rejects the tendency to separate study of civil rights, black power, and women's liberation. Curtin illuminates how gender analysis unpacked both the masculinism of Black Power and the "variegated experience of black women in nationalist organizations." She notes the greater attention to divisions within black America, including the aspirations of poor and working-class women. To the extent that women's networks and organizations "were the key to the success of grassroots protest," then the problem of civil rights becomes "not that lack of great male leaders to fill King's shoes, but the weakening of female-based community institutions." However, black women's activism "reinvigorated" women's groups across the activist spectrum, including national peace organizations, welfare rights, and women's liberation.

The "political" in U.S. women's history now embraces not only citizenship rights, social movements, electoral politics, and state policy, but also personal and sexual relations. More than other fields within history, this one has gained inspiration from "theory," including the writings of Michael Foucault and more recent queer theory. Leisa D. Meyer emphasizes that sexuality is a discourse which marks and configures "power relations between men and women, different racial/ethnic groups, classes, and states," and thus is a site through which cultural anxiety and political struggle are expressed, whether in terms of immigration restrictions or the "Soviet menace." She repositions the history of reproduction as "a site through which hierarchies of race are mediated and contested," as part of the history of sexualities. As with the New Western History, this historiography defies any unitary or binary categories, but rather embodies multivalent trajectories for exploring the body and the body politic.

A topic familiar to women's history, the women's liberation movement, also belongs to wider discussions of political and social action. Kristin Celello observes that not only has the definition of feminism (or feminisms) expanded, but historians now offer a "nuanced critique of feminism's limitations in a historical context." Lesbian feminists have emerged as key actors, complicating tales of "a strict 'gay-straight split' within the movement." She further examines the historiography of antifeminism and the multiple sources of opposition to the Equal Rights Amendment and reproductive freedom, viewing them within the political climate of recent decades. She begins the task of historicizing "the third wave," a self-definition by a multicultural group of women in their twenties that emerged at the end of the twentieth century. Indeed, she exhorts historians to take the concerns of these new voices seriously in order to better trace the continuities and ruptures in women's activism.

The Practice of U.S. Women's History offers readers an expansive sweep of the field of U.S. women's history with all of the messiness, contradictions, and excitement inherent in recording the human condition. The essays provide a sense of the layering within the historiography of U.S. women's history and an appreciation of specific works in their historical moment. As editors and contributors, we share our joy in finding that one nugget in the archive or reading that one passage that helps us frame our work. Evidence, interpretation, and imagination are the building blocks of historical scholarship, and the chapters that follow represent a rich selection of gendered narratives and the crafting of history.

NOTES

1. Peggy Pascoe, *Relations of Rescue: The Search for Female Moral Authority in the American West, 1874–1939* (New York: Oxford University Press, 1990), xxiii.

2. Valerie J. Matsumoto, *Farming the Home Place: A Japanese American Community in California, 1919–1982* (Ithaca, N.Y.: Cornell University Press, 1993), 224.

3. Aileen S. Kraditor, ed., *Up from the Pedestal: Selected Writings in the History of American Feminism* (Chicago: Quadrangle Books, 1968); Berenice A. Carroll, ed., *Liberating Women's History: Theoretical and Critical Essays* (Urbana: University of Illinois Press, 1976).

4. Quoted in Eileen Boris and Nupur Chaudhuri, "Introduction: Standpoints on Hard Ground," in *Voices of Women Historians: The Personal, the Political, the Professional*, ed. Eileen Boris and Nupur Chaudhuri (Bloomington: Indiana University Press, 1999), xi.

5. Nancy F. Cott, ed., *Root of Bitterness: Documents of the Social History of American Women* (New York: Dutton, 1972); Gerda Lerner, ed., *Black Women in White America: A Documentary History* (New York: Vintage Books, 1972); Berkshire Conference of Women's Historians Web site: http://www.umass.edu/history/berks/history.htm.

6. Ellen Carol DuBois and Vicki L. Ruiz, eds., *Unequal Sisters: A Multicultural Reader in U.S. Women's History* (New York: Routledge, 1990), xi.

7. Gerda Lerner, "The Lady and the Mill Girl: Changes in the Status of Women in the Age of Jackson," *American Studies* 10 (spring 1969), reprinted in *The Majority Finds Its Past* (New York: Oxford University Press, 1979), 15–30; Milton Cantor and Bruce Laurie, eds., *Class, Sex, and the Woman Worker* (Westport, Conn.: Greenwood Press, 1977), which did contain

Elizabeth Jameson, "Imperfect Unions: Class and Gender in Cripple Creek, 1894–1904," 166–202; Meredith Tax, *The Rising of the Women* (New York: Monthly Review Press, 1980).

8. Elizabeth Fox-Genovese, *Within the Plantation Household: Black and White Women of the Old South* (Chapel Hill: University of North Carolina Press, 1988), esp. ch. 1.

9. Deborah Gray White, *Ar'n't I a Woman: Female Slaves in the Plantation South* (New York: Norton, 1985); Paula Giddings, *When and Where I Enter: The Impact of Black Women on Race and Sex in America* (New York: Morrow, 1984).

10. Columbia University Libraries, "The Bancroft Prizes; Previous Awards," http://www. columbia.edu/cu/lweb/eguides/amerihist/bancroftlist.html; Jacqueline Jones, *Labor of Love, Labor of Sorrow: Black Women, Work, and the Family from Slavery to the Present* (New York: Basic Books, 1985). This group of Bancroft winners were neither the first to write on women (as in the case of Dublin) nor the first women to receive the award. In 1956 Elizabeth Stevenson was awarded a Bancroft for her biography of Henry Adams and in 1971 David Kennedy for his work on Margaret Sanger.

11. DuBois and Ruiz, *Unequal Sisters*, xii.

12. Ibid., xiii.

13. Ann Stoler, ed., *Haunted by Empire: Geographies of Intimacy in North American History* (Durham, N.C.: Duke University Press, 2006).

14. For more information, see Alice Fahs and Joan Waugh, eds., *The Memory of the Civil War in American Culture* (Chapel Hill: University of North Carolina Press, 2004).

1

Where the Girls Aren't

Women as Reluctant Migrants but Rational Actors in Early America

TREVOR G. BURNARD

ANN M. LITTLE

The most famous fictive British imagining of the colonial situation in America is Daniel Defoe's *Robinson Crusoe*. Immensely popular in its day, it remains just as popular in a post-modernist, post-colonial age as an exemplary text about individualism, modern capitalism, colonialism, and gender. Through industry, self-mastery, and mastery of the environment and its savage inhabitants, Crusoe creates an improved and civilized world over which he is king, a world in which women are entirely absent. *Robinson Crusoe* is thus a highly gendered metropolitan vision of what contemporaries thought was going on (or should be going on) in Britain's colonizing project in the Americas. Defoe's other most lasting fictional creation — his disorderly heroine, Moll Flanders — resembles Crusoe in being an outsider or loner. She also resembles Crusoe in finding her true identity in a colonial setting as a transplanted felon marrying upwards a handsome and prosperous Virginia planter who cares little for her scandalous past. What intrigues readers about Moll is less her inherent goodness than her evident wickedness, her transgressive qualities, and her archetypal quality as a disruptive, disorderly woman. If Robinson Crusoe's tale is about self-mastery, Moll Flanders's mission is self-fashioning, with both characters using colonial British America as an arena for personal and societal transformation.[1]

What is interesting about *Robinson Crusoe* and *Moll Flanders* is the dissonances between them in Defoe's metropolitan imagining of the colonial project. Written within three years of each other, they seem less part of a similar project than books speaking to different concerns. In both, Defoe asks what it means to be a modern man or woman in a commercializing age. But even though Crusoe the king self-evidently needs a queen to accompany him in his rule, he gets instead the faithful slave, Man Friday — an early example of black labor displacing white women's labor. America is envisaged as a male space or at least a place upon which men make their mark unimpeded by women. But in order to survive over time, a society needs women. It doesn't need, however, women like

Moll Flanders — a self-assertive, sexually and socially disruptive tart who even if she has the proverbial heart of gold is unpromising material with which to found a better Britain abroad. It is not surprising that in his envisioning of his little kingdom, Crusoe can find no place for colonial women. He wants and needs a helpmeet: Defoe's *Moll Flanders* implies he will get a troublesome wench unlikely to comply with his grand plans to establish patriarchal household government in a new land. Man Friday's appearance suggests a more ominous solution to the problem of European women's labor in colonial America.

And yet, the "woman problem" — getting enough of them from Europe, and of the right quality — is utterly ignored by the mythology of the settlement of colonial British America. Gender hardly figures in the great narratives of colonial development, even if gender issues have become increasingly matters of concern to a wide range of historians interested in specific events and movements in early America.[2] In this chapter, we wish to explore briefly why the heightened interest in gender relations in early America has not filtered through to gender being a prime organizing principle in syntheses of colonial development. We also want to investigate what a history of colonial America would look like with gender as a prime organizing principle. If colonial history were reconfigured in this way, the master narrative of early American immigration and settlement would not center on European men's migrations, but rather on the fact that European women found America unattractive and unappealing, and in the main refused to go. Their reluctance to migrate ensured that British America would remain a much more masculine society than the societies from which both European and African migrants had come, and that like other New World colonies, it would depend on forced African migration to fill its need for labor. In order to rewrite this narrative of immigration and settlement, we will consider the gendered experiences of the three most typical colonials: indentured white male servants from southeastern England in the seventeenth century going to plantation colonies; enslaved female Biafrans condemned to plantation labor in the Caribbean between 1680 and 1750; and immigrant and native-born young women in the northern farm colonies to 1750. Examining colonial development from the perspective of these three colonial types allows us to question an unsatisfactory model of the historical evolution of gendered relationships in early America — patriarchy disrupted by migration, entrenched by settlement, and transformed or jettisoned through sentimentalism and revolution.

But first, we must analyze the role of gender — or rather, its absence — in the great narratives of colonial development. More than thirty years since the beginning of a profound literature in women's history, and nearly twenty years after Joan Scott's analysis of "gender as a category of historical analysis," the stuff of women's and gender history has not substantially changed the traditional Whig narrative of colonial British America as charted in survey texts and scholarly syntheses.[3] We can go through any number of ambitious syntheses of colonial development and we see little attention paid to gender as an organizing concept.

The *William and Mary Quarterly*, the most important journal in the field, has published very little in women's and gender history. In a 1993 volume that republished eleven of the journal's most influential articles over the past fifty years, the readership of the journal selected only one article on women's history for inclusion, and the authors of that article insist in a postscript for the commemorative volume that "in writing of the experience of women, we have thought of our work as a part of human history, not as a history of women."[4] In the last fifteen years, it has published only one major interpretive article on gender, Carol Shammas's polemic about making the importance of patriarchal household government in Anglo-America more central than it is now, which she has since expanded into a book, *A History of Household Government in America*.[5] Like Shammas, the only scholars who have attempted to incorporate gender into their syntheses come from women's history backgrounds. Mary Beth Norton is the only major scholar to write a general account that incorporates gender in *Founding Mothers and Fathers*, and she deals only with the early period of settlement and constructs her interpretation around whether colonists emulated or departed from a Filmerian political ideology of the family.[6] To our mind, only one book has been written that seriously considers gender to be a useful category of historical analysis for the whole colonial period: Kathleen Brown's ambitious attempt to rewrite the history of a major colony — Virginia — from a gendered perspective in *Good Wives, Nasty Wenches, and Anxious Patriarchs*.[7]

How would the whole of colonial British American history appear if we tried to make gender central to the grand narrative of early American history? If we were to write a history of early America from a gender perspective, what would it look like? First, we must come to terms with just how masculine a place early America was, especially if we look at the experiences of whites instead of blacks.[8] European women did not like America and did not see in it the opportunities that encouraged many thousands of ambitious or desperate young men to cross the Atlantic. This is a point that has received surprisingly little attention in immigration studies, as many historians and demographers seem, like Defoe, to take for granted and thus naturalize the masculine nature of the immigrant population.[9] We know that women did not like America because so few of them were prepared to move there. Of the approximately 70–80 percent of emigrants who moved from Britain to the plantation colonies, men outnumbered women by between 6 and 8 to 1. Only in New England, which accounted for no more than 3 percent of all migrants, was the number of female migrants roughly equal to those of men, and even there the sex ratio was 3 males for every 2 females. Furthermore, as many as one in three New England immigrants in the seventeenth century arrived as indentured servants, and indentured servants were a population that was notoriously masculine. We would be surprised if as much as 15 percent of European migration to British America in the colonial period was female. The total number of white women moving to British America (including the West Indies) was probably between 100,000 and 150,000 out of a total emigration of nearly 1 million. Such migration rates imply European female migration of between 600 and 900 individuals per annum, with the numbers being considerably greater in the mid-seventeenth century and less in the eighteenth century. Such migration was tiny — the equivalent of the cargo of perhaps three slave ships per annum — and meant that the percentage of women in the population who left Britain never amounted to as much as one-tenth of 1 percent, even at the height of outward migration when the percentage of men in the population departing for the Americas was probably as high as 1 percent per annum.[10]

The implications for this imbalance were far-reaching and long lasting, as we will see. Southwest borderlands historians who have put gender at the center of their analyses have suggested that the possession and control of women and children were central to both Spanish and Indian men's status and honor, and that men were willing to engage in violence and oppression to gain access to women. Ramón A. Gutiérrez's *When Jesus Came, the Corn Mothers Went Away* posits connections between sexual mores, marriage politics, and Indian slavery in Spanish colonial New Mexico. And in *Captives and Cousins,* James Brooks argues that access to women was a major goal of the taking and trading of captives by the late eighteenth century, when Plains Indians populations in particular had been ravaged by disease and warfare. On the seventeenth- and eighteenth-century Atlantic coast, larger numbers and percentages of black women (perhaps 1 million African women or 35 percent of all slaves) came to the Americas, of course, but like Indian slaves and captives of other Indians, they did so unwillingly.[11]

Two questions suggest themselves as topics for further investigation. First, why did women not want to come to America? The "push" factors cited for British men were notably less compelling for their female counterparts. Women had more reasons to want to remain closer to home, given that they were much more likely to be involved in looking after family members. Employment opportunities at home were also likely to be more abundant than for men, especially within domestic service, where women were always needed, even if that work was tedious and ill-paid. Furthermore, emigration to America cut women off from family and neighborhood networks of other women who served to ease their own labors. "Pull" factors proved to be weaker for British women as well. Life as an indentured servant was unappealing to both sexes given the hard physical labor that it entailed — but for women in America, servitude often required field labor that violated customary English understandings of the proper type of work allocated to men and women. (British farms blurred the line between domestic service and women's husbandry, such as dairying and looking after animals, and women were traditionally employed in weeding and stone gathering, but farmers did not rely on women's labor in the fields.)

Colonial masters eager to produce lucrative staple crops, on the other hand, seldom discriminated between male and female workers in the Chesapeake and Barbados.[12] In addition, women faced the possibility and sometimes the probability of sexual abuse. The likelihood of sexual violation engendered a further reason to avoid migrating. Female choices after indentureship were more limited than for men: women continued in the colonial period to be defined by their marital status whereas men were defined by occupation or status. It was true that sex ratio imbalances in the seventeenth century in the Chesapeake and Barbados and throughout the colonial period in the Carolinas and much of the West Indies meant that white women might marry better in the colonies than in Britain. But a good marriage did not make up for the lack of amenities that made running a household less onerous in Britain than in British America: the lack of social and familial institutions, the absence of kin to assist when things went wrong, and the likelihood of early widowhood when young children were still underfoot.[13]

Second, what did the absence of women imply about how society was structured? For the seventeenth century, we have a good idea from the pioneering works of Edmund Morgan and Richard Dunn a generation ago on the histories of early Virginia and Barbados — the two most important seventeenth-century colonies — about the character of societies dominated by young migrant men.[14] Morgan and Dunn demonstrate that these colonies, where the majority of young, unattached indentured servants from southern England went in the first fifty years of settlement, were fast-living, fast-dying societies, highly individualistic to the point of becoming occasionally anarchical, strongly materialistic, crude, and boorish with a maximum emphasis put on white male propertied independence. Recent scholarship has softened Dunn and Morgan's portrait and has stressed how quickly Englishmen and Englishwomen abroad re-established familiar gender patterns in the New World, but the main themes established a generation ago about life in seventeenth-century plantation societies still pertain. As Bernard Bailyn argues, throughout the Atlantic world, the original settlements created by Europeans should be seen as contested marchlands, societies that were literally barbarous, scenes of horrific conflict that differed from conflict in the home continents of the new migrants in being characterized by "authorized brutality without restraint, scorched-earth campaigns, [and] the exuberant desecration of the symbols of civility."[15] So too do the basic demographic and social outlines of life in the northern colonies, although recent scholarship suggests that Puritan and Quaker fathers were not as all-powerful and convincingly authoritarian as we once assumed.[16] Philip Greven's long-lived patriarchs in Andover and Kenneth Lockridge's "Christian Utopian Closed Corporate Community" in Dedham, Massachusetts, may have been exceptions rather than the rule in a region rent by religious schism, Indian warfare and captivity, and unruly families. As Susan Juster and Ann Little have shown, religious and political turmoil were deeply gendered phenomena. Lisa Wilson's portrait of elite New England men in *Ye Heart of a Man* demonstrates that they believed themselves powerless in the face of an indifferent or openly anti-authoritarian culture.[17]

In sum, gender is one area in which sharp regional differences seem to disappear, despite our realization of how large were the demographic differences between regions. In all parts of early America, for example, governments recognized that unbalanced sex ratios constrained both settlement and "improvement." Nevertheless, their efforts to create real incentives to get women to emigrate were weak and underfunded. Most importantly, British and French women did not respond to such exhortations. After all, Moll Flanders did not come willingly to America but was transported there as a convicted felon. We know much less about free migration than we do about unfree migration, but we would be greatly surprised if studies of female free migration show that sizeable numbers of unattached free women willingly paid for their trip across the ocean. Even among unfree migrants who generally made a choice to accept indentureship, the percentage of female indentured servants coming from Britain or France to the Americas was under 10 percent.[18] If migration had been entirely composed of free migrants, then the percentage of women in early America would have been miniscule.[19]

In order to look more closely at the operation of gender in the movement of women to America, we will look at three case studies of specific female migrations to British America. Our first case study, derived from a survey of indentureship records to early America, takes us to the earliest years in the first permanent English colonies.[20] The settlements created by the first migrants in Jamestown or Barbados looked more like a military encampment, or a prison, than any convincing replica of English rural society. However, the fledgling literature on masculinity in early America has focused on the importance of marriage and family relationships to male self- and social identity.[21] This is an incomplete view, given the homosocial nature of the majority of seventeenth-century migration and labor, European and African. Although obtaining more European women for colonial settlement became a matter of great interest to early investors and leaders of settlements from the West Indies to Quebec, further research and analysis of these early all-male settlements will yield interesting new ideas on the nature of male identity and self-fashioning outside of the context of bourgeois marriage. What we do know about these early nearly all-male settlements is that they afforded their denizens a Hobbesian existence: poor, nasty, brutish, and, if they were lucky, mercifully short. The early Virginia colony was a combination of fraternity and prison life, with the added hardships of starvation, malaria, and Indian attacks thrown in for good measure. In addition to asking why the women didn't come, perhaps we should first ask, why did the men bother? Why did thousands upon thousands of young male Britons agree that life or death in the New World was a gamble they were willing to take? We argue that men ventured the risky journey to the Leeward Islands, the Chesapeake Bay, or the Connecticut or St. Lawrence River valleys because they were offered economic incentives. And although these colonies eventually recognized the importance of creating a stable and self-reproducing creole population, they never offered such incentives to women migrants. Furthermore, these societies' want of women did not encourage them to create non-economic incentives to increase female migration.[22]

A gendered history of early America would place the successful transplantation of patriarchy into colonial societies and its adaptations over the ensuing
centuries as absolutely central to understanding family relations, the relation
between men and women, and the relation between masters and slaves. The
dominance of patriarchalism as a social doctrine was unchallenged in the colonial era.[23] It was at its height in the early eighteenth century, when native-born
elites emerged everywhere in British America, except Jamaica and the Leeward
Islands, and when slavery became truly entrenched as a social institution everywhere except New England and New France.[24] What James Horn argues for the
seventeenth century was true for the mid-eighteenth century as well, where men
appear to us to be less anxious, as historians claiming a mid-century crisis in
patriarchy consider them to be, than determined to protect at any cost (even
risking calamitous war with Britain) their vaunted independence and authority —
household authority as much as political authority. We would also emphasize the
flexibility of patriarchal thinking. It was capable of responding to the rise of sentimentality from the mid-eighteenth century onwards as easily as it survived its
own transplantation from England to America in the seventeenth century.[25]

The success of patriarchy, however, as an operational ideology does not
mean that some would-be patriarchs were not anxious. These were not so much
Virginian planters having difficulty with troublesome wives, but were rather
African men moved against their will to American shores, usually to the British
West Indies. The crisis in patriarchy in the eighteenth century was the crisis in
African male authority in the New World. Between 1700 and 1760 an estimated
1,343,000 people went from the Old World to America on British ships, intended
to stay in British colonies. Of this number, 72.3 percent were African, of whom at
least 85 percent went to the British Caribbean and over 45 percent to Jamaica.
The modal migrant was thus an African slave going to Jamaica. Of Africans going
to Jamaica, the dominant ethnic origin overall was Biafran. Biafrans were also the
group of migrants most likely to be female: slave ships from Biafra to Jamaica cus-
tomarily contained proportions of women amounting to between 45 and 50 percent of shipments by the mid-eighteenth century, with a higher percentage
of women retained in Jamaica than men (who were often shipped to Spanish
America).[26]

These women, who comprise our second case study, faced a radically different world in Jamaica to the one they had left behind. One of the biggest cultural
changes was a dramatic shift in the relation of power between black men and
black women. Family organization in the Bight of Biafra, as elsewhere in West
Africa, was highly patriarchal. It was structured around the centrality of kinship
as a means of ordering interpersonal relations.[27] Men, especially powerful men,
who established distinctive family forms based on polygyny and, to a lesser
extent, upon polygamy, dominated it. They exerted at least as much power, probably more, over women in West Africa as European men did over European
women in the same period. To a degree, African patterns of family life were

re-created in the Americas. Certainly, slaves developed over time a form of patri-archal household government that drew on African traditions at the same time as it replicated European patriarchal structures. African influences were stronger where the density of slavery was greatest, notably Lowcountry South Carolina and the West Indies. But, as Philip Morgan argues, "it cannot be claimed that African influence was fundamental to African American familial development."[28] Male power over women was not re-established fully in America, no matter how much black men desired it nor how much white masters tried to impose it upon slaves. Although black men exerted patriarchal dominance over their wives and children — the African world in colonial British America was indubitably not a matriarchal society, contrary to long-established myth — that patriarchal power was severely compromised by the constraints of slavery upon the ability of black men to exercise such patriarchal power. It is noticeable, for instance, that com-mentators were struck by how much more dominant Maroon husbands were over their wives than were slave men.[29]

Of course, black men were not totally powerless. Men maintained a near-monopoly on most skilled positions in the slave economy, save that of household domestics. Their greater opportunities for more varied work meant that men could travel more and have more independence than women. It is hardly surpris-ing, therefore, that the great majority of rebels were men. They had the time and opportunity to plot. The naming practices of families, at least in North America, suggest that it was slave men rather than slave women who named children, although most slave children, in Jamaica in any case, seem to have been named by owners rather than parents.[30] Over time, slave men increased their authority within households, especially in North America, where paternalist doctrine smiled on strong husbands and fathers. To an extent, the seeming equality of black women with black men signified nothing more than the powerlessness that afflicted all slaves. As Lorena Walsh has wryly observed, black women "shared the doubtful advantages of greater equality with black men — usually the equal priv-ilege of working with hoes and axes in the tobacco, corn, and grain fields."[31]

But the realities of slavery restricted male control. They did to a certain extent emasculate black men and give black women some advantages that black men did not have. When women worked alongside men doing the same tasks, it was difficult to see themselves as inferior to men. When men could not exercise the traditional powers of a patriarch over the disposition of property and over how children were to be cared for and educated, when they were not recognized as fathers and were denied a role as providers, then their control over their wives was lessened. The damaging psychological effects of slavery upon men used to exerting power over at least wives and children are still little appreciated. The truly important power dynamic in slave society was between slave masters — less constrained in the colonial period by custom or law over what they could do to their slaves than in the U.S. antebellum period — and between slaves, both male and female. The establishment of black male patriarchal power was always constrained by unrestrained white male authority. White men could punish slave men, women, and children alike with impunity, could interfere in slaves' familial arrangements whenever they wanted to, and could, and did, assault physically and sexually any slave that they chose. The decline in their patriarchal authority may have left black men feeling rudderless and displaced. Of course, both black men and women suffered white assaults all the time. But the dynamics of slavery and the reality that the vast majority of slave owners were male meant the experience of white patriarchal power within slavery was different for men and for women.[32]

Although male slaves had better and more varied work opportunities, black women had a few advantages over men. First, their relative scarcity vis-à-vis black men and their attractiveness as mistresses to white men increased their sexual opportunities (and also, of course, the risk of sexual exploitation). Second, they had considerable economic power within the slave community, being responsible, as in Africa, for marketing agricultural produce and for selling household goods. Women dominated the slave markets that flourished in the Caribbean and probably owned the majority of money that slaves possessed. They supplemented their earnings from market produce with earnings from prostitution. Slave women were sexually vulnerable, meaning that they experienced degradations that most slave men never had to experience, but that vulnerability could sometimes be turned to advantage. Sex could provide money. More importantly, it could also provide possibilities for freedom. A liaison with a white man was the second most common means whereby slaves obtained freedom. The most common was to be the child of such a liaison. Both strategies depended upon the skilful exploitation by a black woman of her sexual and domestic powers, and not a small measure of luck in avoiding cruel masters and viciously exploitative white sexual partners.[33]

In short, a study of the typical female migrant of the eighteenth century — the Biafran woman going to Jamaica — reveals much about the significance of gender within the black Atlantic world. Men were more powerful than women, but some women were able to do things that few black men were able to do, notably, to escape the slave world and become established and occasionally economical prosperous members of free communities.

Our third example leads us to ask about the European women who migrated to the northern colonies not dependent on slave labor. Compared to their numbers in the overall migrant population, they were disproportionately members of religiously oriented immigrant groups: Puritans and other reformed Protestants to New England and Providence Island, Catholics to Maryland, and Quakers and Pietists to Pennsylvania and New Jersey. Thus, religious and ideological concerns drove the only immigration waves that boasted anywhere near an even sex ratio. Other women, for whom economic opportunity would have been key, were clearly disenchanted with the lack of incentives offered them. English common law's tradition of coverture was a major obstacle to female economic advancement.[34]

While their male counterparts were offered headrights, most women who emi-
grated were household dependents (daughters, wives, or servants) and so their
headright went to their household governor. If and when they were widowed,
they were not guaranteed any more than a lifetime share in a third of their family's estate.[35] Historians have overlooked economic incentives — or the lack of
them — as disincentives for European women's migration to the New World.
White men took white women's labors for granted, just as they took as their right
the labor of black men and women. The history of the recruitment and retention
of European women is replete with evidence that colonial proprietors and governors recognized the importance (sooner or later) of achieving an even European
sex ratio for the creation of stable, safe, and profitable colonial societies.
However, they consistently demonstrated a stubborn unwillingness to offer
women real economic incentives or opportunities for social advancement outside of serial marriage and lucky widowhood.[36]

For example, the independent investors of the Virginia Company recognized
that the presence of more women might stabilize the early colony. With wives to
look after them, and children to care for, perhaps the men of Virginia would
make more time for producing the new promising staple crop, tobacco. However,
contrary to inducements to encourage male migration, a 1621 effort to recruit
women for Virginia demonstrates that the focus remained on serving Virginia
men rather than offering enlistees much incentive. The women were clothed,
equipped, and shipped to the New World so as to be useful to their future husbands, but were offered nothing for themselves. It was small wonder that only
fifty-seven English women answered the call, although the company had hoped
to send nearly twice that number.[37] The women resembled many other British
immigrant populations in that they were neither from the top of society nor its
very dregs; they were poor or middling women who were down on their luck and
united by the fact that they had no close family members left alive in Britain.
Their migration to Virginia can hardly be distinguished from that of most indentured servants or even slaves, in that they were to be purchased by their future
husbands. The Virginia Company was apparently concerned about the propriety
of what might rightfully have been deemed a "human auction," and so, in a letter
to the governor and council, they urged that the women be married only to the
best quality of men. Thus, a common theme in the recruitment of English women
for the New World was established very early in the process: women were viewed
more as conveniences for men than as people whose work was valuable and thus
worthy of either pay or dignity. Like servants and slaves, women were expected to
volunteer their labors for the good of their husbands, families, and nation.[38]

French women were even more reluctant migrants than English women
were, and, as in the English colonies, women with strong religious motives were
over-represented in the French female migrant population. Ursuline nuns and
Sisters of the Congregation of Notre Dame, along with other orders, donated crucial female labor and social services in both early Louisiana and the St. Lawrence

River valley.[39] Nevertheless, French colonial governors and officers of the Crown were also concerned about the imbalance in the sex ratio of French immigrants to Canada and Louisiana because there were so few French families. While inter-marriage with Native women was common among the *Coureurs des Bois* and sol-diers in early Mississippi Delta (as compared to the English colonies, where it was almost non-existent), recent scholarship has demonstrated that French colonial elites were not immune to anxieties about race-mixing and the possibilities of French property passing into Indian hands.[40] Canadian officials were especially concerned about the frailty of French family life, as they saw their neighbors to the south in New England rapidly populating expanding colonies. By the end of the seventeenth century, correcting the sex ratio had become a matter of national security, not to mention a surer way to achieve their larger goal, domin-ion over North America. Canadian intendents and governors, with funds from the Crown, attempted to fix the sex ratio through various means: by training Native women in French housewifery, an experiment with dismal results, and by coercing French orphans and hospital inmates to emigrate. French religious and secular authorities were hardly more impressed with this last group of *nouvelles Canadiennes*, whom they unfairly characterized as women of low moral character and "young, vicious, and very ignorant." Apparently, their willingness to migrate to Canada was taken as evidence that they were unfit to be suitable wives and mothers.[41] As in the scholarship on British migration, recent scholarship has debunked this "Moll Flanders" stereotype of the French female migrant, but con-temporaries clung to it. French officials were put off by the frankly ambitious characters of their secular female migrants. Unlike the religious sisters, they did not come to Canada to do volunteer work. Moreover, they wanted to see what the New World could do for them. While this is what European colonizers expected of male migrants, ambition for economic advancement or self-improvement was the mark of unvirtuous, ungovernable women.[42]

New France offered one great advantage to its female migrants: the legal pro-tections of the Custom of Paris, which, contrary to the English common law tra-dition, granted married women equal ownership of the marital estate and guaranteed survivor rights of half of the estate as well. While husbands were still designated the "masters" of the "marriage community," Canadian wives could conduct business on their family's behalf, and their husbands could neither sell property nor attempt to control their families with inheritance law. It was no accident that the women who were most successfully recruited and integrated into *habitant* society were English girls and women taken captive by Indians and redeemed by the French in the imperial wars that dominated the northern fron-tier from 1689 to 1763. Interestingly, the years in which most English girls and women defected to Canada were 1689–1713, the very years in which Canadian offi-cials were experimenting with other means for securing female settlers with European housewifery skills — baking good bread, making sweet butter and cheese, and being able to mend and create garments of cloth and yarn. Since

Indian women had proved so hard to retrain, French officials saw the advantage of purchasing English women from their Indian allies, which served to cement their commercial and military ties to the Indians as well as bringing in crucial female labor. While women were always in the minority of those taken during the border wars (less than a quarter of the captive population), 120 to 145 (or about one-third) of all 392 English female captives remained in Canada, converted to Catholicism, married French men, and thus filled New France's need for European housewifery skills. Given the fact that many of the women that scholars have been able to trace were begged by their families to return to New England and were then disinherited and disowned when they didn't, it is insufficient to suggest that it was simply love that motivated these women to remain in Canada. The strong economic incentives offered by the Custom of Paris show that these women were rational economic actors who saw greater opportunities for economic and social advancement in Canada than in New England.[43] Moving farther south, we can see the opposite experience among Dutch American women in New Netherland caught in the shift from Dutch Roman law to English common law: these women lost economic ground and independence when English common law was instituted by the Duke of York.[44]

Canadians and Dutch women in the Hudson River Valley are interesting if minority examples of women who had an opportunity to live under a different European legal regime. What of the majority of Anglo-American women who remained under English household government and the coverture of common law? The evidence seems clear. Life in British America offered only a marginal existence for most of them, one that grew increasingly difficult to eke out over the course of the colonial period. Anglo-American women's literacy rates improved in the eighteenth century, and most educated girls began to be taught how to write as well as how to read, but these skills were no longer sufficient in the increasingly sophisticated economic and legal world in which they lived. While most eighteenth-century women could probably keep their own account books, as Cornelia Hughes Dayton has argued in *Women before the Bar*, local and regional credit networks excluded both *femes soles* and *femes covertes* and thus stranded them in a primitive barter or cash economy long after the Atlantic World of credit and trade had begun to enrich its lucky investors. Dayton also shows that recourse in both civil and criminal courts became increasingly difficult for women in the eighteenth century, especially for poor or middling women who could not afford the services of a (male) attorney.[45] Emancipated servants found fewer opportunities to escape poverty, and many of them formed a new class of the urban poor in the lying-in hospitals and then on the streets of Boston, Philadelphia, and New York. Colonial recruiters had gone from trying to recruit more women to British America to pleading their factors in England to "send no more women!" As Karin Wulf, Susan Klepp, and Simon Newman have shown, poverty in Philadelphia was increasingly that of unmarried women and their children. Furthermore, as Elaine Forman Crane and Lisa Norling have demonstrated, in communities where women were in the majority as they were in New England's seaport cities, they were unable to leverage their work into real money and influence. These cities relied overwhelmingly on Anglo-American women's labor while men were out to sea with the merchant marine and on whaling expeditions, yet the real money and influence remained in the hands of the male administrators of whaling companies and big investors.[46]

By putting gender front and center of our view of colonial history, we can see that patriarchalism and its assumption that African and female labor should be donated to the colonial effort were central to the English colonial project. We can also see that it wasn't just a simple need for labor, but rather a need for women's labor, that vexed colonial development. The lack of women undoubtedly contributed to the miseries and instability of early colonial societies. Although colonial authorities recognized the problem, they were unwilling to respond rationally by offering economic incentives to European women. Finally, this reconsideration of gender and its role in colonial immigration patterns and early American society suggests that we might see the origins of American slavery not in climate or in patterns of regional development, but rather in England's failures to attract sufficient voluntary female migrants to America. Our modal (unfree) migrant, the eighteenth-century Biafran woman, illustrates our argument that women's labor was desperately needed and, at the same time, outrageously exploited. Because too many European women refused to give their labor to colonial America, colonial men stole the labor of African men and women.

NOTES

1. Daniel Defoe, *The Fortunes and Misfortunes of the Famous Moll Flanders* . . . (London, 1722); idem, *Robinson Crusoe* (London, 1719).

2. For typical examples in important syntheses, see Perry Miller, *The New England Mind: From Colony to Province* (Cambridge, Mass.: Harvard University Press, 1953); idem, *The New England Mind: The Seventeenth Century* (Cambridge, Mass.: Harvard University Press, 1954); Edmund S. Morgan, *American Slavery, American Freedom: The Ordeal of Colonial Virginia* (New York: W. W. Norton and Co., 1975); Richard White, *The Middle Ground: Indians, Empires, and Republics in the Great Lakes Region, 1650–1815* (New York and Cambridge: Cambridge University Press, 1991); Ira Berlin, *Many Thousands Gone: The First Two Centuries of Slavery in America* (Cambridge, Mass.: Harvard University Press, 1998); Alan Taylor, *American Colonies: The Settling of North America* (New York: Viking, 2001). Nevertheless, a bold statement such as this requires a footnote detailing the exceptions to the rule. Four historiographical essays on gender in early America are Linda Kerber, "Separate Spheres, Female Worlds, Woman's Place: The Rhetoric of Women's History," *Journal of American History* 75, no. 1 (1988): 9–39; Kathleen M. Brown, "Brave New Worlds: Women's and Gender History," *William and Mary Quarterly*, 3rd ser., 50, no. 2 (1993): 311–327; idem, "Beyond the Great Debates: Gender and Race," *Reviews in American History* 26, no. 1 (1998): 96–123; and Sarah M. S. Pearsall, "Gender," in *The British Atlantic World, 1500–1800*, ed. David Armitage and Michael J. Braddick (New York: Palgrave Macmillan, 2002), 113–132.

3. Joan Scott, "Gender: A Useful Category of Historical Analysis," *American Historical Review* 91, no. 5 (1986): 1053–1075.

4. *In Search of Early America* (Williamsburg, Va.: Institute for Early American History and Culture, 1993), 208. The women's history article they republished is Lois G. Carr and Lorena S. Walsh, "The Planter's Wife: The Experience of White Women in Seventeenth-Century Maryland," *William and Mary Quarterly*, 3rd ser., 34, no. 3 (1974): 542–571.

5. Carol Shammas, "Anglo-American Household Government in Comparative Perspective," *William and Mary Quarterly*, 3rd ser., 52, no. 1 (1995): 104–144; idem, *A History of Household Government in America* (Charlottesville: University of Virginia Press, 2002). The journal has paid more attention to sexualities; see the special issue devoted to sexuality: 3rd ser., 60, no. 1 (2003): 3–206.

6. Mary Beth Norton, *Founding Mothers and Fathers: Gendered Power and the Forming of American Society* (New York: Alfred A. Knopf, 1996).

7. Kathleen Brown, *Good Wives, Nasty Wenches, and Anxious Patriarchs: Gender, Race, and Power in Colonial Virginia* (Chapel Hill: University of North Carolina Press, 1996). Other important works include Cornelia H. Dayton, *Women before the Bar: Gender, Law, and Society in Connecticut*, 1639–1789 (Chapel Hill: University of North Carolina Press, 1995); Laurel Thatcher Ulrich, *Good Wives: Image and Reality in the Lives of Women in Northern New England*, 1650–1750 (New York: Oxford University Press, 1980); Kirsten Fischer, *Suspect Relations: Sex, Race, and Resistance in Colonial North Carolina* (Ithaca, N.Y.: Cornell University Press, 2002); and Susan Sleeper-Smith, *Indian Women and French Men: Rethinking Cultural Encounter in the Western Great Lakes* (Amherst: University of Massachusetts Press, 2001).

8. There have been few studies of masculinity in colonial America. For New England, see Lisa Wilson, *Ye Heart of a Man: The Domestic Life of Men in Colonial New England* (New Haven: Yale University Press, 1999); and Ann Lombard, *Making Manhood: Growing up Male in Colonial New England* (Cambridge, Mass.: Harvard University Press, 2003). For Virginia, see Kenneth A. Lockridge, *On the Sources of Patriarchal Rage: The Commonplace Books of William Byrd and Thomas Jefferson and the Gendering of Power in the Eighteenth Century* (New York: New York University Press, 1992).

9. With the exception of Jennifer Morgan, *Laboring Women: Reproduction and Gender in New World Slavery* (Philadelphia: University of Pennsylvania Press, 2004), the literature on migration to the Americas is large but seldom deals with women specifically. See Marilyn C. Baseler, *"Asylum for Mankind": America*, 1607–1800 (Ithaca, N.Y.: Cornell University Press, 1998); Alison F. Games, *Migration and the Origins of the English Atlantic World* (Cambridge, Mass.: Harvard University Press, 1999); Nicholas Canny, "English Migration into and across the Atlantic during the Seventeenth Century," in *Europeans on the Move: Studies on European Migration*, 1500–1800, ed. Nicholas Canny (New York: Oxford University Press, 1994), 39–75; and Virginia DeJohn Anderson, *New England's Generation: The Great Migration and the Formation of Society and Culture in the Seventeenth Century* (Cambridge: Cambridge University Press, 1991).

10. For female emigration in general, see David Eltis, *The Rise of African Slavery in the Americas* (Cambridge: Cambridge University Press, 2000), 95–100. For New England, see Gloria L. Main, *Peoples of a Spacious Land: Families and Cultures in Colonial New England* (Cambridge, Mass.: Harvard University Press, 2001), 27–37. For the Chesapeake, see Russell R. Menard, "British Migration to the Chesapeake Colonies in the Seventeenth Century," in *Colonial Chesapeake Society*, ed. Philip D. Morgan, Jean B. Russo, and Lois Green Carr (Chapel Hill: University of North Carolina Press, 1988), 99–132.

11. Ramón A. Gutiérrez, *When Jesus Came, the Corn Mothers Went Away: Marriage, Sexuality, and Power in New Mexico, 1500–1846* (Stanford, Calif.: Stanford University Press, 1991); James F. Brooks, *Captives and Cousins: Slavery, Kinship, and Community in the Southwest Borderlands* (Chapel Hill: University of North Carolina Press, 2002); David Eltis and Stanley L. Engerman, "Was the Slave Trade Dominated by Men?" *Journal of Interdisciplinary History* 23, no. 2 (1992): 237–257; Eltis, *Rise of African Slavery*, 85–113; Farley Grubb, "Servant Auction Records and Immigration into the Delaware Valley, 1745–1831," *Proceedings of the American Philosophical Society* 133 (1989): 154–169.

12. Bridget Hill, *Women, Work, and Sexual Politics in Eighteenth-Century England* (Oxford: Blackwell, 1989), ch. 5. Hill argues in *Women Alone: Spinsters in England, 1660–1850* (New Haven: Yale University Press, 2001), ch. 2, that by the mid-eighteenth century, the need for agricultural labor had declined, and by the end of the century it came to be considered too coarsening for single women, who were urged either to marry or enter domestic service. On women's labor in America, see Carr and Walsh, "The Planter's Wife"; and Laurel Thatcher Ulrich, "Martha Ballard and Her Girls: Women's Work in Eighteenth-Century Maine," in *Work and Labor in Early America,* ed. Stephen Innes (Chapel Hill: University of North Carolina Press, 1998), 70–105.

13. No work deals with this topic explicitly. For useful surveys of the situation of women in seventeenth-century England, see Anthony Fletcher, *Gender, Sex, and Subordination in England, 1500–1800* (New Haven: Yale University Press, 1995); and Amy Louise Erickson, *Women and Property in Early Modern England* (London: Routledge, 1993). For Ireland, see Margaret MacCurtain and Mary O'Dowd, eds., *Women in Early Modern Ireland* (Edinburgh: Edinburgh University Press, 1991). For evidence of the overwhelming dominance of white men in the composition of population in the first years of the Jamestown settlement, see Virginia Bernhard, "'Men, Women, and Children at Jamestown': Population and Gender in Early Virginia, 1607–1610" *Journal of Southern History* 58, no. 4 (1992): 599–618.

14. Edmund S. Morgan, *American Slavery, American Freedom;* Richard S. Dunn, *Sugar and Slaves: The Rise of the Planter Class in the English West Indies* (Chapel Hill: University of North Carolina Press, 1972).

15. See James R. Perry, *The Formation of a Society on Virginia's Eastern Shore, 1615–1655* (Chapel Hill: University of North Carolina Press, 1990); and James Horn, *Adapting to a New World: English Society in the Seventeenth-Century Chesapeake* (Chapel Hill: University of North Carolina Press, 1994). For Barbados see Larry Gragg, *Englishmen Transplanted: The English Colonization of Barbados, 1627–1660* (Oxford: Oxford University Press, 2003). Bailyn's most recent formulation of the savagery of the early Atlantic World is in Bernard Bailyn, *Atlantic History: Concept and Contours* (Cambridge, Mass.: Harvard University Press, 2005), quotation, 63–64.

16. Anderson, *New England's Generation*; Norton, *Founding Mothers and Fathers*. For demographic patterns in early New England, see Main, *Peoples of a Spacious Land.*

17. Philip J. Greven Jr., *Four Generations: Population, Land, and Family in Colonial Andover, Massachusetts* (Ithaca, N.Y.: Cornell University Press, 1970); Kenneth A. Lockridge, *A New England Town the First Hundred Years: Dedham, Massachusetts, 1636–1736* (New York: W. W. Norton, 1970), quotation, 16; Ann M. Little, *Abraham in Arms: War and Gender in Colonial New England* (Philadelphia: University of Pennsylvania Press, 2006); Susan Juster, *Disorderly Women: Sexual Politics and Evangelicalism in Revolutionary New England* (Ithaca, N.Y.: Cornell University Press, 1994); Wilson, *Ye Heart of a Man.*

18. Ida Altman and James Horn, eds., *"To Make America": European Immigration in the Early Modern Period* (Berkeley: University of California Press, 1991).

19. For indentured servant migration to America and the West Indies, see David Galenson, *White Servitude in Colonial America: An Economic Analysis* (Cambridge: Cambridge University Press, 1981). For convicts, see A. Roger Ekirch, *Bound for America: The Transportation of British Convicts to the Colonies, 1718–1775* (New York: Oxford University Press, 1987).

20. Transcription of indentures to British America can be found in Peter Wilson Coldham, *The Complete Book of Emigrants, 1607–1776*, 4 vols. (Baltimore, Md.: Genealogical Pub. Co., 1987–1993).

21. Wilson, *Ye Heart of a Man;* Lombard, *Making Manhood;* Ann M. Little, "Men on Top? The Farmer, the Minister, and Marriage in Early New England," *Pennsylvania History* 64 (Special Supplemental Issue, 1997); Little, " 'Shee would bump his mouldy britch': Authority, Masculinity, and the Harried Husbands of New Haven Colony, 1638–1670," in *Lethal Imagination: Violence and Brutality in American History,* ed. Michael Bellesiles (New York: New York University Press, 1999), 43–68.

22. Leslie Choquette, "Recruitment of French Emigrants to Canada, 1600–1700," in *To Make America*, ed. Altman and Horn, 131–171; Games, *Migration and the Origins of the Atlantic World;* Leslie Choquette, "French and British Emigration to the North American Colonies: A Comparative View," in *New England/New France,* 1600–1850, ed. Peter Benes (Boston: Boston University, 1992), 49–59; Horn, *Adapting to a New World;* Anderson, *New England's Generation;* and Menard, "British Migration to the Chesapeake Colonies in the Seventeenth Century."

23. Philip Morgan, *Slave Counterpoint: Black Culture in the Eighteenth-Century Chesapeake and Lowcountry* (Chapel Hill: University of North Carolina Press, 1998), 273–296; Brown, *Good Wives,* 322–323; Anthony S. Parent Jr., *Foul Means: The Formation of a Slave Society in Virginia,* 1660–1740 (Chapel Hill: University of North Carolina Press, 2003), 197–235. For a good theoretical overview, see Shammas, *A History of Household Government in America.*

24. For a comparison of eighteenth-century elites, see Trevor Burnard, *Creole Gentlemen: The Maryland Elite,* 1691–1776 (New York: Routledge, 2002), 237–264.

25. Horn, *Adapting to a New World,* 429; Sarah M. S. Pearsall, " 'The Late Flagrant Instance of Depravity in My Family': The Story of an Anglo-Jamaican Cuckold," *William and Mary Quarterly,* 3rd ser., 60, no. 3 (2003): 549–582. For powerful arguments regarding the anxiety of eighteenth-century Virginia planters, see Brown, *Good Wives,* Lockridge, *On the Sources of Patriarchal Rage,* and Rhys Isaac, *Landon Carter's Uneasy Kingdom* (Oxford: Oxford University Press, 2004).

26. David Eltis, "The Volume and Structure of the Transatlantic Slave Trade: A Reassessment," *William and Mary Quarterly* 58, no. 1 (2001): 43–46; G. Ugo Nwokeji, "African Concepts of Gender and the Slave Traffic," *William and Mary Quarterly* 58, no. 1 (2001): 47–67. Data on the composition of African emigrants to Jamaica can be found in David Eltis, David Richardson, Stephen D. Behrendt, and Herbert S. Klein, *The Trans-Atlantic Slave Trade: A Database on CD-ROM* (Cambridge: Cambridge University Press, 1999).

27. Paul Lovejoy, *Transformations in Slavery: A History of Slavery in Africa* (Cambridge and New York: Cambridge University Press, 2000).

28. P. Morgan, *Slave Counterpoint,* 555.

29. See Bryan Edwards, *The History, Civil and Commercial, of the British Colonies in the West Indies,* 2 vols. (London: John Stockdale, 1794). See also Michael Mullin, *Africa in America: Slave Acculturation and Resistance in the American South and the British Caribbean, 1736–1831* (Urbana: University of Illinois Press, 1992).

30. Trevor Burnard, "Slave Naming Patterns: Onomastics and the Taxonomy of Race in Eighteenth-Century Jamaica," *Journal of Interdisciplinary History* 31, no. 3 (2001): 325–346.

31. Lorena S. Walsh, "The Experiences and Status of Women in the Chesapeake, 1750–1775," in *The Web of Southern Social Relations: Women, Family, and Education,* ed. Walter J. Fraser Jr. et al. (Athens: University of Georgia Press, 1985), 13.

32. For gender and slavery, see Hilary McD. Beckles, *Centering Women: Gender Discourses in Caribbean Slave Society* (Kingston, Jamaica: Ian Randle Publishers, 1999); Bernard Moitt, *Women and Slavery in the French Antilles, 1635–1838* (Bloomington: Indiana University Press, 2001); Barbara Bush, *Slave Women in Caribbean Society* (Bloomington: Indiana University Press, 1990); and J. Morgan, *Laboring Women.*

33. See Barbara Bush, "White 'Ladies,' Coloured 'Favourites,' and Black 'Wenches': Some Considerations of Sex, Race, and Class Factors in Social Relations in White Creole Society in the British Caribbean," *Slavery and Abolition* 2, no. 2 (1981): 245–262; and Trevor Burnard, *Mastery, Tyranny, and Desire: The Anglo-Jamaican World of Thomas Thistlewood and His Slaves* (Chapel Hill: University of North Carolina Press, 2004).

34. See Susan Staves, *Married Women's Separate Property in England, 1660–1833* (Cambridge, Mass.: Harvard University Press, 1990), 199–205; and Erickson, *Women and Property in Early Modern England.*

35. Linda Sturtz, *Within Her Power: Propertied Women in Colonial Virginia* (New York: Routledge, 2002).

36. Dayton, *Women before the Bar;* Carr and Walsh, "The Planter's Wife;" Deborah A. Rosen, *Courts and Commerce: Gender, Law, and the Market Economy in Colonial New York* (Columbus: Ohio State University Press, 1997); Joan R. Gundersen and Gwen Victor Gampel, "Married Women's Legal Status in Eighteenth-Century New York and Virginia," *William and Mary Quarterly*, 3rd ser., 39, no. 1 (1982): 114–134. For a more positive view, see Linda E. Speth, " 'More than Her Thirds': Wives and Widows in Colonial Virginia," in *Women, Family, and Community in Colonial America: Two Perspectives,* by Linda E. Speth and Alison Duncan Hirsch (New York: Institute for Research in History and the Haworth Press, 1983); and Joan M. Jensen, *Loosening the Bonds: Mid-Atlantic Farm Women, 1750–1850* (New Haven: Yale University Press, 1986).

37. David Ransome, "Wives for Virginia," *William and Mary Quarterly*, 3rd ser., 48, no. 1 (1991): 3–18. See also Suzanne Lebsock, *"A Share of Honour": Virginia Women, 1600–1945* (Richmond, Va.: The Project, 1984), 18.

38. Lebsock, *"A Share of Honour,"* 17.

39. Peter Moogk, "Manon's Fellow Exiles: Emigration from France to North America before 1763," in *Europeans on the Move,* ed. Canny, 236–260; Leslie Choquette, " 'Ces Amazones du Grand Dieu': Women and Mission in Seventeenth-Century Canada," *French Historical Studies* 17, no. 3 (1992): 627–655; Natalie Zemon Davis, "Marie de l'Incarnation: New Worlds," in *Women on the Margins: Three Seventeenth-Century Lives* (Cambridge, Mass.: Harvard University Press, 1995), 63–139; Patricia Simpson, *Marguerite Bourgeoys and Montreal, 1640–1665* (Montreal: McGill-Queen's University Press, 1997); and Emily Clark, " 'By All the Conduct of their Lives': A Laywoman's Confraternity in New Orleans, 1730–1744," *William and Mary Quarterly*, 3rd ser., 54, no. 4 (1997): 769–794.

40. On French men's intermarriage with Indian women, see Sleeper-Smith, *Indian Women and French Men.* On the anxieties of French officials concerning intermarriage, see Jennifer M. Spear, " 'They Need Wives': *Métissage* and the Regulation of Sexuality in French Louisiana, 1699–1730," in *Sex, Love, Race: Crossing Boundaries in North American History,* ed. Martha Elizabeth Hodes (New York: New York University Press, 1999), 35–59.

41. Lettre de M. de Meulles, intendant en Canada, Quebec, November 12, 1684; Lettre de M. de Denonville, Gouverneur general de Canada, Quebec, May 8, 1686, both in the Parkman Papers I: 197–98 and 346 (translation by Annette H. Tomarken), Massachusetts Historical Society, Boston, Mass. See also Little, *Abraham in Arms,* ch. 4.

42. Jan (Janet) Noel, "Les Femmes Favorisées," in *Rethinking Canada: The Promise of Women's History,* 3rd ed., ed. Veronica Strong-Boag and Anita Clair Fellman (Oxford: Oxford University Press, 1997); Noel, *Women in New France* (Ottawa: Canadian Historical Association, 1998).

43. Little, *Abraham in Arms,* ch. 4; and Alden T. Vaughan and Daniel K. Richter, "Crossing the Cultural Divide: Indians and New Englanders, 1605–1763," *American Antiquarian Society Proceedings* 90 (Apr. 16, 1980): 23–99.

44. Linda Briggs Biemer, *Women and Property in Colonial New York: The Transition from Dutch to English Law,* 1643–1727 (Ann Arbor, Mich.: UMI Research Press, 1983).

45. Dayton, *Women before the Bar,* 85, 88.

46. Elaine Forman Crane, *Ebb Tide in New England: Women, Seaports, and Social Change,* 1630–1800 (Boston: Northeastern University Press, 1998); Lisa Norling, *Captain Ahab Had a Wife: New England Women and the Whalefishery,* 1720–1870 (Chapel Hill: University of North Carolina Press, 2000); Sharon Salinger, "Send No More Women: Female Servants in Eighteenth-Century Philadelphia," *Pennsylvania Magazine of History and Biography* 107, no. 1 (1983): 29–48; Simon P. Newman, *Embodied History: The Lives of the Poor in Early Philadelphia* (Philadelphia: University of Pennsylvania Press, 2003), ch. 1; Karin Wulf, *Not All Wives: Women of Colonial Philadelphia* (Ithaca, N.Y.: Cornell University Press, 2000), ch. 5; Billy G. Smith, *Down and Out in Early America* (University Park: Pennsylvania State University Press, 2004), especially the essays by Susan E. Klepp, "Malthusian Miseries and the Working Poor in Philadelphia, 1780–1830: Gender and Infant Mortality," 63–92, and Wulf, "Gender and the Political Economy of Poor Relief in Philadelphia," 163–188.

2

"Your Women Are of No Small Consequence"

Native American Women, Gender, and Early American History

GAIL D. MACLEITCH

In May 1756, at the outset of the French and Indian War, a delegation of Iroquois met with British imperial agent Sir William Johnson. Among them were two Seneca women who came with their male counterparts to discuss matters of war. Their male speaker reminded Johnson that it was customary for Iroquois women to participate in the political affairs of their community. He explained, "As women have a great influence on our young Warriors, I must desire that the women now present in particular may be acquainted with what news you may have." Keen to secure Iroquois allegiance, Johnson assured them, "I am sensible your Women are of no small consequence . . . and I shall be always disposed to consult & inform them."[1] This was not the first nor the last time that Iroquois women made their presence and importance known to Johnson. Throughout the war they attended councils, advised on issues related to warriors and captives, traded goods at forts, and served as spies, messengers, and interpreters. Johnson's own wife, Molly Brant, was a Mohawk woman who assisted his diplomacy. As British need for Iroquois military and political support lessened, however, so too did their willingness to accommodate Iroquois gender norms. Johnson's personal belief that politics was a masculine domain made him increasingly reluctant to tolerate female political participation. A year after the British defeat of New France, Johnson sent word for women not to attend an Anglo-Iroquois conference. Contradicting his earlier statement, he explained that he "really could not Discover any Necessity" for their presence.[2]

Cultural exchanges between women of the Iroquois Confederacy and a British imperial official illuminate the presence and importance of Native women and gender in early American history. Iroquois women, like Native women throughout the colonies, participated in the construction of Anglo-Indian alliances. Their involvement in diplomacy and trade and their sexual unions with white men helped mediate exchanges and strengthen ties between

Indian and colonial worlds. Iroquois women's interactions with William Johnson also reveal much about the presence and importance of gender as an organizing principle in colonial America. When Euro-American and Native gender systems came into contact the result was either negotiation or conflict. That the Iroquois felt a need to justify the inclusion of women at meetings with the British suggests their awareness of opposing gender constructs. Johnson, employed by the Crown to maintain an alliance with the Iroquois, acquiesced to their gendered practices. Putting aside his own patriarchal political etiquette, Johnson initially welcomed female political participation. However, he forced them to accommodate to English norms once Iroquois political and economic clout began to wane. The changing geopolitical order in North America pressured Native peoples to reformulate gender identities. The history of Native American women and gender is a complex story and one that is "of no small consequence" in enriching our understanding of early America.

The historical writing of Native American women has changed substantially over the last three decades. In place of crude images of squaw drudges and Indian princesses that once dominated the literature, a rich body of articles and a handful of book-length studies document varied Native women's experiences across cultures and time.[3] The following chapter reviews trends in the literature of Native women in the colonial era, principally in the eastern colonies. First it examines the issue of human agency. Historians have rejected the once popular declension model, which emphasized the uniform decline of women's power as a consequence of contact. They focus instead on the myriad of ways Indian women ingeniously resisted and adapted to colonization. This literature has many positive traits, but in their quest to find agency scholars sometimes lose sight of the broader material forces determining the historical context in which women lived. The second section examines the impact of gender studies on Native women's history. In particular, historians have explored how ideas about gender informed Indian and European perceptions of one another and the ways they interacted. Acknowledging gender as a historical force that influenced colonial encounters is a fruitful exercise, but scholars must remain mindful that while ideas about gender shaped people's interactions, larger historical forces shaped ideas about gender. The final section considers the place of Native women and gender in early American history. There is a danger of Native women's history becoming relegated into an "exotic" subtopic, when instead it must be integrated into comprehensive historical narratives. Adopting a theoretical framework that remains sensitive to the dialetic between broader material forces and forms of cultural construction will produce inclusive narratives.

Native Women and Human Agency

A key issue confronting scholars who write about Native women is how much human agency to give their subject. Whether consciously or not, historians choose where to place emphasis: on the broader material forces (capitalism and colonization) that structured the world of Native women and shaped their experience or on the cultural practices and values that women drew upon when they responded to their objective reality. At stake is the issue of power. A historical materialist approach highlighting the material constraints in people's lives de-emphasizes their human agency and can often render them as "victims" of impersonal forces beyond their control. By contrast, the focus on cultural constructionism humanizes history. It demonstrates how groups and individuals acted as partial agents of their own destiny. However, this approach can overstate the degree of power humans exercised by downplaying the influence of larger constraints.[4]

Scholars in the 1970s opted for a women-as-victims model, stressing material forces over human action. Their studies promoted a declension thesis, a narrative structure that accentuated themes of female disempowerment and subjugation. Feminist anthropologists, engaged in a debate over the origins and ubiquity of female subordination, influenced their work.[5] Eleanor Leacock's seminal study argued that universal female subordination was neither inevitable nor natural, but a product of colonization. Employing historical materialist analysis, she maintained that the onset of capitalism disrupted egalitarian relations among Montagnais Indians. The new commercial fur trade devalued women's labor and undercut values of "cooperation, reciprocity, and respect for individual autonomy." The erosion of traditional ideals made the Montagnais susceptible to the patriarchal values of Jesuit missionaries. Women's power declined.[6] Early historical studies chronicled a similar downward trajectory: precontact Native society was generally egalitarian. Europeans brought the twin corrosive influences of the market economy and Christian missionaries, precipitating the subjugation of Indian women. A corollary to the declension thesis was a debate over women's responses. While some scholars highlighted the stubborn, but ultimately unsuccessful resistance of Native women, others stressed their rapid assimilation of European cultural norms. Either way, they de-emphasized human agency.[7]

The declension thesis has now lost much of its appeal as an explanatory model. A new generation of scholars keen to empower their subjects and to provide a more complex analysis of events challenged the narrative of decline. This challenge began, in part, with the emergence of the New Social History in the 1970s, which, motivated by a desire to give voice and agency to the marginalized and ignored, highlighted acts of resistance, adaptation, and persistence. Themes of self-determination were also prompted by a reconceptualization of the frontier explicit in the New Indian literature. Historians replaced the older image of the frontier as a strict racial dividing line driven by European conquest and domination with a newer image of a porous zone of cross-cultural interaction and exchange, dependent on negotiation and mutual accommodation.[8] Indians were no longer simply passive onlookers made by history, but makers of history.

Consequently, studies of Native American women have shifted from explaining the impact of colonization on women to examining women's imaginative responses.[9] Scholars now demonstrate greater sensitivity to cultural diversity and resist totalizing theories which argue for universal patterns.[10] Native women did not react to colonization in the same way. Experiences varied across cultures and depended upon which ethnic group of Europeans they encountered, during which period, and in what context. A positive trend since the 1990s has been the widening geographical scope of studies. Moving away from the Great Lakes and eastern seaboard, scholars now examine the lives of Native women in more diverse regions. In the process these works have uncovered multiple perspectives, demonstrating how Native women confronted different challenges under the French, Spanish, and British empires. Works by Ramón A. Gutiérrez, James F. Brooks, and Juliana Barr, for example, have illuminated the particular experiences of Indian women in the colonial southwest, particularly New Mexico and Texas. They demonstrate that the widespread phenomenon of captive-taking, the institutionalization of Indian slavery, and the pressures exerted by patriarchal Franciscan missionaries created a unique set of conditions for Native women and meant that they may have faced less opportunities and greater threats of violence than, for example, women in the Great Lakes region.[11]

Scholars are also more sensitive to differences *within* specific cultural groups. Despite a tendency in the historical literature to portray Native societies as egalitarian, variables of age, kinship, rank, and ethnicity acted as important categories of distinction and hierarchy. In her study of southern New England Indians, Kathleen Bragdon notes that divisions of status and wealth fragmented the female colonial experience. Some high-ranking women were drawn to Christianity because it offered them "a means of maintaining their status and that of their families," while women of lower status found Christianity to be restrictive.[12] Similarly, David Peterson-del Mar found that the Chinookan Indians of the Pacific Northwest were a status-conscious society, which encouraged women of noble birth to seek alliances with European traders to enhance their wealth and social standing.[13]

Part of the failure of the declension thesis was that it centered on an inappropriate debate about power and status. Insisting that Indian women once had "power" and "status" but lost them as a result of colonization is problematic. These concepts need to be interrogated. Power has multiple manifestations and meanings, since women exercised power in different ways and in different spheres of their existence. Status is not absolute or measurable, rather "social positions are really plural, composed of a number of statuses."[14] Thus women could both gain and lose power and status at the same time. Theda Perdue's book on Cherokee women documented such contradictory patterns. As a consequence of the fur trade, Cherokee women became marginalized in the eighteenth-century village economy. Yet their other traditional roles and responsibilities were augmented precisely because men's hunting and war-making kept them away from villages for extended periods.[15] Scholars now construct more complex narratives of Native women's history, contending that it was less a straightforward story of decline than it was "a multilayered, shifting narrative." They also resist simple dichotomies of assimilation versus resistance, asserting instead that Indian women were involved in a "complicated cycle of cultural adaptation, change, and persistence."[16]

New literature has replaced narratives of decline with accounts of human agency. Women responded to colonization by taking advantage of the socioeconomic changes transforming North America. In the early stages of colonization women's position did not deteriorate but actually improved. Christianity served as a vehicle for female empowerment as many Iroquois women and those inhabiting the western Great Lakes converted to this religion because it heightened their autonomy and social status. Rather than being subjugated by patriarchal ideology, women selectively appropriated Christianity in ways that brought meaning and fulfillment to their lives. Catholic female iconography included female saints and the Virgin Mary, providing a positive message for Native women. Indeed, when Jesuit priests were temporarily removed from New France, women practiced their own form of "frontier Catholicism."[17] Marriage to European men, particularly traders, also demonstrates women's agency. It increased their access to European trade goods and enlarged their personal social standing. Kinship networks enabled women to temper the pressure of market forces. By transforming foreign traders into husbands, "exchange remained embedded in social relationships" dependent on notions of reciprocity, generosity, and friendship.[18]

Women's participation in the market economy actually strengthened their independence and promoted their parity with Indian men. Although the male-dominated fur trade structured economic relations between Indians and Europeans in most of the colonies, Native women still engaged in the commercial production and exchange of goods. They avoided subordination to Indian men because they produced their own saleable wares. Bruce M. White's article on the Ojibwa argues that opening economic relations with Europeans "provided more rather than fewer opportunities for men *and* women." Women found their own niche supplying food and commodities to barter.[19] Early nineteenth-century Creek women produced nut oil and cotton and engaged in prostitution to earn a livelihood. Claudio Saunt contends, "The marketplace freed them from their reliance on men and even gave them power over Creek warriors, whose profits in the deerskin trade were beginning to decline."[20] Lucy Murphy examines the economic opportunities Native women enjoyed in the western Great Lakes mining industry, while Theda Perdue details how spinning and weaving provided new cash-earning opportunities for Cherokee women.[21]

However, the focus on self-determination can also produce a distorted view of history. Historians' periodization exaggerates female agency. The first thirty years of contact with Europeans provided certain gains and opportunities for women, but a different picture emerges when their experiences are considered over a longer time frame. As well as opportunity and empowerment, the story was also one of limitation and loss. The evolution of a pervasive racist ideology negated whatever benefits marriage with white men offered Indian women. Interracial unions became less acceptable and were as likely to be marked by violence and abuse as by mutual respect.[22]

The parochial focus of studies also exaggerates human agency by examining specific Indian communities in isolation from the colonial, imperial, and, indeed, transatlantic worlds. Considering Native women as a people caught up in a larger historical process of imperial colonization and market integration makes it apparent that forces beyond their control partially conditioned their lives. Women's involvement in a market economy is a case in point. That Indian women maintained "equality" with Indian men by accessing a commercial marketplace may be true, but the value of this form of equality is questionable when Native peoples as a whole experienced growing inequality with Europeans. The absorption of their land, labor, and resources into a burgeoning mercantile-capitalist economy made many dependent on European goods and cash as a commodity to obtain these goods and eroded Indian self-sufficiency. Women resourcefully adopted new economic roles in petty commodity production, but they adopted innovative roles because they had to. Hence, it is problematic to describe their new commercial behavior solely in terms of empowerment and opportunity. Women made choices over how best to respond, but they made those choices from a limited range of options.

Again we need to remain sensitive to the specific geopolitical context in which these women lived as there was a considerable range of experience. In the early nineteenth century the commercial desire for land to cultivate cotton superseded an economic interest in animal skins in the American Southeast. By contrast the Great Lakes and Northwest Pacific fur trade had greater longevity. Hence women faced a different set of economic opportunities and restrictions in these distinct regions of the United States, which in turn made for dissimilar behaviors and responses.

Illustrating constraints in women's lives is not an attempt to revert back to an Indian-as-victim model, but rather presents a more realistic account of their histories. The era of European colonization was an extremely difficult time for Amerindians, and any examination of female agency needs to be tempered by a consideration of major structural changes. There is a case to be made for revisiting a historical materialist approach. Scholars shy away from this model because they believe it renders humans devoid of power or equate it with economic determinism. Historical materialism analyzes the material world and people's relationship to the means of production. Crudely put, in a society where there is equal access to the means of production — land, resources, tools, and skills — individuals enjoy economic independence and egalitarian social relations. As material conditions shift, however, some people are denied access to the means of production, economic autonomy diminishes, and new social relations based on inequality and hierarchy emerge.

Historical materialism does not claim that people are mere products or prisoners of their material world; they mediate material forces through culturally constructed ideologies and modes of behavior in order to make sense of their material existence. Native peoples did not experience the immediate and radical overhaul of their economic and cultural systems as a consequence of contact with Europeans. Instead, they influenced how change occurred. They "Indianized" European trade goods to enrich their own culture and demanded that trade be embedded in their cultural practice of gift-giving. This constant exchange taking place between the realm of material reality and cultural construction needs to be examined. As Patricia Albers contends "historical materialist methodology is not unidirectional but dialectical." It examines "the socially and ideologically mediated articulations of material forces at particular sites of production."[23] Human beings do not just mediate but also create these material forces. By their own volition Indians became participants and consequently co-creators of a transatlantic fur trade. They both shaped and were shaped by mercantile capitalism. Thus a historical materialists approach not only allows for but necessitates a consideration of human activity. Remaining sensitive to the ongoing dialectic between the material and cultural worlds achieves a more nuanced reading of human agency.

Native Women and Gender

The growth of gender studies generated significant development in the historical literature on Native women. Feminist anthropologists in the 1970s articulated the idea that gender is a cultural construct, not a biological fact.[24] Gender ascribes a particular set of attributes, abilities, and responsibilities to each sex. While some differences between men and women are biological, gender refers to all those which are thought to be culturally and historically determined, behavior that is learned rather than inherent.[25] Scholars examine how Native peoples thought about and constructed gender and how this construction differed or compared with European gender systems. They have also used gender as an analytical lens through which to re-examine the past. Consequently, there has been a marked shift away from focusing on women as a category to a study of gender in and of itself.[26]

The study of Native (women's) history illuminates cultural constructions of gender because Native gender systems differed in some respects from European practices. Many historians contend that at the time of contact, Indian gender roles were generally more egalitarian than those in Europe. Reciprocity, rather than hierarchy, structured relations between the sexes: women and men performed different, but equally valued tasks. Furthermore, whereas European society was patriarchal and patrilineal, many Indian societies were matrilineal and matrilocal.[27] The Iroquois, to take but one example, resided in female-headed households and traced descent and identity through the mother's line, which enhanced women's social position. The high premium Native peoples attached to individual autonomy meant that women engaged freely in premarital sex and could dissolve unsatisfactory marriages. Most Native women had a central economic role as horticulturalists. Producing the bulk of their community's diet and controlling the fruits of their labor granted them economic autonomy and social status.[28]

In a number of western Indian societies men and women adopted the identity of the opposite sex without being ostracized. In his study of the New Mexico Pueblo, Gutiérrez notes the presence of the *berdache*, "biological males who had assumed the dress, occupations, mannerisms, and sexual comportment of females as a result of a sacred vision or community selection." Unable to comprehend the existence of a third gender, Spanish officials denounced them as *putos* (male whores) and *sodomitas* (sodomites). In fact the hostile response of Europeans may explain why the figure of the berdache became less visible in the eighteenth century. The phenomenon of the cross-sex individual is a striking example of the cultural construction of gender.[29]

A gendered approach encourages the study of men as well as women. Examining the social construction of "womanhood" in isolation naturalizes the male gender, but the meaning of masculinity is culturally and historically relative and therefore merits attention.[30] The inclusion of men can also enrich our understanding of women's history. After all, women did not live in isolation. Changes in men's cultural identity *as men* affected women's identity *as women*, and vice versa. Shifting gender identities often generated conflict. Saunt investigated complex gender relations among Creek Indians as increased absorption into a market economy and adoption of private property destabilized earlier understandings of gender. Tensions mounted as men found it no longer tenable to maintain their role as warrior-hunters while women's involvement in commercial pursuits reinforced their autonomy. Saunt argues that there was important gender subtext to the Creek Civil War (1813), which warriors used to re-assert older notions of masculinity.[31] His work demonstrates the value of examining women *in relation to* men because their lives were intimately entangled.

The study of gender also illuminates relations between Indians and non-Indians. Using gender as a lens through which to study the encounter experience has yielded interesting results. Kathleen M. Brown contends that scholars need to "conceive of cultural encounters as occurring along gender frontiers." The gendered perceptions of Indians and Europeans affected how they made sense of one another and influenced their interactions. Brown applied the concept of a gender frontier to her own study of contact between the Algonquian Indians of Virginia and early English settlers. On the eve of colonization Englishmen embraced a gender ideology premised on the concept of a "natural" hierarchy, which furnished them with a model with which to conceptualize their relationship to

America and its indigenous people. English settlers "depicted themselves as warriors capable of dominating a feminized population." By gendering their relations with Algonquian men, deeming them "naturally" submissive, Englishmen justified their colonial domination.[32] In a similar way, Juliana Barr asserts the centrality of gender as the "primary idiom of contact" in her study of the seventeenth-century southwest borderlands. As Spanish settlers and Hasinai Indians struggled to communicate over a cultural and linguistic divide, many "latched onto gender in a search for similarity." But divergent attitudes led to misunderstanding and hostility. "Europeans read Hasinai women's expressive gestures and exposed bodies as an invitation to equate offers of food with offers of sex," leading to violent exchanges. Barr demonstrates that gender was critical to the contact period, not peripheral.[33]

Lucy Murphy's study of the western Great Lakes region argues that ideas about gender fundamentally determined the nature of Indian-white interaction. In ethnically mixed fur trading towns peaceful co-existence, high rates of intermarriage, and cultural syncretism characterized relations between Indian, white, and métis inhabitants. The successful negotiation of gender roles was crucial to creating this benign climate. As culturally diverse women and men embraced contrary ideas about appropriate gender roles, particularly in regards to the sexual division of labor, the potential for conflict was great. Yet they negotiated gender roles through "the spirit of creative accommodation." Women assisted this process by teaching, learning, adapting, and mediating different practices. By contrast, interracial hostility and violence characterized lead mining communities in the same region. Murphy contends that "unsuccessful gender relations were central to the discord." There was little opportunity for Indians and whites to find a common ground upon which to cooperate. The gendered attitude of Anglo-American men that mining was "men's work" deterred them from working with Indian women who initially were the principal miners of the region. The gendered belief of Indian men that mining was "women's work" meant that they refused to mine themselves and therefore had little contact with white men. Had Indians and whites worked together, as in the fur trade, "they might have developed lasting patterns of cooperation." Thus Murphy concludes that "women's actions, gender relations, and the negotiation of gender roles were crucial" to successful cross-cultural relations.[34]

The focus on gender has encouraged historians to explore a fuller range of contact arenas. Colonial contests for power did not take place solely in political, economic, and military spheres, but, more importantly, in the intimate domains of kinship, sexuality, and marriage. Ann Marie Plane contends that a battle to define Indian marriage was at the heart of Indian-white relations in colonial New England. As the institution of marriage was infused with patriarchal beliefs about social order and natural hierachy, Puritan ministers were determined to restructure Indian kinship practices. Plane observes, "Marriage, supposedly one of the most intimate of social relationships, in fact often mirrored, encapsulated, and transformed some of the most public struggles of colonial states and societies." Gutiérrez, examining a dissimilar geographical context, likewise explores how "marriage structured inequality." He exposes Franciscan efforts in colonial New Mexico to reshape the sexual and familial behavior of the matrilineal Pueblos. "The friars injected themselves into the control of marriage," he notes, altered the sexual division of labor, and acquired influence over children. As a consequence Pueblo women underwent an "erosion of power." Gutiérrez offers a far more pessimistic depiction of the effects of colonization than Plane. This may be because life under Spanish rule was harsher, or because Gutiérrez wrote his text ten years earlier when declension narratives were more commoplace.[35]

Focusing on gender carries with it potential pitfalls. Historians need to be careful how they make sense of Native constructions of gender, particularly given the problematic nature of primary sources. Most information on Indian culture has been derived from the writings of European men whose cultural biases informed their observations. They frequently commented on the oppression of "squaw drudges" forced to engage in heavy menial labor, but this perception reflected their belief that agriculture was a masculine pursuit unsuitable for women.[36] Understanding Indian conceptions of gender requires scholars to read primary sources with care, to read between the lines, and to be attentive to what is both visible and invisible.[37] It also requires creativity in the types of documents used. Indian creation stories and political discourse, with their elaborate use of kin and gender metaphors, shed light on Indian conceptions of sexual difference.[38]

Scholars also need to be wary of their own cultural predispositions skewing their perceptions. A tendency to vilify "dead white men" and extol the virtues of the oppressed led to an idealization of precontact indigenous society.[39] Historians have begun to address this bias by paying greater attention to sources of inequality within Amerindian society. Some assert that relations between the sexes were not as egalitarian as once thought. In particular, whether a culture was patrilineal or matrilineal made a key difference. Brown notes that among the Algonquians, the empire-building strategies of the male leader Powhatan "intensified the patriarchal tendencies" of Algonquian society. Researchers have also revised older, idealized depictions of women's power in matrilineal societies.[40] The centrality of gender as an organizing principle also needs to be investigated rather than assumed. Gender was clearly an important factor determining an individual's role and status, but so too were age, rank, kinship, and ability.[41] Susan Sleeper-Smith's study of Indian women in the Great Lakes region largely ignored the concept of gender, instead demonstrating how kinship operated as the key determinant of an individual's identity.[42]

A final potential pitfall is the all-too-easy tendency of treating gender as a timeless and static category. Gender constitutes a site of ongoing cultural contestation and change. While it is important to consider how gender acted as a historical force shaping patterns of Indian-white relations, scholars also need to keep in view the historical forces acting upon and reshaping gender. Gender must be historicized. Particular material conditions gave rise to specific gender practices and values. In the mining and fur trade settlements of the western Great Lakes, the economic arrangements of both communities played a major role in determining whether conflicting gender ideologies could be resolved. The fur-trading economy facilitated co-operation and co-existence because whites depended on Indians for furs. The fur trade did not necessitate interracial marriages, but such unions had significant cultural and economic benefits for both parties. By contrast there was little incentive for white men to marry Indian women in the lead mining economy. Whites preferred Indian removal to Indian assistance since it would grant them sole control of the mines. Ideas about gender do not exist in a vacuum but are shaped in large part by the material conditions and needs of a particular historical moment.

Native Women and Early American History

While the historical literature on Native women is richer than ever before, it retains a marginal status, confined to brief passages in textbooks, articles in lesser-known journals, and a small handful of monographs. Scholars now face the challenge to center Indian women within the larger body of historical literature. The stories of Native women's lives need to be woven into the tapestry of early America history. This is no easy task. Colonial historians, never particularly mindful of the contributions of indigenous cultures in general, have been especially neglectful of Native women. In a popular and recently republished textbook on colonial history covering two centuries and 486 pages, there are only two fleeting references to Native women.[43] Furthermore, even though New Indian scholars may have gone a long way to write Indians back into colonial histories, their Indians continue to be predominantly male.[44] The search to find inclusive narratives in which Native women enjoy a prominent role has led scholars to explore new topics, ask new questions, and adopt new theoretical frameworks.

One way to avoid the segregation and marginalization of Native women is to acknowledge the important contribution they made to colonial society. Although seemingly invisible in the primary documents, women were highly visible in early America. They affected the development of the colonies through their interactions with traders, settlers, missionaries, soldiers, and administrators. Women exerted influence through their role as cultural brokers who traveled between cultures, using their knowledge of the customs and language of each to mediate exchanges. A particular branch of this literature focuses on *notable Indian women*. Pocahontas, Molly Brant, Mary Musgrove, Nancy Ward, and Sacagawea all forged links between Indian and colonial societies.[45]

But, because these women were notable and exceptional, their experience and activities cannot be taken as typical. A broader and perhaps more useful literature examines the contribution of ordinary Indian women who served as a nexus between Native and European worlds. One of the principal ways women facilitated exchange was through their role as wives or consorts to Europeans. The topic of *métissage* has received increased scholarly attention in recent years by historians who uncovered "the hidden history of mestizo America." The absence of a rigid racial ideology for much of the colonial era resulted in white men and Indian women forming sexual unions. Through intermarriage women altered the history of colonial America in fundamental ways. Notably they "linked people of different families, communities and ethnic groups" in new multi-ethnic kinship networks.[46] In addition, women literally transformed the makeup of North America by participating in the creation of a new peoples. The *métis*, who identified as a people distinct from Indians and Europeans, constituted a sizeable portion of the colonial population. Their unique position, literally embodying two or more cultures, made them prime candidates to become cultural brokers themselves.[47]

As cultural brokers women promoted economic, diplomatic, and cultural exchanges. The fur trading world of the Great Lakes region would have been radically different, possibly unfeasible without Native American women. Studies illustrate the varied and significant ways women facilitated the trade in furs: preparing skins for sale and providing food to hunters and traders. Their marriages to traders incorporated Europeans into larger kin networks, ensuring that exchange was determined by kinship rules. Europeans viewed Native women as indispensable. An Indian wife granted them access to a family network of potential customers and provided the cultural and linguistic skills necessary to promote the transaction of goods.[48] Native women also participated in the creation and maintenance of political alliances with colonial powers. They served as translators and spies and encouraged male kin to lend military support during colonial wars.[49] Women also united disparate communities through their role as captives. James F. Brooks details the substantial captive exchange economy that connected Indian and Euroamerican societies in the colonial southwest. "The exchange of women through systems of captivity, adoption, and marriage provided European and Native men with mutually understood symbols of power with which to bridge cultural barriers." Brooks estimates that roughly three thousand Indians entered New Mexico between 1700 and 1850 in a form of captivity or servitude, the majority being women. Many of these female captives "found ways to transcend their subordinate status by exercising skills developed during their 'cross-cultural' experience" and were able to pass down their cultural heritage to their métis offspring and provide a permanent link between two worlds.[50]

Focusing on the brokerage role of American Indian women offers one way of incorporating them into broader historical narratives of early American history. Their presence in North America made an undeniable difference to colonial economic practices, political arrangements, and social exchanges. There is, however, a problem with the *contribution approach*, namely, that it is weighted toward a human-agency reading of history. It documents women's power to affect the course of colonial development. This topic merits investigation, but it should not provide the criteria or rationale for how or why Native women are studied. History is not just the investigation of how individuals created the world, but also how the world created them.

Another way to synthesize Native women's history into broader historical narratives is through a *comparative approach*. In the past decade historians have produced monographs or edited collections of essays in which the lives of Indian women are discussed in relation to, or alongside, other female groups.[51] Much of this literature has lacked theoretical precision. Reviewers critiqued Larry D. Eldridge's method of organizing sixteen essays around a "vaguely defined" concept of "freedom" which served as a "weak link." In the absence of a rigorous theoretical framework, comparative studies can become a collection of disconnected discussions about disparate women. Much of the comparative literature has been driven by a desire to map out the "remarkable diversity" of female experience and thereby de-essentialize the category of "woman." By illustrating how region, race, religion, and class fragmented the female experience, scholars can verify the cultural construction of womanhood. But there is a downside to this approach. Carol Berkin's history of colonial women reflected "a commitment to locate women along the axes of race, region, and social class," but reviewers noted that in the process she failed to provide an "overarching interpretation." The drive to document difference can obscure unifying narratives.[52]

While it remains important to acknowledge diversity, there is also much to gain by identifying commonalties. Daniel K. Richter urges historians to look for "unifying themes" that enable them to combine the histories of diverse groups within a single narrative. "A stress on common processes, experiences, and phenomena that *all*, or nearly all groups who struggled for survival and dominance in early America shared, albeit often in different ways," offers a gateway for constructing inclusive histories.[53] Historians must remain sensitive to the particularities of Indian women's experiences, but they also need to situate them within a broader historical landscape. A fundamental common process in the eighteenth century was the rise of mercantile capitalism. As colonial and Amerindian economies became increasingly connected to a transatlantic marketplace, commercial forms of production, exchange, and labor took precedence over subsistence activities. Understanding how "common economic forces" shaped the lives of diverse groups provides a meaningful way of writing a comprehensive history of early America. There is still much work to be done exploring how different cultural groups of women participated in the burgeoning North American economy and how their increased involvement in commercial activities affected their construction of gender identity and relations with men.[54]

The evolving ideological system of the seventeenth and eighteenth centuries constitutes another common force that contoured the lives of early Americans. Both Kathleen Brown and Kirsten Fischer examine how gender and racial ideologies evolved and intersected to affect the lives of Indian, black, and white women in diverse ways. The language of gender and race legitimated hierarchy and oppression, creating a social order that lumped all women together as an inferior sex, but also separated and ranked them according to their racial and class status.[55] Although Indian women do not occupy a major role in either of these studies, Brown's and Fischer's theoretical approach offers an innovative way of producing an inclusive history.

It is not imperative for historians to adopt a comparative approach. Studies that focus exclusively on Native women are still valid and valuable, especially given that we still have so much to learn about them. Yet, historians must acknowledge the larger world in which Native American women lived and the broader historical forces, both material and ideological, that contoured their existence. By doing so, historians can demonstrate that Native women were not peripheral, peculiar, or solitary, literally positioned on the margins of history, but were part of a larger whole. As inhabitants of North America, they were caught up in the same fundamental processes of historical change as other groups. Once this historical context is established, the uniqueness of their experience can be investigated. The study of Native American women is of "no small consequence" because it expands our understanding of early American history: both the diversity of human experience and transformational power of material and ideological forces common in the lives of all colonial Americans.

NOTES

1. "Journal of Sir William Johnson's Indian Transactions, May 1756," in *Documents Relative to the Colonial History of the State of New York*, 15 vols., ed. E. B. O'Callaghan and Bethold Fernow (Albany, N.Y.: Weed, Parsons and Company, 1856–1887), 7:103.

2. "Indian Proceedings, April 21–28, 1762," in *The Papers of Sir William Johnson*, 14 vols., ed. James Sullivan et al. (Albany, N.Y.: University of the State of New York, 1921–1965), 3:707–708, 711–712; Gail D. Danvers, "Gendered Encounters: Warriors, Women, and William Johnson," *Journal of American Studies* 35, no. 2 (2001): 187–202.

3. On stereotypes of Native women, see Rayna Green, "The Pocahontas Perplex: The Image of Indian Women in American Culture," *Massachusetts Review* 16, no. 4 (1975): 698–714; Pauleena M. MacDougall, "Grandmother, Daughter, Princess, Squaw: Native American Female Stereotypes in Historical Perspective," *Maine History* 34, no. 1 (1994): 22–39. For bibliographies on this literature, see "Bibliography; Native American Women," *Journal of Women's History* 4, no. 3 (1993): 235–240; Jo Ann Woodsum, "Gender and Sexuality in Native American Societies: A Bibliography," *American Indian Quarterly* 19, no. 4 (1995): 527–555.

4. For an outline of historical materialism and cultural constructionism, see Ramona Ford, "Native American Women: Changing Statuses, Changing Interpretations," in *Writing the Range: Race, Class, and Culture in the Women's West*, ed. Elizabeth Jameson and Susan Armitage (Norman: University of Oklahoma Press, 1997), 43–44; Patricia C. Alber, "Marxism and Historical Materialism in American Indian History," in *Clearing a Path: Theoretical Approaches to the Past in Native American Studies*, ed. Nancy Shoemaker (New York: Routledge Press, 2000), 107–136.

5. See, for example, Michelle Zimbalist Rosaldo and Louise Lamphere, eds., *Woman, Culture, and Society* (Stanford, Calif.: Stanford University Press, 1974).

6. Eleanor Burke Leacock, "Montagnais Women and the Jesuit Program for Colonization," in *Women and Colonization: Anthropological Perspectives*, ed. Mona Etienne and Leacock (New York: Praeger, 1980), 25–42. See also Leacock, "Women in an Egalitarian Society: The Montagnais-Naskapi of Canada," in idem, *Myths of Male Dominance: Collected Articles on Women Cross-Culturally* (New York: Monthly Review Press, 1981), 31–81.

7. Richard J. Perry, "The Fur Trade and the Status of Women in the Western Subartic," *Ethnohistory* 26, no. 4 (1979): 363–375; Mary C. Wright, "Economic Development and Native American Women in Early Nineteenth Century," *American Quarterly* 33 (1981): 525–536; Karen Anderson, *Chain Her by One Foot: The Subjugation of Women in Seventeenth-Century New France* (London: Routledge, 1991); Jo-Anne Fiske, "Colonization and the Decline of Women's Status: The Tsimshian Case," *Feminist Studies* 17 (1991): 509–535; Carol Devens, *Countering Colonization: Native American Women and the Great Lakes Missions, 1630–1900* (Berkeley: University of California Press, 1992).

8. See, for example, Richard White, *The Middle Ground: Indian, Empires, and Republics in the Great Lakes Region, 1650–1815* (New York: Cambridge University Press, 1991).

9. Tom Hatley, "Cherokee Women Farmers Hold Their Ground," in *Appalachian Frontiers: Settlement, Society, and Development in the Preindustrial Era*, ed. Robert D. Mitchell (Lexington: University of Kentucky, 1991), 37–51; Nancy Shoemaker, "The Rise or Fall of Iroquois Women," *Journal of Women's History* 2, no. 3 (1991): 39–57; David Peterson-del Mar, "Intermarriage and Agency: A Chinookan Case Study," *Ethnohistory* 42, no. 1 (1995): 1–30; Nancy Shoemaker, ed., *Negotiators of Change: Historical Perspectives on Native American Women* (New York: Routledge, 1995); Jean O'Brien, "Divorced from the Land: Accommodation Strategies of Indian Women in Eighteenth-Century New England," in *Gender, Kinship, and Power: A Comparative and Interdisciplinary History*, ed. Mary Jo Maynes et al. (New York: Routledge, 1996), 319–333; Theda Perdue, *Cherokee Women: Gender and Culture Change, 1700–1835* (Lincoln: University of Nebraska Press, 1998); Claudio Saunt, "'Domestick . . . Quiet Being Broke': Gender Conflict among Creek Indians in the Eighteenth Century," in *Contact Points: American Frontiers from the Mohawk Valley to the Mississippi, 1750–1830, ed. Andrew R. L. Cayton and Fredrika J. Teute* (Chapel Hill: University of North Carolina Press, 1998), 151–174; Susan Sleeper-Smith, "Women, Kin, and Catholicism: New Perspectives on the Fur Trade," *Ethnohistory* 47, no. 2 (2000): 423–452. The declension thesis has not totally lost its appeal; see, for example, Michelene E. Peasantubbee, *Choctaw Women in a Chaotic World: The Clash of Cultures in the Colonial Southeast* (Albuquerque: University of New Mexico Press, 2005).

10. For a criticism of "totalizing analysis" see Pauline Turner Strong, "Feminist Theory and the "Invasion of the Heart" in North America," *Ethnohistory* 43, no. 4 (1996): 683–719, esp. 686–687.

11. Ramón Gutiérrez, *When Jesus Came, the Corn Mothers Went Away: Marriage, Sexuality, and Power in New Mexico, 1500–1846* (Stanford, Calif.: Stanford University Press, 1991); James F. Brooks, "'This Evil Extends Especially to the Feminine Sex': Captivity and Identity in New Mexico, 1700–1846," in *Writing the Range*, ed. Jameson and Armitage, 97–121; Juliana Barr, "From Captives to Slaves: Commodifying Indian Women in the Borderlands," *Journal of American History* 92, no. 1 (2005): 19–46.

12. Kathleen Bragdon, "Gender as a Category in Native Southern New England," *Ethnohistory* 43, no. 4 (1996): 575–592.

13. Peterson-del Mar, "Intermarriage and Agency."

14. Nancy Shoemaker, introduction to her *Negotiators of Change*, 13; Ford, "Native American Women," 46; Laura F. Klein and Lillian A. Ackerman, introduction to *Women and Power in Native North America*, ed. Klein and Ackerman (Norman: University of Oklahoma Press, 1995), 12–15.

15. Perdue, *Cherokee Women*, 10

16. Saunt, "Gender Conflict among Creek Indians," 153; Kathryn E. Holland Braund, "Guardians of Tradition and Handmaidens of Change: Women's Roles in Creek Economic and Social Life during the Eighteenth Century," *American Indian Quarterly* 14, no. 3 (1990): 239–258, quote from 239.

17. Natalie Zemon Davis, "Iroquois Women, European Women," in *Women, "Race," and Writing in the Early Modern Period*, ed. Margo Hendricks and Patricia Parker (London: Routledge, 1994), 243–258; Nancy Shoemaker, "Kateri Tekakwitha's Tortuous Path to Sainthood," in *Negotiators of Change*, ed. Shoemaker, 49–71; Sleeper-Smith, "Women, Kin, and Catholicism," 425; and Susan Sleeper-Smith, *Indian Women and French Men: Rethinking Cultural Encounters in the Western Great Lakes* (Amherst: University of Massachusetts Press, 2001).

18. Jennifer S. H. Brown, *Strangers in Blood: Fur Trade Company Families in Indian Country* (Vancouver: University of British Columbia Press, 1980); Sylvia Van Kirk, *Many Tender Ties: Women in the Fur Trade Society, 1670–1870* (Norman: University of Oklahoma Press, 1980); John Mack Faragher, "The Custom of the Country: Cross-Cultural Marriage in the Far Western Fur Trade," in *Western Women: Their Land, Their Lives*, ed. Lillian Schlissel, Vicki L. Ruiz, and Janice Monk (Albuquerque: University of New Mexico Press, 1988), 199–215; Jacqueline Peterson, "Women Dreaming: The Religiopsychology of Indian-White Marriages and the Rise of Métis Culture," in *Western Women*, ed. Schlissel, Ruiz, and Monk, 49–68; Sleeper-Smith, "Women, Kin, and Catholicism," 433.

19. Bruce M. White, "The Woman Who Married a Beaver: Trade Patterns and Gender Roles in the Ojibwa Fur Trade," *Ethnohistory* 46, no. 1 (1999): 109–147, quote from 117, emphasis added.

20. Saunt, "Gender Conflict among Creek Indians," 164; See also idem, *A New Order of Things: Property, Power, and the Transformation of the Creek Indians, 1733–1816* (New York: Cambridge University Press, 1999), chapter 6.

21. Lucy Eldersveld Murphy, "Autonomy and the Economic Roles of Indian Women of Fox-Wisconsin River Region, 1763–1832," in *Negotiators of Change*, ed. Shoemaker, 72–89; Perdue, *Cherokee Women*, 117–118, 130–131. See also James Taylor Carson, "Dollars Never Fail to Melt Their Hearts: Native Women and the Market Revolution," in *Neither a Lady nor Slave: Working Women of the Old South*, ed. Susanna Delfino and Michele Gillespie (Chapel Hill: University of North Carolina Press, 2002), 15–33.

22. For studies that historicize interracial unions, see Jean Barman, "What a Difference a Border Makes: Aboriginal Racial Intermixture in the Pacific Northwest," *Journal of the West* 38, no. 3 (1999): 14–20; Kirsten Fischer, *Suspect Relations: Sex, Race, and Resistance in Colonial North Carolina* (Ithaca, N.Y.: Cornell University Press, 2002), chapter 2; Richard Goodbeer presents a more nuanced reading of interracial sexual relations, noting that they contained "many possibilities" from "violent coercion to respectful coexistence," in "Eroticizing the Middle Ground: Anglo-Indian Sexual Relations along the Eighteenth-Century Frontier," in *Sex, Love, Race: Crossing Boundaries in North American History*, ed. Martha Hodes (New York: New York University Press, 1999), 91–111. For a study that stresses violence and abuse, see Albert L. Hurtado, "When Strangers Met: Sex and Gender on Three Frontiers," in *Writing the Range*, ed. Jameson and Armitage, 122–142.

23. Albers, "Marxism and Historical Materialism in American Indian History," 110.

24. Sherry B. Ortner, "Is Female to Male as Male Is to Culture?" in *Woman, Culture, and Society*, ed. Rosaldo and Lamphere, 67–88; Michelle Zimbalist Rosaldo, "Women, Culture, and Society: A Theoretical Overview," in ibid., 16–42.

25. Elizabeth H. Pleck, "Women's History: Gender as a Category of Historical Analysis," in *Ordinary People and Everyday Life: Perspectives on the New Social History*, ed. James B. Gardner and George R. Adams (Nashville: American Association for State and Local History, 1983), 51–65; Joan Wallach Scott, "Gender: A Useful Category of Historical Analysis," *American Historical Review*, 91, no. 5 (1986): 1053–1075. Some scholars argue that sex, like gender, is also socially constructed. See Thomas Laqueur, *Making Sex: Body and Gender from the Greeks to Freud* (Cambridge: Cambridge University Press, 1990).

26. For a general discussion of gender and Native American culture, see Nancy Bonvillain, *Women and Men: Cultural Constructions of Gender* (Englewood Cliffs, N.J.: Prentice Hall, 1995); Betty Bell, "Gender in Native America," in *A Companion to Native American History*, ed. Neal Salisbury and Phil Deloria (Oxford: Blackwell, 2002), 307–318; Gunlög Fur, " 'Some Women Are Wiser than Some Men': Gender and Native American History," in *Clearing a Path*, ed. Shoemaker, 75–103.

27. On Indian gender equality, see Gretchen Green, "Gender and the Longhouse: Iroquois Women in a Changing Culture," in *Women and Freedom in Early America*, ed. Larry D. Elridge (New York: New York University Press, 1997), 7–25; Margaret M. Caffrey, "Complementary Power: Men and Women of the Lenni Lenape," *American Indian Quarterly* 24, no. 1 (2000): 44–63. For a useful chart that documents which Indian groups were matrilineal, bilateral, or patrilineal, see Ford, "Native American Women," 48.

28. Judith K. Brown, "Economic Organization and the Position of Women among the Iroquois," *Ethnohistory* 17, no. 3–4 (1970): 151–167.

29. Gutiérrez, *When Jesus Came, the Corn Mothers Went Away*, 33–35, 72. See also Evelyn Blackwood, "Sexuality and Gender in Certain Native American Tribes: The Case of Cross-Gender Females," *Signs* 10 (1984): 27–42; Walter Williams, *The Spirit and the Flesh: Sexual Diversity in American Indian Culture* (Boston: Beacon Press, 1986); Raymond Hauser, "The Berdache and the Illinois Indian Tribe during the Last Half of the Seventeenth Century," *Ethnohistory* 37, no. 1 (1990): 45–65; Will Roscoe, *The Zuni Man-Woman* (Albuquerque: University of New Mexico Press, 1991); Sue-Ellen Jacobs, Wesley Thomas, and Sabine Lang, eds., *Two-Spirit People: Native American Gender Identity, Sexuality, and Spirituality* (Urbana: University of Illinois Press, 1997); Will Roscoe, *Changing Ones: Third and Fourth Genders in Native North America* (New York: St. Martin's Press, 1998); Sabine Lang, *Men as Women, Women as Men: Changing Gender in Native American Cultures*, trans. John L. Vantine (Austin: University of Texas Press, 1998).

30. Kathleen M. Brown argues this point in "Brave New Worlds: Women's and Gender History," *William and Mary Quarterly*, 3rd ser., 50, no. 2 (1993): 325. Only a few scholars have begun to examine Indian constructions of masculinity: Nathaniel Sheidley, "Hunting and the Politics of Masculinity in Cherokee Treaty-Making, 1763–75," in *Empire and Others: British Encounters with Indigenous Peoples, 1600–1850*, ed. Martin Daunton and Rick Halpern (Philadephia: University of Pennsylvania Press, 1998), 167–185; Saunt, "Gender Conflict among Creek Indians"; Nancy Shoemaker, "An Alliance between Men: Gender Metaphors in Eighteenth-Century American Indian Diplomacy East of the Mississippi," *Ethnohistory* 46, no. 2 (1999): 239–264; Danvers, "Gendered Encounters"; R. Todd Romero, " 'Ranging Foresters' and 'Women-Like Men': Physical

Accomplishments, Spiritual Power, and Indian Masculinity in Early-Seventeenth-Century New England," *Ethnohistory* 53, no. 2 (2006): 281–329. Ann M. Little, *Abraham in Arms: War and Gender in Colonial New England* (Philadelphia: University of Pennsylvania Press, 2006).

31. Saunt, "Gender Conflict among Creek Indians."

32. K. Brown, "Brave New Worlds," 317; idem, *Good Wives, Nasty Wenches, and Anxious Patriarchs: Gender, Race and Power in Colonial Virginia* (Chapel Hill: University of North Carolina Press, 1996), ch. 2. For other works that explore how discourses of discovery were gendered, see Louis Montrose, "The Work of Gender in the Discourse of Discovery," *Representations* 33 (1991): 1–41; Margarita Zamora, "Abreast of Columbus: Gender and Discovery," *Cultural Critique* 17 (1990/1991): 127–150; Kirsten Fischer, "The Imperial Gaze: Native American, African American, and Colonial Women in European Eyes," in *A Companion to American Women's History*, ed. Nancy A. Hewitt (Oxford: Blackwell, 2002), 3–19, see esp. 4–9.

33. Juliana Barr, "A Diplomacy of Gender: Rituals of First Contact in the 'Land of the Tejas,'" *William and Mary Quarterly*, 3rd ser., 61, no. 3 (2004): 393–434; idem, *Peace Came in the Form of a Woman: The Power Relations of Spanish and Indian Nations in the Early Southwest Borderlands* (Chapel Hill: University of North Carolina Press, 2007).

34. Lucy Eldersveld Murphy, "To Live among Us: Accommodation, Gender, and Conflict in the Western Lakes Region, 1760–1832," in *Contact Points*, ed. Cayton and Teute, 270–303; idem, *A Gathering of Rivers: Indians, Métis, and Mining in the Western Great Lakes, 1732–1832* (Lincoln: University of Nebraska Press, 2000).

35. Ann Marie Plane, *Colonial Intimacies: Indian Marriage in Early New England* (Ithaca, N.Y.: Cornell University Press, 2000), 4; Gutiérrez, *When Jesus Came, the Corn Mothers Went Away*, 227, 76–79.

36. David Smits documents the persistent image of female drudgery in "The 'Squaw Drudge': A Prime Index of Savagism," *Ethnohistory* 29, no. 4 (1982): 281–306.

37. Fur, "'Some Women Are Wiser than Some Men,'" 81–83.

38. Perdue, *Cherokee Women*, 13–15; Barbara A. Mann, "The Lynx in Time: Haudenosaunee Women's Traditions and History," *American Indian Quarterly* 21, no. 3 (1997): 423–449; Shoemaker, "An Alliance between Men."

39. For a somewhat exaggerated critique of the romanticising tendencies of the New Indian history, see H. C. Porter, "Review Essay: Reflections on the Ethnohistory of Early Colonial North America," *Journal of American Studies* 16, no. 2 (1982): 243–254.

40. K. Brown, *Good Wives, Nasty Wenches, and Anxious Patriarchs*, 53; Elizabeth Tooker, "Women in Iroquois Society," in *Extending the Rafters: Interdisciplinary Approaches to Iroquoian Studies*, ed. Michael K. Foster, Jack Campisi, and Marianne Mithun (Albany: State University of New York Press, 1984), 109–123; Karen Anderson, *Changing Woman: A History of Racial Ethnic Women in Modern America* (New York: Oxford University Press, 1996), 18, 19.

41. Shoemaker, introduction to her *Negotiators of Change*, 5; Fur, "Some Women Are Wiser than Some Men," 78–79.

42. Sleeper-Smith, *Indian Women and French Men*.

43. Richard Middleton, *Colonial America: A History, 1565–1776, 3rd ed.* (1992; Oxford: Blackwell Publishers, 2002).

44. Martha Harroun Foster, "Lost Women of the Matriarchy: Iroquois Women in the Historical Literature," *American Indian Culture and Research Journal* 19, no. 3 (1995): 121–140; Theda Perdue, "Writing the Ethnohistory of Native Women," in *Rethinking*

American Indian History, ed. Donald Fixico (Albuquerque: University of New Mexico Press, 1997), 76.

45. Paula Gunn Allen, *Pocahontas: Medicine Woman, Spy, Entrepreneur, Diplomat* (New York: HarperCollins, 2003); Theda Perdue, "Nancy Ward," in *Portraits of American Women*, ed. C. J. Barker-Benfield and Catherine Clinton (New York: St. Martin's Press, 1991), 83–100; Clara Sue Kidwell, "Indian Women as Cultural Mediators," *Ethnohistory* 39, no. 2 (1992): 97–107; Thomas Earle, *The Three Faces of Molly Brant: A Biography* (Kingston, Ontario: Quarry Press, 1996); Michele Gillespie, "The Sexual Politics of Race and Gender: Mary Musgrove and the Georgia Trustees," in *The Devil's Lane: Sex and Race in the Early South*, ed. Catherine Clinton and Michele Gillespie (New York: Oxford University Press, 1997), 187–201; Lois M. Huey and Bonnie Pulis, *Molly Brant: A Legacy of Her Own* (Youngstown, N.Y.: Old Ford Niagara Association, 1997); Theda Perdue, ed., *Sifters: Native American Women's Lives* (New York: Oxford University Press, 2001).

46. Gary B. Nash, "The Hidden History of Mestizo America," *Journal of American History* 84, no. 3 (1995): 941–964; Murphy, *Gathering of Rivers*, 13. This literature is particularly rich in the Great Lakes region; see footnote 18 above. See also Goodbeer, "Eroticizing the Middle Ground," 91–111; Jennifer M. Spear, "'They Need Wives': Métissage and the Regulation of Sexuality in French Louisiana, 1699–1730," in *Sex, Love, Race*, ed. Hodes, 35–59.

47. Jacqueline Peterson and Jennifer S. H. Brown, eds., *The New Peoples: Being and Becoming Métis in North America* (Lincoln: University of Nebraska Press, 1985); Jennifer Brown and Theresa Schenck, "Métis, Mestizo, and Mixed-Blood," in *Companion to Native American History*, ed. Salisbury and Deloria, 321–338.

48. Jacqueline Peterson, "Prelude to Red River: A Social Portrait of the Great Lakes Métis," *Ethnohistory* 25, no. 1 (1978): 41–67; J.S.H. Brown, *Strangers in Blood*; Van Kirk, *Many Tender Ties*; idem, "The Role of Native Women in the Creation of Fur Trade Society in Western Canada, 1670–1830," in *Writing the Range*, ed. Jameson and Armitage, 53–62; White, "The Woman Who Married a Beaver"; Sleeper-Smith, *Indian Women and French Men*; Tanis Chapman Thorne, *The Many Hands of My Relations: French and Indians on the Lower Missouri* (Columbia: University of Missouri Press, 1996). For a discussion of women's roles as cultural brokers in the middle and southern colonies, see Jane T. Merritt, "Cultural Encounters along a Gender Frontier: Mahican, Delaware, and German Women in Eighteenth-Century Pennsylvania," *Pennsylvania History* 67, no. 4 (2000): 503–532; Nancy L. Hagedorn, "Brokers of Understanding: Interpreters as Agents of Cultural Exchange in Colonial New York," *New York History* 76, no. 4 (1995): 379–408, see esp. 388; Michael P. Morris, *The Bringing of Wonder: Trade and the Indians of the Southeast, 1700–1783* (Westport Conn.: Greenwood Press, 1999), chapters 2–4; Fischer, *Suspect Relations*, chapter 2.

49. Perdue, *Cherokee Women*; Morris, *The Bringing of Wonder*; Danvers, "Gendered Encounters."

50. Brooks, "'This Evil Extends Especially to the Feminine Sex.'" See also idem, *Captives and Cousins: Slavery, Kinship, and Community in the Southwest Borderlands* (Chapel Hill: University of North Carolina Press, 2002).

51. K. Brown calls for a comparative approach in "Brave New Worlds." Other studies that examine the experiences of a variety of women include Teresa L. Amott and Julie A. Mathaei, *Race, Gender, and Work: A Multicultural History of Women in the United States* (Boston: South End Press, 1991); Anderson, *Changing Woman;* Carol Berkin, *First Generations: Women in Colonial America* (New York: Hill and Wang, 1996); Paula A.

Treckel, *To Comfort the Heart: Women in Seventeenth-Century America* (New York: Twayne, 1996). Individual essays on Native American women are including in the following anthologies: Schlissel, Ruiz, and Monk, *Western Women*; Jameson and Armitage, *Writing the Range*; Thomas Dublin and Katherine Kish Sklar, eds., *Women and Power in American History* (Englewood Cliffs, N.J.: Prentice Hall, 1990); Hendricks and Parker, *Women, "Race," and Writing;* Jo Maynes et al., *Gender, Kinship, and Power;* Vicki L. Ruíz and Ellen Carol DuBois, eds., *Unequal Sisters: A Multicultural Reader in U.S. Women's History*, 3rd ed. (New York: Routledge, 2000); Delfino and Gillespie, *Neither a Lady nor Slave*; and Hewitt, *Companion to American Women's History.*

52. Eldridge, *Women and Freedom in Early America*, 3; Berkin, *First Generations*, ix. For reviews on Eldridge and Berkin, see *American Historical Review* 104, no. 1 (1999): 146–147; *William and Mary Quarterly*, 3rd ser., 56, no. 1 (1999): 194–196; *Journal of American History* 74, no. 2 (1997): 621–622.

53. Daniel K. Richter, "Whose Indian History?" *William and Mary Quarterly*, 3rd ser., 50, no. 2 (1993): 379–393, quote from 390.

54. An example of this type of project includes Aileen B. Agnew, "Silent Partners: The Economic Life of Women on the Frontier of Colonial New York" (PhD diss., University of New Hampshire, 1998).

55. K. Brown, *Good Wives, Nasty Wenches and Anxious Patriarchs*; Fischer, *Suspect Relations.*

3

From Daughters of Liberty
to Women of the Republic

American Women in the Era of the American Revolution

SUSAN BRANSON

A notice in the January 1848 issue of *Godey's Lady's Book* informed readers that the author Elizabeth F. Ellet was engaged in the preparation of a work on the women of the American Revolution. It encouraged anyone with anecdotes to contact her. Ellet published her three-volume work, *The Women of the American Revolution* (1848), later that year.[1] The first of its kind, it attempted to recover the activities of individual American women, elites and non-elites alike, who contributed to the Patriot cause. Until recently, Ellet's book resided on the shelves of most university libraries in a dusty and untouched state. This nineteenth-century effort to capture the activities and experiences of women, though widely published and republished in its day, has seemed of little use to modern scholars of women's history. Its style is sentimental, the tone is melodramatic, and some of its information is dubious at best. But one of the hallmarks of scholarship in recent years is a reconsideration of such early chroniclers. This essay reviews the directions the history of women in the American Revolution has taken over the past two hundred years.

As the practice of history has changed over time, so have the questions historians ask about women and the American Revolution. The twentieth-century women's movement has had a significant influence on historical analysis. The title of my chapter reflects this change in perspective. Revolutionary women used the term "daughters of liberty" to describe themselves. Daughters, by eighteenth-century definition, were dependents under the charge and authority of men. "Women of the Republic," on the other hand, were autonomous individuals with a recognized relationship to the state. Although women in the late eighteenth century grappled with these patriarchal and civic identities, scholars from that era and well into the twentieth century still firmly placed Revolutionary women in secondary, even marginal roles in the Revolution. The mid-twentieth century witnessed a sea change in society's attitude toward women, a change reflected in historical scholarship. This chapter begins with an examination of recovered early histories, including Ellet's groundbreaking work. It then explores more recent studies and the influence twentieth-century feminism has had on historical interpretations of women's roles and experiences in the American Revolution. Moving women from the margins to the mainstream is not the only development in the history of women in this era. Attention has shifted from women's roles to gender roles, allowing a more comprehensive perspective on American society. In addition, scholars have expanded their focus beyond white elites to indigenous women and women of color. Historians have recently devoted study to the consequences of war and revolution in the early years of the Republic. The legacy of Revolutionary rhetoric casts long shadows on gender roles in the 1780s and beyond.

Participants on both sides of the conflict had their say about women's roles. Constructions of gender in the late eighteenth century gave women a private, rather than public role in society. Commentators valued women for their piety and devotion to family. Men were actors in the public sphere; women performed their duties within the household and among family members. Politics and war were not the province of the female sex. The first narratives of the Revolutionary era written and published in the 1780s make these assumptions about gender roles evident. Loyalist Peter Oliver, in *The Origin and Progress of the American Rebellion*, recounted Patriot women's participation in the public punishments of Tories. But his rather spiteful depiction suggested women did so as a fashionable pursuit, rather than out of more serious political commitment. In contrast, the histories written by the victors credited American women with more laudable motives. David Ramsey's *History of the Revolution in South Carolina* praised the women of Charleston with patriotism and firmness in light of the 1781 British capture of the city. According to Ramsey these "guardian Angels . . . preserved their husbands from falling in the hour of temptation, when interest and convenience had almost gotten the better of honour and patriotism."[2] William Gordon's *The History of the Rise and Establishment of the Independence of the United States of America* (1788) went even further in its adulation. Gordon argued that the founding of the nation was not solely a male accomplishment. It depended on women embracing republican values usually reserved for men.[3]

Mercy Otis Warren, a contemporary of Ramsey and Gordon, held a very different view of the qualities and characteristics demonstrated by American women. In contrast to histories such as Gordon's that assumed women must abandon their feminine qualities to participate in the public political sphere, Warren's *History of the Rise, and Progress and Termination of the American Revolution Interspersed with Biographical, Political and Moral Observations* (1805) argued just the opposite.[4] Warren's account of the siege of Charleston praised women for their "feminine fortitude," a necessary ingredient in the success of the war effort. In her depiction of the effects of the war on the civilian population, she did not shy away from recounting the dangers women faced, including rape, as both British and American forces occupied towns and countryside. Warren described for her readers the British attack on New Haven in the summer of 1779 when many "hapless females" fell victim to the wanton and riotous appetites of Governor Tryon's troops.[5] She also drew attention to the sacrifices and sufferings of women on both sides of the conflict. During the siege of Charleston, for example, Warren noted that South Carolina women endured "hardships they had never expected; and wept in secret the miseries of their country, and their separation from their tenderest connections."[6] Her description of the wives and mothers of British soldiers wounded and taken prisoner drew attention to the personal toll that conflict took on women regardless of their politics. As Warren's biographer, Rosemarie Zagarri, notes, the suffering of wives and mothers transcended geographical boundaries to bind all women together, even in the throes of war. And unlike Ramsey's angels and Gordon's masculine women, Warren's assessment of American women did not idealize them, nor did it rob women of their essential feminine natures.[7]

Even before Warren's history called attention to collective female experiences, the activities of one woman had already been chronicled. In 1797 Hermann Mann wrote *The Female Review*, which related the details of Deborah Sampson's exploits as a Continental soldier.[8] Sampson herself promoted her story in 1802 when she took to the stage and exhibited her military drills dressed in uniform.[9] Her performance and Mann's text showed a far from ordinary woman. Sampson's transgressive, transvestite activities, many of them elaborated or simply invented by Mann for their shock appeal, defied categorization. For early nineteenth-century readers and audiences she was neither angel nor woman, but a curiosity. Sampson's experiences have caught the attention of several scholars in recent years. Judith Hiltner's essays explore the cultural implications of Mann's text and Sampson's performances. Alfred F. Young's monograph, *Masquerade: The Life and Times of Deborah Sampson, Continental Soldier*, details Sampson's experiences but also considers the history of Mann's text. Both these authors are interested in the context of historical writing and rewriting.[10]

Few truly scholarly works on women were written in the first half of the twentieth century. Elizabeth Cometti's 1947 essay, "Women in the American Revolution," stands out as perhaps the only attempt in this era to discuss women's participation in the war effort in any systematic way. Cometti organized women's activities into three general categories: the home front, where many women took on the role of deputy husbands; public actions such as participating in boycotts and signing non-importation agreements; and domestic production for war — spinning and sewing uniforms.[11]

The occasion of the bicentennial of the Revolution in 1976 produced a bonanza of publications. Most of these works were merely factual rather than analytic, what Carol Berkin, in her summary of scholarship on women and the Revolution, called "historical show-and-tell."[12] Some, like Sally Smith Booth's *The Women of 76*, bear a strong resemblance to Cometti's essay, expanding her categories to a book-length study (though without footnotes).[13] Collections such as

Weathering the Storm: Women of the American Revolution were well-intentioned, if not fully documented, presentations of women's diaries from the Revolutionary era.[14] The bicentennial coincided with the first efforts at recovering women's history to come out of the modern women's movement. The scholarship inspired by this social movement resulted in a generation of scholars who were self-taught in women's history and who then in turn trained younger historians, founded women's studies programs in colleges and universities, and established scholarly journals, such as *Signs, Gender and History,* and the *Journal of Women's History.* This is the context within which most of the modern writing and research on women in the era of the Revolution has been accomplished.

In the acknowledgments to *Remember the Ladies* in 1976, the accompanying volume to a 1976 traveling exhibit on women in the Revolution, the authors described women's history as a fledgling area of scholarship undergoing amazing growth within the preceding decade.[15] In the 1970s scholars such as Linda K. Kerber, Mary Beth Norton, and others published their careful, analytic studies. Norton's essay on Loyalist women, for example, used petitions to reconstruct the colonial and Revolutionary-era lives of women and their families whose continued allegiance to the Crown forced them into exile.[16] Kerber's essay, "The Republican Mother: Women and the Enlightenment, an American Perspective," began her extended engagement with the intellectual aspects of women's Revolutionary history, an interest that would become a major component of her monograph, *Women of the Republic,* published four years later.[17] Joan Hoff Wilson, in contrast to historians who looked to the results of the Revolution for signs of change in the status of American women, argued in her important essay, "The Illusion of Change: Women and the Revolution," that politically, economically, and legally the Revolution had little, if any, lasting effect on women's lives.[18] Ten years later, Elaine Crane confirmed Wilson's assessment in her essay "Dependence in the Era of Independence."[19]

At the end of the 1970s, Carol Berkin assessed the state of scholarship on women in the American Revolution to date. She noted that although the "evangelical phase" of women's history as a field was passing, the reverberation of the Revolutionary experience had not yet been satisfactorily examined or discussed.[20] A year later Mary Beth Norton and Linda Kerber published impressive monographs. These studies, Norton's *Liberty's Daughters* and Kerber's *Women of the Republic,* still stand out as milestones in the history of women in the age of the Revolution.[21] Both works examine gender roles and relations in pre-Revolution America and use this information to explore the impact of the political, legal, social, and cultural developments between the 1760s and the 1790s. Though covering similar issues, Kerber and Norton differ in their assessment of the extent to which the Revolution changed women's private and public lives and the degree to which republican ideology was responsible for those changes. Norton's book is more comprehensive in scope. It surveys the material, emotional, and intellectual aspects of women's lives throughout colonial America. It also encompasses a consideration of not only white women, but African and African American women as well. In her assessment, the Revolution was the driving force for a change in society's view of women. She credits republican ideology with spurring new attitudes about marriage choices, family planning, and divorce rates.

Kerber offers a less sanguine evaluation about the role of ideology as a catalyst for change. Her book addresses the intellectual context of the Revolutionary era more directly, seeing little shift in fundamental beliefs and practices. Kerber views the elevated importance of women's roles during the Revolution as much more transient than Norton does. Both scholars agree, however, that women's educational opportunities were the one area in which change was not only visible, but lasting. Yet even there, the motivation for improving female intellects came from a conservative, rather than progressive tendency — from a republican, rather than liberal strain of ideology. The impetus arose from the now well-known concept of republican motherhood, first articulated by Kerber in "The Republican Mother: Women and the Enlightenment, an American Perspective." Women had an indirect, but nonetheless important, relationship to the state through their influence over their families: mothers reared good future citizens; wives fostered civic duty and right thinking in their spouses. Kerber and other historians have used and modified this concept over the past twenty years but have not completely abandoned it as an explanatory force. Republican motherhood, though now considered less of a prime mover, has continued to receive attention from historians. Rosemarie Zagarri published an essay in 1992 that traces the history of this term.[22]

Since the early 1980s, scholars have built upon foundations first established by Norton, Kerber, and others. In 1979 Carol Berkin noted the absence of biographies — collective and individual — for Revolutionary women. There are now many fine studies of individual women, including Judith Sargent Murray, Mercy Otis Warren, and Deborah Sampson.[23] Abigail Adams holds sway as the most written-about prominent woman of the Revolutionary era. The "Abigail Industry," as Edith Gelles termed it, has produced a mixed bag of work, from traditional narrative accounts to psychological studies. Gelles's book, *Portia: The World of Abigail Adams* (1992), portrays Adams as neither the sentimental heroine of Ellet's world nor a liberal feminist of 1970s vintage. Instead, Gelles evaluates Adams within an eighteenth-century social, cultural, and intellectual context. Summing up the state of study on Adams, Gelles observes that most biographers see Adams only through her husband, John, rather than as a significant or interesting individual in her own right. Gelles's biography corrects this bias. Yet scholars persist in viewing Abigail through her husband's personality and career. David McCullough's recent biography of John Adams makes an effort to see Abigail as her own person, but she still falls well within the shadow of her husband. Catherine Allgor has followed Gelles's call for studies that depict women, within the context of their era, as partners, politicians, and prime movers in their own right. Allgor's biography of Dolley Madison shows a founding mother with her own agenda and with the social and political skills to attain her goals.[24]

If the scholarship of the early twentieth century examined the what, where, and when of women's actions during the Revolution, in the second half of the last century scholars were more concerned with motivations and consequences, gender roles, and gender relations. In exploring women in rebellion and war, for example, Barbara Clark Smith examines the gender roles that underlaid the food riots conducted by women during the war. Alfred Young's essay, "The Women of Boston," is an account of women's collective participation in rebellion and revolution in one important city. Using Cometti's categories, Young analyses their activities in light of the gender roles and gender relations of the era. Studies of individual women such as Pennsylvanian Jane Bartram, New Jerseyite Rachel Wells, and New York Mohawk Molly Brant, to name just a few, also situate experiences within a gendered context.[25]

In the essay collection *Women in Age of the American Revolution*, historians consider issues such as the role played by religion in lives of women, the impact of the Revolution on enslaved and free women of color, and women's property rights (or lack thereof). This collection also contains Linda Kerber's preliminary analysis of a gendered history of the Revolution.[26] Historians have also begun to explore overlooked areas of the history of women of the Revolution: Cynthia A. Kierner's monograph, *Beyond the Household: Women's Place in the Early South, 1700–1835*, includes the Revolutionary decades and adds to our understanding of southern women's experiences first depicted in Norton's *Daughters of Liberty*. Scholars in recent years also devote attention to Loyalist and "disaffected" women, another area of study pioneered by Norton. Judith Van Buskirk's "They Didn't Join the Band: Disaffected Women in Revolutionary Philadelphia" and Susan E. Klepp's "Rough Music in Philadelphia: July 4th, 1778" both document women who chose not to side with the Patriot cause.[27]

Attention to the ideological aspect of gender roles has produced a promising body of scholarship. Jan Lewis, for example, argues against Linda Kerber's suggestion that the concept of republican motherhood helped define a new political role for women. Lewis's essay, "The Republican Wife," asserts that it was the ideal of republican *marriage* and the republican *wife* that exemplified the strengths and weaknesses of the Revolutionary era's notion of woman's role and, indeed, of republicanism itself. In the 1980s and 1990s historians Ruth Bloch, Joan Gundersen, and Rosemarie Zagarri have explored how the concepts of dependence and independence, in the context of republican ideology, defined women's (and men's) relationship to the state.[28] Women were subordinate and dependent. By this definition, they were not autonomous individuals who could make political judgments free from the influence of those above them — their fathers, husbands, and sons.

Historians have also begun to pay particular attention to the circumstances and experiences of Native American and African American women. As Jacqueline

Jones succinctly puts it, African American women, the majority of whom were enslaved at the time of the Revolution, "saw freedom through the prism of family life." Her comprehensive essay on slave women in the Revolutionary era discusses how sex not only determined the experience of slavery, but also influenced choices made and opportunities seized or ignored during the military conflict. The British actively recruited male slaves, but they also ended up with women and children in their army camps. Delegated the most menial of tasks, including street cleaning, these refugees labored for their British employers just as hard as they had for their Patriot owners.[29]

When the opportunity arose, whole families sometimes fled to the protection of a British camp.[30] (See Betty Wood's essay in this collection for additional analysis of this point.) With or without British offers of freedom in exchange for labor, some women took the opportunity to free themselves. In the South they often ran to urban areas such as Charleston or Savannah. In backcountry they sometimes joined groups of runaways who attempted to establish maroon communities, such as the one near Savannah, Georgia, which existed until 1787.[31] In the North, many hid in plain sight, joining free blacks in the process of community formation in cities such as Boston and Philadelphia. Newspaper advertisements provide evidence of these individual women who stole themselves. Billy G. Smith and Richard Wojtowicz's edited collection of these runaway advertisements from the *Pennsylvania Gazette* during the Revolutionary era includes notification that in August 1776 thirty-five-year-old Maria, a mulatto, escaped from her New Jersey owner. She was last seen dressed "in men's clothes," thought to be making her way either to New York or Philadelphia. In 1777, Peg took advantage of the British occupation of Philadelphia to flee Chester County for protection by the British. The ads also provide evidence of families fleeing together, as Toney, his wife, Rachel, and their young child did in 1779. Their owner assumed they would try, like many runaways, to "pass for free Negroes."[32]

But Jones also notes that for many enslaved women, "a stable family life was both their personal strength and their vulnerability." Some chose to stay rather than flee because of family ties. For those women who remained behind, the disruption of plantation life afforded some opportunities, but it also brought with it added oppression. Because so many male slaves fled, women's labor was even more necessary than before. Women seized the opportunity to gain a degree of autonomy (interpreted by whites as insolence), but also they were kept (when possible) under even tighter control as slave masters feared losing their labor force. Jones's assessment of the impact of the Revolution on black women is that it "did little to change the basic work and family obligations that assumed a kaleidoscope of patterns in the lives of different groups of black women. Nevertheless, the conflict made much clearer the cleavage in status (if not in consciousness) between free blacks and slaves, for while almost all of them faced unprecedented hardships, some emerged from the crucible of war free (or at least freer) to labor on behalf of their own families and communities, while others entered a new and brutal slave regime in the Cotton South."[33]

In *Water from the Rock* Sylvia Frey describes the various fates of Georgia and South Carolina black men and women after the war. Not all of those who fled to (and with) the British gained their freedom. Many were taken as war prizes in raids on Patriot plantations. Most of these men and women faced continued enslavement in the West Indies. Those who did gain their freedom, often in return for war service, faced an economically precarious future in Nova Scotia and later in Sierra Leone. Slaves who had not escaped from a southern owner risked continual family separation as slavery expanded into the Cotton South.[34]

After the Revolution slavery became even more entrenched in the lower South, further jeopardizing the cohesion of slave families. At the same time, economic developments in the upper South created new opportunities for men and women to achieve their freedom. T. Stephen Whitman's account of slavery in Maryland explores strategies for gaining freedom from slaveholders who needed "predictable, flexible, and cheap labor, [and] knew that an unvaried reliance on slavery might not meet these objectives." Families came to payment arrangements with slave owners to free wives and children — often over a period of years with children's labor under "term slavery." This innovation made slavery affordable to artisans and manufacturers in Baltimore's growing postwar economy.[35]

There were free communities before the Revolution, but they were small and existed within the context of slavery. The Revolution worked a sea change in northern states, and especially in port cities such as Boston, New York, and Philadelphia. In 1780 Pennsylvania became the first state to pass a gradual emancipation law, hastening the growth and autonomy of Philadelphia's free black community. By 1790, 14 percent of black households were headed by women. Over time, these women joined and supported churches and earned a living. The Philadelphia city directory listed "coloured" residents for the first time in 1811. Most men toiled as laborers or mariners. The directory also listed a handful of female independent producers, including Rachael Ayers, who ran a boardinghouse at the corner of Spruce and Little Dock; laundresses Catherine Bailey, Lydia Black, and Louisa Chapaeau; cake baker Hannah Coyrans; cook Rosetta Green; "manutua" maker Mary Marks; and "segarmaker" Mary Samsusar.[36]

For black women as well as men in the Revolutionary era, much depended on time, place, family structure, and skills. The war years offered some opportunities for potential freedom through either running away during the chaos of conflict or occupation or fleeing to the British with hopes of freedom. But the most significant legacy of the Revolution for blacks was the movement toward emancipation in northern states, where men and women of color seized opportunities to develop free communities in northern cities.

Historian Jan Lewis has noted, "As with slave women, the Revolution affected Indian Women more as Indians than as women." These women, along with their communities, were among the "great losers in the Revolutionary era."[37] Though many scholars have written of the collective experiences of Native Americans during the Revolution, few single out Native American women as a subject of study. The absence of this group of women from historical writing is due in part to the paucity of records by or about Native women. The European American men who authored most contemporary accounts assumed that Native women, like European women, were governed by their men. The records of military engagements and government treaties depict a world where British and American men deal almost exclusively with male representatives of Native American tribes. Recovering the history of Native women, with the exception of a few prominent leaders such as Cherokee Nancy Ward or British captives like Mary Jemison, requires reading between the lines of such accounts. A handful of Native American women have received scholarly attention because of their presence in European American records. Perhaps the most prominent of these is Molly Brant. As the daughter and sister of Mohawk chiefs and wife of the British superintendent for Indian Affairs, Sir William Johnson, Brant was strategically placed to represent her people during the wars years and later in exile in Canada.[38] Martha Foster argues that in some cases, information does exist, but the assumptions and biases of past historians often led historians to ignore or misinterpret evidence of women's activities.[39]

Part of the reason that historical sources for Native women are so rare has to do with the changes that occurred within Native American communities as a result of contact with Europeans. Theda Perdue overcomes this gap in the historical record. Her monograph, *Cherokee Women*, is one of the most comprehensive works to date on Native American women in this era. To recover the experiences of Revolutionary-era women, Perdue used a method she describes as "upstreaming." She draws on later documents and even oral histories to explicate the experiences of Cherokee women in the late eighteenth and early nineteenth centuries. Perdue notes that by the time of the Revolution trade relations had altered women's economic relationships within their communities. Warfare accelerated this change. Women lost their tradition role in warfare. Where previously they often determined the fate of captives, the connection between kin ties and warfare declined. Warfare became more political, less clan-based, and an almost exclusively male domain.[40]

Native women did not give up their traditional roles without a fight. As Gail MacLeitch (in this volume), Diane Rothenberg, and Nancy Shoemaker demonstrate, Native women's involvement in food production and interest and participation in agricultural innovations introduced by Europeans illustrate their determination to retain traditional economic roles. Native women kept control over a variety of enterprises. Lucy Murphy's work on Fox women's mining activities in Wisconsin during the Revolutionary era, for example, shows that women were responsible for many types of production and trade. As Europeans discovered the valuable mineral resources of the Fox-Wisconsin riverway, they negotiated with Native women for mining rights.[41] Ultimately, settlers wrested the mines and agricultural land away from most Native Americans by the middle of the nineteenth century. A catalogue of similar events left Native women, along with their communities, increasingly marginalized by the hegemonic patriarchal society of European Americans who either dispossessed Native tribes, influenced their culture and society, or both.

The thriving field of women's history has generated several narrative text-books and readers in American women's history. Both Sara Evans's *Born for Liberty* and Nancy Cott's *No Small Courage* devote chapters to the Revolutionary era. The readings included in Norton's *Major Problems in American Women's History* and Kerber and DeHart's *Women of America* also devote attention to the Revolutionary era, combining essays and primary source material. Nancy Hewitt's recent comprehensive collection includes a good overview by Jan Lewis: "A Revolution for Whom? Women in the Era of the American Revolution."[42] Two narrative histories, Joan R. Gundersen's *To Be Useful to the World: Women in Revolutionary America, 1740–1790* (1996) and, more recently, Carol Berkin's *Revolutionary Mothers: Women in the Struggle for America's Independence* (2005), include chapters on Native American women and African American women.[43]

There are several recent innovations in Revolutionary scholarship. Historians are now more attuned to ideas and ideologies in a transatlantic perspective. One of the best examples of this is *Women and Politics in the Age of the Democratic Revolution*, a collection that brings together studies of France, Britain, British America, the Netherlands, and German states. Collections like this owe much to Atlantic World studies, whose scholarship demonstrates that the American Revolution was one among many interrelated events in the history of eighteenth-century women.[44]

A second development is a chronological shift. Much of the scholarship on the Revolutionary era has moved away from the Revolution itself and toward the postwar years and the long-term consequences of the Revolution on women's lives. The events and issues of the early Republic, including the Constitution's implications for women's status, now occupy scholars trained within the last twenty years as well as established historians whose early publications dealt more directly with the 1770s and early 1780s. Jan Lewis has written about the ways in which the language as well as the statutes of the Constitution reflects women's invisibility and their status as non-citizens. Linda Kerber's essay detailing the Supreme Court case *Martin vs. Massachusetts* (1805) highlights post-Revolutionary assumptions about women's property rights and the debate about their civic identity. Lewis's essay argues that the Revolution did little to change women's legal or political status, yet in individual cases, and depending on what was at stake, courts, lawyers, and citizens sometimes viewed women in a new way.[45] The concept of "natural rights" dominated the language of the Revolution, with the rights of man invoked, toasted, and celebrated from the 1770s into the early nine-teenth century. Rosemarie Zagarri has shown that the invocation of the "rights of woman" did not mean equality. Men and women possessed different kinds of rights based on the gender ideology of the time. According to Zagarri, such rhetoric attempted to reconcile the equality of the sexes with the subordination of women to men, "an exercise that quickly led to the exclusion of women from politics and to a gendered division of rights."[46]

Although women continued to be legally disqualified from participation in politics, they were often welcomed into the informal practices of political culture in the early Republic. Several studies of popular culture in the late eighteenth century explore the degree to which women were not only present, but sometimes necessary to public celebrations and protests of a political nature. David Waldstreicher's *The Making of American Nationalism: Celebrations and Political Culture, 1776–1820* and, especially, Simon P. Newman's *Parades and the Politics of the Street: Festive Culture in the Early American Republic* chronicle women's participation in local and national ceremonies and parades.[47] My own work, *These Fiery Frenchified Dames: Politics and Culture in Early National Philadelphia*, documents both the politicization of American culture in the 1780s and 1790s and the level of women's engagement in politics. This participation occurred in celebrations, ceremonies, and protests, but also through the theater, print culture, and salons. Catherine Allgor's *Parlor Politics* extends this exploration of the informal, but nonetheless important, role of women in national politics into the early nineteenth century when women increased their activities both as hostesses and effective lobbyists.[48] This attention to political culture broadens our definition of political participation. Women (except in New Jersey for a short while) could not vote. But they made their voices heard in the street, the parlor, and the theater.

Despite the rich harvest of scholarship in the history of women in the Revolution, some areas need more attention. Race has received some consideration in the women's history texts and general works on the Revolution (including Betty Wood's essay in this collection), but as of yet there have been no comprehensive studies of women of color or Native American women during the Revolutionary era.[49] Above all, the need for a gendered analysis of the American Revolution, called for by Linda Kerber almost two decades ago, still does not exist. As she said then, the women of the Revolutionary era remain becalmed in the E208 section of our libraries, wringing their hands like the White Queen in *Through the Looking Glass*, suffering gracefully in otherwise admirable books of otherwise distinguished historians.[50]

What would a gendered history of women in this era look like? Expanding historical investigation into the Early National period has shown the ways in which women were an integral part of the political as well as social and cultural developments of the era. Attention now needs to be directed back to the 1760s and 1770s. Several of the essays and books cited here make a good start. Any study must establish a baseline of what was thought possible for women: when did they stay within prescribed roles, when did they stray across gendered boundaries, and what effect did their straying have? For example, the marshalling of an American army required money, arms, officers, and recruits. But that army needed the assistance of women; no matter how much General Washington might have complained about the women in camp, without them the Patriots would have lost the war. Warfare was neither literally nor figuratively a masculine affair. Similarly, colonial resistance and rebellion must include the activities of women. Did women have different kinds of choices to make than men did? For example, we know that women sometimes initiated and often participated in boycotts. But did boycotts affect women differently from men? Many of these questions are applicable to Native women as well as Anglo-American women. How and when did sex and race complicate events? Again, a more complete analysis of the war's effects on slavery, generally, and individual slaves and slave owners, specifically, must factor in the kinds of concerns raised by Jones and others about the circumstances and choices for black women.

Finally, a gendered consideration of the rebellion, the war, and its aftermath must take into account the fact that American society was (and is) infused with language, behaviors, and ideas derived from our assumptions about gender roles. Women may not have been always and everywhere active presences in the Revolution, but every piece of writing generated by the conflict, the peace, or the nation-building that followed was embedded in a gender ideology. It is the historian's job to write history that uncovers and explains those often hidden beliefs that guided men's and women's actions during that crucial era in America's history.

NOTES

1. Elizabeth F. Ellet, *The Women of the American Revolution* (New York: Baker and Scribner, 1848).

2. Peter Oliver, *The Origin and Progress of the American Rebellion: A Tory View*, ed. Douglass Adair and John A. Schutz (San Marino, Calif.: Huntington Library, 1961); David Ramsey, *History of the Revolution in South Carolina: From a British Province to an Independent State* (Trenton, N.J.; Isaac Collins, 1785), quoted in Peter C. Messer, "Writing Women into History: Defining Gender and Citizenship in Post-Revolutionary America," *Studies in Eighteenth-Century Culture* 28 (1999): 346, 350.

3. Gordon recounted specific instances of female patriotism, such as Esther Reed and Sarah Bache's campaign for donations to supply Washington's army with food and clothing. William Gordon, *The History of the Rise and Establishment of the Independence of the United States of America* (London: Printed for the author, 1788); Messer, "Writing Women into History," 348, 349.

4. Mercy Otis Warren, *History of the Rise, and Progress and Termination of the American Revolution Interspersed with Biographical, Political and Moral Observations* (Boston: Manning and Loring for E. Larkin, 1805). This is Messer's argument in "Writing Women into History," 352–353.

5. Quoted in Rosemarie Zagarri, *A Woman's Dilemma: Mercy Otis Warren and the American Revolution* (Wheeling, Ill.: Harlan Davidson, 1995), 146.

6. Ibid., 147.

7. Ibid., 147. As one of the earliest historians of the Revolution, Warren was able to draw on personal experiences as both the wife of a Patriot leader and the mother of sons

caught up in the war (James Jr. lost his leg while serving in the Navy, and Winslow was imprisoned by the British) and from her knowledge gleaned through newspaper reports of women's activities in Boston and elsewhere. This included protests, tarring and featherings, spinning parties, the signing non-importation agreements, and fund-raising. Warren, *History of the Rise*. For analysis of these early histories, see William Raymond Smith, *History as Argument: Three Patriot Historians of the American Revolution* (The Hague: Mouton, 1966); Arthur Shaffer, *The Politics of History: Writing the History of the American Revolution, 1783–1815* (Chicago: Precedent Publishing, 1975); and Lester Cohen, *The Revolutionary Histories: Contemporary Narratives of the American Revolution* (Ithaca, N.Y.: Cornell University Press, 1980).

8. Hermann Mann, *The Female Review* (Dedham, Mass.: 1797). Her story was reprinted numerous times throughout the nineteenth century. An abridged version of the 1797 text was published in installments in Silliman Pratt's newspaper, the Middleboro, Massachusetts, *Namasket Gazette*, July 1857–January 1858. In 1866 the 1797 text was edited and published in Boston by John Adams Vinton. Vinton's edition was reprinted in 1916 and in 1972.

9. Hermann Mann published the speech he wrote for her: *An Address [sic] Delivered with Applause, at the Federal Street Theater, Boston, four successive nights of the different plays, beginning March 22,* 1802 (Dedham, Mass.: Printed and sold by H. Mann for Mrs. Gannet, 1802).

10. Judith Hiltner, "'The Example of our Heroine': Deborah Sampson and the Legacy of Herman Mann's *The Female Review*," *American Studies* 41, no. 1 (spring 2000): 93–113; Hiltner, "She Bled in Secret: Deborah Sampson, Herman Mann, and the Female Review," *Early American Literature* 34, no. 2, (1999): 190–220; Alfred F. Young's *Masquerade: The Life and Times of Deborah Sampson, Continental Soldier* (New York: Knopf, 2004) is a study of Sampson's life as well as the life of her biography. See also Patrick L. Leonard, "Deborah Sampson: Official Heroine of the State of Massachusetts," *Minerva: Quarterly Report on Women in the Military* 6, no. 3 (1988): 61–66. For other women who served in the war, see Linda Grant DePauw, "Women in Combat: The Revolutionary War Experience," *Armed Forces and Society* 7, no. 2 (1981): 209–226.

11. Elizabeth Cometti, "Women in the American Revolution" *New England Quarterly* 20, no. 3 (1947): 329–346.

12. Carol Ruth Berkin, "Remembering the Ladies: Historians and the Women of the American Revolution," in *The American Revolution: Changing Perspectives*, ed. William M. Fowler Jr. and Wallace Coyle (Boston: Northeastern University Press, 1979), 51–67, 55.

13. Sally Smith Booth, *The Women of 76* (New York: Hastings House, 1973).

14. Elizabeth Evans, *Weathering the Storm: Women of the American Revolution* (New York: Charles Scribner's Sons, 1975).

15. Linda Grant DePauw and Conover Hunt, *Remember the Ladies: Women in America, 1750–1815* (New York: Viking Press, 1976). This is a lovely collection of women's material culture from the eighteenth century.

16. Mary Beth Norton, "Eighteenth-Century American Women in Peace and War: The Case of the Loyalists," *William and Mary Quarterly* 33, no. 3 (1976): 386–409.

17. Linda K. Kerber, "The Republican Mother: Women and the Enlightenment, an American Perspective," *American Quarterly* 28, no. 2 (1976): 187–205. See also Nancy F. Cott, "Divorce and the Changing Status of Women in Eighteenth-Century Massachusetts." *William and Mary Quarterly* 33, no. 4 (1976): 586–614.

18. Joan Hoff Wilson, "The Illusion of Change: Women and the Revolution," in *The American Revolution: Explorations in the History of Radicalism*, ed. Alfred F. Young (Dekalb: Northern Illinois University Press, 1976), 383–446.

19. Elaine F. Crane, "Dependence in the Era of Independence," in *The American Revolution: Its Character and Limits,* ed. Jack Greene (New York: New York University Press, 1987), 253–275.

20. Berkin, "Remembering the Ladies," 51–67. For a slightly earlier bibliography, see Vicki G. Fox and Althea L. Stoeckel, "The Role of Women in the American Revolution: An Annotated Bibliography," *Indiana Social Studies Quarterly* 28, no. 1 (1975): 14–29.

21. Mary Beth Norton, *Liberty's Daughters: The Revolutionary Experience of American Women,* 1750–1850 (Boston: Little, Brown, 1980); Linda K. Kerber, *Women of the Republic: Intellect and Ideology in Revolutionary America* (Chapel Hill: University of North Carolina Press, 1980).

22. Kerber, "Republican Mother"; Rosemarie Zagarri, "The Rights of Man and Woman in Post-Revolutionary America," *William and Mary Quarterly* 55, no. 2 (1998): 203–204, 204.

23. Sheila Skemp, *Judith Sargent Murray: A Brief Biography with Documents* (Boston: Bedford Books, 1988); Zagarri, *A Woman's Dilemma*; Jeffrey H. Richards, *Mercy Otis Warren* (New York: Twayne, 1995); Young, *Masquerade*.

24. Janet Whitney, *Abigail Adams* (Boston: Little, Brown, 1947); Lynne Withey, *Dearest Friend: A Life of Abigail Adams* (New York: Free Press, 1981); Charles Akers, *Abigail Adams: An American Woman* (Boston: Little, Brown, 1980); Paul C. Nagel, *The Adams Women: Abigail and Louisa Adams, Their Sisters and Daughters* (New York: Oxford University Press, 1987); Edith B. Gelles, "Abigail Adams: Domesticity and the American Revolution," *New England Quarterly* 52 (1979): 500–521; Gelles's full-length biography of Abigail Adams is *Portia: The World of Abigail Adams* (Bloomington: Indiana University Press, 1992); Elaine Forman Crane, "Political Dialogue and the Spring of Abigail's Discontent," *William and Mary Quarterly* 56, no. 4 (1999): 745–774. See also Pauline E. Schloesser, "Feminist Interpretation of the American Founding (Mercy Otis Warren, Abigail Smith Adams, Judith Sargent Murray)" (PhD diss., Indiana University, 1994); David McCullough, *John Adams* (New York: Touchstone, 2001); Catherine Allgor, *A Perfect Union: Dolley Madison and the Creation of the American Nation* (New York: Henry Holt, 2006).

25. Barbara Clark Smith, "Food Rioters and the American Revolution," *William and Mary Quarterly* 51, no. 1 (1994): 3–38; Alfred F. Young, "The Women of Boston: Persons of Consequence in the Making of the American Revolution, 1765–76," in *Women and Politics in the Age of the Democratic Revolution*, ed. Harriet Branson Applewhite and Darline G. Levy (Ann Arbor: University of Michigan Press, 1990); Wayne Bodle, "Jane Bartram's 'Application': Her Struggle for Survival, Stability, and Self-Determination in Revolutionary Pennsylvania," *Pennsylvania Magazine of History and Biography* 115, no. 2 (1991): 185–220; Linda K. Kerber, " 'I Have Don . . . Much to Carrey on the War': Women and the Shaping of Republican Ideology after the American Revolution," in *Women and Politics*, ed. Applewhite and Levy; Judith Gross, "Molly Brandt: Textual Representations of Cultural Midwifery," *American Studies* 40, no. 1 (1999): 23–40.

26. Linda K. Kerber, "History Can Do It No Justice: Women and the Reinterpretation of the American Revolution," in *Women in the Age of the American Revolution*, ed. Ronald Hoffman and Peter J. Albert (Charlottesville: University of Virginia Press, 1989), 3–42.

27. Cynthia A. Kierner, *Beyond the Household: Women's Place in the Early South, 1700–1835* (Ithaca, N.Y.: Cornell University Press, 1998). Kierner's other contribution to the literature is a collection of women's petitions from the southern states between 1776 and

1800. See idem, *Southern Women in Revolution, 1776–1800: Personal and Political Narratives* (Charleston: University of South Carolina Press, 1998). Judith Van Buskirk, "They Didn't Join the Band: Disaffected Women in Revolutionary Philadelphia," *Pennsylvania History* 62, no. 3 (1995): 306–329; Susan E. Klepp, "Rough Music in Philadelphia, July 4th, 1778," in *Riot and Revelry in Early America*, ed. William Pencak, Matthew Dennis, and Simon P. Newman (University Park: Pennsylvania State University Press, 2002), 156–176.

28. Jan Lewis, "The Republican Wife: Virtue and Seduction in the Early Republic," *William and Mary Quarterly* 44 (1987): 689–721; Ruth Bloch, "The Gendered Meaning of Virtue in Revolutionary America," *Signs* 13, no. 1 (1987): 37–59; Joan R. Gundersen, "Independence, Citizenship, and the American Revolution," *Signs* 13, no. 1 (1987): 59–77; see also Paula Baker, "The Domestication of Politics: Women and American Political Society, 1780–1920," *American Historical Review* 89, no. 3 (1984): 620–647.

29. Jacqueline Jones, "Race, Sex, and Self-Evident Truths: The Status of Slave Women during the Era of the American Revolution," in *Slavery and Freedom in the Age of the American Revolution,* ed. Ira Berlin and Ronald Hoffman (Charlottesville: University of Virginia Press, 1983), 293–337; 298. Jones wryly notes, "Whatever their political differences, the white male combatants seemed to share similar notions about 'black women's work'" (ibid., 328).

30. Mary Beth Norton, Herbert G. Gutman, and Ira Berlin, "The Afro-American Family in the Age of Revolution," in *Slavery and Freedom in the Age of the American Revolution*, ed. Berlin and Hoffman, 175–191, 189.

31. Betty Wood, "Some Aspects to Female Resistance to Chattel Slavery in Low Country Georgia, 1763–1815," *Historical Journal* 30, no. 3 (1987): 605–622.

32. Billy G. Smith and Richard Wojtowicz, *Blacks Who Stole Themselves: Advertisements for Runaways in the Pennsylvania Gazette, 1728–1790* (Philadelphia: University of Pennsylvania Press, 1989), 131, 136, 135. Gary Nash claims that many of the slaves who fled the Philadelphia area during and after the British occupation in 1777 were women — mostly single and young. Gary Nash, *Forging Freedom: The Formation of Philadelphia's Black Community, 1720–1840* (Cambridge, Mass.: Harvard University Press, 1988), 57. See also Debra L. Newman, "Black Women in the Era of the American Revolution in Pennsylvania," *Journal of Negro History* 61, no. 3 (1976): 276–289.

33. Jones, "Race, Sex, and Self-Evident Truths," 297, 326, 324.

34. Sylvia Frey, *Water from the Rock: Black Resistance in a Revolutionary Age* (Princeton, N.J.: Princeton University Press, 1991).

35. T. Stephen Whitman, *The Price of Freedom: Slavery and Manumission in Baltimore and Early National Maryland* (Lexington: University Press of Kentucky, 1997), 119.

36. *Census Directory for 1811 containing the names, Occupations & Residence of the Inhabitants of the City, Southwark & Northern Liberties, a Separate Division Being allotted to Persons of Colour; to which is annexed An Appendix containing much useful information, and a Perpetual Calendar* (Philadelphia: Printed by Jane Aitken, 1811); the Library Company of Philadelphia has a copy of this directory. Free blacks in Pennsylvania could own real property (unlike in New Jersey and New York). Jean Soderlund gives examples of some successful female blacks who owned real estate and slaves. Jean R. Soderlund, "Black Women in Colonial Pennsylvania," in *African Americans in Pennsylvania: Shifting Historical Perspectives,* ed. Joe William Trotter Jr. and Eric Ledell Smith (University Park: Pennsylvania State University Press, 1997), 73–92, 86.

37. Jan E. Lewis, "A Revolution for Whom? Women in the Era of the American Revolution," in *A Companion to Women's History*, ed. Nancy A. Hewitt (Oxford: Blackwell Publishers, 2002), 83–99, quotes on 95, 97.

38. Judith Gross, "Molly Brandt: Textual Representations of Cultural Midwifery," *American Studies* 40, no. 1(1999): 23–40; James Taylor Carson, "Molly Brandt: From Clan Mother to Loyalist Chief," in *Sifters: Native American Women's Lives*, ed. Theda Perdue (New York: Oxford University Press, 2001), 48–60.

39. Martha Harroun Foster, "Lost Women of the Matriarchy: Iroquois Women in the Historical Literature," *American Indian Culture and Research Journal* 19, no. 3 (1995): 121–140. An excellent study of Native Americans during the war years is Colin Calloway's *The American Revolution in Indian Country* (Oxford: Blackwell Publishers, 1995). Calloway examines several Native American tribes, from the Cherokee in the South to the Iroquois Confederacy in the Northeast. The experiences of Native American women are part of the history of these tribes, but Calloway looks at each group collectively and from the standpoint of their engagement with British Americans. Studies with a regional focus include Claudio Saunt, *A New Order of Things: Property, Power, and the Transformation of the Creek Indians, 1733–1816* (Cambridge: Cambridge University Press, 1999); and Richard White, *The Middle Ground: Indians, Empires, and Republics in the Great Lakes Region, 1650–1815* (Cambridge: Cambridge University Press, 1991).

40. Theda Perdue, *Cherokee Women: Gender and Culture Change, 1700–1835* (Lincoln: University of Nebraska Press, 1998), 8.

41. Diane Rothenberg, "The Mothers of the Nation: Seneca Resistance to Quaker Intervention," in *Women and Colonization: Anthropological Perspectives*, ed. Mona Etiennne and Eleanor Leacock (New York: Praeger, J. F. Bergin, 1980), 63–87; Nancy Shoemaker, "The Rise or Fall of Iroquois Women," *Journal of Women's History* 2, no. 3 (1991): 39–57; Lucy Eldersveld Murphy, "Autonomy and the Economic Roles of the Indian Women of the Fox-Wisconsin Riverway Region, 1763–1832," in *Negotiators of Change: Historical Perspectives on Native American Women*, ed. Nancy Shoemaker (New York: Routledge, 1995), 72–89.

42. Hewitt, *Companion to Women's History*, 83–99. The general studies of the Revolution written in the past twenty years do include, if only briefly, information about women's activities. One of the best examples of this kind is Edward Countryman's *The American Revolution* (New York: Hill and Wang, 1985; rev. ed., 2003).

43. Joan R. Gundersen, *To Be Useful to the World: Women in Revolutionary America, 1740–1790* (New York: Twayne, 1996); Carol Berkin, *Revolutionary Mothers: Women in the Struggle for America's Independence* (New York: Knopf, 2005).

44. Applewhite and Levy, *Women and Politics in the Age of the Democratic Revolution.* See also Susan Branson, *These Fiery Frenchified Dames: Politics and Culture in Early National Philadelphia* (Philadelphia: University of Pennsylvania Press, 2001); Simon P. Newman, *Parades and the Politics of the Street: Festive Culture in the Early American Republic* (Philadelphia: University of Pennsylvania Press, 1997).

45. Jan E. Lewis, "'Of Every Age, Sex, and Condition': The Representation of Women in the Constitution," *Journal of the Early Republic* 15, no. 3 (1995): 359–388; Linda K. Kerber, "The Paradox of Women's Citizenship in the Early Republic: The Case of *Martin vs. Massachusetts,* 1805," *American Historical Review* 97, no. 2 (1992): 349–378; see also Joan Hoff, *Law, Gender, and Injustice: A Legal History of U.S. Women* (New York: New York University Press, 1991).

46. Zagarri, "The Rights of Man and Woman," 203–230, 204.

47. David Waldstreicher, *The Making of American Nationalism: Celebrations and Political Culture, 1776–1820* (Chapel Hill: University of North Carolina Press, 1997); Newman, *Parades.*

48. Branson, *These Fiery Frenchified Dames*; Catherine Allgor, *Parlor Politics: In Which the Ladies of Washington Help Build a City and a Government* (Charlottesville: University Press of Virginia, 2000).

49. Mary Beth Norton did devote a portion of *Liberty's Daughters* to enslaved and free women of color, as did Gundersen in *To Be Useful to the World*.

50. Kerber, " 'History Can Do It No Justice,' " 68.

4

Southern Women of Color and the American Revolution, 1775–1783

BETTY WOOD

During the past twenty or so years our understanding of the American Revolution has been transformed in two very important ways. Thanks to such scholars as David Brion Davis, Ira Berlin, and Sylvia Frey, to name but three of those whose findings have been particularly influential, much closer attention has come to be paid to the complexities of slavery and race relations during this pivotal period in nation-making. Building upon the pioneering work of Benjamin Quarles, Frey has shifted our attention away from the political, moral, and religious problems that the institution of slavery posed for white Americans and emphasized the extent to which the American Revolution was also a black revolution, albeit a failed revolution. Thanks to Frey, historians have moved enslaved African Americans to the center of the historical stage and accorded them the agency so long denied them by most historians of the American Revolution.[1]

Simultaneously, the groundbreaking scholarship of Mary Beth Norton and Linda Kerber during the late 1970s marked the beginning of what has proved to be a torrent of research that has explored and continues to explore the many different dimensions of women's lives and experiences during this same critical period of American history.[2] Unfortunately, and despite the work of Quarles and Frey, these two highly innovative scholarly preoccupations have failed to combine in ways that do anything like full justice to the enslaved and legally free women of color of the Revolutionary South.

Nevertheless, there are a cluster of articles and essays that explore some aspects of these women's lives during the second half of the eighteenth century. For example, Betty Wood has explored the intersections between gender, race, and rank in the Georgia Lowcountry, whilst Cynthia Lynn Lyerly has focused her attention on black Methodist women during the Revolutionary era.[3] However, there is still no full-length study of southern women of color between the mid-eighteenth and the early nineteenth century. To date, only one essay, written by Jacqueline Jones and published in 1989, has attempted to provide an overview of the ways in which the ideas and events of the American Revolution had an impact upon the family, the work, and the religious lives of black women. Most regrettably, Jones's comment that "the history of black women in the second half of the eighteenth century has fallen between the cracks that divide the history of women from the study of slaves" remains as true today as it was in 1989.[4]

The available evidence presents various and often enormous methodological difficulties for those seeking to unravel the experiences of enslaved and free women of color in the Revolutionary South, not least during the War for Independence. However, these difficulties are by no means insurmountable. True, no southern woman of color, free or enslaved, penned an autobiography, kept a diary, or wrote letters during the Revolutionary era.[5] There was no Phillis Wheatley hard at work in the mid- and late eighteenth century South.[6] Largely denied even the most rudimentary formal education, the number of enslaved women (and men) in the Revolutionary and Early National South able to read and/or write was minuscule.[7] Those who possessed the second of these skills tended to put pen to paper in order to forge passes and manumission papers for themselves, their family members, or friends rather than to produce autobiographical accounts of their lives under slavery.

Although we have no choice but to depend upon white and often male-generated evidence of varying degrees of objectivity, nevertheless, there is a tremendous amount of such evidence. Private papers and plantation books, newspapers, church and legal records, as well as the voluminous paperwork created by the British and American governments and their armed forces between 1775 and 1783, all provide us with invaluable insights into the ambitions and experiences of southern women of color.

Two other sources are also particularly revealing: the albeit brief descriptions of the literally thousands of people of color who were evacuated with or by the British from both northern and southern ports at the end of the War for Independence; and postwar Loyalists' claims for compensation from the British government for the property, including the enslaved property, that their political allegiance had cost them. The latter sometimes included information about enslaved women, as well as men, who had run away from them during the war; who had been "stolen" by the Patriots; or who had been maimed or killed whilst contributing — either voluntarily or under compulsion — to the British war effort.

Even the most superficial survey of these materials reveals two patently obvious points. First, there is the sheer diversity of the decisions taken by and the subsequent experiences of southern women of color during the War for Independence. In these respects southern women of color were no more homogenous than their white counterparts were, and neither is there any good reason why they should have been. Second, many southern women of color were active if not always voluntary participants on both sides throughout the War for Independence. This participation could and did have very mixed consequences, indeed, for the women concerned, for their families and friends, as well as for those who claimed legal ownership of them.

It is indisputable that free and enslaved southern women of color displayed agency, and often quite remarkable agency at that, between 1775 and 1783, when the British evacuated many of them. It is also indisputable that this agency displayed itself in diverse and often contradictory ways. Contrary to the impression left by many, if not most, histories of the Revolutionary South, women of color were far from being an invisible or inert presence in the war-torn southern mainland.

During the early 1770s, as the Anglo-American political crisis deepened and the North American mainland was plunged into war, the enslaved people of the southern colonies might have hoped, but in Georgia and South Carolina they could scarcely have expected, that sooner or later they might be the beneficiaries of the political rhetoric of their self-styled Patriot owners and be granted freedom from their legal bondage. Toward the end of 1775, however, a rather more realistic prospect of freedom — albeit one that on the face of it seemed to be limited to enslaved men — presented itself in the shape of an essentially pragmatic British policy designed to bolster that country's military capability in North America.

The story of Lord Dunmore's Proclamation of November 1775 and the raising and arming of what soon became known as his Ethiopian Regiment has been told on a number of occasions, some years ago by Benjamin Quarles and most recently by Sylvia Frey.[8] Much the same is true of General Clinton's Phillipsburg Proclamation of 1779, which resulted in the formation of a regiment that came to be known as the Black Pioneers.[9] What remains to be told in more detail, however, is the gendered story that was more than hinted at in a letter published in the *Virginia Gazette* a fortnight after Dunmore had issued his proclamation. The letter pointed out:

> To none is freedom promised but to such as are able to do Lord Dunmore's service. The aged, the infirm, the women and children, are still to remain the property of their masters, masters who will be provoked to severity, should part of their slaves desert them ... should there be any amongst the Negroes weak enough to believe that Dunmore intends to do them a kindness, and wicked enough to provoke the fury of the Americans against their defenceless fathers and mothers, their wives, their women and children, let them only consider the difficulty of effecting their escape, and what they must expect to suffer if they fall into the hands of the Americans.[10]

We can never be privy to the many conversations that must have taken place between enslaved husbands and wives, parents and children, and friends and relations in the slave quarters, in the public markets, and in the churches of the southern mainland as news of Dunmore's offer spread like wildfire. Could enslaved men belonging to Patriot owners trust their promise of eventual freedom in exchange for military service? Ought those belonging to Loyalist owners to ignore it? Was it worthwhile to run the many physical risks entailed in trying to reach British lines and the certainty of brutal punishment if caught by the Patriots? What would be the British reaction to the arrival not just of would-be slave soldiers but also of their wives and children? Predictably, there was no single or simple answer to these questions.

What we do know from contemporary white accounts is that enslaved people "flocked" to join up with Dunmore. By early 1776 his Ethiopian Regiment numbered somewhere in the order of three hundred men.[11] Less well known and seldom acknowledged by scholars is the fact that those enslaved people who "flocked" to Dunmore's standard included many women. These women either took flight alone or the evidence suggests rather more often fled with their about-to-be-soldier menfolk.[12] One such couple, Harry Gray and his wife, Abby, ran away in 1776 from their owner, Benjamin Churchwell of Rappahannock, Virginia. Both survived the war, and in 1783 they were evacuated with the British to begin a new life in Nova Scotia.[13]

A rather different fate befell Aggy, sometimes known as Great Aggy, an enslaved woman owned by Peyton Randolph of Williamsburg, Virginia. Randolph, who died in October 1775, bequeathed Aggy and her children — Little Aggy, a mulatto, Secordia, and Henry — to his wife, Betsy. Shortly afterwards Aggy, who was then aged about thirty, ran away together with Eve, Lucy, Billy, Sam, George, Henry, and Peter, enslaved adults who also belonged to Randolph. The records are unclear as to whether Aggy, Lucy, and Eve took their children with them, but in all probability, they did. In any event, the runaways achieved their objective of reaching the British lines, but by the summer of 1776 four of them, including Aggy, had returned to the Randolph property in Williamsburg, apparently of their own volition. Why they decided to return remains a mystery, although it might have been in an attempt to escape the outbreak of smallpox that decimated the Ethiopian Regiment in the spring of 1776. Little is known of Aggy's life following her return, but the records reveal that she died, still enslaved, in Williamsburg in 1780.[14]

By early 1776, well before the Phillipsburg Proclamation, the notion of the British as potential liberators had also taken deep root in the South Carolina and Georgia Lowcountry. In January of that year, for example, the eminent merchant and planter Henry Laurens complained that British war ships lying off Charleston had "encouraged Negroes to come to them & gave many protection, 30 or 40 it is said were carried away by the *Scorpion*."[15] Seven months later he acknowledged that "many hundreds" of enslaved people had been taken on board British vessels. He was adamant that they were there against their will, that they had "been stolen & decoyed by the servants of King George" who had no other motive but to "sell them into ten fold worse slavery in the West Indies."[16] At this point, Laurens was unwilling to concede the exercise of agency by enslaved people. Within a year, though, events forced him to admit that enslaved people were "continually deserting the plantations" and making for Charleston, where they hoped to be able to take refuge "in Men of War and other Vessels."[17]

The evidence, such as it is, for both the Chesapeake and the Lowcountry suggests that many of the enslaved women who tried to reach the British lines did so in the company of at least one man, usually but not necessarily their husband. We simply do not know how many women set out alone, or how many were separated from their male traveling companions during the course of their journey by wartime disruptions and dislocations. This was the case, for instance, with Rachel Fox. Rachel was described in the so-called *Book of Negroes,* which listed black evacuees from the port of New York at the end of the war, as being forty-two years old, a "thin, weakly wench" who had formerly belonged to James Moorfield of Norfolk, Virginia. The only other information provided by the British was that she had "come thence with Lord Dunmore."[18] The same was true of Sabinah, who before the war had also lived in Norfolk. She demonstrated that age was no deterrent whatsoever to some enslaved women's quest for freedom. As far as we know Sabinah had been a slave all her life, but in 1779, at the age of sixty-six, she ran away from her owner, James Jolly, and somehow or other managed to reach the British lines. In 1783 Sabinah, who by this time was definitely not accompanied by any member of her family, embarked from New York for Shelburne, Nova Scotia.[19]

The evacuation records for both northern and southern ports remain to be mined in detail, as do those that shed light on the gendered experiences of the émigrés once they reached their new homes in Nova Scotia, Florida, the Caribbean, Britain, and Sierra Leone. Although problematical in some respects, and not least because of their brevity, the evacuation records do offer important clues as to the lives led by many of the female émigrés between the time they took flight from their southern owners and the time they were evacuated by the British from the port of New York in 1783. Many of these women, as well as many of those who left with the British and Loyalist émigrés from the ports of Charleston and Savannah, had spent all or part of that time travelling with British and Loyalist regiments.

With or without their husbands or other male relatives, enslaved and free women of color attached themselves to Dunmore's Ethiopian Regiment, as they would do later in the war to the Black Pioneers. Their names can also be found scattered through the records of several of the regular regiments of the British army that served in North America, as well as in those of some of the Loyalists units that were formed in each of the colonies during the war.

As Holly A. Mayer has emphasized in her recent study of the Revolutionary War, the underclass women who followed the armies — and her concern is mainly with the Patriot armies — were not there simply to satisfy the sexual desires of the military.[20] As was the case with most armies in the early modern Western world, these women were employed in a variety of auxiliary, but essentially domestic activities. And what was true of underclass white women was equally true of those women of color who traveled with the British army during the War for Independence. The nature and significance of their contributions was identical to those made by such underclass white women as Sarah Osborn, who accompanied her Patriot sergeant-husband to war and who was present throughout the siege of Yorktown.[21]

Women of color, like Peg Boden, whose husband, Cato, worked as a carpenter in a British artillery regiment, cooked; they washed clothes; and they tended to the sick, the wounded, and the dying both on and off the battlefield.[22] Each of these services was of crucial significance to the military unit with which these women travelled, if only because the willingness of women to perform them freed up men for combat duty. It is quite clear that, regardless of the sometimes derogatory comments made by the officer class of both armies about the sexual morality of women such as Peg and Sarah, their husbands took enormous and entirely justifiable pride in their wives' work as well as in their physical courage and bravery. Samuel Burke, for example, was a freeman of color, a native of Charleston, South Carolina, who volunteered for service in a Loyalist regiment, the Prince of Wales American Volunteers. He was inordinately proud of the fact that his wife, whom he probably met early on in his military service, "a free Dutch mulatto woman," had abandoned "a very good house and garden situated in New York, with furniture," in order to accompany him, "in all his marches & routes during upwards of eight years hard service in America."[23]

Unfortunately, thus far little evidence has surfaced that enables us to tease out the nature of the relationship between the likes of a Peg Boden, a Sarah Osborn, and Samuel Burke's unnamed wife. Were the life-threatening situations that they and their soldier-husbands encountered and the many physical hardships of army life experiences that helped to forge bonds of mutual friendship and sympathy between women of different ethnicities and legal status or did camp followers self-consciously separate themselves according to these differences? It seems probable that this is a question that can never be answered definitively.

British army records offer tantalizing glimpses not only of the kinds of work performed by women of color during campaigns and at army headquarters but also of the sexual relationships that might be formed between them and British soldiers of different ranks. One such relationship, that between Enoch Plummer, a lieutenant in the Sixty-ninth Regiment of Foot, and a woman of color named Rose, also indicates that by no means all those women of color who performed various services for the British armed forces were or were considered by the British to be legally free from bondage. The records reveal little about Rose. We are not told her age, from whence she came, how long she had been traveling with the regiment, or when her sexual relationship with Plummer began. What we do know is that Plummer claimed her as his slave and that shortly before the end of the war she gave birth to a baby boy who was named James. When James was four months old, Plummer, who presumably was the child's father, signed an affidavit freeing him from bondage, but for reasons that he chose not to elaborate on he retained Rose as a slave, despite "the faithful Services" she had rendered him.[24]

Plummer might well have employed the phrase "faithful Services" as a euphemism for sexual services. But it could also have incorporated the range of domestic services that Rose had performed for him, like any other woman of color or underclass white woman who followed the army. For reasons that will always remain hidden, this woman of color, this enslaved woman of color, chose not to abscond from her owner in search of her own freedom. Possibly by the time Plummer signed the affidavit freeing James she thought that it was only by staying "faithful" to him that she would be able to remain in close touch with her child. Perhaps she had come to rue the fact that she had not made an earlier bid for freedom before she had given birth to James.

In one crucial respect Rose typified not only her sex but also the enslaved people of the southern mainland generally. As Sylvia Frey has pointed out, just like Rose, "thousands" of enslaved women and men in the southern mainland chose not to try to take advantage of wartime conditions in order to make a bid for their freedom.[25] There were several entirely valid reasons why this should have been so, but as far as women were concerned, the most important reason for staying put was maternity.

All the evidence points in exactly the same direction: motherhood shaped enslaved women's decisions as to whether they should stay where they were or take flight. Virtually no enslaved mother, of whatever age, anywhere in the southern mainland, was willing to run away, to set out in quest of her own freedom from bondage, if that meant abandoning her young child or young children. This was as true during the war as it had been during the prewar years and would be again during the postwar period. In Maryland, for example, a twenty-seven-year-old mulatto woman named Pleasant was a rare example of an enslaved mother who, according to her owner, "left a suckling child behind her" when she ran away in the summer of 1780.[26]

Precisely the same was true of enslaved mothers in the Lowcountry. Between 1763 and 1790, for example, only one runaway advertisement placed in the *Georgia Gazette* mentioned that an enslaved mother had taken flight, abandoning "a child at her breast."[27] The majority of mothers were simply unwilling to desert their young children or to expose them to the very real physical dangers that flight would have entailed. When enslaved mothers did run away, and many did during the war years, it was likely as part of a family group that included their husband or in a group that included at least one man of color who might or might not have been related to them.

The rewards of successful flight could be truly enormous, truly life changing; yet these are aspects of black women's lives that have been largely ignored by historians. However, enslaved women, just as much as enslaved men, appreciated that running away and the ever-present possibility of recapture also entailed enormous and arguably life-threatening risks, as did staying put. The risks and benefits of staying put see-sawed over time and differed somewhat between town and countryside.

In 1778 and 1779, as the British armed forces advanced through the Low-country seeking to regain control of the richest region of the North American mainland, enslaved people found themselves caught up in what amounted to the front line. In some instances, enslaved women of color did all that they could to further Britain's military progress. In the Carolina Lowcountry, for example, Eliza Wilkinson, a wealthy widow and a committed Patriot who lived on Yonge's Island, about thirty miles south of Charleston, reported that "a Negro wench" had acted not only as an "informer" to a party of British troops but "also as their conductor" through what to them was an unfamiliar and dangerous terrain.[28]

Sometimes, the arrival of British troops provided enslaved people not only with an ideal opportunity to escape but also with some guarantee of their physical safety, at least in the short term, whilst doing so. This was the case, for example, in the spring of 1780, when fourteen or fifteen British troops descended upon Henry Laurens's Mepkin plantation in what his overseer there described as "a plundering manner." Who made the first approach is not recorded, but when these troops left Mepkin they were accompanied by "Simon mary old Cuffey's daughter ougene Stine and his wife fullow prince and Binah tom Savage and ante-lope." Another enslaved man, Stepney, also "whent off with the kings people" but subsequently returned.[29] There is absolutely no hint in the overseer's report of this episode that these enslaved people had been taken against their will or why it was that Stepney subsequently decided to make his way back to Mepkin.

Yet there were other diametrically different responses to the advancing British forces. Eliza Wilkinson described one woman of color as having acted as a willing guide to the advancing British forces. Ironically, a little later in the same letter Wilkinson reported how she and her friends were alerted to the danger they might face from these troops when "a Negro girl ran in exclaiming, O! The king's people are coming, it must be them for they are all in red."[30] We will never know for certain — and Eliza Wilkinson did not hazard a guess — as to why this particular young woman of color had decided to run away from, rather than toward, these British troops, why she had run toward the slave-owning Eliza Wilkinson rather than away from her.

With or without their husbands and children and regardless of their age the majority of enslaved women of color ran neither toward nor away from the British army as it made its way through the Lowcountry, but stayed where they were. Nevertheless, whether in the Lowcountry or in the Chesapeake, choosing to stay put should not necessarily be equated with disinterest, apathy, fear, or an unthinking loyalty to the interests of owners. Certainly, from late 1775 onwards, when Dunmore unveiled British policy regarding the military employment of enslaved men, individual slave owners and public authorities took steps, and often quite ferocious steps at that, to ensure that enslaved people not only stayed put but also stayed docile. At one point, for example, early on in the war, Henry Laurens and other eminent South Carolinians and Georgians seriously considered shooting in cold blood, without even the pretence of due process, the scores of enslaved men, women, and children who had taken refuge on Tybee Island.[31]

In the Chesapeake, as in the Lowcountry, slave owners employed executions and floggings, as well as the sale of enslaved people to the Caribbean, not only as punishments but also as deterrents, as a means of trying to maintain some semblance of racial control. The virtual certainty of harsh physical retribution and the high probability of permanent separation from their loved ones, should they fail, could not be easily discounted by would-be runaways or by those who thought in terms of making a rather more explicit contribution to the British cause in the hope of thereby securing their eventual freedom from bondage. We will simply never be able to know for certain exactly how many enslaved people of either sex stayed put because they understandably dreaded the consequences of failed bids for freedom.

In practice, though, choosing not to take flight meant many things, by no means all of which were entirely negative. Depending upon the decisions taken by and with others, staying put could mean remaining with friends and family and thereby benefiting from the emotional and material support they provided in such turbulent times. True, this usually meant continuing with familiar gendered domestic and work regimes, but wartime exigencies could significantly enhance enslaved peoples' bargaining power. They could secure important concessions either by threatening to run away or by running away and returning to their owners only when their demands had been met. Toward the end of the war, for instance, an owner told one Lowcountry overseer in no uncertain terms to be particularly circumspect when dealing with an enslaved woman named Ruth because "if you say the least about [her] she will run off, for she is an arch bitch."[32] A little earlier, in 1780, in an explicit and successful attempt at labor bargaining, a group of enslaved runaways belonging to Henry Laurens intimated that they would be "willing to go home" provided that they would no longer have to work under the direction of an overseer named Campbell. Laurens's agent, James Custer, did not mention what Campbell had done to so upset this group, but he noted that he had offered those concerned their choice of plantations upon which to work in the future. He told Laurens that he had been "obliged to make this offer as they openly declared to me that they would never stay with Campbell again."[33]

Predictably, things were rather different in the Lowcountry towns, particularly in Savannah and Charleston, but as the war continued the situations in these urban centers changed dramatically in ways that had enormous implications for enslaved women and men. In 1776 and 1777, as they had done in the late colonial period, enslaved runaways from the countryside often made for Charleston and Savannah in what, if their owners are to be believed, were significantly large numbers. The attraction of these two towns to runaways from the countryside was not so much the quasi-freedom of blending in with the black urban crowd and the possibility of being able to escape by sea as it was of being liberated or, as Henry Laurens insisted, being stolen and removed by the British. Charleston and Savannah offered the prospect of a permanent escape from bondage.

During its initial stages the British occupation or reoccupation of Savannah and Charleston seemed to offer tangible material benefits to free and enslaved women of color, whether they were urban residents or fugitives from the countryside. Sometimes these women performed essentially similar kinds of work to those undertaken by the likes of Peg Boden and other women who had followed their husbands to war. The difference, of course, was that they worked closer to home, indeed, sometimes from their homes, and they did not necessarily do so in the hope of thereby securing their eventual liberation from bondage.

In Savannah, for example, General Clinton employed Phillis George, a free woman of color, as a washerwoman. Phillis's husband, David, who in the postwar years was to achieve fame and notoriety in equal measure for his role in the spread of evangelical Protestantism, was the first to acknowledge that it was her work, and her work alone, that supported them and their three children. "Out of the little she got," he subsequently wrote, "she maintained us."[34] Whatever her political sympathies and hopes for the future, Phillis George worked first and foremost to ensure the survival of her family.

The British occupation of Savannah and Charleston provided some women of color, like Phillis George, with crucially important opportunities for paid domestic employment. Although difficult to document with any degree of precision, it is also likely that the free and enslaved women of color who already dominated the public markets of the two towns benefited materially from this influx of troops and the heightened demand for the foodstuffs and other items they offered for sale on a daily basis.[35]

The situation became very different as the Patriot armed forces regrouped and attempted to retake Savannah and Charleston. These two port towns became less attractive magnets for prospective runaways from the countryside; in fact, if anything, the reverse rapidly became the case. Knowing full well that the advancing Patriot army under the command of General Nathanael Greene was an army of liberation only as far as white South Carolinians and Georgians were concerned, an unknown number of women, as well as men, of color tried to leave Charleston and Savannah before it was too late. Others remained, no doubt clinging to the hope that the British would not abandon them.

Phillis George was one of those who took flight as the Patriot forces began to lay siege to Savannah. It was with enormous difficulty, David George subsequently recounted, that he managed to persuade his wife "to escape, and to take care of the children."[36] For enslaved women of color the dislocations and disruptions as well perhaps as the physical dangers associated with the siege offered the ideal opportunity to take flight from their owners. This was the case, for example, with a teenager named Nancy. The *Book of Negroes* described Nancy as being "formerly slave to Mr. Dove, of Georgia, but left him at the siege of Savannah." Nancy managed to make her way to New York — whether by sea or overland is not recorded — and in 1783 left with the British for Nova Scotia.[37]

For all women of color, regardless of their age and legal status, to remain in towns such as Savannah and Charleston whilst they were under bombardment often meant enduring enormous material hardship and deprivation. It could also mean being confronted by life-threatening situations on a daily, if not on an hourly, basis for as long as the siege continued. For many enslaved women of color it would also mean something else: being conscripted into war work of the most physically taxing and physically threatening kinds.

As had long been the case in the prewar Lowcountry, where able-bodied adult slaves of both sexes had been pressed into the public service, usually for the building and repairing of roads, Loyalists and Patriots alike now demanded a different kind of service from them. In Savannah and Charleston and in some of the smaller Lowcountry towns, both sides drafted enslaved women and men by the score, if not by the hundreds, to perform the often-backbreaking and perilous labor involved in constructing and repairing fortifications. In every respect they were at the front line. We simply have no evidence as to how many of them might have thought that this work they were undertaking was vital to securing a British victory, a victory upon which many of them must have pinned their hopes for freedom.

What we do know is that enslaved women worked alongside enslaved men and sometimes took their children, often their very young children, to work with them. In April 1781, for example, John Douglass was ordered to "furnish all your working Slaves in order to put Fort Cornwallis in a State of Defence. . . . Of this, fail not at your Peril."[38] When Fort Cornwallis fell to the Patriots two months later, Jesse, described by Douglass as "a likely young Man 21 years old," was killed by a cannon ball. Two other enslaved men, Ness and Hannibal, were captured by the Americans, as were two women, Venus and Charlotte, and Charlotte's five-year-old daughter.[39] After the war another Georgia Loyalist, Simon Munro, put in a claim for compensation from the British government to cover the financial loss he had incurred as the result of the deaths of two enslaved men, Bristol Sr. and Bristol Jr., almost certainly father and son, who had been killed during the siege of Sunbury. He also put in a claim for an enslaved woman named Bess, who may or may not have been related to the two Bristols. Bess had not been killed during the siege, but she had been "maim'd . . . & rendered of no service." Munro did not bother to describe what were the obviously horrendous injuries suffered by Bess, and there is no record of her subsequent fate.[40] Their owners either gave the labor of enslaved women such as Venus, Charlotte, and Bess or hired them out to the British armed forces. The same was true of those women who were employed in similar capacities by the Patriots. Enslaved women received no material reward for the dangerous work they performed, and neither were they promised their freedom from bondage should they manage to survive until the end of the war.

Whether or not they volunteered or were conscripted for war work, enslaved women and men in southern towns and cities under siege experienced not only constant physical danger but also, as sieges dragged on, enormous physical suffering. The appalling situation during the siege of Yorktown, the starvation and the smallpox that ravaged the besieged, and the allegedly callous British disregard for the people of color trapped there with them, is very well known. Conditions during the sieges of Savannah and Charleston were just as awful as they were at Yorktown during the days before the British finally surrendered.[41]

Depending upon the ebb and flow of war, a rather different danger might await enslaved women and men who escaped to or chose to remain in the countryside, a danger that could and did result in the enforced separation of families and friends. Even though it might not have been officially sanctioned by their high commands, there is a fair amount of evidence to indicate that soldiers and sailors on both sides in the war snatched slaves and treated them as a form of war booty. As we have already seen, Henry Laurens levied this charge against the British navy early on in the war. Exactly the same charges were made against both the fledgling American navy and private merchantmen.

In addition to the compensation claims he made for those of his slaves wounded and killed at Sunbury, the Georgia Loyalist Simon Munro reported the loss of six other of his enslaved people. In what was by no means an isolated incident in the coastal parishes of the Lowcountry, Munro described how four men and two women, Patty and Leah, together with Leah's child, had been seized by a Patriot, or as Munro put it, a Rebel privateer. As far as Munro knew, they had been "carried into Antigua," where, presumably, they had been sold for private profit into the harsh sugar regime of the British Caribbean. Munro had no idea of what fate had befallen three other of his enslaved women, "Elsey, Fanny, and Fanny's Sister, who had been taken by a Rebel party from Mrs. MUNRO when I was doing duty in Savanna [sic]."[42] We will probably never know for certain how many others found themselves in similar situations or where they ended up.

It is, perhaps, stating the obvious to conclude by emphasizing that during the War of American Independence southern women of color were no more homogeneous in terms of their attitudes, affiliations, and ambitions than were that region's women of European ancestry. But what historians have thus far failed to acknowledge is that both directly and indirectly they made significant contributions to the war efforts of both sides through their work. Many forfeited their lives as a result of making those contributions, and all made what were often agonizing decisions about how they might best exploit wartime conditions for their own ends and, above all else, for the benefit of their children.

Both in the Chesapeake and in the Lowcountry, and often at the most enormous physical risk to themselves, scores of enslaved women sought to take advantage of an essentially pragmatic British military policy in the hope and expectation of thereby securing their permanent liberation from bondage. Every one of the hundreds of women evacuated with and by the British at the end of the war, be it from New York, Charleston, or Savannah, had a different story to tell.

For many of these women claimed by Loyalist owners the end of the war and their evacuation from the newly independent American states would not mean any change in their legal status. It might mean, though, exchanging the work regimes of tobacco and rice production for what were generally regarded by contemporaries as being the even more onerous and brutal sugar-producing regimes of the Caribbean. For other women, those who remained enslaved as well as the much smaller number who could demonstrate that they were legally free, their destination would be Nova Scotia. For some of these women that would be their final destination; for others it would prove to be an unpleasant hiatus before they began the next leg of their journey to Sierra Leone. The stories of these women's lives in their new homes remain to be told in more detail, as do those of the overwhelming majority of women of color, the literally thousands of women in the newly independent southern states, who ended the War for American Independence as they had begun it: as legally enslaved people. Only when those stories are told in detail will we have a full understanding of the gendered character of the Revolutionary South.

NOTES

1. David Brion Davis, *The Problem of Slavery in the Age of Revolution, 1770–1823* (Ithaca, N.Y.: Cornell University Press, 1975); Ira Berlin, *Many Thousands Gone: The First Two Centuries of Slavery in North America* (Cambridge, Mass.: Harvard University Press, 2000); Sylvia R. Frey, *Water from the Rock: Black Resistance in a Revolutionary Age* (Princeton, N.J.: Princeton University Press, 1991); Benjamin Quarles, *The Negro in the American Revolution* (Chapel Hill: University of North Carolina Press, 1961).

2. Mary Beth Norton, *Liberty's Daughters: The Revolutionary Experience of American Women, 1750–1800* (Boston, Mass.: Little, Brown, 1980); Linda K. Kerber, *Women of the Republic: Intellect and Ideology in Revolutionary America* (Chapel Hill: University of North Carolina Press, 1980).

3. Betty Wood, *Gender, Race, and Rank in a Revolutionary Age: The Georgia Lowcountry, 1750–1820* (Athens: University of Georgia Press, 1980); Cynthia Lynn Lyerly, "Religion, Gender, and Identity: Black Methodist Women in a Slave Society, 1770–1810," in *Discovering the Women in Slavery: Emancipating Perspectives on the American Past*, ed. Patricia Morton (Athens: University of Georgia, 1996). See also Betty Wood, "Some Aspects of Female Resistance to Chattel Slavery in Low Country Georgia, 1760–1815," *Historical Journal* 30, no. 3 (1987): 603–622; Suzanne Lebsock, "Free Black Women and the Question of Matriarchy: Petersburg, Virginia, 1784–1820," *Feminist Studies* 8 (1982): 271–292.

4. Jacqueline Jones, "Race, Sex, and Self-Evident Truths: The Status of Slave Women during the Era of the American Revolution," in *Women in the Age of the American Revolution*, ed. Ronald Hoffman and Peter J. Albert (Charlottesville: University Press of Virginia for the United States Capitol History Society, 1989), 298.

5. For a selection of women's narratives that includes some petitions produced by or on behalf of free women of color in the postwar period, usually in order to establish their

claim to legal freedom, see Cynthia A. Kierner, *Southern Women in Revolution, 1776–1800: Personal and Political Narratives* (Columbia: University of South Carolina Press, 1998).

6. For an excellent discussion of the nature and significance of Phillis Wheatley's literary works, see David Grimsted, "Anglo-American Racism and Phillis Wheatley's 'Sable Veil,' 'Lenghtn'd Chain,' and 'Knitted Heart,'" in *Women in the Age of the American Revolution*, ed. Hoffman and Albert, 338–446. For an edition of her poetry, see Julian D. Mason Jr., *The Poems of Phillis Wheatley* (Chapel Hill: University of North Carolina Press, 1966).

7. Between the early 1740s and early 1770s, the Anglican Church and its allied missionary societies opened a handful of schools for black children in Virginia, Georgia, and the Carolinas. Most of these establishments were very short lived and seldom taught more than thirty or so pupils at any one time. For a more detailed discussion see Sylvia R. Frey and Betty Wood, *Come Shouting to Zion: African American Protestantism in the American South and the British Caribbean to 1830* (Chapel Hill: University of North Carolina Press, 1998), 72–75.

8. Benjamin Quarles, "Lord Dunmore as Liberator," William and Mary Quarterly, 3rd ser., 15, no. 4 (1958): 494–507; Quarles, *The Negro in the American Revolution*, 19–32; Frey, *Water from the Rock*, 63, 67–77; Sylvia R. Frey, "Between Slavery and Freedom: Virginia Blacks in the American Revolution," *Journal of Southern History* 49 (1983): 375–398.

9. Frey, *Water from the Rock*, 108–114, 118–119, 121, 141, 175, 192.

10. *Virginia Gazette*, November 5, 1775.

11. Quarles, *The Negro in the American Revolution*, 28.

12. At least fifty women of color, described by the Patriots as forming part of "Lord Dunmore's *black banditti*," were discovered by the American troops when they retook control of Gwyn's Island in the spring of 1776. *Virginia Gazette*, August 31, 1776.

13. "Inspection Roll of Negroes" (also known as "The Book of Negroes") 3 manuscript volumes. Book One, April 23–27, 1783, Ship *Polly* bound for Port Roseway [Shelburne, Nova Scotia]: Captain John Browne at http://collections.ic.gc.ca/blackloyalists/documents/official/book_of_negroes.htm. Last consulted November 15, 2005; hereafter cited as "Book of Negroes."

14. For more details, including the last wills and testaments of Peyton and Betsy Randolph, see http://www.history.org./Almanack/people/bios/bioran.cfm and http://www.history.org/Almanack/people/bios/bioaggy.cfm. Last consulted November 14, 2005.

15. Henry Laurens to James Laurens, Charles Town, January 6, 1776, in George M. Rogers, Philip M. Hamer, David R. Chesnutt, and C. James Taylor, ed., *The Papers of Henry Laurens,* 15 vols. to date (Columbia: University of South Carolina Press, 1968–2006), 11:15.

16. Henry Laurens to James Laurens, Charles Town, August 14, 1776, in *Papers of Henry Laurens*, ed. Rogers et al., 11:223.

17. Henry Laurens to Ralph Izard, Goose Creek, June 9, 1777, in *Papers of Henry Laurens*, ed. Rogers et al., 11:350.

18. "Book of Negroes," Book One, April 23–27, 1783, Ship *Ann* bound for Port Roseway [Shelburne, Nova Scotia]: Joseph Clark, Master.

19. "Book of Negroes," Book One, April 23–27, 1783, Brig *Kingston* bound for Port Roseway [Shelburne, Nova Scotia]: John Atkinson, Master.

20. Holly A. Mayer, *Belonging to the Army: Camp Followers and Community during the American Revolution* (Columbia: University of South Carolina Press, 1996). For a study that focuses on the British army, see Sylvia R. Frey, *The British Soldier in America: A Social History of Military Life in the Revolutionary Period* (Austin: University of Texas Press, 1981).

21. For Sarah's account of her experiences see "Sarah Osborn's Application for a Revolutionary War Pension," in *The Revolution Remembered: Eyewitness Accounts of the War for Independence,* ed. John C. Dann (Chicago: University of Chicago Press, 1980), 242–250.

22. "Book of Negroes," Book One, April 23–17, 1783, Ship *Apollo* bound for Port Roseway [Shelburne, Nova Scotia]: John Adamson, Master.

23. Memorial of Samuel Burke, no date, Great Britain, Public Record Office, Audit Office, Class 13, Vol. 63, folios 401–402, at http://www.royalprovincial.com/genealogy/fems/fams6.shtml. Last consulted November 15, 2005.

24. Affidavit of Enoch Plummer, Lt. 69th Regt., Nova Scotia. Public Archives of Nova Scotia, RG 1, Vol. 170, 350, at http://www.royalprovincial.com/military/black/blkfree.htm. Last consulted November 15, 2005.

25. Frey, *Water from the Rock,* 168–169.

26. *Maryland Gazette,* Annapolis, June 9, 1780.

27. *Georgia Gazette,* April 20, 1786.

28. Caroline Gilman, ed., *Letters of Eliza Wilkinson: During the Invasion and Possession of Charlestown, S.C., by the British in the Revolutionary War* (New York: S. Colman, 1839), letter 3.

29. Samuel Massey to Henry Laurens, Charles Town, June 12, 1780, in *Papers of Henry Laurens,* ed. Rogers et al., 15:305.

30. Gilman, *Letters of Eliza Wilkinson,* letter 3.

31. Frey, *Water from the Rock,* 66.

32. Wm. Snow to Mr. Rhodes, September 9, 1781, cited in Quarles, *The Negro in the American Revolution,* 126.

33. James Custer to Henry Laurens, Charles Town, June 1780, in *Papers of Henry Laurens,* ed. Rogers et al., 15:303–304.

34. AN ACCOUNT OF [THE] LIFE OF Mr. David George from S. L. A. given by himself (unpaginated), at http://collections.ic.gc.ca/blackloyalists/documents/diaries/george-a-life.htm. Last consulted November 15, 2005.

35. For women of color and the public markets of Charleston and Savannah, see Robert Olwell, " 'Loose, Idle, and Disorderly': Slave Women in the Eighteenth-Century Charleston Marketplace," in *More Than Chattel: Black Women and Slavery in the Americas,* ed. David Barry Gaspar and Darlene Clark Hine (Bloomington: Indiana University Press, 1996), 97–110; Betty Wood, *Women's Work, Men's Work: The Informal Slave Economies of Lowcountry Georgia* (Athens: University of Georgia Press, 1995), esp. ch. 5.

36. AN ACCOUNT OF [THE] LIFE OF Mr. David George.

37. "Book of Negroes," Book One, April 23–27, 1783, *London,* Frigate bound for Port Roseway [Shelburne, Nova Scotia]: Hugh Watts, Master, at http://collections.ic.gc.ca/blackloyalists/documents/official/book_of_negroes.htm. Last consulted November 15, 2005.

38. Thos. Brown, Lt. Col. Commt. K Troops at Augusta, to Mr. John Douglass, Augusta, April 12, 1781, Great Britain, Public Record Office, Audit Office, Class 13, Vol. 34, folio 357, at http://royalprovincial.com/military/black/blkords.htm. Last consulted November 15, 2005.

39. Certificate signed by Thos. Brown, Lt. Col. Commt. K Troops at Augusta, Great Britain, Public Record Office, Audit Office, Class 13, Vol. 34, folio 356, at http://www.royalprovincial.com/military/black/blkpris1.htm. Last consulted November 15, 2005.

40. List of Negroes Kill'd and taken of Simon MUNRO's during the Rebellion in America, Great Britain, Public Record Office, Audit Office, Class 13, Vol. 36, folio 793, at

http://www.royalprovincial.com/military/black/blkpris1.htm. Last consulted November 15, 2005.

41. As Sylvia Frey has pointed out, in addition to all the other dangers and hardships associated with the sieges of these two towns, toward the end of 1779 Charleston experienced "a major outbreak" of smallpox. Frey, *Water from the Rock*, 128.

42. List of Negroes Kill'd and taken of Simon MUNRO's during the Rebellion in America, Great Britain, Public Record Office, Audit Office, Class 13, Vol. 36, folio 793, at http://www.royalprovincial.com/military/black/blkpris1.htm. Last consulted November 15, 2005.

5

From Dawn to Dusk

Women's Work in the Antebellum Era

INGE DORNAN

S. JAY KLEINBERG

In the 1960s and 1970s the women's movement, galvanized by civil rights protest and reform, radically altered the agenda of historical inquiry. It brought an increase in the number of female scholars to the discipline of history and, in conjunction with the emergence of the new social history, extended the categories of historical analysis beyond high politics to incorporate, among other subject areas, women and the family.[1] This necessitated an overhaul of the widely held assumption that women's role and status in society, often shaped by domestic and familial concerns as wives and mothers, were unchanging and therefore ahistorical. To this end, in the 1960s and 1970s, pioneer studies by Barbara Welter, Nancy F. Cott, and Carroll Smith-Rosenberg became central to the creation of a new historiographic framework that insisted on the historicity of women's experience in the United States. Barbara Welter's analysis of the Cult of True Womanhood described an ideology of domesticity that encouraged some U.S. women to celebrate the virtues of hearth and home. Domestic ideology, Nancy F. Cott argued, confined women to the private sphere, separated from men and away from the concerns of the public political arena. The scope of women's lives, Carroll Smith-Rosenberg insisted, meant relegation to the household, removal from the interests of the outside world, and subjection to prescriptions on female conduct. At the same time, it encouraged women to develop affirmative bonds of friendship and to provide each other with vital emotional and physical comfort.[2]

The Cult of True Womanhood, an ideology of separate spheres, and the development of a "women's culture" were historical phenomena, these historians argued, that framed women's experience after the American Revolution according to the influences of patriarchal ideology and law. Antebellum women thus became historical actors, variously battling to uphold and protest against the imperatives of a patriarchal society. This "triad of true woman, separate spheres, and women's culture," Nancy Hewitt maintains, "became the most widely used framework for interpreting women's past in the United States."[3] It paved the way for analyses that emphasized the collective oppression of women who suffered from the excesses of patriarchal power, as well as a shared sisterhood amongst women who fought oppression through networks of support and friendship. This paradigm, which accentuated the relationship between women's historical experience and patriarchy, had a direct influence during the 1960s and 1970s on shaping the discourse on the relationship between women and work in the antebellum era. It remained persuasive throughout the 1980s, when historians refined the analytic framework to incorporate race and class and thereby integrated the experience of immigrant women, free black women, and bondswomen into studies on antebellum women's labor in the United States.

In the following decade the direction of historical interest moved to politicize women's labor and heralded, among other works, Jeanne Boydston's *Home and Work.* Boydston charts the change in meaning attached to the term "work" that took place during first few decades of the Republic. Work became identified with male wage-earning in the public sphere. This definition led generations of historians to investigate only men's work experiences and to exclude the value of women's unpaid labor from studies of workers and the workplace. They thus framed women as interlopers in the world of work. Boydston's insistence on the centrality of women's unpaid labor to the family economy highlighted the overlap between public and private and paid and unpaid labor and the implications of this overlap for family and society.[4] Her analysis underscored a dramatic change in the historiographic landscape: the terms "public" and "private," male and female spheres of activity, and politics and household interests became conflated. Thereafter a more nuanced portrait of women's relationship to labor began to emerge which insisted on the complexity of their experiences and muddied the boundaries between autonomy and dependence and victory and defeat in the battle to overcome patriarchal oppression.

By 1812, Boydston argued, "a gendered *definition* of labor" emerged which prioritized wage earning, the public sphere, and the market place, associated with men, and, in the process, devalued the importance of non-wage-earning work, the private sphere, and the household, all associated with women. Definitions of work hence became inseparable from gender and rendered invisible and unworthy the unpaid work that women performed within the household.[5] Boydston thus exposed the historical rationale for women's omission from the study of history. To redress this, she invested women's household labor with profound economic and political importance and revealed how the private, domestic endeavors of antebellum women spilled over to the public sphere.[6] In the early industrial era, women's household work was still crucial to the family economy. It enabled other family members to become wage earners at a time when it was still necessary to have a mixed household economy in which one or more people cooked, sewed, saved, preserved, and maintained, while others brought in the cash required to purchase items that were uneconomic to manufacture at home.[7] Contrary to the ideology of separate spheres and the ideals of patriarchy that buttressed this, women's household labor, Boydston demonstrated, often meant an overlap between the public and private sphere.

By identifying the interconnectedness of private and public, Boydston politicized women's domesticity and thereby refined the analytic framework used by historians to recapture women's historical experience. Rather than define women's experience according to clear-cut expressions of dependence or independence, submission or defiance, victory or defeat, her discourse hinted at a complex, more nuanced understanding of women's experience as both paid and unpaid laborers, inside and outside of the home.

Studies of Native American, African American, Spanish/Mexican, and immigrant women are crucial to this new historiographical paradigm as they further demonstrate the extent to which women's labor in a variety of settings was central to a nuanced understanding of cross-cultural interactions and the development of the American economy.[8] In the twenty-first century historians have continued to emphasize the complexity of antebellum women's historical experience. They insist on the interplay of myriad cultural, social, political, and economic forces in determining the significance of women's labor and their experience as working women in a wide variety of culturally determined locations. This intersectional approach enriches and complicates our understanding of women's work in its different historical moments and meanings. In order to illustrate this development, this chapter follows the historiographic chronology outlined above.

In the 1970s and 1980s studies on the relationship between antebellum women and work began to proliferate. Labor historians focused their analyses on recapturing the lives of New England factory operatives, whose status as young, single, wage-earning women signaled a turning point in women's relationship to work in the United States. Building on the early groundwork laid by pioneering economist Edith Abbott in her study *Women in Industry* in 1910 and Caroline F. Ware's *The Early New England Cotton Manufacture*, among others, Thomas Dublin's study of New England factory workers revealed the ways in which their experience as laborers posed a direct challenge to patriarchal conceptions of womanhood and family.[9]

The first generation of mill workers were overwhelmingly young, single, and from northeastern farming families. Contrary to the popular stereotype of the poor factory girl working to support a destitute widowed mother and siblings, many of the "mill girls" in the 1820s and 1830s grew up in comfortable economic circumstances in male-headed households. They were not, therefore, compelled by family economics to seek factory employment. Instead, they chose to enter the factories to further their desire for social and economic independence.[10] As they revealed in their letters, they yearned for nicer clothes, a better education than rural life afforded, and a larger dowry than their fathers could provide.[11]

Rather than pool their salary back into the family economy, young mill operatives chose to spend their wages on their own individual advancement. Their desire for independence and status as wage earners who lived and worked away from the authority and supervision of their fathers and mothers and their employment outside of the household and domestic sphere distinguished these women as a new class of working women.[12] It also signified their refusal to conform to patriarchal ideals of True Womanhood and separate spheres, which characterized women as dependents who were socially and economically subordinate to their fathers or husbands and labored for their family in a monotony of domestic chores. Observing the gulf that existed between factory women's labor and that of their mothers, Lucy Larcom wrote of the first generation of female factory workers that they cleared the way for "independent labor for other women" so that "no real odium could be attached to any honest toil that any self-respecting woman might undertake."[13] The first generation of factory women was unique in the economic and social freedom they possessed and the benign nature of their working conditions.

Studies including Mary Blewett's writing on single and married shoe workers, Kathryn Kish Sklar's analysis of textile workers' efforts to win a reduction in their working hours, Thomas Dublin's investigation of strike activities among mill workers, and Teresa Ann Murphy's exploration of the role that religion played in women's labor organizing in New England mill towns have all examined women's role in the disputes between labor and capital in early nineteenth-century New England.[14] When factory management began to reduce their wages and increase their hours at the loom many felt compelled to strike to maintain their independence. Their rebellion earned them the derogatory appellation "Amazons."[15] Gerda Lerner's "The Lady and the Mill Girl" and Alice Kessler-Harris's *Out to Work* underlined factory women's struggle to maintain their independence as wage-earning women in a climate that increasingly sought to circumscribe women's role and status in society within the household.[16] Christine Stansell's analysis of New York textile workers depicted young wage-earning women whose social behavior suggested rebellion against patriarchal control outside as well as inside the factory during the antebellum era.[17]

The historiography on factory women dovetailed with the new historiographic framework that insisted on women's historical experience as inextricable from the enduring power of patriarchal law and tradition. The early female operatives thus became symbolic of women's historic struggle to confront patriarchal dominance; their social and economic autonomy, derived from waged labor and mill work, weakened the degree of patriarchal control and authority over their young adult lives.[18]

The other occupation opening to women in large numbers during the antebellum era, teaching, offered the prospect of intellectual freedom from the imperatives of patriarchal ideology. Joan Jensen's analysis of Quaker female teachers in Pennsylvania argued that increased educational opportunities and teaching gave young women the intellectual tools to free themselves from the ideological limitations of patriarchy embedded in marriage and the family household. Many young teachers engaged in reformist activities that led to anti-slavery protest and women's rights campaigning. They also manifested their independence in lower rates of marriage than prevailed for women generally. Notwithstanding Thomas Dublin's caveat that New Hampshire teachers were paid such meager wages that they were unable to establish homes independently of their parents, education and teaching nonetheless gave young female teachers the intellectual means to forge a sisterhood, a community of women, based upon women's activism, which led them to challenge the ideological roots of patriarchal oppression.[19]

Despite labor historians' emphasis upon the social, economic, and intellectual struggle for autonomy waged by factory women and teachers, the majority of paid laborers in the antebellum era did not engage in strikes or have access to advanced education. As early studies of women's work in the late nineteenth and early twentieth centuries remind historians, domestic labor was the largest paid profession for single women in this period.[20] In the 1980s historians redressed the representation of paid domestic labor as a monotonous, unchanging cycle of drudgery, poverty, and oppression. They developed a more nuanced portrait that outlined the evolution of this occupation and the ways in which domestic laborers were not purely victims of their circumstance but, at times, were able to assert their autonomy and strength vis-à-vis their employers. This approach differed considerably from that of Lucy Maynard Salmon's *Domestic Service* (1897), which regarded servants and the "servant problem" from the employers' point of view.[21]

Building on the historiographic framework of the previous two decades, which viewed women's historical experience as a struggle against the forces of patriarchal power, historians of paid domestic labor insisted that class conflict was as central as gendered conflict to the history of household service. Faye Dudden argued that eighteenth-century domestic service in the North tended to be an informal, episodic arrangement, often labeled "help" and embedded within family and community relationships. It was generally performed by a niece, cousin, or neighbor's daughter and was undertaken intermittently in times of illness, death, or during periods of intense workloads in the farming calendar. Nor was it always paid labor; sometimes it was given as a favor or in exchange for other goods and services rendered. Family and kin connections deflected open conflict between employer and employed. During the course of the nineteenth century, however, the term "help" began to disappear from usage as household service became professionalized as "servant" or "domestic" (which had previously been used to denote free black female help). This marked a division by race and class between the serving and the served and underscored the conflict that increasingly hallmarked relations between servant and mistress.[22]

This occurred as the demographic structure of the domestic workforce changed. Yankee women left their families and headed off to the mills or teaching profession, to be replaced by Irish immigrant women and, in lesser numbers, free black women.[23] Hasia Diner argued that Irish immigrant women entered domestic service when other women, with the exception of free blacks, turned away from it, preferring the prestige and wages that accompanied teaching and factory work. But Irish immigrant women were also driven by a desire for social and economic autonomy. Since the Irish famine of the 1840s, Irish women had delayed marriage and motherhood in order to achieve greater economic security for themselves and their families. This attitude accompanied them to America. Domestic service provided Irish immigrant women with the chance to support themselves and, as live-in servants, to claim distance from sometimes violent relations with fathers and husbands.[24]

The historiography on paid domestic labor thus embraced an analytic framework that emphasized the desire and opportunity, however slight when compared to factory women and teachers, for social and economic autonomy among Irish immigrant servants. Moreover, despite the prejudice they experienced and the conflict and drudgery that accompanied their labor, Irish immigrant servants discovered ways to assert their value and worth as laborers in the face of poor perceptions of their work and character. They understood that affluent families needed their labor and they used this as a bargaining tool to raise their wages and improve their conditions; when all else failed, they left their employers. There were, therefore, opportunities for paid domestics to actively shape their own destiny. Studies on paid domestic labor thus followed an intellectual line established by analyses of factory women and teachers as they acknowledged the oppressive force of patriarchal power on servant women's status. Nevertheless, their analyses extended the historiographic framework further to incorporate gender and class conflict in their discourse and to argue for the complexity of their experience as both actors and victims within their occupation.[25]

Throughout the 1980s the historiographic literature on single, wage-earning women, whether as factory workers, teachers, or domestic servants, variously emphasized their struggle to secure social, economic, and intellectual freedom from patriarchal control and authority. Yet it made little mention of one key gendered aspect of industrialization's impact, namely, that it separated the working world of single and married women in a way that it simply did not for men.[26] Studies of married women's work in the Northeast investigated the differing labor perspectives of women according to their marital status. They emphasized the ties that bound women to their families and communities as wives and mothers and the labor they performed for the good of the family economy. Many European American women in the Northeast were outworkers, which was a form of labor that generally failed to deliver any meaningful sense of economic and social autonomy for married women. Not only was it usually performed within the home, but few women had direct control of their wages, which were usually handed over to their husbands.[27] Indeed, married women outworkers in New York City in the garment trades were economically and socially circumscribed, according to Christine Stansell: "The outwork system promoted female depend-ence on the family, both because of the low wages outworkers earned and the form their labor took" within the household or family workshop.[28]

Mary Blewett's analysis of women shoe binders concurred that outwork was not undertaken by married women because they sought social and economic autonomy but rather because they needed to provide a supplement to their hus-band's income. Women shoe binders were motivated to work for familial and not personal gain, Blewett argued; it was "their economic circumstances [that] often forced them to integrate wage-earning into their lives."[29] Underscoring the extent to which outwork was premised on family interests and not individual autonomy, when women shoe-binders in Lynn went on strike in the 1830s, they argued for improved wages not to advance their own status but to make a more significant contribution to the family economy.[30] Only widows and single women sought higher wages to support themselves independently. The single female leaders of the strikes perceived themselves to be part of a "women's community" of shoe binders, based on the "bonds of womanhood both in work and in their domestic sphere," according to Blewett. But most married outworkers labored alone, with their working lives following the rituals and rhythms of family life.[31]

Like their married working-class counterparts, middle-class women, too, labored for the good of their families. Although typically possessing servants and slaves to undertake the most arduous and unpleasant chores, the majority of middle-class and elite women nonetheless engaged in domestic activities as household managers. Historians' analyses of the labor performed by middle-class women in the North have, however, focused on their activities and duties beyond their households. Reaffirming the importance of patriarchy to women's historio-graphy, middle-class women's labors have been framed within the context of female activism and reform and the extent to which their attitudes and conduct conformed to and upheld a patriarchal model of womanhood. Rather than oppose patriarchal power, many middle-class housewives felt duty bound to uphold the ideals of domesticity, separate spheres, and True Womanhood, ideals that appeared to dignify their status as housewives. As Mary P. Ryan argued in her study of Oneida County, New York, middle-class women began in this period to organize themselves into a series of associations for moral reform. The Female Moral Reform Society and the Maternal Association directed their anxiety toward their own sex, most especially to young working-class women who openly dis-played their disregard for bourgeois ideals of womanhood and allegedly engaged in loose sexual conduct and excessive drinking.[32] Middle-class housewives united along class lines to proclaim the virtue of True Woman behavior and assert their worth as housewives, but they distanced themselves from their working-class counterparts in the process and affirmed their allegiance to patri-archal constructions of womanhood.[33]

Stansell's analysis of the household labor of working-class women in New York City reinforced the importance of incorporating class analysis in studies on women's labor and illustrated the gulf that existed between middle-class reformers in New York and their working-class counterparts. Her study revealed how household labor led working-class housewives to develop intricate networks of support, which led to both harmonious and violent relationships. Despite the cramped living conditions and the struggle to find food, water, heat, and light, "tenement neighborhoods were a female form of association and mutual aid, a crucial buffer against the shocks of uprootedness and poverty," she argued.[34] But living in such close contact could also lead to explosive encounters, arguments. and physical conflict among women and between men and women. "Amiability and anger, reciprocity and resentment lent the working class neighborhoods the volatile, contentious, emotionally fierce character that so disturbed polite observers."[35] The importance of household labor lay as much in what was produced, procured, and consumed in the privacy of the home as in the web of supportive and antagonistic relations that it engendered outside the home.

A shared experience of patriarchy also failed to bridge the race and class divide among married women in the South. In the 1980s, the analytic framework deployed by historians in their analyses of the southern mistress once again identified patriarchal power and oppression as central to shaping women's experience and labor. They highlighted the need to incorporate race, class, and gender analysis in their investigations to assess the extent to which white women in the antebellum South bonded with their female slaves and yeoman counterparts against patriarchal dominance and oppression. Elizabeth Fox-Genovese concluded that "there is almost no evidence to suggest that slaveholding women envisioned themselves as the 'sisters' of yeoman women."[36] Neither did they develop a shared sisterhood with their enslaved and free black counterparts: "The gulf imposed by racial discrimination was nearly unbridgeable," observed Catherine Clinton.[37] The fraught relations within plantation households which threw together mistresses, female slaves, and masters in an often violent and sometimes fatal sexual maelstrom threatened any potential bonds of unity between mistresses and slaves.

Moreover the patriarchal model of southern womanhood, enshrined in the ideal of the "Southern Lady," described by Anne Firor Scott, further ensured that mistresses, female slaves, and yeoman wives were kept at an ideological distance and white patriarchal power and authority was maintained. The Southern Lady was considered to be a paragon of virtue, obedience, and refinement, a delicate and frail beauty, who prided herself on her lily white hands and gentle, compassionate demeanor.[38] Of course, this vision of womanhood little resembled the working life of a southern mistress, who despite possessing slaves to perform the most arduous and disagreeable tasks still had to engage in domestic drudgery and management and often found herself in conflict with her husband and slaves.[39] And yet southern white women rarely attacked the institution of slavery publicly or spoke out for reform. The Grimké sisters were a notable exception, although they had to leave the South to pursue their antislavery objectives.[40]

Southern white women did, however, in letters to friends, compare their experience to that of slaves and complain of physical and sexual abuse from their husbands and unceasing domestic toil and conflict.[41]

Viewed through the prism of race, class, and gender, as categories of historical analysis, plantation mistresses were construed as victims of patriarchal oppression. Their experience of the excesses of male power combined with race and class to preclude the emergence of a female community based on a shared experience of patriarchy, domesticity, or reform-inspired activism. According to historians, the imperatives of race, class, and gender ideology ensured that planter wives were, in Clinton's words, "an island" unto themselves.[42]

The working lives of poorer farm women, who possessed only one or two slaves or no slaves at all, were similarly conceived by historians during the 1970s and 1980s according to an analytic framework that accentuated their experience of a gendered division of labor and the negative influence of patriarchy in their lives. The traditional work performed by farmwomen, such as selling eggs and poultry and butter- and cheese-making, was both essential and at times the major source of cash income for rural families. Yet gendered legal systems constrained their ability to move into large-scale commercial agriculture, observed Joan Jensen in her influential study of female agricultural production in the mid-Atlantic region. Because married women could neither own land nor enter into legally binding contracts, it was difficult for them to support themselves outside a male-headed household.[43] Nancy Grey Osterud argued that although the work performed by farmwomen in the Nanticoke Valley, Broome County, New York, was central to the mechanics of farming success, this was not enough to empower them; they remained "legally and materially subordinated to men within farm families."[44] Quaker farm communities evinced similar tensions. According to Jensen, the farm, "embedded in patriarchal legal restrictions, offered women little ultimate control over wealth, property, or even their labor."[45]

John Mack Faragher's analysis of Illinois prairie families, although it drew attention to the bonds formed by farming women, nevertheless emphasized the ways in which farming limited rather than enhanced European American women's status and ability to exert power in their families. Inequitable divisions of labor according to gender, a legal system based on English common law which prevented married women from owning property, and a sphere of activity that ensured "women labored at home with children, cows and chickens," all conspired to guarantee that the "farming household exploited women as wives."[46] All in all, farming women in Illinois lived under the firm yoke of patriarchy with few outlets to challenge or redraw the boundaries of their lives.

The experience of European American women who moved westwards presents an alternative portrait to mid-Atlantic farm women, argued Julie Roy Jeffrey. Contextualizing their labor according to the dynamics of patriarchal ideology revealed that in addition to performing women's traditional household duties of cooking, washing, baking and mending, caring for children, and tending to the sick, these migrating women pitched tents, drove wagons, gathered buffalo dung for fuel, and assisted with the cattle. "The line dividing the activities of men and women became less distinct," observed Jeffrey, "and in some cases, disappeared" on the Overland Trail.[47] Even upon arrival, the division of labor according to gender remained flexible. Women had little choice but to continue to work alongside their husbands, clearing land, digging ditches, and building their new homesteads, even if they had more than enough to do on the female side of the labor/gender divide, as both Sandra Myres and Susan Armitage insist.[48]

Notwithstanding the realities of migration and settlement that altered labor roles for European American women moving west, they nonetheless strove to retain their sense of femininity and domesticity. Indeed, contemporary literature counseled these women to assert their moral and civilizing influence over the wilderness. Rather than fear the harsh effects of the frontier on womanhood, "the goal was to shape the frontier into an image of their own liking," Jeffrey maintained in her investigation of the gendered migration process. To this end, social commentators encouraged women to take on the role of community builders, although this purported civilizing role ignored the cultures of indigenous people already resident in the areas to which European American women migrated.[49]

Far from using the alteration in their labor roles to elevate their position within either their families or communities, white women migrating westwards often acted conservatively to reinstate traditional gender relations. Women were indeed perceived and treated as "co-partners" in the family economy, like their "goodwives" counterparts in the colonial era, Jeffrey argued, but "women were careful to maintain the idea of male superiority." To this end, when possible, they paid lip service to patriarchal ideals of domesticity and womanhood. Frontier life may have altered the work that women undertook, but it did not result in a "dramatic reallocation of power" within pioneer families, a point which Susan Armitage's chapter in this volume also discusses.[50]

Historians in the 1980s began to examine another set of power relationships linking patriarchal ideology, racism, and class in their analysis of the status and experience of enslaved women. Investigations into the sexual economy of slavery emphasized that bondswomen performed much the same work as men in the fields but were also completely subject to their personal whims. Studies by Deborah Gray White and Jacqueline Jones shaped the historiography on bondswomen during this decade by articulating the "double burden" of sexism and racism experienced by bondswomen.[51] Their work shows how malleable a category gender could be in the hands of southern slave owners and underscores the limitations of intellectual paradigms such as True Womanhood or the separation of spheres in explaining the experiences of women of color.

Enslaved women's work as field hands, domestic servants, and reproducers of the slave labor force, rendered through the lash, forced family separation, and sometimes rape, all indicated the extent to which African American women's bodies were the physical site of a race-gender-class system which systematically deprived them of their ability to determine their own lives and rendered their subjugation acceptable to the slavocracy. Beverly Guy-Sheftall explains that both the profit motive and a desire for cheap labor led slave owners to rationalize slave women's "involuntary roles as workers and producers of slave children. Their bodies were literally to be used in the fields from sunup to sundown, exploited to fulfill white men's lust and to give birth to slave children who would keep the plantation system afloat."[52] Legal decisions in southern courts deprived female slaves of any legal protection, placing them in the category of property. "The violation of the person of a female slave carries with it no other punishment than the damages which the master may recover for the trespass upon his property."[53] Thus they were never accorded the same definitions of womanhood and motherhood that applied to southern white women.

Enslaved women ploughed, hoed, sowed, threshed, harvested, picked cotton, and dug ditches from dawn to dusk in conditions and clothing that offended white attitudes toward womanhood in a society which considered black, but not white, women physically suited to such tasks and environment. Jones concludes that "slaveholders had little use for sentimental platitudes about the delicacy of the female [slave] constitution."[54] That slaveholders generally failed to apply the same ideals of womanhood to slave women as they did to white women is, in White's view, affirmed by Sojourner Truth's speech at the Women's Rights Convention at Akron, Ohio, in 1851 in which Truth informed her audience that she worked as hard as men and at the same tasks.[55] For Jones and White what constituted slave women's work also constituted a total disregard of their femininity, even as slaveholders relied upon their childbearing capacity to increase their profits.

Notwithstanding the lack of a gendered division of labor according to the same mores that governed white women's labor and a failure to accord enslaved mothers the same maternal dignity as white mothers, plantation work regimes nevertheless promoted "a high degree of sex consciousness" amongst enslaved women. They did this by requiring "women and girls to work together in groups," which made black women "highly dependent on each other," according to White.[56] Their work patterns inadvertently promoted a female culture and reinforced their bonds to each other. Laboring for their families and community — cooking, cleaning and producing food, washing, making and mending clothes, raising their children, and performing the role of mother-father when the latter were absent or sold — united enslaved women in mutual networks of support and asserted their identity as working women and mothers, despite the cruelty they experienced as bondswomen.[57]

New interpretations of enslaved women's labor have uncovered aspects of women's agency that historians have heretofore overlooked. Although not denying their mistreatment, Sharla Fett's investigation of health on plantations nonetheless revealed that older enslaved women, who became nurses and midwives, were able to garner power and status on plantations. They used their skills to benefit the slave community through their nursing care. "Slave health care, from the planter perspective, was very much an issue of labor control," while from the slave's perspective it was also a tool to resist or momentarily suspend patterns of work. The independent knowledge of enslaved female healers threatened the work system, according to Fett, because it inverted the positions of power and control between planter and enslaved, with the former being dependent on the latter as health worker to ensure the survival of the slave workforce and, at times, the planter's family, too.[58]

Throughout the 1970s and 1980s the historiography on working women in the antebellum era, whether as factory women, housewives, farm women, plantation mistresses, migrating settlers, or enslaved women, articulated women's historical experience in the context of race/gender hierarchy and ideology. Foremost, these studies revealed that the institution of marriage and a gendered division of labor were critical determinants of all women's dependent status and inferior position in patriarchal family and community relations to varying degrees. Race and class subordination further restricted women's social and economic status. Many women may well have derived some pride and satisfaction in their work. Others might have drawn comfort and support from the female communities they established. Nevertheless, the overwhelming emphasis in the historical literature is on the hardship and toil these women suffered and the ways in which patriarchal ideology suffused and limited the scope of their lives.

In the 1990s, as historians continued to explore the relationship between women's status and patriarchal ideology and foreground the interplay of race, class, and gender in their analyses, a reformulation of women's historical experience took place which politicized women's status and role in antebellum America. Stephanie McCurry's study of the southern yeomanry placed gender, defined as the construction of power based on the perceived differences between men and women, at the heart of her analysis. For yeoman farmers to assert themselves as "masters of small worlds," McCurry maintained, wives, children, and all slaves had to be seen to be dependent on the male household head, who by virtue of his manhood and mastery over dependents could claim the mantle of independence and authority. Gender relations were thus crucial in structuring the labor performed within and outside yeoman households and in determining who wielded power in and outside the household. Yeoman women's labor and conduct was not only critical to southern white conceptions of manhood, but vital to sustaining the South's class and race hierarchy.[59]

However, as McCurry's analysis reveals, race, class, and gender ideology collided in discussions on yeoman women's work. According to McCurry, the plantocracy and other white farmers responded with a collusive silence to this contradiction regarding women's work and the racial and class inferences that muddied the status between female field workers.[60] Yeoman women labored for the survival of their families. Planter politicians had little choice but to turn a blind eye to the field work that they performed. Despite undertaking work that belied assumptions about appropriate work for white women in the South, the division of labor in yeoman households depended upon the productive and reproductive capacities of women at the same time that it upheld the mastery and independence of yeoman farmers and underlined the dependent status of yeoman women.

Northern farmers began to question white women's roles in farming in their region during the antebellum era. Sally McMurry's research into the political meaning of women's role and status on cheese dairying farms in the North provides a nuanced portrait of farm women's relationship to patriarchal ideology and the division of labor. Despite the positive evaluation of women's work and place on these farms in the early decades of the nineteenth century, by the 1840s the farming community had begun to raise serious questions about the nature of dairying women's work and their continuing role in the cheese-making industry.[61] Most of the concerns turned on how dairying women's labor affected their families and complemented or challenged new definitions of women's work. Contemporaries asked if it was appropriate for women to undertake milking duties as increased commercialization had transferred this task to men. Was it appropriate that women perform the strenuous work involved in cheese-making? Should farming children, especially girls and young women, be encouraged to obtain an education or attend boarding schools, thereby leaving the family farm and removing their labor? "All three questions," McMurry stated, "represented disagreements within dairying families, and within the farming community, over the division of labor and the goals of the family farm."[62]

Recognizing the complexity of gendered dynamics of power, Xiomara Santamarina's analysis of ex-slaves' and free-born black women's narratives reveals how they challenged contemporary representations of black women's work to lay claim to the value and worth of their labor as field workers and domestic servants. Santamarina contends that Sojourner Truth's declaration that she worked as hard as any man was not a confession of the labor she performed as a woman-man slave or an attack against the failure of southern whites to acknowledge black women's femininity, as White suggested, but rather a proud admission of her abilities and labor. This assertion stood in marked contrast to the goals of abolitionists and free black reformers who simultaneously stressed how slavery violated black women's femininity while they encouraged them to follow white women's codes of domesticity.[63]

As Santamarina observes, for many black women, slave or free, it was impossible to uphold these ideals. Emphasizing pride in black women's work offended white ideals of womanhood, undermined the independence of black men, and threatened to jeopardize the abolitionist enterprise. As such, Truth and her amanuensis, Olive Gilbert, endeavored to present Truth's labor as an enslaved worker in the South and a free waged worker in the North. Truth deliberately described her waged labor in the North as offering little more freedom than as an enslaved worker in the South. If anything, it provided her with less satisfaction and sense of value and worth, an interpretation that Olive Gilbert struggled and failed to reconcile with northern attitudes toward freedom and labor.[64] Santamarina's analysis insists that black women's relationship to labor was far more complex than the "double burden" thesis suggested; the terms through which black women understood their labor were intricate and nuanced, reflecting their sense of self-worth as they reclaimed the value of their work for themselves and the African American community. Through their insistence on the value of their labor they asserted themselves as actors in their own destiny and not solely the victims of patriarchal oppression and sex and race prejudice.[65]

Just as the historiography on women's experience began in the 1960s and 1970s with a focus on white women's labor in the Northeast and developed to include immigrant women, southern women, and enslaved women's working lives, new historiographical directions in the 1980s and 1990s have extended the regional scope of historical interest to acknowledge the impact of different cultural systems on women's economic behavior. This has led to a greater consideration of women's labor in the western and southwestern United States. Reflecting the desire for a more nuanced portrait of women's labor experience, the studies that have emerged trace the tension and conflict in women's labor and articulate the complexity of their experience beyond narrow definitions of victimization and oppression.[66]

The Spanish conquest and the later migration of white Americans to the West disrupted the lives of the indigenous population as new power relations, legal practices, and cosmological systems reordered economic, social, and political structures. Before the arrival of Europeans or European Americans, the Pueblo Indians of present-day New Mexico and Arizona were a horticultural people who practiced both serial monogamy and polygamy. As Ramón Gutiérrez explained in *When Jesus Came, the Corn Mothers Went Away,* their matrilocal, matrilineal society had parallel lines of respect and authority for men and women. Women controlled seeds, fertility, child rearing, and household construction while men were chiefs, communicated with the gods, and controlled public rituals.[67] Women in the small tribal groups of what is present-day California had a diversity of culture and practices that respected women's labor and place in creation stories. Depending upon location, the women of the hundred or so native Californian tribal groups gathered fruit, nuts, seeds, and berries; they dug with simple tools and made the baskets in which they carried their crops. Many engaged in intertribal trade either along the coast or in the interior. They processed acorns (piñons) and built granaries to store the surplus.[68]

Navaho women's wealth derived from sheep farming, their agricultural skills, and the weaving of beautiful blankets. Located in northeastern Arizona and northwestern New Mexico, theirs was a matrilocal society in which husbands and children resided with the maternal family. Men held formal power as war and political leaders, while women had a central role in the "elaborate cycle of raid and retaliation in the multicultural Southwest."[69] Their Ute neighbors in present-day Colorado, Wyoming, Nevada, and New Mexico gathered seeds, berries, and nuts along with hunting small game. Describing pre-reservation, post-contact Southern Ute culture, Katherine M. B. Osburn defines women's familial and societal position as equal to men's. They lived in bilateral extended families, with a preference for matrilocality in recognition of women's crucial contributions to the group's survival.[70]

The imposition of Spanish or U.S. law had serious consequences for indigenous peoples, not least in the alteration of land tenure systems. The conquerors both wrenched land away from its previous occupiers and vested formal ownership of land in men as part of an effort to remake gender relations in a patriarchal mode. Thus, the federal government imposed an allotment system of land tenure on the Utes, effectively alienating women from the land in an attempt to force a male/supporter, wife/dependent model upon them.[71]

Despite a relative decline in Native women's status post-conquest, the mixing of cultural, economic, and legal systems through practices of intermarriage, capture, and adoption could reinforce their central roles in their communities, as James F. Brooks suggests in his study of captivity and identity in New Mexico. Indian societies in the New Mexico/Mexico borderlands adapted to Spanish colonialism, using women both as a source of labor and a bridge between cultures. At times women might carve out opportunities for relative power and influence in their families and communities.[72] Nevertheless, as Ned Blackhawk warns, viewing women as human bridges erases the actual experience of "individual captive women, the majority of whom were young girls" whose bodies were "trafficked and preyed upon both during and after enslavement."[73]

Revisiting the theory of a decline in women's status post-conquest, studies of Spanish/Mexican law reveal a more nuanced and complex picture which mixes issues of race with those of class and gender. Teresa L. Amott and Julie A. Matthaei's analysis of race, gender, and work demonstrates that "women's experiences under Spanish rule were sharply differentiated by race and class," with most women of Indian descent involved in agricultural production. Nevertheless, some women received land grants from the Spanish government and managed to hold on to them even after the United States annexed the southwestern regions.[74]

Women under Spanish law had a fundamentally different set of legal rights than in English common law. In particular, they had more control over property in Spanish New Mexico than they had in Anglo-America, although less than in most Native societies.[75] As Yolanda Chávez Leyva points out, Spanish/Mexican women owned the property they brought to the marriage. They also had a dower right to inherit one-half the property of the marriage. In contrast, English-based law deprived married women of the right to their pre-marital property or property that they inherited during the marriage. As eastern society became more settled, Anglo-American testators left less property to their widows and also increasingly put their sons in charge of the administration of their estates. Historians such as Joan Hoff take this as an indication that women lost economic power in the East during the eighteenth century.[76] They had no legally accepted ability to write wills, in contrast with the Spanish/Mexican women of the Southwest who, like the widow María Martin of Santa Fe, New Mexico, could will her property as she wished. She willed her house and land to her daughter, María, "because she is a woman and because she is poor." While such comparisons can be oversimplified, widows' ability to inherit land and to will it to their daughters gave them a greater measure of access to the main form of wealth in the predominantly agricultural society of the Spanish/Mexican Southwest than their counterparts living under English common law.[77]

Deena González's examination of women's lives in Santa Fe, New Mexico, foregrounds the interaction of gender, race, class, and colonization in shaping their lives. She offers a portrait which acknowledges their efforts to support themselves and their families as legal structures shifted. Frequently shunted into domestic service, sewing, or washing clothes for which they were paid less than their European American counterparts, many Spanish Mexican women had difficulty protecting their own and their children's economic position. González contends that emphasizing the dramatic decline in socioeconomic status of Spanish Mexican women hides the myriad and often contradictory ways that they sought to adapt and survive the negative impact of colonization. Indeed, some women managed successful businesses. Her conclusion recognizes the duality of Spanish Mexican women's experience: they survived colonization, but "it was a survival which to a certain extent was based on poverty and a great deal of expectation or hope that it would be eradicated."[78]

Miroslava Chávez-García's investigation of Spanish Mexican women in California follows the path suggested by González and shows how they adapted to their changing environment by challenging the power of their husbands and Anglo-American legal restraints that prevented them from owning property. They were "active agents contesting and negotiating social and cultural norms pertaining to gender relations in marriage, the family and community."[79] As married women they took abusive husbands to court; as widows they sought to buy land and establish ranchos. But, as in González's portrait of Spanish Mexican women in Santa Fe, the stories of dependency counterbalance those of success and autonomy. Divorce might yield freedom from violent husbands, but it brought little economic security. Spanish-speaking women sought employment in the narrow strata open to women of color as domestic servants, cooks, and washerwomen. All too frequently, women who had once possessed land lost it as Anglo-American law, custom, and prejudice combined to ensure that only European Americans constituted the legitimate agents of power in California society.[80]

Theda Perdue's study of Cherokee women in the Southeast warns that the declension model (a decline in women's status post-European contact) obscures the struggles, continuity, and successes that shaped the lives of Native women. While Cherokee women retained some of their cultural and spiritual influence, they lost economic and political power. Trade and warfare disrupted the balance between men's and women's spheres of influence; the American government's "civilization" program called for Indian men to become farmers, usurping women's economic role. The enforcement of monogamous marriage, which upheld patriarchal, not matrilineal descent, gender, and labor relations, undermined their power within their families. Cherokee women opposed the sale of their lands, insisting on common ownership, but they were unable to retrieve the political and economic power that they once wielded in their communities.[81]

Although the declension model paints the broad brushstrokes of the impact of colonization and conquest on Spanish Mexican and Native American women, Perdue, González, and Chávez-García insist that adaptation rather than annihilation accompanied the conquest. James Brooks's analysis of captive women in the Southwest borderlands affirms the complex ways in which women responded to their environment as productive and reproductive laborers. Trade, warfare, and conquest irrevocably altered the lives of southwestern women, even as they developed strategies for survival and assimilation that insisted on their agency as actors in their own destiny.[82]

This analysis has uncovered the ways in which historians in the last half century have variously explored "women's work" in the early decades of American industrialization. It highlights some of the key interpretative frameworks and questions that historians have deployed and raised in their studies to better understand the experience of working women in this era. Bringing these studies together has revealed the similarities and differences in the ways that historians have approached the study of women of different classes, ethnicities, and races, as well as those who performed paid or unpaid labor, out of desire, coercion, or necessity. Analyzing the intersections of gender, race, region, and class shows the complex interactions that structured women's work in a variety of settings and under a variety of economic systems.

The studies examined here reveal the intimate relationship that exists between women's labor history and the lives and experiences of the historians who, since the 1960s, have worked within this field. This account began by locating the initial imperatives that drove scholars to investigate women's work in this period, primarily the women's movement and the desire to create and celebrate the strength of women's community. This led to a historiographic paradigm that accentuated the negative impact of patriarchal law and ideology on women's lives and their struggles to overcome these forces. Reflecting the politics and experience of a new generation of scholars in the latter decades of the twentieth century, the historiography of the 1980s and 1990s on antebellum women's labor revised the historical meaning attached to work and insisted on the political and economic value of women's unpaid labor within the household. It also highlighted a range of other factors that intersected to shape antebellum women's experiences of labor: legal structures, race, class, ethnicity, region, education, freedom and slavery, colonization, and independence. This development encouraged historians to identify the ways in which women individually and in groups grappled with their destiny and asserted their value and self-worth.

In the twenty-first century, hand in hand with a portrait of "women's community" that insists on a diversity of female actors, historians are beginning to dispense with interpretative frameworks that rely on neat dichotomies that posit women as independent or dependent, free or enslaved, empowered or powerless. Instead, they increasingly recognize the complexity of women's labor and the myriad forces that shaped their experiences. The challenge for future historians lies in balancing celebrations of women's self-assertion and strength with giving due recognition to those who did not overcome poverty and oppression, did not derive a sense of self-worth from their labor, or did not feel part of a women's community or network of support.

As the portrait of women's labor becomes more complex, so the historical tools deployed by historians must, too, become more refined.[83] By acknowledging and further exploring the many ways that women workers responded to the complex factors shaping their social, political, and economic environment, we may better understand the meaning they attached to and derived from their labor for themselves, their families, and their communities and the extent to which they interacted and perceived each other as a community of women who labored from dawn to dusk in antebellum America.

NOTES

1. For a sample of this approach see the essays collected in Milton Cantor and Bruce Laurie, eds., *Class, Sex, and the Woman Worker* (Westport, Conn.: Greenwood Press, 1977); Michael Gordon, ed., *The American Family in Social-Historical Perspective* (New York: St. Martin's Press, 1973); Tamara Hareven, ed., *Transitions: The Family and the Life Course in Historical Perspective* (New York: Academic Press, 1978).

2. Barbara Welter, "The Cult of True Womanhood: 1800–1860," *American Quarterly* 18 (1966): 151–174; Nancy F. Cott, *The Bonds of Womanhood: Women's Sphere in New England, 1780–1835* (New Haven and London: Yale University Press, 1977); Carroll Smith-Rosenberg, "The Female World of Love and Ritual: Relations between Women in Nineteenth-Century America," *Signs* 1 (autumn 1975): 1–29; Carroll Smith-Rosenberg, *Disorderly Conduct: Visions of Gender in Victorian America* (New York: Oxford University Press, 1985).

3. Nancy A. Hewitt, "Beyond the Search for Sisterhood: American Women's History in the 1990s," in *Unequal Sisters: A Multicultural Reader in U.S. Women's History*, ed. Ellen Carol DuBois and Vicki L. Ruiz, 3rd ed. (New York: Routledge, 2000), 5.

4. Jeanne Boydston, *Home and Work: Housework, Wages, and the Ideology of Labor in the Early Republic* (New York: Oxford University Press, 1990).

5. Ibid., 54–55.

6. Ibid., 123.

7. See Kathryn Kish Sklar, *Catharine Beecher: A Study in American Domesticity* (New York: Norton, 1973); Susan Strasser, *Never Done: A History of American Housework* (New York: Pantheon Books, 2000). S. J. Kleinberg, *The Shadow of the Mills: Working Class Families in Pittsburgh, 1870–1907* (Pittsburgh: University of Pittsburgh Press, 1989), shows the extent to which households continued to depend upon women's unpaid labor in the home through the end of the nineteenth and beginning of the twentieth century.

8. For examples of this intersectional approach see the essays in DuBois and Ruiz, *Unequal Sisters*; and Elizabeth Jameson and Susan Armitage, eds., *Writing the Range: Race, Class, and Culture in the Women's West* (Norman: University of Oklahoma Press, 1997).

9. Edith Abbott, *Women in Industry* (New York, D. Appleton, 1910); Caroline F. Ware, *The Early New England Cotton Manufacture: A Study in Industrial Beginnings* (Boston: Houghton Mifflin Co., 1931). Other early investigations into women's place in the economy include Lucy Salmon, *Domestic Service* (New York: Macmillan, 1897); Elizabeth Butler, *Women and the Trades* (New York: Russell Sage Foundation, 1909); and Annie Marion MacLean, *Wage Earning Women* (New York: MacMillan Company, 1910).

10. Thomas Dublin, *Women at Work: The Transformation of Work and Community in Lowell, Massachusetts, 1826–1860* (New York: Columbia University Press, 1979), 25–40.

11. Thomas Dublin, ed., *Farm to Factory: Women's Letters, 1830–1860* (New York: Columbia University Press, 1981). Also see Philip S. Foner, ed., *The Factory Girls* (Urbana: University of Illinois Press, 1977); W. Elliot Brownlee and Mary M. Brownlee, eds., *Women in the American Economy: A Documentary History, 1675 to 1929* (New Haven: Yale University Press, 1976); Mary H. Blewett, ed. *We Will Rise in Our Might: Workingwomen's Voices from Nineteenth Century New England* (Ithaca, N.Y.: Cornell University Press, 1991).

12. Dublin, *Women at Work*, 38–40. Also see Teresa Anne Murphy, *Ten Hours' Labor: Religion, Reform, and Gender in Early New England* (Ithaca, N.Y.: Cornell University Press, 1992), on paternalism in the factories and fathers collecting daughters' wages.

13. Lucy Larcom, *A New England Girlhood* (1889; repr., New York: Corinth Books, 1961), 196.

14. Mary H. Blewett, *Men, Women, and Work: Class, Gender, and Protest in the New England Shoe Industry, 1780–1910* (Urbana: University of Illinois Press, 1988); Kathryn Kish Sklar, "'The Greater Part of the Petitioners Are Female': The Reduction of Women's Working Hours in the Paid Labor Force, 1840–1917," in *Worktime and Industrialization: An International History*, ed. Gary Cross (Philadelphia: Temple University Press, 1988); Dublin, *Women at Work*; Murphy, *Ten Hours' Labor*.

15. Dublin, *Women at Work*, 92.

16. Gerda Lerner, "The Lady and the Mill Girl: Changes in the Status of Women in the Age of Jackson, 1800–1840," reprinted in *A Heritage of Her Own: Toward a New Social History of American Women*, ed. Nancy F. Cott and Elizabeth H. Pleck (New York: Simon and Schuster, 1979), 182–196; Alice Kessler-Harris, *Out to Work: A History of Wage-Earning Women in the United States* (New York: Oxford University Press, 1982); Alice Kessler-Harris, "Where Are the Organized Women Workers?" *Feminist Studies* 3 (autumn 1975): 92–110.

17. Christine Stansell, *City of Women: Sex and Class in New York, 1789–1860* (New York: Random House, 1986), 83.

18. Dublin, *Women at Work*, 40, 57.

19. Joan Jensen, *Loosening the Bonds: Mid-Atlantic Farm Women, 1750–1850* (New Haven: Yale University Press, 1986); Thomas Dublin, *Transforming Women's Work: New England Lives*

in the Industrial Revolution (Ithaca, N.Y.: Cornell University Press, 1994), ch. 6. Also see Sklar, *Catharine Beecher*, on the development of teaching as a profession.

20. Salmon, *Domestic Service*.

21. Nicholas Adams and Bonnie G. Smith, eds., *History and the Texture of Modern Life* (Philadelpia: University of Pennsylvania Press, 2001), contains annotated extracts from Salmon's writings.

22. Faye E. Dudden, *Serving Women: Household Service in Nineteenth-Century America* (Hanover: Wesleyan University Press, 1983). Also see Daniel E. Sutherland, *Americans and Their Servants: Domestic Service in the United States from 1800 to 1920* (Baton Rouge: Louisiana State University Press, 1981).

23. On free black domestic service, see Suzanne Lebsock, *The Free Women of Petersburg: Status and Culture in a Southern Town, 1784–1860* (New York: W. W. Norton & Company, 1985), chs. 4 and 6. On the struggles free women of color experienced to support themselves and their families, see Loren Schweninger, "The Fragile Nature of Freedom: Free Women of Color in the U.S. South," in *Beyond Bondage: Free Women of Color in the Americas*, ed. David Barry Gaspar and Darlene Clark Hine (Urbana: University of Illinois Press, 2004), 106–124.

24. Hasia R. Diner, *Erin's Daughters in America: Irish Immigrant Women in the Nineteenth Century* (Baltimore: Johns Hopkins University Press, 1983), 56–60.

25. Ibid., 84–90; Dudden, *Serving Women*, 47–55.

26. Leonore Davidoff and Catherine Hall, *Family Fortunes: Men and Women of the English Middle Class, 1780 — 1850* (London: Hutchinson, 1987), discuss this point in its English context.

27. Dublin, *Transforming Women's Work*, 54–55.

28. Stansell, *City of Women*, 116.

29. Blewett, *Men, Women, and Work*, 66. Also see Carole Turbin, "Beyond Conventional Wisdom: Women's Wage Work, Household Economic Contribution, and Labor Activism in a Mid-Nineteenth Century Working-Class Community," in *To Toil the Livelong Day: America's Women at Work, 1780–1980*, ed. Carol Groneman and Mary Beth Norton (Ithaca, N.Y.: Cornell University Press, 1987), 47–67.

30. Blewett, *Men, Women, and Work*, 35.

31. Ibid., 41.

32. Mary P. Ryan, *Cradle of the Middle Class: The Family in Oneida County, New York, 1790–1865* (Cambridge: Cambridge University Press, 1981). Also see Kathryn Kish Sklar, *Florence Kelley and the Nation's Work: The Rise of Women's Political Culture, 1830–1900* (New Haven: Yale University Press, 1995); Stansell, *City of Women*, ch. 4.

33. Cott, *The Bonds of Womanhood*.

34. Stansell, *City of Women*, 55.

35. Ibid., 61.

36. Elizabeth Fox-Genovese, *Within the Plantation Household: Black and White Women of the Old South* (Chapel Hill: University of North Carolina Press, 1988), 35.

37. Catherine Clinton, *The Plantation Mistress: Woman's World in the Old South* (New York: Pantheon Books, 1982), 166. Also see, on mistresses and slaves, Marli Wiener, *Mistresses and Slaves: Plantation Women in South Carolina, 1830–1880* (Urbana: University of Illinois Press, 1998).

38. Anne Firor Scott, *The Southern Lady from Pedestal to Politics, 1830–1930* (Chicago: University of Chicago Press, 1970).

39. Clinton, *Plantation Mistress,* 17.

40. Gerda Lerner, *The Grimké Sisters from South Carolina: Rebels against Slavery* (Boston: Houghton Mifflin Company, 1967), explores their motivations and actions.

41. Ibid., chs. 8 and 9.

42. Clinton, 164.

43. Jensen, *Loosening the Bonds,* 79–141.

44. Nancy Grey Osterud, *Bonds of Community: The Lives of Farm Women in Nineteenth-Century New York* (Ithaca, N.Y.: Cornell University Press, 1991).

45. Jensen, *Loosening the Bonds,* 207.

46. John Mack Faragher, *Sugar Creek: Life on the Illinois Prairie* (New Haven: Yale University Press, 1986), 118. Also on farm women see Joan Jensen, *With These Hands: Women Working on the Land* (New York: Feminist Press, 1981).

47. Julie Roy Jeffrey, *Frontier Women: "Civilizing" the West? 1840–1880* (New York: Hill and Wang, 1979), 56. For a later analysis of women in the West who undertook roles outside their traditional sphere, see Sally Zanjani, *A Mine of Her Own: Women Prospectors in the American West, 1850–1950* (Lincoln: University of Nebraska Press, 1997).

48. Glenda Riley, *Frontierswomen: The Iowa Experience* (Ames: Iowa State University Press, 1981); Sandra Myres, *Westering Women and the Frontier Experience, 1800–1915* (Albuquerque: University of New Mexico Press, 1983); Susan Armitage, "Household Work and Childrearing on the Frontier, the Oral History Record," *Sociology and Social Research* 63, no. 3 (April 1979): 467–474. Armitage makes this point in her chapter in this volume.

49. Jeffrey, *Frontier Women,* 34. See Susan Armitage's chapter in this volume for an analysis of the cultural clashes that occurred as European Americans migrated west.

50. Jeffrey, *Frontier Women,* 82–84.

51. Deborah Gray White, *Ar'n't I a Woman? Female Slaves in the Plantation South* (New York: W. W. Norton & Company, 1985); Jacqueline Jones, *Labor of Love, Labor of Sorrow: Black Women, Work, and the Family, from Slavery to the Present* (New York: Vintage Books, 1986); Jennifer L. Morgan, *Laboring Women: Reproduction and Gender in New World Slavery* (Philadelphia: University of Pennsylvania Press, 2004). Also see Scott, *The Southern Lady.*

52. Beverly Guy-Sheftall, "The Body Politic: Black Female Sexuality and the Nineteenth-Century Euro-American Imagination," in *Skin Deep, Spirit Strong: The Black Female Body in American Culture,* ed. Kimberly Wallace-Sanders (Ann Arbor: University of Michigan Press, 2002), 11–35, quote on 23.

53. Adrienne Davis, "Don't Let Nobody Bother Yo' Principle," in *Sister Circle: Black Women and Work,* ed. Sharon Harley (New Brunswick, N.J.: Rutgers University Press, 2002), 113, quoting Thomas Cobb, *An Inquiry into the Law of Negro Slavery in the United States of America* (Philadelphia: T & W Johnson and Co., W. T. Williams, 1858), section 107.

54. Jones, *Labor of Love,* 15.

55. White, *Ar'n't I a Woman?* 14. Nell Painter, *Sojourner Truth: A Life, a Symbol* (New York: Norton, 1996), 125–126, gives a different version of Truth's speech, rooted in contemporary documents.

56. White, *Ar'n't I a Woman?* 22

57. Ibid., 121.

58. Sharla M. Fett, *Working Cures: Healing, Health, and Power on Southern Slave Plantations* (Chapel Hill: University of North Carolina Press, 2002), 191.

59. Stephanie McCurry, *Masters of Small Worlds: Yeoman Households, Gender Relations, and the Political Culture of the Antebellum South Carolina Low Country* (Oxford: Oxford University Press, 1995), 75.

60. Ibid., 80.

61. Sally McMurry, *Transforming Rural Life: Dairying Families and Agricultural Change, 1820–1885* (Baltimore: Johns Hopkins University Press, 1995), 84–102. For a discussion of these issues also see Jensen, *With These Hands;* and Jensen, *Loosening the Bonds.*

62. McMurry, *Transforming Rural Life,* 84–102.

63. Xiomara Santamarina, *Belabored Professions: Narratives of African American Working Womanhood* (Chapel Hill: University of North Carolina Press, 2005), ch. 1; White, *Ar'n't I a Woman?* 13–14. For Painter's version of the speech and her analysis, see her *Sojourner Truth,* 120–151.

64. Santamarina, *Belabored Professions,* ch. 1.

65. Specifically on slave resistance, see Stephanie M. H. Camp, *Closer to Freedom: Enslaved Women and Everyday Resistance in the Plantation South* (Chapel Hill: University of North Carolina Press, 2004); Morgan, *Laboring Women,* ch. 5; White, *Ar'n't I a Woman?*

66. For a discussion of the declension argument, see Jennifer M. Spear, "The Distant Past of North American Women's History," *Journal of Women's History* 16, no. 4 (winter 2004): 41–49.

67. Ramón A. Gutiérrez, *When Jesus Came, the Corn Mothers Went Away: Marriage, Sexuality, and Power in New Mexico, 1500–1846* (Stanford, Calif.: Stanford University Press, 1991), 153.

68. Joan M. Jensen and Gloria Ricci Lothrop, *California Women: A History* (San Francisco: Boyd & Fraser Publishing Company, 1987), 4–6. They held positions as shamans and dream helpers. They also gained respect for their dancing and singing abilities.

69. Carol Douglas Sparks, "The Land Incarnate: Navajo Women and the Dialogues of Colonialism, 1821–1870," in *Negotiators of Change: Historical Perspectives on Native Women,* ed. Nancy Shoemaker (New York: Routledge, 1995), 136.

70. Katherine M. B. Osburn, "'Dear Friend and Ex-Husband:' Marriage, Divorce, and Women's Property Rights on the Southern Ute Reservation, 1887–1930," in *Negotiators of Change,* ed. Shoemaker, 158.

71. Ibid., 160. This took place in 1895.

72. James F. Brooks, "'This Evil Extends Especially to the Feminine Sex': Captivity and Identity in New Mexico, 1700–1846," in *Unequal Sisters: A Multicultural Reader in U.S. Women's History* (New York: Routledge, 1990) ed., Ellen Carol DuBois and Vicki L. Ruiz, 24. For Brooks's full argument see James F. Brooks, *Captives and Cousins: Slavery, Kinship, and Community in the Southwest Borderlands* (Chapel Hill: University of North Carolina Press, 2002).

73. Ned Blackhaw, "Borderlands Redux: The Disquieting Celebration of Hybridity in James Brooks' *Captives and Cousins,*" at http://www.wisc.edu/amindian/Faculty/Homepages/NedBlackhawk/NedDoc2.doc, accessed December 14, 2005.

74. Teresa L. Amott and Julie A. Matthaei, *Race, Gender, and Work: A Multicultural Economic History of Women in the United States* (Boston: South End Press, 1991), 69–70.

75. Carole Shammas, Marylynn Salmon, and Michel Dahlin, *Inheritance in America: From Colonial Times to the Present* (New Brunswick, N.J.: Rutgers University Press, 1987); Marylynn Salmon, *Women and the Law of Property in Early America* (Chapel Hill: University of North Carolina Press, 1987); Michael Grossberg, *Governing the Hearth: Law and the Family in Nineteenth-Century America* (Chapel Hill: University of North Carolina Press, 1985), discusses the legal structures of Anglo-America.

76. Yolanda Chávez Leyva, "'A Poor Widow Burdened with Children': Widows and Land in Colonial New Mexico," in *Writing the Range: Race, Class, and Culture in the Women's West* (Norman: University of Oklahoma Press, 1997) ed. Elizabeth Jameson and Susan Armitage; Joan Hoff, *Law, Gender, and Injustice: A Legal History of U.S. Women* (New York: New York University Press, 1991), 88–89.

77. Chávez Leyva, "'A Poor Widow Burdened with Children,'" 85.

78. Deena J. González, *Refusing the Favor: The Spanish-Mexican Women of Santa Fe, 1820–1880* (Oxford and New York: Oxford University Press, 1999), 105.

79. Miroslava Chávez-García, *Negotiating Conquest: Gender and Power in California, 1770s to 1880s* (Tucson: University of Arizona Press, 2004), 23. Also on violence and conquest and their impact on women in California see Albert L. Hurtado, *Intimate Frontiers: Sex, Gender, and Culture in Old California* (Albuquerque: University of New Mexico Press, 1999).

80. Chávez-García, *Negotiating Conquest*, ch. 4; Jensen and Lothrop, *California Women*, 8–10.

81. Theda Perdue, *Cherokee Women: Gender and Culture Change, 1700–1835* (Lincoln: University of Nebraska Press, 1998), ch. 6; Osburn, "'Dear Friend and Ex-Husband,'" 149–175, depicts a similar loss of economic rights among the Ute.

82. Brooks, *Captives and Cousins,* 30.

83. González, *Refusing the Favor,* 120.

6

To Bind Up the Nation's Wounds

Women and the American Civil War

SUSAN-MARY GRANT

The Civil War is the central event in America's national story. It was the nation's defining conflict, the war whose outcome justified both America's claim to nationhood and the central ideals of freedom and equality supporting that claim. Yet the war established neither freedom in anything but the legal sense for African Americans nor equality in any sense for women. Although historians continue to challenge the image of the Civil War as a "brother's war" that ultimately reaffirmed national unity and, specifically, work to incorporate women into the history of the conflict, our understanding of why women's role in the Civil War has been so downplayed remains incomplete. Only by placing the women's Civil War within the broader context of the U.S. struggle for national identity in the nineteenth and early twentieth centuries can we trace the process that led to women's exclusion from the war's narrative. Such exclusion by no means reflected contemporary perspectives on women's importance to the war effort or their role in sustaining it. Nineteenth-century warfare was a man's game, no doubt, but it was also a woman's business. War work — at home or on the battle-field — presented women with new social and political opportunities, even as traditional social structures altered in men's absence.[1]

Gender boundaries fluctuated during and after the Civil War. Responsibility for running the home, farm, or plantation was just one change in women's circumstances. Many white southern women lost husbands and homes, while the planter class lost a way of life predicated on slavery. African American southern women kept the hope of freedom alive in the face of the brutal reality of physical upheaval, loss of families, and increased workload. They soon realized that northerners could be as racially blinkered as their former owners. The interruption of the Cult of True Womanhood in response to the war's many challenges was primarily an issue for white women since its restrictive precepts rarely applied to former slaves. Both groups, however, needed to re-establish marital relationships unsettled by the male war experience, slavery, or the economic and personal responsibilities involved in facing the future alone.[2]

The war reached its most brutal juncture in 1864, after Abraham Lincoln's re-election. His second inaugural address stressed the need to "strive on to finish the work we are in; to bind up the nation's wounds; to care for him who shall have borne the battle, and for his widow, and his orphan." Lincoln referred to the binding together of a severed nation, the reconstruction of a body politic. Paradoxically, reconstruction's requirements inhibited full recognition of women's war experiences. Binding up the nation's wounds diminished women's role in the war. Although not his intention, Lincoln's words neatly encapsulated the traditional image of Civil War women who, as nurses, literally bound up wounds. If not stereotyped as nurses, historical memory allotted Civil War women the role of grieving dependents, "the weeping widows of the dead" in Elizabeth Leonard's description.[3]

Historians have challenged this paradigm by highlighting women's contributions and exploring the war's impact on women, families, and society. The Civil War reinforced traditional gender roles in theory, but the upheavals of war also reformulated prevailing gender stereotypes. Although constrained by limitations of evidence, the gap between ideal and reality structures the historiography of the women's Civil War. Until recently, that historiography had a tripartite structure. There were works on northern women and the longer-term political implications of their Civil War involvement. Studies of southern women focused on their support for the Confederacy and the development of the Lost Cause. African American women's war and postwar experiences remained somewhat opaque to historians because there were fewer firsthand accounts. Moreover, they were usually described in the context of the changing work patterns and familial structures that freedom introduced. Southern elite white women received the most scholarly attention in part because so many of them left written accounts of their war experience. Crucially, the Lost Cause myth — a response to, a rejection of, and means of coming to terms with defeat — accorded white southern women a central role in the war's aftermath. For all of these reasons, southern women can no longer be termed the "half sisters of history," as Catherine Clinton once described them, even as they overshadowed northern and African American women's Civil War.[4]

In 1992, George Rable noted that traditional Civil War historians dismissed women's history while social historians frequently ignored military history. He suggested that the Civil War might constitute common ground, with its rich sources and possibilities for "studying social definitions of gender and the ways in which real people embraced, lived up to, or rebelled against these ideal types." Yet, despite the shift in Civil War historiography toward what used to be called the "new military history" and the merging of home front and battlefront by many historians, others assert that women's experiences of war could not be as valid as men's. The popular image of the Civil War as a "white man's fight" has been slow to give way to an inclusive picture with many players.[5]

Battlefields: Women and the Union

Elizabeth Young quotes Henry Ward Beecher's declaration that "manhood, — *manhood*, — MANHOOD. . . . made this nation" in her study of women's writing. She observes that Lincoln offered "a fantasy of national self-fathering" with masculinity as the literary lifeblood and "literal canon-fodder of the injured body politic," with no need for mothers. Consequently, Civil War studies focused on male protagonists. Warfare, as Jeanie Attie reminds us, is "naturally gendered," juxtaposing "masculine" qualities of aggressiveness and strength with supposedly more "feminine" nurturing qualities. Thus, the battlefront is a wholly masculine environment, while the home front is feminine. Patriotic propaganda reinforced these distinctions, encouraging men and women to "assume gender-appropriate roles to further nationalist objectives."[6]

Hence, the reluctance to acknowledge that some women served in the ranks or a tendency to dismiss such individuals as cranks. Deanne Blanton and Lauren Cook argue that this is a post–World War I perspective. After the Civil War, there was widespread support for women who adopted a male guise and fought for their cause, so long as their motives were deemed to be romantic and/or patriotic rather than economic. Mid-twentieth-century historians viewed female soldiers less positively. Bell Wiley described the reaction of contemporaries to such "freaks" as "one of amused tolerance." Mary Elizabeth Massey suggested that female soldiers were seen as "mentally unbalanced or immoral" individuals. Contemporary observers rationalized female soldiers' transgressive behavior in terms of moral debasement, love, adventurousness, or patriotism. Historians are only beginning to challenge these stereotypes. Women's absence from Civil War military narrative does not skew the interpretation of tactics and strategy, although it does beg the question of how each side maintained an army in the field in the first place.[7]

The focus of recent work on female combatants is essentially corrective, exploring the implications of women's role in the actual fighting of the Civil War. The following index entry in a recent study of Civil War soldiers suggests that not all historians have changed their approach: "Women, Confederate treatment of; flags made by; military camps visited by; as widows." The number of female combatants remains a moot point. Civil War nurse Mary Ashton Livermore believed that about four hundred women took up arms. Leonard suggests between five hundred to a thousand women fought. In contrast, some twenty thousand women served as nurses or general support staff, with three thousand nurses employed directly by the Union army. Neither Wiley nor Massey dismissed the idea of the female soldier entirely. Wiley thought patriotism inspired women to disguise themselves as men to fight with the Union army. Massey believed Civil War women broke out "in all directions at once, and nothing said to or about them could force them back into the fold." She argued that "instead of talking about their rights they were usurping them under the cloak of patriotism." Union general William Rosecrans exhibited a restrained, but recognizably military sensibility when he expressed his "flagrant outrage" that one of his sergeants gave birth, an act which was "in violation of all military law and of the army regulations."[8]

Historians have identified a number of individual women whose combatant role can be verified, but question some contemporary stories of female valor. Livermore's 1889 *Story of the War* singled out Nadine Turchin and Annie Etheridge, of the Ninetieth Illinois and Third Michigan, respectively. Turchin, according to Livermore, took over command of the regiment when her husband fell ill, while Etheridge "was found in the field, often in the thickest of the fight." Leonard notes the improbability of her assuming command; Turchin's diary indicates that by 1863 she did not join troops on the battlefield. However, she does not dismiss Turchin's complaint that women were "slaves of fatal destiny," not permitted by men to be intelligent or enjoy similar constitutional rights. Etheridge accompanied her husband to war but did not desert when he did. Instead, she became the "daughter" of the regiment. Her battlefield nursing led to the unprecedented honor of being buried in Arlington National Cemetery.[9]

Etheridge's behavior reached but did not exceed the accepted gender boundaries of the day. Yet nurses faced opposition in their attempts to support the soldiers. They entered a violent world deemed unsuitable to their natures and therefore prey to suspicion and censure. Even, perhaps especially, during wartime women were expected to be all things to all men: "brave and strong" but also "loving and refined." Even "weak and frivolous" young women should exhibit "endurance and perseverance." Yet, professionally qualified women met with outright hostility. The medical profession disparaged Dr. Mary Edwards Walker's training. She challenged contemporary gender conventions through her expertise, dress, and determination neither to compromise her ideals nor downplay her abilities. The Union army used her skills in an informal, voluntary way, but neither commissioned nor paid her properly. Walker wrote to Lincoln that she had "been denied a commission, solely on the ground of sex. . . . Had a man been as useful to our country a star would have been taken from the National Heavens and placed upon his shoulder."[10]

Walker's experiences showed the general unwillingness to acknowledge the validity and value of women's services for the cause. Ironically, most historical works neglect the Union's most active woman on the battlefield and beyond. Harriet Tubman, like Walker, sought to wear the more practical bloomers in the course of her work, to which contemporaries objected. Race/gender conventions largely excluded Tubman from the Civil War story. Her flight from slavery, efforts to help others escape via the Underground Railroad, support for John Brown's raid on Harpers Ferry, activities as a Union spy, scout, and nurse, and advocacy of emancipation as an essential Union war aim all made her an important figure. Tubman was one of the nineteenth century's "invented greats," to use Nell Painter's phrase. Her public persona has been available to historians largely through its construction by others, resulting in the loss of much of the complexity of the actual life. Painter also uses this phrase in her analysis of the other prominent African American woman of this period, Sojourner Truth, who was also overlooked in traditional Civil War histories. [11]

Despite her work for the National Freedman's Relief Association and efforts to aid former slaves who had escaped to the North during the Civil War, Truth is, like Tubman, largely missing from the history of the Civil War. Two descriptive biographies about Tubman appeared during World War II, and there have been dramatic tales of her life, mostly intended for junior readers. There are new biographies informed by the recent scholarship on slavery by Catherine Clinton, Kate Clifford Larson, and Jean M. Humez. The role of women like Truth and Etheridge has recently been placed in the broader context of nursing at the front by Jane Schultz, whose study of the world of the (predominantly) Union nurse does not ignore the restrictions imposed by gender and class, nor the strains produced by the racialized environment in which black and white female nurses operated. Yet Truth has not yet become the fixture in Civil War history that her activities as an abolitionist and activist merit. Tubman's and Truth's position on the middle ground between slavery and freedom, North and South, makes it difficult for scholars to place them in the Civil War narrative. The symbolic figure of the strong black female has subsumed the historical individual. Painter highlights the (mis)appropriation of Truth by historians of southern slavery seeking a powerful symbol to stand for women under that institution. In Truth they find it, although she was a northerner who was emancipated before the antebellum era began. Both dominant in but obscured from the historical gaze, Truth and Tubman stand outside the historiography of Civil War women, sidelined by a combination of their own very public histories and by a profession that, as Clinton suggests, prefers "movements, collective identities" rather than individual stories, however significant these may be. [12]

The Civil War underlined the very different relationship that men and women enjoyed with the state. Male volunteers in the army received payment plus a substantial bounty, making economic considerations a prime factor in the decision to enlist. Women, by contrast, were expected to take over men's jobs and encouraged to make goods for distribution among the troops. In this way, Attie points out, the "connection between labor and nationalism was not only brought home, it emanated from the home." Unlike men, women's relationship with the state was not premised on their role as citizens, but on the supposition that they were "apolitical and altruistic members of society." Women sustained this role through the men they supported and cared for, not for their own sake but for that of the nation. Consequently, there was a general expectation that men would direct women's services and patriotism. Women acting for themselves as combatants or as nurses encountered a multitude of difficulties. [13]

Judith Ann Giesberg argues that women's work on behalf of the United States Sanitary Commission (USSC) was the missing link between the localized reform activities of the antebellum period and the national reform movements of the Progressive era. The lessons women learned during the Civil War established the basis for subsequent reform efforts. Attie sees the Civil War as an important arena for the "development of new social theories to justify equality between the sexes," but men would not readily share either authority or responsibility with women. The Civil War brought opportunities for both sexes and clashes between them. In theory, "the professionalization of women as nurses, medical personnel, sanitary agents, and so forth, meant the sharing of a type of public stature and power previously reserved for men." In practice, more was at stake than the care of the wounded. The USSC sought to inculcate nothing less than "a new consciousness, a new national culture," with female benevolence and supposedly disinterested patriotism as a means to that end.[14]

The USSC channeled women's philanthropic impulses in accordance with strict gender divisions of labor and responsibility. Stories "about the disorganized character of female benevolence and the confusion it produced at the warfront" proliferated. These formed "the basis of a narrative about the creation of the USSC that depicted the organization as the embodiment of rational benevolence." Women felt the need to involve what Attie terms, somewhat anachronistically, "non-feminist men" but were powerless to prevent them "from appropriating their organizational ideas and structure to serve a distinctly masculine nationalist agenda." The USSC increasingly came into conflict with women who did not share its view of how their benevolence should be directed nor what forms it should take. Northern women challenged the USSC's nationalizing tendencies. They rejected "the dominant version of female patriotism" and "stressed the parity between their loyalties and those of men." According to Attie, "women tried to make public the nature of their real economic contributions not only to the nation but to their families and local economies as well." Harriet Tubman and Sojourner Truth remind us that the struggles of the elite white women who challenged the USSC represent only the most visible tip of an iceberg of female activism during and after the war.[15]

Beyond the Battlefield: The Confederacy

Fought mainly on southern soil, the Civil War was more total for the Confederacy than for the Union. The historiography of the women's Civil War mostly follows the postbellum pattern by according elite southern white women a central and complex role. Popular Union literature acknowledged women's heroism, self-sacrifice, and patriotic impulses.[16] Yet once the fighting stopped, northern women faded from sight. The outpouring of Civil War reminiscences and stories in publications such as *Century* magazine and *McClure's* between 1887 and 1900 did not acknowledge women's war experiences at all. Only four stories concerning northern women appeared in *McClure's, Harper's Weekly,* and the *Ladies' Home Journal* between 1880 and 1900. As Alice Fahs notes, Louisa May Alcott's *Little*

Women (1868) excepted, "popular literature rarely explored Northern women or girls' experiences on the home front." The popular masculinization of the war's memory should be placed in the broader context of a Civil War memorializing process that was in some senses distinctly feminized, but from a southern perspective.[17]

The general "understanding of white southern women's Civil War as a negotiation between the pull of tradition and the forces of change," Thomas J. Brown observes, "was a powerful framework of memory that would adapt readily to a broader vision of modern womanhood." In 1970 Anne Firor Scott documented the Civil War's role in the emergence of the southern belle from the chrysalis of the antebellum Cult of True Womanhood into the wider social and political world of the New South. Scott emphasized the trauma and upheaval of the war and southern women's resourcefulness in the face of invasion and the loss of homes and husbands. Subsequent historians have focused on the southern woman's contribution to the Confederate war effort and the post-war cult of the Lost Cause. In studies that explore the Civil War as a "crisis in gender" or the persistent post-war influence of "Dixie's daughters," historians have located southern women at the heart of Civil War America.[18]

LeeAnn Whites, Catherine Clinton, and Drew Gilpin Faust, among others, have advanced our understanding of how the pressures of war produced both subtle and obvious shifts in gender relations, especially among elite women. This historiography highlights southern women's role during the war and constructs something positive from their experiences through "a new woman" narrative that interpreted the conflict as liberating more than slaves. The Confederate construction of the women's Civil War story reinforces the broader interpretation of the war as America's bloody transition to modernity, a theme that Faust explores in her study of mortality and its meaning during the war. It provides evidence for the existence of an enduring Confederate/southern nationalism that helped the South come to terms with defeat and entrenched a worldview at odds with that of the nation as a whole. Instead of assessments of women's aid to Confederate troops on the battlefield either as nurses or combatants, the emphasis has been on the gender implications for a society in flux between 1861 and 1865, virtually destroyed by 1865, and seeking to reconstruct itself largely in its antebellum image after the war.[19]

Some southern women did engage in armed conflict. Whites mentions several women warriors whose behavior suggested "an apparent breakdown of gender conventions altogether," but they were isolated cases, as were the exploits of Confederate female spies. Southern nurses achieved official recognition with the 1862 Hospital Bill, "an important statement," Faust observes, "of Confederate policy concerning the relationship of the state to its female citizens." But southern women did not volunteer in the numbers required. Disillusion set in as the war progressed. Increasingly, southern women wanted their husbands or sons back from the army, on grounds of economic need or because the soldier was underage. According to Rable, "Women *had* contributed to the decline of Confederate military power" and "both sustained and undermined the war effort."[20]

Faust suggests that "it may well have been because of its women that the South lost the Civil War." Her point is important, if overstated. In the process of persuading Confederate women to support the war effort, southerners constructed a "discourse about women's place in Confederate society" which emphasized women's patriotism and glorified its sacrificial aspects. The notion of sacrifice produced renewed enthusiasm for the cause rather than defeatism. Jacqueline Campbell's analysis of Confederate women's response to Sherman's march through the Carolinas shows how direct contact with the enemy stiffened their resolve. Women's grief sanctified the Confederate cause and established the centrality of women's role in Confederate national identity. This women-centered narrative, Faust stresses, was as much a fabrication as the exclusively male-focused variant; we need to dispel both in order to better understand Confederate women's experiences.[21]

The reconfiguration of the South's antebellum gender norms can be traced through the rise of women-centered narratives. As Elizabeth Fox-Genovese observes, slaveholding women's identity was wrapped in gender, which was itself wrapped in class and race, but such a self could not be sustained in the face of war. Faust explains that antebellum southern women accepted their subordination in return for class and racial superiority, but the war altered their understanding of this bargain. The absence of men breached the antebellum gender divide. It fell altogether with the emancipation of the slaves, whose labor sustained southern ladyhood. Scott, Clinton, Whites, and Faust trace this process in relation to slave management, to violence, to the rise of female organizations, and especially to burying and commemorating the Confederate dead. The violence in the antebellum South and the war itself excluded women and limited their ability to control slaves previously restrained by threats of violence. Men and women couched initial support for the war within antebellum gender conventions. The domestic cast of Confederate women's patriotism continued and extended normal household tasks. The southern soldier had to recognize that his manhood and independence were social constructions built upon women's service, love, and dependence. As the war progressed sacrifice *for* the family became sacrifice *of* the family. White southern women were forced "toward new understandings of themselves and toward reconstructions of the meanings of southern womanhood that would last well beyond the Confederacy's demise."[22]

This reconstruction had its most visible and lasting impact in the postwar world. By excluding women from the male world, the Confederate commemorative tradition enabled them to construct "an alternative arena for the reconstruction of self-worth in the face of the very real public defeat they had suffered." Whites shows that the Confederate memorial tradition empowered a "particularly *female* experience of the white familial bond. . . . [T]he act of mothering the dead emerged . . . as the basis upon which a viable post-Confederate tradition could be built." Her interpretation of the gendered nature of the commemorative impulse has influenced a range of studies on the United Daughters of the Confederacy, the memorial tradition, and the persistent conservative ideology in postwar South Carolina. The historiography reveals that southern women embodied the "weeping widow" paradigm, but they shed "no tears of penitence," in their sorrow, as Scott Poole observes. Rather they inaugurated a process of "guerrilla warfare through mourning," in William Blair's trenchant analysis. The cause may have been lost, but elite southern females ensured that history would forget neither it nor them.[23]

Emancipation

Southern elite women's identity depended on the interaction between gender, race, and class, but southern black women found their identity defined by conventions that others controlled. Black women were trapped between the gender conventions of white southern society and those of the slave community. The historiography of the black women's Civil War remains at odds with that of the white women's experience and with the historiography of the war as a whole. Catherine Clinton assessed the problems and the opportunities facing historians interested in "reconstructing freedwomen" in *Tara Revisited: Women, War, and the Plantation Legend*, which combines the black and white, male and female worlds that sometimes are explored in isolation from each other. Developing many of the points made in her earlier article, "Bloody Terrain: Freedwomen, Sexuality, and Violence during Reconstruction," the African American women's Civil War, Clinton suggests, can most clearly be located in the interaction, or perhaps clash, of previously distinct antebellum worlds.[24]

The war affected slaves and free blacks in very different ways depending on geographical location, proximity to Union lines, and whether slave owners moved them out of the way of Union troops or sent them to one of the loyal slave-holding border states unaffected by Lincoln's 1863 Emancipation Proclamation. For women who might be single parents or became so when their partners joined the Union army or the Confederacy conscripted them, the number and ages of dependents determined whether they made a bid for freedom. Some black women worked for the Confederate war effort as nurses, cooks, or general support staff; others remained on plantations. Those in cities had to cope with refugees and the breakdown of antebellum social norms. There was, in short, no single definable African American women's Civil War, nor even broad parameters within which it can easily be reconstructed. There are, however, certain dominant themes to the historiography of the black female war experience.[25]

Since the 1960s, the historiography of the Civil War and emancipation process attempted to correct the perception of slaves as passive victims by establishing them as active participants in a process that gradually dismantled the antebellum South's peculiar institution. The Freedmen and Southern Society Project, begun in 1976 at the University of Maryland, reflected this trend and influenced the historiography of black women in the Civil War. Initially a documentary history of emancipation and free labor, the second series explored the black military experience. The most recent volume looks at land, capital, and labor; the fifth series will analyze the black community, families, education, and society during and after the Civil War.[26]

The broader historiography follows a similar pattern. The 1970s and 1980s saw a plethora of monographs focused primarily on the conversion from slave to free labor. Clarence Mohr studied this transition in Civil War Georgia; Roger Ransom and Richard Sutch analyzed the economic consequences of emancipation and the racism that hampered African American economic stability. Women were part of that story but, except for Jacqueline Jones's *Labor of Love, Labor of Sorrow* and Leslie Schwalm's *A Hard Fight for We,* were not its focus. Studies seeking to paint the larger picture of the processes involved in the emergence of the New South sidelined black women's shifting expectations, the gendered nature of those expectations, and the difficulties that changing work patterns caused them and their families.[27]

Contemporary political issues in the late 1960s and 1970s shaped investigations of black women in slavery and freedom. The Moynihan Report of 1965 identified supposedly weak family bonds during slavery as negatively affecting twentieth-century black family structures. As historians challenged and repudiated the matriarchal myth, they examined the composition of and support mechanisms for slave families. The historiography focused on slavery and its aftermath, with more attention paid to the transition from slave labor to the development of free labor systems in the South. More nuanced studies of black southern women's lives within and beyond the family during and after the war are appearing now, yet much work remains to be done on the war itself. The difficulty regarding sources is acute, but there is another problem deriving from the African American war experience as a whole, specifically the challenge it poses to the portrayal of the Civil War as the conflict that transformed a Union into a nation. Historians can trace a process that pitted the white desire for control against the black demand for freedom through letters reproduced in the Freedmen project volumes, accounts of owners attempting to maintain control of enslaved children as a means of stemming slaves' flight, the forcible separation of families by federal troops, and the removal of women from contraband camps back onto plantations. This process depended greatly on black women. The sobering reality of their Civil War conflicts with the image of the war as an emancipatory experience for America as a nation. Incorporating the black women's Civil War into the story means fundamentally changing not just the form but also the substance of the narrative.[28]

Jones and Schwalm highlight the gendered nature of emancipation. The need to sustain the family defined the middle ground between slavery and freedom for enslaved women during the Civil War. The care of the young, old, and infirm combined with the war's upheaval to place heavy burdens on enslaved women. Their problems intensified when partners left to join the Union army, forcing many women to follow them into Union lines, where their reception was mixed, at best. As with many white northern women who followed their menfolk to war, they were branded as prostitutes or vagrants. Work was sometimes difficult to find. There were cases of flagrant and sadistic sexual abuse by Union troops whose brutal attitude toward black women expressed the most negative gender and racial assumptions of the nineteenth century. While black men's value to the Union was obvious even in a non-military capacity, the military regarded black women as a hindrance and drain on federal military resources. As the war progressed, and Union forces penetrated deeper into the South, the responsibilities placed on black women's shoulders increased. The proximity to Union lines made flight an option, but also increased the likelihood of their partners joining Union forces. This left them to either endure the anger of their white owners or face the challenge of leading their families out of slavery alone and into an extremely uncertain future.[29]

Race and gender, Thavolia Glymph stresses, combined to define the African American woman's war experience, establishing rigid demarcation lines "that seemed to rule out any public or quasi-public supporting roles for black women." White northern women's contributions may have been challenged but were usually grudgingly accepted. White southern women defined their own role, up to a point, amidst the confusion of war, and firmly so in the postwar era. Yet black women were viewed as dependents of black men with no contribution of their own to make. Their efforts to help the war effort met little success; neither did the federal government protect them. Their position as women, and specifically as mothers with dependents, exacerbated their situation. As Wilma King reminds us, slave mothers' lives were interlocked with their children's. When the war brought the possibility of freedom, mothers and children often fled together; others remained behind, trying to confront and encourage slavery's disintegration in the domestic arena. Schwalm details this process in her study of the South Carolina Lowcountry. Noralee Frankel used federal records, Civil War soldiers' pension files, and the Freedmen's Bureau records to investigate the war's impact on black women and their families in Mississippi. She presents a story of increasing deprivation as the Union blockade bit and concomitantly increased work loads as goods previously purchased, such as clothing, had to be manufactured by slaves. The removal of men to work on military projects left even more of the fieldwork in women's hands. Elizabeth Regosin's recent exploration of the betrayal of "freedom's promise," a study based on pension claims made by African American families after the war, reinforces Frankel's argument. Regosin's detailed analysis of the pension claims submitted by over one hundred African Americans highlighted the disparity between the reality of their lives and white expectations of family "norms."[30]

Frankel regards federal "arrangements" for providing plantations with female contraband labor as problematic; former slaves were poorly paid and separated from their families. Like Jones and Schwalm, she emphasizes black women's continuing struggle to hold families together as slavery collapsed. Understanding the practicalities of the free labor system is crucial to understanding the emancipation process. "Blacks struggled to weld kin and work relations into a single unit of economic and social welfare so that women could be wives and mothers first and laundresses and cotton pickers second." Yet the odds were against freedwomen achieving that kind of crucial compromise: excluded from the middle-class domestic ideal, former owners and northerners pressured them to return to the fields. Both northerners and defeated white southerners agreed that black women should continue to work outside the home. By the end of the Civil War, Glymph wryly notes, no consensus on the question of contraband women had emerged beyond the debate over "how best to put black women to work." White society perceived white women's war-work then and now as remarkable and frequently as a significant step on the road toward equality. Black women's wartime efforts were assumed to be little more than an extension of the norm. In the transition from slavery to freedom, both their gender and their race remained the constants through which they were understood, by which they were judged, and from which freedom itself offered them only a limited form of escape.[31]

The historiography on postwar African American women's experiences pursues them through the Reconstruction era and beyond. Here, too, the black women's Reconstruction represents not merely one theme in a vast historiography on the 1865–1877 period, but a direct challenge to the interpretation of the period as one defined by the political reconfiguration of the southern states. The sources utilized to uncover the black woman in Reconstruction — Freedmen's Bureau records, pension and legal records — highlight a world in transition if not upheaval, a world that Laura Edwards summed up as one of "gendered strife and confusion." The main thesis of Edwards's monograph — that in the sexual violence perpetrated against poor white and black women and the responses of the women sheds a completely different light not just on the postwar South but on the political environment within and through which North and South sought to reconstruct the nation — was developed in a case study of Granville County, North Carolina.[32]

Edwards's findings and the direction of her analysis, taken together with Victoria Bynum's study of "unruly women," were part of a trend in the scholarship that developed in the late 1980s and through the 1990s, a trend apparently grounded in North Carolina. Not only did Bynum base her argument on material from the Piedmont region of the state, but Glenda Gilmore's exploration of the interaction between "gender and Jim Crow" also had North Carolina as its focus. Although Gilmore's main thesis concerned the later period in the state's interracial clashes and compromises, its opening chapters provide a valuable assessment of the Reconstruction period and the various racial and class issues at play, before moving on to trace the inexorable rise of violence in the establishment of white dominance in the state. Indeed, since Edwards's, Bynum's, and Gilmore's works appeared, several historians have positioned violence — domestic, sexual, and otherwise — as the defining theme not just of the Civil War (obviously enough violence came into that) but of the Reconstruction era. The violence was not all of a piece and included the extreme coercion used by white against black, but also sometimes white against white. Bynum included white women's "unruly" behavior during the war itself, and some of her themes — especially the pressure on women to sustain families that led them to demand the return of their men from the front — were developed by Rable in his study of white women's support, or lack thereof, for the Confederacy. The difference lay in Bynum's identification of persistent and more widespread violence than hitherto supposed as the control mechanism for a society in crisis, not just during but after the war.[33]

This theme was further developed by Tera Hunter, whose study of black women's lives, mainly in Atlanta after the Civil War, highlighted both black reaction against white attempts to control their lives and labor and the increasingly violent white response that met this toward the end of the nineteenth and into the twentieth century. Hannah Rosen focuses more specifically on that violence in her contribution to Martha Hodes's edited collection of essays on sex across the color line that appeared in 1999. Rosen's chapter, "Not That Sort of Woman: Race, Gender, and Sexual Deviance during the Memphis Riot of 1866," traces the frequently uphill struggle black women faced in both challenging and overcoming the conventions of a discourse that positioned them outside the sphere of female virtue. This discourse also sought to diminish many white women as well, but rarely with the accompanying levels of threat and violence that black women experienced. In the same year, Hodes published her own monograph on "illicit sex in the nineteenth-century South," which also highlights the violence of the Reconstruction period and long after. While slavery remained in place, Hodes shows, "white Southerners could respond to sexual liaisons between white women and black men with a measure of toleration; only with black freedom did such liaisons begin to provoke near-inevitable alarm, one that culminated in the tremendous white violence of the 1890s and after." The personal impact of such relationships and the ways in which these played out in gender, class, and racial terms over several generations is the subject of an original and brilliant study of northern Mississippi by Bynum.[34]

Diane Miller Sommerville's study of "rape and race" challenged some of the assumptions about gender, race, and class struggles in the postwar South. Sommerville utilizes court records to bring out the opinions and reactions — and in the process sheds light on the lives — of "ordinary" Southerners to the charged subject of interracial rape. She also situates the South more in line with national trends that developed the "myth of the black rapist" far later in the century than was previously thought. Perhaps one of the most important analyses of black women's lives at the conclusion of the Civil War, however, is Karin Zipf's exploration of the apprenticeship system in North Carolina. Focused on the ways in which "some single black women rejected the political and social conventions of the day that reserved the status of independent household head to men," Zipf offers a challenge to Edwards's argument in *Gendered Strife and Confusion*. Zipf's conclusions are both significant and sobering and complicate much of the scholarship on gender, race, and class in the Reconstruction South.[35]

As Zipf traces the struggle of black women to challenge the apprenticeship laws that sought to re-establish the former masters' hold over their former slaves, she pulls together several strands in the scholarship: the relative position of African American women within the discourse on gender norms, their struggle to reconstruct the family by demanding custody of their children, and the violence — physical, but above all emotional — that was used in the attempt to wrest control and the physical presence of their children from them. "Race prevented black women from achieving privileges associated with white womanhood. Gender restricted them from citizenship, a status that white men jealously preserved and black men fought to acquire. Black women," she asserts, "found themselves in a peerless position, a void where freedwomen's status — unlike that occupied by elite and poor white women — was not yet rigidly defined by law or custom."[36]

Conclusion: A National Vision

As a result of the work done to date on the African American women's Civil War, we are gradually coming closer to hearing black women's historical voices. Yet taken together with those of white women, North and South, they sound a descant chord in the larger historiography of the war still dominated by the battlefield and political and military maneuvers. Part of the explanation for this lies in the impulse behind the construction of the public Civil War narrative and the war's place in America's national story. Leonard takes issue with historians who deny the war's role as "a crucible of change for the interrelationship of men, women, and power." She notes that the construction of the Civil War narrative had a definite purpose: to resurrect a "stable world temporarily battered by strife, a prewar Victorian world to which they would happily return once peace was declared." Women's role in the Civil War was an uncomfortable reminder of the war's cost. In the process of challenging the paradigm of Civil War women as no more than weeping widows, historians sometimes sidelined widows, orphans, and destroyed communities. Victorian Americans, Anne Rose argues, were unwilling "to let suffering stand in war as the final word. The will to recover a positive message threaded equally through peace and war because they perceived the conflict's trials to be spiritual as much as physical." Yet to dwell on the woman's Civil War narrative, especially African American women's war, was to dwell on suffering. Only by avoiding the troubling reminder of that suffering, by removing women from the picture, could a more positive narrative of the Civil War be constructed.[37]

The Civil War was, for many years, the most sanitized of conflicts, fought between two great generals, Ulysses S. Grant and Robert E. Lee, whose troops had heroic ideals. The tendency to portray the Civil War in this way increased over time, as General William Sherman's famous change of heart makes clear. "War is hell," he asserted in 1880, but a decade later he told a group of veterans from Tennessee that the Civil War was "the holiest fight ever fought on God's earth." The process of transforming the Civil War from hell to holy muted the very real suffering that the war involved. The women's war suffered a similar fate because it offered too sharp a reminder of the fact that Sherman had been closer to the mark in 1880 than he was ten years later. Yet historians have sometimes been too concerned to right the wrongs done to women in Civil War historiography to place the problem in its broader context. Leonard, for example, takes issue with Henry Bellow's admittedly dismissive observation that Civil War nurses had received a spiritual reward for their work and sacrifice for the Union cause. His attitude, she argues, "contributed to an early postwar image that cleansed the topic of women in Civil War nursing of its unpleasant and threatening aspects." Yet the Civil War was quickly cleansed of many of its most unpleasant aspects, and the diminution of the work of Civil War nurses comprised only one element in that process.[38]

The problem facing the United States after the war has two segments: the local, involving men and their communities, and the national, involving the war and the nation. Local communities during and after the war had to deal with the troubling issue of what war does, of the changes it effects in those involved in combat. There was, as Reid Mitchell argues, a very real need to avoid confronting the reality of what it is that people actually do in war: kill. Both men and women constructed a narrative that avoided the conflict's fatal reality by portraying the war in almost romantic terms, even as they acknowledged the horrors perpetrated in war's name. Within the context of the times, what Linderman terms the "idiom of elevated sentimentality" made the horrors of war bearable. The "language of heroism," with its vocabulary of brave soldiers, spirited action, and noble sacrifice, became "the foundation of public discourse." In their efforts to translate the war from horrific ordeal to heroic catalyst of national definition, Americans continued to employ this language long after the fighting ended. The gendered nature of its vocabulary, however, excluded women from the war's narrative, even as they employed it to describe their own war experiences.[39]

In national terms, North and South predicated their rather uneasy peace on the battlefield experience, the military heroism of both sides, and stories of the "Blue and the Gray." This process reached a peak during the semi-centennial of the Battle of Gettysburg in 1913, as former enemies shook hands across the stone wall over which they had battled fifty years before. This Civil War was, in the *Nation*'s phrase, a "triumph of brotherhood," and white brotherhood at that. The Gettysburg commemoration ceremony of 1913, David Blight argues, "represented a public avowal of the deeply laid mythology of the Civil War" in which the war was "a tragedy that forged greater unity" through soldiers' sacrifices. Women were not entirely absent from proceedings. The *New York Times* had hired Helen D. Longstreet, the widow of Confederate general James Longstreet, to report on the reunion. She reminded readers of women's sacrifice during the war and called for a tribute to their endeavors to form the theme of a future Blue-Gray reunion. Yet the ceremony really belonged to men. The women's story was not all that was lost in the process of binding up the nation's wounds, but it was a casualty of a process that transformed a brutal and bloody conflict into a war for national unity. Historians' efforts to reintegrate women into the Civil War story and highlight race and gender as crucial determinants of that story are more than a process of recovering the voices of the forgotten or reinstating women as significant players in America's critical national experience. They represent a fundamental challenge to traditional explanations of how war functions as a force for national cohesion. They show that such cohesion is achieved through exclusion as well as inclusion. Integrating black and white women into the war's narrative clarifies some of the reasons for their exclusion in the first place, but more fundamentally, it reveals the racial and gendered constructions that defined and undermined America as a nation.[40]

NOTES

I would like to thank S. Jay Kleinberg for giving me the opportunity to contribute to this volume, for pushing me to revise my own ideas about women and the war, and for all her editorial guidance.

1. Theresa McDevitt, *Women and the American Civil War: An Annotated Bibliography* (Westport, Conn.: Greenwood Press, 2003), offers a comprehensive listing of books, articles, and Web sites on women's war.

2. On the impact of the war on courtship and marriage, see Patricia L. Richard, "'Listen Ladies One and All': Union Soldiers Yearn for the Society of Their 'Fair Cousins of the North'"; and Megan J. McClintock, "The Impact of the Civil War on Nineteenth-Century Marriages," both in *Union Soldiers and the Northern Home Front: Wartime Experiences, Postwar Adjustments*, ed. Paul A. Cimbala and Randall M. Miller (New York: Fordham University Press, 2002), 143–181, and 395–416, respectively. On women pushing against the gender conventions, see Richard, "'Listen Ladies One and All,'" 177–181.

3. Abraham Lincoln, Second Inaugural Address, March 4, 1865, in *The Collected Works of Abraham Lincoln*, ed. Roy F. Basler (New Brunswick: Rutgers University Press, 1953), 8:333; Elizabeth Leonard, *Yankee Women: Gender Battles in the Civil War* (1994; repr., New York: W. W. Norton and Company, 1995), xv.

4. Catherine Clinton, ed., *Half Sisters of History: Southern Women and the American Past* (Durham: Duke University Press, 1994).

5. George C. Rable, "'Missing in Action': Women of the Confederacy," in *Divided Houses: Gender and the Civil War,* ed. Catherine Clinton and Nina Silber (Oxford: Oxford University Press, 1992), 134–146, quote on 134–135.

6. Elizabeth Young, *Disarming the Nation: Women's Writing and the American Civil War* (Chicago: University of Chicago Press, 1999), 1; Jeanie Attie, "Warwork and the Crisis of Domesticity in the North," in *Divided Houses,* ed. Clinton and Silber, 247–259, quote on 247.

7. DeAnne Blanton and Lauren M. Cook, *They Fought like Demons: Women Soldiers of the American Civil War* (Baton Rouge: Louisiana State University Press, 2002). Leonard also notes that "by the time of the First World War women's historical centrality to the military had been all but forgotten." Elizabeth Leonard, *All the Daring of the Soldier: Women of the Civil War Armies* (1999; repr., London and New York: Penguin Books, 2001), 101; Bell Irvin Wiley, *The Life of Billy Yank: The Common Soldier of the Union* (1952, repr., Baton Rouge: Louisiana State University Press, 1989), 138–139, 339; Mary Elizabeth Massey, *Women in the Civil War* (originally published as *Bonnet Brigades,* New York: Alfred A. Knopf, 1966; repr., Lincoln: University of Nebraska Press, 1994), 78–79, 84; Leonard, *All the Daring of the Soldier,* 248. See also Richard Hall, *Patriots in Disguise: Women Warriors of the Civil War* (New York: Paragon House, 1993).

8. Index entry in Reid Mitchell, *Civil War Soldiers: Their Expectations and Their Experiences* (New York: Simon and Schuster, 1988). It should be noted that an entry of "combatants" appears under "women" in a recent survey study of the Civil War that also acknowledges that women soldiers did exist and that they "fought for many reasons — to uphold political principles, to enjoy the drama of battle, to support themselves, and to accompany their loved ones." David Herbert Donald, Jean Harvey Baker, and Michael F. Holt, *The Civil War and Reconstruction* (New York: W. W. Norton and Company, 2001), 375; Mary A. Livermore, *My Story of the War* (Hartford, Conn.: A. D. Washington and Co., 1889), 120; Leonard, *All the Daring of the Soldier,* 165, 310–311. Figures for nurses are from Leonard, *Yankee Women,* 7–8; Wiley, *The Life of Billy Yank;* Massey, *Women in the Civil War,* 174; Rosecrans quoted in Massey, *Women in the Civil War,* 84.

9. Leonard, *All the Daring of the Soldier,* 168ff and passim; Livermore, *My Story of the War,* 112; Leonard, *All the Daring of the Soldier,* 135–136, Turchin quoted on 140, and on Etheridge see 106ff., esp. 109, 113.

10. Leonard, *Yankee Women,* 13; George C. Rable, *Civil Wars: Women and the Crisis of Southern Nationalism* (Urbana: University of Illinois Press, 1989), 124, 127; Leonard, *Yankee Women,* 157, Walker quoted on 129–130.

11. Nell Irvin Painter, "Representing Truth: Sojourner Truth's Knowing and Becoming Known," *Journal of American History* 81, no. 2 (September 1994): 461–492; quote on 462.

12. Henrietta Buckmaster, *Let My People Go: The Story of the Underground Railroad and the Growth of the Abolition Movement* (New York: Harper, 1941); Earl Conrad, *Harriet Tubman* (Washington, D.C..: Associated Publishers, 1943); for an example of a more popular treatment of Tubman, see Ann Petrey, *Harriet Tubman: Conductor on the Underground Railroad* (New York: Harper Trophy, 1996); Catherine Clinton, *Harriet Tubman: The Road to Freedom* (Boston: Little, Brown and Co., 2004); Jean M. Humez, *Harriet Tubman: The Life and the Life Stories* (Madison: University of Wisconsin Press, 2003); Kate Clifford Larson, *Bound for the Promised Land: Harriet Tubman, Portrait of an American Hero* (New York: Ballantine Books, 2003); Carleton Mabee and Susan Mabee Newhouse, *Sojourner Truth: Slave, Prophet, Legend* (New York: New York University Press, 1993); Painter, "Representing Truth," 464; and Nell Irvin Painter, *Sojourner Truth: A Life, a Symbol* (New York: Norton, 1996), 272–273. In fairness, Truth herself did present herself as the

symbolic southern slave in her public appearances (Painter, *Sojourner Truth*, 140–141); Jane E. Schultz, *Women at the Front: Hospital Workers in Civil War America* (Chapel Hill: University of North Carolina Press, 2004); see also Schultz's article, "Seldom Thanked, Never Praised, and Scarcely Recognized: Gender and Racism in Civil War Hospitals," *Civil War History* 48, no. 3 (2002): 220–236; Clinton quote from Schultz's interview with David Mehegan for the *Boston Globe*, 2004, see: http://www.boston.com/news/globe/living/articles/2004/02/05/up_from_the_ underground/ (May 2, 2005).

13. Jeanie Attie, *Patriotic Toil: Northern Women and the American Civil War* (Ithaca, N.Y.: Cornell University Press, 1998), 37, 1.

14. Judith Ann Giesberg, *Civil War Sisterhood: The U.S. Sanitary Commission and Women's Politics in Transition* (Boston: Northeastern University Press, 2000), 11–12; Attie, "Warwork and the Crisis of Domesticity," 259; Leonard, *Yankee Women*, xxiii; Attie, *Patriotic Toil*, 5, 53.

15. Attie, *Patriotic Toil*, 5, 53; Attie, "Warwork and the Crisis of Domesticity," 259, 253, 255.

16. Examples include John Greenleaf Whittier, "Barbara Freitchie" (1863), numerous short stories published in *Harper's Weekly* and the *Atlantic Monthly*, firsthand accounts such as Louisa May Alcott's *Hospital Sketches* (Boston: James Redpath, 1863), and post-war tribute volumes such as L. P. Brocket, MD, and Mrs. Mary C. Vaughan, *Women's Work in the Civil War: A Record of Heroism, Patriotism, and Patience* (Philadelphia: Zeigler, McCurdy and Co., 1867).

17. Thomas J. Brown, *The Public Art of Civil War Commemoration: A Brief History with Documents* (Boston: Bedford/St. Martins, 2004), 58–59; Alice Fahs, *The Imagined Civil War: Poplar Literature of the North and South, 1861–1865* (Chapel Hill: University of North Carolina Press, 2001), 140, 316–317, and passim.

18. Brown, *The Public Art of Civil War Commemoration*, 58; Anne Firor Scott, *The Southern Lady: From Pedestal to Politics, 1830–1930* (Chicago: University of Chicago Press, 1970), 96; Lee Ann Whites, *The Civil War as a Crisis in Gender: Augusta, Georgia, 1860–1890* (Athens: University of Georgia Press, 1995); Karen L. Cox, *Dixie's Daughters: The United Daughters of the Confederacy and the Preservation of Confederate Culture* (Gainesville: University of Florida Press, 2003).

19. Scott, *The Southern Lady*; Whites, *The Civil War as a Crisis in Gender*; Drew Gilpin Faust, *Mothers of Invention: Women of the Slaveholding South in the American Civil War* (Chapel Hill: University of North Carolina Press, 1996); Catherine Clinton, *Tara Revisited: Women, War, and the Plantation Legend* (New York: Abbeville, 1995).

20. Whites, *The Civil War as a Crisis in Gender*, 39–40; Faust, *Mothers of Invention*, 219, 97–98, 111; Loreta Velazquez's autobiography, *The Woman in Battle* (1876), is available through the Documenting the American South resource at the University of North Carolina, http://docsouth.unc.edu/velazquez/menu.html (May 3, 2005), and has recently been republished with an introduction by Jesse Aleman: Loreta Velazquez, *The Woman in Battle: The Civil War Narrative of Loreta Velazquez, a Cuban Woman and Confederate Soldier* (Madison: University of Wisconsin Press, 2003); Rable, *Civil Wars*, 89.

21. Drew Gilpin Faust, "Altars of Sacrifice: Confederate Women and Narratives of War," in *Divided Houses*, ed. Clinton and Silber, 171–199, quotes on 199, 172, 174, 184; Jacqueline Glass Campbell, *When Sherman Marched North from the Sea: Resistance on the Confederate Home Front* (Chapel Hill: University of North Carolina Press, 2003), passim. Earlier studies that also stress the strengthening of women's resolve in the face of the enemy include Stephen V. Ash, *When the Yankees Came: Conflict and Chaos in the Occupied South, 1861–1865* (1995; repr., Chapel Hill: University of North Carolina Press, 2002), esp. 38ff;

and Gary Gallagher, *The Confederate War* (Cambridge, Mass.: Harvard University Press, 1999), passim.

22. Elizabeth Fox-Genovese, *Within the Plantation Household: Black and White Women of the Old South* (Chapel Hill: University of North Carolina Press, 1988), 372; Faust, *Mothers of Invention*, 247, on violence, 65, on concepts of ladyhood, 7; on plantation mistresses' difficulties with slaves in their husbands' absence, see also Clarence L. Mohr, *On the Threshold of Freedom: Masters and Slaves in Civil War Georgia* (Athens: University of Georgia Press, 186), 221–222; Laura F. Edwards, *Scarlett Doesn't Live Here Anymore: Southern Women in the Civil War Era* (Urbana: University of Illinois Press, 2000) 73; Lee Ann Whites, "The Civil War as a Crisis in Gender," in *Divided Houses*, ed. Clinton and Silber, 3–21, quote on 16; Faust, *Mothers of Invention*, on sacrifice, 17, quote on 6–7.

23. Whites, *Civil War as a Crisis in Gender*, 149, 165–166, 168; Karen L. Cox, *Dixie's Daughters: The United Daughters of the Confederacy and the Preservation of Confederate Culture* (Gainesville: University Press of Florida, 2003); W. Scott Poole, *Never Surrender: Confederate Memory and Conservatism in the South Carolina Upcountry* (Athens: University of Georgia Press, 2004), 67–68, 70; William Blair, *Cities of the Dead: Contesting the Memory of the Civil War in the South, 1865–1914* (Chapel Hill: University of North Carolina Press, 2004), 54.

24. Clinton, *Tara Revisited: Women, War, and the Plantation Legend*; Catherine Clinton, "Bloody Terrain: Freedwomen, Sexuality, and Violence during Reconstruction," *Georgia Historical Quarterly* 76, no. 2 (1992): 313–332.

25. Fox-Genovese, *Within the Plantation Household*, 373; Elizabeth Fox-Genovese, "Reconstructing Freedwomen," in *Divided Houses*, ed. Clinton and Silber, 306–319.

26. For full information on the Freedmen project and the published volumes to date, see the project Web site at http://www.history.umd.edu/Freedmen/fssphome.htm (May 2, 2005).

27. Mohr, *On the Threshold of Freedom*; Roger L. Ransom and Richard Sutch, *One Kind of Freedom: The Economic Consequences of Emancipation* (Cambridge: Cambridge University Press, 1977); Julie Saville, *The Work of Reconstruction: From Slave to Wage Laborer in South Carolina, 1860–1870* (Cambridge: Cambridge University Press, 1994); see also Michael Wayne, *The Reshaping of Plantation Society: The Natchez District, 1860–1880* (Baton Rouge: Louisiana State University Press, 1983); Thavolia Glymph and J. J. Kushma, eds., *Essays on the Post-Bellum Southern Economy* (College Station: Texas A&M University Press, 1985); Jacqueline Jones, *Labor of Love, Labor of Sorrow: Black Women, Work, and the Family from Slavery to the Present* (New York: Basic Books, 1985); Leslie A. Schwalm, *A Hard Fight for We: Women's Transition from Slavery to Freedom in South Carolina* (Urbana: University of Illinois Press, 1997).

28. Daniel Patrick Moynihan, *The Negro Family: The Case for National Action* (Washington, D.C.: Office of Policy Planning and Research, United States Department of Labor, March 1965); see also Lee Rainwater and William L. Yancey, *The Moynihan Report and the Politics of Controversy* (Cambridge, Mass.: MIT Press, 1967).

29. Jones, *Labor of Love*, 48–49; Leon F. Litwack, *Been in the Storm So Long: The Aftermath of Slavery* (1979; repr., New York: Vintage Books, 1980), 129–131; Schwalm, *A Hard Fight for We*.

30. Thavolia Glymph, "'This Species of Property': Female Slave Contrabands in the Civil War," in *A Woman's War: Southern Women, Civil War, and the Confederate Legacy*, ed. Edward D. C. Campbell Jr. and Kym S. Rice (Richmond: Museum of the Confederacy, and Charlottesville: University Press of Virginia, 1996), 55–71, quotes on 59–60, 61; Wilma

King, "'Suffer with Them till Death': Slave Women and Their Children in Nineteenth-Century America," in *More Than Chattel: Black Women and Slavery in the Americas,* ed. David Barry Gaspar and Darlene Clark Hine (Bloomington: Indiana University Press, 1996), 147–168, quote on 161; on this point see also Jones, *Labor of Love,* 47, 51; Glymph, "This Species of Property," 61–62, 64–65; Schwalm, *Hard Fight for We,* 78–79; Noralee Frankel, *Freedom's Women: Black Women and Families in Civil War Era Mississippi* (Bloomington: Indiana University Press, 1999); on her use of sources in reconstructing freedwomen's lives see also Noralee Frankel, "From Slave Women to Free Women: The National Archives and Black Women's History in the Civil War Era," *Prologue* 29, no. 2 (summer 1997) at http://www.archives.gov/publications/prologue/summer_1997_ slave_ women. html (May 3, 2005); Elizabeth Regosin, *Freedom's Promise: Ex-Slave Families and Citizenship in the Age of Emancipation* (Charlottesville: University Press of Virginia, 2002).

31. Jones, *Labor of Love,* 45–46; Frankel, *Freedom's Women,* 48; Glymph, "This Species of Property," 68.

32. Laura Edwards, *Gendered Strife and Confusion: The Political Culture of Reconstruction* (Urbana: University of Illinois Press, 1997); Laura Edwards, "Sexual Violence, Gender, Reconstruction, and the Extension of Patriarchy in Granville County, North Carolina," *North Carolina Historical Review* 68, no. 3 (1991): 237–260.

33. Victoria E. Bynum, *Unruly Women: The Politics of Social and Sexual Control in the Old South* (Chapel Hill: University of North Carolina Press, 1992); see also her earlier article, "'War within a War': Women's Participation in the Revolt of the North Carolina Piedmont, 1863–1865," *Frontiers* 9, no. 3 (1987): 43–49; Glenda Elizabeth Gilmore, *Gender and Jim Crow: Women and the Politics of White Supremacy in North Carolina, 1896–1920* (Chapel Hill: University of North Carolina Press, 1996); Rable, *Civil Wars.*

34. Tera W. Hunter, *To 'Joy My Freedom: Southern Black Women's Lives and Labors after the Civil War* (Cambridge, Mass.: Harvard University Press, 1997); Hannah Rosen, "'Not That Sort of Woman': Race, Gender, and Sexual Violence during the Memphis Riot of 1866," in *Sex, Love, Race: Crossing Boundaries in North American History,* ed. Martha Hodes (New York: New York University Press, 1999), 267–293; Martha Hodes, *White Women, Black Men: Illicit Sex in the Nineteenth-Century South* (New Haven: Yale University Press, 1999), 2–3; Victoria E. Bynum, *The Free State of Jones: Mississippi's Longest Civil War* (Chapel Hill: University of North Carolina Press, 2001).

35. Diane Miller Sommerville, *Rape and Race in the Nineteenth-Century South* (Chapel Hill: University of North Carolina Press, 2004); Karin L. Zipf, "Reconstructing 'Free Woman': African-American Women, Apprenticeship, and Custody Rights during Reconstruction," *Journal of Women's History* 12, no. 1 (spring 2000): 8–31; Edwards, *Gendered Strife and Confusion.*

36. Zipf, "Reconstructing 'Free Woman,'" 8–31, 9.

37. Clinton, *Tara Revisited,* 17; Leonard, *Yankee Women,* 182, 179; Anne C. Rose, *Victorian America and the Civil War* (New York: Cambridge University Press, 1992), 240.

38. William Sherman, quoted in Gerald F. Linderman, *Embattled Courage: The Experience of Combat in the American Civil War* (1987; repr., New York: Macmillan, 1989), 283–284; Leonard, *Yankee Women,* 48–49.

39. Reid Mitchell, *The Vacant Chair: The Northern Soldier Leaves Home* (1993; repr., Oxford: Oxford University Press, 1995), 146–147; Thomas P. Lowry, *The Story the Soldiers Wouldn't Tell: Sex in the Civil War* (Mechanicsburg, Pa.: Stackpole Books, 1994), 4; Linderman, *Embattled Courage,* 98, 99–100.

40. David Blight, *Race and Reunion: The Civil War in American Memory* (Cambridge, Mass.: Harvard University Press, 2001), 381–387.

7

Turner's Ghost

A Personal Retrospective on Western Women's History

SUSAN ARMITAGE

I have spent my academic career haunted by the ghost of America's most famous historian, Frederick Jackson Turner.[1] When I first began my study of western women thirty years ago, I accepted Turner's frontier thesis without question, as did everyone else I knew. Then, when I noticed flaws in the theory, I tried to exorcize Turner by marshaling arguments against his ethnocentrism and triumphalism. Next, I tried to ignore the ghostly remnants. Recently, however, I've become concerned that Turner's lingering aura is creating two western histories divided by whiteness and plagued by popular myths about the West. In this chapter I chart the genesis and development of the two histories and conclude with an effort to gauge the severity of the divergence.

In his 1893 essay, "The Significance of the Frontier in American History," Turner turned American restlessness into a national epic, asserting that the recurring experience of westward movement and settlement shaped Americans into a uniquely democratic and risk-taking people. As Turner himself put it, "This perennial rebirth, this fluidity of American life, this expansion westward with its new opportunities, its continuous touch with the simplicity of primitive society, furnish the forces dominating American Character."[2] According to Turner, each new frontier in turn marked the dividing line between "savagery" and "civilization," and each followed the same stages of development. Successively, the trapper, the cattleman, the miner, and the farmer each used the land for his own purposes in a recurring pattern that began at the Cumberland Gap and ended at the Pacific Ocean. Turner's focus on the westward movement of American pioneers automatically led one to think of all pioneers as white, never considering that later migrants to the West from Asia, Mexico, and elsewhere were equally pioneers in their own eyes. Further, Turner never doubted that westward movement represented the inevitable march of progress, and neither did most of the western historians who followed in his footsteps. They also accepted Turner's chronological framework from the "opening" of the frontier

126

until its close (according to the U.S. Census Bureau) in 1890, with the result that western history became primarily nineteenth-century history.

As the years passed, Turner's academic thesis blended with the popular myth of the West fostered by popular media, among them Buffalo Bill's wildly successful Wild West shows in the 1880s, dime novels featuring Buffalo Bill and other heroes such as Deadwood Dick, Owen Wister's glorification of the cowboy in his 1902 novel *The Virginian,* and on into the multitudes of "westerns" churned out by Hollywood film studios over the years. The result was the identification of the U.S. West with the frontier and the designation of this special place as the home of freedom, opportunity, and adventure. This identification bred the belief that America's best qualities have been — and will forever be — expressed on the frontier. These special qualities of the West, as they came to be epitomized by the worldwide use of the cowboy as a symbol for America, trapped western historians within the Turner thesis and the frontier myth. The wider public and students alike wanted their faith in American values reinforced, not challenged by harsher versions that told the actual history of the western United States.[3] By mid-twentieth century, as *Bonanza* dominated the television screen and academic history was becoming more critical and analytic, western history was dismissed within the American historical profession as nothing more than "cowboy and Indian history."[4]

What, readers may ask, is wrong with a bit of popular romanticism? This chapter seeks to answer that question by tracing the changes in western history over the past quarter century, focusing on western women's history in particular. My professional career as a historian has coincided with these changes. Because I have contributed to the shaping of the field, I draw on my personal experiences in the following account to highlight some particular moments of changing consciousness as western women's history developed. And because I want to highlight the ways my own consciousness has changed, I quote more liberally from my own work than I would in a less personal essay.

When western women's history first took shape in the 1970s, we all started with Turner. After all, westward expansion was our national epic; it seemed perfectly natural to look first to white pioneer women. We all noticed that historical accounts of pioneering were almost exclusively male, but we thought this was an inadvertent oversight, perhaps a lingering legacy of Turner's generation of historians who mistakenly believed that men alone were actors in history. We thought we only needed to document women's activities and the male bias would disappear. The fuss kicked up by two early works on the Overland Trail soon proved us wrong. Christine Stansell and Johnny Faragher's "Women and Their Families on the Overland Trail to California and Oregon" and Lillian Schlissel's *Women's Diaries of the Westward Journey* met hostile reactions because they claimed that gender mattered: women's trail experiences were different from those of men and provided new critical perspectives on men's actions and attitudes.[5] At the same time, these early writers on western women believed that the Turnerian notion of western opportunity applied to women as well as to men and assumed, in good 1970s feminist style, that opportunity for women meant the chance to do men's work. Neither Faragher, Schlissel, nor another early writer, Julie Roy Jeffrey, found this to be the case. Jeffrey, whose *Frontier Women* was based on the papers and letters of white middle-class women, was very frank about it: "My original perspective was feminist: I hoped to find that pioneer women used the frontier as a means of liberating themselves from stereotypes and behaviors which I found constricting and sexist. I discovered that they did not."[6]

Not yet daring to believe that Turner was wrong, we took this evidence to mean either that women were reluctant pioneers, dragged west against their wills, or that their activities were restricted to the domestic by sexist males. Of course, not all female western historians agreed. Sandra Myres vehemently asserted that attitudes toward "westering," as she called it, were individual rather than gendered. She wrote a substantial study, based on considerable archival research, *Westering Women and the Frontier Experience, 1800–1915,* to prove her point.[7] Thus, in the early 1980s historians of western women appeared to face an unhappy choice between tried and true Turnerism, with the addition of a few women, or the much more radical feminist position. Several things soon mitigated the severity of this choice.

First, when John Faragher's carefully researched and documented *Women and Men on the Overland Trail* sustained Schlissel's argument for a female trail experience that was characterized by endurance rather than adventure, a gendered perspective on western history gained its first foothold.[8] Second, localized studies began to confirm Jeffrey's perception that pioneer women's — and men's — eastern training in gender roles persisted in the West. Glenda Riley, working with women's papers in Iowa, and I, doing oral histories with farm and ranch women in Colorado, reached pretty much the same conclusion: western women were not only committed to traditional gender roles, but were too busy doing their own "women's work" of household production to have any desire to take on men's work as well. While the men were figuring out what crops would grow or how they would make a living in a new place, women had their hands full keeping their pioneer families fed and functioning. Far from looking for twentieth-century-style liberation, women used their considerable domestic skills for family survival.[9] To my mind, this insight was a perfect example of Gerda Lerner's famous admonition that we should always ask, "What did women do while the men were doing what the textbook tells us was important?"[10]

At this early stage, historians of western women sought to identify how the experience of white women settlers differed from that of white men, and in so doing roused the ire of many traditional western historians who saw — perhaps before we did — the dangers that gender posed to Turner's universality. As I wrote rather flippantly in the 1980s, "Frederick Jackson Turner was, at best, half right. The frontier thesis does not explain women's experience. We must recognize that there were two Wests: a female and a male one. We know about the male version; now we need to describe women's western sphere."[11] What we believed we were finding was evidence of kinder, gentler attitudes among women settlers, particularly in their encounters with Indians.[12] This early bias in our scholarship occurred because we failed to fully consider race as well as gender. Our focus was on white women; we did not also view these encounters from an Indian perspective. Today most western women's historians accept at least in principle Brigitte Georgia-Findlay's argument that the very domesticity of white women, like that of British women in India, implicated them deeply in the imperial project.[13] Although some white pioneer women in the American West may have felt occasional sympathy with Native American women, most believed that their race and religion made them inherently superior to the Native peoples whose land and lives they invaded without compunction. Their insistence on imposing their version of domesticity on Native peoples marks their motives and their actions as imperialist.

After this first flurry of feminist scholarship, it was obvious that to change western history we had to produce studies about western women that would change the minds of the predominantly male western history profession. Thus began the steady stream of publications about individual women and groups of women that continues unabated today. Among the earliest were Cathy Luchetti's *Women of the West* and Linda Rasmussen's *A Harvest Yet to Reap*, both illustrated with exciting, unposed pictures of western women.[14] We also worked to make existing information about western women more accessible. In 1982 Christiane Fischer chose a wonderful title, *Let Them Speak for Themselves*, for her collection of excerpts from women's accounts, and the University of Nebraska Press hastened to reprint western women's memoirs that had long been out of print.[15] Many of us collaborated on efforts to encourage archivists to identify women's papers that were part of larger collections (usually their husband's) and, until then, not separately indexed.[16] Additionally, realizing that nineteenth-century newspapers were poor sources of information for any but notorious or notable women, we also worked to extend the range of available sources. Women's diaries, many still in private hands, attracted our attention, even though most of them concerned personal and domestic life rather than "historical" events. I turned to women's oral history because the archived material on women in Colorado was poorly indexed, and class and race biased as well. The first article I published, in 1977, was based on oral histories and contributed to the scanty literature on African American women in the West. "Black Women and Their Communities in Colorado" described how early in the twentieth century both rural and urban African Americans created a bit of community and autonomy in the face of persistent poverty and discrimination. It is interesting now to realize that when I thought of race I still thought in black and white. In the 1970s I had no real understanding of the West as the multiracial, multicultural place we now know it has always been.[17]

In the late 1970s I lacked other insights as well. I read many women's diaries and reminiscences, published and unpublished, but in those days before postmodernism I regarded them as straightforward, transparent historical evidence.

Doubtless, I missed a lot. Personal papers now are treated with much more critical sophistication. With the tools I had available then, I teased out the real reasons why women might be reluctant pioneers and tried to link up their pioneer lives with the insights of women's historians of the industrializing East. The lives of the hardworking women I'd discovered in early Colorado made me look askance at the major theory then popular in national women's history, the Cult of True Womanhood.[18] Its middle-class definition of domesticity didn't seem to fit most western women I had studied. Another popular theory, Carroll Smith-Rosenberg's "The Female World of Love and Ritual: Relations between Women in Nineteenth-Century America," seemed almost too appropriate, reinforcing the pitiful image of the lonely western woman longing for female companionship.[19] Most early studies of women pioneers, my own included, were much too short-sighted: focusing on the immediate shock of newness, they almost always cast women as reluctant rather than as the community builders many of them later became. The fact was that eastern theories weren't adequate to describe western women, but we hadn't yet developed homegrown theories of our own.[20]

Gradually, as the scholarship on western women's history accumulated, female figures stepped forward to join Turner's famous quartet of "the trapper, the cattleman, the miner, the farmer." Sometimes they quietly slipped into place, as the stereotype of the female "helpmate" suggested, but more frequently they demanded serious reconsideration of men's activities.[21] Nowhere was this so evident as in the figure of that famous loner, the trapper, who was suddenly discovered to be a family man. Sylvia Van Kirk's examination of the Canadian fur trade, *Many Tender Ties: Women in Fur Trade Society, 1670–1870*, was the first to demonstrate the dependence of the European fur trade on Native women and their kin. Studies by Jennifer Brown and Jacqueline Peterson followed, describing in detail the mixed-race people who were the offspring of those encounters.[22] The masculine images of the cattleman and that of his much-mythologized employee, the cowboy, have proved much harder to change. Fascination with glittering, commercialized rodeo queens and princesses still continues to obscure the lives of hard-working ranch women in spite of valiant efforts like Theresa Jordan's *Cowgirls*.[23] Female residents of western mining towns have fared better. Paula Petrik's *No Step Backward: Women and Family on the Rocky Mountain Mining Frontier* set a high standard in community studies, and Sally Zanjani's appealingly titled *A Mine of Her Own* revealed the unexpected existence of many female prospectors.[24] But the most significant success in stereotype-smashing arose from new studies of prostitution. Marion Goldman's *Gold Diggers and Silver Miners: Prostitution and Social Life on the Comstock Lode* and Ann Butler's *Daughters of Joy, Sisters of Misery: Prostitutes in the American West* showed the stratification of sex work by race and ethnicity. Their careful descriptions of the sordid and dangerous trade forever banished the image of the glamorous whore with a heart of gold from the historical literature (although not, of course, from popular imagination).[25]

The last of Turner's frontier figures, the farmer, acquired a hard-working wife, but western studies of farmwomen have yet to equal the detail and insight of Midwestern studies such as those by Mary Neth and Deborah Fink.[26] The most surprising finding about the rural West was the number of single women who successfully homesteaded on their own. As the research concerning Elinore Stewart (author of the engaging *Letters of a Woman Homesteader*) has shown, however, single filing often served a larger familial purpose, a perspective later confirmed by Elaine Lindgren's *Land in Her Own Name.*[27] In addition to all of these female counterparts to Turnerian figures, the new scholarship also documented the presence in the West of several sizeable and distinctive groups of single women, among them schoolteachers and nuns.[28] In spite of this flood of findings, aside from decidedly token chapters on women in current state-of-the-field anthologies, there was no obvious move by western historians to incorporate the new research on women into the standard narrative.[29] Furthermore, despite the growing concern about its shortcomings, in the early 1980s Turner's frontier was still the accepted theoretical framework for all western historians, we women's historians among them.

When I had a chance to complain about all of this, I did. As one of the speakers at the first Women's West conference in 1983, I gave an address that the local newspaper reported under the headline "Western History Is a Mess, Armitage Asserts." I criticized the male bias of western history by dubbing the region "Hisland" and said that if we were to include *all* women in western history–Native American women before European contact at one end and the many twentieth-century immigrant women on the other — the field needed a longer time line. It also needed a stronger dose of social history rather than more popular heroes, even if they were women.[30]

A few years later, another author said some of the same things to greater effect. Patricia Limerick's *The Legacy of Conquest*, published in 1987, set the field of western history on its ear.[31] By the simple but fundamental step of conceptualizing the American West as a place, not a destination, Limerick sidestepped Turner's frontier thesis entirely and concentrated on the continuities of western history from its beginnings to the very present, the greatest of which has always been the region's ethnic and racial diversity. Thanks to Limerick, we now see the West not primarily as a white frontier but as a multiracial "meeting-ground of peoples." Limerick modestly claimed that she had merely synthesized much of the newer work in western history, but she did it brilliantly and humorously. Unfortunately, the response of many old-style western historians was less generous, and she endured more than five years of bitter controversy, name-calling, and personal attacks. Still, when the dust finally settled it was obvious that the New Western History had won the field, but at a price. Rejecting Turner meant breaking with the popular ideas about the West that most Americans find so hard to give up. The New Western History marked the moment when popular and academic western history parted ways. And in spite of its apparent victory, the subsequent history of western women's history seems to indicate that the New Western History split the field of western history as a whole.

The triumph of the New Western History at first changed very little for western women's historians because gender played a minor role in Limerick's argument. In the early 1980s Limerick herself told me that, in contrast to environmental history and ethnic studies, she could not find anything theoretically distinctive in the published studies of western women. Susan Johnson echoed this criticism with much more edge in 1993, when she described western women's history as consisting of "a delightful disdain for Big Myths and True Heroes and a dogged devotion to the heroics of everyday life."[32] Of course, she was right; her characterization fit my own work with painful accuracy. Johnson realized that despite what she called a "small mountain of scholarship" on western women, mainstream western historians were continuing to blandly leave questions of gender to women's historians.[33] She decided that the best tactic was attack: her article was one of the first to dissect the manliness of the western myth, an effort in which she and many other historians are still engaged. Her Bancroft prize–winning book, *Roaring Camp*, in which the California Gold Rush is viewed as a site of shifting definitions of race and (largely masculine) gender, shows how very effective such a strategy can be. An anthology, edited by Matt Basso, Dee Garceau, and Laura McCall, *Across the Great Divide: Cultures of Manhood in the American West*, began the task of charting the contours of western masculinity.[34]

What Limerick's *The Legacy of Conquest* did accomplish was to open the door to a growing number of studies of ethnic and racial groups in the American West. In fact, racial-ethnic scholars, rarely noticed until then by most western historians, were already determined to push open the door. But because most of the early studies of racial-ethnic communities in the West were male-centered, women historians of color had to fight to be heard not only by white women's historians but by their own male colleagues. On the first front, in 1983 Vicki L. Ruiz collaborated with Lillian Schlissel and Jan Monk to mount a conference, Western Women, Their Land, Their Lives, that was the first to feature multiracial western women's history and to insist that white women's historians pay attention.[35] As Marian Perales documented in "Empowering the Welder," the second struggle within ethnic studies took a while longer; but, unquestionably, the determination of female historians of color has changed the way most racial-ethnic community studies are written today. Instead of the old-style male-dominated community histories that male historians of all races and ethnicities used to write, many of the newer racial-ethnic histories describe the activities of both men and women.[36]

While these new trends in urban history were still emerging, most white historians of western women, in accordance with Turnerian precepts, continued to write about rural women. Ironically, that customary rural focus was at odds with the demographic reality that for much of its history the West has been as much urban as rural.[37] Western women's historians studied rural women in different ways. Paula Nelson's *After the West Was Won: Homesteaders and Town-Builders in Western South Dakota, 1900–1917* carefully distinguished gender roles in her account of how pioneers in South Dakota learned to survive the harsh climate and erratic economy. Perhaps Nelson's most iconoclastic finding was that few women homesteaders stayed on the land long enough to contribute to the agricultural development of the area. In fact, their small, occasionally cultivated holdings attracted weeds such as Russian thistles that plagued larger long-term farmers.[38]

Joan Jensen concentrated on the way race and ethnicity shaped the lives of rural women in two articles she contributed to the anthology *New Mexico Women*, "Canning Comes to New Mexico: Women and the Agricultural Extension Service, 1914–1919" and " 'I've Worked, I'm Not Afraid of Work': Farm Women in New Mexico, 1920–1940."[39] Continuing the rural focus, Glenda Riley's *The Female Frontier: A Comparative View of Women on the Prairie and the Plains* encompassed rural communities as well as farms and ranches. Attempting to make a definitive generalization about western women, she argued that domesticity was the factor that shaped western women's lives differently than those of men, but the point was considered by many (myself among them) to be too general to be very useful.[40] In a later article, Paula Nelson pointed out that many of the most cherished aspects of contemporary western rural life — commitment to family, to hard work, to religion and the local community — are based on values rooted in nineteenth-century economic and social organization. Beginning in the early twentieth century, the continuity of rural values (including, of course, gender roles) was increasingly challenged by new principles originating in differently organized urban life. This point was made clearly by Dee Garceau in *The Important Things of Life: Women, Work, and Family in Sweetwater County, Wyoming, 1880–1929*, published in 1997. In it she contrasted the opportunities and constraints in gender roles of "Old West" women in ranch families with those of women, many of white European ethnic origin, in a modern urban industrial mining center.[41]

By the mid-1980s the field of western women's history had moved into the twentieth century, with greatly sharpened attention to difference (especially racial ethnic difference). Almost all the outstanding work in western women's history since the mid 1980s has been in the field most accurately described as twentieth-century racial-ethnic labor history. Two of the three most influential western women's history books of the 1980s fell into that category. Vicki L. Ruiz's book about Chicana workers in California, *Cannery Women*, was immediately recognized as a major contribution to women's labor history, although only later did the transnational aspects of her study attract notice. Sarah Deutsch's examination of the extended communities of New Mexican Hispanos, *No Separate Refuge*, changed the terms in which many of us defined the word "community" by demonstrating how firmly the "transient" male laborers in Colorado remained connected to their families in New Mexico. The third book, Peggy Pascoe's

Relations of Rescue, although primarily concerned with the nineteenth century, for the first time placed white women reformers within the framework of their relations to the racial-ethnic women they sought to help. Subsequently, Pascoe's influential perspective was carried forward by two fine works, Margaret Jacobs's *Engendered Encounters,* about the interaction between female anthropologists of the 1920s and the Southwest Indian cultures they studied, and Susan Yohn's *A Contest of Faiths: Missionary Women and Pluralism in the American Southwest,* about the ways their experience in the field changed the beliefs of early twentieth-century missionary women. To this particular category one should also add Joan Jensen's unique study of creative artists, *One Foot on the Rockies: Women and Creativity in the Modern American West,* the most valuable part of which was her attention to the interactions between racial-ethnic artists and their white female patrons.[42]

These works took the field of western women's history decisively in the direction of multiculturalism. This direction had been pointed as early 1980 within the mainstream, when Joan Jensen and Darlis Miller published their influential bibliographic essay, "The Gentle Tamers Revisited," in which they challenged the Euro American focus of western history and identified the rich variety of sources for women of many racial and ethnic groups. Similarly, Elizabeth Jameson's 1988 review article, "Toward a Multicultural History of Women in the Western United States," broke new ground because she considered women of different racial-ethnic groups in their own cultural contexts, thereby critiquing the underlying racism of most cross-cultural frameworks. This recognition of differences between western women addressed a key complaint voiced most clearly by Antonia Castañeda, that for white women scholars the study of racial-ethnic women remained merely an "add-on" to our focus on white women.[43]

Castañeda's prizewinning 1992 article, "Women of Color and the Rewriting of Western History: The Discourse, Politics, and Decolonization of History," marked an important turning point in western women's history because it spotlighted the question of what theories were appropriate for the multicultural study of the U.S. West. She easily demonstrated that theories developed by racial-ethnic scholars were more suitable than the lingering Turnerian theories that most western historians still employed. Her article was part of a larger consideration of the field of western women's history that occurred in the early 1990s. In essays published in *Montana: The Magazine of Western History* in 1991 and in the *Pacific Historical Review* in 1992, ten well-known scholars assessed the field and tried to look ahead.[44] There was no unanimity among them, for without Turner to follow (or to rebel against) the range of possible approaches was great indeed. In retrospect, this was the moment when the paths followed by western women's historians began to diverge, presaging the division within western history as a whole.

The 1990s saw the flowering of work by and about women of color in the West. Chicana scholars were the most prolific. Historians Antonia Castañeda and

Deena González took the lead in recovering the history of Spanish colonial California and New Mexico; in *Refusing the Favor: Spanish-Mexican Women of Santa Fe, 1820–1880*, González took the next step by showing how Spanish Mexican women resisted the American economic and political conquest of New Mexico. In *From Out of the Shadows: Mexican Women in Twentieth-Century America*, Vicki L. Ruiz marked the maturation of Chicana/o history by placing women's experience within a historical narrative derived from Chicana experience — the image of emerging from the private world of the household into public space — rather than using theories developed by historians of immigration.[45] Similarly, Asian American historian Judy Yung used a metaphor specific to Chinese women, the image of bound feet, to frame the historical changes she described in *Unbound Feet: A Social History of Chinese Women in San Francisco*. As well, her book documented the importance to San Francisco's Chinatown of sustained transnational links to Chinese culture and politics, another theoretical perspective that had been largely ignored by traditional historians of immigration. A more recent anthology edited by Shirley Hune and Gail Nomura, *Asian/Pacific Islander American Women: A Historical Anthology*, is an ambitious effort to convey the historical experiences of the many diverse groups gathered under the omnibus label of "Asian/Pacific Islander women." Valerie Matsumoto's study of the Japanese farming community of Cortez, California, *Farming the Home Place*, showed the many ways in which the community melded Japanese and American practices, a point that she creatively underscored by including recipes whose ingredients illustrated the fusion.[46] In comparison, there are as yet few historical studies of Native American women, and none are specifically western. Two books by Theda Perdue indicate the current state of research on American Indian women: her 1998 *Cherokee Women: Gender and Culture, 1700–1835* and her edited collection of biographical essays, *Sifters*, on notable American Indian women from all periods and locations in American history. Other recent works by American Indian women's historians, of which Brenda Child's *Boarding School Seasons: American Indian Families, 1900–1940* is an example, focus on the cultural impact and resistance strategies of Native children in boarding schools.[47] Only a small number of historical works focus on African American women in the West, and almost all concern the twentieth century. One exception is Lynn Hudson's *The Making of "Mammy Pleasant": A Black Entrepreneur in Nineteenth-Century San Francisco*, in which she successfully sorted fact from fiction. Two fine community studies, one by Shirley Anne Moore and another by Gretchen Lemke-Santangelo, describe African American women and the communities they built with African American men during World War II in the San Francisco Bay area. The first comprehensive historical anthology, *African American Women Confront the West*, edited by Shirley Ann Moore and Quintard Taylor, is more recent and begins to correct the heavy male bias that marked the earlier historical community studies.[48] Only a handful of scholars is working in each of these fields; it behooves all western historians to encourage and support young students of color to undertake graduate work in history so that eventually the vast variety of racial-ethnic women in the history of the U.S. West will receive the attention they deserve.

Among white western historians, notable gender-balanced community studies have come primarily from female labor historians studying male-dominated western mining towns. One outstanding example of this newer work is Mary Murphy's *Mining Cultures*, an examination of the shifting definitions of leisure in the famous mining town of Butte, Montana, in the early twentieth century.[49] Murphy carefully shows how the community shifted from the two-fisted, hard-drinking male culture, as mining declined, to a consumer culture that included public roles and activities for women. Murphy's study makes a major contribution to the hitherto exclusively eastern labor history work on leisure and consumerism. Similarly, Elizabeth Jameson's *All That Glitters: Class, Conflict, and Community in Cripple Creek* was immediately recognized as a definitive study of labor, gender, and community. Laurie Mercier's study of Irish American men and women in *Anaconda: Labor, Community, and Culture in Montana's Smelter City* shed valuable light on a western union in decline. Again, these are all twentieth-century studies.[50] They all were impelled, at least in part, by the need to puzzle out the very limited public and occupational opportunities for women in mining towns as opposed to their sometimes considerable informal activities as community networkers and organizers. Surprisingly, in contrast to other regions of the country, organized women's groups and women's clubs have so far not received much critical attention. Sandra Haarsager's *Organized Womanhood* surveyed women's activities in the Pacific Northwest, but there has been little detailed follow-up there or in other parts of the West, which is surprising given the possibilities of the topic. As an early book by June Underwood, *Civilizing Kansas,* suggested, women's groups founded the social services by first financing private efforts and then successfully lobbying for permanent local and state funding. This is a topic that deserves more attention.[51]

I had hoped that *Legacy of Conquest* would encourage social histories of the various racial encounters sketched by Limerick in the book and detailed studies of settlement itself. It is still amazing to me that the region where Turner's frontier is so celebrated should have produced so few studies of the actual building of the communities in which the celebrated pioneers lived. Instead, in the wake of *Legacy,* many formerly Turnerian western historians turned to environmental history, thereby evading the task of writing detailed social histories that engaged race, class, and gender and allowing themselves instead the privilege of manly nostalgia for the old, pristine West ruined by their own insensitive forebears. This stream of nostalgia flows endlessly from the pens of western male writers from Wallace Stegner to Larry McMurtry and also appears to be a major motive for popular fascination with the bicentennial of the Lewis and Clark expedition of 1803–06. Only a few sharp-eyed western women writers like Montanan Mary Clearman Blew have named this nostalgia for what it is — an unwillingness to give up the spotlight.[52]

Although *Legacy of Conquest* had offered a new paradigm to replace Turner's, many western historians had difficulty giving up the frontier, Limerick among them. In later writings, she suggested that "frontier" was still a usable word, if one used the Spanish term "frontera," denoting a reciprocal encounter of cultures rather than Turner's notion of a boundary between "savagery" and "civilization."[53] The new two-(or more) sided, inter-related version of the frontier/frontera is much more complex than the old and much more difficult to research and write than the Turnerian version.

So far, only a few studies have successfully traced the complexities of long-term racial interactions (as opposed to brief encounters). All of them, perhaps not surprisingly, are in the field that used to be called Borderlands history, where the *mestizo* consequence of the Spanish conquest of indigenous Mexicans has always been acknowledged. The first and perhaps best known of these inclusive studies was Ramón Gutiérrez's *When Jesus Came the Cornmothers Went Away*, a study of Spanish conquest and Pueblo resistance in what is now New Mexico. This award-winning book was the first to make sexuality a topic of central concern in histories of conquests, thereby establishing a model most closely followed by Albert Hurtado in *Intimate Frontiers*, a study of Indian-white sexual relationships in colonial California. For all of its pioneering qualities, Gutiérrez's book also served as an example of the immense difficulties of evenhanded multiracial scholarship, for a vocal group of Pueblo Indians complained that the author had not accurately used the full range of Pueblo sources available to him. More recent works tracing multiracial encounters include Lizabeth Haas's *Conquests and Historical Identities in California, 1769–1936* and James Brooks's *Captives and Cousins: Slavery, Kinship, and Community in the Southwest Borderlands*, a detailed study of the interracial connections built over time by the captivity practices of Spanish and Indians alike.[54]

In spite of these efforts to make the frontier two-sided, Turner's ghost still lingers in the classroom and in the popular imagination. Textbooks, such as the recently published western text by Robert Hine and John Mack Faragher, are still organized around the concept of a moving Euro American frontier (albeit with much greater interaction with indigenous peoples than Turner considered), and there is an almost obligatory final chapter on "the image of the West."[55] No one seems to have figured out a way to integrate this image chapter into the main text. Surely this is a useful clue: these well-worn images — these ghosts — are no longer relevant to the real history of the region, but few white western historians and their students seem able to ignore them entirely.

The younger generation of scholars had one great advantage over those of us who were older: they had no difficulty at all ignoring Frederick Jackson Turner's frontier. It simply was not relevant to their work. Indeed, most of the best work about western issues and places in the 1990s was done by people who didn't think of themselves as western historians at all. Perhaps the best demonstration of this refreshing irreverence was the anthology edited by Valerie Matsumoto and

Blake Allmendinger, *Over the Edge: Remapping the American West,* which proposed a number of new cultural perspectives. Most older western historians, unfamiliar with cultural theory, simply viewed *Over the Edge* with bafflement, if they thought of it as western history at all.[56]

Today, then, we have the odd situation of a major American region, the West, with two very separate histories. On one side of the Turnerian divide are those historians who find themselves unable to give up the frontier and its implicit white supremacy. Among them one must count a number of white women historians who seem, by and large, to have retreated into biographical studies of nineteenth-century western women. To cite three recent examples, the anthologies titled *By Grit and Grace: Eleven Women Who Shaped the West,* edited by Glenda Riley and Richard Etulain, and *Portraits of Women in the American West,* edited by Dee Garceau-Hagen, and Virginia Scharff's *Twenty Thousand Roads: Women, Movement, and the West* each include more than token numbers of women of color among the profiled women and, indeed, show all the women as important and determined historical actors, but none ventures beyond individual examples. Two other recent demonstrations of recovery and "setting the record straight" were Glenda Riley's study of women in the early conservation movement, *Women and Nature: Saving the "Wild" West,* and Shirley Leckie's *Elizabeth Bacon Custer: The Making of a Legend.* While this ongoing work of recovery is valuable, it rarely addresses the larger issues of racial interaction and larger social organization that characterize the racial-ethnic perspectives of the newer histories.[57]

Another flourishing, largely white topic in western women's history is woman suffrage in the West, where in every state except New Mexico women had the enfranchisement before the passage of the Nineteenth Amendment to the federal Constitution in 1920. Until this recent scholarship, the prevailing explanations for the early success of woman suffrage in the West seemed to fit right into male versions of political history. One could choose either the incredibly patronizing notion that western men enfranchised women in compensation for the hardships women had endured as pioneers, or that they considered giving the vote to women as a matter of political one-upmanship in state legislatures. In either case it seemed once again that men had been the actors and that women were merely their grateful beneficiaries.[58] The truth was much more complicated. After three relatively easy victories in territorial legislatures in Wyoming (1869), Utah (1870), and Washington (1883), western women were initially no more successful than their eastern sisters in obtaining the vote.[59] Two generations of middle-class western women had to learn to organize, lobby, and form effective coalitions with labor groups and reform parties to achieve the string of successes that began with populist victories in Colorado in 1893 and in Idaho in 1896 and continued to Washington in 1910, California in 1911, and Oregon in 1912, culminating in Nevada and Montana in 1914. Carol Stefanco's 1987 article, "Networking on the Frontier: The Colorado Women's Suffrage Movement,

1876–1893," was the first to draw attention to the importance of working-class women in the Colorado victory of 1893, while Gayle Gullett's *Becoming Citizens: The Emergence and Development of the California Women's Movement* showed that in that state women created "a new kind of women's politics" that not only built cross-class alliances but used new publicity techniques to achieve suffrage and to contribute to the wider progressive movement.[60] Most recently, in *How the Vote Was Won*, Rebecca Mead demonstrated that the willingness of western women to adopt new strategies and to ally themselves with reform movements — first populism, then progressivism — differentiated them from more conservative eastern suffragists. Mead's findings validated the frequently heard contemporary protests by western women against interference by eastern women in local campaigns and made the larger point that the western campaigns have not received the recognition they deserve from historians of suffrage. Now that we know more about suffrage in the West, it is time to remedy the oversight.[61]

Returning to the racial-ethnic side of western history, we find a vibrant and growing body of recent works, many of them precisely the kinds of community and cultural studies we need, combining the categories of race, class, and gender in a variety of ways. Many concern people, issues, or events never before studied, so they have the thrill of newness. Almost all study particular racial-ethnic groups in urban locations in the twentieth-century West. Because they study these communities from within, few white people, female or male, play a part in the story except as examples of the dominant white culture that the group is resisting. The use of gender varies widely in these works and is made more difficult to discern by the current reluctance to use the generic term "women" in the index (or often even to list separate female categories by racial-ethnic group). This absence can either denote the deep embeddedness of gender, as in Josh Sides's *L.A. City Limits: African American Los Angeles from the Great Depression to the Present,* which opens with a vivid example of a black woman rebelling against domestic work, to the total (and inexplicable) absence of gender in a recent book titled *Popular Culture in the Age of White Flight: Fear and Fantasy in Suburban Los Angeles.*[62] In both of these books, and in many other new works of western urban history, the crucial category is race; other categories such as gender and class are secondary. The few recent studies where gender is primary are about gay and lesbian sexuality, in books such as Nan Alamillo Boyd's *Wide Open Town: A History of Queer San Francisco to 1965* and Peter Boag's *Same-Sex Affairs: Constructing and Controlling Homosexuality in the Pacific Northwest.*[63] These new studies are all important to the future of western history, for they are beginning to fill in some of the huge holes that Turner's frontier thesis created.

I am worried, however, about this division between a conventionally theorized western history that includes some women who are usually white and, on the other hand, a rapidly developing new racial-ethnic history in which gender, although usually present, is a minor category of analysis. Surely a reasonable goal would be to put these two perspectives together and try to see what a fully inclusive West might look like. Two very different recent attempts, however, show how elusive that goal still remains.

In 1998, Julie Roy Jeffrey published a revised version of her classic *Frontier Women*, first published in 1979. Tellingly, the revised version had a new subtitle: "*Civilizing" the West? 1840–1880*. In her new introduction and conclusion, Jeffrey took full account of the changes wrought by the New Western History, acknowledging western history to be both more complex and more violent than she had thought in 1979. But although she added new short passages on Native American, Chinese, and Hispanic women to the text, this was a revision, not a rewriting of her original work. Because Jeffrey relied primarily on the diaries and letters of white female pioneers, the new material on women of color remained, as Castañeda warned in 1992, only an add-on. This revision demonstrated, at least to me, that the Turnerian framework cannot be expanded to encompass several perspectives.[64]

The other attempt to tell an inclusive story was the 1997 anthology *Writing the Range: Race, Class, and Culture in the Women's West*, edited by Elizabeth Jameson and me.[65] We went for the big picture, proposing a framework built upon the notion of multiple and continuing migrations to the American West and the effect of these migrations on the women of all races, ethnicities, and classes who participated in them. We postulated a series of encounters between newcomers and Natives beginning with the Spanish *entrada* into what is now New Mexico in the sixteenth century and stretching all the way to the present. Although the anthology was well reviewed, it has not been a popular or classroom success. We don't know whether it was the relative novelty of the framework or our primary focus on women of color that was most unacceptable to teachers and students.

For the present, then, it seems that the gap between the two histories is simply too great to be bridged. The new racial-ethnic urban history is too new to be interested in accommodating older notions, and the old western history, although obviously outdated, is too comfortable and familiar for many people to abandon. I blame Frederick Jackson Turner for this division. It seems that his ghost, although a mere shadow of its former self, still lingers. The new vision of the West beginning to emerge from the new historical scholarship makes me confident that before long Turner will be laid completely to rest, but for now his ghostly presence continues to haunt us all.

NOTES

1. Frederick Jackson Turner, 1861–1932, taught at the University of Wisconsin, 1885–1910, Harvard University, 1910–1924, and later was a research associate at the Huntington Library in San Marino, California. His frontier thesis, little noticed when he first proposed it in 1893, deeply influenced two subsequent generations of western historians. One, Ray Allen Billington, was especially prolific and established the "Turner thesis" as the dominant theme in western history. Turner himself published very little but was important as a teacher. In *The Progressive Historians*, Richard Hofstadter credited

Turner with creating the modern seminar format while at Harvard (New York: Vintage, 1968).

2. Frederick Jackson Turner, *The Frontier in American History* (New York: Holt, Rinehart and Winston, 1920), 1.

3. Ann Butler, "Selling the Popular Myth," in *The Oxford History of the American West,* ed. Clyde Milner II, Carol O'Connor, and Martha A. Sandweiss (New York: Oxford University Press, 1994), 771–801.

4. In 1959, of the ten most popular television programs, seven were westerns. Butler, "Selling the Popular Myth," 791.

5. Christine Stansell and Johnny Faragher, "Women and Their Families on the Overland Trail to California and Oregon," *Feminist Studies* 2 (1975): 150–166; Lillian Schlissel, *Women's Diaries of the Westward Journey* (New York: Schocken Books, 1982).

6. Julie Roy Jeffrey, *Frontier Women* (New York: Hill and Wang, 1979).

7. Sandra Myres, *Westering Women and the Frontier Experience, 1800–1915* (Albuquerque: University of New Mexico Press, 1982).

8. John Mack Faragher, *Women and Men on the Overland Trail* (New Haven: Yale University Press, 1979).

9. Glenda Riley, *Frontierswomen: The Iowa Experience,* 2nd ed. (Ames: Iowa State University Press, 1994); Susan Armitage, "Household Work and Childrearing on the Frontier, the Oral History Record," *Sociology and Social Research* 63, no. 3 (April 1979): 467–474.

10. Gerda Lerner, *Teaching Women's History* (Washington, D.C.: American Historical Association, 1982), 67.

11. Susan Armitage, "Beginning to Come into Focus," *Montana, The Magazine of Western History*, summer 1982.

12. Glenda Riley, *Women and Indians on the Frontier* (Albuquerque: University of New Mexico Press, 1984); Susan Armitage, "Women's Literature and the American Frontier: A New Perspective on the Frontier Myth," in *Women, Women Writers, and the West,* ed. L. L. Lee and Merrill Lewis (New York: Whitson Publishing Company, 1979).

13. Brigitte Georgia-Findlay, *The Frontiers of Women's Writing: Women's Narratives and the Rhetoric of Westward Expansion* (Tucson: University of Arizona Press, 1996).

14. Cathy Luchetti and Carol Olwell, *Women of the West* (Salt Lake City, Utah: Antelope Island Press, 1982); Linda Rasmussen et al., *A Harvest Yet to Reap: A History of Prairie Women* (Toronto: Women's Press, 1976).

15. Christiane Fischer, *Let Them Speak for Themselves: Women in the American West, 1849–1900* (Bloomington: Indiana University Press, 1982); two of my favorites among the many Nebraska reprints are Mollie Sanford, *Mollie: The Journal of Mollie Dorsey Sanford in Nebraska and Colorado Territories* (Lincoln: University of Nebraska Press, 1959); and Nannie Alderson and Helena Hunt Jackson, *A Bride Goes West* (Lincoln: University of Nebraska Press, 1969).

16. See Sue Armitage, Helen Bannan, Katherine G. Morrissey, and Vicki L. Ruiz, *A Guide to Archival Sources on Western Women* (New York: Garland Publishers, 1986).

17. Sue Armitage, Theresa Banfield, and Sarah Jacobus, "Black Women and Their Communities in Colorado," *Frontiers* 2, no. 2 (summer 1977): 45–52.

18. Barbara Welter, "The Cult of True Womanhood: 1800–1860," in *Dimity Convictions: The American Woman in the Nineteenth Century,* by Welter (Athens: Ohio University Press, 1976).

19. Susan Armitage, "Reluctant Pioneers," in *Women and Western American Literature,* ed. Helen Stauffer and Susan Rosowski (New York: Whitson Publishers, 1982); Carroll Smith Rosenberg, "The Female World of Love and Ritual," *Signs* 1, no. 1 (autumn 1975): 1–30.

20. Joanna Stratton's initially very popular *Pioneer Women: Voices from the Kansas Frontier* (New York: Simon and Schuster, 1981) is an example of this immediatist perspective. For an early homegrown formulation, see Elizabeth Jameson, "Women as Workers, Women as Civilizers: True Womanhood in the American West," in *The Women's West,* ed. Susan Armitage and Elizabeth Jameson (Norman: University of Oklahoma Press, 1987), 145–164.

21. Beverly Stoeltje, "A Helpmate for Man Indeed: The Image of the Frontier Woman," *Journal of American Folklore* 88, no. 347 (January–March 1975): 25–41.

22. Sylvia Van Kirk, *Many Tender Ties: Women in Fur Trade Society, 1670–1870* (Norman: University of Oklahoma Press, 1983); Jennifer Brown, *Strangers in Blood: Fur Trade Company Families in Indian Country* (Vancouver: University of British Columbia, 1980); Jacqueline Peterson and Jennifer Brown, eds., *The New People: Being and Becoming Métis in North America* (Lincoln: University of Nebraska Press, 1985).

23. Joan Burbick, *Rodeo Queens* (New York: Public Affairs Press, 2002); Theresa Jordan, *Cowgirls: Women of the American West* (New York: Doubleday, 1982).

24. Paula Petrik, *No Step Backward: Women and Family on the Rocky Mountain Mining Frontier, Helena, Montana, 1865–1900* (Helena: Montana Historical Society, 1987); Sally Zanjani, *A Mine of Her Own: Women Prospectors in the American West* (Lincoln: University of Nebraska Press, 1997).

25. Marion S. Goldman, *Gold Diggers and Silver Miners: Prostitution and Social Life on the Comstock Lode* (Ann Arbor: University of Michigan Press, 1981); and Ann Butler, *Daughters of Joy, Sisters of Misery: Prostitutes in the American West* (Urbana: University of Illinois Press, 1985).

26. Mary Neth, *Preserving the Family Farm: Women, Community, and the Foundations of Agribusiness in the Midwest, 1900–1940* (Baltimore: Johns Hopkins University Press, 1995); and Deborah Fink, *Agrarian Women: Wives and Mothers in Rural Nebraska, 1880–1940* (Chapel Hill: University of North Carolina Press, 1992).

27. Elaine Lindgren, *Land in Her Own Name* (Norman: University of Oklahoma Press, 1996); Elinore Stewart, *Letters of a Woman Homesteader* (New York: Macmillan, 1982); Sherry Smith, "Single Woman Homesteaders: The Perplexing Case of Elinore Pruitt Stewart," *Western Historical Quarterly* 22, no. 2 (1991): 163–183.

28. Polly Kaufmann, *Women Teachers on the Frontier* (New Haven: Yale University Press, 1984); Susan Peterson and Courtney Vaughn-Robertson, *Women with Vision: The Presentation Sisters of South Dakota, 1800–1985* (Urbana: University of Illinois Press, 1988).

29. See, for example, two publications of the early 1980s: Michael Malone, ed., *Historians and the American West* (Lincoln: University of Nebraska Press, 1983); and Roger Nichols, ed., *American Frontier and Western Issues: A Historiographical Review* (Westport, Conn.: Greenwood Press, 1986).

30. Susan Armitage, "Through Women's Eyes: A New View of the West," in *The Women's West,* ed. Armitage and Jameson, 9–18.

31. Patricia Nelson Limerick, *The Legacy of Conquest: The Unbroken Past of the American West* (New York: W. W. Norton, 1987).

32. Susan Lee Johnson, " 'A Memory Sweet to Soldiers': The Significance of Gender," in *A New Significance,* ed. Clyde Milner (New York: Oxford University Press, 1996), 266.

33. Ibid., 256.

34. Susan Johnson, *Roaring Camp* (New York: W. W. Norton, 2001); Matthew Basso, Laura McCall, and Dee Garceau, eds., *Across the Great Divide: Cultures of Manhood in the American West* (New York: Routledge, 2001)

35. Lillian Schlissel, Vicki L. Ruiz, and Jan Monk, eds., *Western Women: Their Land, Their Lives* (Albuquerque: University of New Mexico Press, 1988).

36. Marian Perales, "Empowering 'The Welder': A Historical Survey of Women of Color in the West," in *Writing the Range: Race, Class, and Culture in the Women's West,* ed. Elizabeth Jameson and Susan Armitage (Norman: University of Oklahoma Press, 1997).

37. Walter Nugent, *Into the West: The Story of Its People* (New York: Vintage Books, 1999), 132–133.

38. Paula Nelson, *After the West Was Won: Homesteaders and Town-Builders in Western South Dakota,* 1900–1917 (Iowa City: Iowa State Press, 1986), 186.

39. Joan Jensen, "Canning Comes to New Mexico: Women and the Agricultural Extension Service, 1914–1919" and " 'I've Worked, I'm Not Afraid of Work': Farm Women in New Mexico, 1920–1940," in *New Mexico Women*, ed. Joan Jensen and Darlis Miller (Albuquerque: University of New Mexico Press. 1986).

40. Glenda Riley, *The Female Frontier: A Comparative View of Women on the Prairie and the Plains* (Lawrence: University Press of Kansas, 1988).

41. Paula Nelson, "Rural Life and Social Change in the Modern West," in *The Rural West since World War II,* ed. R. Douglas Hurt (Lawrence: University Press of Kansas, 1998); Dee Garceau, *The Important Things of Life: Women, Work, and Family in Sweetwater County, Wyoming,* 1880–1929 (Lincoln: University of Nebraska Press, 1997).

42. Vicki L. Ruiz, *Cannery Women, Cannery Lives* (Albuquerque: University of New Mexico Press, 1987); Sarah Deutsch, *No Separate Refuge* (New York: Oxford University Press, 1987); Peggy Pascoe, *Relations of Rescue* (New York: Oxford University Press, 1990). Margaret Jacobs, *Engendered Encounters: Feminism and Pueblo Cultures, 1879–1934* (Lincoln: University of Nebraska Press, 1999); and Susan Yohn, *A Contest of Faiths: Missionary Women and Pluralism in the American Southwest* (Ithaca, N.Y.: Cornell University Press, 1995) have extended the interactive cultural framework that Pascoe pioneered, as has Joan Jensen, *One Foot on the Rockies: Women and Creativity in the Modern American West* (Albuquerque: University of New Mexico Press, 1995).

43. Joan Jensen and Darlis Miller, "The Gentle Tamers Revisited," *Pacific Historical Review* 49, no. 2 (May 1980): 173–213; Elizabeth Jameson, "Toward a Multicultural History of Women in the Western United States," *Signs* 13, no. 4 (1988): 761–791; Antonia Castañeda, "Women of Color and the Rewriting of Western History, *Pacific Historical Review* 61, no. 4 (November 1992): 501–534. To honor their landmark essay, the Coalition for Western Women's History established the Jensen-Miller Prize in western women's history, and the winners are gathered in a volume edited by Mary Ann Irwin and James F. Brooks, *Women and Gender in the American West* (Albuquerque: University of New Mexico Press, 2004).

44. "The Contributions and Challenges of Western Women's History," *Montana: The Magazine of Western History* 41, no. 2 (spring 1991), contained essays by Sarah Deutsch, Virginia Scharff, Glenda Riley, and John Mack Faragher; *Pacific Historical Review* 61, no. 4 (November 1992), Special Issue: Western Women's History Revisited, contained articles by Judy Nolte Lensink, Karen Anderson, Antonia L. Castañeda ("Women of Color and the Rewriting of Western History: The Discourse, Politics, and Decolonization of History"), and Virginia Scharff, with introduction and afterward by Susan Armitage, Joan Jensen, and Darlis Miller.

45. Antonia Castañeda, "Gender, Race, and Culture: Spanish–Mexican Women in the Historiography of Frontier California," *Frontiers* 11, no. 1 (1990): 8–20; "*Presidarias y Pobladoras*: Spanish-Mexican Women in Frontier Monterey, Alta California, 1770–1821," (PhD diss., Stanford University, 1990); Deena González, *Refusing the Favor: Spanish-Mexican Women of Santa Fe* (New York: Oxford University Press, 1999); Vicki L. Ruiz, *From Out of the Shadows: Mexican Women in Twentieth-Century America* (New York: Oxford University Press, 1998).

46. Judy Yung, *Unbound Feet: A Social History of Chinese Women in San Francisco* (Berkeley: University of California Press, 1995); and its companion book of oral histories and primary materials, Judy Yung, *Unbound Voices: A Documentary History of Chinese Women in San Francisco* (Berkeley: University of California Press, 1999); Shirley Hune and Gail Nomura, eds., *Asian/Pacific Islander American Women: A Historical Anthology* (New York: New York University Press, 2003); Valerie Matsumoto, *Farming the Home Place* (Ithaca, N.Y.; Cornell University Press, 1993).

47. Theda Perdue, *Cherokee Women: Gender and Culture, 1700–1835* (Lincoln: University of Nebraska Press, 1998); Theda Perdue, ed., *Sifters: Native American Women's Lives* (New York: Oxford University Press, 2001); Brenda Child, *Boarding School Seasons: American Indian Families, 1900–1940* (Lincoln: University of Nebraska Press, 1998).

48. Lynn M. Hudson, *The Making of "Mammy Pleasant": A Black Entrepreneur in Nineteenth-Century San Francisco* (Urbana: University of Illinois Press, 2003); Shirley Anne Wilson Moore, *To Place Our Deeds: The African American Community in Richmond California, 1910–1963* (Berkeley: University of California Press, 2000); Gretchen Lemke-Santangelo, *African American Migrant Women and the East Bay Community* (Chapel Hill: University of North Carolina Press, 1996); Shirley Anne Moore and Quintard Taylor, eds., *African American Women Confront the West* (Norman: University of Oklahoma Press, 2003).

49. Mary Murphy, *Mining Cultures* (Urbana: University of Illinois Press, 1999).

50. Elizabeth Jameson, *All That Glitters: Class, Conflict, and Community in Cripple Creek* (Urbana: University of Illinois Press. 1998); Laurie Mercier, *Anaconda: Labor, Community, and Culture in Montana's Smelter City* (Urbana: University of Illinois Press, 2001).

51. There is no western book comparable to Elizabeth Hayes Turner, *Women, Culture, and Community: Religion and Reform in Galveston, 1880–1920* (New York: Oxford University Press, 1997); Sandra Haarsager, *Organized Womanhood* (Norman: University of Oklahoma Press, 1997); June Underwood, *Civilizing Kansas: Women's Organizations, 1880–1920* (Topeka: Kansas State Historical Society, 1985).

52. Mary Clearman Blew, "Growing Up Female in Charlie Russell Country," *Plainswomen* 9, no. 5 (January 1986): 3–4, 18.

53. Patricia Nelson Limerick, "The Adventures of the Frontier in the Twentieth Century," in *The Frontier in American Culture: An Exhibition at the Newberry Library*, ed. Richard White (Berkeley: University of California Press, 1994).

54. Ramón A. Gutiérrez, *When Jesus Came, the Cornmothers Went Away: Marriage, Sexuality, and Power in New Mexico, 1500–1846* (Stanford, Calif.: Stanford University Press, 1990); Albert Hurtado, *Intimate Frontiers: Sex, Gender, and Culture in Old California* (Albuquerque: University of New Mexico Press, 1999); Alison Freese, "Pueblo Responses to Ramón A. Gutiérrez's *When Jesus Came, the Cornmothers Went Away*," *American Indian Culture and Research Journal* 17 (1993): 141–177; Lizbeth Haas, *Conquests and Historical Identities in California, 1769–1936* (Berkeley: University of California, 1995); James Brooks, *Captives and Cousins: Slavery, Kinship, and Community in the Southwest Borderlands* (Chapel Hill: University of North Carolina Press, 2002).

55. Robert Hine and John Mack Faragher, *The American West: A New Interpretive History* (New Haven: Yale University Press, 2000).

56. Valerie Matsumoto and Blake Allmendinger, eds., *Over the Edge: Remapping the American West* (Berkeley: University of California Press, 2001).

57. Glenda Riley and Richard Etulain, eds., *By Grit and Grace* (Albuquerque: University of New Mexico Press, 2000); Dee Garceau-Hagen, ed., *Portraits of Women in the American West* (New York: Routledge, 2005); Virginia Scharff, *Twenty Thousand Roads: Women, Movement, and the West* (Berkeley: University of California Press, 2003); Glenda Riley, *Women and Nature: Saving the "Wild" West* (Lincoln: University of Nebraska Press, 1999); Shirley Leckie, *Elizabeth Bacon Custer: The Making of a Myth* (Norman: University of Oklahoma Press, 1993).

58. T. A. Larson, "Woman Suffrage in Western America," *Utah Historical Quarterly* 38 (winter 1970): 7–19.

59. Only one of these early successes was permanent. Utah women had to wait until statehood in 1896 to be able to vote, and Washington women's victory was voided by the state's Supreme Court in 1888.

60. Carolyn Stefanco, "Networking on the Frontier: The Colorado Women's Suffrage Movement, 1876–1893," in *The Women's West,* ed. Armitage and Jameson; Gayle Gullett, *Becoming Citizens: The Emergence and Development of the California Women's Movement, 1880–1911* (Urbana: University of Illinois Press, 2000). An earlier book, Sherna Gluck's collection of oral histories with western suffragists of a wide range of political positions, *From Parlor to Prison: Five American Suffragists Talk about Their Lives* (New York: Monthly Review Press, 1985), pointed the way.

61. Rebecca J. Mead, *How the Vote Was Won: Woman Suffrage in the Western United States, 1868–1914* (New York: New York University Press, 2004).

62. Josh Sides, *L.A. City Limits: African American Los Angeles from the Great Depression to the Present* (Berkeley: University of California Press, 2003); Eric Avila, *Popular Culture in the Age of White Flight: Fear and Fantasy in Suburban Los Angeles* (Berkeley: University of California Press, 2004).

63. Nan Alamillo Boyd, *Wide Open Town: A History of Queer San Francisco to 1965* (Berkeley: University of California Press, 2003); Peter Boag, *Same-Sex Affairs: Constructing and Controlling Homosexuality in the Pacific Northwest* (Berkeley: University of California Press, 2003).

64. Julie Roy Jeffrey, *Frontier Women: "Civilizing" the West? 1840–1880*, rev. ed. (New York: Hill and Wang, 1998).

65. Jameson and Armitage, *Writing the Range.*

8

Gender and U.S. Imperialism in U.S. Women's History

LAURA BRIGGS

A decade ago, when I went to publish the dissertation that would become *Reproducing Empire*, I got two responses from university presses that in retrospect seem telling and quite funny. I carefully explained in my cover letter that I was writing about women and U.S. colonialism in Puerto Rico, a subject, I argued, that shed light on a host of important questions in U.S. history. One press's acquisition editor wrote back to me saying that while the manuscript was quite interesting, he would like to see two substantive chapters on African Americans before his press considered it. Another suggested I add two chapters on Mexico, since that was the only really substantial market for books in Latin American history. Apparently, U.S. colonialism could be a subtopic under "race in the United States" (which was further reducible to African American history) or "the history of the nations of Latin America" (which meant Mexico), but could never be the subject of a book in itself. Fortunately, I found another press, where the editors were willing to consider a book that was about neither African Americans nor Mexico, but the experience suggests something of the unthinkability of work on women and U.S. colonialism a decade ago.

I cannot imagine that scenario playing out now. Women and imperialism or women and colonialism, long the arena of British (and post-British colonial) historians among those writing in English, has decidedly become the province also of those of us who work on the United States. There are good and obvious reasons for this. First, the term "globalization," trumpeted from the business pages of U.S. newspapers a decade and a half ago as the coming of prosperity for all, has in the hands of anti-globalization protesters become a critique that demands historicization of U.S. empire. Secondly and more startlingly, in the wake of the decision by the Bush administration to go to war in Iraq unilaterally without approval of the United Nations, "Empire" has become the name that the doyens of U.S. foreign policy themselves approvingly give to U.S. actions overseas.[1] As Amy Kaplan has pointed out, this is a significant reversal of decades-long U.S.

aversion to the term.[2] The urgent need to understand these things has, perhaps more than anything else, motivated a resurgence of interest in U.S. imperialism that we have not seen since the era of the U.S. war in Vietnam and Cambodia and the work of historians like William Appleman Williams.

Yet I do not want to understate the significant consciousness of the question of imperialism that has been present in U.S. women's history throughout its forty-year history. There is a version of the historiography of women that I hear a lot from students in which first we were bad, and we ignored questions of race and imperialism, and then we got better. I would like to do away with that conception (although I know all too well that nothing I write here actually will make it go away; progressivist and triumphalist narratives are too deeply rooted in U.S. culture and nationalism, as well as Protestantism). As someone who was a college student in the early and mid-1980s, at the height of this supposed moment of ignorance, I remember it differently. My women's studies curriculum included Frantz Fanon and Edward Said. Our activism was centrally concerned with Central America solidarity (and what we understood as imperial U.S. wars in the region) and South Africa (where, we argued, U.S. corporations were central to upholding the old British and Dutch colonial order of things, that is, apartheid).[3]

On the contrary, then, I would suggest that feminists have long been committed to thinking about imperialism; and the figure of imperialism — sometimes explicitly, more often lurking in the background — has been crucial to feminist historical thought. Linda Gordon's history of birth control, *Woman's Body, Woman's Right* (1977), one of the ur-texts of women's history, wrestled at length with population control as a colonial policy practiced by the United States.[4] Similarly, Gloria Anzaldúa's *Borderlands/La Frontera* (1987), a touchstone for Chicana/o and borderlands historians, opens by describing the border as "*una herida abierta*, where the Third World grates against the First and bleeds."[5] Angela Davis's *Woman, Race, and Class* (1981), a crucial text for black women's history, conceptualized the struggles of African American women as one among many struggles of "Third World women."[6] Other prominent examples from the 1980s and early 1990s include a body of work on women and labor, which took seriously the political efforts of labor organizers to work internationally and the reality of workers' migrations: Nancy Hewitt's study of women workers from the Carribean in South Florida; Annelise Orleck's observations about the extension of the minimum wage to Puerto Rico; Eileen Boris's work on Puerto Rican needle workers and the New Deal; and Vicki L. Ruiz's analysis of Mexican women's organizing in California.[7] Political scientist Cynthia Enloe's scholarship on women and militarism, especially her widely read *Bananas, Beaches, and Bases*, kept cold war imperialism and its effect on women in feminist consciousness. We lose important parts of the story of U.S. women's history when we erase this legacy.[8]

However, I also want to embrace the critical impulse embodied in my students' narrative. Certainly we could have done better. Historians of women have too often accepted a version of U.S. history that is nationalist in effect, if not in intent. We have too often imagined that continental boundaries (or, still worse, the New England states) define a coherent and complete story, and hence missed the ways that the day-to-day life captured by social history is shot through with the imperial story of the United States. Exceptions to this general neglect, like Elaine Tyler May's *Homeward Bound*, which points to how profoundly the cold war constructed family relations in the United States, or Gail Bederman's *Manliness and Civilization*, which calls attention to how discourses of civilization (and savagery) constituted late nineteenth-century masculinity, powerfully suggest how much we may be missing.[9] Similarly, our accounts of the woman suffrage struggle too rarely remember that conceptualizing citizenship was never just a story about gender, or even gender and race, but was a fight also organized in terms of those who were geographically outside of the nation. Again, an exception underscores the importance of this way of conceiving the suffrage struggle. Louise Newman's *White Women's Rights* exposes the significance of scientific discourses of civilization to the idioms of woman suffrage and suggests how attention to the wider world might strengthen our accounts of U.S. women's social movements.[10]

Furthermore, it would be helpful if women's history reliably were to give attention to the ways the boundaries of U.S. history are not so much given as political and historical; the "common sense" that makes the history of California or Florida or the Midwest part of U.S. history rather than French or Spanish colonial history is an ideological production. Indeed, the force of the belief that U.S. history has known and undeniable geographic boundaries is revealed most amusingly when we as historians try to call them into question and bookstores reassert them: Ramón Gutiérrez's history of pre-Hispanic and Spanish New Mexico, *When Jesus Came, the Corn Mothers Went Away*, is generally found in bookstores under U.S. history.[11] More often, however, we historians are in accord with bookstores: the contemporary borders of the United States are taken for granted as the frame of U.S. history. We are also a long way, still, from reliably noticing the ways that histories of imperialism impact our stories about the United States. How many of us teach that in the United States, women won the unrestricted right to vote in 1920, without acknowledging that in territories like the Philippines it was considerably later, or that neither women nor men in Puerto Rico have ever won an unrestricted right to vote? (Or, we could point out, students and people of color of whatever gender on the mainland are engaged in an ongoing and perhaps endless struggle to actualize their "right" to vote, but that is a parallel story.) A surprising amount of otherwise excellent work on the welfare state, labor, race and slavery, family, consumption, social movements, sexuality, and reproduction has been written and is being written as if the United States were hermetically sealed from the rest of the world. Here, I want to notice some exceptions to this general neglect of imperialism in U.S. women's history, to take a stab at characterizing the new writing on U.S. imperialism and suggest some of the ways it is in conversation with other historiographies, and to sketch some of the (many) projects still left to be done.

Where We Are

From the mid-1980s to the mid-1990s, work on imperialism in women's history could sometimes seem like the stepchild of a far more developed project in British history — of marking out the role of women missionaries and other colonials in developing what Valerie Amos and Pratibha Parmar so powerfully called "imperial feminism."[12] Books like Ian Tyrell's *Women's World, Women's Empire,* Jane Hunter's *The Gospel of Gentility,* and Nancy Boyd's *Emissaries* effectively and importantly challenged our feminist assumptions about the radicalism of movements by women. During the "first wave" of the women's movement (and beyond, according to Boyd), far more women were drawn to missionary work than were ever in suffrage organizations. While, as Tyrell showed for the Women's Christian Temperance Union (WCTU), there were internal fights about imperialism and anti-imperialism, the major themes and rhetorics of missionary organizations could be characterized as patronizing at best.[13] But the field one might call feminism and U.S. imperialism was distinctly a minor literature, with all the real action going on in the histories of other imperialisms and postcolonial settings, mostly British, but also Dutch, French, and Belgian, stretching from Asia to Africa to Latin America, a body of work that has continued to grow and expand in smart and exciting ways.[14]

More recently, contributions from U.S. history have been more conspicuous and have taken a different tack. Rather than focusing specifically or exclusively on women and imperialism, they have asked broader questions: How have discourses of gender played a role in imperialism? The growing list of monographs published in the last decade would include Kristin Hoganson's *Fighting for American Manhood* (Spanish American War), Mary Renda's *Taking Haiti,* Melani McAlister's *Epic Encounters* (Middle East), Christina Klein's *Cold War Orientalism* (China/Asia), Mari Yoshihara's *Embracing the East* (Japan), Laura Wexler's *Tender Violence* (Philippines), Catherine Choy's *Empire of Care* (Philippines), Emma Pérez's *The Decolonial Imaginary* (Mexico), and my own *Reproducing Empire* (Puerto Rico).[15] Collectively, these works have struggled to weld together a "hard" language of foreign policy and military expansionism with the "soft" worlds of femininity and masculinity, revealing in the process how oddly committed the field of history had become to an opposition between foreign policy histories and histories of gender.

Two moves have been crucial to the development of this scholarship. One has been to write against the cold war legacy of U.S. area studies in which work on the history of small places like the Philippines, Haiti, Vietnam, or Puerto Rico is treated as a very specialized — and often, frankly, trivial — enterprise, one that sheds little light on the "big" themes and problems of U.S. history. In response, this body of scholarship argues that what happened in these small places recon-figured masculinity, femininity, meanings of race, social movements, and profes-sional expertise in the United States. This is an urgently needed corrective to the academic habit of discounting U.S. imperialism as not particularly important, which is a politically interested refusal to see U.S. violence or the nation's impe-rial and colonial legacy. This historiographical lacuna has had serious effects, enabling recent political discourse such as Michael Ignatieff's statement in the *New York Times* that "in becoming an empire the U.S. risks losing its soul as a republic" (in an article that ultimately argued that U.S. imperialism was a good thing), as if empire were an utterly new question in U.S. history.[16] This body of scholarship takes up Edward Said's argument that *culture* is a key terrain for the propagation of imperialism, not just as an effect, as in a reductionist Marxist "superstructure," but in itself. Amy Kaplan's articulation of this problem as "the absence of culture from the study of U.S. imperialism, and the absence of imperi-alism from the study of culture" has been very influential.[17] The prominence of Kaplan's formulation also reminds us of how important and generative the field of American studies has been in producing this scholarship, suggesting that in the dialectical struggle over whether that field will embody its roots in 1930s radicalism or 1950s cold war conservatism, the radical tradition is resurgent at precisely the moment when its institutional presence in U.S. universities is under threat.

Much of this work starts with an attention to how ideologies of masculinity were a central problem being worked out in U.S. foreign policy. Hoganson, for example, is concerned with idioms of fragile or endangered mas-culinity in the Spanish American War. Renda pays attention to the ways paternal-ism constituted a sturdy rhetoric of the U.S. occupation of Haiti. Wexler suggests how photographs of the intimacies and tenderness of U.S. Navy sailors enabled viewers to forget the accusations that they tortured and murdered Filipino insur-gents. Such studies of masculinities are clearly deeply indebted to women's his-tory and have much to offer our understanding of the tightly interrelated development of femininity. Older questions about women and social movements have not disappeared. Pérez investigates the development of feminism in part in relation to the Mexican Revolution, and my research takes up questions of the development of the birth control and women's movements both on the island of Puerto Rico and the mainland United States. But a broad array of new issues also has been opened up, involving sexuality, film, material culture, and other issues of representation.

There is also another, slightly different tradition that engages with questions of gender and imperialism, one in which Catherine Ceniza Choy's *Empire of Care* perhaps fits more neatly, that of studies of migration. There is a case to be made that migration history and border history have always been in some sense about imperialism. Certainly, the most interesting of such studies, especially in the last decade, consistently refuse the narrative frame that begins the story when migrants arrive in the United States. Some have suggested that the problem with migration history is that it is not transnational *enough*. While I would not disagree with them, it strikes me that reading it for the ways that it *is* transnational yields significant insights and new ways to think the centrality of small places to the big themes of U.S. history. For example, Yen Espiritu and Choy, writing about migration from the Philippines, have both argued that migration from the archipelago is the product, significantly, of its forty-seven years as a U.S. colony. Choy maps the setting up of nursing schools during the colonial period and the organized project of bringing Filipina nurses to the United States for training. She shows this resulted in the production of a racialized nurse labor force on the mainland, little nursing care in the Philippines, and a discourse about the good fortune of immigrants — that they can come to the U.S. — and the side benefits of colonialism that completely misses the point.[18]

Espiritu's *Homebound*, her study of the Filipino community in San Diego, pushes this insight even further, arguing that migration must always be situated in relation to upheaval in the "home" country: U.S. wars, as in Vietnam or El Salvador; imperialism, as in the Philippines or Puerto Rico; economic disruption, as in the creation of low-wage industrial production primarily to satisfy the U.S. consumer market, like in Mexico or Korea. Immigration, she suggests, is not best conceived as voluntary. In the process, she revises the Asian American historiography that describes an arc from the late nineteenth to mid-twentieth century of exclusion of migrants from Asia (from the 1875 Page Act and 1882 Chinese Exclusion Act) to the post-1965 moment of inclusion. Instead, Espiritu suggests, we want to think about "differential inclusion," the folding together of forms of inclusion *and* exclusion simultaneously.[19] Certainly, work like Ji-Yeon Yuh's study of Korean military brides in the United States gives support to that paradigm.[20] So does Choy's discussion of training grants for Filipino nurses, both of which remind us of Asian women's migration to the United States between 1950 and 1965. Mae Ngai's *Impossible Subjects* brings this point into arresting focus by looking at the production of "illegal aliens." She argues that rather than seeing the U.S. as divided into immigrants and non-immigrants, we need to explore more closely the forms of labor and sociality produced by the recruitment and permanently inferior status of undocumented immigrants.[21] Intriguingly, Carmen Whalen makes a similar point in her study of Puerto Rican migration in the 1950s — which, because of the status of the island, is both unrestricted and involves people whose citizenship is unquestionable. She argues that Puerto Ricans' labor was welcome, as long as they did not expect or demand full inclusion, which, of course, they did.[22]

We can read the historiography of migration and ethnic studies as suggesting a corrective to a paradigm that dominates much writing on gender and U.S. imperialism: that white supremacy and/or masculinism ultimately are the impulses and the logic behind colonialism. This paradigm is a side effect of its very strength, the engagement with Said and culture. By focusing on the ways that culture was a cause rather than an effect of colonialism, it has given extraordinary power to very abstract things, like whiteness or masculinity. While this work is persuasive and important, it seems to me potentially to lose track of what the 1970s and '80s scholarship on imperialism understood so well: economic exploitation and military domination. Ramón Gutiérrez raises this point in response to Ann Stoler's important article in the *Journal of American History*. Focusing on the "tender ties" of imperialism, he suggests, evacuates its violence.[23] Stoler responded, rightly, that the violence and intimacies of colonialism are inseparable. For Stoler it has always been a question of who defined, and with what consequences, how knowledge was produced about what "race" a child belonged to or who slept with whom and under what definition: marriage, concubinage, prostitution? Still, I have a lingering uneasiness that our attention to culture, while doing much necessary work to mark out the normal, quotidian character of empire and colonialism, on the one hand, and to push at the duality of such pairs as public/private, male/female, policy/gender, on the other, leaves us still too unenlightened as to how Wal-Mart constructs gendered relations of labor, for example, and the historical roots of these relationships.

It is not that our recent studies forget about economy or military aims altogether, but that they can begin subtly to slip into mistaking race for a *cause* rather than an effect of imperialism and never ask the question about how to measure the relationship of racialization to military or economic goals. This makes me want to be a vulgar Marxist. Is it not at least as possible that colonial difference — race itself — was being produced in order to create hierarchies of exploitable, differentiable labor? But I am also a historian of Puerto Rico, where labor exploitation was actually not the point, or only very occasionally. Rather, it was first the military base, and later, after World War II, the desire to make Puerto Rico a "showcase for development," the place in Latin America where the United States demonstrated that development was a viable alternative to socialism. So my point is not so much to turn back the clock and insist that, at the end of the day, imperialism is about political economy — though I do sometimes think that an infusion of a bit of that sentiment would be a good thing — but rather to suggest that the causes of imperialism must be a question, not something to which we assume we know the answer.

A significant strength of migration and ethnic studies scholarship is that, following Michael Omi and Howard Winant's powerful work, *Racial Formation in the United States*, it can think of racialization as a process that exists in complex relationship to other processes — social movements, economic exploitation, military domination—as neither exclusively cause nor effect.[24] So, for example, when Natalia Molina in *Fit to Be Citizens* looks at the flexible racialization of Japanese, Chinese, and Mexican subjects in Los Angeles, she attends simultaneously to economic, sanitary, and transnational dimensions of these relationships. She draws our attention to the ways that official discourses of the city could hierarchize these relationships differently at diverse moments. The Chinese, for example, were represented as "worse" and more degraded than Mexicans at one moment and the opposite at another time.[25] This is the insight that we need to bring back to studies of colonialism, borrowing not only from Molina but from the entire body of transnational ethnic studies scholarship that she builds on, including George Sánchez, Vicki L. Ruiz, Lisa Lowe, and Nayan Shah, among others, who have given gendered, historical, transnational meaning to the work of understanding how racialization has taken place in a (mostly but not exclusively) U.S. context.[26]

Ann Laura Stoler's edited collection, *Haunted by Empire*, suggests the incredible diversity of work in progress by historians of U.S. imperialism in ethnic studies, American studies, women's and gender studies. The collection traces an eccentric and powerful history of imperialism that charts not so much a narrative of change over time, nor of grand narratives in U.S. history, but of plural and particular moments, places, and events. *Haunted by Empire* suggests that the stories of how creole Louisiana and white Anglo women defined the proper intimacy with slaves, the problems of half-castes in Samoa, the question of whether Hindu marriages count in the United States (and when and for whom), homosexualities, Russian fur traders in Alaska, and the placing for adoption of children of lepers in the Philippines or leftists in Latin America are the intimacies and violences of U.S. colonialism. It plots the coordinates of a marvelously heterogeneous narrative, one in which the question of the politics of U.S. categories of race, sickness, "legitimate" marriage and sexuality, and whose child belongs to whom constitute a fundamental and newly visible component of the daily life of and in the U.S. empire.[27]

Where Do We Go from Here?

It is now possible to say that the question is not so much *whether* U.S. women's history will engage with imperialism, but *how*. With that comes the necessity to raise critical questions. The most important one, I think, is a critique Mary Renda rightly raised about my *Reproducing Empire*. It needed to pay even more detailed attention to the local political terrain in Puerto Rico onto which U.S. imperialism was grafted. Anthropologists and historians of places other than the United States are frequently shocked by what seems to them like a systematic lack of rigor in work by historians of the United States. We often do not even go to the archives in the places we write about, nor work in languages other than English. Multi-sited, multi-lingual, multi-archival work opens up a world (literally) of insights about U.S. imperialism, what it does, and what it means. Feminist scholars in Latin America and elsewhere have persistently raised the point that U.S. scholars need to write a history of gender and U.S. imperialism that is useful to those outside the United States and engage ourselves in the kind of transnational conversations, movements, and world that our books imagine. There are rich historiographies and archives about U.S. imperialism and traditions and movements of opposition to it that are located outside the United States. We need to read and cite the national historiographies of places other than the United States and engage in serious and useful conversation with historians in and of "small" places. Only a handful of U.S. women's history monographs have a bibliography that includes works in languages other than English. U.S. historians need to stop being some of the only people in history departments (besides historians of England and the British Empire) who can get away without a useable knowledge of a second language. We can begin by making space for our students to engage in language study, but also work seriously to get at some of the sources we might otherwise overlook if we limit ourselves to English. If we can learn to read censuses, we can learn other languages. We need to borrow from anthropology the insight that it is extraordinarily important to go to the place you are writing about, that everything changes when you go there.

Another point, and perhaps this is a "language" argument as well, is that historians are only unevenly fluent in the political idioms of anti-imperial movements, including classic liberalism, Marxist historical materialism, subaltern studies, *indigenismo*, postcolonial studies, radical psychoanalysis, critiques of neoliberalism, and globalization. The resistance of historians in the United States to something that gets called "theory" leaves us significantly under-prepared to engage thoughtfully with other analysts and historians of U.S. imperialism. Much smart and useful commentary exists within these rhetorics, and not using it impoverishes our work. Two anthropologists of Latin America, Diane Nelson (*Finger in the Wound*) and Roger Lancaster (*Life Is Hard*), suggest something of what we might be missing.[28] Their long, serious, thoughtful engagement with radical movements in Guatemala and Nicaragua, respectively, yields significant insight about the workings of U.S. imperialism in those two countries in the 1980s.

Other historiographies and other fields suggest projects that have yet to be fully realized in U.S. women's history. For example, Catherine Hall's *Civilizing Subjects*, a history of the antislavery activism of English Methodist missionaries in Jamaica, raises a very pertinent question for historians of women: What are we to make of the abolitionists and nonconformists? What are their investments (affective, career, and so forth) in imperial and anti-imperial projects? Rather than subject our historical subjects to our own desires for good guys and bad guys, white or elite subjects that succeed or fail in our political litmus tests, what about a more nuanced grammar of colonialism? For the abolitionist missionaries are there, just as much as the brutal governors who execute insurrectionists, as in the Morant Bay post-emancipation rebellion that Hall analyzes with such care. This brings us to the broader question that many of us learned to ask from Ann Laura Stoler: How can we write in a way that is sensitive to the divisions among colonizers and colonized that sees the Manicheism of colonialism as itself a colonial ideology? Migration history redirects our attention to the apparently fungible and disappearing historiographical category of labor. Looking at work like Pierrette Hondagneu-Sotelo's *Doméstica*, for example, George Sánchez has made the argument that we need to think of the hiring of especially but not exclusively Latina household labor as the production of colonial households, this time not overseas but on the mainland.[29] What would happen if we took seriously migration as fundamentally about colonialism, just as Hall points out British history has done? Further, following Stoler (via Foucault), can we begin to map nuanced, situated colonial politics of knowledge and biopower?[30]

Another provocative set of models for thinking about imperialism come from India, or the U.S. via India, through subaltern studies. I have found three subaltern studies scholars particularly instructive. The first, Ranajit Guha, in his *Elementary Aspects of Peasant Insurgency*, provides another groundbreaking study of peasant movements from the 1960s forward. Like Frantz Fanon, Eric Wolf, and James Scott, Guha challenges us to think ever more rigorously about what it really means to do "history from below." Guha's particular innovation has been to challenge our persistent assurance (not entirely naïve, after the anti-imperialist movements of Algeria, Vietnam, Cuba, Nicaragua, and Chiapas) that peasant uprisings really belong to the movements we assign them. To put it in aphoristic form, perhaps the peasants in Guha's account do not really want socialism, maybe they really want God. It was the concurrent social movements for socialism that appropriated peasant uprisings. Guha also gives us the important notion of the "prose of counterinsurgency," that is, what we can read, what we can find in the archives, is an account that was always already about putting down the insurgency, that our archival authors were always appropriating, minimizing, or discounting the efforts of the peasants, and our work as scholars is necessarily complicated by this problem.[31]

A second crucial intervention is Dipesh Chakrabarty's *Provincializing Europe*, with its insistence that history writing is itself part of a European cosmology with its own particularistic ascriptions of cause and effect and theories of time. This is productive of foundational questions about the extent to which any historian shares a worldview with the actors in her story.[32]

Finally, feminist theorist Gayatri Chakravorty Spivak, in her widely read "Can the Subaltern Speak," simultaneously comments on subaltern studies, Michel Foucault, Giles Deleuze, and U.S. feminist and ethnic studies. According to Spivak, we all regularly engage in a play for power and authority that she calls a ventriloquist trick of speaking on behalf of female subaltern subjects whose agency cannot be expressed through either contemporaneous political idioms or through current scholarly discourses. Just as surely it cannot be expressed when subaltern women are invited to vote for the candidate of their "choice."[33] Collectively, these radical historical projects invite U.S. historians to be humble about the possibilities of knowing what subaltern women "want" (as if it were singular) and to recognize other such attempts to speak for "Third World" women — as by political parties and so forth — as intrinsically suspicious. I find in this work an invitation much in consonance with what the field has been doing to read history "from above," as it were, figuring out questions like Mary

Renda's: "How does a man imagine himself when he is about to pull a trigger?"[34] But I also read it as an exhortation to do something more, to trace the processes of subalternization and ask how they have eviscerated the conditions of possibility in which certain subjectivities could be legible.

Others have gestured toward more specific projects. For example, Emma Pérez, in her important *Decolonial Imaginary*, suggests that we can understand feminism as a conversation across national borders and between movements, with feminism in the U.S., for example, deepened and radicalized by the Mexican Revolution of 1910–1917.[35] It would enrich our study of social movements if we followed her lead and placed the experience of U.S. women in a more transnational context. We might engage in a study of 1848, for example, to think about how West Indian antislavery movements, the liberal revolt in France, independence movements throughout Latin America, Indian Wars in and beyond the boundaries of the United States, and the Treaty of Guadalupe-Hidalgo in what became the U.S. West collectively impinged on the Seneca Falls declaration. We have thought some about how the abolitionist movement in the United States affected that gathering. How did that become the only major point of comparison? Similarly, it would change our narrative of the birth of the second wave of feminism if we thought of 1968 as not just a confluence of currents in the U.S. antiwar, civil rights, and racial-justice nationalist movements, but simultaneously remembered the student movement (and massacre) of Mexico, the street protests that shook France, the inspiration and provocation of the explicit feminism of the Cuban Revolution, of Mao's China, and of decolonization movements throughout the formerly colonized world. Kevin Gaines has done fascinating work on Richard Wright's efforts to negotiate among African nationalism in Ghana, questions of Pan Africanism, and diaspora to notice the specific contours of transnationalism in U.S. black radicalism.[36] How different would our account of feminism's origins be if we recalled *its* transnationalism?

Finally, I want to take note that there are also distinct epochs in the historiography of U.S. imperialism that I am analyzing here, and these will, in turn, yield to other concerns. In a slightly different context, Nancy Hewitt repeats Benedetto Croce's claim that all history is contemporary history, adding, "that is, all history is written in dialogue with current issues, concerns, and perspectives."[37] In the past decade of history writing and politics we have seen abrupt shifts that give rise to significantly different imperatives. Clinton-era globalization was above all subtle and elusive; it drew our attention to the kinds of racialization, hyperexploitation of workers, and empire-building that dared not speak their names, that were given names like democracy, NGOs, human rights, and free trade. The regime of the Bush cabal is anything but subtle, a grammar of dirty elections, imprisonment of non-citizens without color of law, the flowering of nationalist paramilitaries like the Minutemen on the border, of Abu Ghraib, Guatánamo, and the fashioning of privatized armies of "contractors" not only in Afghanistan and Iraq but also waging a war against an abstract noun, "terrorism," in more than a dozen countries. The conversation between present and past, politics and histo-riography, has necessarily changed between these two very different adminis-trations (albeit with lags because of the protocols of academic publication). Speaking only for myself, during the Clinton administration I wrote about the ways apparently benign projects of development, modernization, birth control, sanitation, and women's rights worked in the service of imperial goals. These days, my archives and research notes seem full of Latin America's dirty wars, ille-galities, imprisoned pregnant women, and kidnapped children. I say this to take note that shifting methodologies, tools, and the saliences of particular kinds of phenomena may have little to do with whether they are right or helpful, but what they are right and helpful *for*. And I trust that we will continue to raise historical questions that shed light and help us think about our changing political moments.

NOTES

1. Michael Ignatieff, "Democratic Providentialism," *New York Times*, December 12, 2004, late edition, sec. 6, 29.

2. Amy Kaplan, "'Left Alone with America': The Absence of Empire in the Study of American Culture," in *Cultures of United States Imperialism,* ed. Amy Kaplan and Donald Pease (Durham: Duke University Press, 1993), 3–21; Amy Kaplan, "Violent Belongings and the Question of Empire Today," *American Quarterly* 56, no. 1 (2004): 1–18.

3. I am thinking here particularly of Edward Said, *Orientalism* (New York: Vintage, 1979); Frantz Fanon, *The Wretched of the Earth* (New York: Grove Press, 1965).

4. Linda Gordon, *Woman's Body, Woman's Right* (1977; repr., New York: Penguin Books, 1988).

5. Gloria Anzaldúa, *Borderlands/La Frontera* (San Francisco: Aunt Lute Books, 1999), 3.

6. Angela Yvonne Davis, *Women, Race, and Class* (New York: Random House, 1981).

7. Nancy Hewitt and Ana Vandewater, "La Independencia: Patriotas y Obreras in Cuba, Puerto Rico, and the United States, 1898–1921," paper presented at the Symposium on the History of Latin Workers, The Meany Archives, Silver Springs, Maryland, February 1993; Eileen Boris, "Needlewomen under the New Deal in Puerto Rico," in *Puerto Rican Women and Work: Bridges in Transnational Labor,* ed. Altagracia Ortiz (Philadelphia: Temple University Press, 1996); Eileen Boris and Elisabeth Prügl, eds., *Homeworkers in Global Perspective* (New York: Routledge, 1996); Vicki L. Ruiz, *From Out of the Shadows: Mexican Women in Twentieth-Century America* (New York: Oxford University Press, 1999); Vicki L. Ruiz, *Cannery Women, Cannery Lives: Mexican Women, Unionization, and the California Food Processing Industry, 1930–1950* (Albuquerque: University of New Mexico Press, 1987); Annelise Orleck, *Common Sense and a Little Fire: Women and Working-Class Politics in the United States, 1900–1965* (Chapel Hill: University of North Carolina Press, 1995).

8. Cynthia Enloe, *Bananas, Beaches, and Bases: Making Feminist Sense of International Politics* (Berkeley: University of California Press, 1990).

9. Elaine Tyler May, *Homeward Bound: American Families in the Cold War Era* (New York: Basic Books, 1988); Gail Bederman, *Manliness and Civilization: A Cultural History of Gender and Race in the United States, 1880–1917* (Chicago: University of Chicago Press, 1995).

10. Louise Michele Newman, *White Women's Rights: The Racial Origins of Feminism in the United States* (New York; Oxford: Oxford University Press, 1999).

11. Ramón A. Gutiérrez, *When Jesus Came, the Corn Mothers Went Away: Marriage, Sexuality, and Power in Colonial New Mexico, 1500–1846* (Stanford, Calif.: Stanford University Press, 1992).

12. Valerie Amos and Pratibha Parmar, "Challenging Imperial Feminism," *Feminist Review* 17 (1984): 3–19.

13. Ian R. Tyrrell, *Woman's World/Woman's Empire: The Woman's Christian Temperance Union in International Perspective, 1800–1930* (Chapel Hill: University of North Carolina Press, 1991); Jane Hunter, *The Gospel of Gentility: American Women Missionaries in Turn-of-the-Century China* (New Haven: Yale University Press, 1984); Nancy Boyd, *Emissaries, the Overseas Work of the American YWCA, 1895–1970* (New York: Woman's Press, 1986). See also Joan Jacobs Brumberg, "The Ethnological Mirror: American Evangelical Women and Their Heathen Sisters, 1870–1910," in *Women and the Structure of Society*, ed. Barbara J. Harris and JoAnn McNamara (Durham: Duke University Press, 1984).

14. To start a partial list, see, e.g., Donna J. Guy, "White Slavery, Public Health, and the Socialist Position on Legalized Prostitution in Argentina, 1913–1936," *Latin America Research Review* 23, no. 3 (1988): 60–80; Eileen J. Suárez Findlay, *Imposing Decency: The Politics of Sexuality and Race in Puerto Rico, 1870–1920* (Durham, N.C.; London: Duke University Press, 1999), Mary Louise Pratt, *Imperial Eyes: Travel Writing and Transculturation* (London; New York: Routledge, 1992); Anne McClintock, *Imperial Leather: Race, Gender, and Sexuality in the Colonial Conquest* (New York: Routledge, 1995); Lata Mani, *Contentious Traditions: The Debate on Sati in Colonial India* (Berkeley: University of California Press, 1998); Philippa Levine, *Prostitution, Race, and Politics: Policing Venereal Disease in the British Empire* (New York; London: Routledge, 2003); Nancy Rose Hunt, *A Colonial Lexicon of Birth Ritual, Medicalization, and Mobility in the Congo* (Durham, N.C.; London: Duke University Press, 1999); Catherine Hall, *Civilising Subjects: Metropole and Colony in the English Imagination, 1830–1867* (Chicago: University of Chicago Press, 2002); Donna J. Guy, Mrinalini Sinha, and Angela Woollacott, *Feminisms and Internationalism* (Oxford: Blackwell, 1999); Antoinette M. Burton, *After the Imperial Turn: Thinking with and Through the Nation* (Durham, N.C.; London: Duke University Press, 2003).

15. Laura Wexler, *Tender Violence: Domestic Visions in an Age of U.S. Imperialism* (Chapel Hill: University of North Carolina Press, 2000); Mary A. Renda, *Taking Haiti: Military Occupation and the Culture of U.S. Imperialism, 1915–1940* (Chapel Hill: University of North Carolina Press, 2001); Emma Pérez, *The Decolonial Imaginary: Writing Chicanas into History* (Bloomington: Indiana University Press, 1999); Melani McAlister, *Epic Encounters: Culture, Media, and U.S. Interests in the Middle East, 1945–2000* (Berkeley: University of California, 2001); Kristin L. Hoganson, *Fighting for American Manhood: How Gender Politics Provoked the Spanish-American and Philippine-American Wars* (New Haven: Yale University Press, 1998), Catherine Ceniza Choy, *Empire of Care: Nursing and Migration in Filipino American History* (Durham, N.C.: Duke University Press, 2003); Laura Briggs, *Reproducing Empire: Race, Sex, Science, and U.S. Imperialism in Puerto Rico* (Berkeley: University of California Press, 2002); Christina Klein, *Cold War Orientalism: Asia in the Middlebrow Imagination* (Berkeley: University of California Press, 1999).

16. Michael Ignatieff, "The American Empire: The Burden," *New York Times Magazine*, January 5, 2003, late edition, sec. 6, 22.

17. Kaplan, "Left Alone with America."

18. Choy, *Empire of Care*.

19. Yen Le Espiritu, *Home Bound: Filipino American Lives across Cultures, Communities, and Countries* (Berkeley: University of California Press, 2003).

20. Ji-Yeon Yuh, *Beyond the Shadow of Camptown: Korean Military Brides in America* (New York: New York University Press, 2002).

21. Mae M. Ngai, *Impossible Subjects: Illegal Aliens and the Making of Modern America* (Princeton, N.J.: Princeton University Press, 2004).

22. Carmen Teresa Whalen, *From Puerto Rico to Philadelphia: Puerto Rican Workers and Postwar Economies* (Philadelphia: Temple University Press, 2001).

23. Ann Laura Stoler, "Tense and Tender Ties: The Politics of Comparison in North American History and (Post) Colonial Studies," *Journal of American History* 88, no. 3 (2001): 829–865, Ramón A. Gutiérrez, "What's Love Got to Do with It?" *Journal of American History* 88, no. 3 (2000): 866–870.

24. Michael Omi and Howard Winant, *Racial Formation in the United States: From the 1960s to the 1990s* (New York: Routledge, 1994).

25. Natalia Molina, *Fit to Be Citizens? Public Health and Race in Los Angeles, 1879–1939* (Berkeley: University of California, 2006).

26. Vicki L. Ruiz, "Star Struck: Acculturation, Adolescence, and Mexican American Women, 1920–1950," in *Unequal Sisters: A Multicultural Reader in U.S. Women's History*, ed. Ellen Carol DuBois and Vicki L. Ruiz (New York: Routledge, 2000); Nayan Shah, *Contagious Divides: Epidemics and Race in San Francisco's Chinatown* (Berkeley: University of California Press, 2001); George J. Sanchez, *Becoming Mexican American: Ethnicity, Culture, and Identity in Chicano Los Angeles, 1900–1945* (New York: Oxford University Press, 1993); Lisa Lowe, *Immigrant Acts: On Asian American Cultural Politics* (Durham, N.C.: Duke University Press, 1996); Lisa Lowe and David Lloyd, *The Politics of Culture in the Shadow of Capital* (Durham, N.C.: Duke University Press, 1997).

27. Ann Laura Stoler, ed., *Haunted by Empire: Geographies of Intimacy in North American History* (Durham, N.C.: Duke University Press, 2006).

28. Diane Nelson, *Finger in the Wound: Body Politics in Quincentennial Guatemala* (Berkeley: University of California Press, 1999); Roger Lancaster, *Life Is Hard: Machismo, Danger, and the Intimacy of Power in Nicaragua* (Berkeley: University of California Press, 1992).

29. Pierrette Hondagneu-Sotelo, *Doméstica: Immigrant Workers Cleaning and Caring in the Shadows of Affluence* (Berkeley: University of California Press, 2001). George Sánchez, "Roundtable, 1965 Remembered: The 1965 Immigration and Nationality Act — Race, Gender, and Sexuality," at Berkshire Conference on the History of Women, June 2–5, 2005, Scripps College.

30. Ann Laura Stoler, *Carnal Knowledge and Imperial Power: Race and the Intimate in Colonial Rule* (Berkeley: University of California Press, 2002).

31. Ranajit Guha, *Elementary Aspects of Peasant Insurgency in Colonial India* (Durham, N.C.: Duke University Press, 1999); Eric Woolf, *Europe and the People without History* (1982; repr., Berkeley: University of California Press, 1997); James Scott, *Domination and the Arts of Resistance: Hidden Transcripts* (New Haven: Yale University Press, 1990); James Scott, *Weapons of the Weak: Everyday Forms of Peasant Resistance* (New Haven: Yale University Press, 1985); Frantz Fanon, *A Dying Colonialism* (New York: Grove Press, 1967); Fanon, *Wretched of the Earth*; Stoler, *Haunted by Empire*.

32. Dipesh Chakrabarty, *Provincializing Europe: Postcolonial Thought and Historical Difference* (Princeton, N.J.: Princeton University Press, 2000).

33. Gayatri Chakravorty Spivak, "Can the Subaltern Speak?" in *Marxism and the Interpretation of Culture*, ed. Cary Nelson and Lawrence Grossberg (Urbana: University of Illinois Press, 1988, 271–313).

34. Renda, *Taking Haiti*, 3.

35. Pérez, *The Decolonial Imaginary*.

36. Kevin Gaines, "Revisiting Richard Wright in Ghana: Black Radicalism and the Dialectics of Diaspora," *Social Text* 19, no. 2 (2001): 75–101.

37. Nancy Hewitt, quoted in Nancy F. Cott et al., "Considering the State of U.S. Women's History," *Journal of Women's History* 15, no. 1 (2003): 145–163.

9

Chinese American Women in U.S. History

Explaining Representations of Exotic Others, Passive Objects, and Active Subjects

SHIRLEY HUNE

The first sighting that Americans likely had of a Chinese woman was in 1834 as a "curiosity" in New York City, where Afong Moy was elaborately staged as "the Chinese Lady" at the American Museum, owned by showman Phineas T. Barnum. Dressed in silk Qing Dynasty robes and dainty, pointed slippers, she was seated in a chair against an "orientalist" set decorated with carvings, lanterns, and tea accessories. During the 1830s and 1840s, Moy appeared on a variety of stages speaking in Chinese and eating with chopsticks. As "Ah" or "A" is a prefix commonly used in the Cantonese dialect to address a person, Afong is a familiar name and not the proper one given to her by her family. Hence, her true identity is unknown to us.[1]

Barnum also opened the Chinese Museum in New York City and in 1850 featured a Miss Pwan-ye-koo as the headliner of a "Living Chinese Family," complete with maidservant with unbound feet. Such was the attraction (and promotion) of Miss Pwan as a refined young "lady" who had traveled from her "Celestial empire" family to learn more about "outside barbarians" that Barnum reported twenty thousand people had viewed the exhibit over six days. Public accounts made note of her two-and-one-half-inch feet. We do not know what became of Miss Pwan and the other family members after their appearance of a few weeks. We do know that Barnum, taking advantage of the country's fascination with the "Orient," made substantial profits from their display.[2]

Chinese women in their custom and dress, in this case, as cultured ladies, were not alone in being exhibited in this period as living curiosities for mass entertainment.[3] But it was in this manner as racialized and sexualized exotic others that Chinese women entered U.S. history. Such a representation of Chinese American women can still be found, especially in popular culture, and has only recently been revised in historical studies. As subjects of history, we know nothing more at this time about Afong Moy and Miss Pwan and her unnamed maidservant other than the newspaper accounts. By today's historical standards, we also would want to know what they thought or felt as they "performed" their "Chineseness" for U.S. audiences.[4]

This chapter examines how the history of Chinese American women has been explained, past and present. The first part discusses their historiography and the role that historians, their worldviews, and changes in academia, notably ethnic studies and women's studies, have played in Chinese American women's history. The second section considers the historical construction of Chinese American women and the influence of particular frameworks on what we know about them. Here I highlight the long-standing representation of Chinese American women as exotic objects and deviants, notably as prostitutes in the American West, and contrast that to contemporary efforts to center them in history. The last section focuses on revisionist studies that view Chinese women as historical actors with agency. Here I emphasize works that re-interpret long-standing questions in Chinese American history and new studies that incorporate feminist and gendered perspectives, new methodologies, and underutilized resources to document and advance the significance of Chinese American women. The collective result is a re-envisioning of Chinese American women in history as active subjects with vibrant and complicated lives, negotiating hierarchies of power as they struggle to create new opportunities for themselves and others.

This chapter asks: What do we know about Chinese women in the history of the United States and how have we come to know them? Why have their historical interpretations been revised so dramatically over the past three decades? How have new historical practices and resources changed the study of Chinese American women? In what ways have Asian American studies and women's studies contributed to Chinese American women's history? And how do the lived experiences and new representations of Chinese American women influence the incorporation of gender in Asian American studies and revise our thinking about U.S. women's history?

Historiography and Historians

Historiography is an understudied topic in Chinese American history. My early (1977) monograph and Sucheng Chan's 1996 article note that non-historians, especially missionaries, diplomats, journalists, and social scientists, provide most of the early writings on Chinese/Asian Americans. The historical writings of the first period, 1870s to the early 1920s, were heavily biased. Most of the literature was fervently anti-Chinese and anti other Asian immigrants. Social scientists dominated the second period, the 1920s to the early 1960s. Their studies analyzed the cultural adaptation of Asian immigrants and questioned the capacity of the Chinese to fully assimilate. Revisionist works appear in the third period. In the 1960s, scholars begin to write about Asian Americans as a racialized minority group. Some studies assessed Chinese/Asian American history through a lens of racial and class oppression, while others sought to recover their history by documenting the many ways in which Chinese/Asian Americans contributed to U.S. culture and society. Chan identifies a fourth period beginning in the early 1980s when Asian American history came of age with the appearance of professional historians in the field. While publications on Chinese American women with a feminist perspective had appeared by 1996, she concludes that Chinese/Asian American women's history was still "relatively undeveloped."[5]

Focusing specifically on Chinese American women's history, Huping Ling suggests three periods of historiography. In the first period, the late nineteenth century to the 1960s, historians neglected Chinese American women as being historically insignificant and stereotyped and maligned them when they were mentioned. In the second period, the 1960s and 1970s, Chinese American women's experiences begin to be considered as part of Chinese American history. By the 1980s and 1990s, works emerged solely about Chinese American women. While Ling notes that attention to Chinese American women is very recent, she writes with more confidence than Chan about new studies, historical findings, and interpretations on the topic.[6]

How do we explain these changes in historiography? A primary explanation is the historians themselves and their ideological perspectives and training. The early historiography of Chinese women in the United States is intertwined with their being female and members of a racially distinct group whose ancestral homeland is Asia and whose history and peoples have been "orientalized" by Westerners as culturally and politically inferior.[7] Stereotypes of women in Asia as "shy," "submissive," and "exotic" and of their homelands and cultures as "backward," "heathen," and "despotic" have been applied to Asians in the United States as well, whether as immigrants, refugees, or U.S. born.[8]

From the mid-nineteenth century to the 1960s, Anglo American male historians dominated the discourse on Chinese Americans; some would argue that they continue to do so today. They interpreted the Chinese in the United States largely through orientalist, Eurocentric, and male-biased lenses. Nation building became defined by the country's relationship with Europe, despite the extensive China trade and U.S. aggressive expansion in the Pacific region. Such historical undertakings merged with myth making. The nation's unique character, Frederick Jackson Turner argued, had sprung from its experiences in the western territories and European American settlers' efforts to develop the frontier. To maintain this widely heralded U.S. historiography based on an Atlantic migration, a Pacific migration with Asian settlers in the U.S. West had to be erased or rendered invisible. When the Chinese presence could not be ignored, they were treated as a political problem best resolved by exclusion or, given the nation's fixation with racial and cultural differences, as permanent foreigners.[9]

New historical interpretations have stemmed from changes in the academy. The rewriting of Chinese American history must be understood within the larger context of the development of Asian American studies, new historical practices, and demographic changes. As part of a highly contentious period of social change in America during the 1960s and 1970s, marginalized groups and their supporters called for a transformation of U.S. institutions, including universities and colleges. The demands included new curriculum and programs to incorporate the history and culture of groups omitted from the standard college studies of the day and greater access to higher education for people of color, women, and the working class.[10] These changes provided new opportunities for Asian Americans to pursue academic careers.

As a scholarly innovation Asian American studies is an interdisciplinary field that seeks to document and interpret the history, identity, social formation, contributions, and contemporary concerns of Asian Americans and Pacific Islander Americans from their own perspectives. From the late 1960s to the early 1980s, scholars focused on reclaiming the history of Asian Americans within a nationalist framework of U.S. history that had marginalized their presence and contributions. They also placed racism at the center of Asian American history.

Public historians had a role in revising Chinese American history. Through conferences, journals, and exhibits, local historical societies documented the development of Chinese American communities, oftentimes with oral histories and photos. In particular, the rediscovery in the early 1970s of the Angel Island Immigration Station in San Francisco Bay launched a community history project.[11] This site processed more than one million Asian immigrants between 1910 and 1940 with Chinese women receiving the most severe scrutiny from U.S. officials. A significant find was the poetry written or carved on the barrack walls by Chinese men (Chinese women's poetry has not been found). Their words expressed the men's hopes and fears as they awaited their entry or deportation back to China. The publication in 1980 of *Island: Poetry and History of Chinese Immigrants on Angel Island, 1910–1940* increased awareness of the interrogation process, the plight of the detainees, and the agency of Chinese men and women in immigrating and seeking to reunite households.[12] Public historians identified new historical resources and material culture about the Chinese that were later taken up by academic historians. They were also among the first to give attention to Chinese American women.[13]

Women's studies and the Asian American women's movement stimulated interest in Chinese American women's history as well.[14] Asian American women began to teach courses and conduct research on Chinese and other Asian American women.[15] They have challenged traditional disciplines to revise their epistemology, research methods, and knowledge base. An overlapping critique has been the neglect of women in Asian American studies and of women of color in women's studies, especially in each "master" narrative.

Social history with its emphasis on common people and their everyday lives also has done much to recover women. In addition, the increased legitimacy of alternative historical methodologies — for example, oral history, biography, and the use of community documents — has reclaimed and advanced new findings about Chinese American women that have heretofore been hidden or neglected using standard archival practices.[16]

The growth and complexity of the Chinese American community since 1965 in its national origin, gender, social class, and dialect — largely as a result of changes in U.S. immigration and refugee laws, and the increased presence of Chinese international students — has generated additional historical issues as well as policy concerns.[17] The new demographics have brought scholars with different life experiences and perspectives to the study of Chinese American women.

During the past two decades, the Asian American studies field has intensively debated its historic mission and inclusivity (or lack of it). For example, has the field's professionalization displaced its original community-based focus as an agent of social change? And how can Asian American studies better incorporate smaller and more recent Asian American and Pacific Islander American communities and the perspectives of different groupings, such as women, into its narrative?[18] These debates resemble ones in women's studies in which scholars consider the gains and losses from the field's legitimation within the academy and the privileging of theory over consciousness-raising and practice. Women of color pose the problem of essentializing women, because doing so conceals how race, ethnicity, class, sexuality, citizenship, and other factors contribute to their histories and experiences, which are not the same as those of women in the dominant culture.[19] Scholars engaged in transnational and diaspora studies also dispute the use of national boundaries as a framework for analyzing immigrant experiences, in general, and the history of Chinese and other Asian Americans, specifically. Collectively, these factors have challenged the traditional historiography of Chinese American women and contributed to revisionist studies of their history.

Historical Constructions of Chinese American Women

A recognized tenet of feminist scholarship is that one does not simply add in women, stir, and expect to reconstitute history. Feminist scholars have considered phases in which women become integrated into the curriculum and the knowledge base.[20] Here I move beyond the exclusion-to-inclusion continuum and present four frameworks through which Chinese and other Asian/Pacific Islander American women have been constructed in U.S. history.[21] I propose that the way in which historians approach the study of Chinese American women influences how their history is (mis)represented. The discussion that follows illustrates how different frameworks contribute to an incomplete and unbalanced history of Chinese American women, even within revisionist studies. The first two frameworks — *invisibility and visibility as problem, deviant, or victim* — are most prevalent in studies prior to the 1960s. The latter two frameworks — *marginality and centered in history* — reflect the influence of Asian American studies and women's studies.

Omitting, Neglecting, or Making Chinese American Women Invisible

Omitting, neglecting, or making women invisible is a long-standing historical framework for all women's history. When the primary historical narrative centers on the lives, perspectives, and experiences of European Americans and males, Chinese American women are easily omitted as inconsequential in spite of their lived reality and significance. For example, when historians have given attention to the Chinese they have focused on men's immigration, labor, and politics, which reinforces the notion that Chinese American women's lives are less worthy of study. This tendency has been explained away by the worldview of Eurocentric elite males of a previous era and by the small numbers of Chinese women in the United States historically. Although rendering Chinese American women invisible was a central feature of nineteenth-century writings, such a framework still can be found in recently published works despite the increased presence of Chinese American women.[22]

Making Chinese American Women Visible: The Social Construction of the Chinese Female Prostitute as a Moral Problem, Deviant, or Victim

As we have seen, the first Chinese women in America were objectified as "orientalized" curiosities. Their presence on the East Coast during the first half of the nineteenth century was striking, but limited. Significant numbers of Chinese immigrants, mostly men, arrived after 1850 to the western territories and Hawaii, where most worked in low-paying, labor-intensive occupations to support families in China. A few were merchants with households and small businesses in the United States and oftentimes in China as well.

By the 1870s white working men regarded Chinese laborers as unfair competition. Images of Chinese men sharing close quarters and spending their leisure time gambling and in other vices, and of Chinese women as prostitutes, were widely promoted, intensifying negative stereotypes of the Chinese as heathen, unassimilable, and a social danger to U.S. society. Much is known about the violent acts and discriminatory laws against the Chinese and the manipulation of racial and class antagonisms by opportunistic labor and political leaders to fuel an anti-Chinese movement, which culminated in the Chinese Exclusion Act of 1882.[23] This act, which was the first federal legislation to limit U.S. immigration on the basis of race, nationality, and class, restricted the entry of Chinese laborers and denied Chinese residents the right of naturalization.[24] It was renewed, expanded, and not repealed until 1943. Scholars have reinterpreted the critical role of Chinese men in the western territories from economic threat to that of pioneers and major contributors to the region's development.[25] But what do we know about Chinese women in this period through past and present studies?

The dominant view of Chinese women in U.S. history is as prostitutes, and their representation as exotics lingers in contemporary popular culture. Chinese women did not emigrate at the same level as Chinese men, resulting in an enormously skewed sex ratio. There were eighteen Chinese males for every Chinese female in 1880.[26] Large numbers of unmarried Chinese women in the United States in this period did work as prostitutes, a situation that most did not choose. They often had been kidnapped or bribed or sold into the trade. The actual numbers of Chinese prostitutes were small compared to those of women of other nationalities on the U.S. frontier. Most women faced limited employment opportunities in the West, but it was the Chinese woman as prostitute who was most harshly criticized and sensationalized in nineteenth-century U.S. history and publicly scorned by politicians, missionaries, public health officials, and journalists. Consequently, California in 1870 and the U.S. government in the 1875 Page Law denied entry to Chinese and other Asian female prostitutes. The argument that Chinese women contributed to sexual slavery, brought disease and degradation to communities, and threatened the sanctity of the family and its Christian foundation, at a time when the western frontier needed to be settled and civilized, galvanized support for the subsequent Chinese Exclusion Act of 1882.[27]

When Chinese women were not being demonized, they were portrayed in U.S. magazine articles, travelers' accounts, and other popular writings as unfortunate victims of patriarchy, whether as prostitutes or as wives and daughters of merchants. Their situation attracted the attention of social reformers of the day. White Presbyterian mission women made Chinese females the object of their reform zeal. Through their widely publicized efforts to liberate Chinese female prostitutes from brothels and Chinese wives and girls from their cultural constrictions and protect them in mission homes where they could be indoctrinated in appropriate Christian notions of womanhood, marriage, and domesticity, the white mission women have left a remarkable historical record of their motivations and accomplishments.[28] This portrait of Chinese women also defined them as a problem, deviant, or victim and took away their voice. Only recently has attention been given to the views and aspirations of the Chinese women they "rescued."

Marginalizing Chinese American Women

Revisionist academic works on Chinese Americans appeared in the 1970s with the beginnings of Asian American studies. Such works substituted marginalization for absence by recognizing the presence, activities, and contributions of Chinese women, but also judging them to be tangential to the main narrative. Chinese men became the principal actors. For example, scholarship focused on the "bachelor society," a situation forced upon Chinese men by discriminatory U.S. immigration laws from the mid-nineteenth century until World War II that separated families sometimes for decades.[29] Chinese American men gained much sympathy for living for long periods without their wives and children or the lack of opportunity to establish families in their new homeland.[30] Historians gave scant attention to Chinese women, whether in the United States, China, or elsewhere, and their plight of being separated from their menfolk. This representation reflects a masculinist perspective. In general, women's lives were peripheral or collapsed into men's lives rather than being seen as significant in their own right.

Centering Chinese American Women

A few scholars have considered what Chinese/Asian American history would look like if reconceptualized with women at the center.[31] But the notion of centering women is more complicated than generally presented. At least three distinct constructions have emerged within the larger framework of centering Chinese American women; each contributes somewhat differently to articulating their history.

One construction is centering, but within traditional parameters. An imprecise portrayal of Chinese American women's lives occurs when they are centered, but viewed within preferred strictures, namely, through a white or Asian Americanist male lens or a white feminist lens. The tendency of these lenses is to recreate dominant paradigms of what is historically significant. Using male definitions of work or white middle-class women's dichotomy of separate public and private domains, for example, marginalizes, underreports, misunderstands, or renders invisible the economic activities of Chinese American women. Consequently, the historic and contemporary role of Chinese American women in small family businesses, whether as paid or unpaid workers moving between so-called public and private spheres, juggling work with child care and housekeeping, or sometimes as entrepreneurs in their own right or in the informal economy, is not fully documented. Further, in this framework, such activities are not fully appreciated for their originality and impact on gender roles, or as an economic survival strategy for the family, which, in turn, often increased a Chinese American woman's decision-making power in the household and enabled her to exercise a range of talents and skills.

Another construction is centering, but as objects of history. Much research that focuses on Chinese American women as historical subjects interprets them as historical objects.[32] In this context, Chinese women, whether as immigrants, prostitutes, or workers in family businesses, for example, appear as passive actors, often as victims of larger social forces, namely, colonialism, capitalism, and sexist family practices. I do not dismiss the power of multiple intersecting layers of hierarchy that constrain the lives and choices of Chinese American women. This framework, however, tells us more about patriarchy, racism, class exploitation, and heterosexuality as normative and how these factors impact the lives of Chinese American women than about the women themselves, their perspectives, survival strategies, and forms of resistance.

Centering as active subjects of history is yet another construction. A fuller form of Chinese American women's history, as with all women's history, views women as agents of social change who negotiate complex power structures and create new cultural formations within a set of constraints. This perspective provides a very different history, a more robust, complicated, and nuanced interpretation of Chinese American women as family members, workers, or community activists whose lives comprise resistance, oppression, and ambiguities. This framework considers women's perspectives, voices, and experiences as multifaceted, dynamic, and meaningful. Although some struggles for a new life resemble those of Chinese American men, Chinese American women often have different motivations, experiences, and goals, and they are involved in activities, social networks, and organizations distinct from those of their male counterparts. Such an approach began in the late 1970s in revisionist writings from a feminist perspective and with the appearance of a critical mass of Chinese American and other Asian American women scholars.[33] Their findings have begun to transform what we know about Chinese American women in U.S. history.

Re-envisioning Chinese American Women's History

Revisionist studies of Chinese American women begin in the late 1970s and divide into two broad areas: works that (1) reinterpret topics that have dominated Chinese American historiography, namely, prostitution, the scarcity of women, and Chinese exclusion, and (2) examine new or less studied topics about Chinese American women. They also use new approaches, methodologies, and resources to recover and rebalance Chinese American women's history.

Old Questions Revisited: New Interpretations

Chinese prostitution has been revisited. Was the situation of Chinese female prostitutes as depicted by Western journalists, policy makers, and others accurate? Sociologist Lucie Cheng Hirata in a classic 1979 study utilized economic data and prostitute contracts to challenge the notion of Chinese prostitution as a moral problem. She has reinterpreted prostitution as an economic issue involving two aspects: the harsh conditions of peasant life in China, where girls were so devalued that they were often abandoned or sold, sometimes into prostitution, and the material value of prostitution in the U.S. West, which like other frontiers had a large male surplus, making the sex trade an especially lucrative business.[34]

Without question a semi-feudal Chinese patriarchy and a multitude of exploitative groups in the U.S. western territories victimized Chinese women. In describing the daily existence of prostitutes, however, Cheng Hirata discovers agency. Chinese female prostitutes were not simply hapless, although many were much abused. They were also laborers with varied working conditions: a few were free agents, some were enslaved, and others were contract workers. Many women made active choices to support their families in China through prostitution. Some found men to buy out their contract or purchased their own way out of prostitution into other lives. A few became successful brothel owners themselves. They generated wealth for procurers, brothel owners, landlords, and state officials by way of protection fees collected by the police who looked the other way as well as for the state through tax revenues. Cheng Hirata shows Chinese female prostitution as a critical component of economic development.[35]

The scarcity of Chinese women has also been given another look. The scarcity of Chinese women in the United States during the nineteenth century is another perplexing question, and until the mid 1980s its prevailing explanation centered on Chinese values and practices. The long-standing argument is that because the Chinese were patriarchal, patrilineal, and patrilocal, wives remained in the homeland to take care of family members, the farm, or other responsibilities while husbands went overseas to find work. A women's place was with her children and in-laws, especially since her husband was expected to return. This cultural explanation judged Chinese women as wholly subordinate, dutifully fulfilling filial obligations. It also justified the mistreatment of the Chinese in the United States because they were deemed culturally peculiar and inassimilable.

Revisionist scholarship has challenged this interpretation for being culturally biased in its perpetuation of an orientalizing stereotype of the Chinese and for its lack of attention to other mitigating factors. George Anthony Peffer and Sucheng Chan both identify the 1875 Page Law for the lack of Chinese women. Historians had previously ignored this law, which denied entry to Chinese and other Asian female prostitutes. Peffer and Chan conclude that the practices of state officials in carrying out the Page Law limited the entry of all Chinese women, including wives and daughters. Prior to the 1882 Chinese Exclusion Act that restricted Chinese male workers, the Page Law treated Chinese women as unacceptable immigrants because of the sex trade, a component of frontier life not of their making. Chan also explored state and federal statutes and court cases from the 1860s to the 1940s for their role in the exclusion and deportation of Chinese women and uncovered concerns on the part of Chinese men about bringing their families to the United States. Even if the men had the funds to send for their wives, they feared for the women's safety and were reluctant to expose them to the kinds of discrimination that the Chinese faced in America. Chan does not dismiss the influence of cultural customs on the small numbers of Chinese women, but like Peffer finds an additional and more compelling explanation for their scarcity in discriminatory U.S. laws and other practices.[36]

Scholars who adopt a global or transnational perspective have reassessed Peffer's and Chan's interpretation of the scarcity of Chinese women and find serious weaknesses in the nation-based framework of immigration studies. Adam McKeown argues that the transnational household with men being sent overseas to work and remit funds home was a more economically viable strategy for the survival of Chinese families than cohabitation. Hence Chinese wives and husbands living apart was an acceptable practice at this time. For Sucheta Mazumdar, women's economic role was central. Taking into account the extensive agricultural activities assumed by women in China, she concludes that male rather than female emigration was typical in Guangdong's Pearl River Delta because the loss of women's labor would have been most detrimental to the household economy. Both challenge the notion that nuclear families were typical of immigrant families in the United States, including those from European countries, and note that male immigration and the high rate of their return to the homeland was the dominant pattern in this period. Hence, small numbers of women were not unusual for the vast majority of immigrant groups, although it was the Chinese who were singled out as being different and unnatural and who also faced the Page Law.[37]

By situating U.S. immigration studies beyond national borders, global and transnational scholars complicate our understanding of Chinese immigrant experiences. They uncover a different history of Chinese women, shed new light on their challenges and the value of their activities, critique the narrow conception of Chinese patriarchal culture as the sole explanation for women's lack of emigration, and highlight the survival strategies of Chinese households during a difficult economic and political period in both the United States and China. Recasting the question of Chinese women's scarcity more broadly, deeply, and geographically uncovers new areas of their significance.

Chinese exclusion has been revisited as well. Chinese exclusion — six decades of U.S. laws, from 1882 to 1943, that restricted Chinese male laborers, and subsequently their wives and children, but permitted the entry of Chinese merchants, teachers, students, diplomats, and travelers and their wives and children — remains a central question for Chinese American historiography. No other U.S. immigrant group was restricted to the same extent. As a result of these laws, the Chinese American population declined precipitously from 105,465 in 1880 to 61,639 by 1920.[38]

Typically, the study of Chinese exclusion has been male-centered and interpreted as a race and class issue. Revisionist studies that foreground Chinese women and utilize gender as well as race and class as organizing principles uncover new details about Chinese women's creativity, initiatives, and strategies to immigrate and stay. The new scholarship documents the multiple ways in which Chinese women (and Chinese men) took risks, resisted, and were not passive victims during the exclusion era. Since the 1990s, works such as those of Jennifer Gee, Erika Lee, and Judy Yung (I discuss Yung's work in a later section) apply gendered or feminist perspectives to the exclusion era and offer different analyses. Their studies make use of ethnic, community, and family materials, including Chinese-language sources and U.S. Immigration and Naturalization Service (INS) arrival files, which became available in the late 1980s and early 1990s. There is new information about the interrogation process and rich details about Chinese families through letters, photos, interview transcripts, and other documents submitted as part of entry applications.

Gee argues that Asian immigration to the United States must be treated as a gendered phenomenon and not solely as a racial matter and provides new insights on the gender ideology and expectations held by U.S. officials. By comparing how immigration officials treated Chinese and Japanese women, Gee finds that interrogators articulated white middle-class notions of female domesticity and morality in probing a woman's demeanor and reason for entry. For example, officials persistently asked questions about a woman's respectability in seeking to uncover an illicit reason, i.e., prostitution, for immigrating. Japanese women who came as picture brides were generally viewed as prospective housewives, a role deemed appropriate for women. As dependents of men they gained admittance with greater ease than Chinese women, especially laborers' wives, who were seen as more "likely to become a public charge." Although Chinese merchants' wives were exempt from exclusion laws, they were not exempt from heavy scrutiny, as all Chinese women were suspect of entry for prostitution.[39]

Erika Lee's reframing challenges the ease of establishing and maintaining transnational households. She seeks to balance and integrate two foci: studies on the excluded with those of the excluders and acts of resistance in conjunction with acts of exclusion. She focuses on the Chinese who persisted in seeking entry despite exclusion laws and finds that 300,955 Chinese gained admittance as new or return entrants, a number greater than during the prior pre-exclusion period (258,210 between 1849 and 1882). The vast majority were men.[40] Lee concludes that gendered inequities in both the United States and China contributed to a continuing small presence of Chinese women. U.S. officials continued to believe the stereotype of Chinese women as prostitutes. Women were interrogated more harshly than men, resulting in many applicants being rejected for entry, which concurs with Gee's findings. Utilizing her own family history and other documents, Lee argues that male privilege among the Chinese resulted in priority being given to the sending for sons and other male relatives rather than daughters and other womenfolk. Still, many Chinese women actively strategized to ensure their entry. For example, they conformed to the appearance and behavior of the merchant class by displaying small (non-laboring) feet to officials or by using scarce funds to arrive by first-class passage as would be expected of merchant wives. Nonetheless, Lee notes how vulnerable Chinese women remained in this period. Their admission and well-being in the United States were largely dependent on the will and status of their menfolk. Furthermore, INS forces could continue to pursue and deport Chinese immigrants years after their arrival.[41] Studies like these that re-open long-standing questions in Chinese American history play an important role in recovering Chinese American women.

New Studies, Approaches, and Findings

The historiography of Chinese American women shifts dramatically in the 1990s with a focus on their agency, the twentieth-century period, and individuals as well as specific groups, such as the second generation, post-1940s immigrants, and lesbians. Chinese American women's history no longer revolves around immigration, dependency, or prostitution. Reflecting the growth of women's studies, feminist scholarship and perspectives are prominent as researchers consider women's everyday lived realities, gender roles, social, cultural, and political formations in addition to economic activities, and the multiple ways in which Chinese American women adapt to and seek to change their circumstances. These shifts have benefited from the use of oral history and the tapping of multiple primary materials generated from the state, including census, INS, and court records, other government documents, and a wide range of women's and community sources, such as photographs, women's writings and speeches, ethnic newspapers, and related community publications, many of them in the Chinese language.

Marking this new history is Judy Yung's *Unbound Feet*, a social history of Chinese women in San Francisco from the Gold Rush era to World War II. Yung discusses the making of a Chinese American community with a focus on women's contributions in a city that was the entry point of most Chinese in this period. She portrays Chinese American women as actively shaping and reshaping — at times accommodating, at other times resisting, or both simultaneously — gender roles and relations while effecting social change outside their home and community. In contrast to the previous emphasis on the immigrant generation, Yung gives equal attention to the everyday lives of American-born or second-generation Chinese women. In featuring their agency from the 1920s to the 1940s, an understudied period, she analyzes how women negotiated both gender and racial discrimination within U.S. society and the male privilege of Chinese culture in their own community to expand their life choices.[42]

Yung adopts the metaphor of Chinese women unbinding their feet and taking larger steps toward personal development to illustrate their increasing socioeconomic and civic involvement over five decades. They developed social services in Chinatown, sought more education, labored in jobs from which they had previously been excluded, and struck for better work conditions. By 1945 they were "in step" with their community and U.S. society in working in the war industry and serving in the armed forces, much like other women. Yung identifies the emergence of middle-class Chinese Americans, chronicles women-initiated and -governed groups during the first half of the twentieth century, such as the YWCA (Young Women's Christian Association) and Square and Circle Club, and discovers the strivings of most second-generation Chinese American women to be bicultural. At the same time, Chinese American women did not divest themselves of connections with the homeland. Many were active in political organizations to advance nation building in China. Yung's research suggests that there are many more primary sources to be explored if investigators would only look for Chinese women in documents, including community materials, and seek them out for interviews.[43]

Huping Ling's *Surviving on the Gold Mountain* surveys 150 years of Chinese American women's history from the 1840s to the 1990s. In contrast to the West Coast orientation of most scholarship, she incorporates the lives of Chinese women in different parts of the United States, especially those in small towns, and provides coverage of the post–World War II period. Ling explodes the notion of homogeneity through portraits of a range of women, including early immigrant pioneer women in Butte, Montana, second-generation high school girls in 1920s Honolulu, World War II war brides, professional women and garment workers, and recognized notables, such as newscaster Connie Chung, architect Maya Lin, and figure skater Michelle Kwan. Unlike Yung, she finds that Chinese American women did not move into the mainstream in significant numbers until after the 1960s and concludes that they still experience discrimination despite socioeconomic gains.[44]

Particularly significant is Ling's reassessment of marital relations and family and community formation, regardless of social class. She rebalances the long-standing interpretation of Chinese America as a "bachelor society" by drawing attention to the early existence of Chinese American families and noting their changing family and marriage patterns. Chinese American women played a significant economic and social role in their households. They were "co-providers" and shared in decision-making with their husbands, she shows, thus again challenging notions of their subservience.[45] Ling further expands the categories of Chinese women by finding historical counterparts to her own former status as an international student. In recovering female students from China, Taiwan, and Hong Kong from the 1880s to the 1990s, she discusses their experiences in becoming academics and other professionals. Intellectual women generally immigrated independent of men. They tended to come from relatively privileged, oftentimes Westernized households, had different motivations to emigrate than other Chinese women, and were advantaged in their adaptation to U.S. life in comparison to other Chinese women.[46]

Some of the new scholarship on the twentieth century gives attention to U.S.-born Chinese women and the challenges they have confronted in forging their Chinese American identity and in creating new cultural formations that are gendered in addition to being race and class based. Judy Wu introduces us to Chinese American women as beauty contestants in the Miss Chinatown U.S.A. pageant from the 1950s to the 1970s. The male leadership of San Francisco's Chinatown promoted this annual event as a cultural marker of the Chinese American community's Americanness, modernity, and normalizaton as a family society much like middle America and as a counter to the negative "bachelor society" image. Wu reveals how female contestants both accommodated and resisted the commercial and political use of their bodies. Young Chinese American women had their own goals about their representation, which often differed from the idealized notions of womanhood articulated both by their ethnic community and by mainstream U.S. society.[47]

Other scholars introduce additional understudied groups of Chinese women. Xiaojian Zhao recovers war brides in *Remaking Chinese America*. U.S. legislative reforms adopted in 1945 and 1946 for the first time eased the entry of Chinese women who were the wives, new brides, and fiancées of Chinese American war veterans. Consequently, the Chinese sex ratio in the United States changed from

2.9 men to 1 woman in 1940 to 1.35 to 1 in 1960.[48] For Zhao, the presence and role of the war brides was critical in transforming Chinese Americans into a family-centered ethnic community between 1940 and 1965. She also highlights the influential role of women in family and community formation and closes a circle in documenting the reunions of wives and husbands who were separated, sometimes for decades, during the exclusion era. Many of these reunions were fraught with confusion and conflict, especially over the different views of gender relations held by husbands and wives.[49]

Xiaolan Bao identifies the significance of a new group of immigrant working-class Chinese women, most of whom entered the United States after 1965. She emphasizes the critical importance of Chinese women as a labor force in New York City's garment industry and in the economic support of their households. These women's income and health benefits proved essential for their families' survival. Most importantly, Bao documents how the women, faced with the need to work and with the demands of motherhood, became politicized and organized. The women actively campaigned to secure day-care centers from their union, the International Ladies' Garment Workers' Union (ILGWU). After several years of having their appeals dismissed by the union, twenty thousand of them took to the streets to strike in 1982 and held up the pending labor contract. Their persistence and organizing skills paid off. The first Chinatown day-care center for their children opened in 1984. Nonetheless, there remain insufficient child-care centers for the garment workers and other women in Chinatown.[50]

Historical studies of Chinese lesbians are also part of the new scholarship. Trinity Ordona analyzes the role of Chinese and other Asian women in contemporary gay, lesbian, bisexual, transgender, and queer (GLBTQ) movements. Based on her own participatory history, oral interviews, and community documents, such as newsletters and flyers, Ordona describes the marginalization of women of color by the dominant GLBTQ community, the cultural and political formations undertaken by Chinese and other Asian lesbians during the 1970s and 1980s to develop a safe space for themselves, and the difficulties the women faced in sustaining their community in the midst of both internal and external challenges.[51]

Finally, an explosion of biography characterizes the new revisionist history. Largely because of limited sources, the vast majority of Chinese American women remain unnamed and unknown. But a wide range of cultural materials available for twentieth-century studies allows for biographies of notable Chinese American women. For example, there are now multifaceted biographical studies of journalist and fiction writer Sui Sin Far/Edith Maude Eaton (1865–1914), daughter of a Chinese mother and British father, who wrote about Chinese North American life with empathy and a keen eye in opposition to stereotypical depictions;[52] Dr. Margaret Chung (1889–1951), the first known American-born Chinese woman physician, political celebrity, and surrogate mother of more than a thousand U.S. servicemen during the 1930s and 1940s;[53] and Hollywood star and internationally known actress Anna May Wong (1905–1961).[54] As women pioneering in new professions and new ways of being Chinese and American, they negotiated multiple boundaries of race, gender, class, sexuality, and nationality at a time when their aspirations reached far beyond what the nation and their community deemed appropriate and possible for women of Chinese descent in the United States. Chung's gender bending, such as her choice of clothing, and Wong's movie-star life, and their friendships with women, all of which raise issues about their sexuality, as well as Eaton's biraciality and binational experiences (she spent her upbringing and early working years in Quebec, Canada), yield new understandings of the diverse experiences of Chinese American women. This includes the disapproval of their ethnic communities for stepping outside traditional boundaries of Chinese American womanhood. Through the use of biography, these works reveal the complex lives and relations of Chinese American women as women of color in U.S. history.

The recent studies on Chinese American women also find continuities as well as pioneering attributes. They still were vulnerable to larger social and political forces, including gender ideologies of women's roles, stereotypes of Chinese women, U.S. immigration laws, male-centered community goals, and the vagaries of U.S.-China relations. But Chinese American women's resistance to exploitation, racism, patriarchy, and traditional notions of womanhood and their efforts to advance new opportunities for themselves and others have emerged as prominent features of contemporary scholarship. In the re-envisioning of their history, Chinese American women are no longer cardboard figures. Their historical construction has shifted over the decades from exotic others, seen as passive objects of history, to historical subjects with agency. Invisibility and marginalization have given way to centrality and complexity largely through the incorporation of Chinese American women's perspectives, voices, and writings.

How can the reinterpretations of Chinese American women contribute to new understandings of Asian American history? Race has been and continues to be the dominant organizing principle in Asian American history, while gender is generally treated as neutral, that is, there is no difference between men's and women's lives, or as separate, namely, women's experiences, at best. To date, gender as a category of analysis has focused predominantly on feminist critiques of Chinese American women's lives. More attention needs to be given to gender roles and their dynamics in Asian American communities. For example, how did Chinese American men negotiate their manhood during the nineteenth and early twentieth centuries when they were often limited to "feminized" occupations, especially domestic work as household servants, cooks, and laundrymen? What were the forms of men's and women's resistance to racist laws and practices that restricted their civil and political rights and made it difficult to for them to provide for their families and, therefore, altered gender roles as well? And, how did Chinese men and women collaborate to create community?[55]

Re-envisioning Asian American history requires more than adding women into the master narrative. It involves the incorporation simultaneously of the new critiques of gender, race, and class analyses as well as nationhood and a reappraisal of the historical constructions of Asian American femininities and masculinities, the intersections of women and men in all aspects of public and private life and spaces in-between, and the ideologies and institutional structures that contribute to gender formation in multiple locations, such as the United States, Asian American communities, their respective original homelands, and in transnational spaces.[56]

The lived experiences and new representations of Chinese American women also can contribute to our rethinking U.S. women's history. Incorporating Chinese American women's lives dismantles the notion of a universal monocultural U.S. women's experience. Chinese/Asian American women have not led lives of protected domesticity and privilege in a distinct private/public dichotomy, which is a dominant theme in contemporary analyses of U.S. women's history. They have, by necessity, worked not only inside the home, but outside of it often as wage workers or small entrepreneurs. Frequently, they occupy that in-between space of the family business where they can be found negotiating work responsibilities with household duties, child care, and sometimes elder care. They are also part of the informal economy where their activities go unrecorded in U.S. national statistics. Hence, incorporating the work history of Chinese American women broadens our knowledge of U.S. women's participation in economic development and gives significance to the role of women in ethnic enterprises. Having neither benefited from nor been confined by a cult of domesticity, Chinese American women's lives complicate our understanding of American womanhood.

Another example lies in our understanding of family formations and gender practices within them. Feminist studies often have identified the nuclear family as a primary enforcer of traditional gender roles and as a site of oppression for women's development. Like other women of color, Chinese American women do not necessarily view the nuclear family as wholly oppressive. It is also a site of refuge and personal fulfillment that has supported women's development. A central feature of Asian American history is the struggle to establish and sustain families in the face of discriminatory immigration laws and other practices. One outcome is the creation of new family forms, such as the transnational family or split household, which despite the strains on family members became an adaptive economic strategy for survival and a social strategy to maintain families across geographical space and time. Such a family form was shaped in part by the women themselves. In turn, the transnational household shaped Chinese women's lives, in many cases, providing them with greater autonomy and responsibility. Transnational households, it should be noted, are part of the landscape of current Pacific Rim capitalist developments, with Chinese corporate fathers jetting back and forth to families in Asia, the United States, and elsewhere.[57]

We also gain new knowledge about gender roles and their dynamics within the household. Adapting to life in America contributed to new types of households for Asian Americans. The idealized multigenerational Asian family and its patriarchy did not manifest itself in the United States because the traditional authority that men possessed in Asia could not be replicated. At the same time, as previously noted, Chinese American women's economic and reproductive power enhanced their influence in the household. Cut off from their extended families and excluded from full participation in U.S. society during the late nineteenth century and much of the twentieth century, Chinese American men and women negotiated more egalitarian marriage partnerships that were different from those in their homelands and from those developed by the dominant culture. Still there were tensions as many women and men sought to hold onto their traditional roles while forming new ones. The outcome was the creation of an interdependent and cooperative family structure with fluid gender roles long before this form became recognized as a desired one in middle-class white America.

Chinese American women's history also informs U.S. immigration studies. Their history demonstrates the courage and initiatives of female immigrants and the difficulties faced by women of color in their integration into U.S. culture and society over many generations. Although U.S. immigrant women, and women in general, share commonalities, Chinese American women's lives also illuminate the influences of race, ethnicity, class, and other differences on their experiences, including their strategies, both accommodating and oppositional, as they sought to define their own identity and sensibilities about being female, ethnic, and American. Viewing immigrant communities within a transnational and global perspective also provides new perspectives of U.S. history, in general, and women in U.S. history, specifically.

A central core of U.S. history is the agency of its people in establishing a new life and opportunities for themselves and their communities in a society often very different from their homeland. U.S. history, including U.S. women's history, has largely been defined within a black-white paradigm whereby the values, actions, and experiences of European Americans and African Americans are the norm. The incorporation of Chinese American women, who are neither black nor white, sheds new light on women's goals, types of oppression, and struggles for full participation. The ways in which Chinese American women have juggled their multiple roles also cause us to rethink commonalities, differences, and complexities in the lives of American women.

A reassessment of Chinese American women's history is an ongoing process. However, a larger step is the incorporation of their lives from their perspectives and with their voices within a U.S. women's history that is multicultural. Valuing and including the feminist approaches of women of color in the ways in which they represent Chinese American women, along with aspects of ethnic studies in this rethinking and, ultimately, the reconstruction of U.S. women's history, would advance this endeavor.

NOTES

The author thanks Judy Yung and Huping Ling for their helpful comments on an earlier draft.

1. John Kuo Wei Tchen, *New York before Chinatown: Orientalism and the Shaping of American Culture, 1776–1882* (Baltimore: Johns Hopkins University Press, 1999), 101–106.

2. Tchen, *New York before Chinatown.* 117–123.

3. For a more detailed discussion of other human exhibits from Asia and the Pacific region, some with physical talents, others with physical abnormalities, and still others who were frauds or costumed, see Tchen, *New York before Chinatown*, chap. 5.

4. Robert G. Lee, *Orientals: Asian Americans in Popular Culture* (Philadelphia: Temple University Press, 1999), 50.

5. Sucheng Chan, "Asian American Historiography," *Pacific Historical Review* 65, no. 3 (1996): 363–399; and Shirley Hune, *Pacific Migration to the United States: Trends and Themes in Historical and Sociological Literature* (Washington, D.C.: Smithsonian Institution, 1977). See also Roger Daniels, "Westerners from the East: Oriental Immigrants Reappraised," *Pacific Historical Review* 35 (November 1966): 373–383; and Roger Daniels, "American Historians and East Asian Immigrants," *Pacific Historical Review* 43 (November 1974): 449–472.

6. Huping Ling, *Surviving on the Gold Mountain: A History of Chinese American Women and Their Lives* (Albany: State University of New York Press, 1998), 6.

7. Edward W. Said's *Orientalism* (New York: Vintage, 1976) and *Culture and Imperialism* (New York: Vintage, 1993) focus on the power of the West, notably, the influence of elitist writings during the rise of modern imperialism, to inscribe the culture and peoples of the Near or Middle East as inferior, passive, despotic, and sexualized. His conceptual framework has been applied to Asia and the Pacific regions and other parts of the world as well.

8. On the influence of western colonial, gendered ideology on interpretations of Asian cultures and households, especially the promotion of Asian women's subservience to the neglect of a more complicated discussion of their status, including women's oppositional strategies, and the implications of such stereotyping on images of Asian women in the United States, see Kathleen Uno, "Unlearning Orientalism: Locating Asian and Asian American Women in Family History," in *Asian/Pacific Islander American Women: A Historical Anthology*, ed. Shirley Hune and Gail M. Nomura (New York: New York University Press, 2003), 42–57.

9. Hune, *Pacific Migration*, 1–8. See also Sucheng Chan, "Introduction: Western American Historiography and Peoples of Color," in *Peoples of Color in the American West*, ed. Sucheng Chan, Douglas Henry Daniels, Mario T. García, and Terry P. Wilson (Lexington: Mass.: D. C. Heath and Co., 1994), 1–4.

10. Sucheng Chan and Ling-Chi Wang, "Racism and the Model Minority: Asian-Americans in Higher Education," in *The Racial Crisis in American Higher Education*, ed. Philip G. Altbach and Kofi Lomotey (Albany: State University of New York Press, 1991), 43–67; Shirley Hune, "Opening the American Mind and Body: The Role of Asian American Studies," *Change* (November/December 1989): 56–63; and Karen Umemoto, "On Strike!

San Francisco State College Strike, 1968–69: The Role of Asian American Students," *Amerasia Journal* 15, no. 1 (1989): 3–41. On Asian American social activism in the 1960s and 1970s, see William Wei, *The Asian American Movement* (Philadelphia: Temple University Press, 1993), ch. 1. Chapters in Fred Ho, ed., with Carolyn Antonio, Diane Fujino, and Steve Yip, *Legacy to Liberation* (Brooklyn, N.Y.: Big Red Media; and San Francisco: AK Press, 2000) emphasize the radical and revolutionary components of the Asian Pacific American movement in this period.

11. "Paul Chow, 69; Helped Save Immigration Site," *New York Times Obituaries*, July 15, 1998, C24. The immigration station was restored as a National Historic Landmark in the early 1980s at the urging of Chinese American community members.

12. Him Mark Lai, Genny Lim, and Judy Yung, *Island: Poetry and History of Chinese Immigrants on Angel Island, 1910–1940 (San Francisco: HOC DOI, 1980).*

13. Early classic works on Chinese American women written as public history include Ai-Li W. Chin, "Adaptive Roles of Chinese Women in the U.S.," *Bulletin: Chinese Historical Society of America* 14, no. 1 (January 1979); *Linking Our Lives: Chinese American Women of Los Angeles* (Los Angeles: Chinese Historical Society of Southern California, 1984); and Judy Yung, *Chinese Women of America: A Pictorial History* (Seattle: University of Washington Press, 1986).

14. Discussions of the Asian American women's movement in this period include Susie Ling, "The Mountain Movers: Asian American Women's Movement in Los Angeles," *Amerasia Journal* 15, no. 1 (1989): 51–67; and Wei, *The Asian American Movement*, 3. On the creation and impact of women's studies, see Marilyn Jacoby Boxer, *When Women Ask the Questions* (Baltimore: The Johns Hopkins University Press, 1998), for example.

15. Nancy I. Kim discusses the course content, pedagogy, and theoretical approaches of the general survey course on Asian American women taught within Asian American studies at a number of universities from the 1970s to 1998. See Nancy I. Kim, "The General Survey Course on Asian American Women: Transformative Education and Asian American Feminist Pedagogy," *Journal of Asian American Studies* 3, no. 1 (February 2000): 37–65.

16. See Hune and Nomura, *Asian/Pacific Islander American Women*, for examples of research approaches using social history, oral history, biography, participatory case studies, and ethnic/community-based resources. Some of the chapters also reframe Chinese/Asian American women's history within a transnational or global perspective.

17. On policy matters, see Kenyon S. Chan, "U.S.-born, Immigrant, Refugee, or Indigenous Status: Public Policy Implications for Asian Pacific American Families," in *Asian Americans and Politics: Perspectives, Experiences, Prospects*, ed. Gordon H. Chang (Washington, D.C.: Woodrow Wilson Center Press; and Stanford, Calif.: Stanford University Press, 2001), 197–229.

18. For example, Kenyon S. Chan, "Rethinking the Asian American Studies Project: Bridging the Divide between 'Campus' and 'Community,'" *Journal of Asian American Studies* 3, no. 1 (February 2000): 17–36; Shilpa Davé, Pawan Dhingra, Sunaina Maira, Partha Mazumdar, Lavina Shankar, Jaideep Singh, and Rajini Srikanth, "De-Privileging Positions: Indian Americans, South Asian Americans, and the Politics of Asian American Studies," *Journal of Asian American Studies* 3, no. 1 (February 2000): 67–100; and Lane Ryo Hirabayashi and Marilyn Caballero Alquizola, "Whither the Asian American Subject?" in *Color-line to Borderlands: The Matrix of American Ethnic Studies*, ed. Johnnella E. Butler (Seattle: University of Washington Press, 2001), 169–202.

19. For example, see *differences* 9, no. 3 (fall 1997), special issue, "Women's Studies on the Edge."

20. The phrases of Peggy McIntoch and those of Susan R. Van Dyne and Marilyn R. Schuster are discussed in Boxer, *When Women Ask the Questions*, 62–64.

21. These frameworks are drawn, in part, from a larger study. See my chapter, "Introduction: Through 'Our 'Eyes: Asian/Pacific Islander American Women's History," in *Asian/Pacific Islander American Women*, ed. Hune and Nomura, 4–6 and 14, n.12.

22. On the absence of studies on Chinese women (with the exception of chapters on literary works), see Susie Lan Cassel, ed., *The Chinese in America: A History from Gold Mountain to the New Millennium* (Walnut Creek, Calif.: Altamira Press, 2002).

23. Two classic older works on the anti-Chinese movement are Mary Roberts Coolidge, *Chinese Immigration* (New York: Holt, 1909); and Elmer Clarence Sandmeyer, *The Anti-Chinese Movement in California* (Urbana: University of Illinois Press, 1939). More recent studies include Stuart Creighton Miller, *The Unwelcome Immigrant: The American Image of the Chinese, 1785–1882* (Berkeley: University of California Press, 1969); and Alexander Saxton, *The Indispensable Enemy: Labor and the Anti-Chinese Movement in California* (Berkeley: University of California Press, 1971).

24. Chinese exclusion is more precisely Chinese immigration restriction and is a series of acts and court cases. The 1882 act suspended the entry of new Chinese laborers for ten years, while exempting merchants, teachers, students, diplomats, and travelers. Acts that followed renewed the initial act and denied the re-entry of laborers into the United States who had returned to China to visit. Court cases determined that the status of wives and children followed the status of men. Therefore, the wives and children of the laboring class also fell under Chinese restriction, while the wives and children of the exempted classes were given more opportunities to enter. For a discussion of the enforcement of Chinese exclusion acts and the multiple efforts of the Chinese to challenge their immigration status through the courts, see Lucy E. Salyer, *Laws Harsh as Tigers: Chinese Immigrants and the Shaping of Modern Immigration Law* (Chapel Hill: University of North Carolina Press, 1995).

25. On economic activities in California, see Sucheng Chan, *This Bitter-Sweet Soil: The Chinese in California Agriculture, 1860–1910* (Berkeley: University of California Press, 1986). Chapters in Arif Dirlik, ed., *Chinese on the American Frontier* (Lanham: Rowman and Littlefield, 2001), provide details of Chinese activities and contributions in the Southwest, Northwest, and Rocky Mountain states.

26. The sex ratio is calculated from Lucie Cheng Hirata, "Free, Indentured, Enslaved: Chinese Prostitutes in Nineteenth-Century America," *Signs* 5, no. 11 (1979): 5, table 1.

27. Lee, *Orientals*, 89–91; and Nayan Shah, *Contagious Divides: Epidemics and Race in San Francisco's Chinatown* (Berkeley: University of California Press, 2001), 79–90, 107–108.

28. Peggy Pascoe, *Relations of Rescue: The Search for Female Moral Authority in the American West, 1874–1939* (New York: Oxford University Press, 1990).

29. For example, see the exclusive focus on the treatment of Chinese men in San Francisco's Chinatown: Victor G. Nee and Brett de Bary Nee, "The Bachelor Society," in *Longtime Californ': A Documentary Study of an American Chinatown*, ed. Victor G. Nee and Brett de Bary Nee (New York: Pantheon Books, 1972), one of the first revisionist studies to portray the Chinese American community with humanity and from their viewpoints and with their voices.

30. Studies on Chinese men's family formations with women of other national, racial, and ethnic backgrounds dispute the notion of a "bachelor society" as the all-encompassing

feature of Chinese American men's lives. Although most working-class Chinese men were denied opportunities to establish Chinese households in the United States, many persisted and did. Others established families with women from other racial and ethnic communities and produced mixed-race offspring. For example, John Tchen's *New York before Chinatown* uncovers Chinese Irish families in New York City during the mid-nineteenth century; James W. Loewen's *The Mississippi Chinese: Between Black and White*, 2nd ed. (Prospect Heights, Ill.: Waveland Press, 1988), assesses the formation and transformation of Chinese black families in the Mississippi Delta between the 1870s and the 1940s; and Lucy M. Cohen's *Chinese in the Post–Civil War South* (Baton Rouge: Louisiana State University Press, 1984) discloses marriages between Chinese men and white, black, creole, and Indian women in the South during Reconstruction, whose descendants became part of the "mixed nation" of the U.S. South and have largely disappeared from history. For one Chinese family's century-old saga of intermarriage over several generations that intertwined with developments in Los Angeles' Chinatown, see Lisa See, *On Gold Mountain* (New York: St. Martin's Press, 1995).

31. For example, see Shirley Hune, *Teaching Asian American Women's History* (Washington, D.C.: American Historical Association, 1997); Shirley Hune, "Doing Gender with a Feminist Gaze: Toward a Historical Reconstruction of Asian America," in *Contemporary Asian American*, ed. Min Zhou and James V. Gatewood (New York: New York University Press, 2000), 413–430; Sucheta Mazumdar, "Beyond Bound Feet: Relocating Asian American Women," *Magazine of History* 10, no. 4 (summer 1996): 23–27; and Sucheta Mazumdar, "General Introduction: A Woman-Centered Perspective on Asian American History," in *Making Waves*, by Asian Women United of California (Boston: Beacon Press, 1989), 1–22; and Gary Okihiro, *Margins and Mainstreams* (Seattle: University of Washington Press, 1994), chap. 3.

32. Women of color are treated as objects in other fields as well. Sociologist Patricia Hill Collins discusses the ways in which African American women have been treated as objects of sociological knowledge in *Fighting Words* (Minneapolis: University of Minnesota Press, 1998), chap. 3. She finds that it is not until after 1970, when black women become a critical mass as sociologists, that African American women are treated as subjects and agents of sociological knowledge.

33. See note 32. I make the same observation as Patricia Hills Collins. It is with the appearance of a critical mass of Asian American women historians after the 1980s that Chinese American and other Asian American women are increasingly treated as subjects and agents of history.

34. Cheng Hirata, "Free, Indentured, Enslaved." See also her chapter, "Chinese Immigrant Women in Nineteenth-Century California," in *Women of America: A History*, ed. Carol Berkin and Mary Beth Norton (Boston: Houghton Mifflin Co., 1979), 223–244.

35. Ibid.

36. George Anthony Peffer was the first to emphasize the significance of the Page Law. See his works, "Forbidden Families: Emigration Experiences of Chinese Women under the Page Law, 1875–1882," *Journal of American Ethnic History* 6 (fall 1986): 28–46; "From under the Sojourner's Shadow: A Historiographical Study of Chinese Female Immigration to America, 1852–1882," *Journal of American Ethnic History* 11 (spring 1992): 41–67; and *If They Don't Bring Their Women Here: Chinese Female Immigration before Exclusion* (Urbana: University of Illinois Press, 1999). See Sucheng Chan, "The Exclusion of Chinese Women, 1870–1943," in *Entry Denied: Exclusion and the Chinese Community in America, 1882–1943*, ed. Sucheng Chan (Philadelphia: Temple University Press, 1991), 94–146.

37. Sucheta Mazumdar, "What Happened to the Women? Chinese and Indian Male Migration to the United States in Global Perspective," in *Asian/Pacific Islander American Women*, ed. Hune and Nomura, 58–74; and Adam McKeown, "Transnational Chinese Families and Chinese Exclusion, 1875–1943," *Journal of American Ethnic History* 18, no. 2 (winter 1999): 73–110. See also Madeline Y. Hsu, *Dreaming of Gold, Dreaming of Home: Transnationalism and Migration between the United States and South China, 1882–1943* (Stanford, Calif.: Stanford University Press, 2000), for new findings on the ways in which Chinese men in the United States and Chinese women in rural China adapted to their prolonged long-distance separation from one another.

38. Ronald Takaki, *Strangers from a Different Shore: A History of Asian Americans* (New York: Penguin Books, 1989), 111–112.

39. Jennifer Gee, "Housewives, Men's Villages, Sexual Respectability: Gender and the Interrogation of Asian Women at the Angel Island Immigration Station," in *Asian/Pacific Islander American Women*, ed. Hune and Nomura, 90–105.

40. Erika Lee, *At America's Gates: Chinese Immigration during the Exclusion Era, 1882–1943* (Chapel Hill: University of North Carolina Press, 2003), 12. She addresses Chinese women specifically in "Exclusion Acts: Chinese Women during the Chinese Exclusion Era, 1882–1943," in *Asian/Pacific Islander American Women*, ed. Hune and Nomura, 77–89.

41. Lee, "Exclusion Acts."

42. Judy Yung, *Unbound Feet: A Social History of Chinese Women in San Francisco* (Berkeley: University of California Press, 1995).

43. Yung, *Unbound Feet*. In the complementary volume, *Unbound Voices* (Berkeley: University of California Press, 1999), Judy Yung brings together many of the oral histories, women's testimonies and writings, and related materials upon which *Unbound Feet* was based to allow the women to speak for themselves directly through their own documents.

44. Ling, *Surviving on the Gold Mountain*. See also Huping Ling's "'Hop Alley': Myth and Reality of the St. Louis Chinatown, 1860s–1930s," *Journal of Urban History* 28, no. 2 (January 2002): 184–219.

45. Ling, *Surviving on the Gold Mountain*; and Huping Ling, "Family and Marriage of Late-Nineteenth and Early-Twentieth Century Chinese Immigrant Women," *Journal of American Ethnic History* 19, no. 2 (winter 2000): 43–63. See also an earlier work on the economic strategies of Chinese American families by sociologist Evelyn Nakano Glenn, "Split Household, Small Producer, and Dual Wage Earner," *Journal of Marriage and Family* 45, no. 1 (February 1983): 35–48.

46. Ling, *Surviving on the Gold Mountain*; and Huping Ling, "A History of Chinese Female Students in the United States, 1880s–1990s," *Journal of American Ethnic History* 16, no. 3 (spring 1997): 81–109.

47. Judy Tzu-Chun Wu, "'Loveliest Daughter of Our Ancient Cathay!' Representations of Ethnic and Gender Identity in the Miss Chinatown U.S.A. Beauty Pageant," *Journal of Social History* (fall 1997): 5–31. See also Shirley Jennifer Lim, "Contested Beauty: Asian American Women's Cultural Citizenship during the Early Cold War Era," in *Asian/Pacific Islander American Women*, ed. Hune and Nomura, 188–204.

48. Alien dependents of World War II veterans, which included Chinese American veterans, were admitted without quota limits through the 1945 War Brides Act. This was extended to fiancées and fiancés of war veterans in 1946. The Chinese Alien Wives of American Citizens Act in 1946 allowed for additional entrees outside the quota that applied to

Chinese wives of U.S. citizens. Xiaojian Zhao, *Remaking Chinese America: Immigration, Family, and Community, 1940–1965* (New Brunswick, N.J.: Rutgers University Press, 2002), 1.

49. Zhao, *Remaking Chinese America*, especially chap. 6.

50. Xiaolan Bao, *Holding Up More than Half the Sky: Chinese Women Garment Workers in New York City, 1948–1992* (Urbana: University of Illinois Press, 2001). See also Bao's "Politicizing Motherhood: Chinese Garment Workers' Campaign for Daycare Centers in New York City, 1977–1982," in *Asian/Pacific Islander American Women*, ed. Hune and Nomura, 286–300.

51. Trinity A. Ordona, "Asian Lesbians in San Francisco: Struggles to Create a Safe Space, 1970s–1980s," in *Asian/Pacific Islander American Women*, ed. Hune and Nomura, 319–334.

52. Annette White-Parks, *Sui Sin Far/Edith Maude Eaton: A Literary Biography* (Urbana: University of Illinois Press, 1995).

53. Judy Tzu-Chun Wu, *Doctor Mom Chung of the Fair-Haired Bastards: The Life of a Wartime Celebrity* (Berkeley: University of California Press, 2005).

54. See Anthony B. Chan, *Perpetually Cool: The Many Lives of Anna May Wong (1905–1961)* (Lanham, Md.: Scarecrow Press, 2003); and Graham Russell Gao Hodges, *Anna May Wong: From Laundryman's Daughter to Hollywood Legend* (New York: Palgrave Macmillan, 2004).

55. Sociologists have given more attention to analyzing how gender, race, and class together influence the lives and relationships of Asian American women and men. One such work grounded in history is Yen Le Espiritu's *Asian American Women and Men: Labor, Laws, and Love* (Thousand Oaks: Sage Publications, 1997).

56. For examples, see Hune, "Doing Gender with a Feminist Gaze."

57. Aihwa Ong, *Flexible Citizenship* (Durham: Duke University, 1999).

10

Migrations and Destinations

Reflections on the Histories of U.S. Immigrant Women

DONNA R. GABACCIA
VICKI L. RUIZ

In the 1975 motion picture *Hester Street* Carol Kane earned an Oscar nomination for her role as Gitl, a young Eastern European Jewish matron who struggled to make a place for herself in New York's Lower East Side and in the process win back the affections of her thoroughly Americanized husband, Jake. Based on a story by Abraham Cahan, the founder of the *Jewish Daily Forward*, the film captured everyday life and tensions over acculturation and gendered expectations set against the backdrop of a gritty, turn-of-the-twentieth-century New York neighborhood.[1] Feature films that portray immigration through women's eyes are few, yet even the critically acclaimed *Hester Street* was shown primarily at art house venues. At the time of its opening, *Hester Street*'s main themes — of accommodation, Americanization, wage work, commercialized leisure, and family — were becoming the focus of study for an emerging new generation of feminist historians. But like the motion picture itself, this scholarship on gender and migration seemed to attract limited notice.

In 1991, co-author Donna Gabaccia asked readers of the *Journal of American Ethnic History* to ponder why the by-then large and still growing literature on immigrant women in the United States had had such limited recognition and impact on both immigration and women's history. She argued that studies of immigrant women, like many immigrant women themselves, seemed "nowhere at home."[2] In this chapter, we revisit that question, offering both a more positive assessment of the continued vigor of scholarship on immigrant women in the United States and a preliminary assessment of the research that has appeared in the intervening fifteen years. Rather than attempt to summarize both gendered and women-centered studies, we focus on studies on immigrant women in the United States written by historians (and a few historically minded social scientists). We acknowledge the transnational approaches that have sought to "internationalize" U.S. history while also identifying four themes that we believe best characterize recent historical work on immigrant women in the

United States: making a home, community building, memory, and citizenship. These themes that have emerged in studies of women across many different backgrounds might in the near future provide a firm basis for satisfying work of synthesis.

Transnational Analysis

The movie *Hester Street* begins with Gitl's arrival in Ellis Island. Most U.S. historians, too, have concentrated on immigrants once they land on American soil. Their focus is decidedly on the peopling of America, not on human mobility. During the early 1990s, scholars began to assert that such narratives failed to capture the experiences of contemporary immigrants whose lives could not be articulated solely within national boundaries. Feminist anthropologists interested in migration to the United States from the Caribbean were among the first to theorize transnationalism as both a new methodology for the study of immigration and as an apt descriptor for migrants who maintained as a matter of course communication, social ties, and identities between more than one nation.[3]

Of course, even before theories of transnationalism were elaborated, some historians of immigration had voiced incisive critiques of assimilationist paradigms. Indeed, historians of immigration from Theodore Blegen in the 1920s to Frank Thistlethwaite in the 1960s had argued for analysis of migration as a form of lived connection between nations. In his benchmark 1964 essay in the *Journal of American History*, Rudolph Vecoli soundly rejected Oscar Handlin's portraits of immigrants as uprooted.[4] High rates of return and of transience among earlier migrants had become well known already by the 1980s.

Nevertheless, analysis of migrants' transnational lives definitely increased during the 1990s as discussions of globalization became ever more heated. Some of the most extensive work on immigrant women from a transnational gaze has focused on Italians, a group that scattered widely around the world for over a century; studies of "Italians everywhere" helped create models for scholars to problematize, to refine, and to place in comparative perspective the growing numbers of studies on U.S. immigrant women. Italianists, for example, studied women who did not become subjects of scrutiny by traditional immigration historians either because the women had remained in Italy while the men migrated or because they had journeyed to other European or Latin American nations as single parents or in the company of other women or as family members. Many of the chapters in Donna Gabaccia and Franca Iacovetta's *Women, Gender, and Transnational Lives* also trace the movement of ideas of female emancipation and revolutionary activism through anarchist and anarcho-syndicalist migratory networks, linking women's activism in cities as scattered as Buenos Aires, New York, and the mining towns of Illinois.[5]

Transnational analysis reveals how migration transforms as well as connects the United States and other countries around the world. Much scholarship has focused on the recruitment abroad of men's labor for heavy industry, transportation, and agriculture — from forging steel in Pittsburgh to repairing railroad tracks near Topeka to picking cotton outside of Fresno.[6] But under what conditions have women been recruited transnationally for their labor? Catherine Ceniza Choy's study of nurses, *Empire of Care*, elucidates how women's migration has had long-term consequences in both sending and receiving societies. Although Filipina nurses were recruited to alleviate an American "shortage" of nurses, in fact, the ratios of nurses per residents in the United States were already six to seven times higher than they were in the Philippines.[7]

In short, transnational lives and consequences were scarcely new in the 1990s, even though new forms of communications and transportation technologies have made connections easier and more widespread than in the past. It seems unlikely, however, that many U.S. immigration historians will choose to explore world history, to expand their geographies of research, to master new languages, and to delve into archives beyond the United States. Throughout the 1990s the majority of scholars preferred to remain closer to their training and teaching in American history and often turned their attention to micro-level studies (e.g., of specific neighborhoods and/or work spaces). An awareness of the transnational frame around such local places, however, forced historians of immigrant women to problematize even the meaning of home among mobile people who arrive as immigrants in the United States.

Where Is Home?

The task for a woman, like Gitl in *Hester Street*, was as much to make a home as to find one. This theme is cogently captured in Yen Le Espiritu's benchmark book, *Home Bound: Filipino American Lives across Cultures, Communities, and Countries.* In analyzing the diachronous images of home among Filipino immigrants and their families, she describes home making as "the processes by which diverse subjects imagine and make themselves at home in various geographic locations." Similarly, Donna Gabaccia notes elements of both permanence and transiency within Italian communities over a century ago as individuals and households engaged in shifting transnational journeys.[8] More than a metaphor, making home also required enormous investments of women's physical and emotional labor, as Suzanne Sinke's study of nineteenth-century Dutch immigrant women confirms.[9]

Building homes could require rather than negate transnational connections. Lili M. Kim's study of Korean picture brides to Hawaii makes clear the transnational bonds women cherished, especially in their fund-raising efforts for the cause of Korean independence. Some immigrant women reached beyond their racial/ethnic communities. Rumi Yasutake's *Transnational Women's Activism* recounts how women in Japan formed their own chapters of the Women's Christian Temperance Union. When some of these club women journeyed east, they joined their Euro American allies in proselytizing for the cause of temperance in addition to offering social services for their compatriots in California.[10]

Sorting through these varied narrative threads about home and place has invigorated the field of gender and migration studies in part by turning it toward cultural history. Into her study of working-class Mexican women in Chicago during the 1920s and 1930s, Gabriela Arredondo introduces the concept of "lived regionalities" in which women's past experiences and knowledge "shape the lens through which they live and understand their lives." Through the use of demography, archival research, and oral interviews, Carmen Teresa Whalen deftly connects Philadelphia and Puerto Rico through individual stories of migration, community histories of organizations, and the impact of global assembly lines. Her monograph *From Puerto Rico to Philadelphia* provides an astute gendered exploration of transnationalism as lived experience with women's wage and civic labor at the forefront of creating communities and making home.[11]

For many second-generation teenagers across gender, race, ethnicity, and region, popular culture also looms large in defining their own social locations as comfortable and home-like. Though she erases ethnicity, Nan Enstad in *Ladies of Labor, Girls of Adventure* imaginatively interprets the power of mass fiction, fashion, and film in the lives of Jewish and Italian dressmakers. She examines the contradictions and possibilities inherent in the everyday life of a typical garment worker in New York City at the turn of the century: a young woman could hold a picket sign in one hand while adjusting her feathered hat with the other.[12] Race and ethnicity, however, were hardly silent partners in this dance of cultural negotiations and formations.[13] Taking the debate over racial/ethnic women's consumer consciousness into the cold war, Shirley Jennifer Lim in *A Feeling of Belonging: Asian American Women's Public Culture, 1930–1960* contends that young women "claimed a place in the nation" through participation in beauty contests, sororities, and other mainstream heteronormative pursuits typical of 1950s adolescents.[14]

While a "feeling of belonging" can be performed through consumer culture, this sense of affiliation can also be discerned through moments of political activism, art, and paid employment. For example, chronicling Chicana participation in the 1975 International Women's Year Conference in Mexico City, Marisela R. Chávez elaborates on the development of a global consciousness among these young feminists, but a consciousness tempered for them at the time by the disconcerting realization that they were, in fact, Americans. Rather than being accepted as sisters in the struggle by third world participants, they found themselves unflatteringly lumped together with the majority of the U.S. delegation who ignored them. Seeking to fuse sexual and cultural identities within her avant-garde work that combined photography, drama, and raw natural materials, Cuban American performance artist Ana Mendieta enacted a feminist consciousness that incorporated indigenous and Afro-Cuban beliefs.[15]

Elaborating on the elasticity of identity, class, and employment, Yen Le Espirtu emphasizes the impact of differential inclusion that leaves even affluent Filipinos subject to nativism and uncertain about where they belong. Indeed, the immigrant woman as a middle-class professional or entrepreneur complicates standard ethnic migration narratives of upward mobility as providing direct entry into mainstream America. As Diane Vecchio notes in her study of Italians in Milwaukee, Wisconsin, and Endicott, New York, women instead created niches for themselves within ethnic communities through their gendered roles as midwives and merchants.[16] In contrast, Mary Ann Villarreal explores the lives of Mexican American women in Texas who operated local cantinas and dance halls, appropriating for profit a very male-identified public space, albeit one still within the ethnic group itself. The preservation of reputation emerges as a salient theme even for women with prestigious professions; they were never above community scrutiny. Dr. Margaret Chung, the first Chinese American woman physician, was not welcomed by the club women profiled in Judy Yung's *Unbound Feet*. As Judy Wu reveals in her fascinating biography of Chung, the good doctor, as a single female with no local family connections, found a chilly reception in San Francisco; however, undaunted, she built a lucrative practice by catering to Euro Americans who ventured into Chinatown as medical tourists.[17] This sampling of recent scholarship on immigrant ethnic women as entrepreneurs and professionals offers fresh direction by imbricating gender and migration within the new business history. The most recent studies of immigrant women have been particularly effective in demonstrating how communities of mobile people meld interior, exterior, and imagined spaces into homes where work, family, business, and identity formation intersect.

Communities in Motion

In a sense the marriage of *Hester Street's* Gitl and her husband, Jake, foundered on their differing definitions and expectations of themselves in relation to their compatriots. In exploring the creation of communities (whether rooted in place, culture, religion, a shared past, or contemporary interests) social historians of immigrant women for the past fifteen years have continued to rely on the building blocks of race, class, and gender. Within immigrant communities, scholars now seek clues to the construction of ethnic understandings of manhood and womanhood that supplement or even sometimes undermine gendered notions of American individualism. Immigrant communities inevitably link private and public worlds, making them ideal sites for exploring how men and women negotiate and evaluate the connections and cross-currents of sexuality, family, and work in communal ways across generations.

Two monographs published during the early 1980s foreshadowed many of the new directions in gender and American migration studies. Virginia Sánchez Korrol's *From Colonia to Community* and Judith Smith's *Family Connections* illuminated the ways in which women, in partnership and conflict with men, built local institutions in New York and Providence neighborhoods, engaged in politics, and worked in the formal and informal economies while simultaneously seemingly adhering to traditional familial roles.[18] Other studies focused primarily on women's experiences, turning the tables on earlier works in ethnic and immigration studies where women appeared only as domestic scenery. Vicki L. Ruiz's *Cannery Women, Cannery Lives* tells the story of how Mexican women in East Los Angeles made common cause with their Euro American (predominantly Jewish) co-workers and neighbors to nurture a grassroots union that substantively improved their wages and working conditions. Also from a community studies perspective rich in oral history, Judy Yung's *Unbound Feet* provides an engaging gendered generational history demonstrating how Chinese American women in San Francisco during the early decades of the twentieth century created their own personal spaces and how they forged with one another a network of clubs and associations that contributed to a cohesive ethos predicated on family, culture, and social location.[19]

Most immigrant women and their daughters, while visible within their own neighborhoods, received scant public notice. In *Common Sense and a Little Fire*, Annelise Orleck offers rich biographical portraits of Jewish labor activists Clara Lemlich, Rosa Schneiderman, Pauline Newman, and Fannia Cohn, who captured the public imagination during the New York City Shirtwaist Strike of 1909 and two years later the Triangle Fire. In concert with Alice Wexler's path-breaking biography of Emma Goldman, *Common Sense and a Little Fire* brings out women's political consciousness, attributed, in part, to the lessons they learned in their villages in Eastern Europe and in New York's Lower East Side.[20] Of course, women's leadership extended beyond the shop floor, local clubs, and noted individuals. Joyce Antler's *The Journey Home: How Jewish Women Shaped Modern America* encompasses a sweeping survey of political activism among Jewish women during the twentieth century, couching struggles for social justice within a Jewish American domestic sensibility. Social justice as intertwined with feminism, Chicano nationalism, and liberation theology emerges in Lara Medina's *Las Hermanas*. This innovative national group of nuns and laywomen strive to meet the spiritual and material needs of their neighbors though Alinsky-style political mobilization.[21]

Whether understood as physical locale, organizational space, or transnational imaginary, community as it appears in these works is never static but instead constantly fluid, dynamic, and shifting in unanticipated directions. In *Farming the Home Place*, Valerie J. Matsumoto underscores the calibrations of change among Japanese Americans within Cortez, a tightly knit community in rural California. From the years of initial settlement to the tragedy of internment to the suburbanization of the San Joaquin Valley, Matsumoto offers an intricately detailed study of economic and cultural adaptations by four generations of women and men who have called Cortez home.[22]

For well over half a century, scholars of U.S. immigration also have interrogated generational cleavages within communities and, particularly, the tensions that arose between parents and children. In *Southern Discomfort*, Nancy A. Hewitt explains how constructions of race influenced ethnic identification among the children of Cuban immigrants. While these Spanish-speaking immigrants of varying complexions built ethnic community networks, trade unions, and political associations, their children's sense of themselves became predicated on their own racial location in the Jim Crow South where, not surprisingly, Afro-Cubans developed a greater affiliation and kinship with African Americans. Generational conflicts extend beyond individual families. Matt García in *A World of Its Own* reveals the fault lines of generation, gender, and citizenship in the suburbs of southern California, especially tensions between Mexican *braceros* and Mexican American men. Conversely, García smartly delineates a Mexican American youth culture of the 1940s and 1950s where Mexican American teenagers mixed and mingled with their Euro American and African American peers through popular music.[23]

Situating migration, settlement, and generational change through the lens of gender, Carol McKibben in *Beyond Cannery Row* demonstrates that women were the primary decision makers for the migration process, for the building of ethnic community institutions, and in the second and third generations for entrepreneurship that enabled families to stay in Monterey, California, after the collapse of the fishing industry. Her thick descriptions of cannery work are so vivid that the reader can almost smell the fish and shiver in the foggy dampness of the open-air plant. In elaborating on the intertwined nature of public and private obligations, McKibben teases out the ways in which perception and reputation influence the community standing of women as much as occupation and family background.[24]

Recent studies of community-building and activism, much like recent studies of home-building and transnationalism, have continued to draw on the methods and insights of earlier social histories, while also adding insights from cultural studies and biography. The cultural turn, in particular, has also introduced a new dimension to discussions of the immigrant experience, notably, the way in which immigrants have remembered and attempted to preserve their own histories, both in the United States and abroad.

Memory

Hester Street not only obliterates Gitl's and Jake's lives in Russia, prior to migration, but leaves us without a clear sense of how they will remember their conflicted marriage once they have spent a lifetime in America. In interrogating the multivalent strands of making community, home, and a living, memory must also be taken into account as an increasingly central element in our understanding of the impact of mobility on human lives. Many of the books mentioned in this chapter imbricate oral narratives in ways that provide prescient, intimate descriptions of gender in the every day as well as insight into how individuals create meaning in their own lives and shape the lives of others. In linking intertexuality and mobility, historians often rely on memory, personal and collective, as conveyed through speech and written texts or as embedded in buildings and landmarks. Public historian Lydia Otero chronicles the efforts to salvage from urban redevelopment La Placita in Tucson, Arizona, by Mexican American preservationists, for as local leader Alva Torres explained, "The buildings are not the people but they are part of the story that you try to save."[25]

Physical spaces, when layered with personal, cultural, or religious associations, loom large in the memories and experiences of immigrant women. In *Memories and Migrations*, a group of Latina historians, including Otero, examine the reciprocal relationships between memory and place, the ways in which region itself and memories of region mold individual and collective identities. The relationship between physical place and memory lends to a fuller recounting of the lives of immigrant women, one that ventures beyond the level of observed experience.

While often personal and culturally specific, the making of communities, homes, and memories also shapes conceptions and practices of citizenship. Social historians have tended to privilege the agency of individuals, but other scholars, influenced by law and political science, emphasize the critical point that foreigners, while diverse among themselves, are also a distinctive group within American law. Providing a path toward synthesis, histories that tackle legislation, public policy, and the law provide a powerful conceptual counterweight to micro-level community studies, especially around issues of citizenship.

Citizenship

The development of whiteness studies and critical race studies in the 1990s alerted scholars to the fundamental ways in which the American nation has been racialized since its origins.[26] That observation, in turn, has encouraged scholars to recognize women newcomers as a distinctive group of aliens and thus as a logical choice for analyzing citizenship, borders, and U.S. policies such as admission and naturalization. Studies of citizenship, naturalization, and immigration policies helped to reveal what the foreign and female of diverse backgrounds shared, as well as pointing to the ways in which race and class complicated the gendering of American law and the implementation of law as policy both at the boundaries of the United States and in the regulation of everyday immigrant life within the United States.

Studies of immigrant populations have made special contributions to our changing understandings of American citizenship as a mode of incorporation or assimilation. No longer do scholars treat citizenship as a timeless legal and juridical concept based on a sense and obligation of civic culture and enfranchisement. With case studies set in the South, Southwest, California, and Hawaii during the Gilded Age and Progressive eras, Evelyn Nakano Glenn's *Unequal Freedom* demonstrates how gender, race, and class constructed boundaries around American citizenship, creating fundamentally different routes to the privileges of citizenship for immigrant men and women from differing parts of the world.[27] Still, the promise of full citizenship also has provided the grounds for immigrant women, like other disenfranchised groups, to mobilize for civil rights and social justice.

Much like Glenn, Candice Bredbenner, Alexandra Stern, and Natalia Molina in their recent books have focused on issues of citizenship and belonging in the American nation as they have affected the foreign-born and especially female minorities racialized as non-white. In *A Nationality of Her Own*, Bredbenner contrasts how changing notions of the attainment of citizenship through marriage affected foreign-born and native-born women. The former sometimes became American citizens without wanting to do so while the latter on occasion could even lose their status as birthright citizens and become stateless. For example, a woman born on U.S. soil could lose her citizenship if she married a man ineligible for naturalization and citizenship, as were all men from Asia before 1943. Bredbenner traces women's mobilization against these inequities, putting into comparative and global perspective U.S. policies. She provides ample evidence of the complicated ways that the laws of citizenship, the practices of both American and immigrant patriarchy, and the low wages paid women could render foreign-born women vulnerable to deportation.[28]

Alexandra Stern's *Eugenic Nation* and Natalia Molina's *Fit to Be Citizens?* are more interested in nation and nation-building and in cultural and social location than in juridical status or citizenship per se. Both point to how widely the American nation was understood to be as a biologically reproducing human group. Building on Gary Gerstle's distinction between "racial" and civic nationalism, *Eugenic Nation* deepens our knowledge of eugenics in the day-to-day as Stern narrates how immigrants, especially Mexican immigrants, are framed within a discourse of disease and intellectual dimness. From the border disinfecting stations (even spraying *braceros* with DDT during World War II) to the massive repatriations and deportations of the 1930s to the sterilization cases in Los Angeles during the 1970s and beyond, Mexicans have borne the brunt of eugenic-infused public health, education, and social welfare policies. Similarly, Natalia Molina not only examines the ways in which racial ideologies become wrapped in the language of scientific objectivity of public health but also the impact of these ideologies as public health praxis. She creatively uncovers how Mexican, Chinese, and Japanese immigrants both utilized and avoided public health services, historicizing their individual agency within a larger framework of social and economic stratification in Los Angeles.[29]

Equally innovative work has explored the gendering of U.S. borders, with some of the most prescient studies focusing on the exclusion of people from Asia.

Erika Lee interrogates meanings of manhood among the Chinese, including both the perspectives of the immigrants themselves and those of U.S. policy makers and politicians. She is especially mindful of the power of the state in shaping the contours of entry. At the gates, so to speak, in the naturalization and regulation of citizenship, women's sexuality, morality, and reproductive capacity have also been central concerns of immigration officials. Sensitive to the moral discourses evoked in the name of border security, Eithne Luibhéid argues that immigration control has been even more important in actively reproducing heterosexual identities as normative and in reinforcing the gendered consequences of class and race for immigrant women who are not married. She seems especially concerned with how immigration policy helped to make heterosexuality "official" and the ways that border agents maintain considerable discretion on whom to exclude.[30]

Martha Gardner's *The Qualities of a Citizen* digs deep into U.S. law and the case files of the Immigration and Naturalization Service, extending and enriching Luibhéid's observations about how immigration and naturalization laws create racial and gender categories. But while Luibhéid focuses mainly on sexuality, Gardner traces linkages among work, morality, marriage, and childbearing. The book is especially helpful in understanding the ambiguities surrounding immigration restrictions and provisions for family reunification. It provides readers with detailed case studies on the complex relationship among fears of women becoming "public charges," their high rates of detention and exclusion, and the enforcement of heterosexuality and marriage through restrictive immigration policies.[31]

By focusing attention on the borders needed to define nations, scholarship on women immigrants as aliens and potential citizens reminds readers that the long-standing issue of the relationship between pluralism and unity persists down to the present as a major theme in American nation-building. While historians of immigrant women have continued to emphasize diversity among the many groups of immigrants in the United States, the new scholarship on citizenship also can be juxtaposed with commonalities emerging from studies of home, community, and memory across race and ethnicity to suggest not one but many new paths toward synthesis.

The One and the Many

Most specialists in immigration history have emphasized how ethnic pluralism in American history was rooted in the legacy of diversity among immigrants. For much of the 1970s and 1980s, immigration historians seemed interested mainly in documenting and explaining the proliferation of and distinctions among ethnic groups and identities among European immigrants of differing backgrounds. By contrast, during the 1970s many cultural feminists assumed that women shared a number of key experiences across cultures, regardless of race, class, or ethnicity. By the 1990s, such assumptions had fallen to critiques undertaken by specialists on race and racialization; increasingly, historians of women became interested in how ethnicity along with race, nationality, and gender had been constructed and how these changed over time.[32]

Not surprisingly, then, a larger synthesis remains elusive. Studies of particular groups of immigrant women, often in particular places, have burgeoned, but few scholars have attempted to pull these studies together into a national narrative. After a flurry of interdisciplinary anthologies and review essays in the late 1980s and early 1990s, few scholars have even bothered to review the newest historical research.[33] The few books on immigrant women that have drawn on women of many origins most often have collected primary sources and oral histories. Such approaches — popular in women's history since the 1970s — offer vibrant but at times poorly contextualized portraits of individual women. Only Maxine Seller's second edition of *Immigrant Women* (which added sources and narratives by newer immigrants) was organized around broad themes.[34]

One study that did attempt synthesis was Donna Gabaccia's *From the Other Side*. Breaking with the then-current models of immigration history (studies of immigrant life in East Coast cities or encyclopedic accounts of individual ethnic groups), this book compared the lives of all immigrant women, past and present. It showed how global economic change and nation- and empire-building sparked a transition from male- to female-majority migrations and called attention to the gendered impacts of U.S. migration policies on immigrant women. Furthermore, Gabaccia challenged readers to consider women's adjustment to life in the United States not as a form of "emancipation" but rather as "domestication" and highlighted the points of contact among foreign-born women and between immigrants and native-born black and white women. *From the Other Side* also devoted an entire chapter to middle-class immigrants, a group that grew proportionately across the twentieth century. But at a time when most historians and social scientists believed that contemporary immigrations diverged sharply from past patterns, *From the Other Side* seemed well outside the mainstream.[35]

Studies of Asian and Asian American women offer exciting possibilities for studying the long term, comparing successive waves of immigration, past and present, and across national and ethnic groups. Here scholars could usefully build on the volume compiled by Shirley Hune and Gail Nomura to tackle the ways in which the very diverse class and educational backgrounds of immigrant women from Asia over time have reinforced, challenged, and confounded older notions of women as part of the generalized immigrant trope of "huddled masses."[36] The possibilities for interdisciplinary dialogue with the many social scientists and literary scholars interested in women's narratives generated by Asia's diasporas seem particularly rich.

Still, other recent studies have suggested ways to generate useful generalizations on a smaller scale. Studies of East Coast working-class women focused on immigrant women of various backgrounds. A collaborative research project by historians from Europe, led by Christiane Harzig, examined four groups of immigrant women in Chicago — a method Nancy Green has labeled "convergent comparison."[37] Increasingly, too, the burgeoning field of whiteness studies, which focused on how European immigrants acquired white identities, offered an interpretively powerful opportunity to draw together histories of many groups. Unfortunately, among the proliferating studies of Italians, Irish, and Jewish whiteness, only a handful tackled systematically the gendering of racialization itself.[38] In a chapter included in this volume, Vicki L. Ruiz traces the racialized yet gendered contours of Chicana/o history over the last twenty years, problematizing notions of *mestizaje* (*morena/o*), whiteness (*blanca/o*), and cultural coalescence (*café con leche*), teasing out the situational nature of racial constructs in the historical (and the historians') moment.[39]

The reclamation in recent scholarship of belonging — whether in community networks or transnational imaginaries — also has addressed a fundamental and persisting concern in historical discourse about immigration: the tension between structure and agency. Richard Ivan Jobs and Patrick McDevitt posit that the "agency/structure divide is not really a dichotomy . . . [but] an ongoing process of negotiation. Instead of looking away, this Janus confronts itself in conversation, argument, and dialogue." They continue, "We as historians have the challenge of accounting for the manner in which individuals acted within the constraints and possibilities of their broader social world to fashion their own sense of place and community through interpersonal relationships."[40] That challenge has remained at the heart of U.S. immigrant and ethnic women's history over the last two decades.

With increasingly diverse student populations in our classrooms, the field of immigration history remains more salient than ever. Whether in Berlin, New York, North Carolina, Pennsylvania, Minnesota, Texas, Arizona, or California (the places where the two of us have taught over the course of the past twenty-five years), our undergraduates embody both the journeys of transnational migration and an enduring belief in American opportunities. Even when contemporary structures — of economic inequality, immigration policy, or crowded universities — sharply constrain their choices (as they often do), our students' desires for home and for belonging remain strong. They continually generate new experiences that redefine them as "Americans."

Works of synthesis could, it seems, draw on many of these common themes. While daunted by the task of actually co-authoring a big book on immigrant women, we might point at least to a collection of essays that we, ourselves, recently edited (with the evocative title *American Dreaming, Global Realities: Re-Thinking U.S. Immigration History*) as one possible route forward. Placing gender at its center, *American Dreaming, Global Realities* explores the ways in which immigrants and their children are shaped simultaneously by transnational bonds, globalization, family loyalties, and personal choices. In shifting the debate away from models of linear assimilation, we consider how the many pluralities — the very specific historical, economic, regional, familial, and cultural contexts of immigrants' lives — encourage interaction, connection, and a sense of belonging. In laying a foundation for a future synthesis, we must interrogate the many individual and collective journeys that cross the boundaries of national states, while recognizing the shared yearnings that motivate human mobility.[41]

NOTES

Vicki L. Ruiz thanks Victor Becerra for his many years of love, laughter, encouragement, patience, support, and marvelous meals. Donna Gabaccia thanks the other members of the SSRC Working Group on Gender and Migration — Katharine Donato, Jennifer Holdaway, Martin Manalansan, and Patricia Pessar — who inspired some of the thoughts reflected here. We extend our gratitude to John J. Bukowczyk at the *Journal of American Ethnic History* for allowing us to reprint our essay.

1. *Hester Street* (1975), produced by Raphael D. Silver, 90 minutes, videocassette.

2. Donna R. Gabaccia, "Immigrant Women: Nowhere at Home?" *Journal of American Ethnic History* 10, no. 4 (summer 1991): 61–87.

3. Most historians who have adopted the transnational paradigm cite as inspiration two collected volumes co-edited by anthropologists of the Caribbean, Nina Glick Schiller, Linda Basch, and Cristina Szanton Blach. See Nina Glick Schiller et al., eds., *Towards a Transnational Perspective on Migration: Race, Class, Ethnicity, and Nationalism Reconsidered* (New York: New York Academy of Sciences, 1992); and Nina Glick Schiller et al., eds., *Nations Unbound: Transnational Projects, Postcolonial Predicaments, and Deterritorialized Nation-States* (Langhorne, Pa.: Gordon and Breach, 1994). Other path-breaking references would include Eugenia Georges, *The Making of a Transnational Community: Migration, Development, and Cultural Change in the Dominican Republic* (New York: Columbia University Press, 1990); and Patricia R. Pessar and Sherri Grasmuck, *Between Two Islands: Dominican International Migration* (Berkeley: University of California Press, 1991).

4. Theodore C. Blegen, *Norwegian Migration to America* (Northfield, Minn.: Norwegian American Historical Association, 1931–1940); Frank Thistlethwaite, "Migration from Europe Overseas in the Nineteenth and Twentieth Centuries," XIe Congrès Internationa des Sciences Historiques, *Rapports*, vol. 5 (Uppsala, 1960), 32–60; Rudolph Vecoli, "Contadini in Chicago: A Critique of The Uprooted," *Journal of American History* 51, no. 3 (December 1964): 404–417.

5. Donna R. Gabaccia and Franca Iacovetta, eds., *Women, Gender, and Transnational Lives: Italian Workers of the World* (Toronto: University of Toronto Press, 2002); Linda Reeder, *Widows in White: Migration and the Transformation of Rural Italian Women, Sicily, 1880–1920* (Toronto: University of Toronto Press, 2003).

6. Recent examples of this literature include Gunther Peck, *Reinventing Free Labor: Padrones and Immigrant Workers in the North American West, 1880–1930* (New York: Cambridge University Press, 2000); and Gilbert G. González, *Culture of Empire: American Writers, Mexico, and Mexican Immigrants, 1880–1930* (Austin: University of Texas Press, 2004).

7. Catherine Ceniza Choy, *Empire of Care: Nursing and Migration in Filipino American History* (Durham: Duke University Press, 2003).

8. Yen Le Espiritu, *Home Bound: Filipino American Lives across Cultures, Communities, and Countries* (Berkeley: University of California Press, 2003), esp. 2; Donna Gabaccia, "When the Migrants Are Men: Italy's Women and Transnationalism as a Working-Class

Way of Life," in *Women, Gender, and Labour Migration: Historical and Global Perspectives*, ed. Pamela Sharpe (London and New York: Routlege, 2001), 190–208.

9. Suzanne M. Sinke, *Dutch Immigrant Women in the United States, 1880–1920* (Urbana: University of Illinois Press, 2002).

10. Lili M. Kim, "Redefining the Boundaries of Traditional Roles: Korean Picture Brides, Pioneer Immigrant Women, and Their Benevolent Nationalism in Hawai'i," in *Asian/Pacific Islander American Women: A Historical Anthology*, ed. Shirley Hune and Gail M. Nomura (New York: New York University Press, 2003), 106–119; Rumi Yasutake, *Transnational Women's Activism: The United States, Japan, and Japanese Immigrant Communities in California, 1859–1920* (New York: New York University Press, 2004).

11. Gabriela F. Arredondo, "Lived Regionalities: Mujeridad in Chicago, 1920–1940," in *Memories and Migrations: Mapping Boricua and Chicana Histories*, ed. Vicki L. Ruiz and John R. Chávez (Urbana: University of Illinois Press, forthcoming); Carmen Teresa Whalen, *From Puerto Rico to Philadelphia: Puerto Rican Workers and Postwar Economies* (Philadelphia: Temple University Press, 2001).

12. Nan Enstad, *Ladies of Labor, Girls of Adventure: Working Women, Popular Culture, and Labor Politics at the Turn of the Twentieth Century* (New York: Columbia University Press, 1999).

13. A plethora of literature addresses the tensions and transformations in racial/ethnic communities over "American" cultural norms and consumer pursuits, especially among young women. As an example, see Vicki L. Ruiz, *From Out of the Shadows: Mexican Women in Twentieth-Century America* (New York: Oxford University Press, 1998), esp. 51–71, "The Flapper and the Chaperone."

14. Shirley Jennifer Lim, *A Feeling of Belonging: Asian American Women's Public Culture, 1930–1960* (New York: New York University Press, 2006).

15. Marisela R.Chávez, "Pilgrimage to the Homeland: California Chicanas and International Women's Year, Mexico City, 1975,"in *Memories and Migrations*, ed. Ruiz and Chávez; Carlos A. Cruz, "Ana Mendieta's Art: A Journey through Her Life," in *Latina Legacies: Identity, Biography, and Community*, ed. Vicki L. Ruiz and Virginia Sánchez Korrol (New York: Oxford University Press, 2005), 225–239.

16. Espiritu, *Home Bound*; Diane C. Vecchio, *Merchants, Midwives, and Laboring Women: Italian Migrant Women in Urban America* (Urbana: University of Illinois Press, 2006).

17. Mary Ann Villarreal, "*Cantantes y Cantineras*: Mexican American Communities and the Mapping of Public Space" (PhD diss., Arizona State University, 2003); Judy Tzu-Chun Wu, *Doctor Mom Chung of the Fair-Haired Bastards: The Life of a Wartime Celebrity* (Berkeley: University of California Press, 2005).

18. Virginia Sánchez Korrol, *From Colonia to Community: The History of Puerto Ricans in New York City, 1917–1948* (Westport, Conn.: Greenwood Press, 1983); Judith E. Smith, *Family Connections: A History of Italian and Jewish Immigrant Lives in Providence, Rhode Island, 1900–1940* (Albany: State University of New York Press, 1985).

19. Vicki L. Ruiz, *Cannery Women, Cannery Lives: Mexican Women, Unionization, and the California Food Processing Industry, 1930–1950* (Albuquerque: University of New Mexico Press, 1987); Judy Yung, *Unbound Feet: A Social History of Chinese Women in San Francisco* (Berkeley: University of California Press, 1995).

20. Annelise Orleck, *Common Sense and a Little Fire: Women and Working-Class Politics in the United States, 1900–1965* (Chapel Hill: University of North Carolina Press, 1995); Alice Wexler, *Emma Goldman: An Intimate Life* (New York: Pantheon Books 1984).

21. Joyce Antler, *The Journey Home: How Jewish Women Shaped Modern America* (New York: Schocken Books, 1997); Lara Medina, *Las Hermanas: Chicana/Latina Religious-Political Activism in the U.S. Catholic Church* (Philadelphia: Temple University Press 2004).

22. Valerie J. Matsumoto, *Farming the Home Place: A Japanese American Community in California, 1919–1982* (Ithaca, N.Y.: Cornell University Press, 1993).

23. Nancy A. Hewitt, *Southern Discomfort: Women's Activism in Tampa Florida, 1880s to 1920s* (Urbana: University of Illinois Press, 2001); Matt García, *A World of Its Own: Race, Labor, and Class in the Making of Greater Los Angeles, 1900–1970* (Chapel Hill: University of North Carolina Press, 2002).

24. Carol McKibben, *Beyond Cannery Row: Sicilian Women, Immigration, and Community in Monterey, California, 1915–1999* (Urbana: University of Illinois Press, 2006).

25. Alva Torres quoted in Lydia R. Otero, "La Placita Committee: Claiming Place and History," in *Memories and Migrations*, ed. Ruiz and Chávez.

26. Gary Gerstle, *American Crucible: Race and Nation in the Twentieth Century* (Princeton: Princeton University Press, 2001).

27. Evelyn Nakano Glenn, *Unequal Freedom: How Race and Gender Shaped American Citizenship and Labor* (Cambridge, Mass.: Harvard University Press, 2002).

28. Candice Lewis Bredbenner, *A Nationality of Her Own: Women, Marriage, and the Law of Citizenship* (Berkeley: University of California Press, 1998).

29. Alexandra Stern, *Eugenic Nation: Faults and Frontiers of Better Breeding in Modern America* (Berkeley: University of California Press, 2005); Natalia Molina, *Fit to Be Citizens? Public Health and Race in Los Angeles, 1879–1939* (Berkeley: University of California Press, 2006).

30. As examples of this rich literature, see George Anthony Peffer, *If They Don't Bring Their Women Here: Chinese Female Immigration before Exclusion* (Urbana: University of Illinois Press, 1999); Erika Lee, *At America's Gates: Chinese Immigration during the Exclusion Era, 1882–1943* (Chapel Hill: University of North Carolina Press, 2003); and Eithne Luibhéid, *Entry Denied: Controlling Sexuality at the Border* (Minneapolis: University of Minnesota Press, 2002). See also Eithne Luibéid and Lionel Cantú Jr., eds., *Queer Migrations: Sexuality, U.S. Citizenship, and Border Crossings*, (Minneapolis: University of Minnesota Press, 2005).

31. Martha Mabie Gardner, *The Qualities of a Citizen: Women, Immigration, and Citizenship, 1870–1975* (Princeton: Princeton University Press, 2005).

32. Werner Sollors, ed., *The Invention of Ethnicity* (New York: Oxford University Press, 1991); Kathleen Neils Conzen et al., "The Invention of Ethnicity: A Perspective from the USA," *Journal of American Ethnic History* 12, no. 1 (fall 1992): 3–43. For a prescient critique of cultural feminism, see Peggy Pascoe, *Relations of Rescue: The Search for Female Moral Authority in the American West, 1874–1939* (New York: Oxford University Press, 1990), xiii–xxiii.

33. For an early effort, see Doris Weatherford, *Foreign and Female: Immigrant Women in America, 1840–1930* (New York: Schocken Books, 1986). An exception, of course, is this volume.

34. Maxine Schwartz Seller, ed., *Immigrant Women*, 2nd ed. (Albany: State University of New York, 1994). Kristine Leach's *In Search of a Common Ground: Nineteenth and Twentieth Century Immigrant Women in America* (San Francisco: Austin & Winfield, 1995) is an exceptionally short work based almost exclusively on oral histories and the author's interviews. An innovative if largely policy-oriented work that compares resiliency and duality of identity and orientation in immigrant women's narratives is Roni Berger's *Immigrant Women Tell Their Stories* (New York: Haworth Press, 2004).

35. Donna Gabaccia, *From the Other Side: Women, Gender, and Immigrant Life in the United States* (Bloomington: Indiana University Press, 1994). Social scientists who bother to read the work of historians more recently have reached different conclusions. See Nancy Foner, *In a New Land: A Comparative View of Immigration* (New York: New York University Press, 2005).

36. See Hune and Nomura, *Asian/Pacific Islander American Women*.

37. Randy D. McBee, *Dance Hall Days: Intimacy and Leisure among Working-Class Immigrants in the United States* (New York: New York University Press, 2000); Daniel Soyer, ed., *A Coat of Many Colors: Immigration, Globalism, and Reform in the New York City Garment Industry* (New York: Fordham University Press, 2005); Robyn Burnett and Ken Luebbering, *Immigrant Women in the Settlement of Missouri* (Columbia: University of Missouri Press, 2005); Christiane Harzig, ed., *Peasant Maids, City Women: From the European Countryside to Urban America* (Ithaca, N.Y.: Cornell University Press, 1997); Nancy Green, "The Comparative Method and Post-structural Structuralism: New Perspectives for Migration Studies," *Journal of American Ethnic History* 13, no. 4 (summer 1994): 3–22.

38. Here the starting place remains Ruth Frankenberg, *White Women, Race Matters: The Social Construction of Whiteness* (Minneapolis: University of Minnesota Press, 1993). See also Karen Brodkin, *How Jews Became White and What That Says about Race in America* (New Brunswick: Rutgers University Press, 1998).

39. Vicki L. Ruiz, "*Morena/o, Blanca/o, y Café con Leche*: Racial Constructions in Chicana/o Historiography" in this volume.

40. Richard Ivan Jobs and Patrick McDevitt, "Introduction: Where the Hell Are the People?" *Journal of Social History* 39, no. 2 (winter 2005): 309–314, esp. 310–311.

41. Donna R. Gabaccia and Vicki L. Ruiz, eds., *American Dreaming, Global Realities: Re-Thinking U.S. Immigration History* (Urbana: University of Illinois Press, 2006).

11

African American Women and Migration

LESLIE BROWN

Theresa Jan Cameron Lyons was born on the Cameron Plantation, near Durham, North Carolina, the granddaughter of slaves. Her grandfather's death left her uncles as the only men on the farm, and when the sheriff arrested them, she recalled, "The landlord made us move because we didn't have anyone to plow with the mules." The family — now all women and girls — moved to another place. Lyons's mother, Janie Riley, took in laundry to supplement their income, and Lyons was hired as a day laborer at a neighboring farm. Giving up the land, the family moved to the city of Durham in the late 1930s, where Riley found work as a domestic for a local merchant. In the 1940s, a new option opened, and Riley moved to Portsmouth, Virginia, where she got a job in a shipyard. She kept in touch by letter and package, but did not return to Durham until the war ended and women were sent back home.[1]

Corinne Mable Browne's recently widowed mother went to New York in 1918, right after Browne was born, encouraged by her sister. Browne and her six siblings stayed behind with her grandparents, who farmed on St. Helena Island, South Carolina. Browne's mother found employment, like her sister, as a household worker. When Browne's grandmother passed away in 1924, the seven children were divided among friends and family to be raised. Browne was brought up by her grandfather. Her memories of her mother were tied to holidays and special occasions, times when her mother sent gifts. "I looked forward to boxes coming down for Christmas. I remember when I was baptized she sent me this little velvet outfit." Browne married and remained on St. Helena.[2]

In a groundbreaking essay, "The Great Migration to the Midwest: The Gender Dimension," historian Darlene Clark Hine revived a discourse about the Great Migration with a research agenda that considered the experiences of black women as migrants. Noting "an egregious void" in the scholarship, Hine pointed out that African American woman are missing from most studies of this significant upheaval of people, even though they played fundamental roles. That

African Americans traded their southern rural roots for northern urban residences was one of the most striking transformations to occur in the history of black people in the United States. Migration not only fundamentally reshaped the African American experience, it also changed the nation. At its height, the Great Migrations of the 1910s and the 1940s witnessed more men than women leave the South for the urban north. But it seems historically imprecise that migration studies have excluded women altogether or written them into only ancillary parts of the narrative. "Until the differences between the processes and consequences of migration to black men and to black women are fully researched," Hine reasoned, "no comprehensive synthesis or portrait of the migrants is possible."[3]

By problematizing this significant historical process, Hine challenges scholars in African American history, African American women's history, and urban history to ask new questions about black migration and to consider its implications with regard to family, community, core institutions, and gender relations. Looking beyond the period between World War I and World War II, reviewing historiographies of migration, reinterpreting familiar sources, drawing on oral history, and rereading the census, this essay complicates the narrative of black migration by centering women. Mobility, I argue, has existed as a gendered exercise of freedom, and the conditions that encouraged black women's migration differed from those that facilitated black men's migration. Women's perspectives, furthermore, speak to black migrations as other than South to North movements that happened only over a short span of time.

Rising to the challenges of womanist scholarship, an array of community studies and monographs has expanded the depth and breadth of black history and black women's history in particular.[4] Among them complex analyses of race, gender, class, sexuality, religiosity, and other themes complement accounts of social and political activism at the local and national level and finely textured community studies that capture discord and unity.[5] By writing its own theory of multiple jeopardies and reading racial metalanguages, black women's history has succeeded — some would say has led the field of women's history — in addressing multiple perspectives. And, in virtually all of the most recent work of African American women's history, migration runs like a common strand or, if we might return to Elsa Barkley Brown's metaphor of quilting to describe African American women's history, like a thread stitching together pieces of the story. Big loose stitches of migration material hold an unfinished quilt of African American women and migration together while allowing each piece to stand out individually.[6] Tightly drawn, however, the thread facilitates our ability to view a pattern emerging within the patchwork of black women's stories.[7]

Because contemporary researchers surveyed men as the head of the household, they rarely asked black women about their reasons for relocating. Thus the research on African American women's migration requires its students to identify and even create sources, to preserve them as well as study them, but also to listen for the silences and the reasoning related to black women's lives within debates on gender and history. Accordingly, some of the most recent work on women and migration — for example, Beverly Bunch-Lyon's study of migration to Cincinnati, Elizabeth Clark-Lewis's book on black domestic workers in Washington, D.C., and Gretchen Lemke-Santangelo's analysis of women and work in wartime California — utilize oral history to capture the stories of women and their migrations. Oral history collections like the Behind the Veil Project Collection at Duke University and the Southern Oral History Project Collection at University of North Carolina at Chapel Hill document the details of women's everyday lives in the South. The Black Women in the Midwest Oral Project at the Indiana Historical Society provides a store of materials on the daily and organizational lives of black women in Illinois and Indiana. Also revealing are the interviews with those who made significant contributions in professional or voluntary work collected as the Black Women Oral History Project, conducted by the Schlesinger Library. These sources of women's voices offer intricate clues to how migrations proceeded.[8]

Missing Women Found

Scholars — contemporary and current — generally have looked to the Great Migration as a singular demographic turning point in the black American story. As an internal labor migration of low-wage workers, the Great Migration was, according to sociologist Carole Marks, "the first mass movement out of the South, the beginning of significant industrial employment, and the initial exercising of the rights of citizenship." Shaped by the wartime forces of urbanization, industrialization, and opportunity, on the one hand, and discrimination, violence, and economic insecurity, on the other, African Americans looked to the promise of enhanced economic, political, and social freedoms in the North. Marks describes the typical migrant as "a black male between the ages of twenty-five and thirty-four, resident of a medium sized southern city who had worked between five and ten years at one of two industrial enterprises, usually as an unskilled laborer."[9]

Marks makes a point of critiquing the absence of women from the historiography of migration, but she gives them very little attention in her analysis. Yet she is not alone in portraying the Great Migration essentially as a men's movement that linked increased employment among black males to their role as the family breadwinner and male leadership of the race. By focusing on the World War I and II eras, on the industrialized North, and on labor and union organizing, scholars like James R. Grossman on Chicago and Kenneth Kusmer on Cleveland draw attention to the drama of the movement, the travel across great distances, and the conflict inherent to labor relations between white and black male workers. Joe William Trotter Jr.'s study of Milwaukee opens the door to the class dimension of migration studies; yet, his portrait of proletarianization reflects little about women. Similarly, in exploring effects of the Great Migration on the black church and its leaders, Milton C. Sernett analyzes this core institution as an oft-overlooked yet vital component of the migration picture, but he makes only passing reference to women, either as migrants or as congregants.[10]

The virtual absence of women from migration studies is curious in light of the many familiar texts where women and migration appear. Ida B. Wells, for instance, left Holly Springs, Mississippi, for Memphis, and when banned from that city, she moved to Chicago. Madame C. J. Walker, born Sarah Breedlove, left Louisiana with her sister to work the cotton fields of the Mississippi Delta. From there she moved to St. Louis, Denver, Indianapolis, and finally New York City. Charlotte Hawkins Brown, born in Henderson, North Carolina, went north for her education and then returned to the Tar Heel State to open her school, Palmer Memorial Institute. Jane Edna Hunter, from Pendleton, South Carolina, received advanced training in nursing and a law degree. In Cleveland, where she settled, she founded the Working Girls Association (later the Phillis Wheatley Association) to assist other black women who migrated from the South to the North. In New York City, Victoria Earle Matthews established the White Rose Mission with the same purpose in mind, to train and support the young black women who moved to the city in search of work. The theme of women's migration comes out repeatedly in literature as well: Helga Crane leaves Naxos in the South for Chicago, then Harlem, and then back to Alabama in Nella Larsen's *Quicksand;* Mary Rambo had moved North and settled in New York City several years before she takes in Ralph Ellison's protagonist in *Invisible Man*, a novel of the Great Migration. In Gloria Naylor's *The Women of Brewster Place*, Mattie Michael and her best friend, Etta Mae Johnson, leave the South, the former after a beating by her father and the latter to start again after so many failed relationships. Zora Neale Hurston herself left Florida in time to catch the closing years of the Harlem Renaissance. Black women migrants are captured in "Ironers," in the art of Jacob Lawrence, who himself migrated with his mother to Philadelphia and then New York; and migration underlies Langston Hughes's poems about "Madam" ("Madam and Her Madam" and "Madam and the Census Man," for example, from *The Selected Poems of Langston Hughes*). And notably, blues women like Bessie Smith and Ma Rainey left behind tedious lives in the South, seeking the excitement, opportunity, and challenges of new fields in entertainment.[11]

Indeed, relooking at the standard narrative shows that women always numbered among the migrants of the African diaspora, the enslaved who traveled to the New World, the runaways who looked north to freedom, those sold away to the Deep South at the height of the antebellum period, those who were freed by masters or families, and those who freed themselves. Writing about black women, Jacqueline Jones argues that migration was always central to African American women's economic lives. In a similar vein, Tera W. Hunter observes that one way that black women exercised freedom after emancipation was to move from plantations to farms and from rural districts to the South's expanding towns and cities. Freedwomen looked to nearby cities not only seeking work, but also searching for family, safety, community, the Freedmen's Bureau, and a place to sell their wares, a process that continued well beyond Reconstruction.[12] Nell Irvin Painter describes their travels westward with the Exoduster movement after Reconstruction to Kansas, Nebraska, Indiana, and Oklahoma with their families. By the end of the nineteenth century, African American women also had streamed westward to the Pacific coast, to California, Oregon, and Washington, according to Quintard Taylor and Shirley Ann Wilson Moore, as well as northward to the Midwest and the Northeast. The flow of women's migration, then, had begun well before the First Great Migration of the World War I years.[13]

One of the most remarkable and repetitive themes of migration scholarship points to the remarkable consistency of black women's migration experiences over time, despite changes in the nation's economic, political, and cultural life. For example, African American women who migrated for economic reasons found their options limited even outside of the South. Household labor as cooks, laundresses, maids, nurses, and domestic servants remained the most common employment options available, even if those jobs were the least desirable. In fact, as David M. Katzman details, the number of black women working in service increased while the number of white women in the same occupational category declined. In 1920, African American women held over 60 percent of the domestic workers' jobs in Chicago, 70 percent of those in New York City, and 80 percent in Philadelphia. By 1950 almost half of all black women workers still were employed as domestics, and as late as 1970, a quarter of black women laborers worked in service. In exceptional cases, during World War I and II and in the southern tobacco industry, African American women's urban employment shifted to include some positions in manufacturing. Yet even these jobs reiterated the antebellum structure they had always known, the subservient work of service and industry.[14]

In addition, census data record the constant movement of black women out of the rural South. The census provides only a rough measure of how many black women relocated, where they migrated from or to, or their proportion among migrating populations at various points in time. But the data leave little doubt that African American women moved away from rural districts and toward the cities of the South and the North in greater numbers than men, as long-term analyses surmise. To quote one 1960 census monograph, "cumulatively, Negro females have evidenced slightly higher out-migration rates from the rural Secessionist South than Negro males" and "levels of in-migration to the urban regions of the Northeast and Midwest as well as the South were greater for Negro females than for Negro males." Given their proportional dominance in black urban populations, then, this transition bears investigation.[15]

Correspondingly, African American females have outnumbered males in urban populations for about as long as there have been cities. As both Richard C. Wade and Leonard P. Curry found, during the antebellum period black female slaves and freedwomen outnumbered male slaves and freedmen in urban areas, including Baltimore, Charleston, Mobile, New Orleans, Norfolk, Richmond, St. Louis, Savannah, and Washington, D.C. W.E.B. Du Bois writing in 1899 and Leslie M. Harris writing a century later found the same demographic, respectively, in Philadelphia and New York City.[16]

Southern cities swelled with the black female population, but a world of better employment and living conditions also drew women northward at the end of the nineteenth century, a trend that did not escape the notice of black scholars at the time. By 1900, it was clear that black female predominance in the African American urban population was the usual pattern.[17] According to the 1910 census, women formed the majority in two-thirds of the major cities of the North and West, and in 87 percent of large southern cities. A glance toward the five American cities with the largest black populations in 1930 (those with a population of over 50,000 of whom at least 10,000 were black) reveals that in New York, Philadelphia, Baltimore, and Washington women attained statistical advantage. Chicago was the one exception of the five, but its position as the site of exhaustive migration studies undoubtedly helped distort the demographic pattern. By 1930 black females outnumbered males in all but one southern city (Wilmington, Delaware); and although they briefly lost their numerical predominance in some northern cities at the 1920 census, they regained it by the end of that decade, outnumbering men in 60 percent of the major cities of the North, Midwest, and West. Those cities where males numerically dominated tended to be sites where men could find significant employment in heavy industry such as shipping, steel and automobile making, or meat packing: Akron, Cincinnati, Cleveland, Columbus, Dayton, Toledo, and Youngstown, Ohio; Camden, New Jersey; Buffalo, New York; Gary, Indiana; Omaha, Nebraska; and Pittsburgh, Pennsylvania.[18]

This demography challenges several conventional generalizations about black migration. First, as Earl Lewis indicates, most African Americans did not leave the South, and as late as 1970 more than half of the country's black population resided below the Mason-Dixon Line.[19] Second, following the path of women migrants, it is clear that intra-regional migrations carried African Americans to southern cities as well as to northern ones. Third, when seen in the broader context of black migration since Emancipation, the Great Migration periods, the 1910s and 1940s, were anomalous events set against a steadily increasing outflow of a mostly female population. Finally, it was not mostly men, but generally women, who left the land and the family behind; men maintained a remarkable statistical advantage in the rural South.

The census records suggest, then, that women carved out the migration streams that flowed in subsequent years and forged the migration chains that linked family and community across regions. As pioneers in the cities, women laid the foundations for black community development and institution building. They built the cross-regional networks of kith and kin that continue to link black people throughout the nation. One result of women's migration was what Hine calls "the southernization" of the urban North, as migrants brought with them their own food, folkways, patterns of speech, cultural forms, and social networks. And while many women connected with relatives and friends from their old home in their new home, many others managed alone, finding their way by knocking on doors for housing and work. Historian Deborah Gray White asserts that because many members had made the arduous trip themselves, women's church groups, women's clubs, literary societies, and branches of the Young Women's Christian Association — institutions where black women played significant roles — attended to female migrants' adjustment to urban life by providing information, encouraging literacy, and sometimes enforcing community standards of decorum. Among national organizations founded in this context, Dorothy Salem notes the Association for the Protection of Colored Women (AFPCW) and the National League for Protection of Colored Women, which were started by white reformer Frances A. Kellor, were the forerunners of the National Urban League, whose purpose it became to address migration issues. As this assemblage, meshed it contributed to black women's expanding participation in community politics, according to Evelyn Brooks Higginbotham, and after the passage of the Nineteenth Amendment in 1920, African American women migrants increased black voter rolls, especially in northern cities.[20]

The Women Problem

In short, black urbanization from migration to settlement was a feminized process, a cause of consternation for social scientists of the era. The purpose of black social science work was to contend that African Americans could effectively negotiate dominant gender norms and mainstream values. For early twentieth-century scholars sensitive to whites' criticism of black people, a focus on women's migration highlighted a female-centered family paradigm that implied men's inaction or fallibility. These social scientists' considerations of women's migration spoke to the dangers posed by city life for women alone and the uncertainties, ambiguities, and disruptions to family life and home, precariously accruing with the concentration of women among the urban population migration. Social scientists thus connected the over-population of black women with the origins of urban problems. For if women were not central to scholarly analyses of black migration of the time, they were central to discussions about urban problems: black family dysfunction, social disruption, juvenile delinquency, and dependency. As Jonathan Scott Holloway observes in his book about Abram Harris, E. Franklin Frazier, and Ralph Bunche, black social scientists of the era asserted that the plight of African American women was due to flaws in their moral character.[21] Writing about Philadelphia, for instance, Du Bois argued that "lack of respect for the marriage bond, inconsiderate entrance into it, and bad household economy and family government" encouraged illicit sexual arrangements and immoral behavior.[22]

Obsessed with urban morality, unattached women, and female headed-households, scholars and observers of the era signaled an early alarm regarding the skewed sex ratio between black men and women. "The predominance of the female element is perhaps the most striking phenomenon of the urban Negro population," wrote Dean Kelly Miller of Howard University in 1905. Indeed, as Hazel Carby points out, the preponderance of female migration provoked such commentators to declare a "moral crisis," a social problem central to race relations at the beginning of the twentieth century. Miller, for instance, was not pleased. Ostensibly single and without male supervision, "these left-over, or to-be-left-over Negro women," Miller judged, "falling as they do in large part in the lower stratum of society, miss the inhibitive restraint of culture and social pride, and, especially if they be comely of appearance, become the easy prey of the evil designs of both races."[23]

The census raised contemporary activists' anxieties, particularly over sex ratios. By the beginning of the twentieth century, urban progressives like Miller viewed gendered urbanization as an unfavorable harbinger of overcrowding, unemployment, poverty, and strained class and race relations that were sure to grow and spread as migration increased. "These surplus women present a pressing social problem which calls for immediate and special treatment," Miller cautioned. At the same time, he recognized that economic push and pull factors encouraged female migration. "Negro women rush to the city in disproportionate numbers because in the country there is little demand for such services as they can render." Meanwhile, back at home, "the compensation of rural workers is so meager that the man alone cannot earn a reasonable livelihood for the whole family." In a similar analysis coming at the end of the First Great Migration, Du Bois argued, "The Negroes are put in a particularly difficult position, because the wage of the male breadwinner is below standard, while the openings for colored women in certain lines of domestic work, and now in industries are many. Thus while toil holds the father and brother in the country and town at low wages, the sisters and mothers are called to the city." Matching his observations with the census trend, Du Bois observed, "Negro women outnumber men nine or ten to eight in many cities."[24]

Reading the Census, Again

Coupled with the comments of W.E.B. Du Bois and Kelly Miller, the census provides a particularly interesting way to contest the assumption that men left the farm and the women behind. Measuring the number of males per one hundred females, the sex ratio indicates the statistical balance between the number of males and females in a given population. A ratio of less than 100 indicates that females outnumber males and, conversely, a ratio that exceeds 100 denotes a male majority of the population. For African Americans in the South in 1930, the urban sex ratio was 86.2; for rural areas it was 100.8. In the West-South central (into the Black Belt states of Louisiana, Mississippi, and Alabama), the ratio was 102.5, leaning toward men; and in rural farm areas, specifically, it tilted toward males even more at 103.1.[25]

As they should, scholars of the African American experience look at the census with skepticism, arguing that black men were undercounted, thus creating the skewed sex ratio for African Americans. For instance, between 1910 and 1930, the sex ratio for blacks declined from 99 to 97, suggesting that as migration streams flowed, the mobile male population made men more difficult to enumerate. If this is the case, the 1930 census missed some 180,000 black males in the count. Added to the urban population, this figure still would not bring the black population to a statistically even sex ratio in the cities. The recalculation, moreover, does not explain the wide disparity between males and females in rural areas. In addition, social scientists have suggested that the undercounted men could be found among transients, street corner men, and lodgers, which may be true. It could also be argued, however, that women also were transient, women also were lodgers, and many a street corner man belonged to a family who counted him.[26] And, too, African American women, especially southern migrants, were cautious about white male officials — census takers — and did not necessarily give their full cooperation in counting the number of people actually living in their households, relatives or roomers.

In other words, it is likely that women were also undercounted. Census data alone do not capture the complexities and subtleties in African American household and family arrangements, historian Kimberly L. Phillips reasons, as migration of family members scattered and returned. "What census enumerator," she asks, "could recreate the route and meanings of family ties and boarding relationships" that characterized black family and community links? Phillips provides an excellent example of kith and kin networks in action. William Davenport left Montgomery, Alabama, for Cleveland, where he settled with his father's brother and wife, who had previously made the trip. "Four years later the household included not only Davenport, but pregnant and recently widowed Ocelie Johnson and her two small children as well. This expanded household, however, was apparently not simply an impersonal economic arrangement: Johnson had known the family of Davenport's uncle's wife. By 1924, Johnson had married William Davenport."[27]

At the time and on the ground, however, black migration demanded that black leaders, scholars, and theorists respond to questions that had no straightforward answer. In 1917 W.T.B. Williams, black advisor to a number of white philanthropic organizations, admitted confusion about the process underway. Unable to decipher an exact pattern of movement, he acknowledged: "The abnormal movement among the colored people is striking in many ways. It seems to be a general response to the call of better economic and social opportunities. The movement is without organization or leadership. The negroes [sic] just quietly move away without taking their recognized leaders into their confidence any more than they do the white people about them. . . . They rarely consult the white people, and never those who may exercise some control over their actions. They will not allow their own leaders to advise them against going North."[28]

Migration Activity

Williams's bewilderment suggests a portrait of black people carried away by unfathomable forces and overlooks a logic that caused women to lay down the patterns of black migration off the farms. The Great Migration and its constituent parts were mass self-movements and voluntary displacements that exemplified African Americans' self-activity. Both individuals and families decided which members should take the first step, when to move, and under what circumstances.[29] Black migration, furthermore, reflected the constraints and flexibilities of gender roles among families. For that reason, women's migrations were not necessarily linear, nor did economics provide the only reason they moved. Moreover, the migration stream did not necessarily run from South to North. Writing about professional working women, Stephanie Shaw discovered that because educated African American women from the North could not find suitable positions at home, they looked southward, accepting jobs in the black businesses and segregated institutions of the South where they could find work. Historian Francille Rusan Wilson makes this case for Sadie T. Mossell Alexander, the first black woman awarded a PhD in economics (from University of Pennsylvania). Alexander found her first job in the South, where she worked until she returned to Philadelphia to marry and attend law school. Dorothy Fletcher Steele, interviewed for the Behind the Veil Project, averred about her home town, "I knew I had to get out, [it] was stifling. Suffocating." Ironically, "in the Jim Crow car" Steele moved to Charlotte, North Carolina, where she taught for some fifty years. Going in the opposite direction, Mary Bodie and Addie Marie Faulk, two North Carolina teachers, described traveling to New York in the summer during the 1940s. There they worked as waitresses and found factory jobs to earn additional wages.[30]

Other narratives of women's nonlinear migration begin on the farm, but point toward multiple migrations, schemes made possible by a range of factors. Although they faced more limited job opportunities than white women or black men, black women from rural areas were the principal migrants to cities because cities provided them with wage options they could not find in the country. For example, because few rural landlords would rent to single women or to families who lacked adult male kin, female-headed households and families with mostly girls were especially likely to leave the farm. Widowhood, often brought about suddenly, presented particularly difficult economic circumstances. Given the high death rate among adult African American males, exacerbated by the heavy and dangerous work of those occupations where black men dominated — farming and unskilled industrial labor — it is not surprising that black urban populations included a high concentration of African American widows. Cities provided more viable economic options than rural areas for black women on their own.[31]

The vast majority of rural black families retained their status as sharecroppers and tenant farmers, rather than landowners, perpetually in debt. Women's farm labor provided little relief. The financial incentives that loosened women from the land differed from those that loosened men and favored female migration over male migration. In farming, the entire family operated as an economic unit to sustain self-sufficiency, but farming also functioned as an age- and gender-segregated enterprise where adaptable gender roles provided enough elasticity for members to play more than one part. Each member of the family, including youngsters and the elderly, contributed to the family's sustenance. Yet, farming traditions assigned men, women, and children to separate tasks. Although women could and did do any task required, the heavy work of plowing and harvesting was considered men's responsibility. All family members worked the fields, but women and children were assigned to the lighter tasks of making seedbeds, hand weeding and transplanting in the spring, the repetitive work of chopping and picking cotton, or the hand work of separating and drying tobacco leaves in the fall. Women's other work centered on the home, tending to family gardens and doing domestic chores. Women also carried the burdens of reproductive labor, bearing and caring for children, nursing the ill, and burying the dead. If the value of women's labor as a farmer failed to keep pace with the rising costs of seed, feed, fertilizer, tools, and other needs, family members could shift their labor resources to create alternatives. By assigning to males some female farm work, black folk who struggled to make a living on the land could lend female family members to urban areas to pursue other earnings.[32]

Delores Janiewski details how factories in the tobacco regions of Virginia, North Carolina, Tennessee, and Kentucky drew women to them. Black female workers provided the core workforce, providing an industrial option to domestic work. The agricultural cycle actually facilitated female migration — seasonal and long-term — from the country. The industrial calendar meshed with the agricultural calendar to favor women's migration during the farming lull. In the tobacco industry, green season — the time of year when the factories processed new tobacco — lasted from early May through mid-July, after the tobacco fields were plowed, planted, and thinned and before the crop was harvested. Growing up in Durham County, Mary Mebane recalled that during green season tobacco factories hired more than half of their workers, including African American women by the thousands. Conversely, the slow season at the factory, early spring, coincided with planting time on the farm, when all members' labor was necessary. After settling time, when whites had money and blacks had none, provisional positions for domestic workers expanded as white families hired black women who needed the income to do their household labor. Female factory workers who remained in the city shifted to fill the ranks of domestic laborers.[33]

Therefore, it was not unusual for black women to move back and forth between rural and urban areas in tune with the rhythm of family need, the labor market, and the agricultural seasons. Women who stayed on the farm might temporarily move to the city during factory season; just as women who had moved into town might return home to the farm to assist with planting. Tobacco towns like Durham and Winston-Salem, port cities like Charleston, New Orleans, and Memphis, and industrial centers like Birmingham and Richmond provided flexibility for black families from the surrounding countryside to sustain both their rural and urban labor efforts. Migration to nearby cities also enabled families to stay connected, even as members moved further on. Southern cities, then, presented viable, flexible, and familiar options for migration, allowing families to use multiple forms of labor. For those families who remained tethered to the land, the proximity of an urban center made it possible to accomplish several objectives.

Whether they moved to the North or remained in the South, however, black women's flexibility as laborers created a form of gender oppression that distanced them from their closest kin, subjected most of them to exploitation at low-wage, low-status jobs in service and industry, and marked them undesirable as migrants despite the demand for their labor. Work away from home doubled women's duties in the home or shifted the burdens of housework onto children, whose learned skills later transposed to paid household labor positions. Elizabeth Clark-Lewis describes the well-known pattern where older women, mothers, aunts, and sisters trained younger girls in household chores, laundry, food preparation, canning and preserving, and nurturing children. Considered "near-trained" by age seven, daughters could be called upon to migrate from farms to cities to assist in the households of female kin who had already migrated. It was not unusual to send girl children to northern cities to assist family members who had already moved or to take live-in positions as household workers.[34]

Many African American women migrants to both northern and southern cities found their hopes dashed. In terms of employment options, they discovered fewer economic opportunities than black men and faced greater economic discrimination than other women. For those who looked northward, unscrupulous labor agents replaced unscrupulous landlords; factory bosses replaced farm bosses. Incomes might have surpassed the earnings potential of the South, but the increasing costs of city living challenged the most frugal migrant's ability to save. North and South, employment patterns changed little; only a small number of positions in light factory work or the needle trades greeted black female workers who traveled to New York. African American women worked doing the same kinds of household labors they had done throughout their history. As late as the 1950s, most African American female laborers still worked as domestics regardless of the region where they lived.[35]

Because the kind of employment circumstances that African American women faced in northern and southern cities changed little over time and barely differed from place to place, other issues must have factored into their decisions to move. In addition to economic rationales for moving, African American women moved to escape sexual assault and exploitation by white men and domestic violence from male kin, to seek education for their children and for themselves, and to relieve the harsh labor of farm work. Although economics may have provided the impetus — women often spoke of "want[ing] to better [their] condition" — other reasons entered into the decision. Some traveled for the adventure and exploration, not planning to stay. Others who felt left behind joined friends who had gone ahead. Some moved in order to find marriageable men. As a form of liberation, African American women's migration represented their determination to protect themselves, to exercise independence, and to become agents of social change, as well as to manage their productive and reproductive capacities, evidenced by the decline of urban birthrates.

Out of this process black women developed what Hine calls a "culture of dissemblance," a form of personal secrecy wherein black women divulged little information about themselves to outsiders as a strategy of protection.[36] Remaining an enigma to many, black women's migration engaged economic issues as related to the family, but also resisted incursions on their personal lives by revealing scant private information.[37] Ephemeral, transient, and difficult to track, African American women's migration was itself a culture of dissemblance, enabling women migrants to reclaim a certain amount of autonomy and to undercut the kinds of gender exploitation they had known in the past.

This more specific and complex consideration of women's migration not only modifies a narrative of African American history, but contributes to a further understanding of current urban issues, the persistence of poverty, and concerns about the economic and social situations of black families. The focus on northern cities, furthermore, overlooks similar problems plaguing southern cities and the rural South as well. Current social scientists, like sociologist William Julius Wilson and the conservative Charles Murray, would do well to note that the black family has always been a multiple-worker, elastic institution that stretched across regions in order to sustain itself. Women's predominance in the urban population is not a new phenomenon. Moreover, social scientists who have worried about the problem of female-headed households, illegitimacy, and absent males have suggested that increased employment for men is a solution to the problem. Bringing a historical context to bear on current issues, Jacqueline Jones is quick to point out that working-class black women also lost ground in industry and domestic work due to white flight. Black families have always depended on those wages, and that absence has exacerbated their already fragile economic positions. Yet, the lamented loss of industrial employment from the cities disregards the historical position of working black women, both married and single, who accounted for the majority of migrants from the rural South and a significant portion of the black urban labor force.[38]

The movement of women from place to place suggests that an even greater migration occurred than the phenomenon of the war years, not simply because of the numbers of women as migrants but because of their significance in the migration narrative. The economic, social, and political roles that black women shaped as part of the migration scheme continue to illuminate their importance in the dynamics of changing black communities and sustaining families. The outcome of migration for African American women raises compelling questions about the historical implications of the current state of black urban life; a grasp of those implications that looks to gender may lend itself to greater understanding of the complexities of the nation's inner cities.

NOTES

1. Theresa Jan Cameron Lyons, interview by author, August 16, 1995, Behind the Veil Collection, John Hope Franklin Collection of African and African American Documentary, Special Collections Library, Duke University (hereinafter cited as BTV).

2. Corinne Mable Browne, interviewed by Tunga White, July 26, 1994, St. Helena Island, S.C., unedited transcript, BTV.

3. Darlene Clark Hine, "Black Migration to the Urban Midwest: The Gender Dimension," in *The Great Migration in Historical Perspective: New Dimensions of Race, Class, and Gender*, ed. Joe William Trotter, Jr. (Bloomington: Indiana University Press, 1991), 127–146.

4. Among community studies that include discussions of migration, see Sundiata Cha-Jua, *America's First Black Town: Brooklyn, IL, 1830–1915* (Urbana: University of Illinois Press, 2000); Allison Dorsey, *To Build Our Lives Together: Community Formation in Black Atlanta, 1875–1906* (Athens: University of Georgia Press, 2004); Kimberly L. Phillips, *Alabama North: African-American Migrants, Community, and Working-Class Activism in Cleveland, 1915–1945* (Urbana: University of Illinois Press, 1999); Jacqueline A. Rouse, *Lugenia Burns Hope: Black Southern Reformer* (Athens: University of Georgia Press, 1989); Victoria W. Wolcott, *Remaking Respectability: African American Women in Interwar Detroit* (Chapel Hill: University of North Carolina Press, 2000); Joe William Trotter, Jr., *Black Milwaukee: The Making of an Industrial Proletariat, 1915–1945* (Urbana: University of Illinois Press, 1985); Shirley Ann Wilson Moore, *To Place Our Deeds: The African American Community in Richmond, California, 1910–1963* (Berkeley: University of California Press, 2000); Quintard Taylor and Shirley Ann Wilson Moore, eds., *African American Women Confront the West, 1600–2000* (Norman: University of Oklahoma Press, 2004); Earl Lewis, *In Their Own Interests: Race, Class, and Power in Twentieth-Century Norfolk, Virginia* (Berkeley: University of California Press, 1993); Elsa Barkley Brown, "Negotiating and Transforming the Public Sphere: African American Political Life in the Transition from Slavery to Freedom," *Public Culture* 7 (1994): 107–146; Gretchen Lemke-Santangelo, *Abiding Courage: African American Migrant Women and the East Bay Community* (Chapel Hill: University of North Carolina Press, 1996); Beverly A. Bunch-Lyons, *Contested Terrain: African American Women Migrate from the South to Cincinnati, Ohio, 1900–1950* (New York: Routledge,

2002); Robert Gregg, *Sparks from the Anvil of Oppression: Philadelphia's African Methodists and Southern Migrants, 1890–1940* (Philadelphia: Temple University Press, 1993).

5. Some of the most recent works in African American women's history include Melinda Chateauvert, *Marching Together: Women of the Brotherhood of Sleeping Car Porters* (Urbana: University of Illinois Press, 1998); Deborah Gray White, *Too Heavy a Load: Black Women in Defense of Themselves, 1894–1994*; (New York: W. W. Norton, 1999); Angela Y. Davis, *Blues Legacies and Black Feminism: Gertrude "Ma" Rainey, Bessie Smith, and Billie Holiday* (New York: Vintage Books, 1999); Wolcott, *Remaking Respectability;* Yevette Richards, *Maida Springer: Pan-Africanist and International Labor Leader* (Pittsburgh: University of Pittsburgh Press, 2000); Lynn M. Hudson, *The Making of "Mammy Pleasant": A Black Entrepreneur in Nineteenth-Century San Francisco* (Urbana: University of Illinois Press, 2002); Barbara Ramsey, *Ella Baker and the Black Freedom Movement: A Radical Democratic Vision* (Chapel Hill: University of North Carolina Press, 2002); Julia Kirk Blackwelder, *Styling Jim Crow: African American Beauty Training during Segregation* (College Station: Texas A&M University Press, 2003); Michele Mitchell, *Righteous Propagation: African Americans and the Politics of Racial Destiny* (Chapel Hill: University of North Carolina Press, 2004); Annelise Orleck, *Storming Caesar's Palace: How Black Mothers Fought Their Own War on Poverty* (Boston: Beacon Press, 2005); Premilla Nadasen, *Welfare Warriors: The Welfare Rights Movement in the United* States (New York: Routledge Press, 2005); Christina Greene, *Our Separate Ways: Women and the Black Freedom Movement in Durham, North Carolina* (Chapel Hill: University of North Carolina Press, 2005); Kimberly Springer, *Living for the Revolution: Black Feminist Organizations, 1968–1980* (Durham, N.C.: Duke University Press, 2005); Buzzy Jackson, *A Bad Woman Feeling Good: Blues and the Women Who Sing Them* (New York: W. W. Norton, 2005); Kali N. Gross, *Colored Amazons: Crime, Violence, and Black Women in the City of Brotherly Love, 1880–1910* (Durham, N.C.: Duke University Press, 2006); Wilma King, *The Essence of Liberty: Free Black Women during the Slave Era* (Columbia: University of Missouri Press, 2006); Leslie Brown, *Upbuilding Black Durham: Gender, Class, and Black Community Development* (Chapel Hill: University of North Carolina Press, 2008).

6. Deborah K. King, "Multiple Jeopardy, Multiple Consciousness: The Context of Black Feminist Ideology," *Signs* 13 (autumn 1988): 42–72; Elsa Barkley Brown, "What Has Happened Here: The Politics of Difference in Women's History and Feminist Politics," *Feminist Studies* 18 (summer 1992): 295–312; Evelyn Brooks Higginbotham, "African American Women's History and the Metalanguage of Race," *Signs* 14, no. 2 (winter 1992): 251–274; Elsa Barkley Brown, "African-American Women's Quilting: A Framework for Conceptualizing and Teaching African-American Women's History," *Signs* 14, no. 4 (summer 1989): 921–929; Elsa Barkley Brown, "Womanist Consciousness: Maggie Lena Walker and the Independent Order of Saint Luke," Signs 14, no. 3 (spring 1989): 610–633; Jacquelyn Dowd Hall, "Partial Truths," *Signs* 14 (summer 1989): 902–911.

7. Histories that look at black women's migration specifically include Jacqueline Jones, *Labor of Love, Labor of Sorrow: Black Women, Families, and Work from Slavery to Present* (New York: Basic Books, 1985); Dolores E. Janiewski, *Sisterhood Denied: Race, Gender, and Class in a New South Community* (Philadelphia: Temple University Press, 1985); Lewis, *In Their Own Interests;* Earl Lewis, "Expectations, Economic Opportunities, and Life in the Industrial Age: Black Migration to Norfolk, Virginia, 1910–1945," in *The Great Migration in Historical Perspective,* ed. Trotter, 22–45; Elizabeth Clark-Lewis, *Living In, Living Out: African American Domestics in Washington, DC, 1910–1940* (Washington, D.C.: Smithsonian

Press, 1994); Lemke-Santangelo, *Abiding Courage;* Leslie Schwalm, *A Hard Fight for We: Women's Transition from Slavery to Freedom in South Carolina* (Urbana: University of Illinois Press, 1997); Tera W. Hunter, *To 'Joy My Freedom: Southern Black Women's Lives and Labors after the Civil War* (Cambridge, Mass.: Harvard University Press, 1997); Tera W. Hunter, "Domination and Resistance: The Politics of Wage Household Labor in New South Atlanta," *Labor History* 34 (spring/summer 1993): 205–255; Tera W. Hunter, " 'The Brotherly Love for Which This City Is Proverbial, Should Extend to All': The Everyday Lives of Working-Class Women in Philadelphia and Atlanta in the 1890s," in *The African American Urban Experience: Perspectives from the Colonial Period to the Present,* ed. Joe W. Trotter, Jr., with Earl Lewis and Tera W. Hunter (New York: Palgrave MacMillan, 2004), 76–98; Bunch-Lyons, *Contested Terrain.*

8. Clark-Lewis, *Living In, Living Out;* Lemke-Santangelo, *Abiding Courage;* Bunch-Lyons, *Contested Terrain.* Among recently published collections of oral history interviews with African Americans, see William H. Chafe et al., eds., *Remembering Jim Crow: African Americans Tell about Life in the Segregated South* (New York: New Press, 2001); and Timuel D. Black Jr., *Bridges of Memory: Chicago's First Wave of Black Migration* (Evanston: Northwestern University Press, 2003).

9. Carole Marks, *Farewell — We're Good and Gone: The Great Black Migration* (Bloomington: University of Indiana Press, 1989), 44.

10. James R. Grossman, *Land of Hope: Chicago, Black Southerners, and the Great Migration* (Chicago: University of Chicago Press, 1989); Kenneth Kusmer, *A Ghetto Takes Shape: Black Cleveland, 1870–1930* (Urbana: University of Illinois Press, 1976); Trotter, *Black Milwaukee;* Milton C. Sernett, *Bound for the Promised Land: African American Religion and the Great Migration* (Durham, N.C.: Duke University Press, 1997). Also see James Borchert, *Alley Life in Washington: Family, Community, Religion, and Folklife in the City, 1850–1970* (Urbana: University of Illinois Press, 1980); James N. Gregory, *The Southern Diaspora: How the Great Migrations of Black and White Southerners Transformed America* (Chapel Hill: University of North Carolina Press, 2005); Albert S. Broussard, *Black San Francisco: The Struggle for Racial Equality in the West, 1900–1954* (Lawrence: University Press of Kansas, 1993); Quintard Taylor, *In Search of the Racial Frontier: African Americans in the American West, 1828–1990* (New York: W. W. Norton, 1998); Peter Rachleff, *Black Labor in Richmond, 1865–1890* (repr., Urbana: University of Illinois Press, 1989); Peter Gottlieb, *Making Their Own Way: Southern Black Migration to Pittsburgh, 1916–1930* (Urbana: University of Illinois Press, 1987); Ira Katznelson, *Black Men, White Cities* (Chicago: University of Chicago Press, 1973); Heather Ann Thompson, *Whose Detroit? Politics, Labor, and Race in a Modern American City* (Ithaca, N.Y.: Cornell University Press, 2001); Nicholas Lemann, *The Promised Land: The Great Black Migration and How It Changed America* (New York: A. A. Knopf, 1991); Alferdteen Harrison, ed., *Black Exodus: The Great Migration from the American South* (Jackson: University Press of Mississippi, 1991); Elliott M. Rudwick, *Race Riot at East St. Louis, July 2, 1917* (Carbondale: Southern Illinois University Press, 1964).

11. On representations of migration in literature and art, see Farah Jasmine Griffin, *"Who Set You Flowin'?" The African American Migration Narrative* (New York: Oxford University Press, 1995); and Malaike Adero, ed., *Up South: Studies and Letters of This Century's African-American Migration* (New York: New Press, 1993). See also Nella Larsen, *Quicksand* (New York: A. A. Knopf, 1928); Ralph Ellison, *Invisible Man* (New York: Random House, 1952); Gloria Naylor, *The Women of Brewster Place* (New York: Viking Press, 1982).

12. Jones, *Labor of Love, Labor of Sorrow,* 73–78; Hunter, *To 'Joy My Freedom,* I, 21–22; Schwalm, *A Hard Fight for We,* 152. My thanks to Leslie Schwalm for pointing out that women would have been familiar with the city from moving back and forth with slave owners and that migration to cities would have occurred after emancipation and through Reconstruction. See also Deborah Gray White, *Ar'n't I a Woman? Female Slaves in the Antebellum South* (New York: W. W. Norton, 1985); Claudia Goldin, "Female Labor Force Participation: The Origins of Black and White Differences," *Journal of Economic History* 37, no. I (March 1977): 87–108; and Janice L. Reiff, Michele Dahlin, and Daniel Scott Smith, "Rural Push and Urban Pull: Work and Family Experiences of Older Black Women in Southern Cities, 1880–1900," *Journal of Social History* 15, no. 4 (summer 1983): 39–48.

13. Nell Irvin Painter, *The Exodusters: Black Migration to Kansas after Reconstruction* (New York, Alfred A. Knopf, 1976); Taylor and Moore, *African American Women Confront the West;* Moore, *To Place Our Deeds;* Janiewski, *Sisterhood Denied;* Hunter, *To 'Joy My Freedom;* Lemke-Santangelo, *Abiding Courage;* Clark-Lewis, *Living In, Living Out.*

14. David M. Katzman, *Seven Days a Week: Women in Domestic Service in Industrializing America* (New York: Oxford University Press, 1978), 65–78; Joe William Trotter, Jr., "Blacks in the Urban North: 'The Underclass Question' in Historical Perspective," in *The Underclass Debate: Views from History,* ed. Michael B. Katz (Princeton, N.J.: Princeton University Press, 1993), 55–84; Sharon Harley et al., introduction to *Sister Circle: Black Women and Work,* ed. Sharon Harley and the Black Women and Work Collective (New Brunswick, N.J.: Rutgers University Press, 2002), 6–9; Darlene Clark Hine, "Rape and the Inner Lives of Black Women in the Middle West: Preliminary Thoughts on the Culture of Dissemblance," Signs 14, no. 4 (summer 1989): 911–932; Elizabeth Ross Haynes, "Negroes in Domestic Service in the United States," *Journal of Negro History* 8 (October 1923): 384–442.

15. U.S. Department of Commerce, Bureau of the Census, *Changing Characteristics of the Negro Population: A 1960 Census Monograph,* by Daniel O. Price, in Cooperation with the Social Science Research Council (Washington, D.C.: Government Printing Office, 1969), 17–40; also *U.S. Census of the Population: 1960, Subject Reports, State of Birth,* 52–59, Sixteenth Census of the United States: *1940, Population, Internal Migration, 1935–1940,* Age of Migrants, 256–257, and Color and Sex of Migrants, 18–19. The census did not detail migration by sex until 1940 when the bureau published detailed reports based on county of residence in 1935 compared to residence in 1940, and identified more women than men as migrants, but even earlier census documents made this observation. Also see U.S. Department of Commerce, Bureau of the Census, *Negroes in the United States, 1920–1932* (Washington D.C.: Government Printing Office, 1935), 78–86; and *Negro Population in the United States, 1790–1915* (Washington D.C.: Government Printing Office, 1918).

16. Leonard P. Curry, *The Free Black in Urban America: The Shadow of the Dream* (Chicago: University of Chicago Press, 1985); Richard C. Wade, *Slavery in the Cities: The South, 1820–1860* (New York: Oxford University Press, 1964), 329; W.E.B. Du Bois, *The Philadelphia Negro: A Social Study* (1899; repr., Philadelphia: University of Pennsylvania Press, 1996), 46–55; Leslie M. Harris, *In the Shadow of Slavery: African Americans in New York City, 1626–1863* (Chicago: University of Chicago Press, 2003), 99.

17. Du Bois, *The Philadelphia Negro,* 53–55 and fn 2.

18. Unless otherwise noted, all population data for this chapter are compiled from the U.S. Department of Commerce, Bureau of the Census, *Eleventh Census of the United States Taken in the Year 1890 Population, Part I* (Washington, D.C.: Government Printing Office, 1895); Census Report Vol. I: *Twelfth Census of the United States, Taken in the Year 1900,*

Population, Part I (Washington, D.C.: Government Printing Office, 1901); Thirteenth Census of the United States, Taken in the Year 1910, *Population,* Vol. 3 (Washington, D.C.: Government Printing Office, 1913); Fourteenth Census of the United States, Taken in the Year 1920, Vol. III, *Population, Composition, and Characteristics* (Washington, D.C.: Government Printing Office, 1922); Fifteenth Census of the United States, *Population,* Vol. III, Part 2 (Washington, D.C.: Government Printing Office, 1932); Sixteenth Census of the United States: 1940, *Population, Characteristics of the Population,* Vol. II, Part 5, *by States, New York-Oregon* (Washington, D.C.: Government Printing Office, 1943); Report of the Seventeenth Decennial Census of the United States, *Census of the Population: 1950, Part 33, North Carolina* (Washington, D.C.: Government Printing Office, 1952); Negro Population, *1790–1915*; and *Negroes in the United States, 1920–1932*.

19. Lewis, "Expectations, Economic Opportunities," 22–45.

20. Darlene Clark Hine, "Black Migration to the Urban Midwest: The Gender Dimension, 1915–1945," in her *HineSight: Black Women and the Reconstruction of American History* (Bloomington: Indiana University Press, 1997), 95; White, *Too Heavy a Load*; Stephanie J. Shaw, *What a Woman Ought to Be and to Do: Black Professional Women Workers during the Jim Crow Era* (Chicago: University of Chicago Press, 1994); Frances A. Kellor, "Associations for Protection of Colored Women," *Colored American Magazine* 9 (December 1905): 695–699; Dorothy Salem, *To Better Our World: Black Women in Organized Reform, 1890–1920* (Brooklyn, N.Y.: Carlson Publishing, 1990); Evelyn Brooks Higginbotham, *Righteous Discontent: The Women's Movement in the Black Baptist Church, 1880–1920* (Cambridge, Mass.: Harvard University Press, 1993); Evelyn Brooks Higginbotham, "Clubwomen and Electoral Politics in the 1920s," in *African American Women and the Vote, 1837–1965*, ed. Ann Gordon et al. (Amherst: University of Massachusetts Press, 1997), 134–155.

21. Jonathan Scott Holloway, *Confronting the Veil: Abram Harris, Jr., E. Franklin Frazier, and Ralph Bunche, 1919–1941* (Chapel Hill: University of North Carolina Press, 2002), 19 and 29; Marks, *"Farewell — We're Good and Gone,"* 45–48. The contemporary literature on the Great Migration is extensive. See, for example, Donald Henderson, "The Negro Migration of 1916–1918," *Journal of Negro History* 6 (October 1921): 383–499; Lorenzo Greene and Carter G. Woodson, *The Negro Wage Earner* (Washington, D.C.: Association for the Study of Negro Life and History, 1930); George E. Haynes, *Negro Migration in 1916–1917* (Washington, D.C.: Department of Labor, Division of Negro Economics, Government Printing Office, 1919); Louise V. Kennedy, *The Negro Peasant Turns Cityward* (New York: Columbia University Press, 1930); Florette Henri, *Black Migration: Movement North* (Garden City, N.Y.: Doubleday, 1975); Emmett J. Scott, *Negro Migration during the War* (repr., New York: Arno Press and The New York Times, 1969); Sterling Spero and Abram L. Harris, *The Black Worker: The Negro Labor Movement* (New York: Antheneum Press, 1961); Carter G. Woodson, *A Century of Negro Migration* (repr., New York: Russell and Russell, 1969).

22. Du Bois, *The Philadelphia Negro,* 74 and 166; also see E. Franklin Frazier, *The Negro in Chicago* (Chicago: University of Chicago Press, 1932); E. Franklin Frazier, *The Negro Family in the United States* (Chicago: University of Chicago Press, 1939); T. J. Woofter, *Negro Problems in Cities* (Garden City, N.Y.: Doubleday, 1920); St. Clare Drake and Horace Cayton, *Black Metropolis* (New York: Harcourt Brace, 1945); and the less negative Henri, *Black Migration.*

23. Kelly Miller, "Surplus Negro Women," in his *Race Adjustment: Essays on the Negro in America* (New York: Neal Publishing Company, 1908); reprinted as Kelly Miller, *Radicals*

and Conservatives: And Other Essays on the Negro in America (New York: Schocken Books, 1968), 182–192; Hazel V. Carby, "Policing the Black Woman's Body in an Urban Context," *Critical Inquiry* 18 (summer 1992): 738–757.

24. Miller, "Surplus Negro Women," 185; W.E.B. Du Bois, "The Damnation of Women," in his *Darkwater: Voices from within the Veil* (New York: Harcourt Brace and Howe, 1920), 180–181.

25. *Negroes in the United States, 1920–1932*, 80. On the social consequences of the sex ratio from the point of view of men, see Marcia Gutentag and Paul F. Secord, *Too Many Women? The Sex Ratio Question* (Beverly Hills: Sage Publications, 1983), 200–215.

26. Consider here the differences between *Talley's Corner* and *Slim's Table* — two very different portrays of African American men. Eliot Liebowitz, *Talley's Corner: A Study of Negro Street Corner Men* (Boston: Little, Brown, 1967); and Mitchell Duneier, *Slim's Table: Race, Respectability, and Masculinity* (Chicago: Chicago University Press, 1992).

27. Kimberly L. Phillips, " 'But It Is a Fine Place to Make Money': Migration and African American Families in Cleveland, 1915–1929," *Journal of Social History* 30, no. 2 (December 1996): 395–415; Joe William Trotter, Jr., *Coal, Class, and Color: Blacks in Southern West Virginia, 1915–1932* (Urbana: University of Illinois Press, 1990), 63–101. Elizabeth Clark-Lewis illustrated the complex family connections from the South to the North (Clark-Lewis, *Living In, Living Out*).

28. W.T.B. Williams, *Negro Migration, 1915–1917*, (Washington, D.C.: Government Printing Office, 1919), 94.

29. Lewis, "Expectations, Economic Opportunities," 22–25 and fn 19.

30. Shaw, *What a Woman Ought to Be and to Do*, 118; Francille Rusan Wilson, " 'All of the Glory . . . Faded . . . Quickly': Sadie T. M. Alexander and Black Professional Women, 1920–1950," in *Sister Circle*, ed. Harley et al., 164–183; Dorothy Fletcher Steele, interview by author, June 1993, Charlotte, N.C.; Addie Marie Faulk, interview with author, October 27, 1995, Durham, N.C.; Mary Bodie, interview by Karen Ferguson, June 25, 1993, Enfield, N.C., BTV.

31. *Negroes in the United States, 1920–1932*, 183; Goldin, "Female Labor Force Participation," 110; Reiff, Dahlin, and Smith, "Rural Push and Urban Pull," 39–48; S. J. Kleinberg, *Widows and Orphans First: The Family Economy and Social Welfare Policy, 1880–1939* (Urbana: University of Illinois Press, 2006).

32. Janiewski, *Sisterhood Denied*, 27–54; Brown, *Upbuilding Black Durham*; Ila Blue, interviewed by Kisha Turner and Blair Murphy, June 2, 1995, Durham, N.C., BTV; Theresa Jan Cameron Lyons, interview by author, August 16, 1995, BTV.

33. Janiewski *Sisterhood Denied*; Mary Mebane, *Mary* (repr., Chapel Hill: University of North Carolina Press, 1999).

34. Clark-Lewis, *Living In, Living Out*, 56–57;

35. Jones, Labor of *Love, Labor of Sorrow*, 262.

36. Darlene Clark Hine, "Rape and the Inner Lives of Black Women in the Middle West."

37. Marks, *Farewell — We're Good and Gone*, 45.

38. The literature of social sciences and urban problems is vast. For example, William Julius Wilson, *The Declining Significance of Race: Blacks and Changing American Institutions* (Chicago: University of Chicago Press, 1980); William Julius Wilson, *When Work Disappears, the World of the New Urban* (New York: Vintage Books, 1997); Charles Murray,

Losing Ground: American Social Policy, 1950–1980 (1984; repr., New York: Basic Books, 1994), 124–134; Jacqueline Jones, "Southern Diaspora: Origins of the Northern 'Underclass'" in *The "Underclass" Debate: Views from History*, ed. Michael B. Katz (Princeton: Princeton University Press, 1993, 27–54). Also see Douglass S. Massey and Nancy A Denton, *American Apartheid: Segregation and the Making of the Underclass* (Cambridge, Mass.: Harvard University Press, 1993).

12

Morena/o, Blanca/o, y Café con Leche

Racial Constructions in Chicana/o Historiography

VICKI L. RUIZ

The scene is the Mapping Memories and Migrations: Re-thinking Latina Histories Conference held in February 2004. Before a packed house at the Latino Cultural Center in Dallas, Texas, an elegant Mexican American senior citizen rose from her seat to ask me, the panel moderator, a question: "Can you explain to me the word Chicano?" I offered my standard two-sentence spiel and she seemed satisfied with my answer. During the break, a colleague pulled me aside, inquiring if I had recognized Anita Martínez, the woman who had asked the "Chicano" question. In 1969 Martínez was the first Mexican American woman elected to the Dallas City Council. A long-time community advocate, Anita Martínez had worked closely with her friend and fellow council member Juanita Craft, a leader in the local NAACP. Together they helped make city government more accountable to the needs of all of its residents.[1] Given Ms. Martínez's civil rights credentials, a historian might be tempted to call her a "Chicana"; however, for Anita Martínez, the term held little meaning.

Nomenclature and self-identification remain salient issues. What does naming reveal about our multiple identities, our *mascaras* (masks), our *sueños* (dreams)? People of Mexican birth or descent refer to themselves by many names — *mexicana/o*, Mexican American, and Chicana/o (to name just three). Self-identification speaks volumes about regional, generational, and even political orientations. *Mexicana/o* typically refers to immigrants, with Mexican American signifying U.S. birth. Chicana/o reflects a political consciousness borne of the Chicana/o Student Movement, often a generational marker for those of us coming of age during the 1960s and 1970s. Chicana/o has also been embraced by our elders and our children who share in the political ideals of the movement. Some prefer regional identification such as Tejana/o (Texan) or Hispana/o (New Mexican). Spanish American is also popular in New Mexico and Colorado. Latina/o emphasizes a common bond with all people of Latin American origin in the United States, a politicized Pan-American identity. Even racial location can be discerned by whether one favors an Iberian connection (Hispanic) or an indigenous past (*mestiza/o* or Xicana/o). Multiple identities even surface within individual families. As Salt Lake City housing activist María Garcíaz reflected, "My mother is Spanish; one brother is Mexican; my sister is Mexican American; I am Chicana. Three brothers are Hispanic; and the youngest is Latino."[2]

Rather than offering a smattering of sources, I intend to sketch out the racial/gendered contours of Chicana/o history over the last twenty years, problematizing notions of *mestizaje* (*morena/o*), whiteness (*blanca/o*), and cultural coalescence (*café con leche*). The situational nature of racial constructs in the historical (and the historians') moment can be discerned by both focused overview and case study. My recent research on school desegregation in the Southwest seeks to interrogate and interpret issues of whiteness from the standpoint of superintendents, Latina/o parents, and their children. For Chicana/o movement stalwarts, claiming identities was woven into the fabric of political action.

Reflecting on the 1969 National Chicano Youth Liberation Conference in Denver, Colorado, activist María Varela revealed: " 'Conference' is a poor word to describe those five days. . . . It was in reality a fiesta: days of celebrating what sings in the blood of a people who, taught to believe they are ugly, discover the true beauty in their souls. . . . Coca Cola, . . . Breck Shampoo, the Playboy Bunny, the Arrow Shirt man, the Marlboro heroes are lies. 'We are beautiful . . . '[T]his affirmation grew into a *grito*, a roar among the people in the auditorium."[3] As the cradle of the Chicano Student Movement, this conference, hosted by Corky Gonzales and the Crusade for Social Justice, offered a potent nationalist vision linking an Aztec past to a Chicano future. The concept of Aztlán as the mythic Aztec homeland reborn in a Chicano nation resonated among the audience over fifteen hundred strong. Certainly Aztec motifs would come to dominate the iconography of the *movimiento* as young militants embraced the hagiography of a pre-Columbian past as their own.[4] This Aztec imaginary was not only front and center in public protests but also in cultural production. Cultural studies theorist Alicia Gaspar de Alba in *Chicano Art Inside/Outside the Master's House* elegantly interpellates the politics of *indigenismo* and social justice as refracted within Chicana/o visual art at the point of production (the artists themselves) and also at the point of retrospection (the CARA exhibit).[5]

The quest for indigenous roots influenced not only students, artists, and creative writers but social scientists as well. The historical stasis of the essentialized Chicana/o emerged in a popular book published in 1979. In *La Chicana: The Mexican American Woman*, Alfredo Mirandé, a sociologist, and Evangelina Enríquez, a doctoral candidate in literature, baldly proclaimed: "Aztec norms of feminine expectation have remained surprisingly intact to the present day. They are relevant for Chicanas because they suggest that prescribed roles for women in the culture are essentially inflexible." What exactly were the precise, unchanging expectations that could be traced from "Aztec models" to the present? According to the authors, these included "being the heart of the home, bearing and rearing children, being clean and tidy, dedicating oneself to a husband, and preserving one's respectability in the eyes of the community."[6] This laundry list of cultural prescriptions could be applied to women across time, region, and culture. For instance, the Cult of True Womanhood in Victorian America comes immediately to mind. The authors blithely ignore over five hundred years of historical change, not the least of which encompass three centuries of Spanish colonial rule, the conquest of the Mexican North, and the successive movements of peoples to the United States (*al otro lado*).

Writing in the 1970s and early 1980s, most historians sidestepped the search for indigenous roots, preferring to document labor market segmentation, inter-generational economic stratification, barrioization, and, at times, trade union organization. Marking with statistical precision the colonial legacies wrought by Manifest Destiny, these pioneering studies by Albert Camarillo, Richard Griswold del Castillo, and Mario García (among others) center on material conditions and structural impediments with identity, whether Chicano or *mexicano*, taken as a given.[7] Identities, whether racial or regional, were assumed rather than theo-rized. Moreover, Chicano history meant just that — emphasis on the masculine ending *o*.

The first monograph in Chicana history, *Cannery Women, Cannery Lives*, appeared in 1987. Incorporating frameworks in labor history and feminist theory and drawing on trade union documents, newspapers, as well as oral histories, I chronicled the stories of union life among California food-processing workers during the 1930s and 1940s. Mexican women in common cause with their Euro American (predominantly Jewish) co-workers created and led a grassroots union in which they achieved unparalleled benefits, especially for the era, such as equal pay for equal work and vacation pay. Racial constructions or self-identification certainly escaped my view, but brief references to the impact of U.S. popular cul-ture and to intergenerational tensions between daughters and their parents would provide the kernel for my second monograph, *From Out of the Shadows: Mexican Women in Twentieth-Century America*.[8]

In 1990 historian Elizabeth Salas in *Soldaderas in the Mexican Military* returned to the concept of *indigenismo* within her overview of women soldiers and caretak-ers during the Mexican Revolution. "*Soldaderas* have marched through most of Mexican history," the author declares as she links Mesoamerican women war-riors (the ancestors) with *las soldaderas* and their symbolic descendants — Chicana student activists. The strong masculine warrior so prevalent in movimiento motifs shows his feminine side, so to speak, in Salas's narrative.[9]

Salas emphasizes that Mexicans carried the soldadera image with them as they journeyed north; and, yes, they carried that and so much more — a whole array of cultural codes, political beliefs, and occupational skills. Chicana/o labor historians writing in the early 1990s charted the development of a "Mexicanist" identity rooted in class, culture, politics, and employment. Community took center stage. Concentrating primarily on male agricultural workers, scholars such as Camille Guérin-Gonzales, Emilio Zamora, and Gilbert González meticulously record the building of community from neighborhood institutions to trade unions, all predicated on *mexicanidad*, a fusion of class and cultural identity.[10] In general, these monographs focus on neither Mesoamerican linkages nor racial constructions per se but instead on the structural factors influencing the everyday lives of Mexican workers and their responses to racism and exploitation. Within this paradigm, Lisbeth Haas in *Conquests and Historical Identities in California, 1769–1936* and Devra Weber in *Dark Sweat, White Gold* interrogate the interplay of gender and memory. Haas imaginatively traces collective, public memory across time and generation while Weber reveals the gendered dialectics of private memory: "Men remembered the strike in terms of wages and conditions; women remembered the events in terms of food."[11] Bolstered by a fervent sense of mexicanidad, worker identities as community builders and proletariats politicized by material circumstances and, at times, Mexican revolutionary ideals serve as the common interpretative threads running throughout Chicana/o labor studies.

Other historians have problematized the moreno by complicating categories of community and identity. Turning on historical constructions of whiteness, this scholarship illuminates the internal tensions within Spanish-speaking communities, especially the ways in which class feeds into racial formations. Color consciousness with white as the hue of privilege is not just a twentieth-century by-product of Americanization, but represents historical consciousness rooted in colonial Latin America. Ramón Gutiérrez in the path-breaking *When Jesus Came, the Corn Mothers Went Away* provides a paradigm for the study of power and stratification across gender, race, and culture. Meticulously researched and cogently argued, this richly textured history of colonial New Mexico elucidates the confluence of power swirling in and around (en)gendered class relations, focusing on how marital choices were interpolated with the environment and the economy to create a diachronous society predicated on notions of honor, shame, color, and conquest.[12]

While Gutiérrez forefronts the rigid construction of caste, James Brooks in the award-winning *Captives and Cousins* emphasizes a greater fluidity of racial locations within intricate "communities of interest" rooted in slavery. Brooks teases out the possibilities through which captives become cousins across Hispano settlements and surrounding Native nations including the Comanche, Apache, and Navajo. But historian Ned Blackhawk adds a cautionary coda. "Forged amid the maelstrom of colonial diseases, warfare, guns, horses, and economic dependency, captivity in the Southwest might have created webs and bridges between peoples, but it did so on the backs of young Indian women and children."[13]

The advent of "pigmentocracy" further complicates categories of color and caste on the Spanish borderlands. Combing an array of colonial documents, including baptismal records, historian Omar Valerio-Jiménez charts the dynamics of economic mobility in determining racial identification for Spanish-speaking villagers in the Rio Grande region of southern Texas and northern Tamaulipas. As he explains in his dissertation, "Individual examples abound of poor vecinos . . . 'whitening' their caste as their wealth increased. Particularly successful individuals not only entered the upper class but also recreated themselves as *españoles*."[14] Indeed, the doxa that money bought color can be applied across the Spanish empire in the New World. Members of the Californio elite after 1848 desperately sought to hold onto their constructed claims of a Spanish heritage. These claims had passed from one generation to the next, rising with a sense of urgency in the wake of the Treaty of Guadalupe Hidalgo, the Gold Rush, and the accompanying political, economic, and cultural dislocations. *Thrown among Strangers,* by historian Douglas Monroy, and *Racial Fault Lines,* by sociologist Tomás Almaguer, document this pattern. While the remaining Native population in southern California "merged with the general Mexican population through marriage," Californios of some standing (*gente de razón*) accentuated their pretensions to "Europeanness."[15]

For Spanish-speaking women, color and class would be crucial in their relations with European and Euro American men. Those with fair skin and elite backgrounds would be courted, while those with darker hues and limited means would be exploited. In 1852, the *Nevada Journal* distinguished between "native California ladies who dressed with a degree of elegance" and the immodest, less refined "Mexican and Chileno females."[16] The use of the terms "ladies" and "females" speaks volumes about prevalent perceptions of color and class. Several scholars have asserted that elite families believed that they stood a greater chance of retaining their land and status if they acquired a European or Euro American son-in-law. Tomás Almaguer refers to these alliances as "symbolic trafficking of upper class Californio women." Conversely, María Raquel Casas contends that daughters were not oblivious pawns to parental machinations. Intermarriage, however, was no insurance policy.[17]

If the elite had options for "whiteness," what about the working class? Were they immune from the *mentalité* of white privilege? Not according to Linda Gordon in her award-winning study, *The Great Arizona Orphan Abduction.* In her provocative touchstone text, she gracefully details how in 1904 New York City Irish foundlings bound for Clifton, Arizona, in an orphan train were given to Mexican parents upon their arrival. Stunned to see white babies in the arms of Mexicans, Euro American women urged their male kin to round up the children by force and in the process intimidate the local French priest as well as the nuns who had escorted the orphans. After the round up, the Catholic religious were literally run out of town and the children were redistributed to Euro American households. The orphanage sued but lost in the Arizona Supreme Court and later the U.S. Supreme Court. Gordon posits that Mexicans had chosen the children precisely because of their complexion and heritage, in part as an investment for their families' future as the young boys would grow up to claim white wages in the mines. Furthermore, as Stephen Lassonde notes in his *New York Times* book review, by " 'taking in a piece of Anglo culture' — each child 'might become a true *americano.*' "[18]

To be an American resonated among middle-class Mexican Americans during the early decades of the twentieth century, most visibly within the League of United Latin American Citizens (LULAC). Founded by Tejanos in 1929, LULAC, a middle-class civil rights organization, struck a chord among Mexican Americans, and by 1939 chapters could be found throughout the Southwest. Envisioning themselves as patriotic "white" Americans pursuing their rights, LULACers restricted membership to English-speaking U.S. citizens. Taking a page from the early NAACP, LULAC stressed the leadership of an "educated elite" who would lift their less fortunate neighbors by their bootstraps. Mario García reiterates how members considered LULAC "an authentic American organization and that each letter in its name expressed patriotism L stood for love of country; U for unity as American citizens; L for loyalty to country; A for advancement; and C for citizenship." With a somewhat different spin, David Gutiérrez, in *Walls and Mirrors: Mexican Americans, Mexican Immigrants, and the Politics of Ethnicity in the Southwest, 1910–1986*, argues that "LULAC members consistently went to great lengths to explain to anyone who would listen that Americans of Mexican descent were different from (and by implication somehow better than) Mexicans from the other side."[19] Moreover, in billing itself as the other white group, LULAC worked hard in "maintaining the color line between its members and African Americans." In his highly acclaimed monograph, *The White Scourge: Mexicans, Blacks, and Poor Whites in Texas Cotton Culture*, Neil Foley beautifully deconstructs how people's perceptions of themselves are based on both who they are and who they are not.[20]

Through the prism of gender, Cynthia Orozco's dissertation provides fresh insights. From LULAC's inception, women participated in numerous grassroots service projects. In Houston, for example, women raised "monies for milk, eye glasses, Christmas toys, and baby clothes." Orozco inscribes their activism as concrete responses to community needs. Their voluntarist politics indicated that there existed less social distance between immigrants and citizens as well as between workers and merchants than the rhetoric of LULAC would lead us to believe. LULAC women were bridge people, simultaneously seeking to meet the material needs of newcomers and neighbors while engaging in direct action for civil rights.[21] Indeed, in evaluating LULAC's legacy Chicana/o historians generally agree with the following assessment given by David Gutiérrez: "From 1929 through World War II LULAC organized successful voter registration and poll tax-drives, actively supported candidates sympathetic to Mexican Americans and aggressively attacked discriminatory laws and practices throughout Texas and the Southwest. More important . . . LULAC also achieved a number of notable legal victories in the area of public education."[22]

Drawing out the dialectics between morena/o and blanca/o, Neil Foley explains, "Mexican identity, like whiteness itself fissured along lines of class, nationality, and culture." In Texas towns, immigrants clung to a Mexicanist identity while their middle-class neighbors and even their own children considered themselves white.[23] Yet, this duality, while important, does not take into full measure the fulcrum of individuals and cultures in motions, the shifting hues of café con leche. The dances of cultural negotiations can be observed throughout Spanish-speaking communities, from Hispano villagers preserving a regional community in northern New Mexico and southern Colorado (Sarah Deutsch's *No Separate Refuge*) to second-generation Mexican American men in Los Angeles who, according to George Sánchez, were becoming Mexican American.[24] Situating women's lives squarely within the "swirls of cultural contradiction,"[25] is a central premise in *From Out of the Shadows*. In tandem with the claiming of public space by women across generation, class, and region, cultural coalescence represents the text's signifying paradigm.

Immigrants and their children pick, borrow, retain, and create distinctive cultural forms. There is not a single hermetic Mexican or Mexican American culture, but rather permeable *cultures* rooted in generation, gender, region, class, and personal experience. People navigate across cultural boundaries and consciously make decisions with regard to the production of culture. However, bear in mind that people of color have not had unlimited choice. Prejudice and discrimination with the accompanying social, political, and economic segmentation have constrained aspirations, expectations, and decision-making.[26]

From the flappers of the 1920s to the riveting Rosies of the 1940s to Chicana Brown Berets of the 1960s to contemporary community and labor leaders, women have made history. This emphasis on the public, however, has cast its own shadows (pardon the pun), including the long shadow of heteronormativity. As Elizabeth Rodríguez Kessler astutely and charitably points out in her review, "Ruiz's devotion to the political struggle consumes the majority of her text; and she devotes only two pages to the struggles Chicana lesbians endure."[27]

Sexuality and power drive much of recent Chicana historiography; and, yes, there exists a significant body of critical scholarship that can, indeed, be characterized as distinctly Chicana, emphasis on the feminine *a*. A bold envisioning of Chicana historical consciousness as a decentered metanarrative, Emma Pérez's *The Decolonial Imaginary: Writing Chicanas into History* breaks open categories of post-structural analysis and queer theory as they apply to select twentieth-century transnational case studies from women's organizations in the Yucatán during the Mexican Revolution to cultural representations of the late Tejana singing sensation Selena. In particular, her discussion of diasporic subjectivities of Mexican immigrant women is a major contribution to Chicana/o history and cultural studies.[28]

Recent imaginative studies bridge and blend a myriad of disciplines from history and literature to sociology and education (to name a few). In exploring identities rooted in occupation, race, and place, Mary Ann Villarreal and Deborah Vargas chronicle the lives of women entertainers in South Texas, musicians and vocalists who traveled with their bands, earning a livelihood and crafting their own sense of self. Mary Ann Villarreal is the first historian to examine the lives of twentieth-century Mexican American women who patronize or operate local cantinas and the ways in which they appropriate or negotiate a very male-identified public space.[29]

Matters of public space have also been analyzed by a group of Chicana studies scholars, including Maylei Blackwell, Dolores Delgado Bernal, and Dionne Espinoza, who have challenged the masculinist memories of the Chicano Student Movement.[30] Marisela Chávez's nuanced interpretation of Chicana activism in California lends a big picture perspective as she interrogates the overlapping strands of nationalism, Marxism, and feminism as refracted through global concerns and grassroots projects. Both Marisela Chávez and Lorena Oropeza offer unvarnished portraits of youthful militancy, revealing moments of both courage and stupidity. In *¡Raza Sí! ¡Guerra No*, Oropeza recounts the hidden costs of activism, for example, how Kathy Davis del Valle, the daughter of a *mexicana* and an African American, was exhorted by Chicano nationalists to change her name to Katarina and to distance herself from her African American father in order to "prove" her commitment to La Raza. This incident was not an aberration as students of blended heritage who came of age during the 1960s and 1970s encountered similar litmus tests.[31]

The Chicano Movement, of course, extended beyond campus activism. In *Las Hermanas: Chicana/Latina Religious-Political Activism in the U.S. Catholic Church*, Lara Medina focuses on the participation of nuns in the Chicano Movement. She examines the ways in which the sisters navigated the Church, Chicano nationalism, and the communities they served. *Las hermanas* have contributed materially and spiritually to their neighborhoods as they have pioneered strategies of empowerment through grassroots organizations based in liberation theology and Alinsky-style organizing techniques.[32]

Studies by senior scholars Rosaura Sánchez, Deena González, and Antonia Castañeda provide poignant *testimonios* of those who came before us in the eighteenth and nineteenth centuries. These *mujeres* challenged patriarchy at various turns, from indigenous women resisting the sexual predations of soldiers to Spanish/Mexican women going to court, exercising public rights, and seeking redress for personal wrongs.[33] Building on these works, a rising generation of Chicana scholars investigates gendered ethno-regional identities through an array of primary sources heretofore unacknowledged or under-utilized. Barbara Reyes's refreshing analysis of women's lives inside and outside the mission walls in Baja and Alta, California, moves beyond the dialectical resistance/accommodation argument as the author illuminates the everyday (as well as the extraordinary) means by which Spanish-speaking women defined and reconnoitered their worlds. María Raquel Casas's *"Married to a Daughter of the Land": Interethnic*

Marriages in California, 1820–1880 provides a fascinating view of the definitions of race, privilege, and social position, especially through the story of a Hispanicized Native American, Victoria Reed, who crossed class and color lines more than once in her lifetime. Drawing on insights from legal history and feminist theory, Miroslava Chávez-García, in *Negotiating Conquest: Gender and Power in California*, documents the ways in which Mexican women availed themselves of the legal system for both securing property and civil rights. Rather than viewing Mexican women as passive victims of Mexican patriarchy and American conquest, Chávez-García presents cases of real women who used the court system to hold onto land, to rid themselves of abusive husbands, and to gain monetary support for their children.[34] Struggles for sexual agency and for autonomy amidst multivalent colonialisms foreground important new directions in Chicana history.

Masculinity must also be problematized. Steven Rosales's study represents the first historical narrative of Mexican American men in the U.S. military from World War II through Vietnam. Conducting extensive life histories with over forty veterans, Rosales carefully sorts out the ideations of masculinity as he frames his narrators' experiences as soldiers, sailors, and pilots. Equally important, he gauges the impact of military service on their civilian lives. In the acclaimed *A World of Its Own: Race, Labor, and Class in the Making of Greater Los Angeles, 1900–1970*, Matt García deftly delineates the fault lines of generation, gender, and citizenship in the suburbs of southern California. He brings out the tensions between Mexican American male citrus workers and Mexican nationals who entered the groves as *braceros*, tensions that arose over wages and women. Asserting a "protective" proprietorship over "their" women, Mexican American men positioned themselves as "a cut above the *braceros*, whom they viewed with suspicion and at times outright hostility." Focusing on youth, García interrogates the lived experiences of Mexican Americans as individuals who traversed and transgressed a sociocultural milieu that included as integral actors Euro Americans, African Americans, and Mexican immigrants. He demonstrates the multiplicity of inherently political intercultural discourses among such groups as aspiring thespians performing at the Padua Hills dinner theater to African American and Latino musicians and their young fans who frequented a popular integrated Pomona dance hall, the aptly named Rainbow Gardens.[35]

Does region matter in racial constructions and cultural coalescence? The overwhelming majority of monographs in Chicana/o historiography have focused on the Southwest (usually California and Texas), although since the early decades of the twentieth century, a significant number of Mexican immigrants and their U.S.-born children, side by side with other Latinos, have called the Midwest home. In her monograph on Chicago's Mexican communities, Gabriela Arredondo offers an intriguing alternative vision to accepted paradigms in immigration history. Taking head-on Lizabeth Cohen's argument in *Making a New Deal*, she asserts that Mexicans in Chicago did not acculturate along the same lines as ethnic Europeans in that consumer culture and working-class consciousness did not translate into an "American" identity. Rather, she traces how Mexican immigrants developed their own brand of mexicanidad, drawing on popular intellectual discourse in Mexico and as a response to big city life and discrimination. For example, instead of sports teams promoting an American identity, they fostered feelings of nationalist solidarity, expressions of pride as Mexicans, not Mexican Americans. This is a fascinating line of analysis and one I would consider more descriptive of the immigrant generation who arrived during World War I and the 1920s than of their children who came of age during World War II.[36]

Like Arredondo, García, Foley, and Gordon (to mention a few), I am fascinated by the interplay of the every day and self-identification. To what extent are constructions of whiteness an individual strategic shift in response to material circumstances (e.g., segregationist policies) or, as in New Mexico and Colorado, a deeply held community identity, an orientation forged by both public memory and cherished family genealogies? Blood quantum is not the issue. As John Nieto-Phillips so astutely notes in his dissertation, historians should not focus on who claims to be Spanish but "examine how that identity evolved and was shaped in various contexts" as well as how it played out over generations.[37]

My research on school desegregation in the Southwest reveals the situational nature of racial constructions. The landmark case *Méndez v. Westminister* (1946) offers a glimpse into a multivalent discourse that often went unspoken over passing, white privilege, and Latina/o identities. No doubt, complexion counted when parents sought to enroll their children in local schools. The *guera* (light-complected) Alice Esperanza Méndez Vidaurri was admitted to the "white" elementary school in rural Orange County, California, while her more *morena* cousin Sylvia Méndez was turned away. Her parents, Gonzálo and Felícitas Méndez, sought legal redress.[38]

In March 1945 Gonzálo Méndez, William Guzmán, Frank Palomino, Thomas Estrada, and Lorenzo Ramírez, with the help of LULAC, sued four local school districts — Westminster, Garden Grove, Santa Ana, and El Modena. They challenged, in part, the common practice of drawing school boundaries around Mexican neighborhoods to ensure de facto segregation. Mexicans who lived in "white" residential areas were also subject to school segregation as the Ayala family found out when eighteen-year-old Isabel was turned away when she tried to enroll her younger siblings at their local school in Garden Grove. To add further insult, according to the preeminent commentator on California life, Carey McWilliams, placement of children was also based on phenotype. In McWilliams's words, "Occasionally the school authorities inspect the children so that the offspring of a Mexican mother whose name may be O'Shaughnessy will not slip into the wrong school."[39]

During the trial, superintendents reiterated well-worn stereotypes, as exemplified by the Garden Grove superintendent's bald assertion that "'Mexicans are inferior in personal hygiene, ability, and in their economic outlook.'"

Furthermore, these youngsters needed separate schools given their lack of English proficiency, that they "were handicapped in 'interpreting English words because their cultural background' prevented them from learning Mother Goose rhymes." The court transcript is replete with images of "dirty" Mexican children. For example, Superintendent Kent recited a laundry list of hygienic deficiencies peculiar to Mexican children that warranted, in part, their segregation. These deficiencies included "lice, impetigo, tuberculosis, generally dirty hands, face, neck, and ears." When the plaintiffs' attorney David Marcus queried, "Are all children dirty?" Kent answered, "No sir." When Marcus pushed the issue, "Do you keep a record of dirty hands and face?" "No" was the response. Kent's testimony persistently portrayed Mexican children as at a marked disadvantage vis-à-vis their "Anglo Saxon" peers to such an extent that he considered it a "shame" to integrate, even it meant the inclusion of only one token Mexican American child into an all European American classroom. "It is very hard for one child to compete with 40 children of another race in a class." His reliance on the term "race" speaks volumes.[40]

Devising a two-fold strategy, Marcus questioned the constitutionality of educational segregation and called in expert witnesses — social scientists who challenged these assumptions about Mexican American children and the supposed need for separate schools. When she took the stand, Felícitas poignantly summed up her family's struggles: "We always tell our children they are Americans." Taking almost a year to formulate his decision, Judge Paul McCormick "ruled that segregation of Mexican youngsters found no justification in the laws of California and furthermore was a clear denial of the 'equal protection' clause of the Fourteenth Amendment."[41]

Méndez v. Westminster assumes national significance through its tangible connections to *Brown v. Board of Education* in four interrelated areas in addition to the direct involvement of NAACP counsel Thurgood Marshall, whose name appears as a co-author of an *amicus curiae* brief for this case. First, according to historian Rubén Flores, the Mendez case influenced a shift in NAACP legal strategy to include "social science arguments"; he calls the links "clear and unmistakable." Second, Judge McCormick in deliberating his decision relied not just on legal precedent but also on social science and education research. As Charles Wollenberg noted, "much of the social and educational theory expressed by Judge McCormick anticipated Earl Warren's historic opinion in the Brown case." Third, "it was the first time that a federal court had concluded that the segregation of Mexican Americans in public schools was a violation of state law" and unconstitutional under the Fourteenth Amendment because of the denial of due process and equal protection. Finally, as the direct result of the *Méndez* case, the Anderson bill (1947) repealed all California school codes mandating segregation and was signed into law by then Governor Earl Warren.[42] And all of this started from a spark of discrimination when Sylvia's cousin Alice gained admittance to the white school while Sylvia was denied.

Resisting segregation through constructions of whiteness may have occurred more frequently than previously thought. Growing up in the rural West Valley near Phoenix, Arizona, during World War II, Corinne Carbajal Heywood, the daughter of a "Mexican-American father and Spanish-American mother," remembered her first day at school.

> My first day of school. I was eager and happy to go. I recall two school buildings standing in direct contrast to each other; one looked nice and the other looked ignored and in disrepair. My mother filled out papers, and we were led out the door toward the sad-looking building. Mother came to a stop, looking angry. We returned to the office. . . . Mother spoke quietly to a man, and then to my relief, we were led out the door again. This time we were going toward the nice building. But I felt a little less confident . . . about going to school. I kept thinking that maybe I was supposed to be in the sad building and I didn't belong in the nice one at all.
>
> . . . The sad-looking building was for Mexican children. Our Spanish heritage had gotten us into the better school.[43]

For Corinne Carbajal Heywood, her feelings of insecurity, the unintended impact of passing, still burned in her memory sixty years later.

Crafting whiteness also transpired outside the Southwest. According to Gabriela Arredondo, light-complected Mexicans in Chicago could capitalize on their skin color to secure better jobs and mainstream social acceptance through acts of passing: "Many of these Mexicans who could 'pass' tried to position themselves as Spanish. In doing so, they worked to gain a European-ness," an identity just a short step away from being *americana/o*.[44] In the preface to *The White Scourge*, Neil Foley poignantly reflects on the racial/ethnic negotiations of his mother, María Trejo: "My mother . . . in seeking to avoid the harsh discrimination that she witnessed against blacks in the District of Columbia and Virginia in the 1940s and 1950s and that sometimes she herself experienced when she was denied service at downtown lunch counters and department stores, sought to convince neighbors, strangers, and lunch counter personnel that she was white — not exactly Anglo, of course, but white nonetheless. For the first time in her life, she could not be what she had always been in the Southwest — a *mexicana*."[45]

For Andrea Pérez, her desire to marry World War II veteran Sylvester Davis met resistance from the state of California. Pérez was the daughter of Mexican immigrants; her fiancé, Davis, was African American. Fully aware that California's anti-miscegenation code prohibited their union, they hired attorney Dan Marshall to challenge this discriminatory law. Indeed, after a Los Angeles County clerk denied the couple a marriage license, Pérez filed suit. In 1949 the California Supreme Court ruled in Pérez's favor, becoming the first state supreme court to strike down an anti-miscegenation law. As Dara Orenstein brilliantly points out, this decision hinged, in part, on *mestizaje*. She argues that the court rendered the statute as "too vague and uncertain" given that the legislation did not take into account people of "mixed ancestry" and that government employees could not consistently determine degrees of whiteness.[46] In addition to this line of reasoning, the California Supreme Court further ruled that the law violated the equal protection clause of the Fourteenth Amendment. From the borderlands era to the present, the fluidities embedded in mestizaje allow for multiple constructions of subjectivities, including morena/o, blanca/o, and café con leche.

In locating meaning in gendered, lived experiences, we should be mindful of our responsibilities to our narrators, to our craft, and to our communities. Or as Valerie J. Matsumoto insightfully comments, "Perhaps scholars should be reminded that we, no less than those we study, are actors in history, making choices that affect the lives of others."[47] Critical of standpoint methodologies that purport to give voice to the voiceless, postcolonial theorist Rosalind O'Hanlon cautions against using "their words [to] address our own concerns, and to render their figures in our self-image."[48] While I concur that we should not recast narrators/subjects into plaster saints or (worse) intellectual replicas, I do believe their words and deeds can provide guidance, comfort, inspiration, or cautionary tales that can be applied to the here and now. At heart, I am probably an unreconstructed social historian who still dreams of a useable past.

NOTES

I would like to thank Professor Valerie Matsumoto at UCLA and Rubén Flores at the University of Kansas for their comments and guidance.

1. Discussion during the first session of Mapping Memories and Migrations: Re-thinking Latina Histories, Latina Cultural Center, Dallas, Texas, February 28, 2004; Roberto Calderón, "Martínez, Anita N.," in *Latinas in the United States: A Historical Encyclopedia*, ed. Vicki L. Ruiz and Virginia Sánchez Korrol (Bloomington: Indiana University Press, 2006); Brian D. Behnken, "Fighting Their Own Battles: Blacks, Mexican Americans, and the Struggle for Civil Rights in Texas, 1950–1975 (PhD diss., University of California, Davis, forthcoming).

2. Interview with María Garcíaz, conducted by the author, October 2, 2004.

3. María Varela quoted in Carlos Muñoz Jr., *Youth, Identity, Power: The Chicano Movement* (New York: Verso, 1989), 78.

4. Ibid., 75–78; Elizabeth Martínez, "Chingón Politics Die Hard: Reflections on the First Chicano Activists Reunion," *Z Magazine* (April 1990): 45.

5. Alicia Gaspar de Alba, *Chicano Art Inside/Outside the Master's House: Cultural Politics and the CARA Exhibit* (Austin: University of Texas Press, 1998). See also the catalog for the CARA exhibit: Richard Griswold del Castillo, Teresa McKenna, and Yvonne Yarbro-Bejaraño, *Chicano Art: Resistance and Affirmation, 1965–1985* (Los Angeles: UCLA Wight Art Gallery, 1991).

6. Alfredo Mirandé and Evangelina Enríquez, *La Chicana: The Mexican-American Woman* (Chicago: University of Chicago Press, 1979), 14–24, quotes on 24 and 15, respectively.

7. Albert Camarillo, *Chicanos in a Changing Society: From Mexican Pueblos to American Barrios in Santa Barbara and Southern California, 1848–1930* (Cambridge, Mass.: Harvard University Press, 1979); Richard Griswold del Castillo, *The Los Angeles Barrio, 1850–1890: A Social History (Berkeley: University of California Press, 1979)*; Mario T. García, *Desert Immigrants: The Mexicans of El Paso, 1880–1920 (New Haven: Yale University Press, 1980)*.

8. Vicki L. Ruiz, *Cannery Women, Cannery Lives: Mexican Women, Unionization, and the California Food Processing Industry, 1930–1950* (Albuquerque: University of New Mexico Press, 1987); Vicki L. Ruiz, *From Out of the Shadows: Mexican Women in Twentieth-Century America* (New York: Oxford University Press, 1998).

9. Elizabeth Salas, *Soldaderas in the Mexican Military: Myth and History* (Austin: University of Texas Press, 1990), 120.

10. Camille Guérin-Gonzales, *Mexican Workers and American Dreams: Immigration, Repatriation, and California Farm Labor, 1900–1939* (New Brunswick, N.J.: Rutgers University Press, 1994); Emilio Zamora, *The World of Mexican Workers in Texas* (College Station: Texas A&M Press, 1993); Gilbert González, *Labor and Community: Mexican Citrus Worker Villages in a Southern California County, 1900–1950* (Urbana: University of Illinois Press, 1994). For an urban perspective, see Zaragosa Vargas, *Proletarians of the North: A History of Mexican Industrial Workers in Detroit and the Midwest, 1917–1933* (Berkeley: University of California Press, 1993).

11. Lisbeth Haas, *Conquests and Historical Identities in California, 1769–1936* (Berkeley: University of California Press, 1995); Devra Weber, *Dark Sweat, White Gold: California Farm Workers, Cotton, and the New Deal* (Berkeley: University of California Press, 1994). Quote is from Devra Weber, "*Raiz Fuerte:* Oral History and Mexicana Farmworkers," in *Unequal Sisters: A Multicultural Reader in U.S. Women's History,* 2nd ed., ed. Vicki L. Ruiz and Ellen Carol DuBois (New York: Routledge, 1994), 399.

12. Ramón A. Gutiérrez, *When Jesus Came, the Corn Mothers Went Away: Marriage, Sexuality, and Power in New Mexico, 1500–1846* (Stanford, Calif.: Stanford University Press, 1991).

13. James F. Brooks, *Captives and Cousins: Slavery, Kinship, and Community in the Southwest Borderlands* (Chapel Hill: University of North Carolina Press, 2002), quote on 79; Ned Blackhawk, "Review of Captives and Cousins," *American Indian Culture and Research Journal* 28, no. 1 (2004): 89–90.

14. Omar Santiago Valerio-Jiménez, "Indios Bárbaros, Divorcées, and Flocks of Vampires: Identity and Nation on the Rio Grande, 1749–1894 (PhD diss., University of California, Los Angeles, 2000), 60–74, quote on 71.

15. Douglas Monroy, *Thrown among Strangers: The Making of Mexican Culture in Frontier California* (Berkeley: University of California Press, 1990); Tomás Almaguer, *Racial Fault Lines: The Historical Origins of White Supremacy in California* (Berkeley: University of California Press, 1994). Quotes are from Monroy, *Thrown among Strangers,* 245, 158, respectively.

16. Almaguer, *Racial Fault Lines,* 57–62; Antonia I. Castañeda, "The Political Economy of Nineteenth-Century Stereotypes of Californianas," in *Between Borders: Essays on Mexicana/Chicana History,* ed. Adelaida R. Del Castillo (Los Angeles: Floricanto Press, 1990), 221–225; *Nevada Journal,* October 25, 1852; the *Nevada Journal* reprinted this piece from a paper noted as the *Courier.*

17. For a review of this literature, see Richard Griswold del Castillo, *La Familia: The Mexican American Family in the Urban Southwest* (Notre Dame: University of Notre Dame Press, 1984), 66–67; Almaguer, *Racial Fault Lines,* 60; María Raquel Casas, *"Married to a Daughter of the Land": Interethnic Marriages in California, 1820–1880* (Reno: University of Nevada Press, 2007).

18. Linda Gordon, *The Great Arizona Orphan Abduction* (Cambridge, Mass.: Harvard University Press, 1999); Stephen Lassonde, "Family Values, 1904 Version," *New York Times Book Review,* January 9, 2000: 7.

19. Mario T. García, *Mexican Americans: Leadership, Ideology, and Identity, 1930–1960* (New Haven: Yale University Press, 1989), 35; David Gutiérrez, *Walls and Mirrors: Mexican Americans, Mexican Immigrants, and the Politics of Ethnicity in the Southwest, 1910–1986* (Berkeley: University of California Press, 1995), 74–87. Quotes from García, *Mexican Americans,* loc. cit; Gutiérrez, *Walls and Mirrors,* 84.

20. Neil Foley, *The White Scourge: Mexicans, Blacks, and Poor Whites in Texas Cotton Culture* (Berkeley: University of California Press, 1997), 209.

21. Cynthia E. Orozco, "The Origins of the League of United Latin American Citizens (LULAC) and the Mexican American Civil Rights Movement in Texas with an Analysis of Women's Political Participation in a Gendered Context, 1919–1927" (PhD diss., University of California, Los Angeles, 1992). Quote is taken from Cynthia E. Orozco, "Beyond Machismo, La Familia, and Ladies Auxiliaries," in *Renato Rosaldo Lecture Series Monograph,* vol. 10 (Tucson: University of Arizona Mexican American Studies and Research Center, 1992–93), 55.

22. Gutiérrez, *Walls and Mirrors,* 78.

23. Foley, *The White Scourge,* 211.

24. Sarah Deutsch, *No Separate Refuge: Culture, Class, and Gender on the Anglo-Hispanic Frontier in the American Southwest, 1880–1949* (New York: Oxford University Press, 1987); George J. Sánchez, *Becoming Mexican American: Ethnicity, Culture, and Identity in Chicano Los Angeles, 1900–1945* (New York: Oxford University Press, 1993).

25. Rubén Martínez, "The Role of the Intellectual Chicano/Latino in Our Communities," talk given at the Graduate Humanities Center, Claremont Graduate School, Claremont, Calif., October 6, 1993.

26. Ruiz, *From Out of the Shadows,* xvi.

27. Elizabeth Rodríguez Kessler, "New Texts in Chicana Studies," *NWSA Journal* 10 (fall 1998): 210.

28. Emma Pérez, *The Decolonial Imaginary: Writing Chicanas into History* (Bloomington: Indiana University Press, 1999).

29. Deborah Rose Ramos Vargas, "*Las Tracaleras:* Texas-Mexican Women, Music, and Place" (PhD diss., University of California, Santa Cruz, 2003); Mary Ann Villarreal, "*Cantantes y Cantineras:* Mexican American Communities and the Mapping of Public Space" (PhD diss., Arizona State University, 2003).

30. Maylei Blackwell, "Geographies of Difference: Mapping Multiple Feminist Insurgencies and Transnational Public Cultures in the Americas," (PhD diss., University of California, Santa Cruz, 2000); Dolores Delgado Bernal, "Chicana School Resistance and Grassroots Leadership: Providing an Alternative History of the 1968 East Los Angeles Blowouts" (PhD diss., University of California, Los Angeles, 1997); Dionne Elaine Espinoza, "Pedagogies of Nationalism and Gender: Cultural Resistance in Selected Representational Practices of Chicano Movement Activists, 1967–1972 (PhD diss., Cornell University, 1996).

31. Marisela R. Chávez. "*Despierten Hermanas y Hermanos:* Women, the Chicano Movement, and Chicana Feminisms in California, 1966–1978" (PhD diss., Stanford University, 2004); Lorena Oropeza, *Raza Sí! Guerra No! Chicano Protest and Patriotism during the Viet Nam War Era* (Berkeley: University of California, Press, 2005).

32. Lara Medina, *Las Hermanas: Chicana/Latina Religious-Political Activism in the U.S. Catholic Church* (Philadelphia: Temple University Press, 2004).

33. Rosaura Sánchez, *Telling Identities: The Californio Testimonios* (Minneapolis: University of Minnesota Press, 1995); Deena J. González, *Refusing the Favor: Spanish-Mexican Women of Santa Fe, 1820–1880* (New York: Oxford University Press, 1999); Antonia I. Castañeda, "*Presidarias y Pobladoras:* Spanish-Mexican Women in Frontier Monterey, Alta, California, 1770–1821" (PhD diss., Stanford University, 1990).

34. Bárbara O. Reyes, "Nineteenth-Century California as Engendered Space: The Public/Private Lives of Women of the Californias" (PhD diss., University of California, San Diego, 2000); Casas, "*Married to a Daughter of the Land*"; Miroslava Chávez-García, *Negotiating Conquest: Gender and Power in California, 1770s to 1880s* (Tucson: University of Arizona Press, 2004).

35. Steven Rosales, "*Soldados Razos:* Chicano Politics, Identity, and Masculinity in the U.S. Military, 1940–1980 (PhD diss., University of California, Irvine, 2007); Matt García, *A World of Its Own: Race, Labor, and Class in the Making of Greater Los Angeles, 1900–1970* (Chapel Hill: University of North Carolina Press, 2002), quote on 13.

36. Gabriela F. Arredondo, *Mexican Chicago: Race, Ethnicity, and Identity, 1916–1939.* (Urbana: University of Illinois Press, 2006).

37. John M. Nieto Phillips, "'No Other Blood': History, Language, and Spanish American Ethnic Identity in New Mexico, 1880s–1920s" (PhD diss., University of California, Los Angeles, 1997).

38. University of California, Irvine, Division of Student Services, Office of the Vice Chancellor, "A Family Changes History: *Méndez v. Westminster,*" a fiftieth anniversary commemorative program book (1998), 6, 30, back cover; Gilbert González, *Chicano Education in the Era of Segregation* (Philadelphia: Balch Institute Press, 1990), 151. To her credit, Soledad Vidaurri refused to enroll her children in the "white" school when her brother Gonzálo's three children were denied access.

39. Frank Barajas, "On Behalf of . . . ," (graduate seminar paper, Claremont Graduate School, 1994), 1, 12, 26; José Pitti et al., "A History of Mexican Americans in California," in *Five Views: An Ethnic History Site Survey for California* (Sacramento: California Department of Parks and Recreation, 1980), 238; *Los Angeles Times,* September 10, 1996; Vicki L. Ruiz, "*Méndez v. Westminster,*" in *Latinas in the United States: A Historical Encyclopedia,* ed. Vicki L. Ruiz and Sánchez Korrol; Carey McWilliams, "Is Your Name Gonzales?" *Nation* 164 (March 15, 1947): 302.

40. *Los Angeles Times,* September 10, 1996; McWilliams, "Is Your Name," 303; "Reporter's Transcript of Proceedings, *Gonzalo Mendez et. al. v. Westminster School District of Orange County, et. al.,*" in File Folders 4292-M, Box# 740, Civil Cases 4285–4292, RG 21-Records of the District Court of the United States for the Southern District of California, Central Division, National Archives and Records Administration (Pacific Region), Laguna Niguel, Calif., 5, 85–87, 116–119, 120, 122–123, 563–565. The exchange between Marcus and Kent can be located on 116–118.

41. McWilliams, "Is Your Name," 302; Charles Wollenberg, *All Deliberate Speed: Segregation and Exclusion in California Schools, 1855–1975* (Berkeley: University of California Press, 1976), 127–128, 131–132; "Proceedings, *Mendez v. Westminster,*" 460, 468.

42. Rubén Flores, "Social Science in the Southwestern Courtroom: A New Understanding of the Development of the NAACP's Legal Strategies in the School Desegregation Cases" (BA thesis, Princeton University, 1994), 105–116; Wollenberg, *All Deliberate Speed,* 128, 131–132; Barajas, "On Behalf of . . . ," 33; Guadalupe San Miguel Jr., "*Let Them All Take Heed": Mexican Americans and the Campaign for Educational Equality in Texas, 1910–1981*

(Austin: University of Texas Press, 1987), 119; Pitti et al., "A History of Mexican Americans," 239. Quotes are taken from Flores, "Social Science," 116; Wollenberg, *All Deliberate Speed,* 132; and San Miguel Jr., *"Let Them All Take Heed,"* loc. cit. For more information on Mexican Americans and school desegregation, see Vicki L. Ruiz, "Tapestries of Resistance: Episodes of School Segregation and Desegregation in the U.S. West," in *From Grassroots to the Supreme Court: Exploration of* Brown v. Board of Education *and American Democracy,* ed. Peter Lau (Durham, N.C.: Duke University Press, 2004), 44–67.

43. *Arizona Republic,* February 4, 2001. Ironically, the title of the article is "Strong heritage staves off prejudice."

44. Gabriela F. Arredondo, "Cartographies of Americanisms: Possibilities for Transnational Identities, Chicago, 1916–1939," in *Geographies of Latinidad: Mapping Latina/o Studies into the 21st Century,* ed. Matt García, Marie Leger, and Angarad Valdivia (Durham, N.C.: Duke University Press, forthcoming).

45. Foley, *The White Scourge,* xiii–xiv.

46. Dara Orenstein, "Void for Vagueness: Mexicans and the Collapse of Miscegenation Law in California," *Pacific Historical Review* 74, no. 3 (August 2005): 367–407; Alex Lubin, "What's Love Got to Do with It? The Politics of Race and Marriage in the California Supreme Court's 1949 *Perez v. Sharp* Decision," *OAH Magazine of History* 18, no. 4 (July 2004): 31–37; Peggy Pascoe, "Miscegenation Law, Court Cases, and Ideologies of 'Race' in Twentieth-Century America," *Journal of American History* 83, no. 1 (June 1996): 44–69. Quotes from Orenstein, "Void for Vagueness," 371 and 370, respectively.

47. Valerie J. Matsumoto, *Farming the Home Place: A Japanese American Community in California, 1919–1982* (Ithaca, N.Y.: Cornell University Press, 1993), 224.

48. Rosalind O'Hanlon, "Recovering the Subject: Subaltern Studies and Histories of Resistance in Colonial South Asia," in *Mapping Subaltern Studies and the Postcolonial,* ed. Vinayak Chaturvedi (London: Verso, 2000), 96.

13

The Woman Suffrage Movement, 1848–1920

ELIZABETH J. CLAPP

The seventy-two-year-long struggle by American women to gain the vote has proved a fertile area of study for women's historians, although the relationship between the practice of women's history and the history of suffrage has not always been straightforward. Histories of the woman suffrage movement in the United States were written by a range of activists long before women's history became an accepted field of academic inquiry.[1] Traditionally, historians viewed the suffrage struggle as part of the history of democracy in the United States, an effort to widen the franchise to all Americans. They wrote organizational histories of the women's rights movement, centering on the campaign for the vote, and biographers included suffragists among their projects. These pioneering histories paid attention to exceptional women who operated in the male world. They characterized them as white, middle class, and mostly living on the East Coast, which reflected little of the diversity and regional variation highlighted by recent studies.[2]

The emphasis on the suffrage movement proved problematic for women's history as it developed during the 1970s. Some historians considered the concentration on the campaign for the vote as focusing too narrowly on women who behaved in ways usually regarded as masculine. Others, notably the new social historians, wished to include women from all backgrounds. They believed that to study women acting politically and collectively in the woman suffrage movement reinforced assumptions that women's actions had significance only if they emulated men.[3] While not wishing to diminish the struggle of women who sought a larger part in the political life of the nation, those constructing a new methodology for women's history have not regarded the suffrage movement as being of primary importance.[4] Nonetheless, studies of the woman suffrage movement continue to draw on and help to develop conceptual frameworks in the field. Thus, as women's historians begin to examine women's political activism as abolitionists, temperance advocates, and social reformers, but also as party activists, new concerns have come to the forefront. The reinvigoration of political history with its emphasis on political culture, popular movements, and a new inclusivity which incorporates gender as well as class, race, and ethnicity has further influenced the practitioners of women's history, who have begun to re-evaluate the history of the suffrage movement in the light of questions raised by this new intersectional focus.[5] As a consequence, the emphasis has shifted, fresh viewpoints have been added, and the traditional story has been reshaped.

The traditional view begins the struggle for woman suffrage in the United States with the Seneca Falls convention of 1848.[6] Certainly, its earliest historians, themselves participants in the movement, offered such origins. Their narrative focused on the national campaign to secure the vote for women during the second half of the nineteenth century. This narrative typically starts with Elizabeth Cady Stanton's Declaration of Sentiments, highlighting it as the essential statement of antebellum women's rights. Early advocates considered suffrage to be the most radical of women's demands, which ranged from property rights to marriage reform. After the Civil War, suffrage became the central issue for women's rights leaders. They split over strategies for accomplishing suffrage into the National Woman Suffrage Association (NWSA) led by Stanton and Susan B. Anthony and the American Woman Suffrage Association (AWSA) led by Lucy Stone. In 1890, these two organizations reconciled their differences, forming the National American Woman Suffrage Association (NAWSA), which shifted the suffrage argument from an insistence on natural justice to one of expediency. While NAWSA acted as a political pressure group and reshaped suffragists' image to fit with the maternalist, traditional ideal of woman, Alice Paul led the National Woman's Party (NWP) in more radical demonstrations and hunger strikes. The organizations' dual effort proved successful, leading to the ratification of the Nineteenth Amendment to the federal Constitution in August 1920.

Participants in the movement compiled the earliest histories of the suffrage movement even before women gained the vote. The six volume *History of Woman Suffrage*, edited by Elizabeth Cady Stanton, Susan B. Anthony, and Matilda Joslyn Gage, published between 1881 and 1922, was a profoundly personal and political work that sought to encourage future generations of women to become involved in the agitation for woman suffrage.[7] The authors emphasized political perspectives and changing organizational frameworks, concentrating on the national campaign. A largely uncritical assessment of the movement, the work glossed over controversies and buried unsavory matters. Written in part as propaganda for the campaign, the later volumes particularly provided a sanitized version of the movement's story, designed to preserve the movement's place in history. These volumes emphasized female progress, the heroism of the pioneers, and the justice of the cause.[8] Other participants also attempted to make the movement respectable and played down the radicalism of some of its early leaders. Histories written during the final years of the suffrage battle, notably by Carrie Chapman Catt, sought to minimize the role of Elizabeth Cady Stanton, among others, whose interests in the more general problem of women's rights proved embarrassing to her successors.[9] Such works emphasized the conservatism of the woman suffrage movement rather than its radicalism.

The years following the ratification of the Nineteenth Amendment saw no comprehensive history of the struggle for the vote. While some of the suffrage activists wrote their memoirs and others wrote histories of state suffrage movements, not until 1959 did a scholar examine the national campaign in its entirety.[10] Upon publication, Eleanor Flexner's *Century of Struggle* quickly gained recognition as a landmark history of the woman's rights movement.[11] Impressive in range, including an analysis which examined the campaign in the South and West as well as nationally, *Century of Struggle* investigated the movement from its first incarnation to the winning of the Nineteenth Amendment. It placed the suffrage movement in its wider context, reflecting Flexner's own radical understanding of social and economic change. She applied an understanding of "the woman question" and "the Negro question," viewing suffrage history from a perspective shaped by her "left feminist" viewpoint.[12] Flexner did not see the eventual gaining of the vote as an inevitable part of the progress of women, but recognized the depth of achievement of the suffrage leaders and the difficulty of the struggle. Later works obscured these accomplishments by emphasizing the limited changes in women's situation wrought by suffrage.[13] Though concluding with an analysis of what the vote did *not* bring women, Flexner concentrated on the campaign itself and its achievements.

The emergence of what has become known as "second wave feminism" in the 1960s transformed perceptions of women's place in American society. It prompted historians to explain why "first wave feminism" and suffrage seemingly did little to change women's subordination in economic and social life. Like Flexner, both Andrew Sinclair and William O'Neill located the fight for the suffrage in the wider movement for women's rights, concentrating on the national leaders and campaign, but criticizing its focus on the single issue of the vote.[14] O'Neill's account was particularly judgmental. Arguing from the vantage point of the feminist movement of the 1960s, he condemned the earlier women's rights movement for its inability to recognize the causes of women's oppression, particularly for its failure to address the issue of women's role in the family. As a consequence, he claimed, the concentration of the women's rights movement on gaining the vote might have helped them to achieve their goal, but it failed to emancipate women.

By contrast, the 1975 documentary history of the movement edited by Anne Firor Scott and Andrew MacKay Scott posited that the vote actually helped women to advance their cause materially and provided the foundation on which future efforts rested.[15] The Scotts' study centered on the suffrage campaign and the tactics of the main suffrage organizations. They gave little sense of opposition or support, arguing that splits in the movement itself might well have contributed to the eventual success of the campaign.

While these works examined the broad sweep of the national woman suffrage movement from its inception before the Civil War until the ratification of the Nineteenth Amendment, they concentrated on the leaders of the movement and its institutional forms. In 1965, Aileen Kraditor took the study of the woman suffrage campaign into new areas. Although deploying a narrow time frame and overall focus, Kraditor investigated the ideas of the suffrage movement during the Progressive era within the broader context of American intellectual history.[16] The ideas of the suffragists reflected their aspirations, acted as weapons, and developed in response to their opponents. The Progressive Era was, for Kraditor, crucial to the suffragists' success as they sought to reposition themselves by shifting their arguments from an insistence upon natural justice to one of expediency and women's special qualities. They also narrowed their definition of democracy to exclude certain groups such as African Americans and new immigrants in order to appeal to more conservative elements and undermine the arguments of their opponents. Thus, according to Kraditor, the woman suffragists rejected their radical egalitarian heritage and agenda. As a result, when the vote was achieved, it brought few visible gains for most women.

The emergence and development of women's history in the early 1970s interrupted the move toward more specialized studies of the suffrage fight. Political history fell out of favor, as those who sought for the origins of feminism researched other matters. Some feminist historians even disputed the significance of the suffrage movement for the history of feminism. Like O'Neill, Sinclair, and Kraditor, they questioned whether the vote really brought women's emancipation, and they found the radicalism of the nineteenth-century suffrage movement to be wanting. Social historians, such as Daniel Scott Smith and Carroll Smith-Rosenberg, located the radical heritage of feminism in challenges to women's traditional position in the home and family.[17] Nonetheless, even in the mid-1970s, suffragism had its defenders, most notably Ellen Carol DuBois, who drew attention to the radicalism of the movement. The woman suffrage movement was significant, she argued, because it took the debate about women's oppression in the family out of the domestic sphere and insisted that women should be admitted to citizenship and thus the public arena. Suffragism was radical precisely because it demanded for women a kind of power and a place in the social order not based on their position in the family.[18]

DuBois carried her arguments further in a book on the creation of an independent women's movement in the aftermath of the Civil War.[19] She both reasserted the centrality of the suffrage movement to the history of feminism and refused to follow the more general move away from political history and studies of the vote. Drawing on the analytical constructs of the developing field of women's history, DuBois made the case that the woman suffrage movement responded to economic developments, the creation of separate spheres, and the reform movements of the 1820s and 1830s. Political activists promised the creation of a truly democratic society, and this drew women to the women's rights campaign. The emergence of the woman suffrage movement after the Civil War marked their commitment to gain increased power over their lives. DuBois suggested that their failure to achieve the vote in the 1870s was less the result of hostilities within the suffrage movement, as earlier historians had argued, than the product of the defeat of Reconstruction radicalism. Indeed, she contended, conflict within the movement during the late 1860s was significant since it decoupled women's rights from efforts to ensure African Americans' rights. In this way white women sought their own emancipation while jettisoning that of black women and men.[20]

If DuBois was unusual in the 1970s in trying to reconcile the suffrage movement with debates about the origins of feminism and the emerging field of women's history, the quest for the vote itself did not cease to be a subject of scholarly attention altogether. Historians continued to examine the demand for the suffrage, but as part of other social reform movements whose main purpose was not necessarily to involve women in the political process. Keith Melder, for instance, argued that the origins of the women's rights movement and the suffrage movement could be found in the reform associations of the antebellum period. Several of these reforms were directed toward the particular problems of women and, for many women activists, the demand for women's rights followed logically from their involvement in reform movements.[21] Similarly, Barbara Berg examined the antebellum women's voluntary associations as the source of demands for women's rights and eventually the suffrage.[22] Others, such as Jack S. Blocker Jr., shifted the spotlight from the origins of women's rights to an examination of women's reform activity. He found that temperance advocates and suffragists held similar commitments to women's role in the public arena, which led many temperance activists ultimately to demand the right to vote.[23] However, while these scholars sought the origins of the suffrage movement in antebellum reform movements, other historians searched for new definitions of the political which went beyond electoral politics.[24]

While women's history developed in new and creative directions, the uneasy relationship between the practice of women's history and the scholarly examination of the woman suffrage movement which had existed in the 1970s persisted into the next decade. The publication during the 1980s of research which looked at women's growing political involvement at the end of the nineteenth century, even if it did not focus directly on the woman suffrage movement, nonetheless, had a considerable impact on subsequent histories of suffrage. Important among these works was Mari Jo Buhle's *Women and American Socialism*. Her focus on the socialist movement documented its often ambivalent attitude toward both the "bourgeois" suffrage movement and the issue of the vote for women, but she also uncovered a great flourishing of working-class radicalism in the late nineteenth century. The interaction of women within such radical organizations as the socialist movement, the Knights of Labor, and farmers' protest groups with the Women's Christian Temperance Union (WCTU) prompted many of these women to support the vote — a factor crucial to the suffrage victories in many western states.[25] Other historians in this period, notably Ruth Bordin in her study of the

WCTU and Karen Blair's work on the women's club movement, revealed that for middle-class women activism outside the suffrage organizations also could produce a demand for the vote which was not restricted to a single issue.[26]

The seventy-fifth anniversary of the ratification of the Nineteenth Amendment, together with projects to collect and make more readily available the papers of some suffrage leaders, has led to a resurgence of interest in the woman suffrage movement over the last fifteen years.[27] There has been a proliferation of books and articles, more specialized, narrower in chronology, themes, and regional focus. This new scholarship takes the history of the woman suffrage movement in different directions, questioning old assumptions and paradigms and developing new areas of interest.

One of these new directions has been an attempt to place women's rights and the woman suffrage movement more firmly in the context of radical politics and to examine the arguments used by the women's rights advocates. In a symposium on the Constitution, DuBois sought to integrate the women's rights movement into a comprehensive history of radical republicanism. At the heart of radical republicanism was the belief that expanded "rights" would lead to a more egalitarian society. DuBois believes that this conviction was pivotal to debates surrounding the Reconstruction amendments, which were themselves central to the women's rights movement. At the basis of the movement's arguments was the belief that natural rights, among them the right to vote, were common to all individuals and that included women. Rather than suggesting that women's need for the franchise was peculiar to them, women's rights advocates regarded any attempt to single out special needs on the grounds of race or sex as highly suspect. The defeat of universal suffrage marked by the Fifteenth Amendment, which enfranchised freedmen, but not freedwomen or women generally, forced the women's rights movement to produce new rationales for women's political rights, and, in a total reversal of their previous arguments, to advocate women's right to vote on the grounds of special qualities. During the 1870s this "New Departure" attempted to interpret the Constitution in such a way as to suggest that it permitted women to vote, although such efforts were defeated in the courts. The legacy of the Reconstruction era for women's rights advocates was, DuBois maintains, an insistence on woman suffrage, at the cost of increasing racial and ethnic antagonism.[28]

Sylvia Hoffert and Nancy Isenberg look specifically at the ideas of the antebellum women's rights movement, emphasizing less its indebtedness to the antislavery movement and more its location in wider debates about the nature of citizenship and individual rights, thus revisiting DuBois's claims for the radicalism of the movement.[29] Despite rather different concerns, both note that the Declaration of Sentiments represented a rejection of roles imputed to women by Republican Motherhood and the Cult of Domesticity. Instead, the Declaration emphasized women as a disabled caste and demanded women's equality. Suzanne Marilley investigates the ideas of the movement over a longer period of time. She concentrates on the adaptation of the early ideas over the century of struggle, identifying three different aspects of liberal feminism: the feminism of equal rights; the feminism of fear; and the feminism of personal development, each prominent at different periods. Although arguments from expediency occasionally dominated the movement, there were always those who argued for the vote based on principle. She maintains, moreover, that winning the Nineteenth Amendment was a considerable achievement because the forces opposed to women's political equality were always greater than those supporting it.[30]

Other recent works that look at the national woman suffrage movement have positioned it in an explicitly political framework, moving away from the social movement paradigm.[31] Linda Lumsden examines the significance of suffrage activism to the history of freedom of expression and the right to assembly, thus locating it in the context of late-nineteenth- and early-twentieth-century expansions of First Amendment rights.[32] Sara Hunter Graham focuses on the important tactical innovations of the National American Woman Suffrage Association. Looking at the period 1896 to 1910, seen by Eleanor Flexner as the "doldrums" of the movement, Graham explores the ways in which the leaders of the NAWSA refocused the organization and aimed at gaining a new membership and image. In doing so, NAWSA became an effective single-issue pressure group with an efficient political organization at national, state, and local levels and a committed lobby in Washington, D.C. In the process, NAWSA also became much more conservative. While its single-mindedness was extremely effective in winning the federal amendment, the organization was unequipped to take a feminist agenda forward afterwards because it had no plan beyond obtaining the vote.[33]

Graham is not the first historian to try to explain why the energy built by the campaign for the federal amendment dissipated so quickly after 1920 and why the women's movement was unable to carry a feminist agenda forward into the 1920s. J. Stanley Lemons, for instance, claimed that while the main current of American feminism, "social feminism," neither failed nor was destroyed after 1920, it did slow down due to the more conservative climate of the times. The National Woman's Party drifted for some time. It reorganized only in 1921 in order to fight for legal equality, a decision that cut it off from the mainstream of women's activism.[34] Paula Baker, on the other hand, posited that the transformation of political culture in the late nineteenth century helped explain the breakdown of separate political spheres after 1920. Notions of female deference enabled women to lobby for social welfare legislation and encouraged them to ask for the vote in order to achieve reform, with the result that the state absorbed women's political culture. Consequently, once women had the vote they no longer had a separate political identity and politicians quickly realized that women did not constitute a voting bloc to whom they had to appeal.[35]

Nancy F. Cott has a more positive view of feminism after the vote was gained. She observes that the younger generation of women in the 1920s was more interested in other aspects of female emancipation, as represented by new consumer products and modes of dress, than they were in older notions of women's rights. Nonetheless, seeing 1920 as a watershed in the politics of women, she contends, is to obscure many of the continuities. Women's voluntary organizations maintained their membership, while discussions about women's rights continued, leading to the attempt to introduce an Equal Rights Amendment in 1923.[36] Like Graham, recent scholarship on the movement following the Nineteenth Amendment has concentrated on its splintering. More radical elements pursued the goal of legal equality for women, while others, as Christine Bolt shows, pursued quite different agendas, including the furtherance of protective industrial legislation for women, the advancement of social welfare reforms, and the pursuit of the international peace campaign.[37]

Other historians have considered women who opposed suffrage. Aileen Kraditor noted that the suffragists adapted their ideas in response to attacks by their opponents, but until recently few studies dealt specifically with female anti-suffragism. Jane Jerome Camhi, Thomas J. Jablonsky, and Susan Marshall, among others, have begun to rectify this omission. Jablonsky examines the major anti-suffrage organizations, their changing concerns and tactics, and their increasing shrillness as the suffrage movement began to gain victories. Camhi is more concerned with the anti-suffragists' ideas and suffragist reaction to them. Both Jablonsky and Camhi note the similarities between the suffragists and the antis; they came from similar backgrounds, were involved in social reform movements and benevolent work, and were well educated. Jablonsky points out, however, that the antis were less likely to be college-educated than the suffragists. They had a different social vision, but they were not the puppets of the liquor industry, as earlier historians charged. Whereas Jablonsky and Camhi looked at anti-suffragism as a national phenomenon, Marshall concentrates on the Massachusetts organization and especially its elitism. Anti-suffragists there insisted on the importance of separate spheres and the dangers of allowing women a more active role in political affairs. Although class and gender had their role to play in the anti-suffrage movement, she concludes that the local political climate largely explained anti-suffrage success in defeating suffrage referenda.[38]

Elna C. Green's study of the anti-suffragists in the southern states is as much about those who campaigned for the vote as those who opposed it.[39] A great variety of opinion existed among southern pro- and anti-suffragists, but class distinctions particularly divided the groups. The antis tended to be from the planter-manufacturing elite, while the suffragists belonged to an urban middle class, whose economic status rested on professional pursuits. Like Marshall, Green acknowledges the importance of local issues, especially in the opposition of some suffrage groups to a federal amendment that occasionally led to allegiance with the anti-suffragists.

The increasing number of regional and local investigations published in the last few years attest to the importance of local and regional issues to understanding the quest for the vote and the reasons getting it did not bring about radical change. This has become one of the most vibrant areas of scholarship on the woman suffrage movement. Yet while such works have the capacity to challenge the conclusions of national studies, they are not in sufficient numbers or depth to fulfill this potential.[40]

This new research takes various forms: examinations of state efforts to amend the state constitution, state campaigns for the federal amendment, and regional explorations. The majority of these works focus on the last ten years of the struggle to secure the federal amendment. Most studies of local battles concentrate on western states, particularly during the last decades of the nineteenth century, asking why these states were the first to give women the vote. Countering Alan Grimes's 1967 argument that white men were responsible for giving women the vote because they saw white women as a stabilizing influence and a counter-balance to the votes of foreign-born settlers, these works focus on the activism and demands of women themselves.[41] Though it is difficult to generalize from such local studies, most recent historians regard women's agency as key to winning the vote.

Studies of western suffrage campaigns contend that the civic activism of middle-class white women working from within voluntary associations was of particular importance in prompting them to seek the vote. They used the alliances created by such activism as a basis from which to fight for suffrage.[42] Gayle Gullett, for instance, shows the importance of organized womanhood in California in building links with male "good government" reformers. This close interaction allowed elite women to forge a new political identity through their public work, forming the basis of the Progressive movement and eventually leading to success in the 1911 California suffrage referendum.[43] In a more regional perspective, Rebecca Mead contends that debates about equal rights for women began in the West during Reconstruction. The particular experience of western states with reform movements such as Populism, Progressivism, and the labor movement gave woman suffragists more opportunities to gain support for their cause than they had in the East.[44]

Western suffragists learned that they had to match their methods to the political environment, transforming their own activism in order to attract male support and showing a much greater degree of flexibility than their eastern counterparts. Other inquiries into western states consider them in the context of the national campaign for the suffrage. These note the importance of the western victories as propaganda for the national campaign and proof that giving women the vote brought benefits to the state.[45] The exception, as both Sarah Barringer Gordon and Rebecca Edwards have shown, was Utah, which proved somewhat of an embarrassment for the leaders of the national movement, who feared that woman suffrage would be tainted by its association with polygamy.[46]

The work of A. Elizabeth Taylor does much to help us understand the suffrage movement in the southern states.[47] Taylor studied virtually every southern state, and her research lays the foundations on which many recent investigations have been built. Marjorie J. Spruill Wheeler's study develops some of Taylor's insights in connecting the rise of the suffrage movement in the South with the issues of race, rights, and reform. The demand for woman suffrage arose in the South at a time when white supremacy was still insecure in the 1890s and declined when blacks were disfranchised after 1910. Through an examination of the lives and ideas of eleven southern suffrage leaders, Wheeler argues that woman suffrage struck at the very basis of southern patriarchy and chivalry by challenging the leadership of elite white men. It was not intended to apply to all women, however, for white suffragists embraced racial and class inequalities. The national movement echoed their racism. Although some southern suffragists accepted the "winning plan" of Carrie Chapman Catt, others opposed a federal amendment because of the threat it might pose to the racial restrictions of state voting laws.[48] Other historians have also noted the tensions between the southern suffrage leaders and the national leaders over tactics. As national leaders contemplated the federal amendment in the early twentieth century, a number of southern leaders raised states' rights arguments and demanded a state-by-state policy.[49]

Research on the northeastern and mid-western states has been less extensive, in part because many of the national leaders came from these parts of the country. In these regions, too, fewer victories for the suffrage movement occurred before the federal amendment. Like other local studies, however, they help to suggest new perspectives on the national campaign. For instance, Sharon Hartman Strom posits that a grassroots effort was responsible for the highly mobilized and efficient movement in Massachusetts, rather than the aggressive leadership of a few prominent individuals. She also sheds new light on the use of militant tactics learned from English suffragettes, which Massachusetts suffragists used some time before Alice Paul took this approach in Washington, D.C.[50] Michael Goldberg's study of Kansas suffragism reveals women's partisanship even before they gained the vote.[51] His work on women in the Populist movement opens up still another area that suffrage historians touched on in the past, but never developed fully.[52]

The proliferation of this scholarship on the states and regions testifies to a renewed interest in the woman suffrage movement and a determination to make it more central to women's history. New departures in women's history, particularly a concern with the impact of race and ethnicity on women's lives, have opened up areas of exploration in woman suffrage history, areas that offer innovative perspectives on the movement.

Developments in the history of African American women have indicated that historians should look more closely at their demand for the vote. Rosalyn Terborg-Penn has been instrumental in uncovering a hidden history of black women's suffrage activity, including that of African American women in the antebellum women's rights movement. Like their white female and black male counterparts, black female abolitionists often were involved in the women's rights movement and may even have been present at the Seneca Falls convention, despite their absence from the record. During the 1850s they were active as speakers, organizers, and audience members in the women's rights conventions and voiced their own arguments during the debates over the Fourteenth and Fifteenth Amendments in the 1860s.[53]

Terborg-Penn's research also draws conscious parallels between black women's suffrage work during the latter half of the nineteenth century and that of white women. African American women had to struggle for another two generations after the passing of the Nineteenth Amendment before they began to enjoy political rights on a level with white women. This would suggest that the traditional narrative of the woman suffrage movement, which sees the struggle for the suffrage ending in 1920, needs revision.[54]

Glenda Elizabeth Gilmore's work on the gendered aspects of Jim Crow and the imposition of white supremacy in North Carolina shows that for black women, as for their white counterparts, the vote was an important goal. Their demand for the vote became a major concern to white supremacists during the debates over the ratification of the Nineteenth Amendment. This was because enfranchisement threatened to bring African Americans back into politics.[55] Gilmore explores black women's attempts to register to vote in 1920, but, like Terborg-Penn, argues that for black women in the South the struggle for enfranchisement continued long after the ratification of the Nineteenth Amendment.

Other works examine how African American women fought for social and political equality with white society and the ways in which the demand for the vote was part of the wider struggle for race advancement. They also emphasize that while black men were not against their wives and daughters demanding the franchise, when black men gained the vote in the aftermath of the Civil War they viewed their vote as a collective asset, rather than as belonging only to men.[56] In her analysis of Richmond, Virginia, after the Civil War, Elsa Barkley Brown interrogates still further the notion of who owned the vote. She suggests that within the black community itself ideas about participation in politics did not remain static, but changed over time as class and gender distinctions developed.[57]

Wanda Hendricks's study of black clubwomen in Illinois highlights the different attitude toward African American women voting in a mid-western state. Despite the continued disputes within the national suffrage organization over black women's participation in marches and public events, black clubwomen in Illinois campaigned for female suffrage and were able to enjoy the fruits of their victory when Illinois granted women the vote first in local elections and then in presidential ones. Unlike the women Gilmore examined, Hendricks's clubwomen were able to use their votes to pursue a political agenda that was racially based and gender inclusive.[58]

These recent works suggest that the campaign for the suffrage was not restricted only to middle-class white women. Other groups were also involved, and their understanding of the meaning of the vote at the end of the nineteenth century was not always the same as that of the white middle-class leaders of the National American Woman's Suffrage Association. While there is a growing interest in African American women's fight for the vote, the suffrage work of white working-class and immigrant women remains largely unexplored.[59] Such women appear as contributors to local campaigns led by the white middle class, but rarely feature as independent actors. This is beginning to be rectified as historians examine the political activities of women's labor organizations. Annelise Orleck, for instance, has traced the involvement of Jewish garment workers in pushing for the suffrage through their labor unions. The research by historians such as Nancy Hewitt and Elizabeth Salas suggests, however, that among certain ethnic groups class solidarity was of more importance to women than the vote. While, as Hewitt indicates, individual women such as Luisa Capetillo recognized the importance of suffrage to immigrant women, few Latin women (or men) embraced the demand for U.S. citizenship, reserving their activism for mutual aid societies and labor organizations. Such studies indicate the need for additional investigation on the independent suffrage activities of racial/ethnic and class groups.[60]

Research into the role of African American women in the struggle for woman suffrage questions the central role of national suffrage organizations by challenging the traditional narrative of suffrage history and suggesting additional areas to explore. In recent years historians have focused on the exclusivity of the suffrage movement, but this has usually concentrated on attempts to exclude African American men from the polls.[61] Native-born white suffragists also frequently sought to exclude immigrant men and women from their demands for the vote, but there has been little work on this aspect and still less on demands made by immigrant women.[62] Some local studies note alliances between white women's clubs and the associations of working-class and immigrant women, but few of these are directly interested in the role of immigrant women, with the partial exception of Nancy Hewitt's examination of the interethnic activism of women in Tampa, Florida.[63]

The field has experienced a new vibrancy in the early twenty-first century. The recent edition of essays edited by Jean Baker highlights new research and revises older interpretations. Together these essays bring women's struggle for the vote into the mainstream not only of women's history but of American history as a whole. As Baker puts it, "suffrage becomes the story of nation-building and citizen-making."[64] Both Judith Wellman and Lori Ginzberg echo this theme. Wellman conducts a detailed study of Elizabeth Cady Stanton and the first women's rights convention. She scrutinizes the origin story of the Seneca Falls meeting and argues that far from being a spontaneous event resulting from the personal frustrations of a small group of women, the convention was, in part, the product of a geography which enabled the coming together of legal reformers, political abolitionists, and radical Quakers who were all committed to the equality of humans and convinced of the power of voting to effect social change.[65]

Particular social, political, economic, and cultural forces converged at Seneca Falls, which, when combined with the leadership of Elizabeth Cady Stanton, created the call for the first women's rights convention. While Wellman questions Stanton's version of events, which characterized the meeting as born out of her own personal story, Lori Ginzberg takes that challenge further by considering the implications of an 1846 petition by six women in rural upstate New York demanding equal rights for women. Ginzberg probes the validity of the conventional narrative, since the petition was signed two years before the Seneca Falls convention. She also considers women's use of petitions to redress their grievances and reactions to the petition. After Ginzberg, we must confront our assumptions about women's political activities and their willingness to discuss women's rights, when faced by the very ordinariness of the farmwomen who presented their petition at the New York state legislature in 1846.[66]

Despite a renewed interest in the origins of the national woman suffrage movement, other areas remain under-explored. One of these is the more militant aspect of the campaign in the early twentieth century. Again, Ellen Carol DuBois has pioneered. Her biography of Elizabeth Cady Stanton's daughter, Harriot Stanton Blatch, explores connections with the militant English suffragettes and Blatch's attempts to involve working-class women in the campaign for the vote, highlighting the comparative neglect by suffrage historians of these aspects of the movement.[67] While there have been examinations of the more militant elements of the national campaign, most notably works on the emergence of the National Woman's Party by Christine Lunardini and Linda Ford, further investigation should explore the full part played by suffrage militancy in gaining the vote and its effects on the post-suffrage women's movement.[68]

Thus, the traditional narrative that focuses on the national leadership and campaign challenges historians to undertake local research, explore state campaigns, and incorporate the different perspectives gained by examining the involvement of African American, working-class, and immigrant women. More research is needed on the latter half of the nineteenth century when splits and rivalry between the National Woman Suffrage Association and the American Woman Suffrage Association seemed to cause stagnation in the campaign. Little research examines the patterns in the states or regions during this period. Similarly, the dominance of the narrative by Elizabeth Cady Stanton and Susan B. Anthony has obscured the work of other leaders and grassroots workers. Their association with radical causes, which traditionally assumes that the demand for the vote was simply too extreme to encourage much of a following, does not recognize that for many women the vote was not as radical a demand as Stanton and Anthony or their opponents maintained. As the scholarship on the states and regions grows and other research places the American movement in an international context, the conclusions that derived solely from national studies and from the traditional narrative are likely to be increasingly questioned.[69]

The great volume of recent work on the woman suffrage movement also suggests that the uneasy relationship between women's history and suffrage history has ceased to be so problematic. This has been a two-way process. On the one hand, most historians of suffrage are now firmly rooted in the analytical constructs of women's history. More importantly, however, historians of women have begun to take a new interest in women's political activity, interpreting it both in the broad sense of involvement in reform and welfare activity and in the narrower sense of electoral politics. Thus, recent scholarship on women and the origins of the welfare state and works on partisan women have suggested that the public sphere was not as closed to women in the past as the rhetoric of the period might suggest.[70] Consequently, women's involvement in the political world no longer seems as aberrant, and their participation in the suffrage movement is now seen as part of the mainstream of women's history. Local studies have examined women's involvement in female associations and reform activity, which often led them to demand the vote. They did so in terms of the traditionally constructed female sphere. The interests of suffrage historians have therefore become the concerns of women's historians. In turn, that fundamental preoccupation of women's historians, the reciprocity between gender and society and the dynamic nature of that relationship, has equally become a focus of historians of the woman suffrage movement.[71]

NOTES

The author would like to thank Jay Kleinberg, her fellow editors, and the anonymous reader for the Press for their helpful comments and suggestions.

1. Most notably, see Elizabeth Cady Stanton, Susan B. Anthony, Matilda Joslyn Gage, and Ida Husted Harper, eds., *The History of Woman Suffrage*, 6 vols. (New York: Fowler & Wells, 1881–1922).

2. See Ann D. Gordon, Mari Jo Buhle, and Nancy Schrom Dye, "The Problem of Women's History," in *Liberating Women's History: Theoretical and Critical Essays,* ed. Berenice A. Carroll (Urbana: University of Illinois Press, 1976), 74–92; and Gerda Lerner, "New Approaches to the Study of Women in American History," in her *The Majority Finds Its Past: Placing Women in History* (New York: Oxford University Press, 1979), 3–14, for critiques of this approach.

3. Gordon, Buhle, and Dye, "The Problem of Women's History," 74–92; Elaine Tyler May, "Expanding the Past: Recent Scholarship on Women in Politics and Work," *Reviews in American History* 10, no. 4 (December 1982): 216–233; Lerner, *The Majority Finds Its Past,* 3–14; Nancy F. Cott and Elizabeth H. Pleck, introduction to *A Heritage of Her Own: Toward a New Social History of American Women,* ed. Nancy F. Cott and Elizabeth H. Pleck (New York: Simon and Schuster, 1979), 9–24.

4. Gordon, Buhle, and Dye, "The Problem of Women's History," 74–92; Gerda Lerner, "New Approaches to the Study of Women in American History," in her *The Majority Finds Its Past,* 3–14. The suffrage movement does not feature in Linda Kerber's call for a new conceptual framework for American women's history: Linda Kerber, "Separate Spheres, Female Worlds, Woman's Place: The Rhetoric of Women's History," *Journal of American History* 75, no. 1 (June 1988): 9–39.

5. Examples of this new political history include Jeffrey L. Pasley, Andrew W. Robertson, and David Waldstreicher, eds., *Beyond the Founders: New Approaches to the Political History of the Early American Republic* (Chapel Hill: University of North Carolina Press, 2004); Sean Wilentz, *The Rise of American Democracy: Jefferson to Lincoln* (New York: W. W. Norton and Company, 2005).

6. See, for instance, Stanton et al., *The History of Woman Suffrage*; Alison M. Parker, "The Case for Reform Antecedents for the Woman's Rights Movement," in *Votes for Women: The Struggle for Suffrage Revisited,* ed. Jean H. Baker (Oxford: Oxford University Press, 2002), 21–41; Miriam Gurko, *The Ladies of Seneca Falls: The Birth of the Women's Rights Movement* (New York: Schocken Books, 1974).

7. Stanton et al., *The History of Woman Suffrage*; Ellen Carol DuBois, "Making Women's History: Historian-Activists of Women's Rights, 1880–1940," in her *Woman Suffrage and Women's Rights* (New York: New York University Press, 1998), 210–238.

8. Mari Jo and Paul Buhle, eds., *The Concise History of Woman Suffrage: Selections from the Classic Work of Stanton, Anthony, Gage, and Harper* (Urbana: University of Illinois Press, 1978), xviii–xxii; Sara Hunter Graham, *Woman Suffrage and the New Democracy* (New Haven: Yale University Press, 1996), 40, 43.

9. Carrie Chapman Catt and Nettie Rogers Shuler, *Woman Suffrage and Politics: The Inner Story of the Suffrage Movement* (first published 1926; repr., Seattle: University of Washington Press, 1969).

10. DuBois, "Making Women's History," 210–238.

11. Gayle Veronica Fischer, "The Seventy-Fifth Anniversary of Woman Suffrage in the United States: A Bibliographic Essay," *Journal of Women's History* 7 (fall 1995): 172–199; Eleanor Flexner, *Century of Struggle: The Woman's Rights Movement in the United States* (Cambridge, Mass.: Belkap Harvard University Press, 1959).

12. The phrase "left feminist" is Ellen Carol Du Bois's; see Ellen Carol DuBois, "Eleanor Flexner and the History of American Feminism," in her *Woman Suffrage and Women's Rights*, 239–251.

13. Works which examine why the vote achieved so little for women include Aileen Kraditor, ed., *Up from the Pedestal: Selected Writings in the History of American Feminism* (New York: Quadrangle/New York Times Book Co., 1986); William O'Neill, "The Fight for Suffrage," *Wilson Quarterly* 10 (autumn 1986): 99–109; Nancy F. Cott, *The Grounding of Modern Feminism* (New Haven, Conn.: Yale University Press, 1987).

14. Andrew Sinclair, *The Better Half: The Emancipation of the American Woman* (London: Jonathan Cape, 1965); William L. O'Neill, *Everyone Was Brave: A History of Feminism in America* (New York: Quadrangle Books, 1969). William O'Neill reiterated his conclusions in a later article: O'Neill, "The Fight for Suffrage," 99–109.

15. Anne Firor Scott and Andrew MacKay Scott, *One Half the People: The Fight for Woman Suffrage* (Urbana: University of Illinois Press, 1975).

16. Aileen S. Kraditor, *The Ideas of the Woman Suffrage Movement, 1890–1920* (New York: W. W. Norton, 1965).

17. See, for instance, Daniel Scott Smith, "Family Limitation, Sexual Control, and Domestic Feminism in Victorian America," *Feminist Studies* 1, no. 3–4 (1973): 40–57; Carroll Smith-Rosenberg, "Beauty, the Beast, and the Militant Woman: Sex Roles and Social Stress in Jacksonian America," *American Quarterly* 23, no. 4 (1971): 562–584.

18. Ellen Carol DuBois, "The Radicalism of the Woman Suffrage Movement: Notes toward the Reconstruction of Nineteenth-Century Feminism," *Feminist Studies* 3, no. 1–2 (1975): 63–71.

19. Ellen Carol DuBois, *Feminism and Suffrage: The Emergence of an Independent Women's Movement in America, 1848–1869* (Ithaca, N.Y.: Cornell University Press, 1978).

20. In addition to DuBois, see Julie Roy Jeffrey, *The Great Silent Army of Abolitionism: Ordinary Women in the Antislavery Movement* (Chapel Hill: University of North Carolina Press, 1998), 228–232, who sketches the beginnings of this split.

21. Keith Melder, *Beginnings of Sisterhood: The American Woman's Rights Movement, 1800–1850* (New York: Schocken Books, 1977).

22. Barbara J. Berg, *The Remembered Gate: Origins of American Feminism, the Woman and the City, 1800–1860* (New York: Oxford University Press, 1978).

23. Jack S. Blocker Jr., "The Politics of Reform: Populists, Prohibition, and Woman Suffrage, 1891–1892," *Historian* 34, no. 4 (1972): 614–632; Jack S. Blocker Jr., "Separate Paths: Suffragists and the Women's Temperance Crusade," *Signs* 10, no. 3 (spring 1985): 460–476.

24. Examples of this literature may be found in the review article by Elaine Tyler May, "Expanding the Past: Recent Scholarship on Women in Politics and Work," *Reviews in American History* 10, no. 4, (December 1982): 216–233.

25. Mari Jo Buhle, *Women and American Socialism, 1870–1920* (Urbana and London: University of Illinois Press, 1981).

26. Ruth Bordin, *Women and Temperance: The Quest for Power and Liberty, 1873–1900* (Philadelphia: Temple University Press, 1981); Karen Blair, *The Clubwoman as Feminist: True Womanhood Redefined, 1868–1914* (New York: Holmes and Meier, 1980).

27. See Ellen Carol DuBois, "The Last Suffragist: An Intellectual and Political Autobiography," in her *Woman Suffrage and Women's Rights*, 1–29.

28. Ellen Carol DuBois, "Outgrowing the Compact of the Fathers: Equal Rights, Woman Suffrage, and the United States Constitution, 1820–1878," *Journal of American History* 74, no. 3 (December 1987): 836–862.

29. Sylvia D. Hoffert, *When Hens Crow: The Woman's Rights Movement in Antebellum America* (Bloomington: Indiana University Press, 1995); Nancy Isenberg, *Sex and Citizenship in Antebellum America* (Chapel Hill: University of North Carolina Press, 1998); DuBois, "The Radicalism of the Woman Suffrage Movement."

30. Suzanne M. Marilley, *Woman Suffrage and the Origins of Liberal Feminism in the United States, 1820–1920* (Cambridge, Mass.: Harvard University Press, 1996).

31. See, for instance, Steven M. Buechler, *Women's Movements in the United States* (New Brunswick, N.J.: Rutgers University Press, 1990). This is discussed further by Laura E. Nym Mayhall, "Review Essay: Reclaiming the Political: Women and the Social History of Suffrage in Great Britain, France, and the United States," *Journal of Women's History* 12, no. 1 (spring 2000): 172–181.

32. Linda J. Lumsden, *Rampant Women: Suffragists and the Right of Assembly* (Knoxville: University of Tennessee Press, 1997).

33. Hunter Graham, *Woman Suffrage and the New Democracy.*

34. J. Stanley Lemons, *The Woman Citizen: Social Feminism in the 1920s* (Urbana: University of Illinois Press, 1973).

35. Paula Baker, "The Domestication of Politics: Women and American Political Society, 1780–1920," *American Historical Review* 89, no. 3 (June 1984): 620–647.

36. Cott, *The Grounding of Modern Feminism*; Nancy F. Cott, "Across the Great Divide: Women in Politics before and after 1920," in *Women, Politics, and Change*, ed. Louise A. Tilly and Patricia Gurin (New York: Russell Sage Foundation, 1990), 153–176.

37. Christine Bolt, *Sisterhood Questioned? Race, Class, and Internationalism in the American and British Women's Movements, c.* 1880s–1970s (London: Routledge, 2004).

38. Jane Jerome Camhi, *Women against Women: American Anti-suffragism* (Brooklyn: Carlson, 1994); Thomas J. Jablonsky, *The Home, Heaven, and the Mother Party: Female Anti-suffrage in the United States,* 1868–1920 (Brooklyn: Carlson, 1994); Thomas Jablonsky, "Female Opposition: The Anti-Suffrage Campaign," in *Votes for Women,* ed. J. Baker, 118–129; Susan E. Marshall, *Splintered Sisterhood: Gender and Class in the Campaign against Woman Suffrage* (Madison: University of Wisconsin Press, 1997).

39. Elna C. Green, *Southern Strategies: Southern Women and the Woman Suffrage Question* (Chapel Hill: University of North Carolina Press, 1997).

40. Fischer, "The Seventy-Fifth Anniversary of Woman Suffrage in the United States," 189–199.

41. Alan P. Grimes, *The Puritan Ethic and Woman Suffrage* (New York: Oxford University Press, 1967).

42. Examples of such studies include Holly K. McCammon and Karen E. Campbell, "Winning the Vote in the West: The Political Successes of the Women's Suffrage Movements, 1866–1919," *Gender and Society* 15, no. 1 (February 2001): 55–82; Ellen Carol DuBois, "Woman Suffrage: The View from the Pacific," *Pacific Historical Review* 69, no. 4 (Special Issue, November 2000): 539–551; Gayle Gullett, "Constructing the Woman Citizen and Struggling for the Vote in California, 1896–1911," *Pacific Historical Review* 69, no. 4 (November 2000): 573–593; John Putnam, "A 'Test of Chiffon Politics': Gender Politics in Seattle, 1897–1917," *Pacific Historical Review* 69, no. 4 (November 2000): 595–616.

43. Gayle Gullett, *Becoming Citizens: The Emergence and Development of the California Women's Movement,* 1880–1911 (Urbana: University of Illinois Press, 2000).

44. Rebecca J. Mead, *How the Vote Was Won: Woman Suffrage in the Western United States,* 1868–1914 (New York: New York University Press, 2004).

45. Beverly Beeton, "How the West Was Won for Woman Suffrage," in *One Woman, One Vote: Rediscovering the Woman Suffrage Movement,* ed. Marjorie Spruill Wheeler (Troutdale, Ore.: New Sage Press, 1995), 99–115.

46. Sarah Barringer Gordon, "The Liberty of Self-Degradation: Polygamy, Woman Suffrage, and Consent in Nineteenth-Century America," *Journal of American History* 83, no. 3 (December 1996): 815–847; Sarah Barringer Gordon, *The Mormon Question: Polygamy and Constitutional Conflict in Nineteenth-Century America* (Chapel Hill: University of North Carolina Press, 2002); Rebecca Edwards, "Pioneers at the Polls: Woman Suffrage in the West," in *Votes for Women,* ed. J. Baker, 90–101.

47. See, for instance, A. Elizabeth Taylor, "Tennessee: The Thirty-Sixth State," in *Votes for Women: The Woman Suffrage Movement in Tennessee, the South, and the Nation,* ed. Marjorie Spruill Wheeler (Knoxville: University of Tennessee Press, 1995), 53–70.

48. Marjorie Spruill Wheeler, *New Women of the New South: The Leaders of the Woman Suffrage Movement in the Southern States* (New York: Oxford University Press, 1993). See also Marjorie Julian Spruill, "Race, Reform, and Reaction at the Turn of the Century: Southern Suffragists, the NAWSA, and the 'Southern Strategy' in Context," in *Votes for Women,* ed. J. Baker, 102–117.

49. Green, *Southern Strategies.* A number of these works are listed by Fischer, "The Seventy-Fifth Anniversary of Woman Suffrage in the United States," 192–194.

50. Sharon Hartman Strom, "Leadership and Tactics in the American Woman Suffrage Movement: A New Perspective from Massachusetts," *Journal of American History* 62, no. 2 (September 1975): 296–315.

51. Michael L. Goldberg, "Non-Partisan and All-Partisan: Rethinking Woman Suffrage and Party Politics in Gilded Age Kansas," *Western Historical Quarterly* 25, no. 1 (spring 1994): 21–44.

52. Michael L. Goldberg, *An Army of Women: Gender and Politics in Gilded Age Kansas* (Baltimore: Johns Hopkins University Press, 1997).

53. Rosalyn Terborg-Penn, *African American Women in the Struggle for the Vote, 1850–1920* (Bloomington: Indiana University Press, 1998), 13–35. See also William Coleman, "Architects of a Vision: Black Women and Their Antebellum Quest for Political and Social Equality" and "Frances Ellen Watkins Harper: Abolitionist and Feminist Reformer, 1825–1911," in *African-American Women and the Vote: 1837–1965*, ed. Ann D. Gordon and Joyce A. Berkman (Amherst.: University of Massachusetts Press, 1997), 24–40, 41–65; Nell Irvin Painter, *Sojourner Truth: A Life, a Symbol* (New York: W. W. Norton, 1996).

54. Terborg-Penn, *African American Women in the Struggle for the Vote*; Mayhall, "Reclaiming the Political," 172–181.

55. Glenda Elizabeth Gilmore, *Gender and Jim Crow: Women and the Politics of White Supremacy in North Carolina, 1896–1920* (Chapel Hill: University of North Carolina Press, 1996).

56. Essays in Gordon and Berkman, eds., *African-American Women and the Vote*, especially Elsa Barkley Brown, "To Catch the Vision of Freedom: Reconstructing Southern Black Women's Political History, 1865–1880," 66–99; Garth E. Pauley, "W.E.B. DuBois on Woman Suffrage: A Critical Analysis of His *Crisis* Writings," *Journal of Black Studies* 30 (January 2000): 383–410. The issue of who owned the vote in the black community is also discussed by Tera Hunter, *To 'Joy My Freedom: Southern Black Women's Lives and Labors after the Civil War* (Cambridge, Mass.: Harvard University Press, 1997)

57. Elsa Barkley Brown, "Negotiating and Transforming the Public Sphere: African American Political Life in the Transition from Slavery to Freedom," *Public Culture* 7 (fall 1994): 107–146.

58. Wanda A. Hendricks, *Gender, Race, and Politics in the Midwest: Black Club Women in Illinois* (Bloomington: Indiana University Press, 1998).

59. Starting in the mid-1980s a number of books and articles looked at immigrant women. These works touched on their participation in suffrage and politics, but this was not their main focus. See Elizabeth Ewen, *Immigrant Women in the Land of Dollars: Life and Culture on the Lower East Side, 1890–1925* (New York: Monthly Review Press, 1985); Susan A. Glenn, *Daughters of the Shtetl: Life and Labor in the Immigrant Generation* (Ithaca, N.Y.: Cornell University Press, 1990); Annelise Orleck, *Common Sense and a Little Fire: Women and Working-Class Politics in the United States, 1900–1965* (Chapel Hill: University of North Carolina Press, 1995).

60. Orleck, *Common Sense and a Little Fire*; Kirsten Delegard, "Women's Movements, 1880s–1920s," in *A Companion to American Women's History*, ed. Nancy A. Hewitt (Oxford: Blackwell Publishers, 2002), 341–344. The contributions of working-class women and immigrant women are noted by Ellen Carol DuBois, "Working Women, Class Relations, and Suffrage Militance: Harriot Stanton Blatch and the New York Woman Suffrage Movement, 1894–1909," *Journal of American History* 74, no. 1 (June 1987): 34–58; Nancy A. Hewitt, *Southern Discomfort: Women's Activism in Tampa, Florida, 1880s–1920s* (Urbana: University of Illinois Press, 2001); Mead, *How the Vote Was Won*; Nancy A. Hewitt, "Luisa Capetillo: Feminist of the Working Class," in *Latina Legacies: Identity, Biography, and Community*, ed. Vicki L. Ruiz and Virginia Sanchez Korrol (New York: Oxford University

Press, 2005), 120–134; Elizabeth Salas, "Adelina Otero Warren: Rural Aristocrat and Modern Feminist," in *Latina Legacies*, ed. Ruiz and Korrol, 135–147.

61. On the importance of racism in the debates over the Fifteenth Amendment, see Andrea Moore Kerr, "White Women's Rights, Black Men's Wrongs, Free Love, Blackmail, and the Formation of the American Woman Suffrage Association," in *One Woman, One Vote*, ed. Wheeler, 61–79.

62. Philip N. Cohen, "Nationalism and Suffrage: Gender Struggle in Nation-Building America," *Signs* 21, no. 3 (spring 1996): 707–727; DuBois, "Working Women, Class Relations, and Suffrage Militance," 34–58.

63. Gullett, "Constructing the Woman Citizen and Struggling for the Vote in California," 573–593; Putnam, "A 'Test of Chiffon Politics,'" 595–616; Hewitt, *Southern Discomfort*.

64. J. Baker, *Votes for Women*, quote on 8.

65. Judith Wellman, *The Road to Seneca Falls: Elizabeth Cady Stanton and the First Woman's Rights Convention* (Urbana: University of Illinois Press, 2004).

66. Lori D. Ginzberg, *Untidy Origins: A Story of Woman's Rights in Antebellum New York* (Chapel Hill: University of North Carolina Press, 2005). On women's petitioning see also Susan Zaeske, *Signatures of Citizenship: Petitioning, Antislavery, and Women's Political Identity* (Chapel Hill: University of North Carolina Press, 2003).

67. Ellen Carol DuBois, *Harriot Stanton Blatch and the Winning of Woman Suffrage* (New Haven: Yale University Press, 1997).

68. Christine A. Lunardini, *From Equal Suffrage to Equal Rights: Alice Paul and the National Woman's Party, 1910–1928* (New York: New York University Press, 1986); Linda G. Ford, *Iron-Jawed Angels: The Suffrage Militancy of the National Woman's Party, 1912–1920* (Lanham, Md.: London University Press of America, 1991).

69. Works that consider the international context of the woman suffrage movement include Bonnie S. Anderson, *Joyous Greetings: The First International Women's Movement, 1830–1860* (Oxford: Oxford University Press, 2000); Leila J. Rupp, *Worlds of Women: The Making of an International Women's Movement* (Princeton, N.J.: Princeton University Press, 1997); DuBois, "Woman Suffrage: The View from the Pacific," 539–551; Bolt, *Sisterhood Questioned?* For comparison with the British suffrage movement see Jane Rendall, *The Origins of Modern Feminism: Women in Britain, France, and the United States, 1780–1860* (1985; repr., Basingstoke and London: Macmillan, 1990); Christine Bolt, *The Women's Movements in the United States and Britain from the 1790s to the 1920s* (New York and London: Harvester Wheatsheaf, 1993); June Purvis, *Emmeline Pankhurst: A Biography* (London: Routledge, 2002); Mayhall, "Reclaiming the Political," 172–181.

70. For an overview of women's welfare work and politics, see Kirsten Delegard, "Women's Movements, 1880s–1920s," 328–347; Elizabeth J. Clapp, "Welfare and the Role of Women: The Juvenile Court Movement," *Journal of American Studies* 28, no. 3 (December 1994): 359–383; Linda Gordon, ed., *Women, the State, and Welfare* (Madison: University of Wisconsin Press, 1990); Sonya Michel and Seth Koven, eds., *Mothers of a New World: Maternalist Politics and the Origins of Welfare States* (New York: Routledge, 1993); P. Baker, "The Domestication of Politics," 620–649. On women's involvement in electoral politics in the nineteenth century see, for instance, Elizabeth Varon, *We Mean to be Counted: White Women and Politics in Antebellum Virginia* (Chapel Hill: University of North Carolina Press, 1998); Catherine Allgor, *Parlor Politics: In Which the Ladies of Washington Help Build a City and a Government* (Charlottesville: University Press of Virginia, 2000); Ronald J. Zboray and Mary Saracino Zboray, "Whig Women, Politics, and Culture in the Campaign of 1840: Three Perspectives from Massachusetts," *Journal of the Early Republic*

17 (summer 1997): 277–315; Rebecca Edwards, *Angels in the Machinery: Gender in American Party Politics from the Civil War to the Progressive Era* (New York: Oxford University Press, 1997); Melanie Gustafson, *Women and the Republican Party, 1854–1924* (Urbana: University of Illinois Press, 2001); Melanie Gustafson, Kriste Miller, and Elizabeth Perry, eds., *We Have Come to Stay: American Women and Political Parties, 1880–1960* (Albuquerque: University of New Mexico Press, 1999).

71. Kerber, "Separate Spheres, Female Worlds, Woman's Place," 9–39.

14

Engendering Social Welfare Policy

EILEEN BORIS
S. JAY KLEINBERG

When Jay Kleinberg and Eileen Boris first collaborated in the mid-1970s on a project using late nineteenth- and early twentieth-century estate records for the Maryland Historical Society, historians of women were focused on daily life and social and cultural history. But soon Ronald Reagan and Margaret Thatcher would put social welfare back onto the intellectual agenda, reawakening our interest in the Progressive era and the New Deal. We joined a growing movement to bring the state back into understanding social and economic life, which for women's historians meant moving from a focus on women's culture to a newly furbished sense of the political that included the enactment and implementation of policy.

Influenced by debates within socialist feminism, Boris first wrote about the historic role of the state in the transformation of patriarchy and, then, the impact of race, gender, and class on social politics. She participated in a growing transatlantic and interdisciplinary conversation engaged with gendering theories of the welfare state, like those of Swedish Social Democrat Gøsta Esping-Andersen and British Laborite T. H. Marshall.[1] To this discussion she brought the concept of racialized gender, gleaned from the intersectionality she was learning from women of color, as a more robust approach to understanding the United States than appeals to "American exceptionalism." Kleinberg, now teaching U.S. history in Great Britain, became attuned to living in a very different type of welfare state in which class and material conditions rather than race dominated conversations over welfare.[2] Thirty years on there has been a convergence in the national dialogues in Britain and the United States, as gender, race, and class now form the backdrop against which scholars in both nations (and others) analyze the welfare state.

Women have long been the objects of philanthropy and public welfare. Unusually, for a topic in American history, they have formed one of the primary subjects of inquiry. Concerned with documenting the activities of previous generations, early historians of philanthropy and welfare rarely interrogated reformers' categories or attitudes. Thus they did not examine the gender constructs that underpinned the development of welfare policy or their own analyses. They focused on the growth of the field itself, the tensions between private and public charity and welfare workers, and the growing body of legislation regulating and providing for those perceived as less fortunate. Theirs might best be described as straightforward narratives of institutional growth.

Such histories concentrated on affluent women as the prime movers in the impetus for private and public social welfare, the institutions they played a key role in founding, and the professionalization of philanthropy. They mostly overlooked the recipients of either charitable largesse or public provision and accepted gender categories as given rather than as constructs of a particular socioeconomic and political era.[3] This is true even for the more recent surveys of social welfare and ideas about poverty.[4] Yet, as political scientist Virginia Sapiro has stated, it is not possible, "to understand the underlying principles, structure, and effects of our social welfare system and policies without understanding their relationship to gender roles and gender ideology."[5] We would add that it is equally impossible to interpret the contours of social welfare without considering race as it exists in relation to gender and social class.

Recent histories of social policy have reinstated the voices of poor women themselves, examined the homosocial networks that sustained much policy innovation, and explored the contributions of women to public and private institutions.[6] This chapter traces the historiography of social welfare from the 1950s and 1960s, when women were included as subject matter but gender as a system of ordering relations between the sexes was not, to the present, when gender has become one of the principal filters through which to sift such history.[7] It pays particular attention to which women have served as the subjects and objects of investigation and which family forms have been given primacy and public support over others.[8]

The Progressive Era

One of the first postwar historians to discuss social welfare policy, Robert Bremner rooted his investigation in the Progressive Era's "awakening to poverty as a social problem" and described as heroes and heroines the " 'do gooders' — the responsible Americans in every generation who have heard and heeded the cry from the depths."[9] Bremner tied the growing concern for the poor across the nineteenth century to the poverty and immiseration attendant upon an industrialization process that reduced the individual workman's bargaining power "almost to the vanishing point; what little he had left was lost in contests with other men — and women and children, too — for jobs which one was as competent to fill as another. The prize in these races nearly always went to the cheapest."[10] Despite the recognition of women's key role in formulating policy, reformers cast the world of employment in an andocentric mold and regarded women and children as interlopers in the labor force.

Social policies in the United States developed along a two-track system in which men received entitlements based upon their labor (unemployment compensation, retirement pensions, etc.).[11] Women typically obtained discretionary "benefits" based upon their relation to men, their purported weaknesses, or their maternal destiny. While early historians described the legislative efforts of Progressive reformers, they rarely explored the values behind reform or resistance to them. Clarke Chambers recognized the twin tracks of the welfare state, but not why they developed.[12] Walter I. Trattner observed that the redistribution of resources from the "haves" to the "have-nots" depended upon a cluster of factors, not just economic ones.[13] Subsequent historians explored reform networks that led from the settlement houses to state social service commissions and federal appointments and simultaneously analyzed reformers' acceptance of a two-tier system of social compensation.[14]

Historians in the 1960s and 1970s who described the development of welfare in the United States concentrated on conflicts between professional social workers and social activists. Roy Lubove provided the classic formulation. "Women active in charitable and club work were outstanding publicists of mothers' pensions," he remarked, criticizing one of the principal lobbyists for pensions in Massachusetts because she "exhibited the romantic, if not fanatic idealization of motherhood and home which pervaded the mothers' pensions movement."[15] Such a description effectively stereotyped the supporters of widows' pensions as quixotic proponents of motherhood without in any way analyzing the reasons for their stance.

Lubove's study of the emergence of social work as a profession concentrated on the conflict between private philanthropy and public expenditure on welfare, of which mothers' pensions were the main example. He described the transition from Bremner's do-gooders to modern social welfare systems as the professionalization of social work, locating the conflict between charity and social work and voluntary and paid employees as a generational issue.[16] Women's historians, like Kathryn Kish Sklar, celebrated social settlement houses as cauldrons of the welfare state, citing Jane Addams's Hull House as a locus of welfare activity, while Ruth Hutchinson Crocker and Vicki L. Ruiz provided nuance by connecting philanthropy with Americanization and racial uplift among Mexican and African American migrants as well as European immigrants. The settlements both maintained older forms of charity and generated newer structures of state provision.[17]

As later historians have shown, volunteers and trained social workers equally penetrated working-class homes, taking careful notes about clients and judging presumed worthiness. Social work was an explicitly gendered occupation. Women, in the view of many practitioners, could go into places where men would not be welcome and could see what men would overlook. They utilized an implicitly maternal model: both volunteers and professionals assumed the right to visit the poor in their own homes; they shared assumptions about the poor as feckless children needing the guidance of meta-mothers who could steer them toward appropriate behavior.[18] Their judgmental view of clients particularly comes through in historical accounts of maternity homes for out-of-wedlock pregnancy, such as Regina Kunzel's critique of how "fallen women" became "problem girls," although this viewpoint was less common in the African American community, especially as regards working mothers.[19]

Both reformers and their historians have concentrated on cities and the urban poor, generally neglecting their rural counterparts.[20] Migration to cities in search of work, large-scale immigration, and poor urban housing and sanitary conditions contributed to the burgeoning disquiet manifested by affluent men and women regarding their less fortunate counterparts.[21] It could be argued that reform efforts were largely city based and, as a result, so were their histories, but this merely compounds the neglect of rural women and racial minorities of both sexes. According to Elna Green, the South increasingly came to resemble the rest of the country in the early twentieth century, although its asylums, orphanages, and other institutions remained segregated or limited to whites.[22] Thus, African Americans, still concentrated in the rural South, engaged in self-help efforts to improve their situation in the face of white indifference to their impoverished conditions.[23] Yet the few agencies dispensing charity in rural areas rarely had sufficient funds to keep families together, although this was a prime goal of many Progressive reformers.[24] The centrality of this goal and its widespread public acceptance helped explain the support for widows' pensions that sustained families in a particular version of domestic motherhood.[25] Later historians found the mothers' pensions movement that Mark Leff, writing in 1974, described as a "consensus for reform" to be more complicated.[26] Joanne Goodwin's study of mothers' pensions in Chicago pointed to the areas where consensus fell short: "race problematizes maternalism's universalist assumptions and feminism's focus on sex equity."[27]

Theda Skocpol has argued that the United States developed a welfare state in which public provision protected a gendered model of behavior where the male role of breadwinner and soldier-veteran counterbalanced the female one of motherhood. Skocpol's "structured polity" approach emphasized the role of politicians and administrators in the creation of social policy. While male trade unionists played a relatively weak role in forming social policy, exclusion from party politics and strong gender-based organizations enhanced middle-class white women's role in welfare policy. Skocpol also correlated mothers' pension provision with educational levels, a tendency to enact child labor laws, and high densities of women's clubs.[28]

Skocpol recognized the variations between states in the enactment of pensions, finding that literacy levels best explained the acceptance of mothers' pensions. Yet, these were a proxy for another crucial factor in explaining social welfare distribution patterns, namely, the racial structure of any given state.[29]

Moreover, distribution of welfare also varied within states, based largely upon local interpretations of gender. Thus, cities dependent upon female labor provided fewer mothers' pensions than those where women found it more difficult to obtain employment. Kleinberg's comparisons of Pittsburgh, Baltimore, and Fall River discovered that state enabling legislation notwithstanding, there were far more pensions given in the steel-based economy (Pittsburgh) than in either Fall River, where women's and children's employment in the textile mills was central to the local labor market, or Baltimore, where few women of color received any assistance.[30] Susan Traverso's analysis of welfare politics in Boston revealed that elite Protestant women's push for mothers' pensions opened up a political space for the city's Irish, Jews, and Italians to win greater benefits for their compatriots. But these immigrant groups thought in terms of the family, rather than the individual, as the unit for welfare; by the 1920s, they pushed for unemployment compensation for men.[31] Social policies in the United States until the 1930s, and arguably thereafter, arose from local situations, leading to highly variable welfare systems dominated by prejudice and idiosyncratic values.

Most historians and social policy analysts have viewed welfare from the family perspective, mimicking practices which provided for women not because of their poverty, but because they fell into a particular category, the presumably "respectable" poor who conformed to social norms. Widows raising young children on their own were the most likely to benefit from public funds, but only if they were white and living in cities. Few women of color obtained mothers' pensions, although even here there were great local variations. Pittsburgh, for example, was more generous to African American widowed mothers than Baltimore, which could be explained by southern racial politics, or Chicago, which could not.[32] Respectability, as seen by the white middle class, became a key criterion of whether one benefited from public or private largesse.[33] Taking a largely family rather than individual perspective, both reformers and their early historians viewed women and children as dependants seemingly unable to protect themselves in the maelstrom of rapid economic growth punctuated by catastrophic depressions.[34]

According to Mimi Abramovitz, one of the first to write a gendered social welfare history, few scholars studied the relationship between poor women and the welfare state.[35] They depicted the urban poor, especially the women and children among them, as passive beneficiaries of reformers' efforts at social betterment. Since the late 1980s scholars have made imaginative use of social agency records to "give" voices back to the poor, exploring their diversity as well as their common problems. Abramovitz herself has reconceptualized welfare history as the development of policies to reinforce both the work ethic and the family ethic; these policies disciplined poor single mothers and others who failed to live by those dictates.[36]

Peggy Pascoe and Sherri Broder have investigated urban social services from the standpoint of female targets as well as the point of view of reformers. Pascoe's examination of rescue homes in the West corrected the tendency to see welfare in terms of black and white as she analyzed intercultural relations between middle-class whites, Mormon, Chinese, and Native American women and questioned recipients' passivity, thus undermining the social control paradigm. Broder deconstructed reformers' and poor people's images of home and family, with particular attention to constructs of illegitimacy, to explain the way social policy developed and provoked resentment.[37] Changing attitudes toward gender and age meant the immigrant, African American, and white Protestant communities regarded employment in quite distinctive fashions and shaped constructs of appropriate family relationships and roles. Maureen Fitzgerald has labeled maternalist approaches as Protestant on the basis of studying Irish Catholic nuns in their forging of a faith-based, public, and institutionalized welfare system.[38] Marxist feminist theorists critiqued the humanitarian school of welfare historiography for not interrogating either gender constructions or capitalist hegemony. For them, Progressive era social welfare policies sustained the state's institutionalization of patriarchy through welfare provisions designed to separate public and private life while at the same time underscoring the distinctiveness of male and female existence.[39]

Even when early social welfare historians focused on race and racialized gender, they described welfare policies aimed largely at the immigrant poor. As a result, while class and sometimes (white) ethnicity became central topics in the historical analysis of public provision for women, the highly charged gendered and racial construction of those services for African Americans received less attention from historians than from sociologists and social workers.[40] Andrew Billingsley and Jeanne M. Giovannoni's *Children of the Storm: Black Children and American Child Welfare* documented the services (or lack of them) available to African American children, the central role black women played in the development of such services within the black community, and the contrasting motivation and philosophy between black and white social activists. They posited that while white reformers wished "to save children from vice and corruption," African American women endeavored to rescue them from a "cruel environment" by founding small institutions that cared for a few children or sometimes housed young and old together.[41]

A number of historians followed Billingsley and Giovannoni's lead in examining the distinctive bases of reform in the black and white communities. Glenda Gilmore revealed how North Carolina African American clubwomen transformed the discourse of good homes, a justification for white supremacy, into demands for public health and child betterment; they sought through church and civic voluntary societies to gain "some recognition and meagre services from the expanding welfare state."[42] Elisabeth Lasch-Quinn documented the limitations of white settlement house reformers who largely excluded African American city dwellers from their efforts to ameliorate the negative consequences of urbanization and industrialization. The self-help ideology prevalent within the black community led to the founding of schools, as well as rural and urban settlements.[43] According to David T. Beito, blacks, whites, immigrants, the native born, and women and men of all groups invested heavily in mutual aid, sick, death, and burial societies answerable only to their members and providing both indoor and outdoor relief. These organizations and institutions defined their own criteria for inclusion and served as a counter to the public and private social services that required conformity to norms outside of the group.[44]

Recent histories of social welfare have represented family preservation as a major reform goal, understanding it in a dialectical way. Mothers became the objects of social reform when husbands and fathers were unable to fulfill their breadwinning duties — whether through industrial accidents, unemployment, low wages, death, or desertion. The cause of male failure determined whether men and their families would receive public aid. Workmen's compensation maintained the dignity of male breadwinners who, just like destitute mothers, had to meet criteria of worth constructed by reformers. Like the retirement pensions developed by private industry, it was an entitlement program based upon men's relation to the labor force and demonstrated the gendered assumptions incorporated into welfare and employment legislation.[45] Reformers simultaneously criminalized male desertion of families, as Michael Willrich and Anna R. Igra have documented. Fear of "male slackers" led Domestic Relations Courts to adopt breadwinner regulations that policed non-support, creating a legal barrier toward obtaining mothers' pensions.[46]

Mothers' pensions, like other social programs aimed at women and children, provided for dependent children based upon their mothers' inscribed social status. As Gwendolyn Mink commented in her analysis of mothers' wages and inequalities in the welfare state, "welfare asked society to honor women's side of the sexual division of labor while naturalizing that division."[47] The widows' pension system incorporated women into the body politic as lobbyists for poor women's welfare but also restricted their political impact. Male-dominated state (and later federal) legislatures gave small appropriations to such programs, undermining the very families they aimed to conserve.[48] The Sheppard-Towner Act, passed by Congress in 1921 just after women got the vote and repealed in 1929 when it became apparent that reforming women lacked the political muscle to implement their programs, showed how politically sensitive an issue public policy toward families actually was.[49] The reforming women who gained a toehold in the federal bureaucracy through their dominance in the Children's Bureau were ultimately too far removed from the levers of power to protect their programs or their reform agenda, as Robyn Muncy has demonstrated.[50] While Julia Lathrop and her colleagues at the Children's Bureau argued that putting children first would benefit women and families, historians Linda Gordon and Sonya Michel both have explained how the interests of mothers and children could be antagonistic.[51]

The small number of pensions prompted lone mothers to seek other solutions to the dilemma of wage-earning and family care, including the use of orphanages as temporary shelters for their children. Late nineteenth-century orphanages developed not to punish mothers or save money — they actually cost more than placing-out schemes — but emerged out of the ethnic and religious communities that built them to look after children from their group, as was true for other social welfare institutions, as Elna Green showed for New Orleans from 1870 through 1920.[52] Beginning in the Progressive era, according to Nurith Zmora, reformers pushed for more individualized treatment financed by the state whether through mothers' pensions or foster care.[53]

Scholars have explored the sentimentalization of motherhood in the late nineteenth and early twentieth centuries as a point of departure for women's social activism and a restraining force on women's employment outside the home. Seth Koven and Sonya Michel began their collection, *Mothers of a New World: Maternalist Politics and the Origins of Welfare States,* with an epigraph by Charlotte Perkins Gilman, proclaiming that "We Will be the New Mothers of a New World" in which women's contributions will be "unloosed, expanded, spread far and wide throughout the world."[54] Reformers, social welfare activists, and social workers justified their actions on that basic premise. Skocpol and Ladd-Taylor, among others, described women's participation in the battle for mothers' pensions as part of a maternalist welfare state in which such diverse organizations as the National Congress of Mothers, the Women's Christian Temperance Union, and many settlement house residents lobbied for the public protection of motherhood.[55]

These analyses have advanced our understanding of a particular construction of motherhood as the basis for public policy, but they do not address one aspect of the issue, namely, why some social workers and charity activists opposed mothers' pensions. Leading Progressive Era charity activist Mary Richmond vigorously objected to supposedly indiscriminate giving. Like Josephine Lowell before her, Richmond favored investigating the individual circumstances of the potential recipient in order to determine worthiness. As the pioneer of the case-work method, she believed in an individual approach to charity. Despite the "sentimental appeal" of mothers' pensions, giving aid to a group, rather than to an individual whose circumstances could be investigated and closely controlled, would be another form of indiscriminate giving and undermine the work ethic among the poor.[56]

The New Deal Order

The New Deal represented a turning point for social welfare. Its direct relief, work programs and other experiments in public provision marked a federal commitment to public assistance. Power shifted from voluntary organizations and state charities to federal programs, some of which depended on state-level agencies for implementation. With the passage of the 1935 Social Security Act, the United States established a limited welfare state more restricted than European social democracies, but nonetheless committed to aiding the elderly, the disabled, and poor children and supporting the unemployed through economic hard times. Against a historiography mired in the debate over whether Roosevelt saved capitalism or transformed the political economy, gender analysis has not only highlighted the political prowess of what Susan Ware called "the New Deal network of women," but also fundamentally reinterpreted the elevation of work over care in the U.S. welfare state.[57]

Based on wage labor and definitions of employability, the New Deal order incorporated inequalities even as it sought to relieve distress. This partial welfare state, according to Boris, relied on concepts of social insurance that privileged full-time employment in the core sectors of the economy over those who labored, often without a wage, in homes, on farms, or for the family. The white male industrial worker and his dependents gained a modicum of security, but men and women of color and white women found themselves inadequately covered by the law and subject to discrimination, thus without full citizenship rights.[58] As Gwendolyn Mink has observed, the newness of the New Deal was its development of paternalist social policies that coupled male economic security to fair wages, unions, and social insurance, in effect, incorporating men as well as women into the welfare state on a gendered basis.[59]

Breadwinner ideology linking benefits to employment and defining workers as male permeated the Social Security Act of 1935. Its major provisions — Old Age Insurance (OAI), Old Age Assistance (OAA), Unemployment Insurance (UI), and Aid to Dependent Children (ADC) — favored certain forms of work over others. It thus reflected social norms even as it intensified the devaluation of carework, whether done for the family or for wages.[60] Women initially received aid based on their family connection to a man, as wife or daughter, rather than on account of their own wage record. Beneficiaries were more likely to be white, married, and U.S. born. Like minority men, who disproportionately suffered from under and unemployment, women went in and out of the labor market, worked part-time, and concentrated in workplaces uncovered by either law or union contract. This system disadvantaged the vast majority of African American, Mexican American, and immigrant women who could rely on neither their men's access nor their own labor histories and found themselves forced to accept either low-waged jobs without pensions or unemployment insurance or turn to public assistance. There was no mandate to provide aid to non-citizens while legislation restricted citizenship, especially among migrants from Asia, and curtailed immigration itself. Social provision for the poor, stigmatized as welfare, rarely came without arbitrariness or discrimination.[61]

For Michael Katz, "the New Deal cemented into American welfare policy a distinction between social insurance and public assistance," even as it substituted public efforts for private charity, as William Block also has emphasized.[62]

While such analysis critiqued the New Deal order for setting a policy path that made it more difficult to obtain universal and comprehensive economic security, it neglected the role of women in forging it. According to Mink, the U.S. version of the modern welfare state was crafted (mostly) by men and preserved their dominance in the labor market. But, women reformers — the maternalists of Progressive Era historiography — were central creators "to the extent" that social welfare developed "from contradictions among work, race, and motherhood."[63]

New Deal relief programs distinguished between men and women, whites and others. According to economic historian Nancy E. Rose, "Although millions of people were put to work, millions more never got on the rolls." New Deal work programs sometimes engaged in production for use and offered fair work at above poverty wages.[64] Assumptions about proper work and proper workers reinforced racial and gender discrimination in both eligibility and compensation when it came to the Civil Works Administration (CWA), the Civilian Conservation Corps (CCC), and the Works Progress Administration (WPA). Welfare bureaucrats assumed that people of color, even when qualified for relief, needed less to live on and thus received lower payments. Despite establishment of women's divisions, more resources went to men.[65] With the one job per family rule and work restricted mostly to sewing rooms, homemaking, or domestic service projects, women were kept at only one-sixth of WPA rolls, despite being nearly a quarter of the labor force. Local histories, such as Elizabeth Faue's on Minneapolis and Julia Kirk Blackwelder's on San Antonio, further document this gendering of relief. In Minneapolis, 1939 cuts in the WPA disproportionately hit women, dismissed because they were eligible for ADC but without consideration of the lengthy waiting period to receive such benefits.[66]

Studies of the WPA sewing rooms showed how the New Deal reinforced traditional divisions of labor even though Ellen Woodward, head of the Women's Division, objected that self- or family-supporting women should undertake any work for which they qualified, including manual labor, and earn a "man's wages" for it.[67] Atlanta's elite clubwomen, according to Georgina Hickey, viewed the sewing rooms as a space for "intelligent rehabilitation, where destitute women could be uplifted."[68] They feared that the sewing rooms could become sweatshops as much for their potential damage to motherhood as for the poor working conditions. Similarly, Texas relief officials may have wished to keep married women at home, but asserted that their projects kept women from "the despair of idleness" and equipped them to meet their home responsibilities.[69] This dual agenda — rehabilitating poor women as mothers as well as workers — anticipated late-century efforts at welfare reform. In recovering the work of voluntary organizations within Detroit's African American community in the 1920s and 1930s, Victoria Wolcott thus noted, "If black female reformers' emphasis on day care programs and work training had been part of New Deal programs, welfare today might look very different."[70]

Historians of women, like Ware, initially recovered women's contributions to the creation of the welfare state. As the essays in the 1984 *Without Precedent: The Life and Career of Eleanor Roosevelt* made clear, the First Lady served as a historiographical lynchpin for this reassessment. Eleanor Roosevelt's championing of social welfare, as well as civil rights and peace, contrasted with the dilatory efforts of her husband, the president.[71] Later, Landon Storrs reinterpreted the National Consumers' League during the 1930s as an "agent" of the New Deal not only for its formulation of labor standards regulation and work on Washington agencies, like the Consumers' Advisory Board of the National Recovery Administration (NRA), but also for spreading the New Deal idea in attempting to organize the South.[72] Stephanie Shaw highlighted the crucial role of black professional women as mediators for a white public administration of public assistance.[73] That an interracial group of social workers under Gay Shepperson was able to federalize relief in Georgia, offering aid to blacks as well as whites, according to Sarah Wilkerson-Freeman, revealed women's creative use of state power beyond maternalist rhetoric.[74]

The advocates of social insurance displaced the maternalist reformers, who still adhered to casework in determining eligibility for social assistance. Social insurance advocates' plan to provide benefits through employment, however, disadvantaged most women, even as it recognized the contributions of the unskilled or semiskilled mothers in their own homes.[75] Historians have differed in their treatment of these changes. Kessler-Harris condemned maternalist reformers for merely sustaining women within the family, while Mink stressed their continuing influence. Gordon judged the Children's Bureau "feminist" for its commitment to improving women's lives despite their diminished influence. They wanted a social insurance program which would protect their clients from stigma and humiliation.[76] Nevertheless, all parties adhered to similar notions of manhood and womanhood. This sustained a gender-divided welfare state, where men earned generous and uniform benefits but women received arbitrary, personalized, and paltry handouts. The institution of survivors' benefits for widows and orphans privileged married women/widows and their children over those in and from other forms of relationships.[77]

Kessler-Harris revealed the gendered assumptions behind "the right to earn." The AFL's philosophy of voluntarism equated breadwinning, self-sufficiency, and independence, eschewing state protection for real men, who instead would engage in collective bargaining. Economists Figart, Mutari, and Power further documented how wage, hour, and unemployment policy established a hierarchy based upon occupation, union status, and race.[78] Social insurance advocates recognized male economic prowess, enhancing their standing through the unemployment insurance system. The 1939 amendments transformed Social Security, Kessler-Harris noted, with a promise of economic security and a "pay as you go" funding formula rather than an insurance program which returned contributions to retired workers.[79] Over the next decades, this necessitated expansion to new groups of workers — including "regularly employed farm and domestic workers" in 1950 and 1954 — and thus turned OAI into the most universal of work and family programs.[80]

Race, ethnicity, and region separated out some women and men from New Deal benefits. The Federal Emergency Relief Administration (FERA) required matching funds from states which a number of southern and western states refused to provide. Work projects for women replicated a racialized division of labor within occupation: segregation by sex, with African American women slotted for household worker training programs while working-class white women became housekeeping aides for relief families needing assistance with illness. Meanwhile, unemployed teachers, nurses, artists, librarians, and other white-collar women, who were mostly white, found appropriate clerical, supervisory, or professional work relief.[81]

Nevertheless, the New Deal expanded the range of mothers who received assistance. As Kleinberg found for Fall River, French Canadian–born and other immigrant widows had a much greater chance of receiving help under ADC than they had when a combination of city and private philanthropy aided a small number of mostly native-born white widows.[82] Northern cities began to dispense more assistance than blacks previously had received anywhere in the country. Lessons in respectability remained, but instead of better-off neighbors uplifting the race, Wolcott concluded, New Dealers worked from racial stereotypes that labeled African American women as slovenly and unskilled.[83] Michael Brown has argued that the New Deal erected a new structure of dependence by not incorporating African Americans into the New Deal as working-class citizens entitled to security along side other low-income people.[84] Because the New Deal never addressed occupational segregation and only during World War II belatedly confronted job discrimination, it relegated African Americans and other minorities to relief rather than social insurance.

While Brown discussed women without a gendered analysis, his political economy complemented the gender perspective of Suzanne Mettler. In contrast to women's historians who focus on ideology and discourse, Mettler stressed the institutional arrangements by which women gained second-class benefits. Those who qualified for uniform federal programs, predominantly white men and their wives, became independent bearers of rights. The rest suffered under the discretionary lens of state-based policies that relied upon ascriptive, personalistic criteria to judge eligibility and discriminated against racial minorities and women outside the norm of heterosexual marriage and chaste domesticity. Thus, exclusion of female-dominated occupations from the Fair Labor Standards Act left women to the vagaries of state-level regulations, "protected" as dependent-mothers rather than entitled as citizen-workers.[85] Furthermore, because policy makers failed to judge caretaking as work, pregnancy and family responsibilities stood outside the criteria for unemployment. Minority men also failed to meet UI's work test, which depended on subjective evaluations of behavior.[86]

According to political scientist Robert Lieberman, nothing in the law necessarily curtailed black eligibility for ADC. While OAI gained an independent board and merit-based personnel, ADC came under patronage-appointed officials beholden to local elites. General revenue financing further subjected it to political whims, including later revolts by middle-class taxpayers against the "undeserving" poor solo mothers coming under its supposed largess. In contrast, OAI built political support among contributors, who promoted the expanded coverage that would lower payroll taxes while maintaining benefits. These contrasting institutional structures explain Lieberman's paradox: despite initial exclusions, policies underwent different evolutions — OAI went from statutory exclusion to nearly color-blindness, and ADC went from statutory inclusion to administrative exclusion to racial degradation through identification as a "black" program.

From ADC to TANF

Of all the aspects of social welfare, ADC (AFDC after 1962 amendments) has garnered the most scholarly attention, undoubtedly because of political challenges during the last decades of the twentieth century that culminated with Clinton's "ending of welfare as we know it" in 1996.[87] Kessler-Harris first highlighted the significance of the 1939 amendments that made "dependent wives and aged widows" eligible for OAI if husbands had been, segregating poor lone mothers into a separate, despised category. That Congress chose to enhance the benefits of those already covered and their families rather than extend coverage to domestics and agricultural workers suggested to Kessler-Harris that gendered notions of fairness trumped over racial equity.[88] Mink and Kleinberg stressed the ways that these amendments distinguished between types of dependency, providing fuller support to widows than those deserted, divorce, or unmarried since ADC originally lacked a caretaker grant.[89] The state's formulation reflected the illiberal assumption that male household heads represented their dependents in the body politic and women without such heads were to become "wards" of the state.

In the midst of the Great Depression, then, crafters of ADC initially assumed traditional gender norms, in which mothers should stay home to care for children. Mothers were considered unavailable for work when the referent for mother was the white widow. But from the start, southern states — beginning with Louisiana in 1943 — passed "employable mother" rules that compelled would-be recipients into the labor market if any form of employment was available. As Joanne Goodwin has argued, "the practice of welfare continued to blur women's dual roles," demanding that poor single mothers earn income as well as care for their children, especially when such mothers were black and not married.[90] Emphasizing the stake of agribusiness during the 1950s, Ellen Reese has determined that "states are likely to experience powerful pressures to restrict welfare coverage when capitalists' demand for low-wage, flexible labor is high, fiscal constraints are great, and/or racism is salient." Thus Georgia in 1949 required stepfathers to support children and mothers to request courts to enforce payments from absent fathers as well as requiring that mothers with children older than eighteen months obtain employment. Additional suitable home and employable mother rules in 1952 and 1953 halted the more equitable coverage of African Americans that had developed during the previous decade.[91]

Work for single mothers became established national policy with the 1956 amendments that began the shift from a right to be a stay-at-home mother to a need to earn. These emphasized the ending of dependency through rehabilitation. Jennifer Mittelstadt has reperiodized the movement toward workfare by pointing to the late 1940s as a generative time for such ideas about work and has highlighted the role of a new group of social welfare experts from the American Public Welfare Association (APWA), consulting firms like Community Research Associates (CRA), and universities. These policy makers and administrators offered a therapeutic approach focused on dysfunctional families and individual psychodynamics that required education, training, and other social services.[92] Responding to changes in the recipient population from white widows to never married, divorced, and minority mothers, advocates argued that families on welfare could become self-supporting through maternal employment.[93] In recent work on the organization of the home care industry, Jennifer Klein and Boris have linked training for personal attendants and health aides, associated with domestic service, with welfare reform.[94]

As Martha Davis has demonstrated, court decisions moved welfare closer to an entitlement in the 1960s by overturning "man in the house" and residency rules and establishing the right to a fair hearing.[95] The new scholarship on welfare has traced how subsequent reforms mandated workfare for mothers who had access to child care, though never providing adequate amounts.[96] The replacement of AFDC with TANF (Temporary Assistance for Needy Families) in 1996 insisted that recipients take any job, even one below minimum wage, kicking them out of higher education as well as out of the home and placing lifetime limits on obtaining social assistance. By then employment had moved from a liberal strategy to increase women's independence to a conservative strategy to punish their sexuality and reinforce the low-wage labor force, as Mink has emphasized.[97] Poor women never really could choose stay-at-home motherhood, but after the end of welfare they lacked a social safety net. As Rickie Solinger contended, the increased participation of married white women in the labor force justified and stigmatized poor mothers who stayed home to look after their children. Only mothers who earned enough, or whose husbands did, could choose full-time motherhood.[98]

But not all poor women suffered such disdain, as Solinger herself first emphasized in charting shifting attitudes toward unwed motherhood.[99] Kenneth J. Neubeck and Noel A. Cazenave have offered a racism-centered perspective to the history of welfare, judging both gender- and state-centered or institutional analyses inadequate precisely because they neglect the ways that white racial hegemony has shaped the U.S. state. They defined "welfare racism" as "the various forms and manifestations of racism associated with means-tested programs of public assistance."[100] From denying benefits to women of color for being "undeserving" to instituting behavioral and other requirements for eligibility to limit their numbers and finally to lessening the value of welfare itself through declining monetary worth and workfare, the racialization of welfare has served political ends as well as disciplined the poor and shored up the low-waged labor supply.[101] The "welfare queen" replaced the worthy widow, her motherhood denied. Comparing Louisiana's 1960 slashing of its rolls with the Newburgh, New York, 1961 campaign against chiselers, Lisa Levenstein has documented the power of rhetorical framing; "child aid" garnered positive public response in contrast to portrayals of "unwed mother aid."[102]

Other scholars have turned to the struggle of poor women themselves. Expanding the thesis set forth in *Regulating the Poor,* Frances Fox Piven and Richard Cloward argued that expansion of welfare benefits developed from social unrest in *Poor People's Movements.*[103] Guida West's 1981 *The National Welfare Rights Movement: The Social Protest of Poor Women* provided the first, and still the most comprehensive, history of an organization central to the fight for welfare justice and gave full recognition to the black women that were at the NWRO's center.[104] Premilla Nadasen, in particular, has claimed the NWRO for the history of black feminism, while Rhonda Y. Williams charted the struggle of Baltimore's poor black women for respect without respectability in their demand for welfare justice.[105] Felicia Kornbluh highlighted campaigns for credit and the right to consume as part of the group's quest for dignity, justice, democracy, and adequate income.[106] Other historians have revealed how activists deployed the rhetoric of motherhood, refused welfare slavery in protesting workfare, and attempted to organize alternative social welfare systems run by poor mothers themselves.[107]

Alliances with the new feminism, however, floundered on the shoals of race and class, as Martha Davis showed in her study "of the trial-and-error approach that NOW and NWRO muddled through in the 1960s." However, "a powerful analytical framework that views poverty as inextricably linked to the common barriers faced by women in society, such as violence, wage discrimination, and disproportionately family responsibilities, and at the same time recognizes the unique challenges facing poor women and the need for social supports to redress these burdens," she claimed, emerged from the politics of coalition.[108] In fact, Marisa Chappell has presented a traditional women's organization — the League of Women Voters — as actually more committed to achieving income support than the National Organization for Women (NOW), whose members were focused on equality in the workplace ,not funding stay-at-home motherhood.[109]

Conclusion: Welfare History as Gender History

In the public-private welfare system that developed over the course of the twentieth century, characteristics of individuals determined access to benefits and the larger social citizenship that such aid signified. Scholarship on America's welfare state has reflected the fragmented nature of social welfare itself. Historians and social science analysts have interpreted individual programs or directed attention to employer benefits, charity, social insurance, ethnic institutions, or public assistance often without connecting all the components. State-centered, institutional, and political approaches have dominated, but historians of women and gender have looked at the impact of social policy on the lives of women and their families. They have re-valued the labor of care to challenge employment as the lynchpin of welfare rights and have focused on women as the providers as well as the recipients of services and income supports. Joining with scholars of race, they have turned a critical lens on the system as a whole to account for inequalities of race, gender, racialized gender, and nation embodied in the structure, implementation, and outcome of social welfare.[110]

NOTES

1. Eileen Boris charted these developments in "On the Importance of Naming: Gender, Race, and the Writing of Policy History," *Journal of Policy History* 17, no. 1 (2005): 72–92.

2. S. Jay Kleinberg examined the importance of class in the welfare state in "The Economic Origins of the Welfare State, 1870–1939," in *Social and Secure? Politics and Culture of the Welfare State: A Comparative Inquiry,* ed. Hans Bak, Frits van Holthoon, and Hans Krabbendam (Amsterdam: VU Press, 1996), 94–116. The inter-European and transatlantic seminars held at the Roosevelt Center in Middelburg, Holland, fostered a transnational approach to the analysis of the welfare state.

3. Robert Bremner, *From the Depths: The Discovery of Poverty in the United States* (New York: New York University Press, 1956); Roy Lubove, *The Professional Altruist: The Emergence of Social Work as a Career, 1880–1930* (Cambridge, Mass.: Harvard University Press, 1965); Clarke A. Chambers, *The Seedtime of Reform: American Social Service and Social Action, 1918–1933* (Minneapolis: University of Minnesota Press, 1963); Walter I. Trattner, *From Poor Law to Welfare State: A History of Social Welfare in America* (New York: Free Press, 1974).

4. James T. Patterson, *America's Struggle against Poverty in the Twentieth Century* (Cambridge, Mass.: Harvard University Press, 2000); Michael B. Katz, *In the Shadow of the Poorhouse: A Social History of Welfare in America* (New York: Basic Books, 1996).

5. Virginia Sapiro, "The Gender Basis of American Social Policy," in *Women, the State, and Welfare,* ed. Linda Gordon (Madison: University of Wisconsin Press, 1990), 37.

6. Linda Gordon, ed., *Women, the State, and Welfare* (Madison: University of Wisconsin Press, 1990); Linda K. Kerber, Alice Kessler-Harris, and Kathryn Kish Sklar, eds., *U.S. History as Women's History: New Feminist Essays* (Chapel Hill: University of North Carolina Press, 1995); Seth Koven and Sonya Michel, eds., *Mothers of a New World: Maternalist Politics and the Origins of Welfare States* (New York: Routledge, 1993); Theda Skocpol, *Protecting Soldiers and Mothers: The Political Origins of Social Policy in the United States* (Cambridge, Mass.: Belknap Press, 1992).

7. In addition to the sources cited above, see Molly Ladd-Taylor, *Mother-Work: Women, Child Welfare, and the State, 1890–1930* (Urbana: University of Illinois Press, 1994); Robyn Muncy, *Creating a Female Dominion in American Reform, 1890–1935* (New York: Oxford University Press, 1991); Ellen Fitzpatrick, *Endless Crusade: Women Social Scientists and Progressive Reform* (New York: Oxford University Press, 1990); Kathleen Laughlin, *Women's Work and Public Policy* (Boston: Northeastern University Press, 2000); Ann Shola Orloff, "Gender in Early United States Social Policy," *Journal of Policy History* 3 (1991): 249–281; Barbara Nelson, "The Gender, Race, and Class Origins of Early Welfare Policy and the Welfare State: A Comparison of Workmen's Compensation and Mothers' Aid," in *Women, Politics, and Change*, ed. Louise A. Tilly and Patricia Gurin (New York, Russell Sage Foundation, 1992), 413–435.

8. Eileen Boris and S. J. Kleinberg, "Mothers and Other Workers: (Re)Conceiving Labor, Maternalism, and the State," *Journal of Women's History* 15 (autumn 2003): 90–117.

9. Bremner, *From the Depths*, xi–xii.

10. Ibid., 3, 15.

11. Roy Lubove, *The Struggle for Social Security, 1900–1935* (Cambridge, Mass.: Harvard University Press, 1968); Lee J. Alston and Joseph P. Ferrie, *Southern Paternalism and the American Welfare State: Economics, Politics, and Institutions in the South, 1865–1965* (Cambridge: Cambridge University Press, 1999).

12. Chambers, *Seedtime of Reform*, 31.

13. Trattner, *From Poor Law to Welfare State*, vii; Frances Fox Piven and Richard Cloward, *Regulating the Poor: The Functions of Public Welfare* (New York: Vintage, 1971), xv.

14. Kathryn Kish Sklar, *Florence Kelley and the Nation's Work: The Rise of Women's Political Culture, 1830–1900* (New Haven: Yale University Press, 1995); Alice O'Connor, *Poverty Knowledge: Social Science, Social Policy, and the Poor in Twentieth-Century U.S. History* (Princeton: Princeton University Press, 2001).

15. Lubove, *The Struggle for Social Security*, 100–101.

16. Lubove, *The Professional Altruist*, 49.

17. Kathryn Kish Sklar, "Hull House in the 1890s: A Community of Women Reformers," *Signs* 10, no. 4 (1985): 658–677; Ruth Hutchisnson Crocker, *Social Work and Social Order: The Settlement Movement in Two Industrial Cities, 1889–1930* (Urbana: University of Illinois Press, 1992); Vicki L. Ruiz, "Dead Ends or Gold Mines? Using Missionary Records in Mexican American Women's History," *Frontiers: A Journal of Women's Studies* 12, no. 1 (1991): 33–56.

18. Leslie Margolin, *Under the Cover of Kindness: The Invention of Social Work* (Charlottesville: University of Virginia Press, 1997), 32, 68.

19. Regina G. Kunzel, *Fallen Women, Problem Girls: Unmarried Mothers and the Professionalization of Social Work, 1890–1945* (New Haven: Yale University Press, 1993); Linda Gordon, "Black and White Visions of Welfare: Women's Welfare Activism, 1890–1945," *Journal of American History* 78, no. 2 (September 1991): 559–590.

20. There are few studies of the rural poor, but see Mark J. Heale, "Patterns of Benevolence: Charity and Morality in Urban and Rural New York," *Societas* 3 (autumn 1973): 337–350.

21. Boris and Kleinberg, "Mothers and Other Workers"; and Eileen Boris, "What about the Working of the Working Mother?" *Journal of Women's History* 5 (fall 1993): 104–109.

22. Elna C. Green, introduction to *Before the New Deal: Social Welfare in the South, 1830–1930*, ed. Elna C. Green (Athens: University of Georgia Press, 1999), xvii.

23. Elisabeth Lasch-Quinn, *Black Neighbors: Race and the Limits of Reform in the American Settlement House Movement, 1890–1945* (Chapel Hill: University of North Carolina Press,

1993); Jacqueline Anne Rouse, *Lugenia Burns Hope: Black Southern Reformer* (Athens: University of Georgia Press, 1989).

24. Marilyn Holt, *The Orphans Trains: Placing Out in America* (Lincoln: University of Nebraska Press, 1992); LeRoy Ashby, *Saving the Waifs: Reformers and Dependent Children, 1890–1917* (Philadelphia: Temple University Press, 1984); Susan Tiffin, *In Whose Best Interest? Child Welfare Reform in the Progressive Era* (Westport, Conn.: Greenwood Press, 1982); Linda Gordon, *The Great Arizona Orphan Abduction* (Cambridge, Mass.: Harvard University Press, 1999); Kleinberg, *Widows and Orphans First: The Family Economy and Social Welfare Policy* (Urbana: University of Illinois Press, 2006) 106–107.

25. Joanne L. Goodwin, *Gender and the Politics of Welfare Reform* (Chicago, University of Chicago Press, 1997); Eileen Boris, "The Power of Motherhood: Black and White Activist Women Redefine the 'Political,'" in *Mothers of a New World*, ed. Koven and Michel, 213–245; Linda Gordon, *Pitied but Not Entitled: Single Mothers and the History of Welfare* (New York: Free Press, 1994); S. J. Kleinberg., *Widows and Orphans First*.

26. Mark Leff, "Consensus for Reform: The Mothers'-Pension Movement in the Progressive Era," *Social Service Quarterly* 47, no. 3 (1973): 397–417.

27. Goodwin, *Gender and the Politics of Welfare Reform*, 10.

28. Skocpol, *Protecting Soldiers and Mothers*, 41–51, 462.

29. Ibid., 459.

30. Kleinberg, *Widows and Orphans First*, ch. 4.

31. Susan Traverso, *Welfare Politics in Boston, 1910–1940* (Amherst: University of Massachusetts Press, 2003).

32. Goodwin, *Gender and the Politics of Welfare Reform*, 162–164; Andrew Billingsley and Jeanne M. Giovannoni, *Children of the Storm: Black Children and American Child Welfare* (New York: Harcourt, Brace, Jovanovich, 1972), 73–75; Kleinberg, *Widows and Orphans First*, ch. 4.

33. Billingsley and Giovannoni, *Children of the Storm*, 53.

34. For example, Trattner, *From Poor Law to Welfare State*, 185; James Leiby, *A History of Social Welfare and Social Work in the United States* (New York: Columbia University Press, 1978).

35. Mimi Abramovitz, *Regulating the Lives of Women* (Boston: South End Press, 1989), 2.

36. Linda Gordon, *Heroes of Their Own Lives: The Politics and History of Family Violence, Boston, 1880–1960* (New York: Viking Press, 1988).

37. Peggy Pascoe, *Relations of Rescue: The Search for Female Moral Authority in the American West, 1874–1939* (New York: Oxford University Press, 1990); Sherri Broder, *Tramps, Unfit Mothers, and Neglected Children: Negotiating the Family in Late Nineteenth-Century Philadelphia* (Philadelphia: University of Pennsylvania Press, 2002); Gordon, *Heroes of Their Own Lives*, 125.

38. Viviana Zelizer, *Pricing the Priceless Child: The Changing Social Value of Children* (New York: Basic Books, 1985); Pamela Barnhouse Walters and Philip J. O'Connell, "The Family Economy, Work, and Educational Participation in the United States, 1890–1940," *American Journal of Sociology* 93 (1988): 116–152; Maureen Fitzgerald, *Habits of Compassion: Irish Catholic Nuns and the Origins of New York's Welfare System, 1830–1900* (Urbana: University of Illinois Press, 2006).

39. Zillah Eisenstein, *Feminism and Sexual Equality: Crisis in Liberal America* (New York: Monthly Review Press, 1984), 92.

40. Gordon, "Black and White Visions of Welfare"; Dorothy C. Salem, *To Better Our World: Black Women in Organized Reform, 1890–1930* (Brooklyn, N.Y.: Carlson, 1990); Eileen Boris, "The Racialized Gendered State: Constructions of Citizenship in the United States,"

Social Politics 2, no. 2 (summer 1995): 160–180; Gwendolyn Mink, "The Lady and the Tramp: Gender, Race, and the Origins of the American Welfare State," in *Women, the State, and Welfare*, ed. Gordon, 92–122.

41. Billingsley and Giovannoni, *Children of the Storm*, 53.

42. Glenda Elizabeth Gilmore, *Gender and Jim Crow: Women and the Politics of White Supremacy in North Carolina, 1896–1920* (Chapel Hill: University of North Carolina Press, 1996), xxi.

43. Lasch-Quinn, *Black Neighbors*; see also Cynthia Neverdon-Morton, *Afro-American Women of the South and the Advancement of the Race, 1895–1925* (Knoxville: University of Tennessee Press, 1989).

44. Daniel T. Beito, *From Mutual Aid to the Welfare State: Fraternal Societies and Social Services, 1890–1967* (Chapel Hill: University of North Carolina Press, 2000), 52.

45. Kathryn Kish Sklar, "Two Political Cultures in the Progressive Era: The National Consumers' League and the American Association for Labor Legislation," in *U.S. History as Women's History*, ed. Kerber, Kessler-Harris, and Sklar, 36; William Graebner, *History of Retirement: The Meaning and Function of an American Institution, 1885–1978* (New Haven: Yale University Press, 1980).

46. Michael Willrich, "Home Slackers: Men, the State, and Welfare in Modern America," *Journal of American History* 87, no. 2 (September 2000): 460–489; Anna R. Igra, "Likely to Become a Public Charge: Deserted Women and the Family Law of the Poor in New York City, 1910–1936," *Journal of Women's History* 11, no. 4 (winter 2000): 59–81. See also Anna R. Igra, *Wives without Husbands: Marriage, Desertion, and Welfare in New York, 1900–1935* (Chapel Hill: University of North Carolina Press, 2006).

47. Gwendolyn Mink, *The Wages of Motherhood: Inequality in the Welfare State, 1917–1942* (Ithaca, N.Y., Cornell University Press, 1995), 3; Sonya Michel, *Children's Interests/Mothers' Rights: The Shaping of America's Child Care Policy* (New Haven: Yale University Press, 1999).

48. Ann Shola Orloff, "The Political Origins of America's Belated Welfare State," in *The Politics of Social Policy in the United States*, ed. Margaret Weir, Ann Shola Orloff, and Theda Skocpol (Princeton, N.J., Princeton University Press, 1988), 37–80; Ann Shola Orloff and Theda Skocpol, "Why Not Equal Protection? Explaining the Politics of Public Social Spending in Britain, 1900–1911, and the United States, 1880s–1920s," *American Sociological Review* 49, no. 6 (December 1984).

49. Ladd-Taylor, *Mother-Work*, 188.

50. Muncy, *Creating a Female Dominion*.

51. Linda Gordon, "Putting Children First: Women, Maternalism, and Welfare in the Early Twentieth Century," in *U.S. History as Women's History*, ed. Kerber, Kessler-Harris, and Sklar, 77; Michel, *Children's Interests*.

52. Elna C. Green, "Local Circumstances: Social Welfare in New Orleans, 1870s–1920s," in *Before the New Deal*, ed. Green, 81–99; Kleinberg, *Widows and Orphans First*, 60–68.

53. Nurith Zmora, *Orphanages Reconsidered: Child-Care Institutions in Progressive Era Baltimore* (Philadelphia: Temple University Press, 1994), 181. See also Matthew A. Crenson, *Building the Invisible Orphanage: A Prehistory of the American Welfare System* (Cambridge, Mass.: Harvard University Press, 1998).

54. Koven and Michel, *Mothers of a New World*, xi; Georgina Hickey, "Disease, Disorder, and Motherhood: Working-Class Women, Social Welfare, and the Process of Urban Development in Atlanta," in *Before the New Deal*, ed. Green, 181–207.

55. Skocpol, *Protecting Soldiers and Mothers*; Ladd-Taylor, *Mother-Work*, 3–8.

56. Lubove, *The Professional Altruist*, 101–106.

57. Susan Ware, *Beyond Suffrage: Women in the New Deal* (Cambridge, Mass.: Harvard University Press, 1981), 87–115.

58. Eileen Boris, "Labor's Welfare State: Defining Workers, Constructing Citizens," in *Cambridge History of American Law*, vol. 3, ed. Michael Grossberg and Christopher Tomlins (New York: Cambridge University Press, 2008).

59. Mink, *The Wages of Motherhood*, 126.

60. Alice Kessler-Harris, *In Pursuit of Equity: Women, Men, and the Quest for Economic Citizenship in Twentieth-Century America* (New York: Oxford University Press, 2001), 64–169.

61. Immigration history is missing from analysis of the New Deal. But see Evelyn Nakano Glenn, *Unequal Freedom: How Race and Gender Shaped American Citizenship and Labor* (Cambridge, Mass.: Harvard University Press, 2002); Sarah Deutsch, *No Separate Refuge: Culture, Class, and Gender on an Anglo-Hispanic Frontier in the American Southwest, 1880–1940* (New York: Oxford University Press, 1987), 162–199; Mae M. Ngai, *Impossible Subjects: Illegal Aliens and the Making of Modern America* (Princeton: Princeton University Press, 2004); Martha Gardner, *The Qualities of a Citizen: Women, Immigration, and Citizenship, 1870–1905* (Princeton: Princeton University Press, 2005).

62. Michael B. Katz, *Improving Poor People: The Welfare State, The "Underclass," and Urban Schools as History* (Princeton: Princeton University Press, 1995), 55–6; William R. Brock, *Welfare, Democracy, and the New Deal* (New York: Cambridge University Press, 1988).

63. Mink, *The Wages of Motherhood*, 127.

64. Nancy E. Rose, *Workfare or Fair Work: Women, Welfare, and Government Work Programs* (New Brunswick: Rutgers University Press, 1995), 31–57.

65. Nancy E. Rose, *Put to Work: Relief Programs in the Great Depression* (New York: Monthly Review Press, 1994), 13, 59–60.

66. Elizabeth Faue, *Community of Suffering and Struggle: Women, Men, and the Labor Movement in Minneapolis, 1915–1945* (Chapel Hill: University of North Carolina Press, 1991), 154; Julia Kirk Blackwelder, *Women of the Depression: Caste and Culture in San Antonio, 1929–1939* (College Station: Texas A&M University Press, 1984), 109–29.

67. Georgina Hickey, " 'The Lowest Form of Work Relief': Authority, Gender, and the State in Atlanta's WPA Sewing Rooms," in *The New Deal and Beyond: Social Welfare in the South Since 1930*, ed. Elna C. Green (Athens: University of Georgia Press, 2003), 13, 15.

68. Hickey, " 'The Lowest Form of Work Relief,' " 13.

69. Blackwelder, *Women of the Depression*, 119.

70. Victoria W. Wolcott, *Remaking Respectability: African American Women in Interwar Detroit* (Chapel Hill: University of North Carolina Press, 2001), 229.

71. Joan Hoff-Wilson and Marjorie Lightman, eds., *Without Precedent: The Life and Career of Eleanor Roosevelt* (Bloomington: Indiana University Press, 1984).

72. Landon R.Y. Storrs, *Civilizing Capitalism: The National Consumers' League, Women's Activism, and Labor Standards in the New Deal Era* (Chapel Hill: University of North Carolina Press, 2000).

73. Stephanie Shaw, *What A Woman Ought to Be and To Do: Black Professional Women Workers during the Jim Crow Era* (Chicago: University of Chicago Press, 1996), 191.

74. Sarah Wilkerson-Freeman, "The Creation of a Subversive Feminist Dominion: Interracialist Social Workers and the Georgia New Deal," *The Journal of Women's History* 13, no. 4 (Winter 2002), 132–54.

75. Edith Abbott, "Mothers' Aid and Public Assistance, 1938," in *From Relief to Social Security*, 263, quoted in Gordon, *Pitied but Not Entitled*, 176.

76. Gordon, *Pitied but Not Entitled*, 268; Kessler-Harris, *In Pursuit of Equity*, 64–169; Mink, *The Wages of Motherhood*, 123–173.

77. Nancy F. Cott, *Public Vows: A History of Marriage and the Nation* (Cambridge, Mass.: Harvard University Press, 2000).

78. Kessler-Harris, *In Pursuit of Equity*; Deborah M. Figart, Ellen Mutari, and Marilyn Power, *Living Wages, Equal Wages: Gender and Labor Market Policies in the United States* (London: Routledge, 2002), 118.

79. Kessler-Harris, *In Pursuit of Equity*, 142, 149.

80. See Social Security Administration, "History of the Provisions of Old-Age, Survivors, and Disability Insurance," http://www.ssa.gov/OACT/HOP/hopi.htm#302, assessed February 3, 2002.

81. Rose calculated that 53% of those on white-collar WPA projects were women. *Put to Work*, 107–8.

82. Kleinberg, *Widows and Orphans First*.

83. Wolcott, *Rethinking Respectability*, 217–39.

84. Michael K. Brown, *Race, Money, and the American Welfare State* (Ithaca: Cornell University Press, 1999), 64. See also Mary Poole, *The Segregated Origins of Social Security: African Americans and the Welfare State* (Chapel Hill: University of North Carolina Press, 2006).

85. Suzanne Mettler, *Dividing Citizens: Gender and Federalism in New Deal Public Policy* (Ithaca: Cornell University Press, 1998), 5–6.

86. Robert C. Lieberman, *Shifting The Color Line: Race and the American Welfare State* (Cambridge, Mass.: Harvard University Press, 1998).

87. William Graebner, "The End of Liberalism: Narrating Welfare's Decline, from the Moynihan Report (1965) to the Personal Responsibility and Work Opportunity Act (1960)," *Journal of Policy History* 14 (Spring 2002), 170–90.

88. Kessler-Harris, *In Pursuit of Equity*, 132.

89. Mink, *Wages of Motherhood*, 137; Kleinberg, *Widows and Orphans First*, ch. 5.

90. Joanne Goodwin, "'Employable Mothers' and 'Suitable Work': A Re-evaluation of Welfare and Wage-Earning for Women in the Twentieth-Century United States," *Journal of Social History* 29 (winter 1995): 545; Rose, *Workfare or Fair Work*, 73–75.

91. Ellen Reese, *Backlash against Welfare Mothers Past and Present* (Berkeley: University of California Press, 2005).

92. Jennifer Mittelstadt, *From Welfare to Workfare: The Unintended Consequences of Liberal Reform, 1945–1965* (Chapel Hill: University of North Carolina Press, 2005).

93. Robert A. Moffitt and Michele Ver Ploeg, eds., *Evaluating Welfare Reform in an Era of Transition* (Washington: National Academy Press, 2001), 16–17.

94. Eileen Boris and Jennifer Klein, "Organizing Home Care: Low-Waged Workers in the Welfare State," *Politics and Society* 34, no. 1 (March 2006).

95. Martha Davis, *Brutal Need: Lawyers and the Welfare Rights Movement, 1960–1973* (New Haven: Yale University Press, 1993).

96. Gwendolyn Mink, ed., *Whose Welfare?* (Ithaca, N.Y.: Cornell University Press, 1999); Randy Albelda and Ann Withorn, eds., *Lost Ground: Welfare Reform, Poverty, and Beyond* (Boston: South End Press, 2002); Sonya Michel, "Child Care and Welfare (In)Justice," *Feminist Studies* 24, no. 1 (spring 1998): 44–54.

97. Gwendolyn Mink, "Violating Women: Rights Abuse in the Welfare Police State," in *Lost Ground*, ed. Albelda and Withorn, 95–112.

98. Rickie Solinger, *Beggars and Choosers: How the Politics of Choice Shapes Adoption, Abortion, and Welfare in the United States* (New York: Hill and Wang, 2001), 193.

99. Ibid.

100. Kenneth J. Neubeck and Noel A. Cazenave, *Welfare Racism: Playing the Race Card against America's Poor* (New York : Routledge, 2001), 35–36.

101. Frances Fox Piven, "Welfare and Work," in *Whose Welfare?* ed. Mink, 83–99. On the welfare queen, see Ange-Marie Hancock, *The Politics of Disgust: The Public Identity of the Welfare Queen* (New York: New York University Press, 2001).

102. Lisa Levenstein, "From Innocent Children to Unwanted Migrants and Unwed Moms: Two Chapters in the Public Discourse on Welfare in the United States, 1960–1961," *Journal of Women's History* 11, no. 4 (winter 2000): 10–33.

103. Fox Piven and Cloward, *Regulating the Poor*; Frances Fox Piven and Richard Cloward, *Poor People's Movements: Why They Succeeded and How They Fail* (New York: Pantheon, 1977); Fox Piven and Cloward, *The Breaking of the American Social Contract* (New York: Free Press, 1997), 213–242.

104. Guida West, *The National Welfare Rights Movement: The Social Protest of Poor Women* (New York: Praeger, 1981).

105. Premilla Nadasen, "Expanding the Boundaries of the Women's Movement: Black Feminism and the Struggle for Welfare Rights," *Feminist Studies* 28, no. 2 (summer 2002): 271–301; Nadasen, *Welfare Warriors: The Welfare Rights Movement in the United States* (New York: Routledge, 2005); Rhonda Y. Williams, *The Politics of Public Housing: Black Women's Struggles against Urban Inequality* (New York: Oxford University Press, 2004).

106. Felicia Kornbluh, "To Fulfill Their 'Rightly Needs': Consumerism and the National Welfare Rights Movement," *Radical History Review* 69 (fall 1997): 76–113; Kornbluh, "The Goals of the National Welfare Rights Movement: Why We Need Them Thirty Years Later," *Feminist Studies* 24, no. 1 (spring 1998): 65–78.

107. Anne M. Valk, "'Mother Power': The Movement for Welfare Rights in Washington, D.C., 1966–1972," *Journal of Women's History* 11, no. 4 (winter 2000): 34–58; Eileen Boris, "When Work Is Slavery," in *Whose Welfare?* ed. Mink, 36–55; Annelise Orleck, *Storming Caesars Palace: How Black Mothers Fought Their Own War on Poverty* (Boston: Beacon Press, 2005).

108. Martha F. Davis, "Welfare Rights and Women's Rights in the 1960s," in *Integrating the Sixties*, ed. Brian Balogh (University Park: Pennsylvania State University Press, 1996), 145.

109. Marisa Chappell, "Rethinking Women's Politics in the 1970s: The League of Women Voters and the National Organization for Women Confront Poverty," *Journal of Women's History* 13, no. 4 (winter 2002): 155–179.

110. Against this literature comes the challenge from queer studies, which names the welfare state heterosexual. See Margot Canaday, "Building a Straight State: Sexuality and Social Citizenship under the 1944 G.I. Bill," *Journal of American History* 90, no. 3 (December 2003): 935–957.

15

Interrupting Norms and Constructing Deviances

Competing Frameworks in the Histories of Sexualities in the United States

LEISA D. MEYER

Most historians locate the emergence of the field of the history of sexuality as part of the new social history of the 1960s. This new focus and methodology of inquiry investigated and prioritized the histories of groups that had been little studied.[1] These new "subfields" were created in the context of powerful social movements for civil rights and social justice. The resulting historical studies, often framed by the boundaries of these movements, defined their subjects generally by race/ethnicity, gender, *or* class and explored and highlighted the lives, experiences, practices, and perspectives of non-elites (non-white, non-heterosexual, non-middle/upper-class men). In doing so, these studies investigated the question of power — how non-elites, as historical subjects and agents, affected and defined their own lives and communities. In offering a different approach to history, these initial works commonly replicated some of the problems of their predecessors in their elision of the multiplicity of identities and experiences of those individuals within the groups on which they focused.

Thus, some women's histories emerging in the 1960s and even into the '80s focused on white and frequently middle-class historical subjects or institutions and did not speak to issues of race/ethnicity or class, while some African American and Spanish/Mexican American histories highlighted men's experiences and did not address those of women. Certainly, such elisions partially came from the process of historical writing itself that requires that we define our parameters, including questions of locality, the exact group, and the specific issues that we will most fully explore, among many others. This same paradox infused the history of sexuality: the moment we began to revise in opposition to previous scholarly logics or common practices, to research and write on previously untouched historical topics, to excavate previously unaddressed historical subjects, we also simultaneously created new problems of omission within our alternative narratives. This work we do cannot be described adequately as a dialectical process — where generalizations (theses) are interrupted by studies of fragments (antitheses) that do not fit, calling into question and contesting the legitimacy of the conclusions of the former and leading, slowly, to syntheses. Rather, these fragments themselves often transmute into new competing generalizations that are then contested by yet another narrative intervention. This chapter focuses on the United States and predominantly concentrates on the twentieth century. In it I explore some of the key narratives that frame our inquiry into the history of sexuality, the generalizations that seem so necessary to the work we do, but which also inevitably invoke the concomitant need for fragmentation.

What is this sexuality that we struggle to historicize and about which we write? And why are such studies so important to understanding modern U.S. history? Is sexuality an essential element of every human being? Is it desire? Is it behavior? Is it a "tangle of bodily sensations, feeling, thoughts, and inter-actions?"[2] Is it a "cultural production" that "represents the appropriation of the human body and of its physiological capacities by an ideological discourse?"[3] The definition of sexuality entails all of the above and more. Sexuality also is a critical site where broader cultural anxieties are manifested. In other words, sexuality is also a discourse within which power relations between men and women, different racial/ethnic groups, classes, and states are expressed and configured. As such the study of sexuality is the study of politics. Sexuality is central to Americans' understandings of themselves.

It is a means to define respectability and propriety and to label some identities as divergent from the norm. It is a means of creating community and defining those outside these communities. And it is a means of defining threats that reflect and shape broader cultural attitudes toward race, ethnicity, class, and gender. Major institutions, governments, courts, religious organizations, and the medical profession have served as arbiters, constructing normative and deviant sexualities and providing criteria for defining the range within each. Yet arbiters' authority has always also been contested by many and for disparate and contradictory reasons. Making sense of these often competing definitions requires that we understand the history of sexuality as far more complicated than a movement from repression to liberation.

The Question of "Repression" — Myths, Interruptions, and Competing Norm Creation

The philosopher and historian Michel Foucault offered some of the earliest commentary on the presumption that the twentieth century witnessed a steady move toward "liberating" sexuality from the confines of the "repressive" Victorian era. Revising assumptions of Sigmund Freud's work as liberating sexuality, Foucault suggested that the Victorian period was more aptly characterized as one of proliferating sexual discourses. As Stephen Garton suggests, we must understand

Foucault's work as a "sustained critique of psychoanalysis." Rather than Freud marking a break with "moralism and superstition, ushering in new enlightened and scientific theories of sexuality," Foucault held that Freud was part of a "longer genealogy of sexual discourse that claimed the mantle of science."[4] As "deviance" was named, studied, and classified, increasing numbers of possibilities for sexual expression became visible. In the hands of scholars of sexuality in the twentieth century, such multiplicities of expression make the "normative" far more apparent as a construction itself. Thus Victorianism, and continuing scientific and scholarly efforts through the twentieth century to decipher the "truth of sex," did not "repress" sexuality, but rather "produced" it.[5]

Some scholars have investigated the creation, influence, and effect of the "myth" of Victorian repression during the early twentieth century. Christina Simmons, for instance, explores shifts in sexual discourses and behavior that characterize what has been identified as the first sexual revolution. This "revolution," portrayed by commentators as a necessary move away from the unreasonable constraints of the Victorian period, was marked by an increased emphasis on heterosociality, a proliferation of venues within which acceptable heterosocial interactions might occur, and a normative acknowledgment of sexual passion as appropriate for white middle-class women. Simmons exposes the opposing images of white middle-class women that were visible during the early twentieth century — the sexually liberated flapper and the asexual matron — as icons of white female power. The former represented the "new" sexually active "modern" woman who seemed to claim the previously male power of sexual expression, while the latter was understood as controlling men through passionlessness. To the "white liberal sexual commentators" whom Simmons studies, these images suggested that women had obtained an "improper advantage over men in modern life."[6] Thus, in Simmons's study, the "myth of Victorian repression" embodied a "reaction against women's power in either form" and the "new sexual discourse of the 1920s and 1930s represented not 'liberation' but a new form of regulation" that "effectively sustained the cultural power of men, focusing that power in the arena of sexuality."[7]

The early twentieth-century shifts in dominant cultural sexual norms and the myth of Victorian repression against which they operated were eminently raced and classed creations. The move to "acceptable" sexual passion for white middle-class women, for instance, had been *the* key marker of sexual deviance presumed by white commentators and instantiated in racialized sexual stereotypes of women and men of color. In speaking out against lynching during this period, Ida B. Wells challenged the dominant white cultural myth of the black male rapist. By questioning prevalent cultural normative depictions of African American male and female sexuality, she simultaneously cast doubt on the sexual respectability of white women and contested contemporary sexualized racial hierarchies. As African American feminist scholars such as Paula Giddings and Darlene Clark Hine demonstrate, Ida B. Wells disputed the late nineteenth-century dominant assumption of rape that rationalized the white lynching of black men and simultaneously questioned the "passionless purity" of white southern women.[8]

The conscious struggle to combat racist images of African American women as licentious and promiscuous became a critical part of African American women's organizing at the turn of the century. In her study of the Women's Convention of the Black Baptist Church during the late nineteenth and early twentieth centuries, Evelyn Brooks Higginbotham coined the term "politics of respectability" to describe the women's promotion of restrained behavior, especially in terms of sexuality, as a "strategy of reform."[9] She suggests that "the politics of respectability constituted a deliberate, highly self-conscious concession to hegemonic values." Through the appropriation of the discourse of "respectability" accepted by white middle-class society, African American women "boldly asserted the will and agency to define themselves outside the parameters of prevailing racist discourses" that were used to justify sexual violence perpetrated by white men against African American women.[10] Thus African American women, ever cognizant of the white gaze, used the normative ideals of white society to both assert respectability for themselves and interrupt dominant cultural racist presumptions. Historian Paisley Harris argues that the politics of respectability "served a gatekeeping function, establishing a behavioral 'entrance fee'" through which African Americans earned the "right to respect" and full membership within their communities.[11] While this "entrance fee" offered some challenge to dominant cultural views of African Americans, it also constructed and maintained "status" distinctions within African American communities.

The challenge to dominant racist narratives represented by the "politics of respectability" has itself been the subject of contestation, interruption, and fragmentation. Historian Mattie Udora Richardson posits that the "exclusion" inherent in such a "politics" has meant an elision of the range of sexualities present in African American culture historically in "favor of a static heterosexual narrative." "Far from being totally invisible," Richardson argues, "the 'queer' is present in Black history as a threat to Black respectability. Black women's sexuality has been discussed as the 'unspeakable thing unspoken' of Black life."[12] Deena González offers a similar critique of this type of silencing as a regular practice in the writings of Chicana/o scholars. In her critique of the anthology, *Criticism in the Borderlands*, González notes the editors' dismissal of "Chicana lesbian writing" as "not quite . . . cutting edge." This same anthology included a review of Cherríe Moraga and Gloria Anzaldúa's anthology, *This Bridge Called My Back*, that "fail[ed]" to recognize the "specific intention" of *Bridge* editors to "compile women-of-color-identified materials in one place. Essentially speaking," González writes, "the lesbian co-editors of *Bridge* 'othered' the straight mainstream. But this conclusion escapes straight critics and is consistently ignored by others who then go on to impose upon these works a heterosexual genealogy."[13] She concludes that "without some of our work in print we face total erasure, and risk not being present in historical or cultural memory. With work in print, but in the hands of disidentified, disembodied straight critics, we stand to be — as we have been in malestream documents across the ages — configured to serve the interests of domination, to be iconographed as the 'minoritized' voice. They now have our words; they think they 'hear' our voices, our languages, but we are still absent. Poor choices."[14]

Similar to Richardson and González, George Chauncey revises generalizations on the histories of homosexuality offered by previous scholars. In his meticulously researched and eloquently written study of "gay male" New York City, Chauncey cautions against the "appeal" of "gay history" as a "progressive. . . . steady movement toward freedom."[15] He uncovers an effervescent and highly visible "gay world" existing in the early twentieth century, years before the 1969 Stonewall rebellion that has symbolized the beginnings of lesbian and gay "liberation." Chauncey challenges three primary generalizations offered by historians in characterizing gay men's lives prior to Stonewall: that they were "isolated," that hostility from the dominant heterosexual culture required that they be invisible to the outside world, and that they had internalized the dominant cultural view of them as deviant and thus self-hating. Instead, Chauncey excavates the neighborhoods within which gay men lived and thrived, the stunningly rendered, highly visible, and well-attended drag balls of the 1920s, and the vibrant "gay world" which men "came out into" during the first third of the twentieth century. He locates the change in dominant perceptions about this "gay world" and the increased public hostility and state regulation in response to it as emerging during the 1930s. In effect, Chauncey argues that the state built the "closet" and forced gay men to live in it partially in reaction to the "growth and visibility of the gay subculture during the Prohibition years of the 1920s and early 1930s."[16] Other historians find this work especially significant in Chauncey's attention to the "power and political salience of social history." As Kathy Peiss notes, while "clearly influenced by post-structuralist readings and queer theory," the most "compelling" aspect of the book comes from "the way he grounds these matters in the daily life of gay men. Their social practices, Chauncey argues, not the medical model or other elite discourses, created gay identity."[17]

Sexual Identities and Subjectivities

The question of "bottom up" or "top down" approaches has been central to works addressing sexuality historically, including those studies examining shifting sexual behaviors, constructions of sexual identities, and the emergence of "modern" and "postmodern" sexual systems and discourses, among other issues. The bottom line question of who or what defines normative and deviant and how such systems are produced continues to be primary in the field. The "top" is defined serially and alternatively as "upper-class," "middle-class," dominant racial/ ethnic/class/sexual culture, white, the "normative," or major authoritarian institutions. "Bottom" is defined as "ordinary people," the non-normative constructed as occupying the bottom of the racial, gender, class, and sexual hierarchies. Contestation over the authority (or lack thereof) to define normative sexualities, claim "appropriate" desires, and act as sexual agents is linked to this broader question of agency and causation.

The emergence of sexuality as a marker of identity, as a critical means of defining personal identity and the "self" in relation to others and the broader world, is one element describing the shift to a modern era. The questions of what constitutes this modern sexual identity, how different sexual identities come to be created and defined, and who or what is responsible for these definitions are critical points of inquiry and contention among historians of sexuality. Foucault suggested that the emergence of a modern sexual subject was embedded in a larger shift in understandings of sexuality — its normative and deviant forms — moving from constructing particular behaviors as "perverse" or "deviant" and discretely punishable to seeing sexual and gender behaviors as defining a species of individuals or a group, the homosexual or the invert, for instance.[18] Moreover, as scientific and medical discourse constructed taxonomies of sexual deviance, so the range of behaviors defining normative sexualities was simultaneously created. As historian Jennifer Terry puts it, "by conceiving homosexuality as transgressive, experts (though seldom with this express purpose) deployed it to conceptualize and delimit . . . a range of acceptable habits, activities, gestures, relationships, identities, and desires."[19] In his discussion of this shift, Foucault implies that scientists and other researchers *created* homosexuality and other non-normative identities or that at least sexual discourses deployed by "experts" were the currency through which homosexuals, among others, articulated their identities. Foucault points to the literature and discourses produced by these experts as constructing the basis for "social controls" of sexual deviance and also offering the possibility of "the formation of a 'reverse' discourse" through which "homosexuality" could "speak in its own behalf . . . often in the same vocabulary, using the same categories by which it was medically disqualified."[20]

This generalization, that sexual identity is created from the top and trickles down to the "masses," has been both clarified and revised in recent years. Jennifer Terry, for instance, argues that Foucault's "semantical intimation" that the "experts spoke first and then homosexuals appropriated, or 'reversed,' the discourse" is "quite simply not the case." She instead contends that "the scientific and medical construction of homosexuality was and is a collaborative process involving sexual dissenters."[21] Through her concept of "variant subjectivity" Terry examines the interaction between homosexuals who were the subjects of scientific inquiry and those studying them. She finds that gay men and lesbians appropriated and more significantly intervened to change the expert discourse about homosexuality to use it on their own behalf. In doing so, she highlights these subjects as sexual actors who "spoke in a language that had multiple sites of origin . . . including the subcultural practices they shared as dissenters from normative regimes of sex, gender, and sexuality," and who "understood medical discourse as a powerful mode for understanding themselves and for achieving some measure of dignity and respect."[22] George Chauncey also challenged "the assumption . . . that nineteenth-century medical discourse constructed the 'homosexual' as a personality type, and that the appearance of the homosexual in medical discourse should be taken as indicative of or synonymous with the homosexual's appearance in the culture as a whole." Seeing the medical literature as "representing simply one of several powerful (and competing) sexual ideologies," Chauncey argued for situating "medical discourse" in the context of shifting "representations of homosexuality" in popular culture and the quotidian, concrete interactions, perspectives, and practices through which "homosexually active men were labeled, understood themselves, and interacted with others."[23] Joanne Meyerowitz particularly documented how "the discourse on transsexuals" came in part from "the people who hoped to change their sex" as well as from "popular culture . . . the courts . . . and the domains of medicine and science." Transsexual people "articulated their senses of self with the language and cultural forms available to them" and in doing so participated in creating and reconfiguring their own identities.[24]

The question of the agency, or lack thereof, of deviant or non-dominant populations in shaping understandings of their own sexual subjectivity and affecting the dominant cultural norms with which they must interact has also been an important terrain of investigation for scholars of sexuality. Studies of working-class ethnic women's sexual and social lives suggest that such women were sexual actors who created their own definitions of the boundaries of appropriate behavior — definitions that were often in tension with those offered by white middle-class, native-born authorities. In her investigation of the lives of New York working-class women in the early twentieth century, Kathy Peiss found that sexual and consumer desire framed by the economic realities of their lives led some of these women to develop the system of "treating," whereby they exchanged varying degrees of sexual favors with young men for access to the urban heterosocial entertainments increasingly available at the time. The heterosocial leisure culture that originated among New York's working classes actually "trickled up" to the middle classes and in doing so influenced the shifting norms of sexual and social behavior for white bourgeois women.[25]

Building on Peiss's work, Elizabeth Clement outlines the process through which the emergence and evolution of treating as a system of heterosexual barter developed by both European ethnic and African American working-class youth created a new and more permissive continuum for female heterosexual behavior. This continuum, always contested and negotiated, worked through the 1940s to change ideas about courtship and the possibilities for "respectable" heterosexual intimacies. Treating and the negotiations it demanded between young working-class women and men had a deep impact on the practice and meanings of prostitution before World War II. In particular, it served as a bridge between systems of courtship (moderated by ethnic and racial communities and families) and the already instantiated symbol of urban vice — prostitution (moderated by state and federal authorities and urban reformers). In doing so, Clement contends, the sexual practices of working-class youth in many ways became the model and set the trajectory for the development of modern American sexual norms and practices.[26]

The question of who or what is responsible for constructing sexual identities and the corollary query of who or what is responsible for creating sexual norms have been of particular interest to scholars seeking to interrupt the dominant white middle-class narrative that framed many early studies of sexuality. The Baptist women Evelyn Brooks Higginbotham analyzes, for instance, used "restraint" to define their sexual identities and through these identities constructed themselves and other African American women as respectable. In doing so, they participated in the creation of subcultural sexual norms for African Americans that were both resistant and accommodating to those deployed by dominant cultural authorities.[27] Historian Darlene Clark Hine also identifies "self-protection" as a central survival strategy for African American women during the twentieth century. She found that some middle-class African American women in the Midwest developed a "culture of dissemblance" to "protect the sanctity of the inner aspects of their lives."[28] This culture of dissemblance, defined by the absence of discussion of sexuality and their private lives, worked not only to "silence and conceal but also to dismantle and deconstruct the dominant society's deployment of race."[29] Thus, both the politics of respectability and the culture of dissemblance must be clarified as frameworks for understanding African American women's sexuality historically, especially in terms of norm construction.

Processes of norm creation, even alternative normative systems emerging among non-dominant groups as strategies of resistance, are always contested. In her work on Ma Rainey and other African American female blues singers, for instance, literary scholar Hazel Carby argues that these women offered explicit commentary about their own and others' sexualities through the lyrics and performance of the blues. Far from embracing the politics of respectability or being consistent with the silences required by the culture of dissemblance, such women gave voice to and embodied African American female subjectivity of a distinctly different type. In speaking same-sex sexual desire as well as heterosexual passion, Carby's subjects contested dominant and emergent subcultural sexual norms as well as affirmed some elements of racist sexual stereotypes evident among the white American population.[30] Literary critic Ann duCille suggests that it is this form of sexual expression, the blues, which has become the "master narrative" of "the black experience." In an intervention to an intervention, duCille argues for the need to "unhinge the fixity" of explaining African American women's sexual subjectivity as either "completely unwritten to avoid endorsing sexual stereotypes or sensationally overwritten to both defy and exploit those stereotypes." She recommends instead the exploration of "other indices, for wider analytical angles that allow us to plot African America expressive geographies in *inclusive* rather than *exclusive* terms (my emphasis)."[31]

The question of identity has been a trying one for historians of sexuality. How do we address the question of sexual subjectivity? How do we accurately and adequately speak not only to sexual norms and their contestation but also to individuals' understandings of sexuality historically? Ann duCille's critique of Carby and other cultural critics' privileging of the blues as the *most* authentic version of African American women's "reality" is based in part on her analysis of another form of cultural expression — the novel. duCille argues that the writings of African American female novelists Jessie Fauset and Nella Larsen through the 1930s were "far from silent on the topic of sexuality, these artists . . . edged the discourse into another realm: a realm precariously balanced on the cusp of the respectable and the risqué; a realm that is at times *neutral*, perhaps, but never *neuter*; a realm in which they, too, participated in reclaiming the black body and in defining African American expressive culture."[32]

In doing so, DuCille joins other African American feminist critics in suggesting the centrality of "discursive forms other than scholarship" as sources through which women of color more often "speak about sexuality." Cultural studies scholar Domna Stanton, for instance, has characterized works like *This Bridge Called My Back* as a "hybrid critical-creative mode" which, she argues, "encompasses theory" and facilitates speech about sexuality. This hybrid mode, which includes, among other forms, poetry, fiction, diary entries, and autobiographical narratives, has been central as a space through which women of color can and have articulated their sexual subjectivity.[33] These modes of articulation serve as both sources for sexual histories and forms through which to express such histories. Thus, historian Emma Pérez calls for the need to more fully investigate theoretically "fictive" sources to "interrogate . . . representations of sexual deviants and track ideologies about sex and sexuality," pointing to *corridos* in addition to "cultural and literary texts" as underused sources for investigating Mexican, Mexican American, and Chicana/o sexualities.[34] Corridos, narrative songs or ballads generated by Mexican and Mexican American people and Chicana/os throughout the nineteenth and twentieth century, speak to significant themes in Mexican and Mexican American history, including immigration, border crossings, and the dangers of love and war, and offer valuable tools for exploring the histories of sexualities heretofore hidden, subtextual, or willfully ignored in these communities.

In Search of Sexual Identity

Scholarly investigations of sexual identity and identity formation have sometimes sought to find continuities with contemporary understandings of sexual practices and identities in the past. In his work on the significance of the berdache identity among the Zuni,[35] for instance, Will Roscoe suggested that We'wha, an *lhamana* (the Zuni term for berdache) who lived during the late nineteenth and early twentieth centuries and "combined the social roles of both men and women ... and dressed, at least in part, in women's clothes," offers "evidence of continuity between traditional berdache roles and contemporary gay American Indians."[36] Roscoe challenges the prevailing anthropological narrative by demonstrating that Zuni lhamanas did not "cross genders" but rather "bridg[ed] or combin[ed] the social roles of men and women" and in doing so contributed to Zuni society through their "variance" which was not "ignored or disguised by the social fiction of gender crossing." Roscoe's definition of the significance of the Zuni lhamana revises previous anthropological models that had characterized the berdache as a cross-gender role that operated as a mechanism of social control, "society's way of constraining individuals to one or another role."[37] Roscoe's characterization of the berdache category as signifying gender and sexual fluidity has been embraced by contemporary American Indian activists who have reclaimed and renamed this category as the "two-spirit" tradition among native peoples.[38]

Some scholars who see the quest for gay roots in Native American culture as deracinating challenge the celebratory, connected, and inclusive vision of the "two-spirit" put forward by Roscoe and others. Ramón Gutiérrez argues, for instance, that historically the numbers of berdaches were "quite small" among North and South American Indian groups and describes the berdache not as an "accepted," culturally sanctioned, and respected position, but rather as a "status ... principally ascribed to defeated enemies." Gutiérrez interprets the wearing of women's clothes by male lhamana among the Zuni not as evidence of an embrace of variance but rather as an exercise meant to humiliate male prisoners and transgressors. He interprets the associations made between the berdache and homosexual intercourse in Spanish narratives, travelers' accounts, and ethnographies not as linked to the racist and ethnocentrist conventions that were part of the colonial enterprise, but rather related to the "universal gender representation of conquest: victors on vanquishing their enemies asserted their virility by transforming the losers into effeminates." Gutiérrez constructs the berdache not as a gender and sexual role "into which someone is socialized" but rather as a "social status a person was pressed into" or was made to "assume."[39] In other words, it was not a respected identity emerging from the desires of individuals themselves in concert with the culture in which they resided. Rather it was an externally imposed, disgraced identity that stigmatized sexual and gender fluidity and women through its association with a feminine gender script. Nonetheless, the "two-spirit" identity claimed by lesbian, gay, bisexual, and transgender Native American activists during the 1990s articulates an alternative gender and sexual identity that offers a far greater number of possibilities than those prescribed by a heterosexual/homosexual binary. Walter Williams concludes that this category reflects the "emphasis of Native Americans ... not to force every person into one box, but to allow for the reality of diversity in gender and sexual identities."[40]

Indeed, the current focus of scholarship on the fluidity of sexual and gender identities and subjectivities is in part a response to the more static hetero-sexual/homosexual binary employed in historical studies of sexuality since the 1970s. The contention by Michel Foucault and others that "homosexuality" and "heterosexuality" are historically specific cultural productions challenged the "naturalness" of these categories of identity and provided a model for such inter-ventions. However, this model has been, as literary critic Eve Sedgwick suggests, "indicatively male."[41] Foucault's very description of the process through which this binary was created clarifies the elision of gender and women from his model: "Homosexuality appeared as one of the forms of sexuality when it was transposed from the practice of sodomy onto a kind of interior androgyny. . . . The sodomite had been a temporary aberration, the homosexual was now a species."[42]

This erasure of gendered understandings of female sexualities in Foucault's formulation has contributed to the creation of generalizations describing shifts in sexual norms or contemporaneous understandings of sexuality based on stud-ies of gay men or male homosexuality under which lesbians do not always fit. Authors framed their initial generalizations with caveats indicating why they did not address women or lesbians in their studies. These caveats, however, are not always referenced in subsequent works that simply repeated the argument as accepted wisdom or scholarly consensus. Thus, sodomy laws, the juridical system that Foucault argues was replaced by a disciplinary regime defining the "species" of "homosexuals," were rarely employed to prosecute female sexual transgres-sors. Instead, local regulations addressing "cross-dressing," "disorderly conduct," "indecent attire," and "lewd vagrancy" were more often brought to bear against "gender-deviant women," especially of the working and lower classes throughout the twentieth century.[43] Marc Stein argues that the consistent claim that lesbians have been less policed than gay men, a claim that flows from a framework focused on the punishment and disciplining of sexuality, is problematic. If polic-ing is "narrowly defined (in terms of sodomy arrests)" this statement might be accurate. However, Stein also notes that if lesbians have "restricted their public activities because the police have not protected them from rapes, and other forms of sexual violence," then lesbians have been policed in the "broadest sense." Other forms of such policing, according to Stein, include "rendering les-bianism invisible in the public sphere, . . . conceptualizing lesbians as less sexual than gay men, . . . economic discrimination against women to the extent that it encourages dependence on men," as well as dismissing greater numbers of les-bians from the military.[44]

In a second example, the oft-repeated generalization that by the mid-twentieth century sexual inversion, and the gender inversion that defined it, gave way to sexual object choice as the key criterion for identifying "homosexuals" is far less adequate a model for understanding lesbian history than that of the gay men on whom the argument is based.[45] Several scholars have argued that gender inversion remained a powerful cultural marker of female homosexuality in the United States throughout the twentieth century. As Susan Cahn and I have demonstrated, the consistent popular perception that U.S. women in sports or the military during the twentieth century were likely to be or become lesbians hinged on these women's challenge to dominant gender hierarchies. By entering the preeminently masculine arenas of sport and military service, women found that they had to engage with popular presumptions that such activity indicated their potential sexual deviance, especially "mannishness." The institutional answer to such presumptions was to present both female athletes and soldiers as "feminine" and avowedly heterosexual. While institutional responses were meant to decrease lesbian visibility, such reactions also made the association between lesbians and gender inversion more culturally salient. Therefore, efforts to repress sexual deviance resulted in heightened public consciousness of particular sexual identities and the community spaces that supported them. Individual servicewomen and female athletes positioned themselves within these discussions by defining themselves or "others" as lesbians. Thus, while many women who were heterosexual found themselves accused of sexual deviance because of military service or sports activity, others flocked to these all-female cultural spaces precisely in order to find others "like themselves," allowing for a common identification among lesbians.[46]

How can we think about lesbians historically, given that they were rarely identified as sexual criminals or left evidence of explicit sexual activity? Martha Vicinus suggests that our current models for understanding same-sex female sexuality historically in the United States "privilege either the visibly marked mannish woman or the self-identified lesbian" and that romantic friendships, once the leading example of a lesbian past, are now either reconfigured in terms to fit these categories or labeled asexual."[47] The model of "romantic friendship" was used to describe and explore intimate relationships between predominantly white middle- and upper-class women from the seventeenth through the twentieth centuries, characterized by declarations of love for one another expressed in poetry and passionate letters replete with references to kissing, cuddling, and sharing a bed. The overall acceptability of these relationships through the late nineteenth century resided in their ostensibly non-sexual nature.[48]

The investigation of archival materials like diaries and letters that suggested "romantic friendships" marked an attempt by historians to address the possibility of same-sex female desire, relations, and practices without the availability of evidence that spoke explicitly to same-sex female sexual subjectivities. The broad question of how we talk about sexual identity cross-culturally or during periods in which the meanings of such behaviors were dramatically different than they are in the early twenty-first century has been central to these early inquiries as well as current work on normative and deviant sexualities. Martha Vicinus argues that lesbian history "has been characterized by a 'not-knowing' that could be its defining core." The related emphasis on "knowing for sure," Vicinus holds, "has inhibited all too many of us from undertaking the painstaking excavational work necessary to understand the variety of women's sexual subjectivities and the ways in which different societies have permitted, forbidden, and interpreted these experiences."[49]

The "variety of women's sexual subjectivities" to which Vicinus refers must include the histories of reproduction, pregnancy, and childbirth. Laura Briggs asks why studies of reproduction are generally not considered part of the field of sexuality studies and why these fields seem not to speak to one another.[50] Histories of reproduction, reproductive struggles for access to information, contraception, and abortion, histories of pregnancy and childbirth, and motherhood have been increasingly marginalized within or considered separate from the broader field of the history of sexuality. Earlier studies that focused on or addressed reproduction were generally defined as belonging to the fields of family and/or women's history.[51] Studies of sexuality in families or within the field of women's history, both of which concentrated more on women, were joined by a focus on lesbian/gay studies/history by the late 1970s, whose center of attention, despite the inclusive title, has been far more fully on male sexuality. Thus, when the focus moved to lesbian and gay studies and, by the 1990s, "queer studies" as defining the history of sexuality or sexuality studies, work on reproduction, including pregnancy, childbirth, and motherhood, was defined as part of women's history or family history but not necessarily the history of sexuality.

The confusion over where histories of reproduction fit is exacerbated by much of the overview literature on the history of sexuality, which states as a fact that the field has been characterized by far greater coverage of women than men. In introducing *Intimate Matters: A History of Sexuality in America,* John D'Emilio and Estelle Freedman note that "the history of masculinity has greatly enriched the literature on sexuality, which had traditionally explored women more often than men."[52] Kathy Peiss in her undergraduate course reader, *Major Problems in the History of American Sexuality,* concurs, stating that "at the present time, more historians focus on women than men."[53] The only way in which these statements are credible is if, in fact, the definition of the history of sexuality as a field includes histories of reproduction.

The relationship between female sexuality (including both practices and norms) and women's access to knowledge about and their ability to control their reproduction has been central to histories of reproduction. Linda Gordon documents the major shifts and contestations over the meanings of reproduction and reproductive control in specific historical periods. She argues that during these periods there were both "hegemonic" and "resistant" meanings embedded in women's struggle for reproductive control; these meanings were/are "socially and politically, not individually constituted" and speak to the "(unstable) balances of political power between different social groups."[54]

Jesse Rodrique analyzes those "unstable balances of political power." She contends that histories that downplay the role of contraception among African Americans or assert that African Americans had "no interest in the control of their own fertility" are simply wrong. Contraception and birth control were "integrated into other health care provisions" within African American communities, rather than treated as a "separate problem." Demonstrating that African Americans operated independently of white "authorities" and were active participants in both birth control debates and the creation of local clinics, Rodrique interrupts a number of dominant presumptions.[55] Most significantly, she suggested that African Americans merged their own traditions of fertility control with knowledge they appropriated from white authorities and "experts." In doing so, they increasingly linked the meanings of birth control to "race consciousness," seeing birth control as "one means of freeing themselves from the oppression and exploitation of white society." Thus, she shows that the period most scholars characterize as marking the "waning" of the birth control movement during the 1920s and 1930s was actually marked by a "growing ferment and support for birth control within African American communities."[56]

Rickie Solinger and Laura Briggs further revise presumptions about the history of reproduction and reproductive control in the twentieth century, highlighting the importance of the study of reproduction as a site through which hierarchies of race are mediated and contested. Solinger, writing on cultural definitions of single pregnancy, explicates the shifting meanings of female sexuality during the 1940s and 1950s. Languages of "blame" and "shame" embodied competing and mutually constitutive constructions of African American and white middle-class single pregnancy. White authorities blamed African American single women for their pregnancies, associating their conditions with racialized constructions of female sexuality, and located African American women as "most deviant." They shamed pregnant white single women (largely middle-class), but granted the possibility of redemption through psychotherapy. Solinger's white, middle-class "girls" can reclaim the protected and privileged status of "respectable womanhood" denied to African American women.[57] Laura Briggs argues that discourses of reproduction, among other sexual discourses focused on women, became "the battleground — symbolic and real — for the meaning of U.S. presence in Puerto Rico."[58] In perhaps her most controversial contention, Briggs revises the mainland American feminist critique of sterilization as an example of U.S. repression of Puerto Rican women. She instead argues that Puerto Rican women understood sterilization as an option, for some a favored one through which to control their fertility. Briggs highlights the agency of Puerto Rican women in making decisions about reproductive control and characterizes as "colonialist" the actions of some American mainland feminists to construct Puerto Rican women as "victims."[59]

Given that white middle- and upper-class, native-born women (with few exceptions) produced the evidence of female sexual subjectivities that has been preserved, the "painstaking excavational work" argued for by Martha Vicinus takes on increased urgency for scholars focused on the sexualities of women of color. This work is framed not only by narrative and theoretical models that often elide gender and women and models for studying female sexuality that have elided race and the experiences of women of color, but also by the contested position of these scholars and their subjects within communities of color. As Chicana historian Ana Castillo has noted, "Sexuality remains a difficult subject for discussion, even among progressive, formally educated women. For many politically minded self-defined Chicanas, it is not seen as a priority issue demanding a direct address in light of our ethnic and gender conflicts with society. This kind of rationale is a reflection of the hierarchical fragmentation of the self in society. All of our conflicts with dominant society, all of the backlashes we receive when attempting to seek some kind of justice from society are ultimately traceable to the repression of our sexuality and our spiritual energies as human beings."[60]

In her memorial tribute to literary scholar Gloria Anzaldúa, Chicana historian Yolanda Leyva speaks to Anzaldúa's "battle" to be taken seriously as both a scholar of Chicana lesbians and a Chicana lesbian. During the 1970s Anzaldúa was "unable to continue her graduate education because her fields of interest were considered unacceptable. . . . [S]cholars such as Anzaldúa often had difficulty getting their work accepted by universities that did not believe that studying Mexican Americans or feminism was valid. As someone who tried to combine both, Anzaldúa often faced such criticism."[61] Leyva has also addressed the disparaging treatment she and other scholars of Chicana lesbians have received from some Chicana/os at activist and professional conferences. She writes of one such incident, "My memories of this great event in Movimiento history are collapsed into that one humiliating and painful moment when my own people dismissed the treatment of gay and lesbian Mexican immigrants with laughter and scorn."[62] "The issue of being a lesbian," literary scholar Carla Trujillo remarks, "is still uncomfortable for many heterosexual Chicanas and Chicanos, even (and especially) those in academic circles. Our culture seeks to diminish us by placing us in a context of Anglo construction, a supposed *vendida* to the race."[63] As historians Vicki L. Ruiz and Emma Pérez have documented, however, the multiple narratives of erasure framing the work of those studying the sexualities of Chicanas have not succeeded in silencing these scholars.[64]

The compound barriers to excavating the sexualities of women of color make clear that while exploring and analyzing the linkages between gender and sexuality are critical, concomitant attention to relations between sexuality and race/ethnicity is equally imperative. Literary critic Siobhan Somerville posits that the " 'crisis of homo/heterosexual definition,' which emerged in the United States in the late nineteenth century, had to do with concurrent conflicts over racial definition and the presumed boundary between 'black' and 'white.' "[65] The "formation of notions of heterosexuality and homosexuality" was simultaneous with the rigidification of distinctions between black and white bodies.

Somerville asserts this was not "coincidence" but rather indicative of the ways in which the production of sexual discourses was "saturated with assumptions about the racialization of bodies."[66] In her analysis, Somerville reads this "saturation" through a number of late nineteenth- and early twentieth-century texts and the dominant discourses they produced — legal, sexological, filmic, and literary popular cultural. Somerville's elegant study cautions against oversimplifying linkages between race and sexuality through the language of analogy. At this particular historical moment, when some activists and historians are pointing to the 1967 Supreme Court decision in *Loving v. Virginia,* which struck down state statutes banning interracial marriage, as one of the key legal precedents supporting "gay marriage," Somerville makes clear that "analogy obscures those who inhabit both identifications." "Rather than suggesting race, gender, and sexual orientation are somehow 'natural' analogies," she defines her study as focused on the "intersections among" and potential mutual constitutiveness of "these categories of identity at a particular cultural moment."[67]

While Somerville challenges approaches to race and sexuality that define these categories as "metaphoric substitutes," she also re-inscribes a black/white racial binary as the dominant discourse for understanding race in the United States. Chicano/a historians have offered a number of challenges to this black/white binary, and Emma Pérez speaks specifically to Somerville in doing so. In revising Somerville's innovations, Pérez posits that it is *also* "not historical coincidence that the classification of homosexual and heterosexual appeared at the same time that the United States began aggressively policing borders between the United States and Mexico." Somerville invokes the 1896 U.S. Supreme Court decision in *Plessy v. Ferguson* and the separate-but-equal doctrine that emerged from this decision as legalizing segregation and critical in the creation of rigid and legally sanctioned boundaries between black and white bodies. Pérez suggests that this decision also "sanctioned the segregation of brown from white" in the Southwest. Pérez asks, "How did the emergent and rigid policing of the border between the United States and Mexico in the early twentieth century reinforce a white colonial heteronormative way of seeing and knowing that fused race with sex?"[68]

Sexual Identities and Subjectivities:
The Interpellation of Queer Theory

Feminist film theorist and cultural critic Teresa de Lauretis defined queer theory in 1991 as "convey[ing] a double emphasis — on the conceptual and speculative work involved in discourse production, and on the necessary and critical work of deconstructing our own discourses and their constructed silences."[69] In her deconstruction of Somerville's approach and its constructed silences, Pérez's response can be seen as fulfilling the promise of some of these initial articulations of queer theory. Since the early 1990s the emphasis of scholars of sexuality on deconstructing the heterosexual/homosexual binary and interrogating the stability of identity categories flowing from this regime has been critical to modes of inquiry identified or self-defined as "queer." As historian William Turner explains, "The basic approach, central to queer theory, is the investigation of foundational, seemingly indisputable concepts."[70] Queer theory shifts the focus away from finding homosexuality in history and concentrates instead on analyzing the construction of the normal and, in the process, "map[ping] the deviant."[71] As central, queer theory posits the instability of identity categories and offers a correlative critique of identity politics as a viable framework for resistance to the dominant intellectual, cultural, and political modes of thought and practice. It is on this point that some historians have had the most difficulty accepting queer (and other postmodern) theoretical approaches because they seem to ignore the experiences of historical subjects. Actually, queer histories do not so much ignore experiences but rather see people's identities as "historically produced" and "experience" as "always already narrativized."[72] In other words, in queer histories the experiences of historical subjects must be understood as themselves narratives and products of contestation; thus, historical subjectivities are fluid, not static — streaming videographies that were constantly being interrupted and revised, not snapshots of moments.

In her work on the turn-of-the-century murder of Freda Ward by her lover Alice Mitchell, Lisa Duggan employs queer theory as a tool through which to comment on the emergence of the "modern desiring subject."[73] She uses mass-circulation newspapers and the trial transcript as texts through which to analyze depictions of the murder as well as the constructions of the female perpetrator, her victim, their families, and friends. The coverage of the murder and trial emerging from these sources "fashion[ed] stories out of living women's relationships" which "sexologists then reappropriate[d] . . . as 'cases' and women themselves reworked . . . as 'identities'" in an "extended battle over the meaning of women's erotic partnerships at the turn of the century. Out of this battle the first publicly visible forms of modern lesbianism were born."[74] The "modern lesbian identity" Duggan analyzes was not simply a product of "self-definition." Rather identity, Duggan suggests, is better understood as a "narrative of a subject's location within social structure." She characterizes the process of identity construction as a process of "contested narration. Contrasting stories are told, appropriated, and retold — as stories of the self, and others — stories of difference — as stories of location in the social world of structural inequalities."[75] In this sense the competing stories told about and by her produced Alice Mitchell's "identity" as a "lesbian," including medical scripts that labeled her as deviant, sexually and psychologically; legal and civic scripts that named her predatory and criminal; and popular scripts that called her "unnatural" for "rejection of the feminine body . . . for herself." Along with Mitchell's "self-presentations," which, Duggan argues, "took her outside the boundaries of the female world (for her, feminine dress and gestures were unnatural)," these scripts, both competing with and accommodating to one another, created "new narratives of lesbian identity" in the early twentieth century. In this process of identity formation, identity is never static but always in flux and in the process of construction and becomes, in the end, the "story or narrative structure that gives meaning to experience."[76]

Turner suggests that it is not possible to understand queer theory without understanding how it was created and by whom. He explains that "Lauretis came to queer theory via questions about the ability of women to speak about and otherwise represent themselves using a language and conceptual framework that men had created in a social and political order that took little account of women, except as commodities for exchange."[77] Lauretis, for instance, speaking implicitly to the process of naming and the construction of identities linked to such names, notes that through the 1980s "North American lesbians . . . rejected . . . terms" like "homosexuality" for themselves not only because of the "stigma still carried by the word homosexual, which many identify as a 'medical' term" but also "precisely because of its close association with male homosexuality and its elision of both sexual specificity and relevant questions of gender."[78] In terms of queer theory and those who employ it in their studies, she further cautioned that they must recognize and address the "continuing failure of representation, an enduring silence on the specificity of lesbianism in the contemporary 'gay and lesbian' discourse."[79] Lauretis's caution is echoed by American Indian activist Beverly Little Thunder, who argued that while the "two-spirit" identity is meant to include both men and women, it remains urgent to "continue to talk specifically about female two-spirits because they have been so invisible in the scholarly literature."[80]

The possibilities of queer theory, then, lie, in its beginning as oppositional to the "predominant modes of intellectual and political culture during the late twentieth century."[81] Turner describes the "motivations" of Lauretis and Judith Butler in their development of queer theoretical approaches as "the concern to maintain the specificity of lesbian experience against the tendency for lesbian lives, voices, and stories to disappear by subsumption into the categories 'woman' and 'gay or homosexual' or even 'gay and lesbian.'"[82] While queer theory began as oppositional, Turner also posits that currently "queer theorists have not arrived at a scheme for what should replace these existing modes. Instead, they seem to agree that the present project should consist primarily of elaborating the problems with existing intellectual and political modes."[83] This reluctance to name, or to narrativize, has resulted, paradoxically, in a tendency to subsume lesbians under the rubric of "queer" without specifying their distinct social location.

Community Studies as Generalization and Fragmentation

The community study has been an especially vibrant and paradoxical method for approaching the history of sexuality. The deep context and historical specificity of many such studies both elucidate and revise dominant understandings of the history of sexuality. Thus, community studies often operate as fragmenting/ fragmentize narratives that interrupt generalizations. The very language of "community," however, also suggests the creation of new generalizations and exclusions.

Among the most dominant generalizations to which recent community studies speak is the presumption that shifts in sexual systems, behaviors, and norms moved from the metropolis to the hinterland. In his study of the gay male world that developed in New York City during the early twentieth century, for instance, George Chauncey insists that, while neither "typical" nor "representative," "nonetheless, New York may well have been *prototypical*, for the urban conditions and cultural changes that allowed the gay world to take shape there, as well as the strategies used to construct that world, were almost surely duplicated elsewhere."[84] John Howard explicitly contests such a presumption in his study of same-sex male sexualities in Mississippi through the twentieth century. Howard shows us that queer sexuality in rural Mississippi did not "come from" these "urban archetypes" but was regionally specific and rooted in local community folkways and institutions.[85] Historian Sharon Ullman's study of turn-of-the-century Sacramento argues similarly that sexual shifts occurring in the early twentieth century did not trickle down from large urban centers. Instead, residents of Sacramento and other smaller communities negotiated their own understanding of sexual transformations that mirrored but did not "copy" developments in urban America.[86]

Community studies have been a method through which some scholars have also illuminated and emphasized the importance of queer daily life, as opposed to a more self-conscious public activism, as critical in the creation of queer culture. Nan Alamilla Boyd calls into question the presumptions that lesbians were not as central to the development of queer public spaces and queer communities as gay men through highlighting the centrality of women in the drag performances of San Francisco that became a language through which to establish a queer presence.[87] In his investigation of the daily lives, neighborhoods, and political activisms of lesbians and gay men in Philadelphia in the post–World War II period, Marc Stein argues that "lesbians and gay men have used same-sex sexualities to set up, invert, multiply, and modify cross-sex relationships." Drawing on Carroll Smith-Rosenberg's work on female romantic friendships, Stein contends that "homosocial culture" is political in its own right and that "everyday relationships among gay men and lesbians are *intrinsically political* (my emphasis) and therefore every bit as political as more formal movements."[88] One reviewer characterizes Stein's work as "mov[ing] the field of gay male and lesbian history into the twenty-first century field of queer history by stressing the redundancy of fixed gender definitions and the malleability and changeability of the object of sexual desire over the life course."[89]

Yet community, defined primarily as based on sexuality, is itself a naming that oversimplifies queer life in America. Nayan Shah's study of Asian immigrants in the early twentieth-century northwest holds that when anti-Asian immigrant sentiment was at its height, arrests of Chinese and Indian men on sodomy charges paradoxically reified the deviance of Asian men, while simultaneously challenging the clear trajectory of white manhood. Shah demonstrates that the "Asian male predator"/"white boy victim" juridical paradigm that developed in northern California and British Columbia in the early twentieth century relied on statutory rape case law focusing on "age of consent" and required the construction of white "boys" (whether ten or twenty-eight years old) as morally innocent and lacking will — therefore unable to consent — and, most importantly, lacking knowledge of the alleged crime. This "lack of knowledge," Shah contends, translated into/as silence for white boys, a silence that enabled their protection and redemption. Thus, while the "path" to manhood was "interrupted" for these white boy "victims," it was not forfeited, while Chinese and Indian men were denied access to the citizenship rights presumed to inhere in white "manhood" status. Shah also suggests, however, that concomitant with rigidly articulated racial boundaries were to be found myriad instances of interracial homosocial and potentially queer relations.[90] Similarly, Horacio Roque Ramírez locates one of the major problems with queer community histories in their failure to analyze the "intersectional complexity of lesbian and gay movements of color." Ramírez urges scholars of queer communities and activism to go beyond the question of how gays and lesbians of color "fit into" or "related" to the "gay movement" (implicitly white) and move to ask and research the equally significant question of how these historical actors operated within their own "racial ethnic communities."[91] In exploring the interactions between and among gay and lesbian Latina/os in the Bay area during the late twentieth century, Ramírez notes that in their daily lives as well as their activism they were "less interested in 'transcending' differences than in incorporating the multiple dimensions of their social experience. They sought to address race, sexuality, class, and gender simultaneously and were often quite conscious of the interplay among them."[92]

Several scholars recently have interrupted the presumption that community is or *should* be the goal for sexual minorities and the implicitly celebratory stance of many studies of sexual communities. Most notably, historian Karen Krahulik in her study of Provincetown, Massachusetts, investigates the interactions between white Yankee residents and Portuguese immigrants and between Portuguese residents and lesbian, gay, and transgender tourists and neighbors through the twentieth century. Exclusion as much as inclusion defined the process of community building. For lesbians, gay men, and transgender people, the act or acts of queering always initially required appropriation, here of beaches, clubs, restaurants, and other entertainment venues located in Provincetown. The claim to such physical spaces concomitantly involved dismantling and reconfiguring the conventional meanings associated with them. The initial forays of effeminate white gay men to Provincetown in the 1950s, for instance, called into question residents' understandings of manhood, and the later presence of white lesbian entrepreneurs in the 1970s fractured presumptions of masculine prerogatives. Simultaneously, however, some white gay men's choices to appear in blackface during local parades in the 1990s maintained and reinvigorated, not displaced, normative racial hierarchies. Krahulik suggests the need to move beyond a simple celebration of the creation of queer community and look to the consequences of such creation. In other words, the creation of a queer community — like the creation of any other community — is always also about constructing boundaries, boundaries that operate *within* communities as well as *between* emergent and existing communities.[93]

Using the term "queer network" instead of "queer community," John Howard criticizes the privileging of "community and subculture" in other queer histories, which he contends makes the history of the "group" an "analogue for the individual."[94] Instead, he focuses on "desire" as an organizing category for explaining and interrogating the many varieties of sexual activities "worked out between two men." "Queerness" was routed through "heteronormative locations," and "silence" became the model for creating such networks.[95] "Gay communities existed alongside and within broader queer networks; self-identified gay men shared spaces with presumably large numbers of non-gay-identified queers," he argues.[96] Howard also challenges the presumption that "queer life necessarily improved" through the 1960s and '70s, since "to the extent that the civil rights movement, in reality and perception, was linked to queer sexualities, massive resistance to the former was accompanied by massive repression of the latter." And in one of his most controversial contentions, Howard suggests that what has been understood as the ever-increasing empowerment of gay men and lesbians through the 1970s actually "foreclosed the quiet accommodation of differences characteristic of the 1940s and 1950s."[97]

Conclusion

The overlapping generalizations and fragmentations that characterize histories of sexualities drawn through community studies suggest the need for more complicated understandings of the enactment of the multifaceted sexual networks and subjectivities that have emerged in specific locations and among particular groups historically. Our scholarship must move beyond comfortable generalizations and return to the historical and geographic specificity of sites within and through which sexual desires emerged and were enacted. Paradoxically, however, our desire not to overgeneralize, to name and narrativize, risks subsuming all non-normative sexual histories and practices into a queer framework.

In a recent seminar on the history of sexuality in the United States, my graduate students developed a mantra in response to virtually all of their readings: Why don't these scholars "do it all?" Getting their degrees at a moment when it is becoming less and less accepted (though ultimately still widely sanctioned) to offer studies that do not at least marginally address race/ethnicity, gender, class, and, I would hope, sexuality in relation to the topic being explored, some are struggling to find a map, model, road sign, or other signifier that might lead them (us) to *the* way to approach history — a route that might fragment, but does not preclude generalization, that might generalize, but does not marginalize or exclude, a route that might theorize, but does not preclude narratives. The "promised land" they (we) seek is always already in motion — not an ends but a means, whose very instability is its greatest strength. And how do we find this route? Is it to be found in joining the beauty of accessibly written theory and the explanatory power of a complicated and accessibly written narrative? Is it to be found in the fragmenting interventions, in studies of the local? In concluding this chapter I would like to offer several possibilities and cautions concerning future routes and subjects of inquiry.

In discussing the reasons why early twentieth-century New York City's vibrant "gay world" seemed to "disappear" from "historical memory," George Chauncey notes, "Until recently nobody looked for it."[98] The necessity of excavating such worlds and the historically specific sexual subjectivities, systems, meanings, discourses, and realities that reside there remain. Archivist and historian Horacio Roque Ramírez highlights several possible approaches to such excavational work. First, the creation of community archives that serve as repositories for collections "chronicling, preserving, and making accessible materials that reflect(ed) the actions, dreams, and lives" of communities, and also whose materials are made available and visible to residents of and visitors to the larger community in which they are housed.[99] Such work should entail making "copies and duplicates of some materials available to various grassroots archives" that might exist within the broader community.[100] Second, Ramírez speaks to the importance of community oral history projects that document the memories of individuals, their lives, and the multiple communities to which they belong. As both historian and archivist Ramírez seeks to make visible and retain what he calls "fragments" of the queer Latina/o community in San Francisco, a community he characterizes as "multi-gender, multi-racial" and facing "multiple disappearances." He notes, "Because memory is about history and history is about survival — mine, my family's, my community's, my peoples' — I know I will never stray too far from oral history as a method and as a practice."[101]

Historian Emma Pérez suggests the need for different ways of seeing and interrogating sources as another possible route for historical inquiries into sexuality. Speaking specifically to and about the lack of attention to the American Southwest and to sexuality on/in the "borderlands," Pérez argues for the importance of "decoloniz[ing] our history and our historical imaginations" as a mode through which we might find evidence to document and uncover multiple sexualities and systems in the Southwest. She suggests we might do so by exposing the "colonial imaginary" that frames regimes of knowing and naming, a colonial imaginary that posits a "normative language, race, culture, gender, class, and sexuality" and through which our perceptions, questions, and historical projects are filtered. "When conceptualized in certain ways, the naming of things already leaves something out, leaves something unsaid, leaves silences and gaps that must be uncovered. . . . To decolonize our history and our historical imaginations, we must uncover the voices from the past that honor multiple experiences, instead of falling prey to that which is easy — allowing the white colonial heteronormative gaze to reconstruct and interpret our past."[102]

In addition to those of Ramírez and Pérez, there have been a number of other potential routes and approaches for historical inquiries into sexualities discussed throughout this chapter. In the end we must each find our own way in this field that is incredibly energizing and deeply frustrating. And we should keep close to hand Teresa de Lauretis's caution to continue to engage in the "critical work of deconstructing our own discourses and their constructed silences."[103]

NOTES

I would like to thank several folks for their help in my work on this piece: my colleague Cindy Hahamovitch for her close reading of a draft of this chapter, my graduate students whose questions helped inform the focus of this essay, and my partner, Maureen Fitzgerald, for her willingness to read and comment on multiple drafts and her constant and unwavering support.

1. For one example of this perspective see Estelle Freedman, "History of the Family and the History of Sexuality," in *The New American History*, rev. and expanded ed., ed. Eric Foner (Philadelphia: Temple University Press, 1997), 285–286.

2. Kathy Peiss, ed. *Major Problems in the History of American Sexuality* (New York: Houghton Mifflin Company, 2002), xv.

3. David Halperin, "Is There a History of Sexuality?" *History and Theory* 28, no. 3 (October 1998): 257.

4. Stephen Garton, *Histories of Sexuality — Antiquity to Sexual Revolution* (New York: Routledge, 2004), 10–11.

5. Michel Foucault, *The History of Sexuality,* vol. 1: *An Introduction*, trans. Robert Hurley (New York: Vintage Books, 1978), 1–13, especially 12–13.

6. Christina Simmons, "Modern Sexuality and the Myth of Victorian Repression," in *Passion and Power: Sexuality in History,* ed. Kathy Peiss and Christina Simmons with Robert A. Padgug (Philadelphia: Temple University Press, 1989), 157.

7. Ibid., 171–172.

8. Paula Giddings, "The Last Taboo," in *Race-ing Justice, En-gendering Power: Essays on Anita Hill, Clarence Thomas, and the Construction of Social Reality,* ed. Toni Morrison (New York: Pantheon Books, 1992), 441–463; Patricia Schechter, *Ida B. Wells-Barnett and American Reform, 1880–1930* (Chapel Hill: University of North Carolina Press, 2001).

9. Evelyn Brooks Higginbotham, *Righteous Discontent: The Women's Movement in the Black Baptist Church, 1880–1920* (Cambridge, Mass.: Harvard University Press, 1993), 187.

10. Ibid., 191–192.

11. Paisley Harris, "Gatekeeping and Remaking: The Politics of Respectability in African American Women's History and Black Feminism," *Journal of Women's History* 15, no. 1 (spring 2003): 213.

12. Mattie Udora Richardson, "No More Secrets, No More Lies: African American History and Compulsory Heterosexuality," *Journal of Women's History* 15, no. 3 (autumn 2003): 63–64.

13. Deena González, "Masquerades: Viewing the New Chicana Lesbian Anthologies," *Out/Look: National Lesbian and Gay Quarterly* 4, no. 4 (winter 1992): 81–82.

14. Ibid., 82–83.

15. George Chauncey, *Gay New York: Gender, Urban Culture, and the Making of the Gay Male World, 1890–1940* (New York: Basic Books, 1994), 9.

16. Ibid., 5–6, 8.

17. See, for instance, Kathy Peiss, Review for *The Nation* 259, no. 9 (September 26, 1994): 316 (4).

18. Foucault, *The History of Sexuality*, 101.

19. Jennifer Terry, *An American Obsession: Science, Medicine, and Homosexuality in Modern Society* (Chicago: University of Chicago Press, 1999), 1.

20. Foucault, *The History of Sexuality*, 1:101.

21. Terry, *An American Obsession*, 17–18.

22. Ibid., 223.

23. Chauncey, *Gay New York*, 26–27.

24. Joanne Meyerowitz, *How Sex Changed: A History of Transsexuality in the United States* (Cambridge, Mass.: Harvard University Press, 2002), 9–10, 12–13.

25. Kathy Peiss, *Cheap Amusements: Working Women and Leisure in Turn-of-the-Century New York* (Philadelphia: Temple University Press, 1986), 7–8. Peiss specifically argues that the "lines of cultural transmission traveled in both directions" (ibid., 8).

26. Elizabeth Clement, *Love for Sale: Courting, Treating, and Prostitution in New York City, 1900–1945* (Chapel Hill: University of North Carolina Press, 2006), 3, 10.

27. Higginbotham, *Righteous Discontent*, 191–192.

28. Darlene Clark Hine, "Rape and the Inner Lives of Black Women in the Middle West: Preliminary Thoughts on the Culture of Dissemblance," *Signs* 14, no. 4 (summer 1989): 915.

29. Evelyn Brooks Higginbotham, "African-American Women's History and the Metalanguage of Race," in *"We Specialize in the Wholly Impossible": A Reader in Black Women's History*, ed. Darlene Clark Hine, Wilma King, and Linda Reed (Brooklyn, N.Y.: Carlson Publishing, 1995), 13.

30. Hazel Carby, " 'It Jus Be's Dat Way Sometime': The Sexual Politics of Black Women's Blues," in *Unequal Sisters: A Multicultural Reader in U.S. Women's History*, ed. Ellen Carol DuBois and Vicki L. Ruiz (New York: Routledge Press, 1990), 239.

31. Ann duCille, "Blues Notes on Black Sexuality: Sex and the Texts of Jessie Fauset and Nella Larsen," in *American Sexual Politics*, ed. John C. Fout and Maura Shaw Tantillo (Chicago: University of Chicago Press, 1993), 217–218.

32. Ibid., 217–218.

33. Domna Stanton, introduction to *Discourses of Sexuality: From Aristotle to AIDS*, ed. Domna Stanton (Ann Arbor: University of Michigan Press, 1992), 20. See also Hortense Spillers, "Interstices: A Small Drama of Words," in ibid., 74.

34. Emma Pérez, "Queering the Borderlands: The Challenges of Excavating the Invisible and Unheard," *Frontiers* 24, nos. 2 and 3 (June–September 2003): 125.

35. I use the word "berdache" here because it was the term used by Will Roscoe and Walter Williams in initial publications concerning this role in Indian cultures. During the

1990s this term was rejected by many Native Americans who saw it as "colonially imposed" and stigmatizing of Native peoples. See Evelyn Blackwood, "Two-Spirit Females," in *The Encyclopedia of Lesbian, Gay, Bisexual, and Transgender History in America*, vol. 3, ed. Marc Stein (New York: Scribners, 2003), 213.

36. Will Roscoe, "The Zuni Man-Woman," *Out/look: National Lesbian and Gay Quarterly* 1, no. 2 (summer 1988): 56, 65. See also Will Roscoe, *The Zuni Man-Woman* (Albuquerque: University of New Mexico Press, 1991).

37. Roscoe, "The Zuni Man-Woman," 64. For an example of the anthropological model that Roscoe challenges, see Harriet Whitehead, "The Bow and the Burden Strap: A New Look at Institutionalized Homosexuality in Native North America," in *The Lesbian and Gay Studies Reader*, ed. Henry Abelove, Michele Aina Barale, and David M. Halperin (New York: Routledge, 1993), 498–527.

38. In fact, Roscoe argues, "some of the individuals who once filled this role might today identify themselves as transsexuals, bisexuals, or transvestites — as well as homosexuals." Roscoe,"The Zuni Man-Woman," 65. According to Evelyn Blackwood, " 'Two-spirit' signifies the presence of both masculine and feminine in one person" (Blackwood, "Two-Spirit Females," 213).

39. Ramón A. Gutiérrez, "Must We Deracinate Indians to Find Gay Roots?" *Out/Look: National Lesbian and Gay Quarterly* 1, no. 4 (winter 1989): 62, 65, 66.

40. Walter Williams, "Two-Spirit Males," in *The Encyclopedia of Lesbian, Gay, Bisexual, and Transgender History in America*, ed. Stein, 215.

41. Eve Kosofsky Sedgwick, *Epistemology of the Closet* (Berkeley: University of California Press, 1990), 1.

42. Foucault, *The History of Sexuality*, 1:43. For historical studies specifically querying this binary see Jonathan Katz, *The Invention of Heterosexuality* (New York: Dutton, 1995); and Chauncey, *Gay New York*.

43. William N. Eskridge Jr., "Crime and Criminalization," in *The Encyclopedia of Lesbian, Gay, Bisexual, and Transgender History in America*, ed. Stein, 264. See also William N. Eskridge Jr., *Gaylaw: Challenging the Apartheid of the Closet* (Cambridge, Mass.: Harvard University Press, 1999); and Elizabeth Lapovsky Kennedy and Madeline Davis, *Boots of Leather, Slippers of Gold: The History of a Lesbian Community* (New York: Routledge, 1993).

44. Marc Stein, "Police and Policing," in *The Encyclopedia of Lesbian, Gay, Bisexual, and Transgender History in America*, ed. Stein, 392–393. See also Allan Bérubé's *Coming Out under Fire: The History of Gay Men and Women in World War II* (New York: Free Press, 1990), in which he argues that lesbians were not as scrutinized or targeted by the military as gay men during World War II (43). In her overview of twentieth-century lesbian history Lillian Faderman accepts and repeats this generalization; see *Odd Girls and Twilight Lovers: A History of Lesbian Life in Twentieth-Century America* (New York: Columbia University Press, 1991), 122–125.

45. See George N. Chauncey, "From Sexual Inversion to Homosexuality: Medicine and Changing Conceptualizations of Female Sexual Deviance," *Salmagundi* (fall–winter 1982): 114–146; and *Gay New York*, in which Chauncey simply states, "By the mid-twentieth century . . . a system categorizing people on the basis of their sexual object choice had largely replaced one categorizing them on the basis of gender style" (49). For an example of accepting and using this generalization see Siobhan Somerville, *Queering the Color Line: Race and the Invention of Homosexuality in American Culture* (Durham, N.C.: Duke University Press, 2000), 15.

46. See Susan Cahn, *Coming on Strong: Gender and Sexuality in Twentieth-Century Women's Sport* (New York: Free Press, 1994), 41; Leisa D. Meyer, *Creating G.I. Jane: Sexuality and*

Power in the Women's Army Corps during World War II (New York: Columbia University Press, 1996), 153.

47. Martha Vicinus, introduction to *Lesbian Subjects: A Feminist Studies Reader*, ed. Martha Vicinus (Bloomington: Indiana University Press, 1996), 2.

48. See Carroll Smith Rosenberg, "The Female World of Love and Ritual," in her *Disorderly Conduct: Visions of Gender in Victorian America* (New York: Alfred A. Knopf, 1985), 53–76.

49. Vicinus, introduction, 2.

50. Laura Briggs, Abstract for Workshop on Reproduction and Sexuality Studies, "Sex and the Body Politic," 13th Annual Cultural Studies Conference, 2004, Kansas State University.

51. See Linda Gordon, "U.S. Women's History," in *The New American History*, ed. Foner, 185–210. For an example of the linkages between histories of reproduction and histories of sexuality during the 1960s, see Estelle Freedman's review essay on the connections between "family history" and the "history of sexuality": Estelle Freedman, "The History of the Family and the History of Sexuality," in *The New American History: Revised and Expanded Edition*, ed. Eric Foner (Philadelphia: Temple University Press, 1997), 285–310. The "history of sexuality" is not covered as a discrete "field" in either edition of the major anthology of review essays exploring the various fields in American history, *The New American History*. In the first edition of this work (1990) the history of sexuality is addressed explicitly in only one chapter, authored by Linda Gordon and titled "U.S. Women's History." In the editor's introduction Eric Foner remarked on the "great expan[sion] of women's history as a field" and noted that women's historians have moved "into such previously ignored realms as the history of sexuality." Eric Foner, introduction to *The New American History* (1990), viii. In the second edition of this anthology, published in 1997, the history of sexuality is covered by Estelle Freedman in a joint essay that also reviews the history of the family.

52. John D'Emilio and Estelle Freedman, *Intimate Matters: A History of Sexuality in America*, 2nd ed. (Chicago: University of Chicago Press, 1997), 5.

53. Peiss, *Major Problems in the History of American Sexuality*, xvi.

54. Linda Gordon, *The Moral Property of Women: A History of Birth Control Politics in America* (Urbana and Chicago: University of Illinois Press, 1974), ix.

55. Jesse Rodrique, "The Black Community and the Birth Control Movement," in *Passion and Power*, ed. Peiss and Simmons, 138, 144.

56. Ibid., 159–160.

57. Rickie Solinger, *Wake Up Little Susie: Single Pregnancy and Race before* Roe v. Wade (New York: Routledge, 1992).

58. Laura Briggs, *Reproducing Empire: Race, Sex, and U.S. Imperialism in Puerto Rico* (Berkeley: University of California Press, 2002), 51.

59. Ibid., 159.

60. Ana Castillo, "La Macha: Toward a Beautiful Whole Self," in *Chicana Lesbians: The Girls Our Mothers Warned Us About*, ed. Carla Trujillo (Berkeley: Third Woman Press, 1991), 40.

61. Gloria Anzaldúa was one of the first scholars to address Chicana lesbians — both historically and in Chicana literature. See Gloria Anzaldúa, *Borderlands/La Frontera: The New Mestiza* (San Francisco: Spinsters Ink/Aunt Lute, 1987); Yolanda Chávez Leyva, "A Woman Who Lived Sin Fronteras," *Progressive* 68, no. 8 (August 2004): 21.

62. Yolanda Chávez Leyva, "'There Is Great Good in Returning': A Testimonio from the Borderlands," *Frontiers: A Journal of Women's Studies* 24, nos. 2–3, part 1: "Claiming" (June–September 2003): 2–3.

63. Trujillo, *Chicana Lesbians*, ix. For a discussion of this issue in relation to African American communities and scholars, see Richardson, "No More Secrets, No More Lies."

64. Vicki L. Ruiz, *From out of the Shadows: Mexican Women in Twentieth-Century America* (New York: Oxford University Press, 1998), 119–123; Emma Pérez, "Queering the Borderlands: The Challenges of Excavating the Invisible and Unheard," *Frontiers: A Journal of Women's Studies*, 24, nos. 2 and 3, part 4: "Excavating" (June–September 2003): 127–128. Yolanda Retter, "On the Side of Angels: Lesbian Activism in Los Angeles, 1970–1990" (PhD diss., University of New Mexico, 1999).

65. Somerville, *Queering the Color Line*, 3

66. Ibid., 3–4.

67. Ibid., 7–8; *Loving v. Virginia*, 1967 (388 U.S. 1).

68. Pérez, "Queering the Borderlands," 126; *Plessy v. Ferguson*, 1896 (163 U.S. 537).

69. Teresa de Lauretis, "Queer Theory: Lesbian and Gay Sexualities, an Introduction," *Differences* 5, no. 2 (summer 1991): iv.

70. William Turner, *A Genealogy of Queer Theory* (Philadelphia: Temple University Press, 2000), 3.

71. Donna Penn, "Queer: Theorizing Politics and History," *Radical History Review* 62 (spring 1995): 34.

72. For a commentary on this distinction see Laura Briggs, "In Contested Territory," *Women's Review of Books* 17, no. 6 (March 2000): 20–21.

73. Lisa Duggan, "The Trials of Alice Mitchell: Sensationalism, Sexology, and Lesbian Subjects in Turn of the Century America," in *Queer Studies: An Interdisciplinary Reader*, ed. Robert J. Corber and Stephen Valocchi (Malden, Mass.: Blackwell Publishing Ltd., 2003), 73–87.

74. Ibid., 73–87. See also Lisa Duggan, *Sapphic Slashers: Sex, Violence, and American Modernity* (Durham, N.C.: Duke University Press, 2000).

75. Duggan, "The Trials of Alice Mitchell," 73–74.

76. Ibid., 73–74, 76, 84.

77. Turner, *A Genealogy of Queer Theory*, 5.

78. Lauretis, "Queer Theory," v.

79. Ibid., vi–vii.

80. Beverly Little Thunder, quoted in Blackwood, "Two-Spirit Females," 213. See also Sue-Ellen Jacobs and Sabine Lang, eds., *Two-Spirit People: Native American Gender Identity, Sexuality, and Spirituality* (Urbana: University of Illinois Press, 1997).

81. Turner, *A Genealogy of Queer Theory*, 9–10.

82. Ibid., 5.

83. Ibid., 10.

84. Chauncey, *Gay New York*, 29.

85. John Howard, *Men like That: A Southern Queer History* (Chicago: University of Chicago Press, 1999).

86. Sharon Ullman, *Sex Seen: The Emergence of Modern Sexuality in America* (Berkeley: University of California Press, 1997), 10–11.

87. Nan Alamilla Boyd, *Wide-Open Town: A History of Queer San Francisco to 1965* (Berkeley: University of California Press, 2003).

88. Marc Stein, *City of Sisterly and Brotherly Loves: Lesbian and Gay Philadelphia, 1945–1972* (Chicago: University of Chicago Press, 2000), 2, 6.

89. Kevin White, review of Mark Stein's *City of Sisterly and Brotherly Love, Journal of Social History* 35, no. 3 (2002): 710–712.

90. Nyan Shah, "Between 'Oriental Depravity' and 'Natural Degenerates': Spatial Borderlands and the Making of Ordinary Americans," *American Quarterly* 57, no. 3 (September 2005): 703–725.

91. Horacio Roque Ramírez, "Communities of Desire: Queer Latina/Latino History and Memory, San Francisco Bay Area, 1960s–1990s" (PhD diss., University of California, Berkeley, 2001). See also Horacio Roque Ramírez, " 'That's My Place!' Negotiating Racial, Sexual, and Gender Politics in San Francisco's Gay Latino Alliance, 1975–1984," *Journal of the History of Sexuality* 12, no. 2 (April 2003): 258.

92. Ramírez, " 'That's My Place!' " 225.

93. Karen Krahulik, *Provincetown: From Pilgrim Landing to Gay Resort* (New York: NYU Press, 2005).

94. Howard, *Men like That,* 12.

95. Ibid., 32.

96. Ibid., 78.

97. Ibid., xviii.

98. Chauncey, *Gay New York*, 9–10.

99. Horacio Roque Ramírez, "Queer Community and the Evidence of Desire: The Archivo Rodrigo Reyes, A Gay and Lesbian Latino Archives," in *The Power of Language/El Poder de la Palabra: Selected Papers from the Second Reforma National Conference,* ed. Lilian Castillo (Englewood, Colo.: Libraries Unlimited, 2000), 185, 187.

100. Ibid., 191.

101. Horacio Roque Ramírez, "My Community, My History, My Practice," *Oral History Review* 29, no. 2 (summer–fall 2002): 91.

102. Perez, "Queering the Borderlands," 123.

103. Lauretis, "Queer Theory," iv.

16

Strong People and Strong Leaders

African American Women and the Modern Black Freedom Struggle

MARY ELLEN CURTIN

"It is good that the stories of black women in the civil rights movement are finally being told," remarked Stephanie Shaw when reviewing Jo Ann Robinson's memoir of the Montgomery bus boycott, a key event in the history of the civil rights movement that was initiated, organized, and largely sustained by black women.[1] Indeed, a spate of recent monographs, biographies, memoirs, and articles explore the role of African American women in the modern black freedom struggle, illuminating how their organizational skills, leadership, and spiritual energy drove the movement forward.[2] What can we learn from this literature other than that women were there too? Historians typically consider black women's activism in the civil rights, black power, and women's liberation movements discretely. The most challenging books in this area, however, urge us to rethink the interconnectedness and periodization of these movements. In assessing the significance of black women's involvement in the pursuit of equality, it is essential to go beyond the restricted chronology and geography of the classical civil rights movement to explore the earlier decades of the black freedom struggle.

Too often the African American women who participated in the movement remain "invisible, elusive, or unappreciated."[3] Historians have sometimes assumed that the lack of high-profile black female leaders in civil rights organizations such as the National Association for the Advancement of Colored People (NAACP) or the Southern Christian Leadership Council (SCLC) diminished the significance of women's participation. For example, Manning Marable argues that rigid, patriarchal hierarchies in black political organizations modeled on African American churches confined women to "lower-level organizational tasks."[4] Women's importance in fostering grassroots organizing has perhaps obscured their equally important contributions to black leadership. Civil rights activist and organizer Ella Baker famously asserted "strong people don't need strong leaders."[5] Nevertheless, African American women served as leaders as well as organizers, activists, tacticians, theoreticians, and demonstrators in the long struggle to end segregation and extend the meaning of freedom into uncharted waters of American life.

The roots of organized women's leadership among African Americans lay in the late nineteenth century, when an educated middle class of teachers, business people, and homemakers formed in the wake of emancipation and Reconstruction.[6] Glenda Gilmore, Stephanie Shaw, and Rosalyn Terborg-Penn all write about the entry of such women into the public sphere, describing their participation in Republican politics, the temperance movement, and benevolent associations.[7] Evelyn Brooks Higginbotham demonstrates how women Baptists, despite male monopoly of ministerial leadership, carved out a significant role within the black Baptist Church by organizing missionary, charitable, and educational projects. Mary Mcleod Bethune, founder of the National Council of Negro Women, college president, and presidential advisor, personified the feeling of divine calling that energized black women's commitment to racial "uplift." "Instinctively I felt that leadership was needed," Bethune told interviewer Charles S. Johnson in 1940, "someone to inspire and build a program to tell the people something else aside from this very scanty life we were called upon to live."[8]

The history of the National Association of Colored Women's Clubs (NACWC), organized in 1892, which became the principal organizational vehicle of middle-class activists, has inspired a large scholarly literature.[9] Studies of the NACW delineate the broad, multifaceted character of the black club women's movement and its local components as well as its roots in antebellum black women's organizations. During the Progressive era, as Deborah Gray White's overview illustrates, black women promoted racial uplift through interracial cooperation, improved education, care of orphans, and insistence upon respectability.[10] Their commitment to service and leadership made them natural allies in the fight against the scourge of lynching, peonage, and the convict leasing system.[11] Prominent club women honored and supported Ida B. Wells for her courageous journalism exposing the horrors of lynching and shaming of the hypocritical business elites of the South.[12] Wells's call to oppose white supremacy through boycotts, political pressure, the press, and armed self-defense surely anticipated the future path that African American protest would take. As her biographers illustrate, however, Wells's singular achievements existed alongside her difficult personal relations with wealthier club women.

Extended formal education or wealth was hardly a prerequisite for black women's activism. As Elsa Barkley Brown shows, after emancipation poor black women embraced politics even though they lacked the formal power of the ballot.[13] Tera Hunter outlines how even the poorest black female laundry workers in post-bellum Atlanta engaged in strikes and labor organizing.[14] Jacqueline Jones delineates the pivotal role of black women's labor in fields and factory for supporting black families and communities after emancipation.[15]

Historians are only beginning to explore how poor and working-class African American women merged their organizations with their aspirations. Community activism could bring women together through their shared identity as mothers. "Black activist mothering" is a term employed to describe the work of black women throughout the late nineteenth and twentieth centuries.[16] Linda Gordon has also shown the distinctive community-based nature of black women's welfare activism in this period.[17] Darlene Clark Hine in Detroit, Gretchen Lemke-Santangelo in Oakland, and Ann Meis Knupfer in Chicago all explore black women's efforts to build new communities in the aftermath of migration from the South.[18] Black women were also instrumental in the Garvey movement, building black nationalism through community-building in northern urban settings.[19] Melinda Chateauvert's study of the women's auxiliary of the Brotherhood of Sleeping Car Porters and Gerald Horne's biography of the writer and communist Shirley Graham DuBois explore their presence in the labor movement and left wing politics of the 1930s. Other historians such as Rosalyn Terborg-Penn argue that black women's labor organizations hardly needed to convert their members to radicalism as their origins rested upon long-standing traditions of community organizing and self-help.[20] Martha Biondi contends that mass protests led by left-leaning white and black radicals in New York succeeded in dismantling racist practices among some of that city's established corporations, universities, and segregated public housing and garnered significant victories for economic and political equality and for civil rights.[21]

Indeed, as most of these studies suggest, the term "civil rights" is increasingly slippery: Does it apply everywhere or nowhere? The southern context of the movement was unique in at least two respects: the high level of violent social control exercised against African Americans in order to subordinate a cheap labor force and the simultaneous creation of closely knit black communities focused on church and family. William Chafe, historian and director of the "Behind the Veil" oral history project documenting life under segregation, notes that black community institutions provided the "rallying point for movements toward social change."[22]

In retrospect, it is difficult to distinguish between a civil rights organization devoted to bringing about racial equality and a typical women's organization devoted to racial uplift. Stewart Burns regards the Women's Political Council of Montgomery, Alabama, as "the largest best organized and most assertive black civic organization in the Alabama capital." Yet its struggle to promote black voting and welfare would now designate it as a civil rights organization. The goals of black freedom were broad and included sexual respect. Danielle Maguire demonstrates that civil rights organizations protested the rape of black women as evidence of egregious racial oppression.[23] Clearly, the term "civil rights" limits the broader vision contained in the modern southern movement for black freedom.[24]

Recent books by Christina Greene and Megan Shockley redefine the contours of the civil rights movement with a focus on local women's organizations and class. Shockley's unique comparative study of black women in Detroit and Richmond between 1940 and 1954 distinguishes between middle- and working-class women's organizations, illuminating how class influenced the language of protest as well as practical demands. Women employed in industries pressed the state for equal opportunity and equal treatment; they also fought for welfare rights and better housing. Shockley acknowledges that such activism failed to dismantle segregation. She argues, nevertheless, that prior to 1954 black women's organizations provided a new language of dissent and protest, "based upon their status as citizens within the state," and set the stage for the later movement. She concludes, "If the modern civil rights movement can be defined as a time when large numbers of people directly confronted symbols of oppressions by staging sit ins and filing suit, . . . the women (of) . . . Richmond and Detroit from 1940 to 1954 played an important role in that movement."[25]

Christina Greene's study of black women's activism in Durham, North Carolina, takes an even longer view, challenging the accepted periodization of the movement. Her study spans the 1930s to 1970s, charting the trajectory of women's activism over time. She investigates racial and class tensions among women's organizations, civic groups, and civil rights groups in Durham, offering an illuminating perspective on how the freedom movement depended upon local networks to thrive and succeed. Spurred on by events during World War II, African American women's organizations blossomed in Durham. These organizations included "occupational associations, social clubs, neighborhood groups, charity organizations, and church groups." Greene shows that this explosion of black women's organizations dovetailed with the expansion of the NAACP, whose membership increased from 50,000 to 450,000 between 1940 and 1945. She maintains that African American women used their tradition of community work and networking to generate the foundation of mass community protest.[26]

Greene takes a closer look at definitions of protest and leadership. The relative paucity of black women in formal positions of leadership disguises a greater truth, according to Greene, in that black women "frequently were the majority of participants in a wide range of protest and civil rights activities in the late 1950s and 1960s."[27] Her study intriguingly suggests that black women reinvigorated white women's organizations, such as the Women's International League of Peace and Freedom and the American Association of University Women, by insisting upon equality within those organizations. Black female activists in Durham had a broad view of what comprised work necessary for freedom. Greene painstakingly shows the complex links between civil rights, welfare rights, housing rights, and integrated education. Her examples of class-based fissures among black women activists challenge "essentialized notions of racial solidarity." The black women she studied kept their eye on their ultimate aims, finding alliances with both black power advocates and white women.[28]

Green's analysis has far-reaching implications, for if female-dominated community networks were the key to the success of grassroots protest, then the demise of these groups has dire implications for any promise of a similar movement in the future. The problem, in other words, is not that lack of great male leaders to fill King's shoes, but the weakening of female-based community institutions. Lacking that fabric and local leadership, mass protest will in all likelihood fail to achieve the longevity or cohesion witnessed in the South during the 1940s, '50s, and '60s.

Histories of black women in the movement tend to gravitate toward biography, but these works often amplify the importance of community institutions rather than the individual. Although biographies can clarify why individuals chose to be involved in movement activities, they also demonstrate that for many ordinary women, such as Odette Harper Hines, a Louisiana native who housed young civil rights workers, community activism spanned a lifetime.[29] Biographer Barbara Ransby's study of Ella Baker illustrates the protean nature of black women's activism.[30] During a half century of organizing, Baker worked in many different organizations, sometimes in the background, sometimes exercising important leadership roles. Both in the NAACP and the Southern Christian Leadership Council (SCLC), Ransby argues, Baker built grassroots support for black freedom by empowering others to act. She influenced the Student Non-violent Coordinating Committee's (SNCC) unorthodox, non-hierarchical approach to political organizing and leadership.[31]

According to Ransby, Ella Baker's difficulties finding a place within SCLC's minister-centered leadership illustrate the male chauvinism embedded within the organizational structure of the civil rights movement.[32] But sexism was not the only difference between the two leaders, as Baker believed that King's charisma inhibited individuals rather than empowered them. She encouraged students to reject the control of the NAACP and the SCLC and form their own organization, the Student Non-violent Coordinating Committee (SNCC). Other black women also criticized SCLC's hierarchical, autocratic leadership style. Historian Jacqueline Rouse stresses the significance of what she calls "participatory Leadership" pioneered by Septima Clark and her schools for citizenship."[33]

Biography also enables us to see that women dubbed "civil rights" activists possessed a far broader dream. Chana Kai Lee, Fannie Lou Hamer's most recent biographer, emphasizes how a life of poverty influenced the economic dimension to Hamer's vision. "The primary political mission for Hamer was the end of racial *and* economic injustice. Indeed, as a product of the Jim Crow South, she was a race woman, but she was also a very poor woman, and she remained so throughout her life. These two conditions — racism and poverty — shaped her political aspirations "[34] Because of SNCC and the grassroots approach pioneered by Baker, this Mississippi sharecropper emerged as a national figure who spoke directly to the public via television and newspapers about the realities of segregation, poverty, and white violence. When Hamer testified on national television that she was beaten for attempting to vote, her refrain of "I question America" spoke to the nation, not just to her white male jailers. Hamer ran for public office and became an outspoken advocate of a war on poverty; she continued as one of the most inspiring voices of the movement. Her dedicated service to the poor demonstrates the entrenched, institutional nature of southern poverty as well as the lack of economic parity for blacks in the South. But black women never gave up on attaining higher ideals. Constance Curry's studies of Mississippi activists Mae Bertha Carter and Winson Hudson highlight the importance of courageous, and often lone, black women in isolated southern communities who overcame violent threats to fight for rights as large as voting and education and as quotidian as telephone service.[35]

The memoirs of women activists throw new light on familiar events, such as school integration and other protests that the public only glimpsed on television.[36] For example, standard accounts of the 1963 March on Washington focus on the controversy over John Lewis's speech or the power of Martin Luther King's "I Have a Dream" oration. The autobiography of Dorothy Height, head of the National Council of Negro Women, however, emphasizes the way male civil rights leaders ignored and belittled black women: "Nothing that women said or did broke the impasse blocking their participation. I've never seen a more immovable force. We could not get women's participation taken seriously." According to Height, black women from a range of organizations found their exclusion from the speaker's podium humiliating and troubling.[37] Some black women made their discontent known. Pauli Murray, civil rights lawyer and later one of the founders of the National Organization for Women (NOW), pointed to the black women's subordination within the civil rights hierarchy. They held subsidiary roles rather than being the partners that "their courage, intelligence and dedication" warranted. "Not a single woman was invited to make one of the major speeches or to be part of the delegation of leaders who went to the White House. The omission was deliberate." Murray's speech brought a "new awakening" among black women activists tired of being "behind the scenes."[38]

Can an overall pattern of black women's involvement in the civil rights struggle be discerned? Based on his study of local organizing in Mississippi, Charles Payne argues that among people between the ages of thirty and fifty, black women were three to four times more likely than men to support the movement. Payne concluded that black women felt empowered by religion. They either lacked fear or they possessed faith, which he believes is the key to understanding gender differences among activists. Their participation in church-related community activities accustomed black women in the Mississippi Delta to creating organizations and doing the everyday work upon which most successful organizations depend. Payne's argument that the civil rights movement was "men led, but women organized" has been highly influential.[39]

Belinda Robnett also investigates whether there was a pattern to women's participation. She examines how organizational structure encouraged or discouraged women's leadership in the civil rights movement. Robnett introduced the concept of "bridge leaders," women who had leadership positions but whose strength lay in their ties with local organizations rather than widespread recognition. Bridge leaders were not national leaders; instead, they connected local organizations to national movements and engaged in one-on-one community-based interaction. Robnett observes that "while formal leaders may also work in this manner it is neither a sufficient nor an efficient means of mass mobilization." She finds that men could also be bridge leaders, "but it was the most accessible and acceptable form of leadership available" to women.[40] A crucial difference between Robnett's "bridge leaders" and Payne's "organizers" is that bridge leaders were "critical mobilizers of civil rights activities." Nevertheless, female bridge leaders differed from primary formal leaders as well as from secondary leaders, who were also part of an inner circle of formal leadership. Bridge leaders were primarily concerned with grassroots constituencies, "while the latter were concerned with the organization's credibility, image and relationship with the state."[41]

Disputing the notion that movement participation consisted of leaders and followers, Robnett offers a more complex portrait of mobilization in which local bridge leaders "extended and transformed" the movement's message. Bridge leaders might be more radical than formal leaders, often challenging the conservatism or conventional thinking of the latter.[42] Robnett rejects the notion that "movement leaders begin movements and mobilize the masses." Instead, "leaders are often mobilized by the masses they will eventually come to lead."[43] She questions conventional views of leadership: "Leaders have been generally defined as those who hold titled positions, have power over members, make decisions on behalf of the organization and are perceived by the public and the state as the leaders." In contrast, Robnett draws on the observations of activist Victoria Gray, whose admiration for women leaders such as Ella Baker rests upon "that effectiveness, of the loyalty of those who work with and around them. It was a lot to do with a kind of loyalty and influence that you are able to elicit from the people around you."[44]

Robnett refutes Payne's belief that women's involvement can be relegated to the realm of local organizing. She argues that this term cannot capture how women's participation in grassroots activism extended into communities and sustained crucial momentum, longevity, and efficacy. "Often the purveyors of the movement's message were women."[45] In a particularly intriguing section, Robnett suggests that female emotion was critical for sustaining the movement, validating action, and spurring on courage.[46]

Robnett concedes that sexism in the movement, particularly among ministers, obstructed black women's access to formal leadership. When Diane Nash submitted a plan to shut down Montgomery in the aftermath of the Sixteenth Street church bombings, Dr. King laughed. Ministers deemed similar plans by other women as outlandish, "emotional," or undermining of their authority.[47]

She depicts King as a leader concerned with reinforcing a strong male image, who envisaged women primarily as wives and mothers. In the leadership hierarchy of an organization dominated by ministers, women could only go so far. They were "often channeled away from formal leadership positions and confined to the informal level of leadership."[48] Memoirs of women activists confirmed the sexism of the SCLC. Septima Clark, for example, who headed SCLC's Citizenship Education Project, recalled that "those men didn't have any faith in women, none whatsoever. They just thought that women were sex symbols and had no contribution to make. That's why Rev. Abernathy would say continuously, 'why is Mrs. Clark on this staff?'"[49]

Ironically, on one level, Robnett's analysis reinforces Marable's male-centered, charismatic paradigm in that it acknowledges the power of the black church to define leadership and exclude women. However, Robnett insists that black women considered themselves as leaders and resisted the sexist assumptions of male ministers. She gives credence and legitimacy to the activities of women, highlighting their achievements and detailing the sexism that prevented them from attaining more. She concludes that black women were interested in national leadership, but because of the context of the times and because of gender exclusion, they more readily became bridge leaders. She even argues that, paradoxically, the exclusion of talented black women from formal positions of church leadership turned out to be a benefit to the movement. Black women's exclusion from formal positions of power meant that highly talented people were channeled into local positions of leadership. Once there, these women strengthened and enhanced the grassroots base that gave the movement its momentum and power.

It should be emphasized that secular civil rights organizations, notably the NAACP, did not shut African American women out of formal leadership positions. Although NAACP leaders were from male-dominated or male-only occupations such as ministers, postal workers, Pullman car porters, physicians, dentists, and pharmacists, the growth of the NAACP in this period depended, in part, on the support it received from black women. Many of the Atlanta members were teachers.[50] In Durham, black women's groups often purchased bloc memberships. Indeed, some social and fraternal groups made NAACP membership mandatory. Nevertheless, men still dominated NAACP leadership positions. Historians posit a number of reasons for this. Barbara Woods's study of Modjeska Simpkins shows the NAACP purged some female leaders because of their alleged ties with communism.[51] More local and regional studies of NAACP activism would perhaps shed light on the difference a secular organization made upon the level of women's ability to be accepted by men as a leader.

A recent study of Lulu White of Houston, Texas, suggests that the 1930s and '40s may have been more accepting of women's formal leadership. Historian Merline Pitre chronicles Lulu White's journey to becoming the first black woman in the South to hold the paid position of president and executive secretary of an

NAACP chapter. White revitalized the Houston NAACP when, in 1937, she resigned as a public school teacher to work full time for the organization. The Rev. A. A. Lucas, elected branch president in 1939, recognized White's abilities and encouraged her. In 1943, a Houston chapter that previously was notorious for infighting offered Lulu White the position of executive secretary. In six years she increased the membership of Houston's NAACP from two thousand to twelve thousand members. She led the fight to elect more blacks, gain economic parity, and integrate the University of Texas. She mounted a campaign to get African Americans to pay poll taxes and worked closely with ministers to increase voter registration. It was Lulu White, Pitre argues, who energized Houston's NAACP into a mass-based organization.[52]

White's rise within the NAACP hierarchy stemmed from her alliances with unions and support for integration rather than from traditional black women's organizations. Her association with left-leaning labor lawyers Arthur J. Mandell and Herman Wright prompted Houston newspaper owner Carter Wesley, who favored the creation of a segregated black university in Houston, to label White a communist. White was no communist, but her support for Henry Wallace made her vulnerable to the charge. White's marriage to Julius White, a self-made Houston businessman, gave her economic independence from white Houstonians. Her sociability and ambition also contributed to her effectiveness as a political leader.[53] Pitre's account offers many tantalizing questions: Did the influence of inter-racial alliances or left-wing ties during the 1930s and '40s make women's leadership acceptable in a way that Dr. King could never envision in the 1950s and '60s? Was there a time when black ministers were more accepting of black women as leaders?

Historian John Kirk downplays the role that traditional community organizations, religion, and women's groups played in the political evolution of Daisy Bates, leader of an NAACP chapter in Arkansas. As a child, Bates saw the women in her neighborhood as "a lazy conniving bunch of porch sitters" who sent children on errands they should have done themselves. According to Kirk, Daisy Bates had little time for religion or the church, and she eschewed black women's groups.[54] Throughout her life, Bates had no associations with female-dominated networks such as the NCNW or the YWCA. She rejected anodyne interracialism. When asked to join the Little Rock Urban League in 1939, Bates said no, calling the executive board "just a bunch of niggers who want to sit next to white folks once every two weeks."[55] Bates despised any accommodation to segregation and viewed black women's groups that focused on uplift as too complacent.

According to Kirk, Bates's uncompromising stance stemmed from two sources: the brutal, unpunished rape and murder of her mother by three local white men and her experiences as a journalist during the Second World War. Her controversial reporting included a story of the 1942 murder of a black army sergeant in downtown Little Rock by a white police officer. This story prompted an investigation, a mass meeting of black Arkansans, and concessions that included the hiring of black police officers. Bates used the pages of the *State Press* to lash the shortcomings of complacent black middle-class leadership and deride halfway measures that failed to challenge the principle of segregation. She called for a complete end to racial discrimination.[56]

These accounts of Bates and White suggest that a rethinking of stages of women's activism is called for; instead of steady progress, there appear to be peaks and troughs. As in Houston, the NAACP in Little Rock had a long history but was dormant in the 1930s largely through the lack of direction amongst the middle-class male leadership. The lack of action frustrated female branch secretaries. In 1933, one described male professionals as egotistical talkers who accomplished little. The divisions between the militants and the conservatives in the state NAACP threatened to destroy the organization and were only resolved when Bates took charge in 1952. Supported by Arkansas NAACP members, Bates voiced very public, unpopular, and even dangerous positions on integration. Like Lulu White, Bates enjoyed financial independence from whites because of her marriage to an older, financially secure husband. Like White, Bates put herself at risk for the ideal of equality.[57]

The example of Gloria Richardson, who headed a direct action campaign in Cambridge, Maryland, between 1960 and 1962, also challenges the notion that black women were largely confined to the role of bridge leaders. The subject of three biographers, Richardson was educated at Howard University and came from a well-off, politically influential family. Until 1946, her grandfather had served on the city council of Cambridge. Token political representation, however, did not bring power to African Americans in Cambridge who suffered debilitating economic and social deprivations. Richardson's organization demanded a complete end to segregation in the community and programs to address unemployment, poor health, and inferior housing. Annette K. Brock interprets Richardson's militancy as key to her leadership style. "Seeing that voting failed to effect change, Richardson would embrace direct action instead."[58]

Richardson's group courted arrest and picketed segregated theaters and bowling alleys; they boycotted local stores that did not hire blacks. Some segregationists resisted their demands by launching arson and gun attacks. Police cordoned off the black district of Cambridge. The Governor of Maryland called in Richardson, city officials, businessmen, and NAACP representatives to discuss a compromise. When Richardson would not agree to a moratorium on demonstrations, the mayor imposed martial law. Despite confrontations with the police and the National Guard, hundreds of blacks continued the protest, forcing Robert Kennedy's Justice Department to intervene. Richardson's militancy placed her at odds with both Martin Luther King and the NAACP. Historian Sharon Harley has questioned Belinda Robnett's depiction of Richardson as a "bridge" leader who came into her leadership position by default, that is, because no one else wanted it. Like White and Bates, Richardson did not "fill a vacuum" but was requested to lead by people who respected her abilities. Her courage, willingness to stand up against moderates, and unflinching principles garnered her much support among African Americans in Cambridge.[59]

Still, sexist assumptions about women's abilities abounded in society during the 1960s, influencing all civil rights groups. The Student Non-violent Coordinating Committee was no exception.[60] However, as Belinda Robnett argues, SNCC differed from SCLC in offering more opportunities for leadership. SNCC did not begin as an explicitly feminist organization, but, according to Robnett, it succeeded in cultivating women leaders because of the non-traditional, non-hierarchical style of the organization itself. SNCC's belief in participatory democracy discouraged centralized leadership and thereby encouraged women. "Through an ideology of inclusion, cooperation and individualism, as opposed to self interest, SNCC broke down barriers to participation seeking not to indoctrinate, but to engage. Consequently, its organizational form, as created by its ideology, was able to incorporate women leaders into its leadership structure."[61]

Many historians argue that the black power movement represented a retrograde step in black women's participation in SNCC. Its leadership became more patriarchal and authoritarian, while the turnover of staff and expulsion of whites "damaged the distinctive esprit de corps that southern war zones had inculcated at SNCC." Decentralization and spontaneity had facilitated women's involvement, but such "open spaces" were closing up. Historian Clay Carson summarizes the changes in SNCC's ideology: "Instead of immersing themselves in protest activity and deriving their insights from an ongoing mass struggle, SNCC workers in 1966 stressed the need to inculcate among urban blacks a new racial consciousness as a foundation for future struggles." The rise of black nationalism, Robnett argues, led to so-called gender norms, an emphasis upon male leadership just for the sake of appearance, a priority of the movement. Power became centralized, and followers became "acolytes." Similarly, Paula Giddings suggests that the struggle in the urban North made the posturing of young black men fashionable. The rhetoric of black nationalism emphasized a new black masculinity; women were asked to "step back."[62]

Was there an inevitable conflict between black women's leadership and black power? Cynthia Fleming's biography of SNCC worker Ruby Doris Smith Robinson illuminates the personal crisis and personal confusion of black women working within an organization dedicated to black power.[63] Smith was absolutely essential to the daily running of SNCC; self-effacing and hard working, her dedication won her the admiration of both men and women alike. In 1966 she succeeded James Forman as SNCC's executive secretary. Nevertheless, Smith felt compelled to justify her leadership. At the height of black power, black women were being asked to step aside to make room for men, allegedly the main victims of white supremacy. In an interview with *Ebony* magazine, Smith admitted that black women had been effective leaders but suggested that "the crusade for racial justice was really men's work after all." In the future, she hoped, black women "would not be needed for movement work anymore, but that change would come slowly."[64]

Historians have been at pains to show that variegated experience of black women in nationalist organizations. Ula Taylor, for example, examines how women in the Nation of Islam interpreted the contradictions between their participation and subordination. For these women, any sexual discrimination they may have experienced was secondary to being accorded respect and recognition by the men in their group.[65] The testimonies of former Black Panther Party members amply illustrate the sexism of that organization. The party exhorted women to have babies for the revolution and to eat after the men had had their fill. Historians have sometimes sidestepped the issue of sexism within the civil rights movement, suggesting, for example, that King was simply a man of his time. A comparison of his views as a black minister on the place of women with those voiced by black nationalists and members of the Nation of Islam, however, would be illuminating.

Despite the male-centered rhetoric of nationalist organizations, historians have found that many black women also remember opportunities for leadership.[66] Traceye Matthews argues that the Black Panther Party (BPP) was unique in affording women opportunities for full participation on a basis of equality. According to former member Assata Shakur, "The other organizations at the time were so sexist . . . [that] joining the BPP was one of the best options at the time."[67] Although women had to fight against sexist assumptions, the Black Panthers, like SNCC, seemed to have open spaces for women to take effective action and to lead. Kathleen Cleaver was the first female to serve on the Central Committee of the Black Panther Party and spent years in exile avoiding the FBI. She and Angela Davis were outspoken revolutionaries of the period. Elaine Brown became the first and only woman to lead the Black Panther Party.[68]

Margo Perkins has analyzed the autobiographies of Angela Davis, Assata Shakur, and Elaine Brown as reflections of the era of their writing. Shakur and Davis, writing close to the period of their activism in the 1960s, wrote to promote their cause, whereas Brown's work is purposefully more reflective. Brown's autobiography in particular, she argues, offers a new narrative of black female sexuality in the period; it also shows, without judging or condemning, the contradictory nature of the Panther's relationship to power and sexuality, as the new sexual freedoms affected men and women differently. Perkins employs psychology to interpret how the Panther's organization reflected and exaggerated the hierarchical power relations of the dominant society. Perkins concluded that the rigid, and at times sado-masochistic, hierarchy of the Panthers was a destructive force for both men and women.[69]

Historians have begun to recast the relationship of black women to the story of "second wave" feminism. In 1980 Sara Evans argued that the movement for black freedom in the South birthed the modern feminist movement.[70] Many black women supported the National Organization for Women (NOW); indeed, three of NOW's founders were women of color: Aileen Hernandez, a former commissioner of the EEOC, attorney Pauli Murray, and Democratic congresswoman Shirley Chisholm. These civil rights veterans joined with upper-middle-class women who "drew an analogy between sexism and racism, . . . declaring that they wanted to form an 'NAACP for Women.'"[71]

However, others countered that racism among mainstream white feminists isolated black women from the feminist movement.[72] Toni Morrison's 1971 article, "What the Black Woman Thinks about Women's Lib," stated that race had been a greater problem than sex for black women, who did not share the same concerns as white women. Betty Friedan had urged women to get paid employment, but Morrison and others pointed out that dire economic circumstance had long compelled the majority of black women to work for low wages while simultaneously taking care of families. "We don't find these roles mutually exclusive. That's one of the differences." Morrison also wrote honestly about the personal and class antagonisms between black women and the white women who employed them to work in their homes. She saw no reason for black women to support a movement that excluded them or to align themselves with women who had hitherto oppressed them.[73] Numerous black female writers and activists of the early 1970s criticized feminism as, in the words of Ann Ida Lewis, editor of *Essence*, "a family quarrel." Michele Wallace wrote that "there was some low key directionless complaining and grumbling among black women in the sixties. But they put more energy into their fight against Women's Liberation than into anything else. Hardly a week passed during the late sixties and early seventies when there wasn't an article on how black women felt that women's liberation was irrelevant to them because they were already liberated."[74]

Some argue that the emergence of black power strangled discussion of feminism among black women. Wallace states that the black nationalist movement rendered black women invisible, excluding them from political planning. They were not allowed to go to the "hairdresser or church, to attend most clubs, or to participate in sororities, all of which had been declared counter-revolutionary."[75] Later, however, Wallace reconsidered her position, acknowledging the feminist writings of Alice Walker, and downplayed the impact of black nationalism on women's behavior.[76] Nevertheless, as Paula Giddings notes, it is difficult to reconcile black power with women's equality. In the 1960s, black feminists seemed "invisible." Historian William L. Van Deburg saw no challenge to the sexist posturing of black male militants until 1972 or 1973, with the formation of the New York–based National Black Feminist Organization.[77]

Recently, however, historians have begun to see the relationship between black women and feminism in a different light. A new consensus is emerging that black feminism, born out of the legacy of black women's organizing as well as the civil rights movement, developed organizations with a coherent, independent ideology. Benita Roth, Kimberly Springer, and Becky Thompson challenge the notion that black women rejected women's liberation.[78] They point to a far less publicized movement among black women activists occurring in the 1960s and gathering steam and momentum throughout the 1980s. In 1970 journalist Charlayne Hunter observed that "while liberation is being discussed by black women — in workshops, liberation groups and privately — it is usually in a context different from that of white women."[79] Kristin Anderson-Brinker details how black women in SNCC founded the Black Women's Liberation Committee (BWLC) in 1968, which became the home of activists Frances Beale and Toni Cade. Both she and Hunter denounced sexism in black organizations and urged black women not to forsake their public role as activists simply because of what the Moynihan report said about the alleged black "matriarchy." Toni Cade wrote that "racism and chauvinism are anti-people. And a man cannot be politically correct and a chauvinist too."[80] The BWLC also took an internationalist perspective. From this group came the Black Women's Alliance, then the Third World Woman's Alliance.[81] Far from being an offshoot of white feminism, then, these black feminists organizations emerged out of the black nationalist/civil rights struggle and specifically included the plight of third world women in their analysis.

According to Benita Roth, there was not a single feminist movement but several "feminisms" that grew out of diverse political communities. Roth argues that black feminists redefined notions of women's freedom. For example, they transformed the movement to legalize abortion into a broader and more inclusive campaign for reproductive rights.[82] In her study of the reproductive rights movement, Jennifer Nelson argues that black women rejected the argument that birth control and abortion were race genocide but also "criticized abortion rights feminists for their narrow focus."[83] Premilla Nadasen shows how black women's civil rights activism led to the welfare rights movement.[84] Black women, in Roth's view, constituted a "vanguard center" that persuaded the women's movement to be more concerned with the poor, third world women, and women of color. Still, as Kimberly Springer notes, black feminist organizations were caught between the "blind spots" of white feminists and most of black liberation. Like many other social movements, black feminism rose with the waters of the 1960s and sank slowly in the era of the Reagan backlash. Springer argues that although these groups may have developed in tandem with those dominated by white women, they originated from a distinctive set of concerns and problems.[85]

What these studies suggest is that the notion of what Jacquelyn Dowd Hall has called "the Long Civil Rights Movement" applies to the activism of black women from the time of emancipation to the emergence of modern black feminism.[86] A consensus seems to be emerging that modern black female activism and feminism was the culmination of a deeply rooted struggle among black women who had historically worked in both single-gender and gender-mixed organizations for freedom, equality, and opportunity. Black women, it is being suggested, provided a large part of the popular base for the modern civil rights movement through their church and community networks. They then took the movement's message of social justice into housing, education, employment, and the personal realms of reproductive rights and sexual equality. However, greater attention now needs to be paid to delineating the shifts in their struggles and opportunities over time. We also need further research into black women's organizations and networks and a more complicated history of black women, politics, and leadership.

NOTES

1. Jo Ann Robinson, *The Montgomery Bus Boycott and the Women Who Started It: The Memoir of Jo Ann Gibson Robinson*, ed. David J. Garrow (Knoxville: University of Tennessee Press, 1987); Stephanie Shaw, "Review of *The Montgomery Bus Boycott and the Women Who Started It*," *Journal of Southern History* 54, no. 4 (November 1988): 687–689; Douglas Brinkley, *Rosa Parks* (New York: Viking, 2000); Rosa Parks and Jim Haskins, *Rosa Parks: My Story* (New York: Dial Books, 1992).

2. Paula Giddings, *When and Where I Enter: The Impact of Black Women on Race and Sex in America* (New York: Bantam Books, 1984); Bernice McNair Barnett, "Invisible Southern Black Women Leaders in the Civil Rights Movement: The Triple Constraints of Gender, Race, and Class," *Gender and Society* 7, no. 2 (June 1993): 162–181; Belinda Robnett, "African American Women in the Civil Rights Movement, 1954–1965: Gender, Leadership, and Micromobilization," *American Journal of Sociology* 101, no. 6 (May 1996): 1661–1693; Belinda Robnett, *How Long? How Long? African American Women in the Struggle for Civil Rights* (New York: Oxford University Press, 1997); Lynn Olson, *Freedom's Daughters: The Unsung Heroines of the Civil Rights Movement from 1830–1970* (New York: Scribner, 2001, 2002). Edited collections include Vicki Crawford, Jacqueline Rouse, and Barbara Woods, eds., *Women in the Civil Rights Movement: Trailblazers and Torchbearers, 1941–1965*, vol. 16: *Black Women in United States History*, Darlene Clark Hine, ed. (Brooklyn: Carlson Publishing, 1990); Ann D. Gordon, Bettye Collier-Thomas, et al., eds., *African American Women and the Vote, 1837–1965* (Amherst: University of Massachusetts Press, 1997); Peter J. Ling and Sharon Monteith, eds., *Gender in the Civil Rights Movement* (New York: Garland Publishing, 1999); Kimberly Springer, ed., *Still Lifting, Still Climbing: African American Women's Contemporary Activism* (New York: New York University Press, 1999); Bettye Collier-Thomas and V. P. Franklin, eds., *Sisters in the Struggle: African American Women in the Civil Rights–Black Power Movement* (New York: New York University Press, 2001).

3. Christina Greene, *Our Separate Ways: Women and the Black Freedom Movement in Durham, North Carolina* (Chapel Hill: University of North Carolina Press, 2005), 5.

4. Manning Marable, *Black Leadership* (New York: Columbia University Press, 1998), xvi and xiii–xiv.

5. Quoted in Ellen Cantarow and Susan O'Mally, *Moving the Mountain: Women Working for Social Change* (Old Westbury: Feminist Press, 1980), 55.

6. Audrey Thomas McCluskey, "We Specialize in the Wholly Impossible: Black Women School Founders and Their Mission," *Signs* 22, no. 2 (winter 1997): 403–426; Jacqueline Ann Rouse, "Out of the Shadow of Tuskegee: Margaret Murray Washington, Social Activism, and Race Vindication," *Journal of Negro History* 81, no. 1–4 (winter–autumn 1996): 31–46; Ann Short Chirhart, *Torches of Light: Georgia Teachers and the Coming of the Modern South* (Athens: University of Georgia Press, 2005); Elsa Barkley-Brown,

"Womanist Consciousness: Maggie Lena Walker and the Independent Order of St. Luke," *Signs* 14, no. 3 (spring 1989): 610–633.

7. Stephanie Shaw, *What a Woman Ought to Be and to Do: Black Professional Women Workers during the Jim Crow Era* (Chicago: University of Chicago Press, 1996); Glenda Gilmore, *Gender and Jim Crow: Women and the Politics of White Supremacy in North Carolina, 1896–1920* (Chapel Hill: University of North Carolina Press, 1996); Rosalyn Terborg-Penn, *African American Women and the Struggle for the Vote, 1850–1920* (Bloomington: Indiana University Press, 1998).

8. Audrey Thomas McCluskey and Elaine M. Smith, eds., *Mary McLeod Bethune: Building a Better World* (Bloomington: Indiana University Press, 1999) 40–41; Joyce A. Hanson, *Mary McLeod Bethune and Black Women's Political Activism* (Colombia: University of Missouri Press, 2003); Evelyn Brooks Higginbotham, *Righteous Discontent: The Women's Movement in the Black Baptist Church, 1880–1920* (Cambridge, Mass.: Harvard University Press, 1993); Cheryl Gilkes, *"If It Wasn't for the Women" — Black Women's Experience and Womanist Culture in Church and Community* (Maryknoll, N.Y.: Orbis Books, 2001)

9. Stephanie Shaw, "The Creation of the National Association of Colored Women," in *We Specialize in the Wholly Impossible: A Reader in Black Women's History,* ed. Darlene Clark Hine, Wilma King, and Linda Reed (New York: Carlson Publishing, 1995), 433–447; Beverly Jones, *Quest for Equality: The Life and Writings of Mary Eliza Church Terrell, 1863–1954* (Brooklyn, N.Y.: Carlson Publishing, 1990); Gerda Lerner, "Early Community Work of Black Club Women," *Journal of Negro History* 59, no. 2 (April 1974): 158–167; Darlene Clark Hine, *When the Truth Is Told: A History of Black Women's Culture and Community in Indiana, 1875–1900* (Indianapolis: National Council of Negro Women Indianapolis Section, 1981); Sharon Harley, "Beyond the Classroom: The Organizational Lives of Black Female Educators in the District of Columbia, 1890–1930," *Journal of Negro Education* 51, no. 3 (summer 1982): 254–265; Lynda F. Dickson, "Toward a Broader Angle of Vision in Uncovering Women's History: Black Women's Clubs Revisited," *Frontiers: A Journal of Women Studies* 9, no. 2 (1987): 62–68; Anne Firor Scott, "Most Invisible of All: Black Women's Voluntary Associations," *Journal of Southern History* 56, no. 1 (February 1990): 3–22; Wanda A. Hendricks, *Gender, Race, and Politics in the Midwest: Black Club Women in Illinois* (Bloomington: Indiana University Press, 1998); Cynthia Neverdon-Morton, *Afro-American Women of the South and the Advancement of the Race, 1895–1925* (Knoxville: University of Tennessee Press, 1989); Elizabeth Hayes Turner, *Women, Culture, and Community: Religion and Reform in Galveston, 1888–1920* (New York: Oxford University Press, 1997); Janette Greenwood, *Bittersweet Legacy: The Black and White "Better Classes" in Charlotte, 1850–1910* (Chapel Hill: University of North Carolina Press, 1994).

10. Deborah Gray White, *Too Heavy a Load: Black Women in Defense of Themselves, 1894–1994* (New York: W. W. Norton, 1999), 179; Floris Barnett Cash, *African American Women and Social Action: The Clubwomen and Volunteerism from Jim Crow to the New Deal, 1896–1936* (Westport, Conn.: Greenwood Press, 2001).

11. Mary Church Terrell, *A Colored Woman in a White World* (New York and London: Prentice Hall International, 1996); and Jones, *Quest for Equality.*

12. Patricia A. Schechter, *Ida B. Wells and American Reform, 1880–1930* (Chapel Hill: University of North Carolina Press, 2001); Linda O. McMurray, *To Keep the Waters Troubled: The Life of Ida B. Wells* (New York: Oxford University Press, 1998); Jacqueline Jones Royster, ed., *Southern Horrors and Other Writings: The Anti-Lynching Campaign of Ida B. Wells, 1892–1900* (Boston: Bedford Books, 1997); Dorothy Sterling, *Black Foremothers: Three Lives,* 2nd ed. (New York: Feminist Press, 1988); Alfreda M. Duster, ed., *Crusade for Justice: The Autobiography of Ida B. Wells* (Chicago: University of Chicago Press, 1970);

Rosalyn Terborg-Penn, "African American Women's Networks in the Anti-lynching Crusade," in *Gender, Class, Race, and Reform in the Progressive Era*, ed. Noralee Frankel and Nancy Schrom Dye (Lexington: University of Kentucky Press, 1991).

13. Elsa Barkley Brown, "To Catch the Vision of Freedom: Reconstructing Southern Black Women's Political History, 1865–1880," in *Unequal Sisters: A Multicultural Reader in U.S. Women's History*, 3rd ed., ed. Ellen Carol DuBois and Vicki L. Ruiz (New York: Routledge, 2000), 124–146; Elsa Barkley Brown, "Negotiating and Transforming the Public Sphere: African American Political Life in the Transition from Slavery to Freedom," in *Jumpin' Jim Crow: Southern Politics from Civil War to Civil Rights*, ed. Jane Dailey, Glenda Gilmore, and Bryant Simon (Princeton, N.J.: Princeton University Press, 2000), 28–66.

14. Tera W. Hunter, *To 'Joy My Freedom: Southern Black Women's Lives and Labors after the Civil War* (Cambridge, Mass.: Harvard University Press, 1997).

15. Jacqueline Jones, *Labor of Love, Labor of Sorrow: Black Women, Work, and the Family from Slavery to the Present* (New York: Basic Books, 1985).

16. Katrina Bell McDonald, "Black Activist Mothering: A Historical Intersection of Race, Gender, and Class," *Gender and Society* 11, no. 6 (December 1997): 773–795; Jenny Irons, "The Shaping of Activist Recruitment and Participation: A Study of Women in the Mississippi Civil Rights Movement," *Gender and Society* 12, no. 6 (December 1998): 692–709; Nancy A. Naples, ed., *Community Activism and Feminist Politics: Organizing across Race, Class, and Gender* (New York: Routledge, 1998); Nancy A. Naples, *Grassroots Warriors: Activist Mothering Community Work and the War on Poverty* (New York: Routledge, 1998); Nancy Naples, "Activist Mothering: Cross-Generational Continuity in the Community Work of Women from Low Income Neighborhoods," *Gender and Society* 6, no. 3 (September 1992): 441–463; Eileen Boris, "The Power of Motherhood: Black and White Women Redefine the 'Political,'" in *Mothers of a New World: Maternalist Politics and the Origins of Welfare States*, ed. Seth Koven and Sonya Michel (New York: Routledge, 1993), 207–225.

17. Linda Gordon, "Black and White Visions of Welfare: Women's Welfare Activism, 1890–1945," *Journal of American History* 78, no. 2 (September 1991): 559–590.

18. Gretchen Lemke-Santangelo, *Abiding Courage: African American Migrant Women and the East Bay Community* (Chapel Hill: University of North Carolina Press, 1996); Darlene Clark Hine, "Rape and the Inner Lives of Black Women in the Middle West," *Signs* 14, no. 4 (summer 1989): 912–920; Darlene Clark Hine, *Hine Sight: Black Women and the Re-construction of American History* (Brooklyn, N.Y.: Carlson Publishers, 1994); Ann Meis Knupfer, *The Chicago Black Renaissance and Women's Activism* (Urbana: University of Illinois Press, 2006).

19. Karen S Adler, "Always Leading Our Men in Service and Sacrifice: Amy Jacques Garvey, Black Feminist Nationalist," *Gender and Society* 6, no. 3 (September 1992): 346–375; Ula Yvette Taylor, *The Veiled Garvey: The Life and Times of Amy Jacques Garvey* (Chapel Hill: University of North Carolina Press, 2002); Kathy L. Glass, *Courting Communities: Black Female Nationalism and "Syncre-Nationalism" in the Nineteenth-Century North* (New York: Routledge, 2006).

20. Melinda Chateauvert, *Marching Together: Women of the Brotherhood of Sleeping Car Porters* (Urbana: University of Illinois Press, 1998); Gerald Horne, *Race Woman: The Lives of Shirley Graham DuBois* (New York: New York University Press, 2000); Rosalyn Terborg-Penn, "Survival Strategies among African American Women Workers — a Continuing Process," in *Women, Work, and Protest: A Century of U.S. Women's Labor History*, ed. Ruth Milkman (New York and London: Routledge and Kegan Paul, 1988), 139–155.

21. Martha Biondi, *To Stand and Fight: The Struggle for Civil Rights in Post-War New York City* (Cambridge, Mass.: Harvard University Press, 2003).

22. William H. Chafe, "The Gods Bring Threads to Webs Begun," *Journal of American History* 86, no. 4 (March 2000): 1531–1551, 1531.

23. Stewart Burns, ed., *Daybreak of Freedom: The Montgomery Bus Boycott* (Chapel Hill: University of North Carolina Press, 1997), 7; Danielle McGuire, "It Was Like All of Us Had Been Raped: Sexual Violence, Community Mobilization, and the African American Freedom Struggle," *Journal of American History* (December 2004): 906–931.

24. Constance Curry, *Silver Rights* (New York: Harvest Books, 1996), preface; Christina Greene, *Our Separate Ways: Women and the Black Freedom Struggle in Durham, North Carolina* (Chapel Hill: University of North Carolina Press, 2005), 223.

25. Megan Taylor Shockley, "*We Too Are Americans: African American Women in Detroit and Richmond, 1940–1954* (Urbana: University of Illinois Press, 2004), 204, 206–207.

26. Christina Greene, *Our Separate Ways: Women and the Black Freedom Movement in Durham, North Carolina, 1940s–1970s* (Chapel Hill: University of North Carolina Press, 2005), 7–32.

27. Ibid., 219.

28. Ibid., 42–61.

29. Kathryn L. Nasstrom, "Beginnings and Endings: Life Stories and the Periodization of the Civil Rights Movement," *Journal of American History* 86, no. 2 (September 1999): 700–711, 700; Judith Rollins, *All Is Never Said: The Narrative of Odette Harper Hines* (Philadelphia: Temple University Press, 1995); Richard A. Pride, *The Confession of Dorothy Danner: Telling a Life* (Nashville: Vanderbilt University Press, 1995).

30. Barbara Ransby, "Behind-the-Scenes View of a Behind-the-Scenes Organizer: The Roots of Ella Baker's Political Passions," in *Sisters in the Struggle,* ed. Collier-Thomas and Franklin, 42–57; Joanne Grant, *Ella Baker: Freedom Bound* (New York: John Wiley & Sons, 1998).

31. Ransby, "Behind-the-Scenes View of a Behind-the-Scenes Organizer"; Carol Mueller, "Ella Baker and the Origins of 'Participatory Democracy,'" in *Women in the Civil Rights Movement,* ed. Crawford, Rouse, and Woods, 51–70, 51–52.

32. Barbara Ransby, *Ella Baker and the Black Freedom Movement: A Radical Democratic Vision* (Chapel Hill: University of North Carolina Press, 2003), 187 and chap. 6, "The Preacher and the Organizer," 170–195.

33. Jacqueline A. Rouse, "We Seek to Know . . . in Order to Speak the Truth," in *Sisters in the Struggle,* ed. Collier-Thomas and Franklin, 98–119; Septima Clark, *Echo in My Soul* (New York: Dutton, 1962); Cynthia Stokes Brown, ed., *Ready from Within: Septima Clark and the Civil Rights Movement* (Navarro, Calif.: Wild Tree Press, 1986).

34. Chana Kai Lee, *For Freedom's Sake: The Life of Fannie Lou Hamer* (Urbana: University of Illinois Press, 1999), 140; Kay Mills, *This Little Light of Mine: The Life of Fannie Lou Hamer* (New York: Plume Books, 1993).

35. Curry, *Silver Rights;* Constance Curry, *Mississippi Harmony: Memoirs of a Freedom Fighter* (New York: Palgrave, Macmillan, 2002).

36. Charlayne Hunter Gault, *In My Place* (New York: Vintage, 1993); Melba Patillo Beals, *Warriors Don't Cry: A Searing Memoir of the Battle to Integrate Little Rock's Central High* (New York: Pocket Books, 1994). Other memoirs written by black women include Daisy Bates, *The Long Shadow of Little Rock: A Memoir* (1962; repr., Fayetteville: University of Arkansas Press, 1986); and Anne Moody, *Coming of Age in Mississippi* (New York: Dial Press, 1968).

37. Dorothy Height, "We Wanted the Voice of a Woman to Be Heard," in *Sisters in the Struggle,* ed. Collier-Thomas and Franklin, 85; and Dorothy Height, *Open Wide the Freedom Gates: A Memoir* (New York: Public Affairs, 2003).

38. Pauli Murray, "The Negro Woman in the Quest for Equality," speech delivered at the National Council of Negro Women's Leadership Conference, November 14, 1963, quoted in Height, "We Wanted the Voice of a Woman to Be Heard," 89–90. See also Pauli Murray, *The Autobiography of a Black Activist, Feminist, Lawyer, Priest, and Poet* (Knoxville: University of Tennessee Press, 1989), 353.

39. Charles Payne, "Men Led, but Women Organized: Movement Participation of Women in the Mississippi Delta," in *Women in the Civil Rights Movement,* ed. Crawford, Rouse, and Woods, 1–13; and Charles Payne, *I've Got the Light of Freedom: The Organizing Tradition and the Mississippi Freedom Struggle* (Berkeley: University of California Press, 1995), chap. 9.

40. Robnett, *How Long,* 21 and 19.

41. Ibid., 20.

42. Robnett, "African American Women in the Civil Rights Movement," 1661–1693, 1664.

43. Ibid., 1664.

44. Ibid., 1665.

45. Ibid., 1663.

46. Robnett, *How Long,* 192–193.

47. Ibid., 166–167, 93–97.

48. Robnett, "African American Women in the Civil Rights Movement," 1667.

49. Ibid., 1671.

50. Kathryn L. Nasstrom, "Down to Now: Gender, Memory, and Women's Leadership in the Civil Rights Movement in Atlanta, Georgia," *Gender and History* 11, no. 1 (April 1999): 113–144.

51. Modjeska Simkins lost her post as secretary of the South Carolina NAACP because she worked with the Southern Negro Youth Congress, the Southern Conference on Human Welfare, and the Southern Conference Educational Fund, all branded by HUAC as communist fronts. Barbara Woods, "Modjeska Simkins and the South Carolina Conference of the NAACP, 1939–1957," in *Women in the Civil Rights Movement,* ed. Crawford, Rouse, and Woods, 115–116.

52. Merline Pitre, *In Struggle against Jim Crow: Lulu B. White and the NAACP, 1900–1957* (College Station: Texas A & M Press, 1999), xi, 36–37.

53. Ibid., 15.

54. John Kirk, "Daisy Bates, the National Association for the Advancement of Colored People, and the 1957 Little Rock School Crisis: A Gendered Perspective," in *Gender and the Civil Rights Movement,* ed. Peter J. Ling and Sharon Monteith (New York: Garland Publishing, 1999), 23; Grif Stockley, *Daisy Bates: Civil Rights Crusader from Arkansas* (Jackson: University Press of Mississippi, 2005).

55. Kirk, "Daisy Bates," 31.

56. Ibid., 21, 29, 30.

57. Ibid., 34.

58. Annette K. Brock, "Gloria Richardson and the Cambridge Movement," in *Women in the Civil Rights Movement,* ed. Crawford, Rouse, and Woods, 121–144, 123.

59. Jenny Walker, "The Gun-Totin' Gloria Richardson: Black Violence in Cambridge, Maryland," in *Gender and the Civil Rights Movement,* ed. Ling and Monteith, 169–186; Sharon Harley, " 'Chronicle of a Death Foretold': Gloria Richardson, the Cambridge

Movement; and the Radical Black Activist Tradition," in *Sisters in the Struggle,* ed. Collier-Thomas and Franklin, 174–196, 176–177.

60. Robnett, "African American Women in the Civil Rights Movement," 1673–1674.

61. Belinda Robnett, "Women in the Student Non-violent Coordinating Committee: Ideology, Organizational Structure, and Leadership," in *Gender and the Civil Rights Movement,* ed. Ling and Monteith, 131–167, 163.

62. Quoted in Robnett, "Women in the Student Non-violent Coordinating Committee," 162; Paula Giddings, *When and Where I Enter: The Impact of Black Women on Race and Sex in America* (New York: William Morrow, 1984).

63. Cynthia Griggs Fleming, *Soon We Will Not Cry: The Liberation of Ruby Doris Smith Robinson* (New York: Rowman & Littlefield, 1998).

64. Ibid., 166.

65. Ula Taylor, "Elijah Muhammad's Nation of Islam: Separatism, Regendering, and a Secular Approach to Black Power after Malcolm X (1965–1975)," in *Freedom North: Black Freedom Struggles outside the South, 1940–1980,* ed. Jeanne F. Theoharis and Komozi Woodard (New York: Palgrave Macmillan, 2003), 177–198.

66. For a summary see Deborah Gray White, *Too Heavy a Load: Black Women in Defense of Themselves, 1894–1994* (New York: Norton, 1999), 216–223; Margo Perkins, "Inside Our Dangerous Ranks: The Autobiography of Elaine Brown and the Black Panther Party," in *Still Lifting, Still Climbing,* ed. Springer, 91–106.

67. Tracye A. Matthews, "'No One Ever Asks What a Man's Role in the Revolution Is': Gender Politics and Leadership in the Black Panther Party, 1966–1971," in *Sisters in the Struggle,* ed. Collier-Thomas and Franklin, 231–256, 249.

68. Della Scott, "An Interview with Kathleen Neal Cleaver," *ABAFAZI: The Simmons College Review of Women of African Descent* 6, no. 2 (spring–summer 1996): 26–33, 28. See also Elaine Brown, *A Taste of Power: A Black Woman's Story* (New York: Pantheon Books, 1992); and Angela Davis, *An Autobiography* (1974; repr., New York: International Publishers, 1988).

69. Margo V. Perkins, *Autobiography as Activism: Three Black Women of the Sixties* (Jackson: University of Mississippi Press, 2000).

70. Sara Evans, *Personal Politics: The Roots of Women's Liberation in the Civil Rights Movement and the New Left* (New York: Alfred A. Knopf, 1979).

71. Duchess Harris, "From the Kennedy Commission to the Combahee Collective: Black Feminist Organizing, 1960–1980," in *Sisters in the* Struggle, ed. Collier-Thomas and Franklin, 280–305, 287.

72. Nancie Carraway, *Segregated Sisterhood: Racism and the Politics of American Feminism* (Knoxville: University of Tennessee Press, 1991); Winifred Breines, *The Trouble between Us: An Uneasy History of White and Black Women in the Feminist Movement* (New York, Oxford: Oxford University Press, 2006); Gloria Joseph and Jill Lewis, *Common Differences: Conflicts in Black and White Feminist Perspectives* (New York: Anchor Press, Doubleday, 1981); Gloria T. Hull, Patricia Bell Scott, and Barbara Smith, eds., *All the Women Are White, All the Blacks Are Men, but Some of Us Are Brave* (Old Westbury, N.Y.: Feminist Press, 1982).

73. Toni Morrison, "What the Black Woman Thinks about Women's Lib," *New York Times Magazine,* August 22, 1971, 14–15, 63–64, 66..

74. Ann Ida Lewis, quoted in Michele Wallace, *Black Macho and the Myth of the Superwoman* (New York: Dial Press, 1978), 169.

75. Wallace, *Black Macho and the Myth of the Superwoman,* 169–170.

76. Michele Wallace, *Invisibility Blues* (London: Verso, 1990). See Alice Walker's criticisms of Wallace in Alice Walker, *Search of Our Mother's Gardens: Womanist Prose* (1983; repr., New York: Harvest, 2003).

77. William Van Deburg, *New Day in Babylon: The Black Power Movement and American Culture, 1965–1975* (Chicago: University of Chicago Press, 1992), 297–298.

78. Becky Thompson, "Multi-racial Feminism: Recasting the Chronology of Second Wave Feminism," *Feminist Studies* 28, no. 2 (2002): 337–360; Benita Roth, *Separate Roads to Feminism: Back Chicana, and White Feminist Movements in America's Second Wave* (Cambridge: Cambridge University Press, 2004); Kimberly Springer, *Living for the Revolution: Black Feminist Organizations, 1968–1980* (Durham: Duke University Press, 2005). See also Angela Davis, *Blues Legacies and Black Feminism: Gertrude "Ma" Rainey, Bessie Smith, and Billie Holiday* (New York: Pantheon Books, 1998).

79. Charlayne Hunter, "Many Blacks Wary of Women's Liberation Movement in U.S.," *New York Times,* November 17, 1970, 47, 60.

80. Kristin Anderson-Brinker, "On the Issue of Roles," in *The Black Woman: An Anthology,* ed. Toni Cade (New York: Signet, 1970), 99, 107; and Kristin Anderson-Bricker, " 'Triple Jeopardy': Black Women and the Growth of Feminist Consciousness in SNCC, 1964–1975," in *Still Lifting, Still Climbing,* ed. Springer, 49–69.

81. Anderson-Bricker, " 'Triple Jeopardy,' " 49–69.

82. Roth, *Separate Roads to Feminism,* 3; and Jennifer Nelson, *Women of Color and the Reproductive Rights Movement* (New York: New York University Press, 2003).

83. Nelson, *Women of Color and the Reproductive Rights Movement,* 56; see also Jessie M. Rodrique, "The Black Community and the Birth Control Movement," in *Unequal Sisters,* ed. DuBois and Ruiz; and Loretta J. Ross, "African American Women and Abortion," in *Abortion Wars: A Half Century of Struggle, 1950–2000,* ed. Rickie Sollinger (Berkeley: University of California Press, 1998).

84. Premilla Nadasen, "Expanding the Boundaries of the Women's Movement: Black Feminism and the Struggle of Welfare Rights," *Feminist Studies* 28, no. 2 (summer 2002): 271–301; and Premilla Nadasen, *Welfare Warriors: The Welfare Rights Movement in the United States* (New York: Routledge, 2005).

85. Roth, *Separate Roads to Feminism,* 76; Kimberly Springer, "Third Wave Black Feminism?" *Signs* 27, no. 4 (summer 2002): 1059–1082; Kimberly Springer, *Living for the Revolution: Black Feminist Organizations, 1968–1980* (Durham: Duke University Press, 2005).

86. Jacquelyn Dowd Hall, "The Long Civil Rights Movement and the Political Uses of the Past," *Journal of American History* 91, no. 4 (March 2005): 1233–1263.

17

A New Century of Struggle

Feminism and Antifeminism in the United States, 1920–Present

KRISTIN CELELLO

The project of uncovering the origins, ideas, and nature of post-suffrage feminist activism in the United States has been an important area of study for women's historians over the past thirty years. Indeed, the link between the history of post-suffrage feminism and its chroniclers is unique because the renaissance of the women's history field coincided with, and can in part be attributed to, their very area of inquiry: the upsurge of feminist activity in the 1960s and 1970s. Many of the architects of modern women's history, in other words, were passionate participants in this movement. Subsequent generations of scholars, including myself, were first exposed to feminism in women's history courses.

Much of the early scholarship about feminism, in turn, focused intensely on the ongoing "second wave."[1] But while this focus remained central to the historiography throughout the 1980s and 1990s, other historians began to question whether it obscured as much as it explained. At the center of this debate was an ostensibly basic question: What was (and is) feminism? The answers to this question, in turn, challenged the view that feminist activity only occurred during the aforementioned "waves" and also brought attention to feminist efforts from beyond a white, middle-class perspective. One of the most striking developments in the historiography, therefore, has been the expansion of the definition of feminism (and some might even say "feminisms") as well as a nuanced critique of feminism's limitations in a historical context.

The study of antifeminism has been a relative latecomer to the scholarship, following a larger, but changing, historiographical trend in which scholars choose to study progressive activism more frequently than they analyze attempts to maintain the status quo or to return to "simpler times." Not surprisingly, defining antifeminism has proven to be as problematic as defining feminism. Should it be construed narrowly, so that only women and men who explicitly define themselves as opposed to feminist ideology and programs are included in this category? Or, more broadly, is antifeminism best understood as any beliefs and actions that attempt to uphold "traditional" notions of womanhood? The latter approach, in particular, has effectively challenged the notion that all women, by simple virtue of their sex, have been committed to what feminists viewed as the advancement of women and their causes in the post-suffrage United States.

In its examination of the historiography of post-suffrage feminism and antifeminism, therefore, this chapter pays close attention to the shifting definitions and understandings of feminism and antifeminism over the past several decades. Studies of the second wave provide a strong interpretive framework because the contributions of these works, as well as the reactions to them, have guided much of the evolution of this scholarship. But by casting a wider net from the 1920s through the rise of what some contemporary commentators have labeled a "third wave," this chapter illustrates the many ways in which feminism and its history have been embraced, transformed, and resisted for the better part of the past century.

Between the "Waves"

The question, What happened to feminism? has long framed the scholarship of women's activism between the achievement of suffrage in 1919 and the social movements of the 1960s and 1970s. Historians have investigated both the causes of feminism's alleged decline as well as examples of feminist activism that seemingly contradicted this trend. Much of this work has focused upon the efforts of white, upper- and middle-class women to advance broadly defined "feminist" goals — often predicated upon the premise of female difference, rather than equality — in the face of internal disputes and a relatively hostile social and political climate. Considering this evidence in tandem with a growing literature on working-class feminism, it becomes clear that the period "between the waves" was not a dormant time for feminism (or antifeminism), but rather one of important activity that would significantly shape the future trajectory of the movement.

The analysis of how women in the United States successfully gained the right to vote was a relatively early topic of inquiry for historians of women and certainly one that remains popular to this day. The historiography of suffrage from the 1950s and 1960s, however, generally relegated the fate of women's activism after winning the vote to impressionistic closing remarks. In the conclusions of their respective monographs, for instance, Eleanor Flexner and Aileen S. Kraditor readily acknowledged that many American women continued to live politically active lives — some even with the explicit goal of improving women's place in American society — in the post-suffrage era. But a note of melancholy accompanied these acknowledgments, especially because women seemingly had made nominal progress as a result of winning the vote.[2] "It is doubtful," Kraditor wrote, "whether Mrs. Stanton or Miss Anthony, returning to the scene of their labors, would take more comfort if they looked elsewhere than politics to see how their sex was faring."[3]

Such assertions, in turn, were a welcome corrective to arguments made by previous historians of the 1920s that women, best characterized as "flappers," had made great strides toward equality in the decade after suffrage.[4] By challenging such narratives, historians such as Flexner and Kraditor also contributed to a growing understanding, which coalesced in the 1970s and the 1980s, that the period between the achievement of suffrage and the rise of the second wave was a relative low point in the history of American feminism. Thus did William O'Neill frame an entire book around the question: "Why did feminism disappear after 1920, even though the Nineteenth Amendment gave women only a symbol of equality rather than the real thing?"[5] While few historians agreed with O'Neill that feminism had altogether disappeared, and, as Nancy F. Cott pointed out, his usage of the term "feminism" to describe most suffrage activity was inaccurate, given that the word did not enter common parlance until the 1910s, they did not dispute that feminists often failed to forward a unified, coherent agenda in the 1920s.[6]

Feminists, in fact, openly disagreed about the best direction for their movement after the passage of the Nineteenth Amendment. This situation was hardly surprising, given that only the firm belief that women should have the right to vote had held the suffrage coalition intact. After suffrage, many women, whom J. Stanley Lemons referred to as "social feminists," favored fighting for broad social reforms, including special protective legislation for women and children. This agenda, which had its intellectual roots in the Progressive tradition, was adamantly opposed by "hard-core" feminists, like Alice Paul, who lobbied for the passage of a federal Equal Rights Amendment (ERA) that would guarantee that women had the same rights and obligations of citizenship as men.[7] This internal debate between "difference" and "equality" clearly divided the white feminist community of the 1920s. But while the second wave's preference for equality led some historians to criticize the feminists who made the case for difference, Amy Butler recently argued for the importance of placing both visions in the social and legal context of their time. Feminists on each side of this divide, Butler contends, ultimately wanted to achieve full equality for women. Those women who supported protective legislation, such as Ethel M. Smith of the National Women's Trade Union League, however, were also keenly aware of the real class (if not racial) barriers faced by women in the 1920s. In their eyes, then, the ERA was not a panacea, but rather had the potential to improve the status of some (primarily white, upper- and middle-class) women at the expense of others.[8]

Largely absent from this discussion was the question of race. According to Rosalyn Terborg-Penn, this omission led many "discontented" black feminists in the 1920s to focus their attention solely upon the fight to end racial oppression.[9] Deborah Gray White establishes, however, that African American women continued to push for feminist causes within male-dominated organizations such as Marcus Garvey's Universal Negro Improvement Association (UNIA). Garvey's second wife, Amy Jacques Garvey, became the "feminist conscience" of the UNIA, insisting that black women had a right to equality with black men and that they should not be afraid to lead their race if the men failed to do so. In doing so, she and other supporters resisted the idea that the establishment of a strong patriarchy was necessary in the battle for black rights.[10]

External pressures, most notably a socially conservative climate, also impeded feminists' ability to make substantive gains in the 1920s. This climate also contributed to the rise of significant antifeminist and extremist activity. The War Department, for example, considered feminist organizations to be a threat to national security and actively sought to discredit their activities.[11] Indeed, Kim E. Nielsen persuasively argues that the Red Scare context allowed for a thriving antiradical and antifeminist culture. These conservative women and men feared the growth of the state and the undermining of patriarchal authority, specifically as they related to women's changing citizenship status after they gained suffrage.[12]

During these years, as well, an estimated half million women joined the Ku Klux Klan (KKK). Kathleen Blee demonstrates that female KKK members in Indiana were often more effective than their male counterparts in forwarding the Klan's message. Furthermore, these Klanswomen did not believe that there was a tension between their organization's stated goal of protecting white womanhood and the participation of white Protestant women in the public sphere and electoral politics. While Klansmen tried to reassert their masculinity through the maintenance and celebration of traditional gender roles, in other words, Klanswomen actively stepped outside of their prescribed sphere in order to promote the KKK's agenda.[13]

If feminists and their opponents thus remained active in the 1920s, what happened to their agendas as the nation sank into the Great Depression? While Lois Scharf maintains that feminism disappeared in the 1930s because public, and even feminist, support for married women's workforce participation dwindled during the Depression, Susan Ware paints a more positive picture by examining a women's "network" that made important contributions, especially in the realm of social welfare, to the New Deal government of Franklin Delano Roosevelt.[14] Further biographical research into the lives of these women — notably, Ware's book on Molly Dewson, Blanche Wiesen Cook's work on Eleanor Roosevelt, and Martha H. Swain's study of Ellen S. Woodward — emphasizes their attempts to move within existing political structures to forward women's issues and to place women in positions of influence in the federal government and political parties. These works also recognize the social and political realities, such as growing congressional and public opposition to the reform programs championed by these women in the latter years of the Depression, which constrained their efforts.[15]

It is clear, however, that feminists found a place not only in the upper eche-lons of the federal government, but also in progressive organizations, such as the National Consumers' League (NCL). Whereas historians previously assumed that voluntary organizations like the NCL had experienced their peak of influence during the Progressive Era, Landon R. Y. Storrs establishes the persistence of their advocacy for women workers as well as the important role played by the NCL in influencing the New Deal's approach to labor standards for both men and women. Indeed, the NCL was in many ways a victim of its own success, as male experts co-opted its authority on such issues following the 1938 passage of the Fair Labor Standards Act.[16]

Similarly, the 1930s and early 1940s also witnessed the ascendance of a vari-ety of right-wing women's organizations. According to June Melby Benowitz, the women who formed such groups drew upon the tradition of women's activism not in search of a role in the New Deal state, but rather to protest the approaches that their government was taking on a range of issues from unemployment to for-eign policy. While their hatred of New Dealers and Jews was extreme, it is notable that most right-wing women were not explicitly antifeminist in their rhetoric.[17] Benowitz and Glen Jeansonne both contend that women of the right were, in fact, acutely aware of their position as women and mothers. As such, they used the language of traditional women's roles in order to recruit thousands of women into a mothers' movement that sought to keep the United States out of World War II and that opposed the war throughout its duration. It seems unlikely, how-ever, that most of the American women who joined this movement understood the extremist views of the organization's leaders.[18]

Feminists during the second wave, as well as many historians of the move-ment, often regard the postwar years as a period in which reactionary views of womanhood prevailed and feminism languished. Upon closer examination, it is evident that the feminist impulse clearly was not dead, even during the 1950s. Leila J. Rupp and Verta Taylor indicate that the elite women affiliated with the National Women's Party (NWP), many of whom had been active in the latter years of the suffrage movement, continued the feminist tradition as they single-mindedly campaigned for the passage of the ERA between 1945 and the early 1960s.[19] Susan Lynn's study of women's involvement in progressive organizations such as the YWCA and the American Friends Service Committee as well as Susan Levine's work on the American Association of University Women broaden this discussion. Lynn's analysis, for example, reveals that while many women in the 1950s did not identify as feminists because they disagreed with the "racist, anti-Semitic, and right-wing leanings of some members of the NWP," they neverthe-less supported a number of feminist issues from the right of married women to work to the elimination of gender inequality in politics.[20] In fact, participation in progressive, although not explicitly "feminist" organizations, such as Women Strike for Peace in the early 1960s, often led otherwise "traditional mothers" to become supportive of or involved in feminist causes.[21]

Clearly, then, feminism amongst white middle- and upper-class women did not simply disappear between the early 1920s and the late 1960s. Many of these narratives, however, neglect the development and persistence of feminism amongst women of the working class, especially in the decades after the Great Depression. Ruth Milkman's study of women in the auto and electrical manufacturing industries during World War II, for example, finds that working women both participated in campaigns for gender equality in workplace and protested (albeit unsuccessfully) their expulsion from jobs traditionally held by men at the end of the war.[22] Taking a longer view, Nancy F. Gabin establishes that the female membership of the United Auto Workers (UAW) consistently worked to eradicate the sexual division of labor in the workplace from the 1940s through the 1970s. While tensions between male and female unionists often ran high in these years, working-class feminists in the UAW did succeed in convincing the union "at least to acknowledge the legitimacy of their goals and purposes."[23] Similarly, Dennis A. Deslippe's case studies of the United Packinghouse Workers of America and the International Union of Electrical Workers indicate that while a variety of circumstances influenced how union leadership responded to demands for gender equality, working-class feminists employed a number of strategies to protest workplace discrimination, especially after the passage of Title VII of the Civil Rights Act of 1964.[24]

While such investigations, by their very nature, tended to emphasize the exceptional nature of each case, Dorothy Sue Cobble's recent synthetic approach to the subject of what she termed "labor feminism" observes the far-reaching effects of working-class women's activism.[25] Cobble argues that the multiracial coalition of labor feminists could not easily be classified within the "equality" versus "difference" debate because they did not view the push to end workplace discrimination and concurrent demands for special treatment as inherently incompatible. Furthermore, labor feminists championed issues such as the need for fair wages and the accommodation of women's caretaking roles with their families well before the second wave claimed them as their own in the 1960s and 1970s. By forwarding such an agenda — and achieving some degree of success with the legislative victories in the early to mid-1960s — labor feminists helped to open the path for the new movement that arose later in the decade.[26]

The Second Wave: Origins and Ideologies

As Cobble's work makes clear, historians have blurred the line between the search for feminist activity between the waves and the examination of the origins and ideologies of the second wave. Through this process, they have come to realize that Betty Friedan, to paraphrase Linda K. Kerber, did not simply write a book.[27] Friedan herself, after all, took a much more complicated path to feminism than she publicly proclaimed.[28] The recognition of the multiple sources of the second wave, in turn, has allowed for the emergence of a significantly more nuanced portrait of the movement, especially as it has pushed historians to move beyond the narrow, white, middle-class focus that dominated much of the earlier literature.

Writing in the mid-1970s, Jo Freeman identified two separate groups of women — virtually all of them "white, middle-class, college-educated, profession-ally employed women" — as the originators of the women's liberation movement. The first, an "older branch," had its roots in the realm of federal- and state-level politics, whereas the second, a "younger branch," emerged from the civil rights movement and the New Left.[29] On the former group, Cynthia Harrison's research explains how they came to fight for the legal and economic rights of women, detailing how laborite Esther Peterson — with an able legal assist from African American civil rights activist Pauli Murray — helped to table divisions between pro-ERA and anti-ERA feminists in the early 1960s. The discussions about American women's fundamental lack of equal opportunity sparked by the national and state commissions on the status of women, paired with a lack of fed-eral responsiveness to women's concerns, led to the 1966 founding of the National Organization for Women (NOW), which would grow to an important feminist organization.[30] Sara Evans argues that the sexism encountered by Jo Freeman's younger group, especially those of the white middle class, in the social movements of the 1960s prompted them to articulate a thorough critique of women's devalued place in American society. Meeting in small groups, these women realized that what they perceived to be personal problems were, in fact, endemic. They could only be solved, therefore, by a drastic reorientation of women's personal relationships and their interactions with the larger world.[31]

By the 1990s, it was clear that these interpretations, while central to the his-tory of second-wave feminism, did not tell the entire story. Susan Hartmann observes, for instance, that men and women in mixed-sex liberal organizations, such as the ACLU and the National Council of Churches, actually pushed for fem-inist reforms, such as abortion rights, sex equity, and recognition of the prob-lems associated with male dominance in settings like the church, before liberal or radical feminist organizations raised these issues.[32] Other historians contend that ties to the Old Left, as well as the New Left, influenced the women of the sec-ond wave. Daniel Horowitz's biography of Betty Friedan establishes that in spite of her protestations to the contrary, Friedan's career as an activist and labor jour-nalist in the 1940s and early 1950s led her to be sensitive to women's and other social justice issues long before she discovered "the problem that has no name" as a suburban housewife.[33] In a similar vein, Kate Weigand notes that feminists working within the American Communist Party in the postwar years compelled the party to be cognizant of women's issues. These women effectively argued that social and cultural issues, and not economics alone, were at the root of women's oppression and also demonstrated an understanding of the "interdependence of gender, race and class" that provided second-wave feminists with an important intellectual heritage.[34]

The scholarship on the activities and beliefs of white second-wave feminists follows a similar trajectory as the discussion of the movement's origins. In the 1970s and 1980s, historians identified two distinctive strands of second-wave feminism. Liberal feminists, on the one hand, organized bureaucratically (notably through NOW) and worked within the traditional political system. Radical feminists, on the other hand, challenged and often acted to overthrow the existing system, primarily on the grassroots level. In this construction, liberal feminism emerged first and was pushed to the left by the more radical wing of the movement.[35]

Radical feminism, in particular, received scholarly attention in the late 1980s and 1990s. Alice Echols details what she views as the relatively rapid rise and fall of radical feminism in major urban areas in the United States. Radical feminists successfully introduced the idea that sexism was a form of oppression in the larger American discourse, developed consciousness-raising, and "articulated the earliest and most provocative critiques of the family, marriage, love, normative heterosexuality, and rape." But, in Echols's view, the movement's insistence upon a leaderless structure, as well as internal debates on issues ranging from class differences to lesbianism, led to its displacement by cultural feminism.[36] Nancy Whittier, however, disputes this latter point in her case study of radical feminism in Columbus, Ohio. According to Whittier, radical feminism persisted in a variety of forms and venues — from rape crisis centers to feminist bookstores — after the mid-1970s, but this history was often hidden from view because radical feminists did not organize in a structured fashion on the national level.[37]

Recently, historians have begun to challenge the idea of a stark radical/liberal divide in the second wave. At the same time, they have drawn attention to the fact that feminist activism did not take place only in major American cities. Judith Ezekiel's study of second-wave activism in Dayton, Ohio, for instance, observes that a liberationist, radical strain of feminism, grounded in the proliferation of consciousness-raising groups, emerged well before liberal feminism in this heartland town.[38] Stephanie Gilmore similarly argues that scholars need to play close attention to the question of location in their studies of the second wave. Her analysis of the Memphis, Tennessee, chapter of NOW finds that the group participated in activities that fell under both the liberal and radical rubric, thereby occupying the space between these two categories and suggesting a heretofore unrecognized dynamism within the movement.[39]

Historians also began to take a closer look at the intellectual history of the second wave, examining the specific issues that were important (and frequently divisive) to feminists as well as the reasons that they dwelt on these issues. Mari Jo Buhle makes the case that feminists throughout the twentieth century vacillated between the poles of equality and difference because of their complicated relationship with Freudianism and psychoanalysis.[40] Jane Gerhard explains why white second-wave feminists came to view questions of sexuality as the "source of both women's oppression and their liberation," as well as the limitations that this interpretation placed upon the movement.[41] Just as Gerhard endeavors to counter the frequent misperception that radical feminists were antisex, so do Lauri Umansky, Susan Douglas, and Meredith Michaels, who challenge the dual myths that second-wave feminists ignored motherhood, on the one hand, and were anti-family, on the other. Umansky also points to the critical role played by race in these discussions: both the influence of black feminist thought on the discourse about motherhood and the attempts by white feminists to posit motherhood as a universal bond between women.[42]

Many of these misperceptions about second-wave feminism, in turn, arose from the complicated relationship shared by feminists and the mass media. Susan Douglas investigates how the representations of women in popular culture in the 1950s and early 1960s, paired with the recognition that teenaged girls were an untapped market, had the subversive potential to convince women of the need for feminist action. The news media's coverage of the women's liberation movement, in turn, helped to create the contradictory conditions in which many women by the late 1970s and 1980s identified with feminist causes but adamantly rejected the label "feminist."[43] Amy Erdman Farrell, in turn, examines the history of the movement's most visible publication, *Ms.*, and exposes the difficulties inherent in "forging an oppositional politics within the context of commercial culture." *Ms.*, in other words, quickly became one of the most recognizable products of second-wave feminism, but the editors engaged in a constant negotiation between the conflicting demands of its readership, other factions within the movement, and the need to produce a profitable magazine that appealed to advertisers.[44]

Just as the media anointed Gloria Steinem, *Ms.*'s white, heterosexual, apparently middle-class editor, as a leader of the movement, so many accounts of the second wave tend to focus upon the experiences and ideas of this select group of women. Historians in the 1990s and early twenty-first century, however, worked to correct this trend. Lillian Faderman, for example, explores the rancor that accompanied NOW's slow recognition of lesbians as well as the radical feminist stance that lesbianism was a necessary political choice for women who were committed to their cause. Through the 1970s, many lesbians sought to create new, often separatist, institutions and a culture that celebrated values that they identified as "essentially" female, such as nurturing.[45] While some historians, notably, Alice Echols, blame this trend for the rise of cultural feminism and the depoliticization of radical feminism, others, such as Verta Taylor and Leila J. Rupp, maintain that lesbian feminists actually ensured the continued political character of the movement.[46] Nancy Whittier similarly presents evidence that complicates the notion of a strict "gay-straight split" within the movement and highlights the role played by lesbians in Columbus in maintaining an active feminist agenda during the relatively hostile 1980s.[47]

Historians also began to explore the activities of feminists of color, both within the white women's movement and in their own organizations. By examining black women's participation within the former, they effectively challenge the idea that women of color were uninterested in the second wave.[48] Paula Giddings, for example, observes that some black women were active members of NOW — notably Aileen Hernandez, who became president of the organization after Betty Friedan. Yet, they also had reasons to be skeptical of their place in a movement dominated by white women and their concerns.[49] Susan Hartmann contends that African American women played an essential role in advancing the cause of feminism in liberal institutions such as the Ford Foundation and additionally promoted the inclusion of racial justice issues within the second-wave agenda.[50]

Recent scholarship additionally makes clear that that many women of color did not organize simply in reaction to white women's activism. Such accounts clearly heeded Sherna Berger Gluck's call to destabilize the traditional narrative of a single, easily identifiable second wave.[51] Benita Roth, for instance, argues that African American, Chicana, and white women each took "separate roads" to their own distinctive feminist movements.[52] Unlike the white women who felt it necessary to break away from the civil rights movement and the New Left, for instance, Chicana women remained close with their "parent" movement, arguing from their own organizations and from within that feminism was necessary for their larger community's liberation.[53]

Both Roth's work and Kimberly Springer's comprehensive examination of five black feminist organizations, in turn, locate the black feminist movement's origins in the reaction to the changing, more masculinist nature of the civil rights movement as well the negative portrayal of black women in public policy documents such as the Moynihan Report. Black feminists, then, were among the first women to articulate an activist position that recognized the multiple sources of oppression.[54] Premilla Nadasen's study of black women in the welfare rights movement in the 1960s and 1970s, for example, demonstrates how these women "incorporated aspects of class empowerment, racial liberation, gender equity, and sexual autonomy" into their agenda.[55] Indeed, according to Winifred Breines, the early failures of white socialist feminists to act upon similar convictions exacerbated the already deep divide between white and black women. Only in understanding the impossibility of a unified women's movement could socialist feminists of both races begin to work together and to transcend, at times, their recognized differences.[56]

Integrating the history of feminists of color into the history of the second wave calls for a reexamination of not only the origins of the movement, but also the idea that feminism waned in the late 1970s and 1980s. Becky Thompson maintains that from the perspective of multiracial feminism practiced by both women of color and white antiracist feminists "the best days of feminism were yet to come" in the early 1980s.[57] The influence of such analyses is evident in the new documentary collections and syntheses of the movement that have appeared in the last decade.[58] Rosalyn Baxandall and Linda Gordon's collection,

for example, studiously avoids portraying the origins of the second wave as a predominantly white phenomenon and includes voices from a broad range of feminists of color.[59] Sara M. Evans makes the case that, in spite of the changed
political landscape, "feminism not only persisted but flowed into new channels"
in the 1980s.[60] Evans and Ruth Rosen call attention to the vast array of positive
changes that feminism brought to the United States. (Their books are subtitled
How Women Changed America at Century's End and *How the Modern Women's
Movement Changed America*, respectively.)[61] Estelle B. Freedman expands this
trend, placing the feminist "revolution" in global perspective.[62] In doing so, these
historians work to counteract several decades — and, in Freedman's estimation,
several centuries — of negative responses to feminist activism.

Antifeminism and the Second Wave: Origins and Ideologies

The negative responses to the second wave were tied specifically to the emergence of a strong, explicitly antifeminist movement in the 1970s. This movement
was one of the more visible manifestations of the resurgent conservatism in the
latter decades of the twentieth century. According to Lisa McGirr, suburban
women, as well as men, had played an important, grassroots role in the reshaping
of conservatism in the 1960s. By the latter part of the decade, spurred by the rising tide of evangelicalism, their attention had turned from anticommunism to
"single-issue campaigns" such as the fight against the teaching of sexual education in schools.[63] Indeed, much of the scholarship about antifeminism focuses
intensely upon such campaigns, especially the battles over the Equal Rights
Amendment (ERA) and abortion. In the process, scholars have started to understand the complex motivations that prompted antifeminist activism, while recognizing that antifeminism was not always all conservative women's primary
concern.[64] Indeed, Donald T. Critchlow's recent and largely flattering biography
of right-wing "sweetheart" Phyllis Schlafly argues that Schlafly's career as a grassroots activist was important exactly because it offered a window into the
"remarkable changes that took place in the larger politics of the last half of the
twentieth century."[65]

Scholars assessing the failed passage of the ERA tend to take a dual approach,
examining both the shortcomings of pro-ERA activists and the successes of their
opponents, including Schlafly. Mary Frances Berry, for example, observes that
supporters of the amendment did not appreciate the importance of building consensus on the state as well as the federal level.[66] Jane J. Mansbridge demonstrates
that public support for the ERA was frequently "superficial" and, in fact, declined
as the ratification process was prolonged. Both sides of the ERA debate, she
holds, exaggerated the effects that ratification would have upon the place of
women in American society, and the amendment's detractors successfully dis-
credited the idea that it would benefit all women.[67] Donald G. Matthews and Jane
Sherron De Hart expand upon this latter analysis in their case study of the ERA in

North Carolina. They claim that the supporters and the opponents of the amendment had fundamentally different world views, demonstrated by their understanding of "sex." As such, the former group "was comfortable with modern social analysis and challenges to tradition," whereas the latter "believed such critiques eroded the foundations of self and community."[68]

The issue of abortion continued to mobilize feminists and antifeminists long after the demise of the ERA. The scholarship on this topic largely mirrors that of the ERA, examining what drew men and women to both sides of the debate.[69] Kristin Luker asserts that the abortion controversy often stood in for a larger discourse about women's place in American society. Women who supported abortion, in other words, believed that they should have control over their reproductive choices so that they did not have to be defined solely as wives and mothers. The women who defined themselves as "pro-life," in turn, reacted to this perceived devaluing of motherhood and argued that childbearing was a key component in women's social role.[70] Faye D. Ginsburg's case study of the conflicts surrounding an abortion clinic in Fargo, North Dakota, similarly insists that abortion activists were motivated by drastically different views about the place of women and nurturing in contemporary American society.[71] It is also clear that by employing increasingly violent tactics throughout the 1980s, anti-abortion supporters effectively succeeded in limiting access to abortion, even if they failed in their campaigns to overturn *Roe v. Wade*.[72]

Another Wave?

Altogether, it is clear that antifeminism helped to shape what Susan Faludi referred to as a "backlash" against women in the 1980s.[73] As Evans, Whittier, and others argue, however, feminism certainly did not die nor fade away after the 1970s. Still, starting in the 1990s, some young feminists declared themselves to be members of a "third wave." According to Barbara Findlen, this was "the first generation for whom feminism has been entwined in the fabric of our lives."[74] The presence of feminism, however, appeared to have contradictory effects upon the young women who came of age during and after the 1980s. On the one hand, it seemed natural for them to embrace feminism and to recognize the opportunities that previous activism had brought into their lives. On the other hand, some women — especially those of the white, middle and upper classes — felt that feminism had accomplished all that it needed to and were unwilling to align themselves with a movement (and a word) that had long been maligned and caricatured in much of the national discourse.

Many of the earliest works of the third wave are anthologies that give voice to the issues and concerns that were relevant in young women's lives. As a whole, these collections suggest that the interests of second-wave feminists do not always coincide with those of the next generation and that the latter clearly object to being told how to conceive of or to confront their issues. Third-wave anthologies indicate awareness of the pitfalls of expressing a single-mindedly white, heterosexual feminist perspective, and writings by young women of color, in particular, emphasize the global scope and multiplicity of concerns that fell under the feminist umbrella.[75] Moving beyond these personal narratives, third-wave writers Jennifer Baumgardner and Amy Richards celebrate the movement's vitality and spell out the persistent problems facing women both outside and inside the feminist movement. In doing so, they offer a plan of action, their "manifesta" for bringing about equality and feminist-inspired change.[76]

It is particularly ironic that young women posit the existence of a third wave at the same time that many scholars have begun the question the usefulness of the wave analogy. Third-wave feminists' insistence upon differentiating their movement from that of the previous generation reminds scholars that, even if they put this analogy to the side, activists themselves find it to be a useful tool in identifying themselves and in mobilizing participants. Of course, the history of the third wave and the reactions against it is yet to be written. When historians turn their attention to this history, they will likely confront many of the same challenges that historians of twentieth-century feminism and antifeminism have faced. How will they decide what to include in their analyses of this activism and how will they assess its successes and failures? Taking a cue from the third wave, historians will assuredly continue to incorporate analyses of the intersections of race, class, gender, and sexuality into their studies of feminism and antifeminism. In doing so, they will further illuminate the connections — and disconnections — that defined women's activism in the twentieth-century United States.

NOTES

1. Historians generally consider the "first wave" to be the campaign to win women the vote. Some also include the unsuccessful fight from the 1920s through the 1960s to achieve congressional and popular support for an Equal Rights Amendment.

2. Eleanor Flexner, *Century of Struggle: The Women's Rights Movement in the United States*, 2nd ed. (Cambridge, Mass.: Belknap Press of Harvard University Press, 1966), conclusion; Aileen S. Kraditor, *The Ideas of the Woman Suffrage Movement* (New York: Columbia University Press, 1965), ch. 9.

3. Flexner, *Century of Struggle*, 326.

4. On this perception, see Estelle B. Freedman, "The New Woman: Changing Views of Women in the 1920s," in *Decades of Discontent: The Women's Movement, 1920–1940*, ed. Lois Scharf and Joan M. Jensen (Westport, Conn.: Greenwood Press, 1983), 21–22.

5. William O'Neill, *Feminism in America: A History*, 2nd rev. ed. (New Brunswick, N.J.: Transaction Publishers, 1989), xiii.

6. Nancy F. Cott, *The Grounding of Modern Feminism* (New Haven: Yale University Press, 1987).

7. J. Stanley Lemons, *The Woman Citizen: Social Feminism in the 1920s* (Urbana: University of Illinois Press, 1973). On the activities of Paul and the National Women's Party, see also Susan D. Becker, *The Origins of the Equal Rights Amendment: American Feminism between the Wars* (Westport, Conn.: Greenwood Press, 1981).

8. Amy Butler, *Two Paths to Equality: Alice Paul and Ethel M. Smith in the ERA Debate, 1921–1929* (Albany: State University of New York Press, 2002).

9. Rosalyn Terborg-Penn, "Discontented Black Feminists: Prelude and Postscript to the Passage of the Nineteenth Amendment," in *Decades of Discontent*, ed. Scharf and Jensen, 261–278.

10. Deborah Gray White, *Too Heavy a Load: Black Women in Defense of Themselves, 1894–1994* (New York: W. W. Norton, 1999), ch. 4.

11. Joan M. Jensen, "All Pink Sisters: The War Department and the Feminist Movement in the 1920s," in *Decades of Discontent*, ed. Scharf and Jensen, 199–222. See also Lemons, *The Woman Citizen*, 209–225; and Cott, *The Grounding of Modern Feminism*, esp. ch. 8.

12. Kim E. Nielsen, *Un-American Womanhood: Antiradicalism, Antifeminism, and the First Red Scare* (Columbus: Ohio State University Press, 2001).

13. Kathleen Blee, *Women of the Klan: Racism and Gender in the 1920s* (Berkeley: University of California Press, 1991). On the centrality of gender to the rise of the Second Klan, see Nancy MacLean, *Behind the Mask of Chivalry: The Making of the Second Ku Klux Klan* (Oxford: Oxford University Press, 1994).

14. Lois Scharf, *To Work and to Wed: Female Employment, Feminism, and the Great Depression* (Westport, Conn.: Greenwood Press, 1980); Susan Ware, *Beyond Suffrage: Women in the New Deal* (Cambridge, Mass.: Harvard University Press, 1981).

15. Susan Ware, *Partner and I: Molly Dewson, Feminism, and New Deal Politics* (New Haven: Yale University Press, 1987); Blanche Wiesen Cook, *Eleanor Roosevelt*, vol. 2: *The Defining Years, 1933–1938* (New York: Viking, 1999); Martha H. Swain, *Ellen S. Woodward: New Deal Advocate for Women* (Jackson: University Press of Mississippi, 1995).

16. Landon R. Y. Storrs, *Civilizing Capitalism: The National Consumers' League, Women's Activism, and Labor Standards in the New Deal Era* (Chapel Hill: University of North Carolina Press, 2000).

17. June Melby Benowitz, *Days of Discontent: American Women and Right-Wing Politics, 1933–1945* (Dekalb: Northern Illinois University Press, 2002).

18. Glen Jeansonne, *Women of the Far Right: The Mothers' Movement and World War II* (Chicago: University of Chicago Press, 1996); Benowitz, *Days of Discontent*.

19. Leila J. Rupp and Verta Taylor, *Survival in the Doldrums: The American Women's Rights Movement, 1945 to the 1960s* (New York: Oxford University Press, 1987).

20. Susan Lynn, *Progressive Women in Conservative Times: Racial Justice, Peace, and Feminism, 1945 to the 1960s* (New Brunswick: Rutgers University Press, 1992), 2 and ch. 5; Susan Levine, *Degrees of Equality: The American Association of University Women and the Challenge of Twentieth-Century Feminism* (Philadelphia: Temple University Press, 1995).

21. Amy Swerdlow, *Women Strike for Peace: Traditional Motherhood and Radical Politics in the 1960s* (Chicago: University of Chicago Press, 1993). On women's involvement in a variety of social justice causes, including the peace movement, in the 1950s and early 1960s, see the essays in part 2 of Joanne Meyerowitz, ed., *Not June Cleaver: Women and Gender in Postwar America, 1945–1960* (Philadelphia: Temple University Press, 1994).

22. Ruth Milkman, *Gender at Work: The Dynamics of Job Segregation by Sex during World War II* (Urbana: University of Illinois Press, 1987).

23. Nancy F. Gabin, *Feminism in the Labor Movement: Women and the United Auto Workers, 1935–1975* (Ithaca, N.Y.: Cornell University Press, 1990), 6. Alternately, Annelise Orleck's study of four industrial feminists finds evidence of decline in the 1950s. Much of her analysis can be attributed to the fact that these women were getting older and to the specific case of the Women's Trade Union League. Annelise Orleck, *Common

Sense and a Little Fire: Women and Working-Class Politics in the United States, 1900–1965 (Chapel Hill: University of North Carolina Press, 1995), ch. 7.

24. Dennis A. Deslippe, *"Rights, Not Roses": Unions and the Rise of Working-Class Feminism* (Urbana: University of Illinois Press, 2000).

25. Cobble herself wrote such a case study. See Dorothy Sue Cobble, *Dishing It Out: Waitresses and Their Unions in the Twentieth Century* (Urbana: University of Illinois Press, 1991).

26. Dorothy Sue Cobble, *The Other Women's Movement: Workplace Justice and Social Rights in Modern America* (Princeton: Princeton University Press, 2004).

27. Linda K. Kerber, "'I Was Appalled': The Invisible Antecedents of Second-Wave Feminism," *Journal of Women's History* 14, no. 2 (summer 2002): 93.

28. Daniel Horowitz, *Betty Friedan and the Making of* The Feminine Mystique*: The American Left, the Cold War, and Modern Feminism* (Amherst: University of Massachusetts Press, 1998).

29. Jo Freeman, *The Politics of Women's Liberation: A Case Study of an Emerging Social Movement and Its Relation to the Policy Process* (New York: David McKay Company, 1975), 9 and chap. 2.

30. Cynthia Harrison, *On Account of Sex: The Politics of Women's Issues, 1945–1968* (Berkeley: University of California Press, 1988). On the specific role of the Women's Bureau in this process, see Kathleen A. Laughlin, *Women's Work and Public Policy: A History of the Women's Bureau, U.S. Department of Labor, 1945–1970* (Boston: Northeastern University Press, 2000).

31. Sara Evans, *Personal Politics: The Roots of Women's Liberation in the Civil Rights Movement and the New Left* (New York: Alfred A. Knopf, 1979).

32. Susan M. Hartmann, *The Other Feminists: Activists in the Liberal Establishment* (New Haven: Yale University Press, 1998), esp. ch. 3 and 4.

33. Horowitz, *Betty Friedan and the Making of* The Feminist Mystique. Friedan's protestations were clearly related to her fear of red baiting. On the effects of McCarthyism on left-wing feminists, see Landon R. Y. Storrs, "Red Scare Politics and the Suppression of Popular Front Feminism: The Loyalty Investigation of Mary Dublin Keyserling," *Journal of American History* 90, no. 2 (September 2003): 491–524.

34. Kate Weigand, *Red Feminism: American Communism and the Making of Women's Liberation* (Baltimore: Johns Hopkins University Press, 2001), 3.

35. A good overview of NOW is Winifred D. Wandersee's *On the Move: American Women in the 1970s* (Boston: Twayne Publishers, 1988), chap. 3. On the specific role of older women within the organization, see Patricia Huckle, *Tish Summers, Activist, and the Founding of the Older Women's League* (Knoxville: University of Tennessee Press, 1991).

36. Alice Echols, *Daring to Be Bad: Radical Feminism in America, 1967–1975* (Minneapolis: University of Minnesota Press, 1989), 3–4.

37. Nancy Whittier, *Feminist Generations: The Persistence of the Radical Women's Movement* (Philadelphia: Temple University Press, 1995).

38. Judith Ezekiel, *Feminism in the Heartland* (Columbus: Ohio State University Press, 2002). See also Beth Bailey, *Sex in the Heartland* (Cambridge, Mass.: Harvard University Press, 1999), ch. 6 and 7.

39. Stephanie Gilmore, "The Dynamics of Second-Wave Feminist Activism in Memphis, 1971–1982: Rethinking the Liberal/Radical Divide," *NWSA Journal* 15, no. 1 (spring 2003): 94–117.

40. Mari Jo Buhle, *Feminism and Its Discontents: A Century of Struggle with Psychoanalysis* (Cambridge, Mass.: Harvard University Press, 1998). For an interpretation of the equality/difference debate from a legal perspective, see Deborah L. Rhode, *Justice and Gender: Sex Discrimination and the Law* (Cambridge, Mass.: Harvard University Press, 1989), esp. ch. 3–5.

41. Jane Gerhard, *Desiring Revolution: Second-Wave Feminism and the Rewriting of American Sexual Thought, 1920 to 1982* (New York: Columbia University Press, 2001), 3.

42. Lauri Umansky, *Motherhood Reconceived: Feminism and the Legacies of the Sixties* (New York: New York University Press, 1996); Susan J. Douglas and Meredith Michaels, *The Mommy Myth: The Idealization of Motherhood and How It Has Undermined Women* (New York: Free Press, 2004).

43. Susan J. Douglas, *Where the Girls Are: Growing Up Female with the Mass Media* (New York: Times Books, 1994).

44. Amy Erdman Farrell, *Yours in Sisterhood*: Ms. *Magazine and the Promise of Popular Feminism* (Chapel Hill: University of North Carolina Press, 1998), 2.

45. Lillian Faderman, *Odd Girls and Twilight Lovers: A History of Lesbian Life in Twentieth-Century America* (New York: Columbia University Press, 1991), ch. 8–10.

46. Echols, *Daring to Be Bad*; Verta Taylor and Leila J. Rupp, "Women's Culture and Lesbian Feminist Activism: A Reconsideration of Cultural Feminism," *Signs* 19 (autumn 1993): 32–61.

47. Whittier, *Feminist Generations*, chap. 3.

48. On this perception, see, for instance, Freeman, *The Politics of Women's Liberation;* and Steven M. Buechler, *Women's Movements in the United States: Woman Suffrage, Equal Rights, and Beyond* (New Brunswick, N.J.: Rutgers University Press, 1990), 131–135.

49. Paula Giddings, *When and Where I Enter: The Impact of Black Women on Race and Sex in America* (New York: William Morrow and Company, 1984), ch. 17.

50. Hartmann, *The Other Feminists*, ch. 6.

51. Sherna Berger Gluck in collaboration with Maylei Blackwell, Sharon Cotrell, and Karen S. Harper, "Whose Feminism, Whose History? Reflections on Excavating the History of (the) U.S. Women's Movement(s)," in *Community Activism and Feminist Politics,* ed. Nancy A. Naples (New York: Routledge, 1998), 31–56.

52. Benita Roth, *Separate Roads to Feminism: Black, Chicana, and White Feminist Movements in America's Second Wave* (Cambridge, Mass.: Cambridge University Press, 2004).

53. Ibid., ch. 4. One of the first descriptive examinations of the history of Chicana feminism is Vicki L. Ruiz, *From Out of the Shadows: Mexican Women in Twentieth-Century America* (New York: Oxford University Press, 1998), ch. 5.

54. Kimberly Springer, *Living for the Revolution: Black Feminist Organizations, 1968–1980* (Durham: Duke University Press, 2005). See also, White, *Too Heavy a Load*, ch. 7.

55. Premilla Nadasen, "Expanding the Boundaries of the Women's Movement: Black Feminism and the Struggle of Welfare Rights," *Feminist Studies* 28, no. 2 (summer 2002): 294.

56. Winifred Breines, *The Trouble between Us: An Uneasy History of White and Black Women in the Feminist Movement* (New York: Oxford University Press, 2006).

57. Becky Thompson, "Multiracial Feminism: Recasting the Chronology of Second Wave Feminism," *Feminist Studies* 28, no. 2 (summer 2002): 344.

58. Syntheses that presented the more traditional narrative include Flora Davis, *Moving the Mountain: The Women's Movement in American since 1960* (New York: Simon and Schuster,

1991); Barbara Ryan, *Feminism and the Women's Movement: Dynamics of Change in Social Movement Ideology and Activism* (New York: Routledge, 1992); Sheila Tobias, *Faces of Feminism: An Activist's Reflections on the Women's Movement* (Boulder: Westview Press, 1997).

59. Rosalyn Baxandall and Linda Gordon, eds., *Dear Sisters: Dispatches from the Women's Liberation Movement* (New York: Basic Books, 2000).

60. Sara M. Evans, *Tidal Wave: How Women Changed America at Century's End* (New York: Free Press, 2003), 176.

61. Ibid.; and Ruth Rosen, *The World Split Open: How the Modern Women's Movement Changed America* (New York: Free Press, 2000).

62. Estelle B. Freedman, *No Turning Back: The History of Feminism and the Future of Women* (New York: Ballantine Books, 2002). See also Myra Marx Ferree and Beth B. Hess, *Controversy and Coalition: The New Feminist Movement across Three Decades of Change*, 3rd ed. (New York: Routledge, 2000), introduction.

63. Lisa McGirr, *Suburban Warriors: The Origins of the New American Right* (Princeton: Princeton University Press, 2001).

64. Rebecca E. Klatch, *Women of the New Right* (Philadelphia: Temple University Press, 1987).

65. Carol Felsenthal, *The Sweetheart of the Silent Majority: The Biography of Phyllis Schlafly* (Garden City, N.Y.: Doubleday & Company, 1981); Donald T. Critchlow, *Phyllis Schlafly and Grassroots Conservatism: A Woman's Crusade* (Princeton: Princeton University Press, 2005), 3.

66. Mary Frances Berry, *Why ERA Failed: Politics, Women's Rights, and the Amending Process of the Constitution* (Bloomington: Indiana University Press, 1986).

67. Jane J. Mansbridge, *Why We Lost the ERA* (Chicago: University of Chicago Press, 1986), 2.

68. Donald G. Matthews and Jane Sherron De Hart, *Sex, Gender, and the Politics of ERA: A State and the Nation* (New York: Oxford University Press, 1990), xi.

69. An exception, which focuses primarily on the anti-abortion side, is Dallas A. Blanchard, *The Anti-Abortion Movement and the Rise of the Religious Right* (New York: Twayne Publishers, 1994).

70. Kristin Luker, *Abortion and the Politics of Motherhood* (Berkeley: University of California Press, 1984).

71. Faye D. Ginsburg, *Contested Lives: The Abortion Debate in an American Community* (Berkeley: University of California Press, 1989).

72. Marcy J. Wilder, "The Rule of Law, the Rise of Violence, and the Role of Morality: Reframing America's Abortion Debate," in *Abortion Wars: A Half Century of Struggle, 1950–2000*, ed. Rickie Solinger (Berkeley: University of California Press, 1998), 73–94.

73. Susan Faludi, *Backlash: The Undeclared War against American Women* (New York: Anchor Books, 1991).

74. Barbara Findlen, introduction to *Listen Up! Voices from the Next Feminist Generation*, ed. Barbara Findlen (Seattle: Seal Press, 1995), xii.

75. See, for instance, Rebecca Walker, ed., *To Be Real: Telling the Truth and Changing the Face of Feminism* (New York: Anchor Books, 1995); Daisy Hernandez and Bushra Rehman, eds., *Colonize This! Young Women of Color on Today's Feminism* (New York: Seal Press, 2002).

76. Jennifer Baumgardner and Amy Richards, *Manifesta: Young Women, Feminism, and the Future* (New York: Farrar, Straus, and Giroux, 2000). *Manifesta* also includes a useful bibliography of other third-wave works.

CONTRIBUTORS

SUSAN ARMITAGE is Claudius O. and Mary W. Johnson Distinguished Professor of History at Washington State University, where she has taught since 1978. She is the co-editor, with Elizabeth Jameson, of *The Women's West* (1987) and *Writing the Range: Race, Class, and Culture in the Women's West* (1997). With Ruth Moynihan and Christiane Fischer Dichamp, she edited *So Much to Be Done: Women Settlers on the Mining and Ranching Frontier* (1990) and, with Patricia Hart and Karen Weatherman, *Women's Oral History* (2002). She was editor of *Frontiers: A Journal of Women Studies* from 1996 to 2003. She has written a number of articles about western women's history and is currently at work on a history of women in the greater Pacific Northwest (Washington, Oregon, Idaho, western Montana, and British Columbia).

EILEEN BORIS is the Hull Professor of Women's Studies at the University of California, Santa Barbara and chair of women's studies. Her research focuses on women's labors in the home and other workplaces and the racialized gendered state in the United States. Her publications include *Home to Work: Motherhood and the Politics of Industrial Homework in the United States* (1994), winner of the Philip Taft Prize in Labor History, and *Voices of Women's Historians: The Personal, the Political, the Professional*, co-edited with Nupur Chaudhuri (1999). Among her fellowships have been awards from the National Endowment for the Humanities, the Woodrow Wilson Center, and the Fulbright Foundation. She was co-chair of the Thirteenth Berkshire Conference on the History of Women (2005) and is president of the board of trustees of the *Journal of Women's History*. Her current book project with Jennifer Klein gives health aides, personal attendants, and in-home supportive service workers a history, intervening in debates over care-work, racialization, and the welfare state.

SUSAN BRANSON is an associate professor in the American Studies Program at Syracuse University. She is the author of *"These Fiery Frenchified Dames": Women, Politics, and Culture in Early National Philadelphia* (2001). Her recent book is a shift from political culture to criminal culture. *Dangerous to Know: Women, Crime, and Notoriety in the Early Nineteenth Century* (forthcoming) investigates the activities (and crimes) of a woman who attempted to kidnap the governor of Pennsylvania in 1816. She was awarded a National Endowment for the Humanities Fellowship for 2005–2006.

LAURA BRIGGS received her Ph.D. in American civilization from Brown University. She is the author of *Reproducing Empire: Race, Sex, Science, and U.S. Imperialism in Puerto Rico* (2002). She is currently working on a history of transracial and transnational adoption. She is an associate professor of women's studies at the University of Arizona, where she teaches classes in gender and imperialism, cultural studies of science, and the history of race/gender in the United States. She has published articles on race, reproduction, and international politics in numerous journals, including *Gender and History*, *Social Text*, *American Quarterly*, *Debate Feminista* (Mexico City), and *Centro: Journal of the Center for Puerto Rican Studies*.

LESLIE BROWN is an expert in African American history, especially the history of African American women. She attended graduate school at Duke University in Durham, North Carolina, where she earned her Ph.D. in history. From 1990 to 1995 she co-coordinated "Behind the Veil: Documenting African American Life in the Jim Crow South," a collaborative research and curriculum project. She teaches in the History Department at Washington University, St. Louis. Her recent journal articles include "The Sisters and Mothers Are Called to the City: Black Women, Migration, and Work," "Race, Place, Gender," and "Space: The City as a Site of African American Women's History." She is the author of *Upbuilding Black Durham: Gender, Class, and Black Community Development in the Urban South*.

TREVOR G. BURNARD, co-organizer of the Re-visioning Women's History Conference in London in 2001, is professor of American history at the University of Warwick, where he teaches courses on early American history. He is the author of *Mastery, Tyranny, and Desire: Thomas Thistlewood and His Slaves in the Anglo-Jamaican World* (2004) and *Creole Gentlemen: The Maryland Elite, 1691–1776* (2002). His current projects include a social and demographic history of black and white society in Jamaica, 1655–1780; the history of Kingston, Jamaica, 1745–1770; and women in Atlantic port towns.

KRISTIN CELELLO received her Ph.D. in history from the University of Virginia in 2004. She was a postdoctoral fellow at Emory University's Center for Myth and Ritual in American Life, where she revised her manuscript, *Making Marriage Work: Marital Success and Failure in the Twentieth-Century United States*. She has taught at the University of Virginia and the University of Toronto at Mississauga and was senior associate editor of the *Dolley Madison Digital Edition*. She now teaches at Queens College, CUNY.

ELIZABETH J. CLAPP is senior lecturer in American history at the University of Leicester, where she teaches courses on ideals of womanhood in nineteenth-century America, American religious history, the history of the family, and American history to the Civil War. She is a fellow of the Royal Historical Society. Her research interests are in nineteenth-century American women and their roles in partisan and welfare politics. She is the author of *Mothers of All Children: Women Reformers and the Rise of the Juvenile Courts in Progressive Era America* (1998) and articles on women in the nineteenth century. She is just completing a book-length study of Anne Royall and the political culture of Jacksonian America.

MARY ELLEN CURTIN received her Ph.D. from Duke University. She was a fellow at the Carter G. Woodson Institute for Afro-American Studies, located at the University of Virginia. She is the author of *Black Prisoners and Their World, Alabama, 1865–1900* (2000), a study of the convict leasing system and its consequences in the postbellum South. She teaches African American and American women's history at the University of Essex in England. She is a fellow at the Woodrow Wilson center, where she is writing a biography of former Congresswoman Barbara Jordan of Texas.

INGE DORNAN is a lecturer in American history and a member of the Centre for American, Transatlantic, and Caribbean History at Brunel University, West London. She received her doctorate from Girton College, University of Cambridge, supported by a postgraduate research award from the Economic and Social Research Council. Her research interests lie in colonial slavery and the Atlantic slave trade. She has published articles on colonial women and slavery and women's work in the colonial South, including "Masterful Women: Colonial Women Slaveholders in the Urban Low Country" in the *Journal of American Studies* and "The Rise and Fall of Womanhood: Ideal and Reality in Women's Status and Experience in the Colonial Low Country." She was one of the organizers of the Re-visioning Women's History Conference in London in 2001.

DONNA R. GABACCIA is the Rudolph J. Vecoli Professor of Immigration History and director of the Immigration History Research Center at the University of Minnesota. She is the author of many books and articles on immigration to the United States and Italian migration worldwide, including *From the Other Side: Women, Gender, and Immigrant Life in the United States, 1820–1990* (1994) and (co-edited with Franca Iacovetta) *Women, Gender, and Transnational Life: Italian Workers of the World* (2002). She is co-editor, with Vicki L. Ruiz, of *American Dreaming, Global Realities* (2006) and recently edited a special issue, "Gender and Migration," for *International Migration Review*.

SUSAN-MARY GRANT is professor of American history at Newcastle University, England. She is the author of *The War for a Nation: The American Civil War* (2006) and *North over South: Northern Nationalism and American Identity in the Antebellum Era* (2000) and editor of *Legacy of Disunion: The Enduring Legacy of the American Civil War* (2003). She is editor of *American Nineteenth-Century History* and serves on the boards of *Nations and Nationalism*, the Association for the Study of Race and Ethnicity in the Americas (ARENA), and *H-Nationalism*.

SHIRLEY HUNE is professor of urban planning and faculty affiliate of Asian American studies and the Center for the Study of Women at the University of California, Los Angeles. Since 1992, she has served as associate dean for graduate programs, Graduate Division. Her current research focuses on Asian American women's history and access and equity issues of women and people of color in higher education. Previously, she examined the human rights of international migrant workers and the global concerns of postcolonial states while conducting research at the United Nations. Recent publications include *Asian/Pacific Islander American Women: A Historical Anthology* (2003) and *Women's Realities, Women's Choices: An Introduction to Women's Studies* (2005). She has held the position of president of the Association for Asian American Studies.

S. JAY KLEINBERG is director of the Centre for American, Transatlantic, and Caribbean History at Brunel University, West London, a fellow of the Royal Society for the Arts, and an academician of the Academy of Social Sciences. She co-organized the Re-visioning Women's History Conference in London in 2001. Her research centers on the impact of economic change on women and family life, women's work, and social welfare. She is the author of many books and articles, including *Widows and Orphans First: The Family Economy and Social Welfare Policy, 1880–1939* (2006), *Women in the United States, 1830–1945* (1999), and *The Shadow of the Mills: Working-Class Families in Pittsburgh, 1870–1907* (1989). She edited *Retrieving Women's History* (1988) and *How Did the Debate about Widows' Pensions Shape Relief Programs for Single Mothers, 1900–1940?* (2005). She was editor and associate editor of the *Journal of American Studies* from 1996 to 2006 and is currently researching middle-aged women in the twentieth century.

ANN M. LITTLE is an associate professor of history at Colorado State University in Fort Collins, Colorado, where she teaches early American history. She is the author of *Abraham in Arms: War and Gender in Colonial New England* (2006). She has written numerous book chapters and articles on women's and gender history, New England family history, northeastern borderlands history, and monastic women's history in journals such as the *New England Quarterly* and *Eighteenth-Century Studies*. She is also the U.S. and Canadian History Program Committee co-chair for the 2008 Berkshire Conference on the History of Women.

GAIL D. MACLEITCH completed her Ph.D. in 2002 at the University of Sussex. She teaches at King's College, London, where she researches and teaches history of Native Americans, frontiers and borderlands, and the social construction of identity from the colonial period to the late nineteenth century. Her forthcoming monograph, *Imperial Entanglements*, explores the reconfiguration of Iroquois economic practices and cultural identities resulting from a commercial and territorially expansive British empire. Her article on Indians in the market economy, which appeared in *Labor: Studies of Working-Class History of the Americas*, won the 2004 award for best journal article published in the field of early American economic history, from the Program in Early American Economy and Society at the Library Company of Philadelphia.

LEISA D. MEYER is an associate professor of history and acting director of women's studies at the College of William and Mary. She is the author of *Creating*

G.I. Jane: Sexuality and Power in the Women's Army Corps during World War II (1997) and is currently working on "Talking Sex: A History of Sexuality in American since World War II." She was also an associate editor for the *Encyclopedia of Lesbian, Gay, Bisexual, and Transgender History and Culture* (2003) and is a member of the editorial collective for the journal *Feminist Studies*. Her research interests include women's, gender, and sexuality studies/history, popular culture, and cultural history.

VICKI L. RUIZ is professor of history and Chicano/Latino studies at the University of California, Irvine and chair of the history department. She is the author of *Cannery Women, Cannery Lives* (1987) and *From Out of the Shadows: Mexican Women in Twentieth-Century America* (1998). She is the co-editor of *Unequal Sisters* (with Ellen Carol DuBois) and *American Dreaming, Global Realities* (with Donna R. Gabaccia). With Virginia Sánchez Korrol, she co-edited *Latina Legacies: Identity, Biography, and Community* (2005) and *Latinas in the United States: A Historical Encyclopedia* (2006). She is president of the American Studies Association and past president of the Organization of American Historians and the Berkshire Conference of Women's Historians.

BETTY WOOD is reader in American history in the Faculty of History at the University of Cambridge. She writes on the history of slavery, race relations, and gender in the eighteenth- and early nineteenth-century southern United States. Her publications include *Slavery in Colonial Georgia, 1730–1775* (1985); *Women's Work, Men's Work: The Informal Slave Economies of Lowcountry Georgia, 1750–1830* (1995); *Come Shouting to Zion: African American Protestantism in the American South and British Caribbean to 1830* (1998, with Sylvia R. Frey); *The Origins of American Slavery* (1998); *Gender, Race, and Rank in a Revolutionary Age: The Georgia Lowcountry, 1750–1820* (2000); and *Slavery in Colonial America, 1619–1776* (2005). She is currently working on a book provisionally entitled "'Notions of Freedom': Enslaved Southern Women during the Era of the American Revolution."

Index